D1265397

The Hangman and His Wife

The Hangman and His Wife

The Life and Death
of Reinhard Heydrich

NANCY DOUGHERTY

Edited and with a Foreword by

Christopher Lehmann-Haupt

ALFRED A. KNOPF | NEW YORK | 2022

THIS IS A BORZOI BOOK
PUBLISHED BY ALFRED A. KNOPF

Copyright © 2022 by James D. Dougherty;
Foreword copyright © 2022 by the Estate of Christopher Lehmann-Haupt

All rights reserved. Published in the United States by Alfred A. Knopf,
a division of Penguin Random House LLC, New York, and distributed in Canada
by Penguin Random House Canada Limited, Toronto.

www.aaknopf.com

Knopf, Borzoi Books, and the colophon
are registered trademarks of Penguin Random House LLC.

Library of Congress Cataloging-in-Publication Data
Names: Dougherty, Nancy, 1939–2013, author. | Lehmann-Haupt, Christopher, other.
Title: The hangman and his wife : the life and death of Reinhard Heydrich /
Nancy Dougherty ; foreword by Christopher Lehmann-Haupt.
Other titles: Life and death of Reinhard Heydrich
Description: New York : Alfred A. Knopf, [2022] | Includes bibliographical references and index.
Identifiers: LCCN 2021024236 (print) | LCCN 2021024237 (ebook) |
ISBN 9780394543413 (hardcover) | ISBN 9780593534137 (ebook)
Subjects: LCSH: Heydrich, Reinhard, 1904-1942. | Nationalsozialistische Deutsche
Arbeiter-Partei. Schutzstaffel—Biography. | Nazis—Biography. | Heydrich, Lina,
1911–1985—Interviews. | Germany—Politics and government—1933–1945.
Classification: LCC DD247.H42 D68 2022 (print) | LCC DD247.H42 (ebook) |
DDC 943.086092/2 [B]—dc23
LC record available at https://lccn.loc.gov/2021024236
LC ebook record available at https://lccn.loc.gov/2021024237

Jacket photograph from the author's collection
Jacket design by Jenny Carrow

Manufactured in the United States of America
First Edition

CONTENTS

FOREWORD

by Christopher Lehmann-Haupt

Nancy Dougherty traveled a long and circuitous route to arrive at the writing of *The Hangman and His Wife*—admittedly yet another among thousands of books about Nazi Germany as well as one of several dozen volumes on Reinhard Heydrich, whom Adolf Hitler himself called "the man with the iron heart," and who as Reichsprotektor of Bohemia and Moravia was the top Nazi trusted by Hitler most with the leadership of another country. Yet this book is unique in being a portrait of a leading Nazi figure based in part on interviews with his wife, Lina von Osten Heydrich, who survived him by more than four decades, well into the latter half of the twentieth century.

Nancy Dougherty's long journey into the heart of Nazi evil began with her childhood experience of World War II on the remote home front of midwestern America. Then, as an eleven-year-old in 1950, she was shocked by the war's physical damage by seeing firsthand the bombed remains of Cologne, Germany.

Much later, in college, as a student of modern European history, she searched for why wars were fought at all, which prompted her to write her senior thesis on the Nuremberg war trials. From there her dismayed curiosity led her to the German concentration camps, to the guards who manned them, to their boss Adolf Eichmann, to *his* boss the enigmatic Heydrich, and finally to the Baltic island of Fehmarn, where Heydrich's widow agreed to be interviewed at length.

True, while Frau Heydrich loved and supported the man who can be described as the designer and executor of the Holocaust and was called "the Butcher of Prague," she was never herself even socially part of the Nazi leadership's inner circle. And though she must have seen him change over the years, she did not ever participate in or even witness at first hand the process of decision-making that defined the horrors of the Nazi era. Still, her presence in these pages as Heydrich's spouse, domestic partner, and mother of his children casts light by her very existence on the course of Heydrich's career and the nature of his monstrous evil.

During the three occasions in the 1970s and 1980s that Nancy Dougherty visited and interviewed Lina Heydrich at her various homes, she succeeded in peeling away the many layers of her subject's personality, slowly exposing her shocking, if unsurprising, interior.

Sadly, Nancy Dougherty succumbed to Alzheimer's disease before completing a final draft of her biography. So my task as the editor engaged by her husband after her death has been to sharpen and highlight her all-but-tragic vision of Heydrich's descent into profound evil. At the time I was approached, I was in the midst of writing a book about a year living in Berlin right after World War II. There, as a twelve-year-old, I became physically familiar with the Wannsee, the large lake in Berlin's suburbs, by learning to sail on it. But I never once heard of the meeting held nearby five years earlier, the so-called Wannsee Conference, purportedly intended to settle on a "Final Solution of the Jewish Question," and presided over by Heydrich. Many years later, when I finally learned of the conference and discovered Heydrich's role as an enemy of anyone even partly Jewish, I was prompted by my own German-Jewish ancestry to write a memoir.

Oddly enough, whenever I would mention Heydrich as the reason I had interrupted work on that memoir, I was often greeted by silence. At first, I interpreted this as stunned horror at the very thought of the man, but after a time I found that in a surprisingly large number of cases, people either hadn't heard of Heydrich or weren't quite sure who exactly he was. This is puzzling, because while Hitler, Göring, Goebbels, and Himmler remain vividly grotesque images of evil in the minds even of people born after these barbarians ceased to bestride Europe, Reinhard Tristan Eugen Heydrich in a number of respects surpassed them in frightfulness. Dubbed "the Blond Beast" (as well as "the Butcher of Prague" and "the Hangman") and evincing a chiseled physiognomy— blond hair, blue eyes, aquiline nose—Heydrich possessed also athletic skills (he was a near Olympic-level fencer and an able pilot), musical talent (he played the violin well), a photographic memory (his subordinates characterized him as a human filing cabinet), and a keen sense of German culture (his father was a composer and opera singer good enough to study with Richard Wagner's widow, Cosima, at the Wagner Festival House in Bayreuth).

Moreover, while at various times during the Nazi era, Hermann Göring, Martin Bormann, Albert Speer, Joseph Goebbels, and Karl Dönitz each became a candidate to succeed Hitler, Heydrich, as the leader of Bohemia and Moravia and about to be put in charge of Nazi-occupied France when he was assassinated in the spring of 1942, possessed possibly better credentials to become Nazi Germany's next Führer.

In the pages of *The Hangman and His Wife*, we come face-to-face with the embodiment of the Nazi ideal of the Aryan master race.

In Nancy Dougherty's handling of Heydrich's career—particularly in her treatment of the Wannsee Conference, held on January 20, 1942, a few months before Heydrich would be assassinated—we come to grips with the existential question of whether the Nazis embodied evil in their very being, or whether they were human beings who turned bad.

In telling Reinhard Heydrich's story, largely in her own words, but with commentary by his widow, we meet someone who at first appears to be a quintessentially cultured and talented German who was buffeted by the storms of twentieth-century history and bit by circumstantial bit turned from an ambitious and talented naval officer into the architect and engineer of Hitler's Holocaust.

Yet one searches in vain for a rational explanation of Heydrich's descent into evil. No single biographical fragment satisfies. Not his awkward, ugly-duckling childhood and adolescence. Not the sudden flameout of his promising naval career. Not the seemingly hopeless job prospects he suddenly faced in 1931 as an untrained civilian, what with the deadly combination of hyperinflation and unemployment corroding Germany's economy. Not the attraction to Nazism of his fiancée and her father. Not the rising contempt for the Weimar Constitution's experiment in democracy. Not Heydrich's experience fighting in the Freikorps (Free Corps), the right-wing paramilitary volunteer group that fought leftist elements during the Weimar period. Not the rumor of a strain of Jewishness inherited from his father's side—the rumor at that time amounting for all intents and purposes to established fact.

Not even the inclination in the German character to excel at any job, regardless of its purpose. Not one of these details suffices—not singly nor as a symphony of evidence orchestrated in cacophonic discord.

Reinhard Heydrich's monstrosity surpasses experiential evidence. His career puts one finally in mind of the controversial experiment designed in the 1960s by Stanley Milgram, a Yale University social psychologist, and described in his book *Obedience to Authority: An Experimental View*. Here it was determined that under carefully controlled circumstances where subjects were ordered to administer what they believed to be extremely painful electric shocks in order to teach "victims" random word associations, 60 percent of the subjects continued to obey the experimenter's commands, despite the evident and increasing suffering of the "victims."

Except that in imagining Heydrich as a subject, one sees him falling through some trapdoor in his mind, and not only administering the maximum electric voltage but then breaking into the glass chamber where the "victim" is pretending to suffer and proceeding to strangle him to death with his bare hands.

Or in a similarly well-known undertaking, the so-called Stanford Prison Experiment, conducted by Philip G. Zimbardo in 1971, where people pretending to be guarding prisoners found themselves resorting to physical violence, one imagines Heydrich going even further and exterminating the playacting subjects with Zyklon-B gas.

There is simply no accounting for the nature or extent of his evil.

In Primo Levi's *Survival in Auschwitz*, the author famously tells of reaching for an icicle to slake an awful thirst and having it knocked from his hands to the ground by a concentration camp guard. When Levi asks the universal Holocaust question, "Warum?," meaning, simply, "Why?," the guard answers, now famously, "Hier gibt es kein Warum!"—"Here, there is no why!"

In a system created and executed by the strivings of incomprehensibly evil genius, the answer to millions of victims' "Why?" is no more than Reinhard Heydrich.

INTRODUCTION: THE HANGMAN'S WIFE

"I think that even if it is very difficult, the old National Socialists should be incorporated into the unity of history."

—LINA VON OSTEN HEYDRICH

This book provides an intimate glimpse into the political and social life of one of history's most notorious, dreaded, and least understood organizations, the Nazi SS, short for Schutzstaffel (literally Defense Squad, though known as Black Shirts). Its story focuses on two people who were both members of the Nazi Party. One of them—Reinhard Heydrich, who, as SS Commander Heinrich Himmler's chief assistant, was second in command of the SS—was a remarkable man by any reckoning, and was responsible for a remarkable amount of suffering. The other, Heydrich's wife, Lina, represented the other side of the Nazi coin, the quiet supporters of the leadership. She was "responsible" for nothing, except that she built a household for her husband and did her best to back him in every way possible.

Their stories flow together, break apart, and converge again. Some things they shared; in more ways their lives were parallel, but barely touched. Reinhard Heydrich died in 1942; Lina Heydrich in 1985. She spent much of the forty-two years following Reinhard's death trying to come to terms with what her husband had done almost two generations earlier.

The world at large, of course, is also still attempting to come to terms with what her husband did, generally through reliance on convenient stereotypes that teach us little and usually prevent us from learning anything else. In Reinhard and Lina Heydrich our two most widespread myths—the diamond-hard, fanatic SS monster and the "ordinary" camp follower who weakly acquiesces to the dictates of an evil regime—join hands and lives. And, like all real people, one of the things they have to tell us is that nothing is as simple as clichés would make it seem.

The history that this book recounts is mainly devoted to Reinhard Heydrich—his remarkable rise in the Nazi hierarchy from almost nowhere, and his precipitous fall from a high place. How I discovered him began with my stunned apprehension of the Holocaust, its incomprehensible statistics, the racial fanaticism behind it, the concentration camps, the SS and Gestapo (or Secret State Police), and eventually the places and people involved.

When, in the early 1960s, I was studying sociology at the University of California at Berkeley, and reading about social change and organizational leadership, I put on my reading list a book on the history of the SS. I was less concerned with victims of Nazi Germany and more with the way the persecutors had organized their activities, with what sociologists might call "integration, adaptation, goal attainment, and pattern maintenance"—as far from suffering people as the jargon of sociology is from the language of everyday life.

From this perspective, the individual is important only when he occupies a pivotal position, where many strands of the social network converge. As I read about the SS, I was surprised to discover that the man with the gun who greeted the camp prisoners, and who held the power of life and death in his hands, did not occupy a pivotal position in the sociological sense; in fact, he represented just about the bottom rung of the huge SS hierarchy. He and his victims had reached the end of the line together.

As the leaders of the SS bureaucracy had learned, intense pressure was ordinarily required to induce a man to participate in mass murder, and so they seem to have searched systematically for weak and desperate people. For instance, the man who designed the training programs for the Death's Head Legions, SS Obergruppenführer Theodor "Papa" Eicke, had once been hospitalized for mental illness; the commandant of Auschwitz had been jailed for murder.

Franz Stangl, commandant of the death camps of Sobibor and Treblinka, perhaps had a more typical career. As a police official in Austria, he had incurred the displeasure of his boss, and as a way out of the situation had accepted service in an "experimental" euthanasia program. This was in 1938, and Stangl's willingness to participate in the killing of 100,000 physically sick and mentally disabled Germans must have been entered in a file somewhere. In 1942, he was sent to Sobibor, along with many of his fellow workers from the earlier "program." But Stangl had been reluctant in 1938; in 1942, when he found out what his assignment was to be, he immediately applied for a transfer. He received many promises, but no ticket home. Week after week, Stangl sent desperate pleas to various higher SS leaders, but week after week, he stayed on the job.

After the war, he told an interviewer that one of his methods of coping with his inner conflict was to avoid spending much time in the areas where the exterminations occurred. That was not as difficult as it may have seemed: as much as possible, the SS tried to arrange for the actual dirty work to be done by the inmates themselves, or failing that, by guards in SS uniform who were citizens of an occupied country. From the SS point of view, the ideal death camp guard was not a German, but an "inferior" foreigner, someone who couldn't even talk to most of the inmates, and who was already in fear for his own life. Many of the guards drank heavily when they could, and the higher officials were no models of self-discipline either. Attempting to explain how he struggled to anesthetize his conscience, Stangl admitted, "I took a large glass of brandy to bed with me each night and I drank."

Heinrich Himmler, the leader, or Reichsführer, of the SS, often made speeches glorifying the "courage" and "sacrifices" of men like Stangl, but he spent relatively little time with these "brave" camp commanders. The brightest stars within the organization's hierarchy tended to be more resourceful, more polished, and much more calculating. Where the camps were concerned, they followed Himmler's lead. It was all right to accompany him on one of his brief visits to selected sites (which were inevitably spruced up for his arrival, since everyone knew the sight of blood made Himmler ill) but only a fool would get involved in running those sites.

The real leaders of the SS sat behind desks all day, were whisked to and fro in limousines, went to elegant dinner receptions in their glittering paramilitary uniforms. And so it could happen that Adolf Eichmann, the administrator of the death camps, who had always wanted to become one of these real leaders, could sit in his bulletproof booth in Jerusalem in 1961 and profess amazement that he was regarded as a common murderer. Again and again, he asserted that he, personally, had never killed anyone, or ordered them killed, or even held a gun in his hand.

From the man on the railroad platform to the man in the glass booth, no one seems to have felt himself responsible for anything.

Adolf Eichmann's superior officer, the man he tried so hard to please, was Reinhard Heydrich; and with Heydrich at last, we arrive at someone with character and responsibility comparable to his terrible power. Heydrich was the official custodian of the new morality. Neither his career nor his personality could be described as banal; in fact, so many elements of social significance collided at his desk that one historian has labeled him "a symbol and perhaps *the* representative figure of the Third Reich at the peak of its internal and external power."

It is easy to see why: if ever a man killed in cold blood, that man was Reinhard Heydrich; if ever a man lived his life with a reckless, almost demonic intensity, that man too was Heydrich. This is the stuff of legend and of nightmare, of philosophical speculation and psychological schlock, of B movies and high drama—and, unfortunately, of the gravest historical consequence.

What we know of the SS and its members comes largely from the works of historians, journalists, political philosophers—and the purveyors of what might kindly be described as trash. As I read about Heydrich, and about the outlandish stories and speculations that always swirled about him (and still do), I thought that someone with training in the social sciences should try to do a study that analyzed his role as a "technologist of power," and also sought to understand how, as a human being, he could have become so inhuman.

Alas; perhaps I should not have been surprised to discover that the man who is the emblem of all we mean by "Nazi" was also the most enigmatic of their leaders. Heydrich's actions, taken individually, seem as clear, as obvious, as the stabs of a knife, but the man himself tends to flicker out of focus and evade our grasp.

Every effort to describe even the major events or the most important relationships of his life becomes a complicated historical problem. From his family origins, through his real opinions about Adolf Hitler or Heinrich Himmler or the Holocaust, to the reasons why he died in Prague; from, in fact, the cradle to the grave, Reinhard Heydrich remains a controversial figure. And that, unfortunately, makes it easier for everyone else to relapse into the convenient, conventional stereotype of the Nazi leaders who, as George Orwell put it, "think in slogans and speak in bullets."

Reinhard Heydrich will be speaking in words as well throughout this book, but the reader should take note that his voice comes from far away, and there is sometimes static on the line. Like most young men who die suddenly in the middle of a war, he did not have time to write his memoirs. And Heydrich, unlike Himmler, kept no diary, and wrote few letters. Most of our knowledge of his behavior comes from the testimony of men who were clever enough to survive both the war and the war crimes trials that followed it. Professional survivors have their uses, but they tend to make flawed historians.

In addition, there are the scattered documents that remained after the Nazis' last-minute efforts to destroy incriminating evidence. In them Heydrich speaks as a high government official, giving orders or analyzing troubling situations, yet those are often memos, written down by someone else, and so they give us policies and arguments but little concrete speech. After he became Reichsprotektor of Bohemia and Moravia, Heydrich made formal speeches to his new subjects, as well as to his subordinates, but these cover only the last eight months of his life, and only the public side of that.

And so it has happened that for details of his personal life, many investigators wound up in the same place, the small, windy island of Fehmarn, in the Baltic Sea between Denmark and Schleswig-Holstein, where Heydrich's wife spent her childhood and where she returned in 1945.

Most wives of former Nazi leaders, particularly of major war criminals, do not give interviews, and tend to live in deepest seclusion surrounded by a cordon of watchful family members. But Lina Heydrich was never quite like other Nazi wives. After her husband's death in 1942, she elected to remain in Czechoslovakia, and led such an active life from her thirty-two-room country villa that Himmler (who had assumed the role of her legal guardian) reprimanded her for being that almost unimaginable thing, "a politicizing widow."

After the war, and a wildly adventurous flight before the advancing Allied armies, Frau Heydrich settled back in Fehmarn with her children, to emerge only in the early 1960s when she actually tried to claim the pension to which widows of soldiers "fallen in battle" were entitled under West German law. Her lawsuit made headlines when the court ruled that no one who had "profited" from the Nazi regime could claim such a pension. It was after this that the widow of "Heydrich the Hangman" began to grant occasional interviews to historians, journalists, and sifters of wartime documents. In 1976, she published her own book of memoirs, *Life with a War Criminal* (an intentionally ironic title she came to regret because, for the obvious reason her husband, had he lived, would have been judged a war criminal, the irony was lost on many); and a few years later, when the TV film *Holocaust* was broadcast on German television, she appeared in a TV interview to denounce the way her husband, played by the English actor David Warner, had been depicted in that drama.

From all of this, one might assume that interviewing Lina Heydrich would be a little like listening to a Germanic version of one of the propaganda broadcasts of Tokyo Rose. I had had no trouble getting in touch with her by telephone, nor in securing her agreement to receive me at her home, where she ran a small pension, or rooming house, for an interview late in 1974, two years preceding the publication of her memoirs and a decade before her death in 1985. As I rode in a rented car on one of Hitler's autobahns past the quaint villages and thatched houses of Schleswig-Holstein toward the new bridge to Fehmarn, I anticipated a cold, guarded, brittle, and fanatic Valkyrie—but then never in this exploration have I quite found what I expected.

By the time I arrived at her house, in the twilight of a cold and windy evening, it was not a propitious moment for either of us. Unknown to her, I was exhausted, having already conducted one interview that morning in Hamburg, and unknown to me, I had arrived on June 4, the anniversary of Reinhard Heydrich's death.

My husband had come along with me, as, to be frank, a sort of bodyguard, though unlike me he spoke no German. The woman who greeted us in the driveway, before a rectangular, two-storied, white-brick house, had obviously been crying. Inside, the first thing she did was offer me some cognac; the first thing I did was accept it. We sat nervously on a flowered couch while Frau Heydrich cooked dinner in a little, hidden kitchen into which we were not invited.

The room in which we sat, where my future interviews—three more following this one, over a span of seven years—were to be conducted, would have been a rather spacious rectangle were it not so crowded with furniture. There were a variety of tables, always with something on them—a bowl of apples, a vase of ferns—as well as a large cupboard made of highly polished, carved wood, an ancient seaman's trunk embellished with wrought iron scrollwork, a few bits of pink porcelain in a niche in the wall, and other cozy or elegant objects that appeared and disappeared from day to day. In contrast, one other item was always there—a bronze death mask of her late husband.

This was, to say the least, a commanding presence. The Nazis thought so much of this incarnation of Reinhard Heydrich that in 1943 they issued a commemorative postage stamp based on a photograph of it.

Glowing in tarnished golden metal, with his eyes closed and a faint smile calling to mind statues of the ancient Pharaohs, he looked, literally, magnificent. The effect was unearthly and unnerving, and seemed at odds with the room around it—except, perhaps, at night.

On the evening we arrived, Frau Heydrich's living room was lit only by a few candles on the dinner table. The room seemed dark and, somehow, clammy. I felt I had wandered into an underwater grotto, clogged with chimeras and shadows. The only thing in the world I wanted to do, in the beginning, was leave. But we stayed for five hours, sipping cognac, drifting away from pools of real controversy, carefully avoiding anything that could be construed as a formal interview question. I spoke with her in German, which, possibly aided by my father's background, I had learned well enough to be reasonably comfortable communicating with her. I recorded our conversations on a voice-activated tape recorder, so as to be certain I understood her correctly.

Lina Mathilde von Osten Heydrich Manninen was small and a bit *zaftig* (a word that, when it sprang into my mind as the perfect description of a master anti-Semite's widow, momentarily shocked me with its irony, given that its meaning as "appealingly plump and juicy" is Yiddish, but in German means merely "juicy"). She looked a little like Simone Signoret—her eyes had that same worldly shrewdness—but Lina seemed both less refined and more emotional. She seemed, generally, to express what she felt at the moment. She could tell elaborate (often funny) stories in earthy words, and her command of the language of gestures was good enough to make my silent bodyguard feel a part of our conversation. She was interested in how other people lived; she

"The Final Solution had nothing to do with my husband,"
said Lina Heydrich (1911–85), widow of Reinhard Heydrich
(1904–42), to *The New York Times* in 1979. "That was something
falsely attributed to him."

seemed uncertain of almost everything else, except how she felt (still)
about her husband. When we finally got around to the subject I had
come so far to discuss with her, I mistranslated the word for leadership,
using *Leiterschaft* (there is actually no such word) instead of *Leitung*. She
understandably thought I had said *Leidenschaft*, the word for passion.

"Oh, how wonderful!" she said. "What a really important thing to
write a book about!" And she clapped her hands together in front of
her smiling face. After I explained the misunderstanding, she put her
hands down on the table and looked at them. "Of course," she said, very
quietly, "leadership is significant too."

It seems fair to say in retrospect that the effort of reconciling these
two hopelessly incompatible things, her love for her husband and her
knowledge of the hateful consequences of his leadership, was the great,
insoluble dilemma of Lina Heydrich's life. As I talked to her, I realized
that the woman who lived with the man who carried the kind of "gun"
that really mattered was both a cause and a casualty of the destruction
I myself had worried about so many years earlier, as a child thinking
about the ruins of Nazi Germany. She was also one of the few participants prepared to discuss the question I had asked as a child—what did
the Nazis think they were doing?

I have come to believe that this question is more important now than
it was when I was a child, in the 1950s.

But what has been, for me, only an infrequent experience of the nightmare side of life was, for Lina Heydrich, entwined with the substance of her everyday existence, the most horrifying and the most mundane personal events. The commentary she gave me brings her famous, myth-shrouded husband down to earth—and adds a surprisingly feminine point of view (though it is, to say the least, politically incorrect). And this, it should be noted, is a woman urbane enough to have waltzed with Rudolf Hess, argued with Heinrich Himmler, feuded with Hermann Göring, and drunk vintage wine with Albert Speer.

Of course, her perspective had pronounced limitations, as she and her husband were never part of Hitler's inner circle, where she might have had more opportunity to listen in when ideology and wartime news might have been discussed. And in any case, women were not allowed to get involved in Nazi politics.

Moreover, on the subjects with which Lina was familiar, she was often difficult to pin down. "She is confused," one of Heydrich's biographers told me before I went to see her for the first time (though he still quoted her extensively in his footnotes). "You must be very careful," another researcher told me. "Things only began to work for me after I had been there four or five days."

When I had been on Fehmarn that length of time, Frau Heydrich and I had had every sort of encounter, from tears to shouting matches. But then, I was the rare woman visitor—and perhaps the only historian to focus as much on her own opinions as those of Reinhard Heydrich. It is obvious that for her, as for most of us, the path to truth was a journey through a series of successive approximations toward an end never entirely attained. She might have been "confused," yet very often, that seemed to suit her purposes. What I found was not so much confusion as a tendency to shift among the layers of reality that lay behind her husband's image. This almost mercurial talent reflected her way of dealing with the complexity of the past.

Yet for all the confusion of her utterances, what she did offer was the framing perspective of Heydrich's homemaker. Here was the woman who reared his children, who preserved his memory, who remained forever loyal to him, who even helped him to get his start. However distant her life was from his, she was always there, for better or worse.

While Frau Heydrich and I disagreed on almost everything, we reached total accord on this: "I think," she said, "that even if it is very difficult, the old National Socialists should be incorporated into the unity of history. You should not shut them out! For you can learn much from them; at the least, you can learn what you should not do, no?"

Yes. The Nazis' greatest failing, I believe, was the refusal or inability to make connections—between the various implications of their own actions, between their pretensions and their realities, and between themselves and other people. This last omission may also be described as a failure of empathy: they simply refused to regard inconvenient or troublesome people—mainly Jews—as human beings.

It seems to me that these sins are not confined to the population of Germany between 1933 and 1945. To treat the Nazis as less than human is to repeat a sickening mistake.

The organizational scheme of this book is derived from categories alien neither to universal experience nor to that of Reinhard and Lina Heydrich: there are chapters on, among other things, love, honor, fear, social life, and sex, as well as power, violence, war, and death. If their lives were only fiction, they would make an exciting cautionary tale, a sort of fable combining passion and horror, mystery and tragedy.

But because this story is true, I am focusing on the historical issues, as well as the compelling narrative, on the things to which a woman can bear witness, and both from her own perspective and beyond, on the rise and fall of a powerful, ruthless man.

| PART I |

STARTING OUT

STARTING OUT

1

THE FACE OF NATIONAL SOCIALISM

"The position of my man is always overrated. Just look at the photographs of him. There he's shown where he really belongs, always in the second rank."

—LINA HEYDRICH

O N JANUARY 20, 1942—a dark snowy Tuesday morning—Obergruppenführer Reinhard Tristan Eugen Heydrich strode through the porticoed entrance of a grand villa at 56–58 Am Grossen Wannsee, in the prosperous west Berlin suburb of Wannsee. There, in a residence overlooking the larger of two bodies of water known collectively as Lake Wannsee, fifteen men waited for Heydrich to convene a brief meeting, which later came to be known as the Wannsee Conference. Its stated intention was to arrive at a Final Solution of the Jewish Question.

Given that the mass murder of Jews had already begun and that the death camps were already under construction, the true purpose of the meeting is still a subject of scholarly debate. But Heydrich's lofty status as the meeting's leader was unambiguous. By January 1942 he had reached a pinnacle of power in the Nazi hierarchy. To arrive at the meeting, he had flown his own private plane from Prague, where, as of three months earlier, he held the position of Reichsprotektor of Bohemia and Moravia. He was scheduled shortly to take over the Nazi occupation of France.

Heydrich's career is often described as a "skyrocket," perhaps because there was an explosion at its end, in the form of his assassination three months after the Wannsee Conference. The rocket's igniting occurred

Reinhard Heydrich was frequently described as the physical embodiment of the Aryan ideal: "a tall, impressive figure with a broad, unusually high forehead [and] small restless eyes as crafty as an animal's and of uncanny power," according to his deputy in the SS, Walter Schellenberg, who further noted, "His hands were slender and rather too long—they made one think of the legs of a spider."

obscurely, in the summer of 1931, when at age twenty-seven, Heydrich joined Heinrich Himmler's new, small, elite bodyguard, the SS. His job was to take over the "intelligence" files, consisting of a shoebox full of the names of Himmler's enemies within the Nazi Party.

In 1933, Adolf Hitler came to power, and rewarded Himmler with the post of chief of the Bavarian Political Police, a not very important assignment. Himmler immediately appointed Heydrich as his assistant. Thirteen months later, the SS had gained control of every political police unit in Germany and united them into one organization, the Gestapo, short for Geheime Staatspolizei (Secret State Police), with Heydrich as the acting chief. By 1934, as well, his intelligence and counterespionage network, the SD, for Sicherheitsdienst (Security Service), became the official Secret Service of the National Socialist German Workers' Party (the Nationalsozialistische Deutsche Arbeiter Partei, NSDAP, or Nazi Party).

In 1936, Heydrich took over the regular Criminal Police, known as the Kripo, short for Kriminalpolizei. In 1939, he combined these organizations, along with four other divisions, to form the RSHA, or Reichssicherheitshauptamt (Reich Security Main Office), which was estimated to have employed 100,000 men.

Heydrich's formal powers over the SD, the Kripo, and even the Gestapo had been based on his abilities to control and coerce the German citizens of his own nation. What he said he wanted was nothing less than "the total and permanent check on the situation of each individual."

But in 1939, Germany went to war, and responsibility for racial policies began to pass from the hands of the party's propaganda machinery into those of the already militarized SS. In that same year, and again in 1941, Heydrich received a completely different grant of authority, based on a "Führer order," which bypassed all organizations, including his own, and went directly from Hitler to the individual recipient of his commands. A second Führer order to Heydrich directed him in a few terse words to "make all necessary organizational, functional, and material preparations for a complete solution of the Jewish Question in Europe." In 1939 that usually meant deportation; by the time of Heydrich's death three years later, it certainly meant annihilation. Reinhard Heydrich had been chosen by the Nazis as the responsible official, the man with the mandate who arranges for the arrival of the man with the gun.

Heydrich (foreground, in 1940) was placed in command of the Security Police force when Himmler officially merged the unit with the Security Service.

The Final Solution was neither Heydrich's idea nor his primary responsibility: his orders came from Hitler, Himmler, or Göring; Himmler alone controlled the network of death camps that oozed across eastern Europe, and Adolf Eichmann handled the so-called business details. Heydrich's expertise lay in translating vaguely formulated commands into orderly, clever directives that other officials could then handle on their own. One of his former subordinates has called him "the puppet master of the Third Reich," and he is often regarded today as the Nazis' preeminent "technologist of power." The most dreadful crime in modern history thus represented only one of his many-faceted concerns.

In September 1941, Heydrich acquired still another kind of power, when he was appointed Reichsprotektor of Bohemia and Moravia, the strategic heartland of Czechoslovakia, which had been incorporated into the Reich. This appointment gave him the status of a government minister, as well as Hradčany Castle as his official residence, and meant that for this one function he outranked Heinrich Himmler himself. In the light of the increasing responsibility with which he was entrusted (including the leadership of the French occupation), Heydrich can plausibly be thought of as a candidate to succeed Hitler.

And that is far from the whole story. In addition to an inscrutability and prodigal nature, Reinhard Heydrich possessed high intelligence, a photographic memory, considerable athletic skill, a striking physical appearance, strong musical aptitude, and a store of sheer physical energy that few of his contemporaries could match. He skied and sailed and hunted and played tennis. He rode horseback in the mornings with Admiral Wilhelm Canaris, his rival as chief of military intelligence. He played the violin well enough to have considered it as a career; he fenced well enough to win international competitions. He had countless love affairs, yet he seems to have had a deep affection for his wife, and it is clear that she loved him. They had four healthy, attractive children.

As a high administrative official, Heydrich was exempted from combat, but he nevertheless went off to battle, incognito, in the uniform of the Luftwaffe, the German Air Force. He had learned in his spare time to pilot a plane, and flew nearly a hundred reconnaissance missions, including one in which his aircraft was shot down and he was forced to crawl, injured, through enemy territory. He won the Iron Cross.

In late May 1942, Heydrich was mortally wounded by a bomb

Circa 1943, Lina (top row, center) with the Heydrich children: from left, Klaus (age ten), Silke (age four), Marte (age one), and Heider (age nine). By age ten, boys were expected to join the Hitler Youth, while girls were fed their propaganda in the League of German Maidens.

From left, Silke, Klaus, Marte, and Heider Heydrich. The family's French-style chateau near Prague had since 1909 belonged to the Jewish sugar industrialist Ferdinand Bloch-Bauer and his wife, Adele, until Austria was annexed by the Nazis.

thrown into the back seat of the unescorted, open convertible in which he regularly drove through the streets of conquered Prague. Before he collapsed, he managed to leap from his car and fire several shots at his fleeing assailants.

Reinhard Heydrich received a hero's burial in Berlin, to the inevitable accompaniment of the funeral march from Wagner's *Götterdämmerung*. Martin Bormann, deputy chief of the Nazi Party, and Heinrich Himmler both gave emotional eulogies, and the short funeral oration was delivered by Adolf Hitler himself. "He was one of the best National Socialists," the Führer declared, "one of the strongest defenders of the idea of the German Reich."

The Führer also personally selected a suitable monument to Heydrich's memory—the total destruction of the inhabitants and buildings of the Czech village of Lidice, on suspicion of having harbored local resistance partisans. Later, in an aside to his entourage, Hitler murmured in a shaking voice, "Heydrich . . . He was the man with the iron heart." On the very day of the funeral, the mythologizing of the Nazi's leading candidate for the role of metallic, inhuman Superman had already begun.

But none of Heydrich's multifarious qualities were unambiguous to his widow, Lina von Osten Heydrich. Consider, for a prime example, our talks about the very faces that she and her husband presented to the world.

Lina said she had met Adolf Hitler for the first time in 1937, when she accompanied her husband to a reception at the Reich chancellery. That was eight years after she herself had joined the Nazi Party, six years after Reinhard joined the SS, and one year after he became chief of the Secret Police and the Security Service. She no longer remembered the occasion, but she did recall the Führer saying "spontaneously" as he greeted them, "What a handsome couple!"

Reinhard Heydrich was tall, blond, blue-eyed, and good-looking in the harshly angular, rawboned style so cherished by the Nazis. Lina Heydrich was blue-eyed, blond, a little severe, and a little sad, the perfect Germanic beauty of her era.

Appearances are deceiving. Still, what better way to make the acquaintance of myth-shrouded people than to observe the faces they presented to the outside world.

Nazi Germany was unique among modern societies in its obsession with the ideal human form; for an equal concern with perfect physique one must go back to the Italian Renaissance or to ancient Greece. In Adolf Hitler's Third Reich, artistic subjects were chosen for their ability to function as archetypes of such things as "leaders" and "followers," "men and women in their basic duties of combat and fertility," and, most of all, "ideal biological form."

For art was linked with the achievement of another goal, the creation of a racially disproportionate, totally Aryan Reich, out of whose purified gene pool would arise a fabulous creature that Nazi propagandists called "the New Man." (There was rather less talk about the "New Woman," probably because the role envisioned for her was already familiar: women were to do the breeding and provide domestic comfort, while the men did everything else.) But what, exactly, was the New Man to be like?

Most of the party leaders were too busy preparing first for power, and then for war, to give much thought to this problem; but Heinrich Himmler, leader of the SS (which he described as "a formation of German men in the Nordic mold"), was obsessed by it. It was easy enough to devise an ideal physical model on which Himmler's so-called racial experts could agree. As enunciated, for example, by Paul Schultze-Naumburg, an artist who also lectured on the subject of physiognomic racial fitness, the perfect Aryan prototype would have a high and receding forehead, a strongly protrusive nose, thin lips, a jutting chin, pale gray or blue eyes (the latter could be either pale or dark), and undulant, fine, blond hair. A long neck, a tall, long-legged body, long slender hands, a clearly discernible pelvis, and a spinal column rising "vertically, like a jet of water," were also deemed desirable.

Unfortunately, this ideal was not everywhere in evidence, especially among the leadership. To compensate, Hitler took the long view. Confronted with the obvious fact that the major Nazi figures—fat Göring, clubfooted Goebbels, the puny, myopic Himmler, and even Hitler himself, with his swarthy visage—were hardly cast in the Nordic mold, the Führer liked to talk of the generations it would take to shape the New Man.

Himmler, however, could not rationalize so easily. His SS was supposed to be an elite, the vanguard and emblem of the new order to come. Every SS man was supposed to be able to trace his ancestry backward through two hundred years of Teutonic racial purity, and to be in good health. Each was supposed to be able to pass rigorous tests of physical fitness, to see without glasses, to be at least 1.70 meters (five feet six inches) tall.

In fact, however, most SS men resembled their Reichsführer more closely than their ideal. Year after year, Himmler tried and failed to pass the physical exams he himself had designed, until finally his officers agreed to fake the results. And, in the end, Himmler was always forced to extend the same tolerance to the generality of his men.

SS racial specialists eventually produced a chart of genetically acceptable German types—only one of which was actually called "Nordic." Included were such categories as "Dinaric" (darker than the Aryans) and "Eastern" (usually Germans from the Baltic area). Within these types, there was an even larger range of physique, beginning with "ideal" and ending with "deformed," which, of course, was not acceptable. But in the intermediate categories, "good bearing" and desirable personal characteristics might override physical deficiencies. Thus, space was made for exceptions, for selection among traits, and for a rather confused adaptation to the old, old reality that a "good" man (however defined) is hard to find.

Despite his many compromises, Himmler never quite overcame his early conviction that blond was best. This sometimes took him to the extremes of tragic lunacy. During one of his periodic inspections of the concentration camps, Himmler spied a blond and blue-eyed man wearing the yellow triangle designating a Jew. Thinking a mistake had been made, the Reichsführer asked if he was really Jewish. "Yes," the prisoner replied with magnificent courage. "Then I can't help you," Himmler said sadly, and walked away. On another occasion, he met an impressive-looking blond SS man on the street and promoted him on the spot. (He later turned out to be a pimp, and had to be dismissed.)

In the long term, however, Himmler intended to recruit primarily from among the children of his own SS men. No member of his elite guard could marry without obtaining a permit, a difficult process requiring the woman to pass an athletic test, submit to a physical exam, and provide, in addition to the obligatory proof of Aryan ancestry, a photo of herself in a bathing suit. The Reichsführer himself scrutinized the pictures of potential wives: "I looked at the photographs of all of them, and asked myself, can I see infusions of foreign blood?"

He must have seen a lot of something, for between 1932 and 1940,

106,304 marriage applications were submitted, but only 7,518 of these were judged entirely satisfactory. Of the remainder, 40,388 received "provisional clearance in default of documentation."

Yet however intractable real people may be, in art everything is possible. Official portraits and formal photographs of the leaders, as well as glossy mass-produced pictures of perfect, Nordic followers, abounded during the Third Reich. What the real world lacked, propaganda would furnish. Hitler often rewarded deserving underlings with pictures of himself, and these seemed to set the trend. The Führer always appeared larger than life, posed against a flag or a large group of trees, or on horseback, wearing armor. The artists tried to catch a "spiritual emanation," that necessary whiff of blood and iron that revealed a true leader, and which usually meant that Göring, Hess, et al. were shown with gaze directed outward or upward, staring resolutely into the future.

Within the SS, and especially on the walls of the great labyrinth of bureaucratic offices under its control, another style of portraiture prevailed. Hitler once said he wanted to breed a youth from which "the world will shrink in trepidation." There could be "nothing weak and tender about it. Its eyes must glow once more with the freedom and splendor of the beast of prey." Perhaps conscious of their role as instruments of trepidation, the officers of the SS were usually celebrated by means of an official photograph, dressed in the most imposing of their uniforms, looking bleak-eyed and relentless beneath their death's-head visors.

There is a famous photograph of Himmler with Reinhard Heydrich on the day the Nazis announced Austria's forced *Anschluss* with Germany. This was on March 12, 1938, and it must have been cold weather: both men are wearing military greatcoats, and striding along decisively in their polished black boots. Himmler, walking a little in front of his second in command, is bending backward slightly toward him, talking, smiling. Heydrich, however, is staring straight into the camera, unsmiling. He looks restless, predatory, ready to spring forward at the slightest rustling in the underbrush. He looks, in fact, like a wolf in a fancy uniform; what Himmler was always trying, and failing, to achieve came naturally to Reinhard Heydrich.

Few people, when confronted by the founder of the SS Security Service, can have wondered what was meant by the New Man: he seems to have sprung, perfectly formed, straight out of the pages of Schultze-

Heinrich Himmler, as Reichsführer of the SS (left, outside a Vienna hotel, in 1938), hired Heydrich to serve as his chief of SS Intelligence. Physically, the two were complete opposites: Himmler (1900–1945) slouched and appeared soft, while Heydrich exuded athleticism and sexual prowess.

Naumburg's book of Aryan physiognomy. Indeed, as one writer has said, "If National Socialism had looked in the mirror, Reinhard Heydrich would have looked back."

There is no question that Heydrich's persona had a strong impact on those whose path he crossed. His own men called him "the blond beast," although one of his closest associates thought he more closely resembled Siegfried and other classic Wagnerian warrior-heroes. A Nazi police official investigating Heydrich's assassination saw him shortly after he died and commented that his facial expression betrayed the "perverted beauty of a Renaissance cardinal." One companion at a dinner party recalled Heydrich's "pre-Raphaelite, lily-white hands, formed for slow strangling."

No Nazi leader, excepting Hitler, has been surrounded by such a cloud of hyperbole, both pro and con. The simplest terms used to describe the chief of the SD are "iciness" and "like polished steel." Heydrich has also been likened to a spider, to a cat playing with its victims, to the tip of a sword. The historian Joachim Fest sums Heydrich up: "In his Luciferian coldness, amorality, and insatiable greed for power he was comparable only to the great criminals of the Renaissance, with whom he shared a conscious awareness of the omnipotence of man."

One cynical observer, Wilhelm Höttl, who served under Heydrich in the SD, compared him to Cesare Borgia: "Both men," he said, "were imbued with the same complete disregard for all ethical values, both possessed the same passion for power, the same cold intelligence, the same frigidity of heart, the same systematically calculated ambition, and even the same physical beauty of a fallen angel."

SS recruits appear to have seen the better side. A young cadet remarked that Heydrich's photograph was pasted on the footlockers of nearly all of his comrades, and added, "There were many more of him than of the Reichsführer."

Heydrich's appearances in the limelight, however, were carefully calculated by his superiors to begin where Himmler's ended, in the "private" world of athletic achievement, where official titles could be regarded as secondary. It was Himmler who walked with Hitler through the long lines of silent soldiers on the party Day of Honor at Nuremburg, while Heydrich would be shown as a member of the prize-winning German fencing team, or as leader of the annual SS route march.

Predictably, Heydrich's striking physical gifts may have affected his SS career most decisively at its very beginning, on the day he met Heinrich Himmler for the first time, June 14, 1931. Neither man ever talked publicly about that meeting, which was decisive for the development of the SS and hence for the fate of millions of people. All that's known is that after a conversation that lasted less than an hour, Himmler impulsively offered his tall blond guest the position of chief of SS Intelligence, and it seems likely that he was strongly influenced simply by the way Heydrich would look in his new uniform.

Heydrich, also, was not what he appeared to be, yet while the Nazis didn't officially value those other qualities he possessed, they nevertheless rather desperately needed them. In a regime that exalted brawn over brains, doctrinal loyalty over technical skill, and the "big lie" over the search for truth, Heydrich valued other traits. He chose his assistants on the basis of their intelligence, rewarded technical expertise, promoted men known for pragmatic cynicism, and insisted on factual accuracy.

"It doesn't matter what happens," he told his subordinates, "as long as you know about it, but you *have* to know about it." What good is blackmail, after all, if you get the facts wrong? And how can you claim responsibility for the security of the Führer, and then the SS, and then the party, and then the Reich, if you don't know what is actually going on? Unlike Himmler, Heydrich didn't let himself be fooled by appearances.

Sometime after Heydrich created the Reich Security Main Office in 1939, he emerged from his official obscurity to pose for a portrait that was exhibited in 1941 by the SS at the House of German Art, in Munich. Artistically, the oil painting, by Josef Vietze, a Sudeten (German-Czech) artist, is unexceptional, unless one is willing, as the Nazis were, to judge art purely by its impact. Even in reproduction, the portrait is a startling picture, and perfectly mirrors Heydrich's dual roles as the embodiment of the fantastical stereotype of the Nordic warrior-hero and the grimly realistic chief of a vast and malevolent bureaucracy.

The image has some of the trappings and all of the exquisite calculation of late Renaissance paintings of such figures as Machiavelli or the Borgia popes. The young leader of the RSHA is portrayed sitting down, in a shadowy setting that is inescapably a government office. And the face of National Socialism is gazing not off into the blue, but right back at the viewer. It is disquieting to look at it.

An oil portrait of Heydrich (1941) by Josef Vietze shows a figurine to the left, *Der Fecter* (*The Fencer*), by Ottmar Obermaier. The statuette, representing that Heydrich was Germany's greatest fencer of 1937, was produced by forced-labor inmates from Dachau.

For once, a Nazi artist felt no need to be flattering, and Vietze paints his subject's head from a deliberately distorting angle, a three-quarters view that emphasizes the harsh planes of his face, the jutting line of his high forehead, the protruding bones of his nose. Heydrich's soft, pale blond hair is lost in the shadows. This is a face as an architect might have constructed it, all intersecting angles and planes, with the outlines of the skull showing through.

Reinhard Heydrich's eyes were rather small and set a little too close together, and one might expect them to be eclipsed by the abundance of architectonic detail, but it doesn't work out that way. Instead, his face becomes a gothic rigging apparatus, designed to let the eyes send their message to the outside world.

In contrast with Heydrich's slightly upward curving lips, his eyes contain a mixture of two elements not usually considered compatible—cool contemplation and warm contempt, approaching almost a sneer.

This is the kind of expression one sometimes encounters, even in a democracy, on the faces of government officials from whom one needs something but who feel the need is not mutual. Heydrich's distillation of the look, however, is no more similar to the normal version than a file clerk is to the Grand Inquisitor. Every element of the picture's compelling iconography, in which Heydrich himself no doubt had a hand, seems designed to emphasize his personal scale of values. The chief of Imperial Security chose to be painted, not in the black and silver dress uniform of the SS, but in the workaday field gray costume of the SD, the one party agency that was his alone. The uniform is festooned with a few eagles and medals, but nothing to indicate his stewardship (in Himmler's name) of the Secret State Police. Dimly, very dimly, shown on part of his right shoulder, merged into the shadowy background, is a vague pattern that is probably the V-shaped "old-fighter" chevron worn as a badge of honor by Nazis who joined the party before Hitler came to power. Heydrich had barely qualified for this mark of esteem and was doing his best to consign the old fighters to the shadows.

In his right hand, the lord of the SD is holding a rather crinkled piece of paper, and, nestled casually between his lightly clenched fingers, a pencil. This is probably the way he would have appeared to someone—an underling, perhaps, or a suspect—summoned to see him at his office.

For example, when the SS took control of the Gestapo, it inherited a group of officials who were, for the most part, bitterly hostile to the Nazi newcomers. After Heydrich had reviewed their records, he decided to retain almost everyone who would agree to cooperate. One by one, the police officials were called for an interview. One, Franz Josef Huber, whose name was the same as at least one other member, recalled his surprise when confronted by Heydrich, who was sitting calmly behind his desk, holding a piece of paper.

This Huber had been a prominent anti-Nazi, and expected dismissal or imprisonment. Instead, his interlocutor pointed to the paper, which contained a list of names, Huber's apparently among them. Some of the names had checkmarks in front of them indicating political reliability; others had a little zero. Heydrich picked up a pencil, and let it hover over the names. "Which Huber are you?" he asked. It was all he needed to say. Huber knew that by asking the question when he perfectly well knew the answer, Heydrich was saying that he didn't care. He could use Huber, despite his questionable past.

There can be something quite threatening about the mutability a pencil implies. Everything that is can be altered; everything that has come into being can be erased.

Sometimes, however, a pencil is not enough. In the Vietze portrait, on a line directly above Heydrich's right hand, stands an object with a different connotation. It is a small statue of a man, dressed in fencing costume, his right hand resting on a gracefully arched foil. The light shines on this statuette so strongly it is almost bleached white: only Heydrich's forehead, shirt collar, and hands, and parts of the paper in his hand, are as brightly illuminated.

As one's eyes are pulled along the inevitable pathway from statue to paper to Heydrich's arrogant, challenging eyes, it is impossible to miss the symbolic message of Vietze's work. This is a portrait of a man who will never have to decide whether the pen(cil) is mightier than the sword, because he can avail himself of both. The same hand that writes the letter of denunciation can pick up the executioner's weapon. The picture is really a police state icon for the worship of totalitarian power: what it is, what it feels like to have it, and, most effectively of all, what it is like to be confronted by it.

When I mentioned the Vietze portrait to Frau Heydrich on my first visit to her pension on Fehmarn, she was dismissive. She remembered it, of course, as anyone would. "Yes," she said, "it somehow happened in Prague. Vietze was a Praguer. I don't find much in the painting."

Not to find much in it! Perhaps Vietze painted several pictures, and we are not talking about the same one.

"You mean the one with the fencer?" I asked.

"The fencer is Schulder, a very good sabre fencer in the SS called Schulder. He was a very chic figure. And a plaster statue was made; we had it at home; it was really beautiful. And Vietze had this statue in the foreground . . . But I found that Vietze couldn't do much."

"Yet your husband looks so . . . Nordic in the picture."

She was silent for a long time. Perhaps I had gotten the word wrong. I was, after all, the enemy's child. And I'd already learned that nothing served her better than a long pause to remind us of the war and the blood, the opinions, experiences, age, and culture we did not share.

"He appears very Nordic," I repeated. (Better inanity than nothing.)

"Yes, but he has a very strange look on his face. That is not him."

Yet we did not really disagree on the symbolism of Vietze's painting. She knew exactly what sort of threat it represented: "The position of my man is always overrated. Just look at the photographs of him. There he's shown where he really belongs, always in the second rank."

In Lina Heydrich's talk of her ten and a half years with Reinhard, the black thread of power in the fabric of his career seems to obsess her, and to be what she would like to pluck out and be rid of. She would talk of murder (though she didn't usually call it that), but Lina Heydrich acted as if her husband after all hadn't had that much power, really.

And by the way, she had had absolutely none over him.

"Did you ever, ever try to influence your husband's decisions?" I asked.

"Oh, no. My husband tolerated no interference in the service sphere. If I had tried to suggest anything to him, he would have said, 'Go back to your kitchen cupboard!' "

On the subject of art and her own painted image, Heydrich's widow was even harder to pin down. Something else I had learned that Reinhard Heydrich used to say sums up her conversational style. When some goal of his could not be achieved by direct means, he would advise his men, "Find some back door!"

Lina von Osten was adept at finding many back doors. And so it happened that as she and I spoke further of art and artists, the specter of power, which she had tried to throw out the front door in our discussions of Vietze's painting, crept silently in through the back door. But this wasn't the fierce imperial force we saw in the face of the chief of Reich Security (depending on whether she or I was looking at it). This was a different phenomenon, involving subtle influence as well as naked force, involving power thwarted as well as power displayed, and involving a female form of power as well as a male one. In art, there is room for everything.

Wolfgang Willrich was one of Nazi Germany's best-known artists, primarily because his pastel-hued portraits of earnest, almost identical, blond Aryans lent themselves so well to reproduction in magazines, posters, postcards, and on the pages of *Das schwarze Korps*, the official newspaper of the SS. Willrich was a protégé of Walther Darré, a fuzzy-minded theorist of eugenics who was also a friend of Heinrich Himmler's. Like them, Willrich equated salvation with the reestablishment of the racial ideal.

In 1936, he was appointed to a special commission whose task it was to tour every major German museum, confiscating examples of "degenerate" art, such as works by Georg Grosz, Paul Klee, and Willi Baumeister, among German artists, and such foreigners as Pablo Picasso, Piet Mondrian, Marc Chagall, and Wassily Kandinsky. Willrich decided to use the opportunity to paint his way across the Reich, culling illustrations of racially pure Germans from every region and province. Sometime in 1936, he painted several pictures of Lina Heydrich. The results pleased her husband no better than the portrait of him had suited her.

In File MA 286 of the Institute of Contemporary History in Munich, incongruous amid a pile of captured Nazi documents, is a reproduction of one of Wolfgang Willrich's more elaborate works. At its center sits a fair-haired woman with a spare, strong face, looking down at a child suckling at her breast. She is naked from the waist up. Next to her sits a handsome, blond man. Clustered around them are two flaxen-haired little girls. Kneeling before them is a teenage boy. In the background, behind a huge, golden sunflower, is a white brick wall supported by chunky wooden beams, thick as railway trestles. They form a sort of Y with the vertical line thrust upward between the two raised "arms." In its solidity and massive strength, it also has some similarity to a cross, just as the grouping of mother and child with a respectful male attendant resembles a conventional depiction of the Holy Family.

The woman in the painting is really a sort of pagan Madonna. But

The Aryan Family, a 1938–39 propaganda painting, depicted a
perfect example of Nazi domesticity, though its artist, Wolfgang
Willrich, was more widely known for his "Soldiers of the Reich"
postcards. This work featured a nursing Madonna figure thought
to bear more than a passing resemblance to Frau Heydrich.

is she also Lina Heydrich? It's just as well that Reinhard Heydrich can
speak for himself on this point, since his wife emphatically disagreed
with him.

In January 1937, Reinhard Heydrich tried to block the reproduction
of the painting as an article of mass culture. He seems to have assumed
not only that the scantily clad woman was his wife but also that she
would be easily recognizable. Willrich's painting of the severe, fruitful
mother seems to have caused Himmler's second in command no end of
trouble, which is why it found its way into files usually devoted to international intrigues, the fight against ideological enemies, and the maintenance of domestic order. The chief of the Reich Security Main Office
took time off from all of this to write a personal letter to Wolfgang
Willrich that is interesting in part because of the insecurity it betrays.

As always, Heydrich got right to the point:

After long hesitation, I permitted you to use the picture of my wife, without giving her name, in one of the articles that you put together for the magazine *Volk und Rasse*. Yet, when this edition appeared, I was astounded to see that you misused the picture of my wife . . . as the cover picture.

You know exactly how very much I resisted publication at first, and then I only agreed under the conditions mentioned above. I must express my sharpest displeasure, and request you to send me immediately all of the reproductions of plates and pictures of my family which are still in your possession. I am going to make an appropriate report to the Reichsführer SS.

Reinhard Heydrich rarely admitted either to hesitation or astonishment: "sharp displeasure" is hardly strong enough to account for the anger he must have felt at such a betrayal of his trust. Yet his approach to Willrich is surprisingly mild for a man who had been known to threaten his enemies with "the grave." The remark about reporting to Himmler was, of course, a threat of a sort; but it was also an admission that Heydrich could not solve the problem on his own.

"My husband was a loner," Frau Heydrich once told me. "He was not a man for, as you say in English, 'teamwork.'" Yet he had to sit by for three months while his letter, with its embarrassing personal revelations, made the rounds of the various SS offices.

Among other places, it crossed the desk of Himmler's chief of staff, Karl Wolff, perhaps Heydrich's biggest rival within the SS. Wolff agreed to stop Willrich from publishing more copies of the picture, but the order seems to have been delayed for some time, because "Herr Willrich was traveling." Apparently, the resources of the SS were not sufficient to locate him—even though by 1937, Wolfgang Willrich had become a fellow member of the order.

Heydrich's letter was forwarded to the chief of the Race and Settlement Office, Richard Hildebrandt, who was on close personal terms with both him and his wife. Hildebrandt agreed to block further publication. On April 8, he also sent a note to Himmler reminding him that Willrich was not a real SS Obersturmführer, but was only allowed to wear the uniform in exchange for rendering some service to the organization. Himmler had created this new category of "furthering members," so if anyone was responsible for them, he was. Hildebrandt, with his note to Himmler, was merely tossing the hot potato back into the Reichsführer's lap.

Whereupon, as was his wont, Himmler paused awhile. No doubt, he rather enjoyed his subordinate's discomfiture. The previous year, he had been so troubled by Lina Heydrich that he had tried to persuade Heydrich to divorce his wife—and here she was again, causing more trouble.

Yet in the end, knowing he needed Heydrich's wholehearted support in the battle for authority that had now replaced the old parliamentary debates, Himmler acceded to his subordinate's pleas. The chain of correspondence may end with a note from Heydrich to his boss: "I request most obediently that you instruct the Race and Settlement Office to forbid the painter, Willrich, from publishing and making use of all of his pictures—which, certainly, *were* ultimately produced under the auspices of the RUSHA [Rasse- und Siedlingshauptamt]—without express permission from the RUSHA."

But this memo was undoubtedly designed to formalize something that had already occurred: in Nazi Germany, officials often acted first, and made documents later. Further evidence is that Heydrich has reverted to his customary style of mixing commands with polite requests: in one paragraph, he uses "instruct" and "forbid," and rather touchily insists on fixing responsibility on the Race and Settlement Office. The little note has something of the tone of a grumpy staff officer trying to get his unit into shape—except for that "most obediently," so strategically placed at the beginning, like the master key that opens all doors.

It is understandable that Reinhard Heydrich would not want his wife to appear scantily clad on the cover of a national magazine; yet one can guess why he managed to overcome his initial "hesitation" about more discreet usage of her image within the magazine if not on the cover: unlike many SS wives, Lina's racial credentials were perfect—and by that time it was becoming known through possible revelations about his family's background that his own might not be. A little help from his wife might have seemed in order.

The real surprise is Heydrich's sanctioning at all of this particular type of painting. Of course, the SS was the ideological vanguard, and the Nazis certainly had no compunctions about baring the (anonymous) body beautiful. In photos of state festivals, nearly naked young women are sometimes shown, standing in rows, holding torches, or participating in sports rallies. Yet, according to Berthold Hinz in his book *Art in the Third Reich*, portraits of the wives of leading Nazis as a rule "show no trace of the image of woman dictated by the National Socialist ideology . . . The image projected is that of a 'lady.' She is shown standing or sitting, in either full or three-quarter figure, and wearing a formal evening dress with décolleté."

I hoped Frau Heydrich might resolve the confusion over her husband's attitude toward Willrich's painting. "Willrich!" she said. "Oh, Willrich! Ha! Ha!" Her laughter cut sharp, staccato stabs in the air between us. "He was a terrible man! Today, there are many Willrichs. They paint in order to be *Zeitgerecht*, in the taste of the present time. Today, they are cubists, and so forth. They paint in that style without caring what people think of the significance, which only they know anyway. Willrich could not paint at all! It was trash! And he was also a horrible fellow.

"We lived for weeks on Fehmarn, and Willrich was always trying to paint me, but it was never right. And then, finally, he painted me in Fehmarn costume with a shawl around my shoulders, and then it was over."

"But wasn't it in a magazine?"

"Oh, yes . . . yes . . . I saw that once. But there was one man who *could* paint, and he drew all my children—that is Professor Petersen, Wilhelm Petersen. And, I still correspond with him today."

To the widow of the chief of SS Intelligence, all things seemed in some way related to all other things. Her conversations were full of reverberations, cross-connections, and, sometimes, contradictions. We had just taken a sharp turn away from my intended topic—but also away from her presentation of herself as a cloistered *Hausfrau*, not to mention the sacred Aryan Woman of Wilhelm Willrich's imagination.

"Willrich was a *Knillstepper*," she continued, "a little man. But Professor Petersen—that was a man!

"And Wilhelm Petersen had an exhibition in Berlin, in the Tiergartenstrasse, and I went and looked at it, and I was so enthusiastic! At that time, I had founded a sports club, a squad of women. I found it so bo-o-ring when my husband's subordinates were invited to coffee, and we ate cookies and talked much too much, and so, as I said, I founded an athletic club. We did gymnastics, and we swam, and I found that much nicer. And at the next meeting—we had them every

Wednesday—I told my women that I had been to an exhibition of a man called Wilhelm Petersen and I found it so beautiful!"

Unlike Willrich, Wilhelm Petersen never seems to have painted Lina Heydrich's portrait, but a small drawing by him of her eldest son, Klaus, sat on the table she used for a desk. He looks about ten, around the age when he attended his father's funeral, holding Heinrich Himmler's hand. He appears handsome, solemn, a little troubled, vulnerable. The drawing is done in red chalk, but it seems full of colors.

Indeed, Wilhelm Petersen seems to have represented Lina's ideal vision of man. She always spoke of him in the superlative mode (a favor accorded neither Reinhard nor Hitler), and she loved to tell her version of his story.

Petersen's exhibition was "a sensation," she said. "He was invited to [Alfred] Rosenberg's! To Goebbels's! Into the highest circles!" (Rosenberg [1893–1946] was an influential Nazi racial theorist and author, in 1930, of *The Myth of the Twentieth Century*.)

Suddenly, her tone slid an octave downward, each word and person

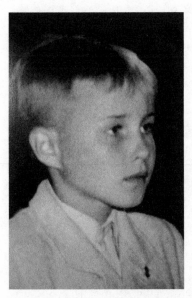 

Lina Heydrich extolled the work of the artist Wilhelm Petersen (1900–1987), who had sketched a small portrait of the Heydrichs' eldest son, Klaus (right; his photo, left). Petersen also specialized in depictions of Vikings, ancient Teutons, and female nudes. Hitler encouraged "Aryan art" as a means to promote the physical and military might of the Fatherland and the Nordic race.

emphasized carefully—as if she were reciting a litany. "And he didn't at all know how it happened to him. He came from Schleswig-Holstein, so he was from the country. He lived in a village, in a thatched-roof house. And they kept buying his works again and again. And then one day, he was invited to Hitler's! To tea! And he *didn't go*!

"The next morning, I received a letter from him in which he explained it: he had to find himself again. He was unable to motivate himself anymore. There had been so much admiration for him. And now, he was afraid he wouldn't become great. And so he wrote to me, and said— I would like you to grasp this—he had upset Herr Himmler. Invited to tea at the Führer's! And, with a clear head, he did not go! And then I spoke to my husband and said he must understand that this is an artist, this man is not a soldier, and he must understand that. And so my husband saw to it that he was left in peace, and nothing happened to him.

"In fact, he was somehow especially prominent since he wouldn't go to tea with Hitler, but he also was not persecuted. That was everything, after all."

I tried to pull her back to the subject of Willrich's portrait of her. "Wasn't it a scandal to be on the cover of *Volk und Rasse*? I had the impression that your husband was unhappy over that picture."

Frau Heydrich refused to take the bait. She took the time to pour us each a glass of wine. Then: "Yes . . . yes . . . yes . . . You mean the one by Vietze?"

"No. Willrich."

"Yes, but my husband found Willrich abominable, detestable. He was an opportunist. He had, I believe, drawn all the generals . . . Yes, painting is a special thing. Sometimes it is toil, and sometimes it is dabbling . . ."

There was no way to pin her down.

Four years later, in 1980, I arranged for the subject to come up again, and this time Lina seemed to acknowledge that Willrich had painted more than just the picture of Lina in Fehmarn costume. That one was suggested by Reinhard, but, nevertheless, she never liked it: "I found it not good at all."

"But the other picture? Was that the naked one?"

"Ah, the other picture . . . I cannot remember. You know, that must perhaps have been a symbolic picture. It was perhaps called 'The Family' . . . That was someone else . . . Frau Jessen. And Frau Jessen had also been drawn by Willrich but he had also made a symbolic figure of her, as the Mother, or I don't know what. And that picture remained here."

"But your husband wrote about giving permission to paint privately but not for a magazine cover, and he used the words *my wife*."

But Frau Heydrich was not willing to reveal an open confrontation with Reinhard. The flow of her conversation broke into fragments, as if it had plunged over a ledge, onto rocks.

"Ah, well," she concluded briskly. "Willrich had to live; he was only a poor wretch. While Professor Petersen—*he* was gifted."

And so Frau Heydrich glided along on her stream of consciousness, as it carried her away from dangerous waters, not so much confused as evasive.

"And, imagine, Professor Petersen is now blind. A painter who is blind, it is terrible, *nicht wahr*? He wrote to me recently, and he used such large letters, because he had to do it that way. He can't make out even the largest shapes anymore . . ."

Sometimes even the largest shapes of the past, when the refusal of an invitation to tea was a seditious act, when Reinhard Heydrich could decide whether a man was an artist or a traitor, when the intervention of his young wife could save her favorite painter from persecution, are more manageable when reduced to fragments of unexamined recollection.

An examination of those fragments makes one thing clear, however: confusion was never Lina Heydrich's difficulty.

2

CHILD OF UNCERTAINTY

"There is nothing worse than uncertainty."

—REINHARD HEYDRICH

LTHOUGH HIS SUPERIOR, Heinrich Himmler, loved to talk about his own childhood and "origins," Reinhard Heydrich was notably silent on the subject. In the case of Himmler's second in command, the past was passed over; one lived in the moment—deciding, fighting, achieving—moving from event to event with swift ferocity, concentrating totally on the here and now.

Much of Heydrich's incessant activity had to do with the gathering, analyzing, and processing of information about other people. "Do you know what the inscription over this house ought to be?" he once asked a subordinate at police headquarters. The startled man could only think of Dante's depiction of the gates of hell. "'Abandon hope, all ye who enter here'?" he said. "No," said Heydrich. "You have misunderstood my question. I mean a motto that will fit not only the involuntary visitors to this house, but all of us . . . I am thinking of 'Knowledge is power.'"

The man who built his SS career on the skillful manipulation of secret files did his best to ensure that posterity's portfolio on his own life remained virtually empty. If we relied on information provided by Heydrich, a chapter about his childhood experiences would run less than a paragraph. This is what he told the SS in a brief vita written in 1937, most of which reads:

Heydrich's earliest known official SS photo, March 1933, two months after the Nazis gained control of the German state. Within a year, Heydrich, age thirty, would take command of the Gestapo while remaining chief of the security elite that oversaw the safety of Hitler and other senior Nazi officials.

I, Reinhard Heydrich, was born on March 7, 1904, as the son of Conservatory-Director Bruno Heydrich, in Halle/Salle. I attended the Reform *Gymnasium* in Halle, passed my exams at Easter, 1922, and entered the Reich Navy . . .

History, however, abhors a vacuum. The gap that Heydrich left has been filled several times over, but, generally, not with hard facts. Rumors abound—impossible to disprove—of altered church records, missing gravestones, vanished dossiers. Everyone knew that if the chief of the Security Service and the Security Police had wanted to eliminate evidence of any kind, he could certainly have done so. All his silence achieved was the further obfuscation of an already complicated story, full of disjunctions, contradictions, and peculiar reversals of identity and fortune. The file on Reinhard Heydrich has never yet been closed.

In later years, many Nazis thought of Heydrich as the consummate Prussian officer, but he was actually born in Saxony. In contrast to the bleak plains of Prussia, dominated by huge, hardscrabble farms on which lived an arrogant nobility whose real business was warfare, Saxony, to the south, was a center of manufacturing and handicrafts, a land of beautiful ancient cities and quaint "tinkling valleys," where villagers created some of Germany's finest musical instruments.

Saxony also maintained a strong regional identity, stressing attributes quite different from dour Prussian discipline. "Never trust a Saxon," runs an old German proverb. "They love to trap each other with elaborate but amazingly childish practical jokes," wrote a foreign visitor in 1939, citing the example of a Saxon host who found it amusing to remove the wheels from his guests' carriage during the night. In the morning, he claimed thieves had stolen them, forcing his visitors to stay longer.

April Fool's Day was a gleeful Saxon holiday, but daily conversation was also filled with verbal sleights of hand, designed to entrap others in some kind of error. (Adolf Hitler tried to avoid giving speeches in Saxony, because the wary inhabitants sometimes failed to succumb to his oratory.)

Lina Heydrich told me that her husband had a fund "of typical Saxon stories" he liked to tell on festive occasions. Unfortunately, she couldn't remember any of them "at the moment." However, Madeleine Kent, an Englishwoman who lived in Saxony with her German husband, recalled many tales of trickery, generally perpetrated by mean-spirited dwarves said to dwell in the mountains separating Saxony from Czechoslovakia. A typical story tells of a village musician so talented he was asked to entertain at every social occasion. One day a dwarf appeared and begged him to descend to the depths of the mountains to play at the wedding of the king of the dwarves. Only after he was promised untold wealth did the reluctant fiddler agree. He did his job, expecting to receive a hatful of gold. Instead, he was paid with burning coals—and a single piece of gold that immediately turned to ashes.

There is, of course, another side to Saxon culture, one that stresses genuine appreciation for the arts. Leipzig, the largest Saxon city, lies on the old trade routes between the feudal nobles of North Germany and the wealthy kingdom of Bohemia. (Prague, where Reinhard Heydrich was to rule and die, is less than a hundred miles to the east.) A market town since the tenth century, Leipzig was also the center of the German book trade, and home to at least five hundred newspapers and periodicals. Bach played the organ in Leipzig, Mendelssohn founded a music conservatory, and Richard Wagner was born there in 1813. In 1891, Heydrich's father, Bruno, played the lead roles in *Faust* and *Tannhäuser* at the Leipzig Opera House. His bravura performances were so controversial the theater was said to have become a "battleground" of conflicting opinions.

The administrative center of Saxony, the capital and former seat of the royal court, is Dresden. Until World War II, when it was razed by Allied bombers, the city was famous for its art galleries, museums, and magnificent rococo buildings. (The city has since been restored to its former state.) Dresdners were also intensely *musikalisch*. According to Kent, they were almost too sophisticated, attending concerts "with ears a-cock to determine whether or not the first horn played a false note in the ninth bar of the scherzo."

Reinhard Heydrich's mother, Elisabeth Maria Anna Amalie Krantz, was born in Dresden in 1871. She belonged to a family that had worked its way up from poverty: first shoemaking, then painting and designing, and finally the teaching of music. By the middle of the nineteenth century, her father, Eugen Krantz, had made it all the way to the top of his profession, founding the Royal Saxon Conservatory of Music, and in the process becoming a Hofrat (privy councillor) at the Dresden court.

Professor Krantz also managed to marry well: his wife, Maria Mautsch, was the daughter of a wealthy businessman. In Lina Heydrich's view, "Herr Krantz had music in his head, but not money," whereas, "the Mautsches knew that power and money go together."

After his musician father, Bruno Heydrich—right, with Heydrich's mother, the former Elisabeth Maria Anna Amalie Krantz—died in 1938, Elisabeth married the mechanic Gustav Süss. To many, the surname sounded suspiciously Jewish.

Sociologists call the Krantzes' climbing "upward social mobility," and have given it great attention, particularly in the United States, for it is the essence of what we take to be the American experience. Many Americans do not even know their great-grandfather's first name, so little do we value bygone history and outworn statuses.

This has rarely been the case in Europe, however, and certainly not in Saxony, sitting squarely in the middle of the continent's conservative heartland. To compensate for her lower-class background, Heydrich's mother, Elisabeth Krantz, was taught exquisite manners and rigid adherence to social forms. Of course, she also learned a great deal about music. Then, she was sent for "finishing" to a convent school in Switzerland. All her life, she remained a devout Catholic, insisting her family attend mass at least once a week. She thus ensured their membership in what we now call a minority group, since Saxony was at least 90 percent Protestant. The royal family at Dresden, however, was historically Catholic, so she was in the best of company—which was always the company she preferred.

When Elisabeth Krantz married the well-known opera star Bruno Heydrich, it must have looked as if she were continuing to rise in the world. He was a talented musician like her father, and a man whose story also turned around the atypical axis of social mobility. There, however, the similarities ended.

Her new husband came from the small, obscure village of Lom-

Bruno Heydrich, age thirty (circa 1895), fell short when it came
to achieving the goal his wife had mapped out for him: leadership
of her parents' prestigious Dresden music conservatory.

matzsch, and his forebears remained impoverished during the generations the Krantzes spent rising to better things. Bruno, born in 1862,
was the eldest of six children. His father, a carpenter, died young, leaving the family destitute. Bruno later claimed he spent "a difficult youth"
trying to provide for his siblings. Luckily, he possessed two exceptional
qualities—a prodigious musical talent, and the ability to call it to the
attention of people who mattered.

By the time he was twelve, Bruno Heydrich was already known as a
child prodigy, performing solos with the Meissen Boys Orchestra. Soon
he won a scholarship to study various musical instruments, playing the
violin, the tenor horn, the double bass, and the tuba. Three years later,
he earned another scholarship—to the Royal Conservatory in Dresden,
where he must, in passing, have met his future wife, then a six-year-old
girl.

While at the conservatory, the teenage Bruno tried his hand at com-
position. More than a few of his early works were devoted to the joys
of kissing. (He was always a great man for the ladies.) After one of his
professors discovered he had a powerful, dramatic voice, he enrolled
in singing classes, paying for them by playing what he later described
vaguely as "not very dignifying music."

Bruno Heydrich was always to straddle the dignity divide, with one
foot on the plain of high culture and the other rooted in the peasant commonality from which he had sprung. He was tall and swarthy,
something of a braggart, and given to flamboyant, exaggerated gestures.
In a rigidly status-conscious society, he was foolish enough to boast of
being a self-made man, though he didn't talk about his family much,
other than joking about his origins.

At first, this seemed to make no difference to anyone. His teachers
recommended him to others in the musical community, who helped
him in their turn. He became a noted opera singer, specializing in
heroic-tenor roles. In 1890, he was invited to spend the summer studying at Bayreuth with Cosima Wagner, widow of the composer. He
became a confessed "absolute Wagnerian."

Few listeners are neutral on the subject of Wagner's work, but most
would agree that its central theme is passion, both human and divine,
both sacred and profane; and many would also concede that he depicts
it brilliantly. One student of Wagner has argued that the love duets in
Tristan und Isolde are the most graphic possible description of sexual

Bruno Heydrich, age forty-one (in 1906), gave up any hope of financially supporting his wife and three children after Germany's hyperinflation of 1923.

ecstasy—and were deliberately intended to be. Wagner's music has an intoxicating effect on many listeners, most famously, perhaps, on an unemployed Austrian drifter named Adolf Hitler.

But there is another, more disciplined, side to Wagner's work: beneath the soaring, surging music lies an intricate structure of calculated design. Aiming at nothing less than the creation of a new, "total" form of art, Wagner averred that his poetry was as important as his music. He spent twenty years collecting ancient Germanic myths and forging them into the libretto of *Der Ring des Nibelungen*.

Revolutionary in his art, Wagner also led a wild private life—in and out of debt, adulterous affairs, and public controversies over his anti-Semitic writings or his interest in vegetarianism, anti-alcoholism, vivisection, and "the regeneration of man" by some hazy synthesis of humanism, Christianity, Buddhism, and theosophy.

Obviously, it is possible to draw many different things from the life and works of Richard Wagner. We are not really certain what Bruno Heydrich saw in the operas he loved to perform, but we do know his children were exposed to them early and often. Later on, many who encountered the tall, blond, fiercely blue-eyed chief of the Security Service immediately thought of the "conquering heroes of earlier times." As one subordinate observed, "Heydrich's father played Wagner's heroes in front of the footlights," but his son played them on the world's stage. Yet nothing in Heydrich's life was ever to be that simple. For one thing, he didn't actually like Wagner much.

"Who were your husband's favorite composers?" I once asked Lina Heydrich.

"Bach, Haydn, Mozart," she said flatly.

"Not Wagner?"

"My husband crawled enough in front of Wagner when he was a little boy!" she snapped.

Bruno Heydrich had already performed in *Lohengrin;* now he went on to star as Tristan, Siegmund, Siegfried. Despite the controversy he provoked in Leipzig, he was generally well received, particularly in Cologne, where his fee for one night's performance rose to a peak of 1,000 marks. His attraction lay not so much in his voice, which inclined to harshness, as in his acting, gestures, and mime—that lifelong talent for compelling attention.

Bruno was also hardworking and extremely ambitious. Almost as if he were trying to conquer the entire field of music, he began to compose operas in Wagner's grandiose style. His first work, *Amen*, had its premiere in Cologne in 1895, where it was enthusiastically greeted by the critics. Bruno Heydrich continued to compose with substantial success for many years. He wrote two more operas, as well as enough string quartets, orchestral pieces, patriotic marches, and love songs to give him an honorable place in the history of German music.

Honorable, however, is not necessarily the same as absolutely first-rate. Although Reinhard Heydrich's father was a multitalented man, importantly involved in the artistic activity of his age, he was not a perfect success. He waited in vain for official royal patronage, for his music to be performed by the Berlin Philharmonic, and for an invitation to sing at Bayreuth. His application to be a state-certified professor like his father-in-law was turned down. After Professor Krantz died, his wife's two brothers refused to let him take over the famed Dresden Conservatory, causing a rift between the two families that was never really healed. Bruno Heydrich had to settle for local celebrity, rather than national renown.

This would no longer be of interest to anyone, if it hadn't seemed to matter to his son Reinhard. When Lina von Osten met Bruno Heydrich for the first time she noticed that a diamond brooch in the shape of a swan was given pride of place among his mementos. Herr Heydrich told her Cosima Wagner had given it to him during that formative summer in Bayreuth.

But his son disagreed, saying the brooch had actually been attached to a bouquet thrown onstage after one of his father's performances. Such an adoring admirer would almost certainly have been a woman, probably one of the many who seemed willing to give more intimate gifts to a celebrated star of his day.

The tradition of extramarital adventures was one of the things Reinhard Heydrich inherited from his father. "His mother was always jealous—and, I presume, with good reason!" Lina told me once in a moment of unusual candor. Generally, she preferred to ignore the problem of infidelity, whichever Heydrich it seemed to involve. "I am inclined to believe his father's version was correct," she wrote tersely of the brooch in her memoirs. (Yet, if logic alone is considered, it seems unlikely that the imposing, world-renowned Frau Wagner would give such a gift to a mere student, a man far younger than she.)

In either case, the question of the origins of the jeweled swan should not be allowed to obscure the essential story of a son disputing the word of his father. Of course, like all tales of Heydrich's childhood and youth, this has been filtered through the sensibilities of someone else, someone whose attention was largely elsewhere at the time. Still, it suggests a clash of orientations extending far beyond a single episode. Reinhard Heydrich was always to be obsessed with distinguishing truth from falsehood, with finding out how things *really* were. His father was more concerned with what *sounded* interesting, admirable, appealing, amusing, with how things could be made to play.

Pondering the flamboyant, cosmopolitan, and complicated Herr Heydrich, we may well wonder what pains he took to encourage the proper development of his children. Performances as a father are not announced in tall, black letters.

Bruno Heydrich was already middle-aged before he tried his hand at family life. As the century approached its close, his career seemed to have peaked. He was now thirty-five, and after twenty richly rewarded vagabond years, he finally decided to settle down. Returning to Dresden, to one of the men who had helped him the most, Professor Eugen Krantz, he asked for his daughter's hand in marriage.

Whatever else may have been involved, the proposed union was convenient for both parties. Elisabeth Krantz was still unmarried at twenty-six. She was considered beautiful, though also a little arrogant, and something of a snob. Yet she was a good musician, a capable manager, and a hard worker. Bruno Heydrich hoped to capitalize on the craze for amateur musicales sweeping through the newly united, newly rich Second German Reich. He and Elisabeth decided to take up teaching, and to try their luck in the little manufacturing city of Halle, which boasted of a university but, as yet, no music conservatory.

A truly accomplished singer would be an interesting novelty in such a place, and could use his reputation to attract students. Until his engagement, Bruno Heydrich had been a rather lax member of the Protestant Evangelical Church. To please his fiancée, however, he converted to Catholicism. They were married in December 1897. By 1899, they had already started their school, and by 1901 were expanding so rapidly they decided to call it the Halle "Conservatorium."

There is no question that Bruno and Elisabeth Heydrich made an effective professional team. With his wife's help, Bruno continued his astounding climb up the social ladder. While he taught classes in music and the language of gesture, she kept the books. When he sang, she accompanied him on the piano. Perhaps most important of all, while he cultivated male authority figures within the community, she gained access to the higher social circles that might have been closed to him alone. Soon the local newspaper was enthusiastically reviewing his concerts. Through his music, he got to know the mayor and other city notables, such as the influential Freiherr (Baron) von Eberstein, a Prussian army officer and a fellow Wagnerian. Bruno became active in local charities, including the Red Cross (which his son Reinhard would one day suspect of being a nest of international spies). He was a good fencer, and was appointed "honorary fencing instructor" at the German Imperial Fencing School. He also joined a Masonic lodge, the "Three Daggers."

Soon, Bruno Heydrich was a well-known and popular figure in the town, celebrated for his broad Saxon wit and ability to imitate almost anyone. Sometimes he pretended to be a Jew, mimicking a Yiddish accent. This did not prevent him from welcoming Jews to his conservatory, however, or from numbering them among his many friends. Indeed, one of his wife's brothers married a Jewish woman from Hungary, whom Lina Heydrich knew as "Aunt Iza," and remembered as beautiful, with flaming red hair.

. . .

Lina met the Heydrichs for the first time in 1931, but her description of the relationship between restrained, pious Elisabeth and carefree, extroverted Bruno expresses the viewpoint of virtually all observers: "Never have I seen two people who lived together their whole lives long who revealed such differences as my in-laws did." She described Elisabeth Heydrich as delicate, blond, blue-eyed, and cultivated. Bruno, on the other hand, was very tall and dark, "a man of the people . . . of the kind who makes jokes in social gatherings."

Elisabeth Heydrich apparently did not go in for joke making; she is invariably described as *zurückhaltend*, literally "holding back," and usually translated as "reserved." According to Lina, her mother-in-law was "always trying to dam up the over-showiness, the over-loudness of her marital partner."

It didn't work. Even forty years after his death, Lina Heydrich said she remembered Bruno's distinctive way of speaking. Suddenly, she slid into another persona, chin tucked tightly into her neck, chest thrust pompously outward.

"My father-in-law was an *artist*," she intoned, "and he was taught as a singer to project his voice. There were no microphones then; they had to reach a whole room. So he would talk as if he were in a theater, and when he did that, someone would say, 'From the breast, Papa!' and everyone would laugh. It is what you say to a singer, you see, when you are learning to project. And they would all laugh, and he would laugh, too!"

She returned to her former self. "Now *there* was a charming man!" she said.

The odd coupling of Bruno's jaunty gregariousness with Elisabeth's sober respectability proved highly profitable in the world of musical instruction. By 1904, the Heydrichs had 190 pupils; employed eleven teachers, a secretary, a librarian, two housemaids, and a porter; lived in an elegantly large house, which also provided space for the conservatory classrooms; and had been endorsed for a state charter by the city school committee, which found their establishment worthy of recommendation "in every respect."

. . .

The children of Bruno and Elisabeth Heydrich (circa 1910): clockwise from top, Reinhard (age six), Maria, nicknamed "Mausi" (age nine), and Heinz (age five). The boys, reared in a household governed by Catholicism and nationalism, played mock military games as youths.

It was into these comfortable circumstances that Reinhard Tristan Eugen Heydrich was born on March 7, 1904, allegedly to the strains of a music class being conducted at the same time.

In biographies, it has been fashionable to call him a "child of music." Yet along with an undoubted aptitude for chords and harmony, Reinhard also acquired at home the seeds of diverse personal conflicts. The very factors that made the Heydrichs such an effective musical team also made their household both disharmonious and unique. There was simply no one else like them in town. In his own family, there was no one much like Reinhard Heydrich, either. He was thus to start out in life as something of a misfit, never sure precisely where he belonged. It might, therefore, be more accurate to describe him as a child of uncertainty—which usually begins at home.

He was the first son, but not the first child. A daughter, Maria, had been born three years earlier, and, eighteen months later, a second son, Heinz Siegfried, completed the family.

Reinhard—which in German is a melting together of the words "pure" and "hard"—was, as the middle child, the one on whom the greatest hopes for the future were always placed. His mother picked his first name to honor the hero of her husband's opera, *Amen*. His father chose "Tristan" in homage to Wagner and his own favorite operatic hero; and "Eugen" was an act of deference to Elisabeth's father. (Bruno's own family was accorded no filial recognition.)

The choice of Eugen Krantz seemed immediately prophetic: everyone in the family agreed that Reinhard was "the only real Krantz" among the children. What everyone meant is that the other two were beautiful, outgoing, and good-humored. "They were sunshine children," Lina said, "like their father."

By contrast, Reinhard Heydrich was regarded as moody and withdrawn, much more introspective, and either shy (said Lina) or self-pitying and sullen (in the view of both his sister and sister-in-law). The man who was to become the very model of "hardness" for the SS began life as a frail child. He had a high, piping voice at which other children laughed; sometimes they also attacked him on the playground. Lina told me he took up fencing at a very young age, and at his father's suggestion, in order to gain more physical strength. Like Bruno, young Reinhard was to grow very tall; like his mother, he was very blond.

Frau Heydrich mentioned that she had no photographs of her husband as a little boy, and none of his parents either. ("The Allies took all that away after the war.") Many years later, however, in the home of one of their grandchildren I saw a group photo of the children of Elisabeth and Bruno Heydrich. All three looked strikingly attractive. Compared to his siblings, Reinhard seemed more serious and more sensitive, a child of around ten, as grave, and almost as beautiful, as an angel.

No one has ever said little "Reini" (as he was called within the family) was an easygoing child, or charming, like his father. But it is clear that he had the same overwhelming need for attention, merely seeking other means to achieve it. He is remembered as smart—and also as something of a smart aleck—full of a reckless bravado that seemed to have nothing to do with intelligence.

One day he scaled the high roof of the schoolhouse and paraded precariously across the top, allegedly to show his courage. Down on the ground, he would yield his position on the sidewalk to no one, even if it meant they had to step out of his way. And once, when he didn't get an

A in chemistry, he had the nerve to protest the grade—something rarely done in that era in a good German school by a good German student. And he was a good student, making excellent grades, especially in science, and always more ambitious than his brother and sister. (Like his father, he was to wind up supporting his siblings.)

The children attended the "reform" *Gymnasium* in Halle, which featured science and literature in addition to the traditional classics. (The term *Gymnasium* refers to Germany's traditional, nine-year secondary schools to prepare students for higher academic learning by the age of nineteen or twenty, with those seeking to pursue a vocational path allowed to transfer to a trade school at age sixteen.) German schools were notoriously strict, with an emphasis on discipline, rote learning, and reverence for authority, yet young Reinhard was also capable of using his intellect in more questing ways. The few surviving family members who have talked to historians don't remember his reading anything besides mystery stories, but a childhood friend told Günther Deschner, the right-wing German journalist and historian, that he and Reinhard spent one summer holiday in the country, working their way through a book about the history of French civilization—in French. This was after the outbreak of the First World War, and the two boys also became interested in talking to Russian war prisoners working in the area. Soon they were fantasizing about the joys of travel, especially at sea, to which they dreamed of running away. Outside of his family—and out of town—Reinhard relaxed and lost some of his shyness and most of the arrogant posturing he adopted to cover it.

Back at home, Elisabeth Heydrich was said to favor the lonely boy who so resembled her, and may even have spoiled him a little. Lina Heydrich emphatically disagreed. In her view, the Frau Direktor was too busy to spoil anybody: "My mother-in-law was, so to say, one of the very first *career* women! She was the pianist! She was the teacher! And she always accompanied her husband. The children had a nursemaid. I never met her. She was really their mother. She was always with them. She darned his stockings, made the food, oversaw the schoolwork."

"I have heard that your husband did not have a happy childhood. Is that true?" I asked.

"My husband submitted to the artistic consciousness of his father. The children suffered . . . There was no—"

She interrupted herself, and thought for a while before continuing.

"You know, it is just like that today. The artist marries . . . the artist is an egotist. He *must* be. And the entire family must regulate itself according to him.

"And my father-in-law had to go to the theater at six. It wouldn't do to eat; he couldn't sing on a full stomach. And when the theater was over, then the parents went somewhere to eat. And the children sat in the house with the service personnel. When the parents came home, they went once again into the children's room. But the children were not the *main thing*! And that is what they should *always* be!"

"The children, the brothers and sisters. Were they very close to each other?" I asked.

"They were all three very different in their nature . . . My husband's sister, Mausi—she was named Maria, but called Mausi—she was very dumb. Really stupid! She looked good, though; she was a beautiful woman. And she always ordered them around. And because of that, the younger ones always united against their sister.

"And when my first child was born, my husband said, 'Thank God, it's a boy! He isn't going to be ordering his little brothers and sisters around!' He was afraid it would be a girl, and would lead to a change in the childhood of the rest of the children."

As she began to guffaw with laughter, it occurred to me that the only time Frau Heydrich ever told an anecdote about her husband was if it happened to well up spontaneously, a little freshet amid the flow of conversation.

"Did the family ever play music together in their childhood?"

"Well, they would play for fifteen minutes and that would be that. Mausi played the piano, my husband played the violin, and Heinz played cello. And Heinz tried to follow as well as he could. And my husband played first violin. The one playing first violin sets the tempo, and the piano is the accompaniment. But my sister-in-law would say, 'No, the piano is the dominant instrument.' And that's when the fighting would start.

"And then my mother-in-law would get into it: Some years earlier, she had had an infection in her little finger and it had to be operated on. And after the operation the finger was no longer straight but was crooked. It was shriveled. But this was just the finger she always made use of. Every time she wanted to get attention, she lifted this misshapen finger. 'Permit me!' she would say."

In Lina's telling, Elisabeth Heydrich radiates slight overtones of witchiness. By contrast, Bruno is a cheerful figure of fun: "He belonged to a lodge, for artists. And his lodge name was Bosco. The members had a special name they called each other—Lulu. So whenever he walked into the meeting, they would say, 'Lulu, Bosco!' And the family started doing it, too. 'Lulu, Bosco!' they would say when he came in at night.

"Lulu, Bosco!" she laughed. "The lodge was harmless. Later they dissolved it. They dissolved all the lodges, but it was all harmless, really . . ."

Her voice trailed off, as well it might. The amorphous "they" who disbanded Reinhard's father's lodge was actually Reinhard himself, acting as agent of the notion that there was something subversive in the type of social gatherings in which his father had thrived.

It is easy to conclude from all this that Reinhard Heydrich was in some way at war with his father. Such a development is not an unfamiliar story in Germany. A common theme in the folklore of German childhood depicts a strong, demanding father whose harsh discipline is only softened by the entreaties of a gentle mother, perceived as both good and also somehow "weak." According to the psychiatrist Erik Erikson, this was the "legend" that Hitler exploited in *Mein Kampf,* offering a life story designed to appeal to the masses of his countrymen. In the end, the future Führer claimed, he had to rebel against his father's cruelty and go off to find his own way.

Hitler's version of his "struggle" proved seductive precisely because it reflected the dominant pattern of child-rearing in imperial Germany. The father ruled the home much as the Kaiser ruled the nation, with a stern and often authoritarian hand.

The household of Bruno and Elisabeth Heydrich, however, blurred this common pattern, and indeed, almost reversed it. Bruno Heydrich, busy with performing, composing, teaching, and the numerous social activities he so enjoyed, seems to have played only a fitful and flickering role in the life of his children. His wife supervised their upbringing, as she did the financial affairs of the conservatory, trying deliberately to create an atmosphere of Catholic virtue and personal discipline. As Lina Heydrich described it, "Inside the house, she led a regiment [*sic*] that was so strict in a bourgeois way, that the bohemian lifestyle toward which her husband . . . very much inclined, could not even begin to develop."

Lina told me Reinhard venerated his mother, and had in effect chosen her side in a house divided at the core. Yet, in fact, Bruno and Elisabeth's middle child seems to have been perpetually trapped in the middle, oscillating between his mother's bourgeois "regiment" and his father's chaotic creativity. Reinhard Heydrich's interest in sports, intense ambition to excel in everything, and highly active imagination can very likely be traced back to his male parent. So can his love of the violin, which Bruno had encouraged by giving him a special, child-sized instrument before he even went to school. For the rest of his life, Reinhard continued to play the violin. Lina Heydrich said that she might not have married her husband at all if he had not played the violin so well. As she wrote wistfully in her memoirs, "I might today be known as the wife of a violin genius, rather than a war criminal."

Frau Heydrich placed music and politics in separate, incompatible categories, as if unaware that Reinhard and his violin—like Nero and his fiddle—have become part of the legendary exotica of evil. In his childhood, however, the violin was merely one of the many varieties of discipline he was expected to master. When he failed to meet his mother's expectations, she would apply the classic Germanic remedy of physical punishment, giving us one of the tiny store of anecdotes repeated by biographers: one day when Frau Elisabeth had been beating her son for a while, he turned to her and said, "Please, try the other side."

Several authors have interpreted this as the first youthful budding of a special "code of honor," combining cynicism, arrogance, a sardonic sense of humor, and a tough, combative response to adversity. Later, Heydrich's personal style would be both nourished and imitated within the barracks atmosphere of the SS. In his youth, however, these traits were also acts of adolescent resistance against the rigorous piety of a woman who both punished and protected him.

Elisabeth Heydrich's greatest contribution to her son's education may have been not the use of physical punishment (which was commonplace at the time), but the force of her example as leader of her household. Despite the extreme misogyny of Nazism, Reinhard Heydrich always maintained a certain respect for strong women. Indeed, like his father, he married one.

Perhaps Heydrich *was* a child of music in the sense that the development of his character reveals a variety of motifs appearing, fading, sometimes conflicting. No doubt this is true of almost everyone.

Nazism, however, was so firmly based on denial of complexity, and hence of reality itself, that individual Nazis often seem to be hiding an unacknowledged multiplicity of selves behind the masks they held out to the world. Instead they saw themselves as supermen, splendidly invariant animals, or, even, as pieces of machinery ("Get yourself back in working order!" Heydrich once told a subordinate).

Whoever wishes to explore the human faces of Reinhard and Lina Heydrich and their circle of associates will therefore have to become a temporary Wagnerian, weaving together a great many ill-assorted themes.

One leitmotif, in particular, must recurrently compel our attention. It is another of the themes first associated with Heydrich's father, and it always sounds tones of disaster. When Lina von Osten met her fiancé's parents in 1931, Bruno was sixty-eight, and in failing health. The conservatory was failing, too. After over a decade of revolution, foreign occupation, inflation, and then depression, who could afford music lessons? Nevertheless, Elisabeth Heydrich was trying desperately to maintain both her school and home.

"It made me sick to see how hard she had to work," Lina wrote in her memoirs. Even Heinz, who still lived at home, helped out with the domestic chores, a fact she thought worthy of note. (Young German men of that era and social class did not often help with the housework.)

Several times Frau Heydrich told me a story whose central points suggest the outlines of a family myth: Reinhard's mother is sitting at a kitchen table, adding up figures with a pencil, trying to find enough money for food. And then his father bursts into the room. He has been to the hairdresser and has returned with his arms full of bundles—gifts for everyone. And such gifts! Perfumes, and perfumed soap and lotions for the body. Useless gifts! "Of course, they had to take it all back!" the story always ends.

In earlier times, Lina claimed, nothing was taken back: "Every year, my mother-in-law received 20,000 gold marks from the conservatory in Dresden. Twenty thousand gold marks and they simply spent it! They managed to just use it up. They had parties; full blast—they lived full blast!"

Lina Heydrich saw a lesson in the misfortunes of her husband's family: "Neither the Heydrichs nor the Krantzes had the correct feeling for material property. They relied on their talents, on what they could

Bruno Heydrich (circa 1935, age seventy, three years before his death) supplemented his career as an opera singer by composing five operas. While not particularly distinguished, the works were nonetheless often programmed along with those by Beethoven, Strauss, Mendelssohn, and Bruno's personal role model, Wagner.

do . . . What they earned themselves, they gave away through generosity or indifference."

As she saw it, Bruno Heydrich also managed to give away his family's birthright.

The cause, as usual, was an excess of generosity. While Bruno had been busy building a career, his mother married for the second time, to a man named Gustav Süss. He was poor, as Bruno's father had been, and, like him, was a member of the Protestant Evangelical Church. In Germany, however, Süss has been regarded as a Jewish name since at least 1827, when Wilhelm Hauff, the German poet and novelist, wrote a famous anti-Semitic semi-fictional novella called *Jud Süss*, about the rise and fall of the financier Joseph Süss Oppenheimer.

Of course, Bruno Heydrich had no blood tie to his stepfather. But he was a generous man: after he became established in Halle, he went every month to the post office and arranged to send his mother a gift of 300 marks. This was a good sum of money, and the postmaster noticed it and gossiped about it—along with the name to which it was sent. Herr Heydrich was a newcomer, a "striver," and he joked about being a Jew. But what if it wasn't a joke at all?

It wasn't very long before rumors were flying, and once aloft, they could not be put to rest. Swiftly, they made their way to the school courtyard, where the Heydrich boys were taunted by classmates who called them "Isi." (Isidore was a generic first name used as an insult by anti-Semites of the era.) Heinz Heydrich once pulled a knife to make them stop; Reinhard Heydrich didn't try to fight them directly.

At first Bruno Heydrich did little to defend himself, either. Of course, he denied the ill-founded rumors. But what did it matter, really? He was an artist, and an important community figure, a friend of Freiherr von Eberstein, a local member of the nobility and an early member of the Nazi Party. That was what mattered. A bit of gossip didn't count for much against his ever-increasing wealth and success. Characteristically, he made light of the whole thing.

"Can you believe it?" Lina Heydrich said. "He actually *laughed* about it! He made *jokes*!"

Speculating that the state's refusal to grant Bruno a professorship was related to the rumors, Elisabeth Heydrich advised her children not to talk about their father's background, which she herself had rarely mentioned. A veil of silence smothered the Heydrich household. If a little boy was not sure what the truth was, he wouldn't find out at home.

In 1916, the outside world got its answer. In that year's edition of *Riemann's Musik Lexicon*, a sort of who's who in the world of music, Bruno's achievements appeared as usual, but after his name came a parenthesis ("Really Süss") as if the lexicon were imparting a juicy secret. The Heydrichs believed that a disgruntled former student at the conservatory had taken this way to retaliate for supposed slights. This time, Bruno Heydrich sprang into action, launching an official protest and a lawsuit, which he won. But it was already too late. The First World War had begun in 1914 in a wave of exhilarating patriotism. Almost everyone thought the fighting would be over in a few weeks. After these hopes were brutally exploded, naive excitement hardened into an intolerant, narrow-minded nationalism sweeping everything else before it—including Germany's liberal heritage and civil liberties. By 1916, the country had succumbed to martial law, under the sway of the aristocratic Prussian generals von Ludendorff and von Hindenburg.

Bruno Heydrich had been a proud mixture of bohemian and businessman—"half-liberal, half-conservative." Now his enlightened lifestyle merely seemed less than German. He and his family had been caught up in the tides of war. Engulfed by forces beyond anyone's control, his story ceased to be merely his own, and the Heydrichs' personal and familial problems merged with much larger social and political dilemmas.

When the tides receded in 1918, Reinhard Heydrich was fourteen, and the comfortable, cosmopolitan world of his childhood had vanished forever. Only the rumors lingered on, persisting long after political and financial collapse had destroyed everything else.

3

THE HONOR OF AN OFFICER

"I always look at things from the psychological point of view. The politics that everyone is so interested in, that came last. First came the development of character."

—LINA HEYDRICH

I N THE SPRING OF 1922, Reinhard Heydrich turned his back on his parents' music conservatory, and on the university career to which his excellent high school grades entitled him, and became a cadet in the German Navy, the Kriegsmarine. He had just turned eighteen.

Nine years later, in 1931, he left the navy—or more precisely, was thrown out of it for dishonorable conduct—and found that in a country wracked by depression and unemployment there wasn't much interest in his tainted credentials.

Lina Heydrich's voice throbbed with bitterness when she talked about the scandal that radically changed her life as well as her husband's: "If someone wants to have something propagandistic where they can say, 'This is what the man was like!'—then they have this departure from the Kriegsmarine. Oh, they have made so much *theater* out of that!"

She was right: it is a dramatic story, full of anguish and conflict, allowing many different interpretations—a perfect piece of theater. But good theater does not always make good history. Heydrich's biographers tend to dismiss his time in the navy primarily as a melodramatic interlude, a sort of decorative arabesque preceding the stark and deadly upward thrust of the rest of his career.

Charles Wighton, author of the first book about the man he called "Hitler's most evil henchman," summarized the whole period in a few swift clichés: "Heydrich took to naval life like a duck to water" and "Reinhard Heydrich was an admirable staff officer—both of the democratic days of Weimar and in the days of Adolf Hitler's SS."

In the next few decades, the Israeli historian Shlomo Aronson concluded Heydrich was a mediocre misfit whose essentially "gangster" character development merely "took a different turn" during his years in the navy. Whereas Eduard Čalić, the Yugoslav journalist and historian, asserted that Heydrich's service in the Kriegsmarine was actually a well-planned step along the road toward Hitler's Brown House in Munich. Finally, the German journalist Günther Deschner has argued that Heydrich was a brilliant but essentially apolitical and amoral "technocrat of power" who might well have become admiral if he hadn't run into some very bad luck.

These assessments differ from one another radically, but all share the assumption that nine years of grueling military service and agonizing personal conflict can somehow be dismissed as essentially unimportant. This is all the more surprising since developmental psychologists often argue that young adulthood is a pivotal time in life, during which decisions determining ideological preference are frequently made.

Yet only Lina Heydrich—the very opposite of an unbiased social observer—saw his time in the navy as a turning point in the evolution of her husband's character. In her view, Heydrich was transformed from a "sensitive son of an artistic family" into a tough, disciplined man who had learned to hide his emotions and "think like a soldier": "You see, Frau Dougherty, I always look at things from the psychological point of view. First came the development of character, and that happened during navy time. Politics always comes later: it is a reaction to historical circumstances. It is what you have to do, or not do, every day in order to survive. But the foundation for this must lie in ideas about honor or courage or self-respect. That is character, and that comes first."

Frau Heydrich's opinions about Reinhard's naval experiences are particularly interesting since he himself rarely mentioned them. His SS colleagues soon learned to avoid the topic. A close associate (who was also a district judge, and writes like one) summarized all that the Nazis knew about it: "His relationship to the navy became, on account of his withdrawal, a purely negative thing, so that it was difficult in later times to discern his original attitude toward the career of a naval officer."

If we believe Frau Heydrich, however, his original attitude is one of the few things that are clear: he thought the navy was "wonderful"—until he actually became a member of it.

Even though Reinhard Heydrich grew up in landlocked Saxony, little bits of naval lore seem to have been strewn throughout his early life. An occasional visitor to Heydrich's parents' home was a man known in German history as the "sea devil," Felix Graf von Luckner, a celebrated hero of World War I for his exploits in command of the SMS *Sea Eagle*. And Heydrich and a school chum used to fantasize about running away to sea. Young Reinhard, however, wasn't supposed to search out a new pathway in life. He had been taking music lessons since he was five; he was supposed to inherit his father's music academy.

"Did your husband ever consider becoming a teacher of music?" I asked Frau Heydrich. When she answered, her voice was sad. "My mother-in-law would have liked very much to see my husband take over the conservatory. But it was just impossible at the time. By then the radio was discovered. And the people, instead of attending a conservatory and learning to play an instrument, they just turned on the radio, and didn't make house music anymore, *nicht wahr*?"

"Why do you think he decided to go into the navy?"

"He wanted to have order in his life. He wanted to eat dinner *every day* at seven in the evening!"

But how did Heydrich know what kind of order he wanted? Possibly the locale of Lina's own background and upbringing made her sympathetic to his joining the navy. Fehmarn, lying in the Baltic Sea between Denmark to the north and Germany to the south, has always been on the path of the Trans-Europe Express, and Lina Heydrich believed these geographical circumstances not only affected the character of the inhabitants but also made them superior in some way: "We have always lived on the frontier, and all such people have an entirely different attitude toward life from those who live in the center of a state. It is the same everywhere. We border inhabitants have always had something soldierly in us."

She thought this was one reason why Reinhard Heydrich found both herself and the navy attractive. Though he himself had come from landlocked Saxony, he had moved to the frontier, metaphorically, through his decision to join the navy.

I tried another approach, not quite accepting the equation between Lina's appeal and the navy's. "Perhaps the Freikorps were also an influence?" I suggested, referring to her husband's involvement following World War I in paramilitary volunteer units that had existed since the eighteenth century, and in the 1920s had resisted the Weimar Republic.

In attempting to explain her husband's motivations, Frau Heydrich had completely ignored the impact of the First World War. He was ten when it began in August 1914, and barely fifteen when the German government finally collapsed in the autumn of 1918.

If the war years had been difficult for his family, their aftermath was devastating. Amid the near anarchy of defeat, Communists attempted revolution in several provinces, including Saxony, where a workers' revolt was accompanied by intermittent flashes of bitter civil war. The conservatory had always drawn its students from the middle and upper classes, and the upwardly mobile Heydrichs had no use for radicalism. They supported the use of counter-revolutionary violence, including the vigilante right-wing murders of supposed leftists that continued after the uprising itself had been put down. They also joined the nationalistic German Volkspartei, or People's Party, a right-wing political party during the Weimar Republic.

Meanwhile, Reinhard had begun to play a minor role in some of the paramilitary groups springing up like poisonous mushrooms in the rank soil of civil unrest. Later, he claimed membership in the famous Freikorps Märcker, a unit formed by an anti-Semitic former World War I general, Georg Ludwig Rudolf Märcker, which had fought a fierce battle near Halle in March 1919. In fact, such a seasoned unit of battle-scarred war veterans would likely have had little use for an untried youth. A year later, however, Heydrich's entire class was conscripted into the new Halle Freikorps. By then, however, there was little to do aside from a bit of drilling in their free time.

Reinhard Heydrich's family later claimed he was not really interested in politics at that time, though he enjoyed the excitement of dressing up in a steel helmet to have his picture taken. Nevertheless, the boy had certainly been exposed to both violence and militant nationalism—and he had met them in the glamorous, swashbuckling form of "political soldiers" prepared to kill and to die for their cause.

Two childhood acquaintances remembered him as an ardent and probably anti-Semitic nationalist, and that is certainly how he later presented himself to the SS, claiming to have joined various rightist groups, including the "German Offensive and Defensive Alliance," a cluster of fanatics who blamed "alien" races for destroying Germany, and who sported a badge featuring a black swastika against a background of cornflower blue.

Since the end of the war, anti-Semitism had increased and was developing a virulent edge. The most famous leaders of the Communist uprising, Rosa Luxemburg and Karl Liebknecht, were Jewish. Moreover, many thousands of Polish Jews had fled into the liberal Weimar Republic from the collapsing tsarist empire to the east. For the first time, Germans were confronted by large numbers of poor, "foreign" Jews, many of whom didn't speak their language or know their customs.

The Jews made convenient scapegoats for the fear and rage felt by almost everyone as the German economy spun out of control. But it was really the punitive fiscal policies of the Allied victors, added to the severe disruptions of defeat and sudden social and political change, that caused Germany's troubles, in particular the runaway inflation so democratically sweeping away both humble savings accounts and great fortunes.

By 1922, the Halle Conservatory was on the brink of bankruptcy. In desperation, Bruno Heydrich wrote the authorities of Halle, begging for money. In the process, he also felt obliged to refute "the erroneous assumption . . . that the leader and founder is a Jew and has raked in a fortune with the school." On the contrary, Bruno argued, both he and his wife had put their own money into it, thus enriching the community.

The community fathers nevertheless rejected his plea, sending Bruno into a mood of despair from which he never really recovered. The conservatory, like its founder, continued to slide toward ruin, as both the quality of the teaching and the number of students declined.

It is against this background that young Reinhard Heydrich made his decision to join the German Navy. According to the mythologist Joseph Campbell, the donning of a military uniform signifies a drastic change of identity, and may even be considered a form of rebirth. More pragmatically, to do so offers the ideal second chance, the classic way of securing an honorable discharge from the difficulties of one's previous life.

"The Freikorps? Oh, no, no," Lina Heydrich exclaimed in reaction to speculation about one possible reason for her husband's joining the navy. "I have read that, but the Heydrich family went every summer to Swinemünde, to the baths. Swinemünde, today one would say that that was 'high society.'" (Surprisingly, these last two words emerged in English, though Frau Heydrich said she didn't know the language.) "The Heydrich family," she continued, "everyone, the nursemaids, the hangers-on, they went every year to Swinemünde. And that was when the children were still little. And every year in Swinemünde, there was a Kaiser parade, that is, a boat show when all the warships came, and it was a great sight. And my husband as a little boy, he obviously found that *wonderful*." Frau Heydrich laughed. "He was so little—it is understandable! But he was also yearning toward an ordered life. For a *feste Stellung*." She bore down heavily on the last words, which may be variously translated as a "fixed" or "secure" "position." "A *feste Stellung*, that is what he wanted!"

Given the consequences of this yearning, one is reminded of the ancient curse "May you get what you think you wish for!"

Once his decision was made, the seventeen-year-old boy had little trouble securing the agreement of his parents. Reinhard would be the first professional military man in the family, and to have "an officer in the house" was still regarded in the circles in which the Heydrichs moved as a sign of secure and exalted status. Unfortunately, it was also a great expense. Lina Heydrich explained: "You see, this was no lucrative career; it was more a position of honor. And to that belonged the assumption that there was a monetary foundation, a financial cushion. But my husband didn't have that. That was all lost."

Still, Heydrich's mother realized that an officer's career made a promising investment. After serving ten years, he would be entitled to a substantial pension. And there was always the possibility he would meet the "right" sort of people, particularly the right sort of woman—one with money. As the woman who finally did become his wife imagined Elisabeth's point of view: "Her son would surely make a so-called good match, no? A Leutnant zur See [lieutenant at sea]! One might get a millionaire's daughter with that!"

We are less certain what Heydrich's father, unwell and preoccupied with the collapse of the family's fortunes, thought of his son's decision, but we know that he gave the young man a fine violin as a farewell gift.

Young Reinhard took this instrument with him when he reported for

Heydrich (here in 1924), at the time of his 1922 enlistment, entered a German Navy that was still operating under restrictions imposed by the Treaty of Versailles, including a prohibition against the building of submarines.

training on board the battleship *Braunschweig*. Metaphorically speaking, the violin was only one of three inappropriate pieces of baggage he took on board that day, the first of three things that led to disastrous consequences.

A violin, on board a ship? As the Heydrich biographer G. S. Graber has commented, if Heydrich had brought an accordion or a banjo, this would have been in keeping with naval tradition, and "would have been assets at any dormitory party." But the flagrantly "artistic" violin was merely a sign of how little was known in his parents' high-culture household of actual military lore. Lina knew better, having herself descended from a family of seafarers, and having grown up on an island most of whose citizens made their living from the sea. As she commented, "A violin, on a warship? Surely, there had *never* been a cadet in the navy who came onto a warship with a violin!"

Lina described the atmosphere within which Heydrich's early naval training occurred: "I know, certainly, various crew comrades who laughed at Reinhard because he played the violin. You see, there always exists certain types who can get their diplomas without trouble and yet remain spiritually primitive. And so one cannot say that all *Jahrgänge* [loosely translated, "peers"] of the navy who in 1922 were sent to be broken in, that they were similar people. They came out of various milieus, *nicht wahr*?

"And in the navy, they had to be, so to say, towed off one by one and then built into a homogeneous mass. But when my husband came along with his violin there was certainly no homogeneous sameness then. There were people there whose parents were farmers or artisans, and they had an entirely different educational development and an entirely different childhood atmosphere, and they *naturally* had to reject my husband, because he was an exception. He was an exception from the start."

Lina Heydrich may have been playing an old and easy tune—one that insists a person who does not succeed at something never had a chance in the first place. Yet it is certainly true that her husband had some bad luck at the outset, when he was assigned to the second of two types of training squad. The first was commanded by an "elite" drillmaster, but Heydrich's unit was the result of an innovative experiment in which future officers and regular crew members were mingled indiscriminately.

Before the war, an aspiring officer would not have had to fraternize with the sons of farmers and artisans. At that time, the navy was rigidly stratified, and battleships were like huge, floating factories with underpaid, underfed crews serving groups of officers from wealthy families who were themselves divided into rigid hierarchies. In 1918, German sailors at Kiel had mutinied rather than obey their officers' efforts to launch one last, hopeless attack against the English fleet. The rebellious sailors were soon joined in other cities by workers' soviets, touching off a year of revolutionary violence.

Once peace was restored, the new Weimar democracy launched a program of naval reform designed to lessen class conflict in the existing training regimen. But most of the old ways—and ways of thinking—were not abandoned.

Thus, it was not only in relation to the lower classes that young Reinhard Heydrich was "different." In her memoir, Frau Heydrich contrasted his background with that of the children of the great bourgeois families who still made up the bulk of the officer class: "For them there had been no fears about the success of [their] performances . . . probably for most of them, none of the financial risks bound up with these things." The result of this disparity, she says in her laconic, elliptical writing style—so different from the way she talked—was that "it became difficult for Reinhard to enter into this circle."

That's one way to put it. Another might be to say that the youthful Heydrich became involved in a situation that is every adolescent's nightmare. Far from taking to the navy like a duck to water, he was hardly on board before he began to be singled out as the ugly duckling among a bevy of relentlessly pecking swans.

In 1964, the Israeli historian Shlomo Aronson obtained written statements from four naval officers who served in the same crew as Heydrich—almost the only evidence about this period that does not come from his family or acquaintances. All four agreed on one thing: they didn't like Reinhard Heydrich, and no one else did either. He was, according to Captain Heinrich Beucke, "the only one out of the entire class of new recruits not to have a friend."

Why not? First, there was the way he looked. However imposing Heydrich may have appeared later in his tailor-made SS uniform, at eighteen he cut a very different figure. Aronson's respondents remember his physical appearance with a remarkable, almost obsessive, grasp of detail. Beucke's statement illustrates the general tone:

The exterior of Heydrich is best described as a peculiar disharmony. His limbs somehow did not match. A long neck, a much too small head with short blond hair, a long nose, mostly pinched and mistrusting eyes, and a small mouth with pouting lips, always pinched. A long upper part of the body with especially long ape-like arms on a low and wide pelvis . . . gangling, somehow womanly and effeminate.

It did not help that Heydrich still had a high-pitched voice, which went oddly with his tall, lanky frame. (His laughter reminded his comrades of the bleating of a goat.) At that time, he did not smoke or drink, and this, too, was regarded as unusual.

And then, of course, there was the violin.

As he had since childhood, Heydrich turned to it for consolation. Lina Heydrich said that "everything that he found strange, that he rejected, but also everything that he loved, that he longed for, that he could not say to any person, he confided to his violin. It was his best comrade, as he called it; many times, it was his only friend."

Nevertheless, one would think he must have been at times very, very tempted to throw his friend overboard. A warship offers no real privacy. Heydrich's other comrades soon discovered what he was doing, and began to tease him about it.

One of them reports that "on certain occasions" Heydrich used to play the same Italian serenade again and again on his violin, and he describes a lampoon in the ship's newspaper that ended with the lines "to musical glory was opened the road for a bleating goat." The nature of the "occasions" at which Heydrich played is not mentioned, but these were usually instigated by one of his drill instructors, a Pole from West Prussia. He was a small, plump, stocky man, who liked to bully the recruits. He particularly enjoyed the "test of courage," in which participants had to kneel, arms folded behind their back, then fall straight forward. The fat little instructor fell on his stomach, but the skinny young recruits slammed down hard, on their faces.

At night, the drill sergeant liked to have a drink or two. Then, he would often feel overcome by a desire for music and would have Heydrich roused from bed, ordering him to play "something sentimental" on his violin. A particular favorite was the Serenade by Enrico Toselli. Night after night Heydrich played this and other songs until he was dismissed with the remark, "You have given me peace."

What treatment like this gave to the future deputy chief of the Gestapo is not clearly known, but Lina said that after leaving the navy, he never played the Toselli Serenade again—and turned it off whenever it was played on the radio. As a result of his experience with the drill sergeant, Heydrich also took "an informed interest" in the "little, fat, round-headed racial types of the East."

For a man later legendary for aggressive dynamism, however, his response at the time seems almost bafflingly passive. As one moves onward from the violin, one comes to the second unacceptable piece of "baggage" Heydrich brought on board—his methods of dealing with conflict. Initially, he relied on the strategies of his childhood: when people attacked him, he got angry, and if that didn't work, he withdrew into the defensive defiance of the loner. But this type of personal style was ill-adapted to a society where men were valued as much for their ability to work in teams as for their technical skills.

Nor did it help that Heydrich's abilities at that time were undistinguished. His grades were mediocre, and, except in swimming, his athletic performance was clumsy. Whenever he made a mistake, his peers marked the occasion by bleating like goats in imitation of his laugh. Such malign attention could hardly have enhanced his confidence in public, but it did seem to strengthen his private resolve. Refusing to give up, he practiced alone the fencing, riding, shooting, swimming, and sailing that would one day impress his SS comrades.

He did not talk much about politics, though, not even after the assassination in 1922 of Walter Rathenau, one of the most able foreign ministers in the short history of the Weimar Republic; and not even when it was discovered that a member of his naval squad had driven the car carrying the murderers.

According to Captain Hans Rehm, another of Heydrich's fellow cadets, Heydrich showed "no inner sympathy" when his bunkmates exulted in this event. (They were not the only ones: an early Nazi song contained a refrain roughly translated as "Let's shoot down Walter Rathenau, the God-damned Jewish pig!")

Rehm recalled Heydrich "squabbling" with members of the extreme right and said that he himself, "taking his background and education into consideration, would have classified Heydrich as a liberal."

No matter how one classifies him, however, it is clear that Heydrich was a misfit. "Somehow, he was different," according to Captain Hans Heinrich Lebram, another fellow cadet, who thought his attitude timid and defensive.

Things would have gone far better if Heydrich had behaved like his future mentor Admiral Wilhelm Canaris, who was also teased during his training period seventeen years earlier, but reacted with disarming tolerance and wry humor. Heydrich, however, seems to have become involved in what sociologists call a "reaction process." In this situation, an irritating action by one party to a conflict causes the other to sharpen his response, which then inspires the first party to do the same—and on and on in an escalating spiral that usually ends in some sort of blowup.

In her memoir, Lina Heydrich provided a glimpse of the way the process worked. Her husband apparently told her a great deal about Captain Rehm: "Whenever he ran into Reinhard, he teased and insulted him. For Reinhard, there remained nothing else to do than to act as if he didn't see him, which, however, was generally considered to be arrogance on his part." His mates reacted to the "arrogance," turning the spiral another round.

Once begun, such a reaction process is very difficult to stop. Perception of the nuances of individual behavior becomes distorted: people see only what they are looking for and respond accordingly. Of course, another interpretation is irresistible. Instead of a "reaction process," the behavior of Rehm et al. might have been a response to perceiving little flashes of the demonic they were glimpsing in Heydrich, as if they were somehow divining intimations of his monstrous future.

But according to the Israeli historian Aronson's documents, Heydrich's mates observed in him no trace of unusual interests or attributes aside from music. They saw no devilish hatred or spite—quite the opposite, in fact. One man thought Heydrich tried to be friendly, but was often envious and awkward instead—"but not malicious." Another noted he could be frank, magnanimous, and cooperative, and was "eager to be a good comrade . . . but one could feel that he was not a part of us."

They saw a man who could be vain, sarcastic, and quarrelsome, who gave up if he was not assured of victory, who was a bad loser in an era when it was said of military officers that they did "not need intelligence, but character."

They also saw in him a Jew.

A person has the option not to exercise a talent for the violin. One can also change one's ways of coping with the world. But one cannot alter one's ethnic identity. Race is what sociologists call an "ascriptive trait": one is categorized according to the group into which one is born, and talent and behavior have nothing to do with it. The opposite of ascription, in sociological parlance, is "achievement."

Heydrich's third mistake was to think that by leaving Saxony far behind he could achieve a "secure position" based on achievement alone. In this naive hope, he was very much like his father, and he achieved similar results. Aboard ship was a crew member from Halle who said Heydrich's name had once been Süss. According to Heydrich's roommate Captain Beucke, "Everyone more or less took Heydrich for a Jew." Though Captain Rehm hastened to add that he didn't care whether "one of us was Jewish or not," he betrayed a very different outlook: "I kept away from Heydrich right from the start just instinctively." Then, an incident occurred which he considered "decisive."

Heydrich had gone home to Halle on leave and had been out strolling with a young woman when they met an acquaintance described by Rehm merely as "a student." This "student" jeered, "Look here, Itzig

Süss in a navy uniform!" When Heydrich returned to his ship, he was still concerned enough about the incident to mention it to Rehm, who, in turn, was concerned about Heydrich's response:

> I asked Heydrich about his reaction, and in a rather meek way he said, "What could I do?" That was sufficient reason for me to tell him that this meant a forfeiture of his honor. I cut all my contact with him, never spoke a word to him, and reported, too, my decision to my comrades. As they did not approve of Heydrich anyway, they joined me in my conduct, and for days and weeks he was for us "null and void."
>
> It was an accident that the situation came out into the open: Heydrich was under medical orders to stay in his room [because he was not feeling well]. The officer in charge, looking into his room, asked whether he had already received his food. Heydrich answered, "No." And, when asked whether his comrades did not, out of comradeship, bring in his food, Heydrich answered in the negative, adding verbatim, "They have not spoken a word to me for some time."
>
> The division commander stepped in and handled the situation by himself. There were long and repeated confrontations involving both sides, resulting in an order of the commander that we should settle the affair amicably. At first, I refused to comply, but as the commander threatened that he and I would have to draw the conclusions from a refusal by me I preferred to shake hands with Heydrich than to be cashiered from the service.

One needs to hear this story in Rehm's words to get the flavor of the cool, arrogant ruthlessness of his behavior. Like the youthful Heydrich, he too seems to have longed for a "secure position": a man who had forfeited his honor by refusing to fight a duel to prove he was not a Jew might just as well not exist. Small wonder that Heydrich had fallen ill.

The amazing thing was Heydrich's initial decision to bare his soul to a "comrade" like Rehm. What a spectacular error of judgment for a man whose "fingertip instincts" were to become the envy of his SS subordinates. Heydrich was also to be widely admired for the "lightning speed" of his response to events. This combination of psychological acumen and swift action later became the very essence of Heydrich's leadership style, but if he displayed such qualities during his naval career, there is no record of them. Ridiculed for playing the violin, derided if he made a misstep, teased if he got angry, unable even to laugh without reminding people of a goat, the young cadet might have become so tightly wedged within a constricting box of negative possibilities that he became almost paralyzed.

Nevertheless, Captain Rehm inadvertently provides evidence of a turning point in Heydrich's behavior, a reaction—not very swift, to be sure—to their fateful dispute about the duel.

After a reconciliation ceremony, Heydrich asked to talk with Rehm about his father's origins, having first extracted a pledge of secrecy. He told Rehm a story blending pure fantasy with the actual details of his father Bruno's youth. It seems Bruno had first appeared in Dresden when he was still a small boy, traveling with a band of Romani musicians heading north through Hungary and Bohemia. He played the fiddle for the Romanis, and was thought to be "an infant prodigy." His extraordinary talent so impressed the director of the Dresden Conservatory (Herr Eugen Kranz) that he adopted the lad, who later married his daughter and established his own conservatory in Halle.

Having found his way back to reality, Heydrich ended with an anguish also painfully real: "This is the path through life of my father, and now you will understand why I could do nothing when they insulted me by calling me a Jew-boy. How could I stand up for my father without any counter-evidence?"

Learning of this tale, one begins to see why Heydrich had avoided both fights on the playground and duels on a playing field where his fencing skill might have brought victory: he wasn't sure what the truth was. He had no "counter-evidence."

After the war, the social scientist John M. Steiner interviewed some (unnamed) members of Heydrich's family, who also seemed uncertain of the facts and "did not exclude the possibility" that he might have been partially Jewish. Neither did Peter Thomas Heydrich, son of Heydrich's brother, Heinz, when I spoke with him in October 1993: "All the stories that have been told—such as that my great-grandfather was Jewish—to this day there is not the slightest proof . . . We know that the great-grandfather wasn't. That we know. But for the great-grandmother, the one who had borne Bruno and all the children, there is no documentation . . . No one knows for sure."

How often have imaginative children dreamed of being kidnapped?

Lina said Reinhard's sister, Mausi, pictured here circa 1930, "was very dumb. She looked good, though." As a rule, Nazi life dictated that women appear plain, as traditional German peasants.

Heydrich's version of this fantasy, which so magically disposes of his father's troubled antecedents, doesn't seem very sophisticated, even for a designed effort. The really extraordinary thing is that Rehm seems to have believed it.

But then, he had his reasons. Speculating that Heydrich's "various and contradicting characteristics" might be explained if he were "a possible mixture of Hungarian, Romani, and Jewish blood," he concluded, "I, for my part, could not see . . . a 'pure Aryan,' in spite of his blue eyes, blond hair, and his impressive figure."

As a method of clearing his name, Heydrich's little fairy tale foundered on the rocks of Rehm's racism. But as instruction in the relative merits of the truth versus the Big Lie, it may have taught a different lesson: How hard it is, always, to deal with people's "various and contradicting characteristics." How much easier to find a simple explanation and simply stick to it.

In later years, Heydrich was to tell his subordinates, "Truth is for children."

Heydrich remained in the navy for several years after the incident described by Rehm. The two men spoke only when it was absolutely necessary, and in Lina Heydrich's euphemistic phrase, his contact with the rest of the crew also remained, for a long time at least, "only formally comrade-like, cool."

Several times I asked Frau Heydrich how he could have borne to remain in the navy under such difficult conditions. "He loved the navy, in spite of everything," she sometimes said.

"But what was there to love? If his comrades behaved so badly, how could he—?"

"Don't you understand?" Lina Heydrich said one day. "He would never quit. Never! Everything he did, he always did right down to the last consequence!"

Despite his reputation as a bad sport, Heydrich did not usually give up when he was losing. Certainly, in his later career he rarely turned away from any sort of conflict or difficult enterprise, even when prudence suggested it. Sometimes, indeed, Himmler felt obliged to intervene to prevent him from antagonizing a political colleague.

And so Heydrich persisted, seeking out (in Beucke's phrase) "any kind of achievement that helped to fortify his personality." He bought a motorcycle and, characteristically alone, went off in search of other fields to conquer.

Yet his first conquest came almost by accident, one of those chance meetings behind which imaginative folk can hear the creaking machinery of fate. In 1923, Heydrich and the crew with which he was locked in desperate adolescent combat were assigned to a new training ship, the *Berlin*. And in July 1923, a famous hero of the First World War, Lieutenant Commander Wilhelm Canaris, was also transferred there as chief officer.

Canaris, like Heydrich, was not happy aboard the *Berlin*. His exploits as a spy and daring organizer of U-boat warfare had made headlines a few years earlier, but now, ill health and right-wing political adventurism had combined to dim both his career star and his enthusiasm for the service. "All that occasionally cheered him," writes Heinz Höhne, author of books on both Canaris and the history of the SS, "were the civil, almost servile attentions of a lanky cadet whose personal appearance became indelibly imprinted on his mind and was to haunt him like a nightmare in years to come."

Höhne is referring to Heydrich, and the uncharacteristically florid tone of this passage reflects the baffled fascination with which historians greet one of the most peculiar relationships in the history of espionage.

It would be naive to claim that Canaris—future chief of military intelligence for the Wehrmacht and hero of the German resistance—and Heydrich—future chief of political intelligence for the Nazi Party, and major war criminal—were friends. But it is also too simple to say

Wilhelm Canaris (left, age seventeen, circa 1905, at the time he joined the German Imperial Navy; right, circa 1915), the future head of German military intelligence, first became acquainted with the young Heydrich aboard the latter's training ship, the *Berlin*.

that they were not. In any case, it seems clear that at the beginning, the two men simply enjoyed each other's company.

For commanders of cruisers to invite lowly cadets into their homes for any but the most ritualized of social occasions was not customary, but Canaris was not a conventional man. He was also not very interested in conventional social life; like Heydrich, he is always described as a loner. While Heydrich fled to his violin for companionship, Canaris turned to a more common form of "best friend," lavishing affection on a series of pet dachshunds, and frequently remarking how much more trustworthy they were than people.

Perhaps not surprisingly, Canaris's marriage was not a happy one. His young wife, Erika, was a cultivated woman who disliked the intrigue, psychological speculation, and derring-do on which Canaris had always thrived. She was a talented musician, and liked to organize little evenings of chamber music. As luck would have it, she needed a second violin for a string quartet; Canaris invited Heydrich over to audition for the role. He succeeded in impressing Erika with his musical skills and Canaris with something else, though no one knows exactly what. (Canaris was certainly no lover of music: "Music is just something for musicians, I suppose," he used to say.) Perhaps what impressed him was Heydrich's sheer admiration of him. Canaris's real-life experiences were the sorts of things Heydrich had dreamed of as a boy. The older man probably told him stories of espionage and adventure; certainly he offered him the only words of welcome he had yet received from a man in naval uniform. Soon Heydrich was invited back, and of course accepted the invitations, forging a bond he could hardly have guessed would last for the rest of his life.

His former comrades did not mention this in their statements, and one can only guess what additional yeast his visits to their commander's home added to the already simmering brew of mutual animosity and resentment.

In any case, Canaris soon left the *Berlin*, and Heydrich moved on, gradually making new acquaintances among groups described by Aronson as "music-making intellectuals." By 1926 Heydrich was well enough established in these circles for his peers to notice that he was invited to other officers' homes and treated well there.

A young economics student who met Heydrich on one of these occasions recalled that at first, he seemed conventionally shallow, talking only about sports or his naval duties. When he spoke of music, however, "he changed completely." Then, when the musical interludes ended, he changed back, once more becoming a "polite, amiable, and somehow uncommunicative naval officer."

That Heydrich should transform himself according to the company and the type of activity with which he was engaged is not really surprising, for he had shown the beginnings of this chameleon-like quality in his childhood visits to his friend in the country. "The unpredictable Heydrich," his SS colleagues would call him, describing how they tried to keep up with each manifestation of his multifaceted interests and character. In the navy, as afterward, music was only one of an ever-expanding array of identity-affirming pastimes. Heydrich also continued the more soldierly activity of sport, doggedly "working on himself" as he was later to exhort others to do. He practiced and he practiced and he practiced—swimming, fencing, shooting, sailing, riding, running. Finally, his zeal began to pay off.

Lina Heydrich said that her future husband became German Baltic sailing champion (in the twelve-foot dinghy class) in 1927, and in 1928, also North Sea champion. Indeed, he did so well that the navy sent him to their special sports training school. His erstwhile comrades made no mention of these things, but they did acknowledge that by 1928, he was competing in the naval pentathlon competitions. They said that he placed third in a field of five, and, finding this unsatisfactory, he blamed the referee.

In 1927, Heydrich participated in the Second German Officers' Fencing Tournament in Dresden. His fencing instructor described him as "very good and enthusiastic," but added that he failed to distinguish himself at the tournament: not only did Heydrich lose; he also displayed "lack of self-control" afterward, furiously hurling his rapier to the ground.

In Captain Beucke's opinion, Heydrich overestimated his abilities, was already dreaming of the Olympics, "and was not shy at all in telling us about his performances."

In fact, the formerly reclusive and sullenly shy young man was beginning to reveal qualities later observers would also note. "There is no doubt," said Beucke (who had replaced Rehm as Heydrich's roommate), "that ambition was his characteristic peculiarity . . . On all occasions, he wanted to be outstanding—in the service, in front of his superiors, with the comrades, in sportsmanship, and in bars . . . He is, or he will be, good at everything."

Obviously, Heydrich had not abandoned his parents' reliance on achievement, though he never managed to pursue it with his father's cheerful insouciance. It seemed to one observer that he was convinced "everybody wanted to get him" and set "traps" for him.

We have seen that wariness of traps was an old Saxon habit. It is also, of course, a sign of paranoia—depending on whether the traps are real or only in one's imagination. As the adage has it, real paranoids may also have real enemies.

Heydrich certainly had them in the navy, and it is hard to know what precise degree of mistrust is appropriate in a situation in which comrades wait expectantly for a chance to deride your failures and some of them are perfectly willing to let you starve. Clearly, Heydrich had been more open and trusting of his colleagues at the beginning than he was at the end. After he was promoted to junior officer status he was cold, arrogant, and often insulting to his subordinates, probably, Lebram speculated, because he didn't think he would succeed otherwise.

Yet despite all this, Heydrich's relationships with his shipmates improved during the last part of his service in the navy. "Heydrich changed tremendously," Beucke said. He was beginning to develop some of his father's charm and social self-confidence. Now he sometimes told jokes and sang songs, accompanying himself on the lute (not the violin). Apparently, he was also growing better looking, having lost the stumbling awkwardness of his youth. Certainly, he did not lack feminine companionship.

(He later told his wife that he felt at this stage in his career he had become at least "partially recognized." "I had made my way," he said, and then added, "or perhaps I had just gotten used to it at last.")

In 1928, Heydrich was promoted to first lieutenant—the last hurdle in the training process—and was posted to Kiel as a signals officer. Even before that, he had begun to receive favorable reports from his organizational superiors. One of them, Vice Admiral Gustav Kleikamp, praised his performance as above average, despite the fact that, "convinced of his own abilities, he has always been anxious to put forward his own views." And, Kleikamp added, "without doubt this favorable report will be endorsed by many later superior officers."

Of course, this did not happen. A few years later, Admiral Kleikamp was a member of the court of honor that decreed Heydrich's departure from the navy. In his terse life history prepared for the SS, Heydrich correctly said that he had been "dismissed from the service for nonservice reasons."

It was thus not his professional performance or his personal relations aboard ship that caused his final confrontation with the men of the Kriegsmarine. The immediate cause was a woman (or, rather, two women). The ultimate causes are still being debated. It is clear, however, that Reinhard Heydrich had not quite "gotten used to" the way the navy did things, after all.

4

THE HONOR OF A WOMAN

"What really is love? I believe that the best thing is when one really doesn't know it at all. When everything becomes precisely known, then it becomes dreadfully boring."

—LINA HEYDRICH

O**N DECEMBER** 6, 1930, Reinhard Eugen Tristan Heydrich met Lina Mathilde von Osten at a ball in Kiel. He was twenty-six years old; she—born on June 14, 1911—was nineteen.

An early biographer wrote that they came together in cold northern waters, when her rowboat overturned and he dived in to rescue her. But Lina Heydrich rejected this romantic fantasy, insisting they met more traditionally at a dance. Neither had come alone. Heydrich was with a naval comrade named von Manstein; Lina was part of a delegation from her school, which had just joined the sailing club sponsoring the ball. She agreed to come only to keep a rendezvous with a young beau from Fehmarn. He was a farmer, not a sailor, and at the last minute had to stay home "with his pigs and hens," as Lina later put it.

Arriving at the dance, she saw at a glance that most of the other women were students from a different school, and older besides. Her group remained on the sidelines: Lina and a friend, feeling shy and bored, had just decided to leave when a tall blond man and a short dark one came over and introduced themselves. They were Heydrich and von Manstein.

At first Lina busied herself by silently trying to place von Manstein's name. But it was Heydrich who asked her to dance, bowing stiffly, and speaking tersely in the military style of the time. After dancing, the two naval officers maneuvered the girls to their table; and after that, Heydrich accompanied Lina back to her school.

Three days later, on the 9th of December, Reinhard Heydrich and Lina von Osten became engaged. The date can also be taken as marking the effective end of his naval career. For, unfortunately, it was not the first time Heydrich had met a woman at a ball, or even the first time he had gotten in trouble for doing so. While not exactly a ladies' man, he had an interest in the sexual charms of the opposite sex that may fairly be described as insistent, consistent, and intense.

For Heydrich, as with political leaders in other times and places, self-assertion in the halls of influence and in the intimacy of the bedroom seemed a natural coupling, reflecting a desire to triumph everywhere. According to his former subordinate Werner Best, Heydrich often took time off from the pursuit of personal power to investigate various blond beauties. "In that sphere too," Best added, "he was a conqueror."

Bruno Heydrich had also had his share of amorous escapades, but these seem to have been regarded with some tolerance and amusement, even by his family, as an inevitable aspect of his freewheeling style. This is not the way his son's sexual liaisons are usually presented, however. Like Best, various people recounting Heydrich's peccadilloes tend to want to illustrate a thesis.

For example, his sister-in-law, Gertrude Heydrich, the wife of his younger brother, Heinz, said he behaved arrogantly with social inferiors and added that he used to instruct Heinz on how to take advantage of the maids serving in their house. Heydrich's naval nemesis, Hans Rehm, also expressed the feeling that he was overly interested in females of a lesser class, in "local women" and brothels. Though Heydrich moved gracefully enough through upper bourgeois salons, impressing "elderly ladies especially" with his good manners and knowledge of music, his relationships with women of his own age and class were more problematic.

The public arena of the dance floor, with its elaborate rules of behavior, seems to have brought out a maladaptive, aggressive streak in Reinhard Heydrich. The same man who could perform with perfect politeness in small groups was often undone by this larger-scale setting of music and social demands.

In 1926, when his training ship stopped at the Portuguese island of Madeira on its spring cruise, a group of English officers asked some of the German ensigns, Heydrich included, to a party. After welcoming their guests, the English hosts made no particular effort to make them feel at home. Though the band was playing, no one had yet gotten up to dance. Brushing aside the admonitions of his fellow officers, Heydrich asked an English woman to join him in a turn around the floor.

On the same training cruise in 1926, he was invited to another social gathering, this time sponsored by the German club of Barcelona. There he was correctly introduced to a young lady from a prominent family. He invited her for a walk in the gardens of the club, where he apparently made improper advances. She slapped his face, and then complained to the naval authorities, who forced him to apologize.

On this occasion, it was Heydrich who felt embarrassed. He turned to Captain Hans Heinrich Lebram for advice in handling the situation, just as he had earlier consulted Rehm in the matter of the duel. He seems to have felt some need to correct offensive behavior. Or perhaps merely to justify it: when Lebram told him, "Serves you right," Heydrich left in a rage.

But he may have learned something after all. Later in his naval career he had begun to moderate his abrasiveness. When he met Lina von Osten, Heydrich had been in the Kriegsmarine for eight and a half years. After all, a professional officer in a society still infatuated with militaristic values, Reinhard Heydrich was something of a "catch."

Indeed, he was well on his way to justifying his mother's hopes of a good marriage, having established a close relationship with the daughter of an influential friend of the commander in chief of the navy, Admiral Erich Raeder.

Lina von Osten, on the other hand, was just a schoolgirl away from her impoverished family for the first time, enrolled in a course in commerce that might someday enable her to teach the same subject. She was not a good catch for anyone but a rural Fehmarn lad, free to respond to her cheerful vitality, creamy blond coloring, and electric blue eyes.

In her conversations with me, Lina was rarely forthcoming about her family's background. In her short autobiography, written for a German readership, Lina did give a few particulars of the family genealogy: her father, Jürgen von Osten, was the second son of a North German gentleman farmer who had, in all, six sons and two daughters. As a youth, Jürgen had hoped to take over the family homestead but had to yield this right to his elder brother. Eventually, he became a schoolteacher and moved to Fehmarn, where he met Lina's mother. In sharp contrast to Reinhard Heydrich's father, Jürgen sprang from the nobility (the "von" indicates aristocratic connections), and should have been more secure about his place in the scheme of things. Yet he was as deeply concerned about the "identity" of Fehmarn as if it had not already been part of Germany for forty-five years before his daughter's birth. "He was a real *hater* of Denmark," she recalled. "Outspokenly anti-Dane."

Lina's mother's birth name was Hiss, and she came from an island stock of merchants and seafarers who had lived there for centuries. Like Heydrich's mother, Frau von Osten came from a propertied family. One of her brothers went prospecting in California in the nineteenth century (returning home with a ring of his own gold); another did very well in the coal business.

This is not what Lina chose to emphasize in her conversations with me, however. Her mother had nine sisters, and it is the good times they all had together that seem to have appealed to her most. As a child, she thought it great fun to imitate the various mannerisms of her aunts and to tell amusing stories about them to her schoolmates.

Lina often told me there were no secrets on Fehmarn. Homogenous, intimate, and isolated, it served as her lifelong point of reference and place of refuge. It is worlds away from Halle, where Reinhard Heydrich grew up with no refuge but music, and no reference point aside from ambition and the sort of rootless cosmopolitanism that was soon to go radically out of style.

Even in her published book, though, Lina provided very few anecdotes about her family—except for her father's remark on the day she was born (with neither doctor nor midwife in attendance): "She has come into the world without help, and she will also make her way through the world without help."

In fact, when Lina talked to me about her childhood, she treated poverty as a shared condition of life rather than the devastating personal loss it appeared to Heydrich's family. When she spoke of "us" and "we," the reference was to the whole community. She said "nobody" had any money, and described a woman who had to live with her husband in a henhouse in someone's backyard. "And these were *educated people!*"

There is a tincture of negativity that clings to almost everything she said about her father, as if he were linked in her mind with experiences of adversity. The first thing she told me about him was that he had "lost" not only his own inheritance but also his wife's, in vain efforts to purchase a homestead.

The economic collapse that destroyed so many German fortunes at the end of the First World War wrecked his hopes, and left the family destitute. Lina's brother was reduced to carrying his lunch to school not in a metal box or a basket, but in a wooden pail, a gift from a "peasant." The other children jeered at him, shouting, "Here he comes again with his commode!" Meanwhile, Lina had to wear her brother's shoes. "I was always wearing shoes several sizes too large!" she said, laughing.

Laughing at adversity is a quality Frau Heydrich seems to have admired deeply, but she didn't learn it from her father. Instead, he counseled her not to take risks, to be cautious and "respectable," to hold back.

"Could you turn to your mother?" I asked. "Did she give you advice?"

"Of course, my mother couldn't give me political advice, but she could be supportive in a way not dependent on external realities, but rather, how one *basically* behaves."

The best example of what she meant by basic advice occurred when Lina was seventeen, and wanted to go away to business school. Her father did not approve: "Better that I should have stayed on Fehmarn and married a farmer!"

At this point, Frau von Osten intervened with a compromise: Her daughter should spend one more year at home, learning to cook the local island dishes. "It was the only *lasting* investment I ever made," she wrote in her memoirs (somewhat cryptically, given that she did not mention the many years she ran a pension, preparing the food herself).

Yet from the moment they met, Reinhard Heydrich treated Lina differently from his other female friends—with respect. She was immediately impressed by his good manners, military bearing, and combination of self-assurance and self-restraint. "I felt sympathy for this ambitious yet reserved man," she wrote. "I wanted to get to know him better."

Heydrich obviously felt the same way: after accompanying her to the door of her genteel boarding house, he asked to see her again, thus beginning a very proper—though also very fleet-footed—courtship.

The next day they wandered together through Hohenzollern Park, in the center of Kiel,* "groping toward one another," as Lina later

* Now Schrevenpark.

described it. He told her about his family, revealing a deep affection for his mother. "It seems to me he wants to unfold his whole life to me," Lina later wrote in a breathless first-person reminiscence: "There is nothing of flirtation, of a wish to please, of desire, or certainly, of lust. It is an entirely simple, plain process of making oneself known, with much warmth, much trust."

She remembered his behaving "not as a lover, but as a comrade, as a friend—and that is really much more . . . When I come back home, I am not the same person anymore. I have encountered something wonderful, and it has changed me."

This account was written forty-five years after the fact. Interviewing Lina in person, beyond the confines of written autobiography, I expected a more ambivalent, tempered view of a man now regarded as despicable. (After all, even Magda Goebbels, so devoted that she joined her husband in a family suicide that also included their six children, had nevertheless expressed frequent doubts about Joseph Goebbels's behavior and beliefs.)

When I asked about her initial impression of Reinhard, the question didn't seem to interest her. She sat silently, gazing out of the window.

"I suppose he was very good-looking," I prompted her.

She shrugged. "Oh, I don't know about that."

"What was it about Herr Heydrich that first appealed to you?" I asked, trying to bridge the gulf that had opened between us.

"Yes . . . if one knew that exactly . . . ," she replied in a more interested tone. "What in a man really impresses a woman? Basically, it is either that a woman loves a man because she dominates him or because she is ruled by him, and can rely on him, no?

"And that last was probably it. He always knew exactly what he wanted . . . But finally, what really is love? I believe that the best thing is when one really doesn't know at all. When everything becomes precisely known, then it also becomes dreadfully boring."

The whirlwind courtship of Lina and Reinhard must have been the very opposite of boring. It contained all the proper moves, but drastically speeded up, like a minuet forced into the tempo of a quick march.

After the walk in the park, the next evening the pair went to the theater, the second step in the local ritual of wooing. For the occasion, Heydrich wore his full naval uniform, including ceremonial cape, and Lina arranged to get a front door key to her rooming house. To stay out after the doors were locked required a special interview with the housemother, a Fräulein Pommerenk. "I must have the key, it is terribly important!" Lina told the Fräulein, who thereupon agreed to let her keep it all night. Lina replied that she didn't need it that long; she was only going to the theater.

Afterward, they continued on to the next step in the hallowed courtship process—a visit to that very Germanic institution, a *Weinstube* (tavern). These are usually cozy, informal places, where one comes to talk as much as drink. Young female students were not accustomed to visiting such places, but her older escort treated her protectively, turning the visit into a special occasion. They sat in a corner, she remembered, and having had two days of excited conversation, now didn't talk much. In fact, Lina had the leisure to ask herself questions like, "Who am I really," and to reach the unhappy conclusion that she was just a schoolgirl—"and otherwise nothing."

She thought a sophisticated military officer must surely find her boring. In his presence, she was struck dumb, but why was he so quiet? she wondered.

As it turned out, Reinhard Heydrich was making the decision that would wreck his naval career. Finally, and "very quietly," he said, "Will you be my wife?"

Another silence followed. Lina realized Reinhard knew nothing about her father's background—or her family's poverty. She insisted on telling him all about her parents before she said yes. That moment seems to have been almost the first time she told him anything.

"This engagement happened so quickly, no?" I said on my third trip to Fehmarn, in 1980. This time I had brought along a translator, an American professor of political science who also happened to be a good friend and professional colleague—and a man. (Lina had told me several times that she really preferred the "tension" of talking to men.)

"The engagement went fast, yes! Quickly or not at all!" she replied, breaking into delighted laughter.

"How many days?" I asked. "Only four?"

"Three days."

"We have an expression: love at first sight."

"No, it was not love at first sight; it was simply fate."

"What is the difference?"

"You can't be truly in love with a man at once because you can't get beyond the externals at first. And a man proceeds the same way with a woman. A man can be infatuated on the first view of the woman. That's how it normally goes. And then, much, much later the man arrives at the interior. And much, much later he learns about the woman who at the first moment he had viewed so enthusiastically. That is *entirely* different, no?"

She began to chuckle, a warm earthy bubbling sound not at all like the usual sharp bursts of her laughter. Soon we were all laughing. "And by then, she has her hooks into you!" my professorial friend said, going on to explain in some detail what that expression meant in our country. "You are speaking from *experience*," she joked, "aren't you!"

Just a few days before, I had asked him why he had agreed to come to frowsy, freezing Fehmarn in November. "I want to have a look at the war criminal's widow!" he said.

"*You're* going to have to be polite," I told him. "You're going to have to sit on her sofa and make conversation."

"You're going to make the conversation," he had said. And now here he was, full of courtesy and good humor, explaining our folklore to Frau Heydrich. There was something about her—the intense concentration of her gaze, the constant flickering of feelings playing across her face—that encouraged one to talk. I imagine many people having been gracious to her who hadn't intended to be.

"But," she continued, "in *our* case the external didn't make the decisive impression—or at least, I believe, on me. It was perhaps only one word; perhaps only one hint that the person within had shone through.

"I believe," Frau Heydrich announced, "that I could even today repeat everything that we said to each other at that time. Every word, perhaps. It really wasn't the external picture. It was simply something fateful. We knew from the first sight, from the first moment . . .

"And my husband asked me—it was entirely unmotivated, entirely unfounded—my husband asked me, 'Wollen Sie meine Frau werden?' ['Will you be my wife?'] We did not use the intimate *du* with each other.

"And then I answered him, 'I cannot give you an answer, for you don't know who my father is.' I knew a naval officer cannot marry just any woman; she must be honorable . . . And then he said, 'Even if your father is nothing at all, I want to marry you!'"

Lina Heydrich's voice, expressive as the flight of a bird, dipped low, and wobbled. "That was the decisive word," she said. "And that was really . . . the inscription over our marriage: Even if your father is nothing at all, I want to marry you! I do not believe there are many women who receive such an answer!"

As she said the last words, her eyes filled with tears.

Of Heydrich's inner feelings, we have almost no information, aside from his actions. To me, Lina Heydrich emphasized the romantic, impetuous side of his nature, describing a man much like his namesake, Tristan, who had let nothing stand in the way of love—including prudence, duty, or honor.

To the journalist Günther Deschner she said that her future husband curtly rejected her plea to consider navy protocol: "It is of complete indifference to me what an officer in the German Navy can or cannot do." The note of rebellious defiance is one Heydrich sounded periodically in his childhood, but it had been muted in the navy, where he was trying so desperately to win acceptance. It is noteworthy that a man working ceaselessly to overcome the stigma of his father's antecedents would so grandly ignore those of his future in-laws.

Some have speculated that he actually married Lina to acquire an attractive summer house on Fehmarn, but this is surely far-fetched, since, when it was eventually built, he ended up paying for it himself. Others argue that he wanted a blond, aristocratic wife to enhance his Aryan persona. (Possible, though, as matters stood at the time, there were other available blondes.)

The fact is we will probably never know. Heydrich's namesake Tristan provided as good a conclusion as any when King Mark asked him to explain what he desired: "O Sov'reign, I cannot truly tell you; and what you ask can never have an answer."

"It was very determined of him—" I began, in the silence that had followed Frau Heydrich's emotional outburst. She interrupted me.

"Yes, he knew. He *knew*. On the 6th of December, we met each other. On the 9th of December, we agreed to marry, and on the 24th of December we became engaged."

At first, the would-be couple attempted to keep their betrothal secret. On Lina's part, at least, this was unsuccessful. She herself told me she had a "loose mouth." Soon, most of her school friends had heard the great news.

"And in the meantime," she told me, "my man wrote to my parents in an entirely formal way—you know, this was in *Europe*!—and he asked my father in writing for the hand of his daughter.

"Then my father wrote back this, 'If you don't have any lice in your fur, you are welcome!'

"But he *had* lice in his fur!" she said with a laugh. "My father was of the opinion that all officers had debts, and debts he designated as lice, and my man had debts. A debt of 2,000 marks!"

These were not, Lina emphasized, "sowing-wild-oats debts." Instead, Heydrich owed the money to the navy treasury. Not only were his parents virtually bankrupt, but also he himself had been balancing perilously on the fiscal edge. None of Reinhard's family had "any feeling for money," Lina had told me, and he turned out to be just like them. When she helped him pack after his discharge, she discovered that, rather than sending dirty laundry home to his mother according to established custom, Heydrich had merely bought new uniforms. Lina still remembered precise amounts of soiled clothes: "Thirty-six white shirtfronts! Seventy-two pairs of socks!"

He simply could not live on his salary, she reported. "Today they have more money," she said, referring to naval officers, "an overflowing payment. But it wasn't like that earlier. It was an honorary soldier's pay. And it was also still the Weimar Republic—he was a *Weimar* officer!"

When Frau Heydrich referred to Weimar, she used it as a term of disdain, an almost metaphysical reference to a time of defeat and loss of identity, when everything went wrong. Of course, one does not really expect a Nazi war criminal's widow to be a friend of Germany's faltering first attempt at democracy, which lasted from 1919 until 1933. But it is useful to remember how few friends the Weimar Republic actually had. In fact, almost none of the groups on which democracy usually rests believed in it much. Most people in the propertied middle classes and the professions, including teachers, clergymen, and civil service employees, joined the wealthy industrialists and conservative aristocrats in their longing for some other form of government. (Most hoped for a return of the old monarchy.) Such support as the Weimar democrats obtained came from the industrial workers, and from their party, the Social Democrats, as well as from liberal artists and intellectuals, and diverse members of other classes who feared civil war and accepted democracy as the lesser of the available evils. The writer Thomas Mann summed up the feelings of such people as being reluctant democrats "from the head," but never "from the heart."

Members of the military didn't even have their heads turned in a democratic direction, and their hearts were full of contempt for leaders who had been forced to accept the freezing of the Fatherland's armed forces at 100,000 ill-paid and badly equipped men. German warships—the few that were permitted—could not carry torpedoes; German pilots in training could not fly planes and had to practice with gliders.

Of course, it was convenient for Lina Heydrich to offer up her husband as a victim of the Weimar Navy. By doing so, she was finessing the inconvenient fact that, before Weimer, a man of Heydrich's lately prosperous, overly artistic, uncertain background would have had almost no chance to join the navy at all.

Most of his problems in that service seem in fact to have arisen from his inability to fit into smugly conservative patterns of thought and behavior inherited from the previous era. His maladaptive combination of aggrieved hauteur and insecurity eventually led to his ruin; yet it was just this mixture that appealed so much to Fräulein von Osten. "Bittersweet," she called it.

During his Christmas leave, 1930, Lina's secret fiancé paid a formal visit to the von Ostens. Sitting in the redbrick schoolhouse where her father both taught and lived (an arrangement familiar to Heydrich from his own childhood), the young officer gave a report about his family that was brisk and brief—the *knapp* (terse) style that Lina admired in him. He told of his father's profession, admitting that his family was now poor and kept afloat only by its good name. (Obviously, he did not dwell on the persistent rumors about his racial origins. It was just as well: the von Ostens, like many people in heavily agrarian, economically depressed Schleswig-Holstein, were increasingly drawn to Nazism—and presumably its anti-Semitism—especially because of Hitler's promise to restore the prosperity of rural areas.)

Whatever Heydrich said, it seems to have been successful. Lina's father, who was quite *knapp* himself, told her he was satisfied that her young man would "fit into the landscape."

After this auspicious beginning, Heydrich confessed his various financial failings. Herr von Osten took it in good humor, having himself made some foolish investments. He must have been enthusiastic about the match, for he also promised to pay Heydrich's debt to the navy treasury—and even a small dowry. (Indeed, the marriage announcement was postponed to give the von Ostens time to raise the money.)

This must have surprised Lina, for she said her father was not normally so forgiving of debt. "I first learned from my father, one buys best when one has the money. A responsible man makes no debts! That was my father's principle, and because of that I have always saved." (This may have reflected more of her own attitude toward money. Indeed, when she appears in the folklore of Nazism, it is usually as an acquisitive harpy, seeking lucre as greedily as her husband sought power.) Through the years, Lina admitted, her father did pay for other things, among them not only the debts of her fiancé but also the tuition for her son's education: "He was the angel who stepped in at critical moments—but otherwise, nothing."

Only after Heydrich's financial matters had been discussed did Herr von Osten tell Heydrich about his own life, including the various careers and backgrounds of his eight brothers and sisters, and his wife's nine siblings. Lina had thought her suitor might be bored with this family epic. In fact, he encouraged the flow of talk, and wanted "to know everything."

Frau von Osten, Lina's mother, makes such a scant appearance in this story that I thought she must have been less than impressed. No, said Lina: "They had a *wonderful* time with each other! I never understood it! I couldn't believe it! She would tell him the simplest, the most everyday things, and he would be fascinated. She wrote him letters—what she had eaten for dinner, what she had done all day—and he wrote her back, and this went on until the very end. It was unbelievable!"

From an outsider's point of view, it is quite easy to believe that Reinhard Heydrich might delight in the company of Lina's parents: the father who behaved like a Prussian officer, the mother who was purely and simply domestic—so unlike his own parents, so like the typical Germanic family to which he had never before belonged.

The major opponent of the proposed marriage was not Lina's mother, but Reinhard's.

"I believe his mother was very disappointed," Lina said. "Her son, the officer," was supposed to come home with a "female millionaire. And she always held that against me . . . I, a poor village schoolmaster's daughter, thwarted her entire early plans . . . I was not at all welcome. Not at *all*!"

In late December 1930, Reinhard Heydrich finally told his fiancée a bit about a well-connected young woman he might have married. Lina Heydrich staunchly resisted all of my efforts to discuss this aspect of her husband's fall from grace with the sea. The sum total of her account to me went like this: "Admiral Raeder had a friend, who was on the board of works, and my husband met his daughter at a sailing regatta and I believe she liked him very much, and then she followed him afterward, whenever there was a regatta. And she believed that she had conquered him. And then he met me, and he got engaged to me, and she was entirely unhappy. And, supposedly, she tried to kill herself. Yes, but one doesn't know that exactly, *nicht wahr*?

"But in any case, the father now complained about my husband to Herr Raeder. And then, he was dismissed."

Among the many interesting components of this richly terse account are the very aggressive role assigned to the young woman, and the total omission of any reference to a crucial aspect of the situation: Lieutenant Heydrich was not dismissed by Admiral Raeder but by a military court of honor especially convened for the occasion.

Here was his final confrontation with the German Navy's rigid code of ethics. When his roommates had labeled him a "man without honor" for failing to take arms against the rumors of his Jewish ancestry, Heydrich had been uncertain of the correct course. This time, he was sure he was right—but once again, his peers thought otherwise.

On December 18, 1930, a few days before his first meeting with Lina's family, Reinhard Heydrich wrote her a letter betraying a disquieting mixture of the expected romantic feelings ("Much, much love") and uncomfortably realistic thinking. He says he is busy at work, but when he has a pause for breath, his thoughts are always with her: "You! I can no longer think that it was ever any different. And I know only too well how very much I have given up. That much more do I look forward to the life that lies before us. You! With you, I can survive any trouble!"

Trouble? Given up? (The word he used, *abgestreift*, also means stripped away, divested of, done away with.) Heydrich went on to assert that "the highest demand I have always placed on myself is to be straightforward and upright." He says he is confident he can look her father in the eye. Then he gives Lina a little lecture: "Mark you, *Mädel*, . . . with people I love, there is nothing worse than subterfuge and insincerity. With common people, I do not hesitate to respond in such a manner."

In German, the prose is contorted and the tone stilted—but the whiff of menace comes through in either language. The letter suggests that Heydrich sensed what was coming, had tried to think through the consequences of his impetuous engagement, and was stiffening into the old, arrogantly defensive posture that had never served him well.

Nevertheless, he apparently waited until he had visited Lina's family, and had become officially betrothed, before making the final break with his other flame. Then he did it in the unkindest way possible, as if she were one of the "common people." Apparently, he simply sent her an announcement of his engagement to someone else. (This, of course, is hearsay evidence. The announcement no longer exists, the girl and her father cannot be located, and Heydrich's navy files have mysteriously disappeared.)

At roughly the same time as he was ridding himself of his unwanted girlfriend, Heydrich wrote to his "Dear Parents-in-law," using the familiar form of address and thanking them "from the heart" for making him feel like a son in their house and for permitting an open engagement: "Lina doesn't need to do anything clandestine in Kiel, and we can get to know each other better and better without having to pay any attention to the gossip of our dear fellow creatures."

Heydrich's hatred of gossip—the whispered innuendos that had poisoned his childhood and naval experience—comes through very clearly. He asked the von Ostens to agree to an earlier date than planned for the wedding. "Please, please, permit this," he urged.

Lina's parents did agree, but to little avail. After Heydrich's return to his new job as a signals officer on the mainland, the father of his former girlfriend got in touch with him. His daughter had suffered a nervous breakdown, he said, and if Heydrich were a "man of honor" he would marry her. Heydrich allegedly replied that he was now formally committed to someone else, and thus honor bound to marry her instead. It was after this angry standoff that the father of the scorned woman called in Admiral Raeder. Shortly thereafter, Heydrich was suspended from duty, pending his appearance before a naval court.

Heydrich had obviously not expected such a drastic reaction to his insistence on having honor his own way. When his fiancée returned, full of excitement from her visit home, he met her at the railroad station. "Something terrible has happened," he said.

He gave her a brief report: he was said to have promised to marry a girl and not to have kept the promise. Even this was too much for Lina to grasp all at once; she asked him to explain in more detail. On my first visit to Fehmarn, I naively asked her to do the same thing for me. "I have written about this rather precisely in my book," she replied, knowing that the book wasn't yet published, even in Germany. ("I have written about that!" or "I have already told you!" were her favorite ways of evading difficult questions.)

It turned out that Heydrich's explanation wasn't very satisfactory to Lina either: he had met the girl at the usual place—a dance. Later she "dropped by" his apartment in Kiel. Since she had no quarters for the night, he offered to let her stay at his landlady's house (which, of course, was also his home).

"This report irritated me," Lina wrote, "and I didn't believe so exactly in this version." Heydrich had enlarged his account to present himself as a victim of antiquated naval protocol forbidding female visitors to an officer's lodgings under any circumstances.

In her conversations with me, Frau Heydrich wove in her own variations on this theme: "The commander of the navy, Herr Raeder, was such a little man. He was so moralistic. We say *kleinkariert*. That is, a man who is no more than a schoolmaster. He demanded, for example, that the young officers go to church every Sunday and they had no desire at all to go. They did not always say, '*Jawohl!*'"

Frau Heydrich ended her tirade with a soft sigh. "Today," she said, "today we would *laugh* about it!"

In her youth, however, the reputation of a woman was no laughing matter, and the honor of a man-at-arms was accorded reverent attention. Indeed, the court was far more concerned with Heydrich's behavior than that of the lady in question.

Spectators were barred from the *Ehrengericht*—the court of honor—and the records were kept secret and have subsequently vanished. Thus, we have nothing to rely on aside from "the gossip of our dear fellow creatures." Yet we are richer in data than Heydrich's contemporaries, since it wasn't until after the war that a few people who had participated in the proceedings were willing to talk about them. Until then, the rumor mills created just the sort of "theater" that Lina Heydrich so often derided.

The most widely repeated story has it that Heydrich's former flame was "compromised," and that he refused to make an "honest woman" of her. This tale was repeated by Gerald Reitlinger, the author of the first history of the SS. According to Reitlinger, Heydrich said it would be dishonorable to marry a girl who had given herself beforehand—even to him.

The most widely repeated story also has it that Heydrich's former flame was pregnant. This tale has been repeated by several writers, among them Wilhelm Höttl, an Austrian Nazi and former SS Sturmbannführer writing, after World War II, under the pseudonym Walter Hagen.

Postwar witnesses said, however, that both Heydrich and the young woman denied that they had ever had sexual relations. They disagreed, however, about who was at fault. Turning the story Heydrich told Lina on its head, the girl claimed he pursued her, asking her to visit, failing to book a hotel room so that she was forced to spend the night at his place, then trying—unsuccessfully—to take advantage of his reluctant guest.

All of this may be diverting in a *National Enquirer* sort of way, but it hardly seems grounds for a military court-martial. At first, Heydrich's naval comrades seem to have felt that "a disagreeable affair about a girl" was not that unusual and could even be regarded with a degree of sympathy. Something dramatic must therefore have occurred behind the closed doors of the tribunal. We know roughly what it was—the emergence of the stunning difference between the agreed-on general content of a story and the precise way in which it is told by the parties involved.

Whoever had actually been the instigator of the ill-fated visit, Reinhard Heydrich was clearly supposed to take the blame on himself, profess to be terribly sorry—and contrive to avoid marrying the girl anyway. Many "gentlemen" have gotten away with this, though it often demands cunning maneuvering. But Heydrich was angry at the crude attempt to railroad him into marriage. In addition, of course, he had endured many miserable years in the navy. The convening of the court may have been the last straw, providing a target for accumulated anger and pushing him into an explosion of self-destructive behavior. He refused to say *jawohl* to what Wagner called the "hard laws of hypocritical custom."

According to Günther Deschner, he did not think he had behaved dishonorably, and "attempted to gloss over his actions." Heydrich's old roommate Heinrich Beucke later heard "that he had tried to clear himself *totally* of any guilt." This was a grievous mistake, for the members of the court, like Lina, were suspicious of his story. After the war, one of the participants, Admiral Karl-Jesko von Puttkamer, told an English journalist, "A court of honor is not to be compared with an ordinary court where it is self-evident that the accused may lie."

In his letter to Lina, Heydrich had professed an ability to behave either in a straightforward way or with "subterfuge." In the end, he seems to have chosen a disastrous mixture of both of these approaches, arrogance when he should have adroitly faked contrition, deviously denying what he should have straightforwardly "confessed." To most of the members of the court this seemed an appalling lack of gallantry, incompatible with the exalted position of a military officer. In April 1930, the court decreed his discharge—*cum infamia*—from the navy.

Both Heydrich and Lina were devastated by the decision. But unlike others, they did not feel his own behavior had been the determining factor. By then, Lina had become convinced he had told the truth. She looked for other explanations for the court's decision. Later she wrote that the chairman of the court of honor was a longtime member of his crew, which she found unfair. If one remembers that Heydrich was regarded as an overly abrasive commander by many of his subordinates, she had a certain point. On the other hand, another member of the court was the same Admiral Kleikamp who had written a letter praising Heydrich's fine future in the service. In that light, it seems likely that he got a relatively fair hearing, which he handled more than relatively badly.

But "we didn't think it was that simple," Lina wrote. "We thought of intrigues, professional jealousy . . . Suddenly, everything impossible seemed possible to us. All of that only because of a woman? Even today I don't know."

"So you were not the cause?" I asked her.

"That I don't know . . . I met the girl once at a ball. She was a very pretty girl. And I asked my husband, '*You said*, that is such a pretty girl, why didn't you marry her?' And he said, 'Ah, she was so boring!'"

"We have an expression in America. A 'love match'—a marriage for love."

"Yes?"

"As in a romantic legend."

"Yes, it was a truly great love."

"Still, it was a hard decision to make."

"He didn't make it; it was made for him."

"Still, he had to—"

"He did not *choose*. He was dismissed!"

Perhaps only by absolving Heydrich of any responsibility could either of them face the agonizing consequences of their romantic whirlwind courtship. At the time, both Reinhard and Lina had thought he would someday be an admiral; after the *Ehrengericht*, his future seemed impossibly bleak.

In the end, of course, he found a career open to his talents.

In 1945, Lina Heydrich chanced to meet the man who had been chairman of the court of honor. She had just made her way home across a devastated continent; she found him in an Allied prison camp. "No big words were needed," she wrote. "He said only, 'I am sorry, I am sorry.' What was I supposed to do with that? If Reinhard had not been eliminated from the navy . . . only God knows what would have happened."

"I am sorry, I am sorry." For any bias in the court? For Heydrich's subsequent behavior? For the miscarriage of Lina's hopes, and, no doubt, of his own? Like so many aspects of the story, this remark can be taken more than one way.

5

HEINRICH HIMMLER: THE GREAT ENIGMA

"[Heinrich Himmler] was the originator of the idea of the
SS. He was the head of the entire organization; he was an old
comrade of Hitler's. My husband was only responsible for
security."

—LINA HEYDRICH

WHILE GERMANS OFTEN TALK OF *"das Schicksal"*—the great,
implacable power of destiny that determines the supreme issues
of life—Lina Heydrich did not speak a lot about fate, at least to
me, whom she saw as representing the American faith in democratic
self-determination. When she did finally refer to the operation of destiny in her life I assumed she was about to speak of her husband—the
day he married her perhaps, or the day he died. Instead, she brought up
Heinrich Himmler.

"It was fate," she said. She seemed on the edge of tears. "The day
Reinhard met him was the star hour of my life."

Yet as much as she regarded Heydrich's path crossing that of the
Reichsführer's as fateful, what seemed to impress her even more was the
degree to which Himmler was a puzzle or riddle.

The first time I interviewed Lina Heydrich, she had just finished
reading Albert Speer's memoirs, *Inside the Third Reich*. She was furious.
Not only had Hitler's minister of armaments and war production left
her husband out almost entirely, but also he had dismissed Himmler
as a virtual incompetent, "half schoolmaster and half crank." "I cannot
understand that!" she fumed. "I don't see how people can fail to take
him seriously! He was our biggest problem!"

In small part, Lina's dismay over Speer's dismissal of Himmler may

Chief of Personal Staff Reichsführer SS Karl Wolff (age forty, circa 1940) served as liaison officer between the SS and Hitler's headquarters during the war. Privy to inside information about party members, it was Wolff who suggested that Himmler advise Heydrich to divorce the tactless Lina.

have reflected her lasting dislike of the Reichsführer SS. One incident that fed this feeling came about because even Lina Heydrich was not immune to uttering malevolent whispers. She once wrote that she had never expected to have to live with "secrets, political and otherwise," and told me she had no gift for it: "I have always had a loose tongue." She also loved to administer humorous tongue lashings (behind their backs) to a variety of targets, including Frau Himmler, whom she detested. ("It seems I called her a she-goat or something like that.")

This occurred around the time of the 1936 Summer Olympic games, which that year were held in Berlin. Reinhard Heydrich had helped with propaganda directed at foreign visitors, cleverly ordering the removal of anti-Jewish placards and the addition of posters calling for tolerance of every form of belief—including Nazism. Since Heydrich was also an accomplished sportsman, he received splendid seats for the games, and his wife's place eclipsed even Frau Himmler's. ("Apparently, my car also passed hers on the highway," Lina said disdainfully.)

Meanwhile, Heydrich had become involved in a struggle for power with Karl Wolff, Heinrich Himmler's chief of staff. Though the two men were constantly vying for primacy at Himmler's court, they still enjoyed socializing together with their wives. Lina guessed that "Wolfie" was the one who informed Himmler of her own little struggle with the Frau Reichsführer. One day Himmler called for Heydrich. "If you can't control your own family, how can you run an organization?" raged the Reichsführer SS. He even urged Heydrich to divorce his outspoken wife.

That same day, Karl Wolff's wife, Frieda, had lured Frau Heydrich out of town, inviting her to a regatta near Kiel. Frieda was acting at Karl's behest, but her loyalties were obviously divided. Soon she told Lina that back in Berlin Himmler was trying to convince Reinhard to begin separation proceedings. Frau Heydrich spent the afternoon in tears. That night she called her husband, who laughed, and said he had resolved the situation.

"How?" I asked her. She said he never told her ("We never talked about it. Not once!"), but she guessed he had deflected Himmler's attention toward "whoever" had denounced her, slyly suggesting there must be a conspiracy involved. According to Felix Kersten, Himmler's physical therapist, the Reichsführer believed that

almost every important man is controlled by anonymous forces behind him and is the exponent of these forces.

He puts his information service onto this, making them draw great charts to depict the various influences graphically. He can stand for hours with Heydrich, discussing and pondering . . . Heydrich encourages this basic trait of the Reichsführer's.

Himmler apparently dropped his demands, but he and Frau Heydrich were not on speaking terms until the night they found themselves sitting next to each other at a banquet at Hermann Goering's. Throughout a long dinner, Lina Heydrich continued to say nothing to the man who had the power to destroy her—and her husband. Silence has its own eloquence. Finally, Himmler asked her to dance; then, as the music played, he asked why she was so quiet. "Do you find that surprising?" she answered demurely.

"Well, Frau Heydrich, everything will be all right," the Reichsführer said at last.

"You see, that was typical of Himmler," Lina Heydrich later explained.

A November 1923 Nazi attempt to establish a new order became
known as the Beer Hall Putsch. The unsuccessful coup resulted
in the arrest of nine participants, including Hitler, who was
convicted of treason and sentenced to five years in Landsberg
prison. (He served less than a year, during which time he dictated
his memoir, *Mein Kampf*, and practiced his oratorial skills.)
Pictured here, directly underneath the German imperial flag,
is Heinrich Himmler, who had joined the party three months
earlier.

"On paper, he ordered us to divorce, but when face-to-face with me, his
courage left him. The matter was never referred to again."

"Were you afraid of Himmler?" I asked her.

"I was not afraid of any man!" she snapped, swift as a rap on the
knuckles.

Later, however, she admitted, "I was always afraid of Himmler. I was always afraid I would do something wrong. There was no way to please him."

It took both Reinhard and Lina Heydrich, applying their various skills, to undo most of the ill-effects of Wolff's denunciation. (From that time on, however, Frau Heydrich refused to set foot in Himmler's household.)

In larger part, however, Lina's negative attitude toward Himmler probably reflected a latent desire to shift history's censure from her husband to his leader, or at least make Himmler share the burden. Yet evidence for her puzzlement over Himmler's not being taken seriously goes considerably beyond Speer's dismissal of his competence.

The paradox her dismay seems to mirror is represented by a photo of Himmler taken in Munich on November 9, 1923, the day of the so-called Beer Hall Putsch, when Hitler and his followers tried but failed to seize power in the midst of the political chaos of the early Weimar Republic. In the photo Himmler appears in the thick of the action, carrying a flag (not the swastika but the old imperial standard of the Kaiser Reich). His weak chin is fiercely elevated above his spindly body, his spectacles reflecting back the light of the cold autumn day, masking the expression in his eyes. The image reflects his subsequent reputation in popular history: chilly and opaque, carrying the banner of incomprehensible atrocities—inhuman leader of the SS, sadistic chief of the Gestapo, monstrous creator of Dachau and Auschwitz.

And yet despite being clearly visible in the ranks of the putsch, Himmler was never arrested, as such participants as Hitler himself and his followers Rudolf Hess and Ernst Röhm had been. Moreover, the apparent enormity of Himmler was played down by his associates and by subsequent history, at least for a time. It is almost shocking to read descriptions of Himmler written by people who actually knew him. From his closest associates in the Nazi Party down through enemy agents who met him only briefly, the accounts are similar in their startling blandness. The infamous Reichsführer SS is "ordinary," "mediocre," "polite," "otherworldly," "indecisive." Other observers used a more universal frame of reference: at some point in almost every account, Himmler is compared to a mildly eccentric schoolmaster.

Robert Wolff, chief of the Department of Captured Military Documents at the National Archives, had told me much the same thing: "I don't understand why more people don't write about Himmler; he was the leader, after all." In the 1990s, as if to confirm this point, the computerized references at the New York Public Library listed 18 books under the topic "Reinhard Heydrich," and only 5 under "Heinrich Himmler." It may be that for a time the contrasting images of the satanic Heydrich and the schoolmasterish Himmler affected scholarship, accounting for the imbalance. Yet the "Himmler Enigma," as Lina Heydrich called it, certainly does not stem from any lack of data. Unlike Heydrich, Himmler kept a diary for ten years of his early life. He also ordered extensive investigations into his own past, personally preserving bits of memorabilia to add to his secret files on himself. In addition, numerous files of the offices under his command were recovered after the war. All of this, moreover, is in addition to the "secret speeches," published pamphlets, and reminiscences by subordinates that form the usual store of materials on the rulers of the Third Reich.

In any case, the passage of time seems to have shifted the balance. In 2015, the digital references in the New York Public Library listed 114 books under the subject "Himmler" compared to 72 dealing with "Heydrich."

It is not my intention to resolve the "Himmler Enigma," or even to apportion how much it can be explained by Frau Heydrich's biases and how much by scholarship's. The fact remains, as Lina Heydrich recognized, that Heinrich Himmler was a great, inescapable presence in her husband's life—and in hers. Himmler was Heydrich's mentor, rival, antithesis, fellow criminal, and boss. The fortunes of the two men were constantly interwoven, like lines of contrapuntal music, or interlocking parts of a swiftly moving locomotive. Their careers cannot really be considered apart: biographers of each inevitably wind up devoting great attention to the other. Indeed, the two men together seem to form a whole, both symbolically and in the realities of power that transcend the individual roles they played in Nazi life. At the same time, their immense differences in style and character constantly challenge historians, often providing a launching point for high-flying speculations: as the journalist Günther Deschner put it, "In Heinrich Himmler and Reinhard Heydrich the two great archetypes of the twentieth century confront each other—the true believer and the technologist of power."

When I quoted Deschner's assessment to Lina Heydrich, she disagreed: "It was never so crass as that!" In her view, Himmler was certainly *weltfremd* (a German word meaning "unworldly" or "not of this world"), but far from mediocre: "He was an enormously well-read man. Perhaps he had simply read too much! He could have been a professor. He could have written books; he was a man of truly distinctive makeup."

She also liked to emphasize Himmler's far greater formal power (and criminal responsibility) compared to Heydrich's: "He was the originator of the idea of the SS. He was the head of the entire organization; he was an old comrade of Hitler's. My husband was only responsible for security."

But even after Heydrich's death, Himmler continued to cast a shadow over his adjutant's bereaved family, assuming the role of legal guardian to his wife and four children. Both Reinhard and Lina Heydrich gave Himmler at least equal weight so far as responsibility for the Holocaust is concerned.

The future Reichsführer of the SS was born October 7, 1900. Like Reinhard Heydrich, he was the second of three children. Himmler's few childhood achievements were often overshadowed by those of his older brother, Gebhard Wilhelm, who had been named after his father. There was also a younger brother, Ernst.

Like the Heydrichs, the Himmler family had risen swiftly from social nullity to a position of considerable eminence. Heinrich's paternal grandfather, Johann, was a great family hero, even though he was not entirely a reputable character. An illegitimate child, he had sought his fortune abroad as a mercenary soldier, returning home occasionally for a bit of manly brawling before finally settling down as a royal police official in the Bavarian town of Lindau.

Having married late, Johann sired only one child, Heinrich's father, Gebhard. Encouraged by his ambitious parents, Gebhard spent ten years at the University of Munich studying philology and classical languages. Eventually, he became *Rektor* (similar to principal) of a *Gymnasium* in Munich, a status rivaled by few non-nobles.

Unlike Bruno Heydrich, then, Gebhard Himmler was impeccably successful in his chosen field, largely because he had mastered the skills of the courtier that always eluded Heydrich's flamboyantly self-made father. When he wrote to his idol and favorite student, Prince Heinrich of the ancient monarchial Wittelsbach line, Professor Himmler usually addressed him as "Illustrious Prince, Most Gracious Prince and Lord." (This skill at servility would later creep into Heinrich Himmler's relations with the Führer.)

An incorrigible educator, Professor Himmler personally supervised his children's education. Night after night, he told them stories about their family heritage or read from old German classics. Like Heydrich, young Heinrich Himmler knew about Siegfried, Wotan, et al., from an early age. Unlike little "Reini," however, Heinrich couldn't actually play the Wagnerian music—or any other kind. All during his childhood Himmler struggled with the piano and never mastered it. In his diary, he also lamented his "disastrous" efforts to learn to dance, before concluding the whole enterprise left him "absolutely cold."

Headmaster Himmler tried also to inject reverence for hierarchy and superior authority into his son's worldview. Former Nazi Ernst "Putzi" Hanfstängel studied under Professor Himmler at the Royal Bavarian Gymnasium and recalled him as "a terrible snob, favoring the young titled members of his class and bearing down contemptuously on the commoners." Young Heinrich he remembered as a brat, "always running to his father and other teachers with tales about his fellows."

The historian Bradley F. Smith, who has made an intensive study of Himmler's youthful prose, writes that "the whole pattern of his life was based on conventionality, on a desire to do the right thing and think the right thoughts." It was both Himmler's and posterity's misfortune that he grew up in a time of such turbulence that many misguided souls lost sight of what the right thing so clearly was.

In contrast to Reinhard Heydrich's turbulent bohemian home, the conventional, orderly, patriarchal Himmler household was the very model of the admired family of the period. While it is true that Gebhard Senior was overbearing and pedantic, he was also an apparently loving father, who kept lists of his sons' endearing sayings, as well as many receipts for toys. While Heinrich Himmler might have had reason to detest his harshly schoolmasterish father, the psychohistorian Peter Loewenberg has concluded that in Himmler's youth "his father was the only person he was aware of loving."

Gerald Reitlinger, the first historian to attempt a serious study of the SS, argued that if Himmler's childhood had been "repressed, he would have been less prone in later years to imitate his father . . . constantly relapsing into a Bavarian schoolmaster." Surely, Reitlinger speculates, as if grasping for an alternative view, the problem had to be "a lack of motherly love."

Unfortunately, we know little about Heinrich Himmler's mother, Anna Maria Himmler. (In his diaries, she is mentioned only twice.) Like Elisabeth Heydrich, she married quite late, brought a sizable dowry of money from merchant relatives, and was a devout Catholic. In strong contrast to Heydrich's careerist mother, however, Anna Maria was a full-time *Hausfrau* who fussed over her son's health, sent him packages of food when he was away from home, and cried easily when he hurt her feelings.

In contrast to Reinhard Heydrich, Heinrich Himmler was in no way an unusually talented, pugnacious, or rebellious child. Like him, he was a good student. Often, in fact, he was first in his class, but he still worried about minor infractions, commenting in his diary, "I must admit that I was really very bad."

The only known truly unusual element of Himmler's childhood was his continual ill health. When he was two and a half, he contracted a respiratory infection so serious that the family moved to the healthier atmosphere of the mountains (while his father exchanged worried letters with his idol Prince Heinrich in the flatlands below). In the next few years the boy had trouble with his eyes, his heart, and his stomach; and one cannot help wondering whether these physical infirmities did not somehow foreshadow his later philosophical posture, when he looked with puzzled incomprehension at opponents of his regime, hardened his heart against them, and suffered agonizing stomach cramps after ordering measures whose cruelty he could never quite digest.

In childhood, such weaknesses meant that he made a poor showing at gymnastics and became the butt of his schoolmates' jokes. In similar circumstances, Heydrich had indulged in displays of temper, but Himmler merely maintained the tiny, tight smile he still wore years later in official photographs. Like Heydrich, he worked secretly at self-improvement. Himmler, however, often became deflected before he reached his goal. Among his mementos are little notes in which he urged himself to show "strengthening of the will."

Himmler did not emerge appreciably stronger from these youthful efforts, but he did acquire an almost obsessive reverence for physical grace. Like many other Germans of his era (Thomas Mann, for instance, in his short story "Tonio Kröger"), he equated bodily perfection with blond coloring.

For the young Himmler, the most admirable figures became the "iron man," noble in appearance and action, unyielding in rectitude and valor, who "never concedes loss of control" over himself—no doubt because he himself had so much trouble living up to this ideal.

Yet none of Himmler's views was the slightest bit unusual; his notions of strength and valor were shared by many of his war-torn generation. (Himmler was four years older than Heydrich; World War I began in August 1914, shortly before his fourteenth birthday.) His first reaction was a boyish mixture of excitement over "planes and spies," and patriotism: "The French and Belgians scarcely thought they would be chopped up so fast." By the beginning of 1917, Prince Heinrich was dead, Himmler's older brother was in combat, and he himself would soon be in officer training school.

Heinrich's reaction to the hard realities of barracks life was ambivalent. He loved the rituals of militarism, especially the wearing of uniforms, but was homesick for the little comforts of domesticity. In the end he found a niche as a camp wheeler-dealer, arranging housing for visiting friends, buying foodstuffs for his family, and doing little favors for his superior officers.

These civilian skills turned out to be the most enduring legacy of his military service, for the war ended before his unit got to the front. Himmler felt he had been cheated of his chance for glory, particularly since Gebhard had already won an Iron Cross. During the next war, the Reichsführer SS told a Swedish diplomat that he had led troops into battle in 1916, a maladroit, easily disprovable lie.

"Soldier Heinrich," as he sometimes called himself, returned home in December 1918, and enrolled in a special program for students whose war duties had interrupted their high school education. His father turned out to be his homeroom teacher.

Few teenage veterans could adjust easily to such an embarrassing change of identity. Himmler's diary entries ceased during this period, and offer no clue to the "sudden" decision he made to take up a career in agriculture. Himmler's escape to the countryside was in any case short-lived: after a few months of the grinding labor then customary on German farms he collapsed, and his doctor prescribed a more restful lifestyle.

Heinrich Himmler (circa 1930) was a "narrow-chested, weak-chinned, spectacled man," with eyes "extraordinarily small, and the distance between them narrow, rodent-like," according to Felix Kersten, a physical therapist engaged to alleviate Himmler's chronic stomach cramps. Yet, Kersten conceded, "if you spoke to him, these eyes would never leave your face . . . they would rove over your countenance, fix your eyes, and in them would be an expression of waiting, watching, stealth."

Himmler went back to Munich to study agronomy, but restful it was not. Soon he had joined both right-wing soldiers' organizations and the student fraternity to which his father had belonged. He spent the next three years drifting back and forth between the competing attractions of the militarism he had romanticized but never fully experienced, and his father's crumbling world of bureaucratic punctiliousness and academic objectivity.

In 1921, he began writing in his diary again. Underneath the metronomic ticking of precisely listed schedules (his most frequent activity was scrutinizing the files of the student association) the constant hum of self-doubt is still audible. Continually, he reproaches himself for being too easygoing, too undisciplined, and, especially, too talkative. "I told an awful lot of jokes, talked and mocked a lot," he wrote on one occasion, and then added, "I just can't stop it."

His schoolwork suffered, and so did his relationship with his father. Describing a trip home, he wrote, "Suddenly, Father came in a great state of excitement and in a terrible mood, accusing me, etc." Nevertheless, he did not express anger at his father, but instead placed the blame on himself, writing, for example, "Father is so good, if only I did not have to plague him any longer."

Did Himmler, as Peter Loewenberg insists, attack others for qualities and feelings he was unable to acknowledge in himself? This seems likely, but it is the nature of the "Himmler Enigma" that amid a wealth of material we are rich only in fuel for speculation, remaining poor in clearly established connections and dramatic, emphatic conclusions.

As time went on, the quest for mental clarity became the unacknowledged theme of Himmler's diary. In everything, he sought a moral lesson or a resolution of some pressing dilemma. He was particularly worried about the age-old student custom of recreational dueling, which he felt was contrary to the teachings of the church. Nevertheless, he longed to receive the scars of honorable combat. To add to his problems, he was a poor fencer, and had trouble finding partners.

In the end, he managed to have things both ways. He fought a duel and lost as expected, but stood fast long enough to be wounded five times, garnering visible proof of courage. Now that he had achieved warrior status, he promised himself that he would "always defend" the church. He didn't, of course: a few years later he was contemplating arresting the pope—but then, Himmler was never good at honoring inconvenient promises. He was always better at determining people's weaknesses.

Loewenberg writes that Himmler's cold and critical new demeanor was "armor" donned to defend against a fear of losing control of his impulses, including "inner unconscious sadism." And Bradley Smith maintains that he "constantly retreated behind a mask of conventionality and formality." Both armor and masks have in common a fear of spontaneity. Himmler did not often reveal emotions to others, and those that emerged tended to be shallow and lukewarm, as if filtered through a series of inhibiting barriers.

With his male contemporaries, Himmler strove mightily to maintain a soldierly posture. But the face he turned toward women often revealed more of his inner conflicts. Letters written to his mother from army training camp show he felt entitled to berate, wheedle, and complain, as he would not have dared to do with his intimidating father.

His shrill attempts to get "something" from his mother are reminiscent of a comment Heydrich made to his mother ("No one takes care of me here; you should do it"). It appears as if both men felt they were missing some essential form of feminine nurturance. As they moved further into adolescence, however, their attitudes toward women—particularly as objects of sexual desire—diverged radically. Heydrich always seems to have embraced the prospect of sexual union with aggressive enthusiasm. Himmler, by contrast, approached it with a brittle intensity barely distinguishable from dread.

His family and his church had taught him to believe in premarital chastity for both men and women, but after Heinrich arrived at the university, he began to wonder whether various women he met could be "had." He fantasized about rescuing beautiful girls who might otherwise go wrong. And sometimes, he himself was tempted: "I have experienced what it is like to lie closely together, by couples, body to body, hot; . . . The girls are then so far gone they no longer know what they are doing . . . One has enough to do to struggle with one's self."

Sequestered within the shelter of sexual purity, Himmler sought help for his insecurities in a private program of reading. The man who was later to incorporate book burnings into SS ritual read 270 books between 1919 and 1926. Initially, his choices reveal a certain sense of intellectual inquiry. He read many novels by Jules Verne, as well as *The Odyssey*, Gogol, Dostoevsky, five plays by Ibsen, and even a bit of Émile Zola, whom his father had once warned him explicitly not to read (and he had agreed that he wouldn't).

As time went on, however, he turned increasingly to German authors, and to political themes. He enjoyed the memoirs of General Ludendorff, Richard Wagner, and former kaiser Wilhelm, though he also criticized the latter's book as self-serving. In addition to politics, he also read works on spiritualism and peasant life. Exploring his personal concerns as they were examined in the literature of his time, young Himmler was doing something usually considered admirable. The evolution of his anti-Semitic views, however, illustrates his halting, groping steps toward a disastrous conclusion.

Still uncertain is the orientation that Himmler carried away from his parental home. In 1919, when young Heinrich begins to mention in his diary that he has been having discussions about Jews, we cannot be certain of his initial position. For instance, in 1920, when he read a novel called *The Sin Against the Blood*, a racist diatribe that included an appendix of educational "documents," Himmler described it in his notes: "A book that introduces one to the Jewish Question with shocking clarity and causes one to approach this situation with extreme distrust. However, at the same time . . . to investigate the documents on which the novel is based . . . The author is blinded by his rage against the Jews."

There is no evidence that he actually investigated the documents; instead he took a year off from school, enrolling in a correspondence course designed to enhance his mental powers, as well as a class in Russian. Apparently, he seriously considered emigrating to the new Soviet

Union, though the massive social upheavals there made this unfeasible. Nevertheless, Himmler remained interested in Russia: in future years he would claim, "The East belongs to the SS."

In 1922, when Himmler went back to finish at the university, having found no other alternative, he discovered that student life had become more radicalized in his absence. In that year, too, his family began to feel the effects of the growing economic crisis that had already devastated Heydrich's home.

The embattled leaders of the Weimar Republic were drifting toward financial disaster in their efforts to pay the tremendous, punitive reparations demanded by the Treaty of Versailles. The value of the German mark plunged downward. By the end of the year, Heinrich's father had lost all his savings, a small tragedy mirrored in millions of other families and compounding upward until the government itself couldn't meet its debts and defaulted on its payments to the Allies. In retaliation, France occupied the Ruhr, and in response to *that*, the German government called for a general strike. In the ensuing turmoil, the mark sank into worthlessness, creating the legendary ruinous, humiliating inflation in which a wheelbarrow full of German money purchased a loaf of bread, while rich foreigners could buy a lakeside villa for a few hundred English pounds.

It is against this background (though it should be emphasized that it is not known if it was for this reason) that the entries in Heinrich Himmler's diaries become markedly more strident, intolerant, imbalanced, and racist. Himmler now found that he agreed with Houston Stewart Chamberlain's wildly racist pamphlet "Race and Nation." It was "objective," he thought, "not just hate-filled anti-Semitism . . . these terrible Jews."

A few months after this entry, the German-Jewish statesman Walter Rathenau was assassinated. Reinhard Heydrich, then just beginning his naval training, had refused to join his comrades in celebrating this grisly event. In Munich, however, Heinrich Himmler wrote, "Rathenau is murdered. I am glad." He began to drift away from his old friends and toward the para-militaristic conspirators who were plotting revolution. Himmler was a natural satellite, attracted by the dynamism of a strong source of energy. In Ernst Röhm, he seems to have found the first of several strong authority figures who finally pulled him out of his father's orbit. He followed Röhm into the Nazi Party, and joined Röhm's unit in Hitler's ill-fated putsch of 1923.

After the revolt failed, Himmler wandered around Munich, as if he had been stunned, doing little but loiter in beer halls, talking politics. He had lost his job with a fertilizer firm and was in no rush to find another. It was as if he had been ruined for bourgeois life, though he still retained the middle-class traits of parsimony, impersonal courtesy, and orderliness.

When Röhm went into exile in 1925, Himmler found another Nazi mentor in the Gauleiter of Lower Bavaria, Gregor Strasser, who hired him to be his secretary. A few years later, he moved on, compelled by the greater charisma of Adolf Hitler.

In addition to a leader, the putsch provided Himmler with a way to exert some attraction of his own. An unknown female admirer wrote him a letter "of fervent gratitude," in which she commented invitingly on how "secure" the flag must have felt in his hands. A more red-blooded revolutionary might have sought her out, but this was not Himmler's way. Real women were so difficult and had to be treated accordingly, "as a dear child who must be admonished, perhaps even punished, when she is foolish," as he once told a friend, "though she must also be protected and looked after because she is so weak."

Obviously, mutual pleasure mattered far less than control over the "beloved child" who existed to serve Himmler's convenience and could never be allowed to "shackle" his spirit. Psychologists have speculated that he projected on the "weaker" sex qualities in himself that he regarded as unmanly. Significantly, he was already considering the need to punish the frailer species for its "foolishness."

In 1923, he was granted an opportunity to do just that. The previous year, his brother Gebhard Himmler had become engaged to a spirited woman named Paula Stölzle. Heinrich had never really approved of her, but in 1923, his animosity was intensified when Paula committed an indiscretion with another man. Apparently, Gebhard wasn't sure precisely what she had done, and asked his little brother to help straighten things out. Himmler fell to with a vengeance, writing Paula in an instructive letter, "Since you do not handle yourself strongly and firmly, . . . I feel myself obligated to do it."

Handling herself strongly and firmly, Paula told Himmler to mind his own business. But he was not about to abandon his "obligation." Eventually, he persuaded Herr and Frau Himmler, and then finally Gebhard, that the engagement was an insult to the family honor and must be broken off.

One would expect the story to end here, but it did not: in March 1924, Heinrich Himmler hired a private detective to investigate Paula's family background. He also asked an acquaintance to pass on any tale about her "which you can *prove.*"

Perhaps the investigator had some success, for shortly afterward, Himmler was emboldened enough to return a package of gifts given to his family by Paula's, and rude enough to enclose merely his personal visiting card. When Paula began making unkind remarks about the Himmlers, Heinrich praised his own restraint and threatened, "I will be completely different if anyone forces me into it. Then, I will not be stopped by any false sense of pity until the opponent is socially and morally ousted from the ranks of society."

After Paula had at last been ousted from the Himmler family ranks, a woman acquaintance warned Heinrich against seeing everything in terms of "we" and "us," and placing unconditional faith in a single political faction. But it was too late. By then, Himmler had merged his identity and his fortunes with the Nazi Party, delighting in dividing people into simple categories, reveling in being on the "naturally superior" side.

He had finally completed his long mental journey. For the rest of his life Heinrich Himmler's character was to remain essentially unchanged, confined by the emotional and political commitments he had made in accepting Nazism.

The remaining comments in Himmler's reading notes include an admiring comment about Adolf Hitler and two references to a book called *The State Within a State.* At the time, anti-Semites sometimes referred to the Jews this way; a decade later, the term would be applied to the SS.

The volume Himmler seems to have liked best, however, was called *The Knight, Death, and the Devil.* It described a noble Germanic hero struggling bravely against his enemies and "against fate." Himmler had at last discovered his own fairy-tale kingdom—in that "dark world of priests and knights" that Goethe had ridiculed a century earlier as a threat to enlightenment. "A book which expresses in pleasing words and sentences what I have felt and thought since I began to think," Himmler wrote exultantly in his diary.

A man who could hardly make a decision on his own now found it easy to choose to follow. After all, a knight needs a lord to serve. Subservient to his "betters," insecure with his peers, domineering toward the weak and fallible, Himmler had finally found a place where such traits would prove useful. Professing eternal faith to Hitler, facing his party comrades from behind the protection of a bureaucratic desk, finding in Nazi ideology a justification for merciless actions against opponents, Heinrich Himmler was more than useful, he was deadly.

In 1930, a conversation occurred between Hitler and his cronies that Konrad Heiden recorded in his book *Der Führer*:

> Hitler surprised a circle of his friends by asking them if they had read the just-published autobiography of Leon Trotsky, the great Jewish leader of the Russian Revolution, and what they thought of it. As might have been expected, the answer was, "Yes . . . Loathsome book . . . memoirs of Satan . . ." To which Hitler replied: "Loathsome? Brilliant! I have learned a great deal from it, and so can you." Himmler, however, remarked that he had not only read Trotsky but studied all available literature about the political police in Russia, the Tsarist Ochrana, the Bolshevik Cheka, and the GPU and he believed that if such a task should ever fall to his lot, he could perform it better than the Russians.

In the intervening years Himmler had apparently changed his mind about the merits of Secret Police work in general and Trotsky's views in particular, not to speak of the nature of human barbarity. Where once he had found Bolshevik techniques bestial, he now found them practical. During the interval, he had been appointed Reich leader of the SS, a few hundred ragtag men who often served as Hitler's bodyguards, when they weren't peddling party newspapers or secretly gathering information about their fellow members. The SS was regarded as completely insignificant—as was Himmler himself. ("He's no world-beater, you know," his boss Gregor Strasser said.)

His stewardship of the SS nevertheless turned the schoolmasterly Himmler into an "armed intellectual." Soon, he would be referring to the concentration camps as "a school for good citizenship." But even before the Nazis came to power in 1933, their would-be headmaster realized that he needed an assistant. Once more, Heinrich Himmler was searching for a boost from someone else, someone who would give him the daily infusions of energy his subservience to the remote godlike Hitler could not provide.

6

FATE, OR "WORK IN RELATION TO LIFE'S POSSIBILITIES"

"My husband wasn't at all determined to make a good
impression on Himmler. He wanted only to have a position,
to earn his bread."

—LINA HEYDRICH

I N THE FIRST FEW YEARS after Himmler became Reichsführer, he
spent his energies building up the organization and assisting in the
Nazi struggle for electoral power. His path did not converge with
that of Reinhard Heydrich until the summer of 1931, some two or three
months after the latter received his final dismissal from the navy.

Like Himmler a decade earlier, Heydrich was facing the bleakest
prospects. By the end of 1931, unemployment in Germany had risen
to 6 million men. (The figure in the summer of 1929 was 1.3 million.)
Within this feverishly competitive civilian world, an ex-lieutenant had
few marketable skills.

"What could he do?" Lina Heydrich asked. "What were his possibilities? He had only been trained for one thing."

When the ambitious son who had been the hope of his family came
home in disgrace, he could apparently think of nothing better to do
than remain secluded in his room, giving himself up to tears of despair.
I asked Lina about his feelings at that time, and about her own feelings
as well. She merely shook her head: "It is all a blank in my mind."

In her memoirs, she mentioned a disparaging remark of her father's
("That man has women everywhere!") and she noted that neither of
her parents felt she should marry Reinhard after the situation had been
so unpleasantly transformed. She defied them: "I had not agreed to

Heydrich (age twenty-seven, circa 1931) initiated his intelligence work by ferreting out the "radical opposition": political churches, Freemasons, Marxists, and Jews. Homosexuals and various "mattress affairs" both inside the party and out also came under his purview.

marry a set of job prospects; I had agreed to marry a man"—a man who had given up everything for her, including his honor in the eyes of the world.

Heydrich's own parents also were profoundly unhappy with the situation. They had never approved of their son's plans to wed a penniless girl. And now he had been dismissed just a few months before his pension vested, and would receive next to nothing for his nine and a half years of national service.

Frau Heydrich thought he could never throw off his naval training. "We were once in Kiel," she told me, "and we were going along the old harbor where he had spent a part of his service days and I a part of my school time. And I was in a coat, an open coat—I was just meandering along—and he suddenly said, 'Close your coat!' The sight of a naval ship sufficed to create a defensive posture of decorum in him! He had been an officer for almost ten years, *nicht wahr*?"

In this incident from a time long after Heydrich had achieved power greater even than an admiral's, we can sense a flavor of unrequited passion, as if a rejected suitor were suddenly to come face-to-face with a great love of his past. In 1931, of course, the wounds were still fresh and Reinhard Heydrich seems to have longed with raw fervor for the uniform he had so recently forsworn. Finally emerging from his room, he tried obstinately to build a new life on the old, ruined foundations, but no genuine military service was open to a cashiered officer. All he was offered was a minor position in the merchant marine. Also possible was a job as a sailing instructor in Hamburg, but his fiancée counseled against it: "To spend all day teaching the spoiled children of the rich . . . what future is there in that?"

The young couple had reached the edge of a social abyss before which many others of their era also paused; the only prospects open to them required a plunge downward in social status and personal hopes, into a marginal petit bourgeois world out of which it would be almost impossible to escape.

Lina's background growing up on Fehmarn had prepared her well to face her future husband's dilemma. She had always admired the island population's talent for compromise, and she realized this heritage had given her a personal orientation different from her husband's: "For him, two and two had to make four. I am less demanding; I can live with a situation where they make five."

While her fiancé hesitated, Lina acted. She did not work alone, however. Instead she found an unlikely ally—her prospective mother-in-law, Elisabeth Heydrich. The two women were hardly friends, but both realized that whatever else happened, Reinhard had to have a job. For years, the older woman had been skillfully cultivating the influential folk of Halle. Baron von Eberstein, the Wagnerian admirer of Bruno's music, had a son, Karl, who was more or less Reinhard's age and was rising swiftly in the Nazi Storm Troopers. Perhaps Karl could find "Reini" a job?

Heydrich himself was cool to his mother's project; he would only accept a position as some sort of officer. His future wife found him even less than enthusiastic about that parvenu, Hitler, whom he mistakenly thought to be Czech. "He was wedded to his naval career. He knew nothing about politics," Lina told a British journalist shortly after the war. Later, she boasted to me, "I myself on the island here already knew more about politics then he did. I had to make things clear to him at first!"

"Do you believe your husband would have become a National Socialist if he had—"

"Remained in the navy?" Frau Heydrich finished my sentence, as she often did when the topic was familiar. "No! No! He never would have, because the navy had no relationship to politics. They were not per-

From left: British prime minister Neville Chamberlain, Munich SS chief Friedrich Karl von Eberstein, and German foreign minister Joachim von Ribbentrop, in the Munich airport, September 15, 1938. By month's end, Britain, France, and Italy permitted the German annexation of the Sudetenland, in western Czechoslovakia. By the following March, Hitler annexed the remainder of that country.

mitted to vote. Today it is different. But they were absolutely without civil rights, and they were supposed to be trained entirely apolitically, according to the traditional ethical concepts."

"Then why did he join the SS?" I asked several times. At first, Lina kept herself well out of it: "That was very simple. When my husband separated from the navy, he could only work in a military-soldierly organization, and there was only the SS."

"Wasn't there also the SA?" (Sturmabteilung, or Storm Troopers, better known as Brown Shirts, the paramilitary wing of the Nazi Party.)

"The SA wasn't a military organization," she snapped. (She had told another interviewer that the brown-shirted Storm Troopers were rabble.)

"What did he think of the SS? Did he have a—"

"He had no conception, nothing at all. It was an entirely new sphere for him."

"So you would say that it was an accident that he joined the SS?"

She smiled gnomically and got up to go into the kitchen. "It was not an accident—but it had nothing to do with the SS."

Another time, in another context, Lina told me, "I said to my husband more or less this, which anyway was true, that he should do what he really knew how to do. He was nothing more than a soldier; otherwise he had learned nothing beyond his *Abitur* [high school diploma]. So it had to be in some kind of office or under authorities where something military would be demanded and where prerequisites for this were given. That would be the *natural* thing. And around that time his Halle neighbor von Eberstein wrote back, 'There is an SS under Himmler, the leader, and he is looking for someone.'"

In our second interview, Lina revealed that she advised Reinhard to make an appointment with Reichsführer Himmler, and, for obvious reasons, to join the Nazi Party first.

"Did he become a Nazi to make a career, then?"

"To make his career, you're right. And then, I have, naturally, also felt that for a long time I had been on the right trail. Not so much from politics, but rather, that the things National Socialism proposed lay directly on the path of our economic survival."

Lina knew something of what she spoke. In 1928, more than a year before she first met Reinhard, her father had gone to an election rally to hear an increasingly famous orator named Adolf Hitler. This was at the low point in the fortunes of Nazism (which only really prospered after the depression of 1929), but Herr von Osten came home convinced Hitler represented "the best hope" for Germany. He had joined the Nazi Party—more or less. "He was too cheap to pay the membership fee," his daughter remarked, reverting to one of her conflicting judgments of her father's penuriousness.

Lina herself had joined the party in 1929, shortly after her brother, Jürgen, a member of the SA, had persuaded her to attend a rally where Hitler spoke.

Where others have guessed that Heydrich was already a nationalistic, probably racist, fanatic, his fiancée felt her man needed a wifely little nudge to the right: "In truth, my husband came to his career like a speculator, and was certainly not driven by a [political] goal."

After some delay, Heinrich Himmler agreed to see him on June 14, 1931. Heydrich was living in Hamburg, and didn't look forward to the long train trip to Munich, which he seems to have regarded in true Prussian style as uncongenial southern territory. In the meantime, Himmler also fell prey to second thoughts, having developed a cold that kept him home, in bed. As Lina told it, "And then Karlchen telegraphed back, 'As God is willing, don't go, Himmler is sick!'" Heydrich and Karl von Eberstein agreed there was no rush. Besides, the 14th was Lina's birthday, and Reinhard preferred, romantically, to spend it with her.

Once more his fiancée intervened. Sitting in her cold, cluttered living room, Lina repeated for me the words she told him then: "You are not going to stay with me. Seize the opportunity instead. It is all the same, whether it is my birthday or not! I feel this illness is somehow a refusal. If it is truly important, then being sick is not important.

"Just go anyway!" she urged.

And so Reinhard Heydrich took the train to Munich. He was met there by von Eberstein, who told him the Reichsführer was displeased with his show of independence and preferred to see him another time. But Heydrich would not be dissuaded so easily again. The forceful side of his nature had been reawakened, and he persuaded his childhood friend to take him to Himmler's modest little house (named "Snowflake" because it was full of odd angles and eccentric corners).

They arrived just in time. Himmler had virtually decided to hire another man, and had lost interest in Heydrich. But then he saw him face-to-face. And everything changed.

In the navy, Heydrich had learned to disguise desperation under a coating of discipline glazed with arrogance. He was well over six feet tall—he towered over Himmler—and was always perfectly groomed. Of course, he was also glaringly Aryan in appearance, with the butter-blond hair, sky-blue eyes, and bone-pale skin of Himmler's most elaborate Nordic fantasies. In later group pictures of SS leaders, he always stands out, like a Viking prince on a social visit to a club for officers and bureaucrats. In the lean, drab year of 1931, Himmler must have been dazzled.

But he *was* Reichsführer of the Schutzstaffel, and he had been more or less defied, so in his best schoolmaster style, he created a test for the man who stood powerless before him, giving him twenty minutes to come up with a plan for reorganizing SS Intelligence. According to Lina, Heydrich hadn't known the precise nature of the job for which he was auditioning; suddenly, he realized that Himmler had made a mistake.

Frau Heydrich told me her version of what he did then (actually it is the only version, for neither man survived the war to tell of it): "Himmler said, 'I have heard you are a Nachrichtenoffizier [intelligence officer] and I want to build up an intelligence service, and how do you think that should be done?' But my husband was not an intelligence specialist, he was a Nachrichtenmitteloffizier [information officer], and that is a very big difference! But Himmler either had not grasped this difference or he didn't really hear it. Then my husband fell back on his intelligence, and thought, 'I'll just give it a try. Perhaps I can do what he wants; it is necessary for me to have a career if I want to marry.'

"And then he wrote down things that he himself could not remember afterward. But the navy had always had a good intelligence service, and he had some experience, I don't know what. In any case, he wrote everything possible—what sorts of things were perfect versus what could be improved. (To someone age twenty-eight, there are always some things that need improvement, *nicht wahr?*) And he wrote it all down and then Himmler said, '*Ne prima!* You are the one!'"

The young, dishonorably discharged former officer emerged from the Reichsführer's house transformed into the new head of SS Intelligence. If Himmler ever regretted his impulsive action, it was not until much later; in the next six months, he promoted Heydrich three times. During that period, he must surely have discovered other virtues in his new subordinate, in addition to military bearing, correct physiognomy, and quick intelligence. He must certainly have heard about Heydrich's prowess in sports, particularly fencing. (Himmler had once told a friend he wished he could join the navy, and he had always wanted to be a good fencer himself.) The man who had fumbled ineptly through piano lessons must have found out how many musical instruments Heydrich could play, and how well. Even the stories about loose behavior with women, incidents at dances or in bars, reckless insubordination in the navy, must have added an aura of careless bravado appropriate to both the old Teutonic knights and the new Nazi "elite." Reinhard Heydrich effortlessly must have seemed to embody everything Heinrich Himmler had spent his youth trying—and failing—to become. The Reichsführer does not seem to have thought to request an investigation of Heydrich's racial background, for his assets had already displayed themselves with perfect clarity.

If Himmler was both quickly and deeply impressed, the same cannot be said for Heydrich. When I asked Frau Heydrich to describe his initial impressions of Himmler, she gave me a little lecture: "*Ach* . . . Himmler had lain in bed and he had the flu, *nicht wahr*? No one cuts a good figure like that!

"And anyway," she continued, reversing the direction of my original question, "my husband didn't reflect at all about what this sick man in bed said to him. He only wanted to know, 'What does the man want from me?' That is very basic, right?"

Himmler's offer and Heydrich's acceptance of it marked the beginning of an alliance that was to prove truly fateful for millions of people. The pattern they set on the day of their meeting endured in rough outline until the end of their interlocked careers: Himmler, "unworldly," sickly, and misinformed, nevertheless makes a shrewd choice that will greatly enhance his political power; while Heydrich, clever, cynical, and quick on his feet, uses his skill in anticipating "what the man wants" to advance his own position. Seldom have two men who worked so closely together been so different in temperament and aptitudes; and seldom in modern history has there been such a devastatingly effective team. Separately, neither would have been likely to reach the pinnacle of power; together, they forged what various historians have characterized as two of the more extraordinary careers in the Third Reich.

The vast, malevolent empire of the SS was their joint creation: their very differences made it possible. In a sense they were trapped together, victims of both their own united strength and their complementary weaknesses. As time went on their "primitive" relationship became elaborately complex, its intricate convolutions reflected everywhere in the Orwellian world of clashing values, half-hidden intrigues, and labyrinthine bureaucratic byways they created.

Yet they also had much in common—or at any rate just enough. Both had experienced rejection, failure, and despair, and both had learned to hide their feelings behind masks of toughly "masculine" superiority. Both had shown a capacity to work hard and tenaciously to gain a place in the world commensurate with their dreams—and their dreams were exceedingly ambitious. More than once they had seen others thwart their plans, and both were inclined more to blame those others than themselves, yet they were sensible enough to try to learn from experience. Indeed, their restless inability to "settle," to know when to draw the line and when to quit, was one of the several things

that marked them as outsiders of the world of "bourgeois" content-
ment. Both belonged to that class of men "transformed into soldiers of
fortune by Europe's postwar disorders, and by . . . their incapacity for
satisfaction or resignation, either one." This anxious, stubborn spirit
became a fundamental part of the ethos of the SS.

What they did *not* share was a clearly articulated political philosophy, a sense of the potential of their partnership, or even an awareness
that it would become any such thing. On that fateful June 14, 1931,
Heydrich became merely a minor subordinate of an eccentric leader of
an unimportant organization, submerged within the millions of Storm
Troopers, who were themselves part of a ragtag movement struggling
for its very survival.

One evening, his widow provided me with her definitive reply to the
vexing question of exactly where he began. "My husband was twenty-
eight years old when he left the navy. And at twenty-eight, a man is
formed: he is stamped; his national consciousness, his feeling of duty,
these fundamental rules of conduct—to be clean, to be honest, to stand
up for something, to be loyal—so many things . . . His soldierly life was
stamped in the navy, not in the SS. On the contrary, he carried it over
to the SS so far as it was possible . . .

"His special political attitude was surely formed after he left the navy.
But it was naturally also formed on the basis of factual realities—data,
no? These were not utopian ideas, Spinozan ideas; rather they were real
experiences in real life. And this real life was not especially beautiful
then, *nicht wahr?*"

In June 1931, daily life in Germany had the raw quality of an infected
wound. Reinhard Heydrich, returning to Hamburg, found bands of
armed men clashing in the streets, as the forces of the far right and
far left fought to show their strengths and lure support away from the
irresolute, inept coalition of Prussian conservatives and Catholic businessmen occupying the parliamentary center.

The Nazis and the Communists were more or less evenly matched,
and both were advocating radical social change. It is a sad, old story,
repeated in the natural history of countless revolutions: while the
moderates hesitate, the extremists define things. The Nazis called this
period of expectant tension the *Kampfzeit* (time of struggle) and Heinrich Himmler loved it. Talking later of this era of fervent electioneering
punctuated by violence, conspiratorial meetings, and late-night chats

with Hitler, he called it "the best time" of his life. But there is no evidence that Heydrich shared the general euphoria. For one thing, his new job did not provide the clear "prerequisites" he wanted: he was chief of an organization that did not yet exist. For two months, he remained in Hamburg, and Lina, who was generally on Fehmarn, said she didn't really know what he was doing. In his eulogy at Heydrich's funeral, Himmler said his new subordinate had been active in "propaganda campaigns" in the city's Communist districts. This was a polite way of describing brawls. To a man trained in the rigid disciplines of naval life—not to mention the elegantly ritualized combat of fencing—such roughhousing must have seemed vulgarly déclassé. At any rate, he rarely mentioned it afterward.

Having completed his baptism through violence, Heydrich was sent to Munich, to the SS Supreme Command in the Brown House, the general party headquarters. "Still a small affair at the time," Himmler said in his speech; "indescribable" is the term Heydrich used when he tried to tell a friend about the situation there. His only asset, such as it was, consisted of Himmler's old files—clippings from newspapers and other items cut-and-pasted together. The entire collection filled a few shoeboxes. Heydrich had no separate office, no staff, and no typewriter. He also had no definite budget and no precise organizational title, since, contrary to his promise, Himmler had not relinquished his official position as intelligence chief.

Nevertheless, two weeks after he arrived in Munich, Heydrich gave his first report at a secret meeting of the Nazi bosses. He said merely what all knew anyway: the party was permeated with spies, representing every political faction from the Communists to the Weimar Secret Police. Observing that everyone suspected everyone else of being a possible informer, Heydrich was happy to fan the fumes of paranoia. His information was based on "real evidence," he said. The system must be tightened up. Then Heydrich added the conclusion that marked the beginning of his power: to maintain its purity, SS Intelligence should be screened from public view, and therefore must be moved out of the Brown House. At a stroke, he had cut himself off from Himmler's direct daily supervision, and made clear the separateness and independence of his tiny organization.

Meanwhile, Himmler had become distracted by other responsibilities. He had recently met Richard Walther Darré, an amateur eugenicist

who wanted to breed strong new races through selective mating practices. The Reichsführer was inspired to step up his efforts to create an
Aryan elite; in 1931, he began work on a new marriage code for the SS.
Henceforth, none of the leaders of his New Order was to marry without
his permission, or before proving his bride could meet stringent physical and racial requirements. Preoccupied with these elaborate plans,
he finally handed Heydrich official responsibility for "investigation of
hostile elements." Reinhard Heydrich was now truly chief of the Security Service of the SS, but this was hardly regarded as a pivotal position.
"What he was doing was quite unimportant," Lina said.

Undeterred, the new SD chief moved his skimpy files into rooms he
had rented at 23 Türkenstrasse, the home of "Mother" Viktoria Edrich,
the staunchly Nazi widow who kept hidden in a closet the "blood flag"
carried in the failed putsch of 1923, and who provided cheap lodging
and simple meals for young party comrades. (Over at the nearby university, future Youth Leader Baldur von Schirach sometimes asked Frau
Edrich for a plate of sandwiches to mark a special celebration.)

Once again, a woman helped the neophyte Heydrich find a place
among the Nazis. Now he had to prove his mettle. Hitler admired hard
men, "tough as Krupp steel," eager to demonstrate their strength wherever they were placed. Lina told me her fiancé was desperate to "achieve
something for the SS, since it was now the task giver . . . The people
must know that he was there!"

But how was this to be done? Several years later, Heydrich wrote a
brief article in which he claimed that the difficulties of that time—in
particular, the "lack of fundamental executive power"—had forced him
into "exhaustive rethinking on all fronts." Perhaps, but what he did
at first was borrow, with hasty eclecticism, from a variety of unlikely
sources.

Everyone but Lina Heydrich claims he was a great reader of detective
stories ("Yes, I know they say that, but *I* never saw him read them"),
and that he acquired through these a great respect for the British Secret
Service. His wife thought his model was the well-informed and well-
organized English police. In fact, these differences in organizational
titles didn't mean much to Heydrich, who saw England as a paradise
of espionage, a nation of politely patriotic informers, only too glad
to report any observed irregularities to a Secret Service correctly held
in high esteem. "This wouldn't happen in England!" he would remark

when an inexperienced agent made a mistake. Lina told me he felt it "would take a generation" for Germany to match England's expertise.

Heydrich knew that Germans felt there was something dishonorable in being a spy. Hitler, for instance, despised the "adventurers" who practiced espionage—even though he himself had been an informer for the military in 1919. Heydrich intended to change all that, and to make a career with his Sicherheitsdienst (or SD, as it was abbreviated in German) into a highly honorable position.

For the moment, however, he alone was the SD, and he worked alone on the files, trying to re-create some of the military order he had observed in the navy. Lina said he didn't get his ideas from Nazi practices, but he did certainly adopt his enemies from that source. Of course, he viewed the Communists as hostile, but any organized political party was worthy of scrutiny. Some opponents could be found even closer to home: Heydrich's first task was to build up a dossier on Gregor Strasser, Himmler's former boss, who had criticized Hitler for "betraying" the socialist part of the party platform. Lists of enemies *within* the Nazi Party were soon given the highest priority, because those closest to the Führer were the most potentially dangerous.

Himmler had collected tidbits about the major Nazi leaders; Heydrich now expanded the effort, even maintaining files on the leaders' wives. His vigilant presence began to irk Nazi "Old Fighters," who had signed up in earlier, wilder, days. Erich Wagner, the Gauleiter of Munich, called Heydrich "beer-counter for the party" in contemptuous reference to his unseemly interest in the amount of alcohol consumed at mass meetings.

Eventually, the "beer-counter" would spin a vast network of spies, but at first, he had to do the legwork himself. One day he made a surprise visit to the office of Gunter d'Alquen, a journalist who was later to become editor of the SS newspaper *Das schwarze Korps* (*The Black Corps*). The two men had not met before, d'Alquen told me in an interview.

"Didn't you feel somewhat apprehensive?" I asked.

"Oh, no, no, no!" he said, laughing. "Heydrich was just a little man then. The fact was that I was a rather more important figure at the time. And, anyway, he wanted a favor." Heydrich asked politely if d'Alquen would send him any information about people he knew who might be of interest to the new Security Service.

"And did you agree?"

D'Alquen laughed again. "Oh, yes, why not? I didn't know anything much—I was more interested in working on the newspaper—but it paid to stay on the right side of people. And we were comrades after all—no?"

However much one manipulates the concept of honor to suit special needs, there is still an inherent conflict between serving your country in a noble manner and ratting on your fellow combatants. One wonders if Heydrich knew of the expression, which, like much that he admired, was made famous by an Englishman, Alexander Pope (translating Horace): "Get wealth and power, if possible, with grace; if not—by any means get wealth and place." Heydrich later achieved immense power, but there has always clung about him the notion that he had had to sell his soul to do it. Even the Nazis felt the means he used were dubious. According to a saying of the time, if the Germans won the war, Hitler would become king of the world, Goebbels king of the demimonde, and Heydrich king of the underworld.

Himmler's powers, responsibilities, and crimes were far greater, but this short, bespectacled man could never serve as the symbolic representative for what Gideon Hausner, the head prosecutor in the trial of Adolf Eichmann, has called the "Satanic force" and "fiendish cunning" of Nazism. It is Heydrich who looked the part, and who has been called "a professional criminal of Luciferian magnitude."

The English journalist Charles Wighton writes that Heydrich "bloomed like an exotic flower in the highly artificial atmosphere of the SS . . . Soon the other members of the SS leadership began to be aware that they were faced by a major personality of enormous potential and Heydrich began to take on the shape that within a few years made him the most dreaded man in the Third Reich."

His development was a straggly, uneven sort of growth, at least according to various associates of his I interviewed. A woman who had played in string quartets with him in his naval days happened to meet the new SS officer on a train in the late summer of 1931. He told her that he had gotten a wonderful new job and would soon be in a position to show the world how well he was doing. She thought he looked tired and ill—and so unhappy that his protestations rang false.

A year or so later, he met a friend from his childhood—one of the very few people who are still willing to claim such a relationship—and allegedly told him, "I think I have stood and shouted 'Hurrah!' at the wrong railroad station."

Skeptical of these stories, I thought I would nudge Frau Heydrich into disagreeing with them. "I suppose after your husband joined the SS, he said to himself, 'Now I have found my place . . .'"

She made a grunting sound. "He thought, 'Now at last I have a job. Now I can get married!' *That* is what he thought!"

On December 26, 1931, Reinhard and Lina were finally married. The wedding occurred at Grossenbrode, the small village on the mainland where Herr von Osten taught school, but the nature of the ceremony would have made it clear to Heydrich that he was moving onto a definite political terrain, as well as pledging himself to a particular woman.

Lina was obviously proud of the unusual rituals that occurred, but also strangely loath to talk about them. On the one hand she bragged, "I must say people are still talking of *that* wedding!" On the other, she demurred, "Well, my wedding . . . Oh, well, that was just an ordinary wedding."

"But you did a lot of unusual things, right?"

"Oh no, after all, we were married in thirty-one . . ."

"Yes, but you had a flag in the church, isn't that right? A swastika?"

"Yes, well, that was during the so-called time of struggle [*Kampfzeit*], and the local Frauenschaft [the Ladies' League of the Nazi Party] fashioned a . . . a floral wreath and then they put a swastika in the center, and it was like that."

"But wasn't this considered unusual?"

"Well, yes, but that was during the struggle time."

"You had an honor guard of Storm Troopers, right?"

"Yes, that was the local custom . . . of the local NSDAP [i.e., the Nazis], you might say."

"Did you plan it like this, that it would have a political tone?"

"Oh no, we did nothing at all. And it was not necessary. How should I put it: it was a festive occasion of this area? The people who belonged to the NSDAP, they thought it fashionable to form an honor guard, to play the 'Horst-Wessel-Lied' on the organ . . . and they were always very loyal and tolerant."

"And the people from Fehmarn, what did they think?"

"It was a beautiful wedding, but it was a family wedding."

"But with political—"

"Overtones, yes. But it could just as well have been a social club, I would say."

"Your husband's family was not very politically oriented, were they?"

"No, not at all. They were artists."

"Didn't it rather surprise them? Didn't your husband's mother or father say, 'That's a little too much'?"

"No, if you think about it, my in-laws still belonged to the class of artists who thought as long as your name was mentioned in the papers . . . You know the way these artists were."

In the manner of artists, Bruno Heydrich composed a special piece, which he sang in the ceremony. That is what Lina told me, at any rate; in her book, she says that Heydrich's sister, Maria, sang from a Bach cantata. The groom wore the traditional black morning suit and top hat, but his bride thought he looked awkward and unnatural in it. As the bridal couple left the church, the Storm Troopers sprang into action, forming their honor guard and making an arch of crossed swords under which the Heydrichs walked.

Political action groups had recently been prohibited by the Weimar government, and the SA men accordingly wore only white shirts and black breeches. Nevertheless, they were all arrested afterward by the vigilant authorities—and so was the minister who performed the ceremony.

Frau Heydrich insisted to me, however, that it was not "an SS wedding." Later on, Himmler devised an openly pagan ritual in which the bridal couple exchanged symbolic gifts of bread and salt, and invoked the blessings of the sun and earth on their union. Still, I presumed the Reichsführer SS must have enjoyed the Heydrichs' dramatically politicized ceremony, but as it turned out, he wasn't there: "Nooo, noooo, for heaven's sake! . . . We were just *little* people!"

Instead, Himmler, short of money and notoriously cheap, gave Heydrich as a wedding gift his third promotion since August. (The couple's racial credentials were not investigated, since the new marriage code had not yet gone into effect.)

Heydrich was now a Standartenführer (approximately, colonel); but he could not afford a honeymoon, and so went immediately back to work. After a wedding that had proved transitional in both form and

Lina and Reinhard's December 1931 wedding, where the ceremony included an organ rendition of the SA marching song, the "Horst-Wessel-Lied," also known as "Raise the Flag High." Wessel, a leader of the Brown Shirts, had written lyrics to the anthem in 1929, a year before being fatally shot by two Communists.

significance, he moved with his bride into a house he had amateurishly renovated himself, attempting to hide the cracks in the floorboards with several layers of brown paint.

No one could have imagined that before their third wedding anniversary, the bridegroom would have become even more powerful than the leader of the huge army of Storm Troopers or that he would by then have succeeded in gathering all of the nation's powers of arrest into his own manicured hands.

GATHERING POWER

7

BITTER YOUNG MEN, BRIGHT YOUNG MEN: HEYDRICH'S SD

"He never required that the men who worked for him be
in the Nazi Party. Not at all. He relied essentially on their
intelligence . . . I can't imagine there could be an intelligent man
he didn't find interesting in some way."

—LINA HEYDRICH

L ONG BEFORE REINHARD HEYDRICH himself emerged as the Nazis'
chief of political intelligence, he was recruiting and training a group
of the cleverest assistants he could find—an elite within the elite
SS. Heydrich once described the SD—Sicherheitsdienst, or Security
Service—as "the shock troops of the new worldview," but they were also
his personal brain trust, the nucleus of advisers and underlings fueling
his skyrocket rise to power.

Paradoxically, the organization that is generally known as "Heydrich's
SD" was officially called "the Security Service of the Reichsführer SS,"
meaning, of course, Heinrich Himmler's. Yet after Himmler handed
over to Heydrich his collection of newspaper clippings, his role was
effectively over.

The SD has been called Heydrich's one "idealism." Certainly there
was a glamorous, swashbuckling side to his role as chief of security.
Secret agents may do nasty things, yet almost every country has them
and they are often extolled as heroic patriots. In their day, "Heydrich's
bright young men" were swathed in mystery and sinister prestige. On
June 9, 1934, Party Secretary Rudolf Hess "decreed the SD the sole intelligence service of the Nazi Party," reflecting the widespread view that
the organization was the brain of the party and the state. In less dramatic form, the legend still persists: Heinz Höhne, the German writer

who specialized in intelligence history, has called the SD "the refuge for National Socialism's most intelligent men."

"One hears so much of the SD," I asked Frau Heydrich. "Where did your husband find these people?"

"First, he never required that the men who worked for him be in the Nazi Party. Not at all. He relied essentially on their intelligence. And, naturally, on their preparation. Also that they be without reproach morally."

"In what way, morally?"

"That they be honest. That they had revealed their human qualities . . . I can't imagine there could be an intelligent man he didn't find interesting in some way."

She told me Heydrich sometimes attended the qualifying exams for young lawyers: "To see how the people would appear, and also to ask questions and be asked questions. He would say, 'Place your questions,' and one man asked, 'How much money will I earn?' My husband said—he told me this—'If you really believe you are the man for us, you must ask me, 'What do I have to do! What tasks will I have to perform?' "

Heydrich apparently thought that the gentlemanly leaders of the British Secret Service didn't work for money. Neither did he. A potential SD man therefore had to exert what Frau Heydrich called a certain "radiation, a power of attraction," to which her husband reacted instinctively.

By what objective standards, then, did Heydrich measure the people he recruited for his ultra-elite organization? As is so often the case, history cannot respond speedily with specific answers to such generalized questions. No complete personnel rosters of the SD have survived. However, there does exist a copy of the 1934 *Führerlexikon*, a list of hundreds of high-ranking Nazi leaders that gives one an idea of who was who at the dawn of the Third Reich. Studying the lexicon, the political scientist Daniel Lerner has found that the Nazi leaders, like revolutionaries almost everywhere, were younger than the members of the establishment they sought to supplant. The average age of German military officers at the time was fifty-two, but Nazi officials averaged only forty. And although SD officers were not considered lexicon material in 1934, other documents reveal that almost half of them were under thirty. (Heydrich had turned thirty-one in March; Himmler was all of thirty-four.) This is a generation gap of very large proportions: more than twenty years separated the real military officers from their para-military watchdogs in the SD.

Recalling the adage once popular among Berkeley radicals, "Never trust anyone over thirty," I asked Frau Heydrich if her husband had deliberately sought out young men. No, she replied, but there were more of them available, since so few could find work. Such unemployed recruits to Nazi organizations have been described as "bitter young men," settling for a political movement because they couldn't get jobs commensurate with their training and ambitions. Frau Heydrich put this another way: "It was the young people who could afford to be ide-alistic, to have faith in the future. After all, what did they have to lose?"

Granted that the men of the SD *were* extremely young; they were supposed to be smart as well. Unfortunately, the Nazis, who exalted brawn above brain, did not often test IQs. Scholars must therefore examine such inferential indicators of intelligence as higher education and professional degrees. The American historian George C. Browder has analyzed the records of more than two hundred SD officers who joined before 1934, and found that half had attended university or professional school, twenty-nine had some legal training, and another twenty-nine had obtained a PhD. (Two even described themselves as "theologians.") Statistically speaking, they were indeed bright young men, surpassing both Nazi Party members and their fellow elitists in the SS. Obviously, however, intelligence is not the only quality needed for intelligence work. One-third of the other early officers came from the sparsely educated working class; perhaps they were chosen for some Nazi version of "street smarts."

In fact, the most widely shared attribute of Heydrich's SD recruits was not good education but the nature of their political experience: not one had ever been a member of a Marxist, socialist, or even a liberal party. This is a remarkable statistic, particularly reconsidering that "Nazi" is an abbreviation for "National Socialist," and that no less a person than Himmler had considered moving to the Soviet Union. Yet Heydrich's young men had been involved only with German nationalism.

They also conformed excessively to another aspect of the Nazi ethos—reverence for military experience. Himmler's boss, Ernst Röhm, had wanted to create a corps of "political soldiers" to patrol the New Order. But his millions of unruly Storm Troopers were too numerous, heterogeneous, and undisciplined truly to embody this ideal. By contrast, fifty-eight of the early SD members had, like Heydrich himself, already proved their soldierly credentials in the Freikorps—a far higher percentage than in any other Nazi group. By 1934, Heydrich had already bested Röhm at his own soldierly game.

Obviously, the special criteria Heydrich was using to select his new subordinates far exceeded the needs of the little SS spy network he had been assigned to create. Frau Heydrich often said that by 1932, her husband was already attempting to lay the groundwork for a militarized, centralized, national intelligence service along the lines of Britain's MI5. Available statistics support this claim.

They also reveal a final peculiarity of the SD group picture. In 1932, the year after Heydrich took over, fully half of his staff was from central Germany (where he was born) or northern Germany (where he had been stationed in the navy). By contrast, as Daniel Lerner, the student of the lexicon, found, most of the early Nazi leaders came from the "marginal" parts of the country along its borders—such as Bavaria (Himmler's birthplace) or Austria (Hitler's homeland). By canvassing and drawing from mainstream Germany, Heydrich was apparently recruiting in the areas he knew best, rather than running with the Nazi pack.

One of the earliest SD leaders, Hermann Johann Heinrich Behrends, happened to be in Munich on a social visit, and was promptly signed up. He and Heydrich had been friendly since Heydrich's days in the navy, when Behrends's father had run an inn frequented by officers. Chronically impoverished, Heydrich had often been unable to pay his bills. Perhaps he thought a debt was owed; perhaps he was imitating Hitler's pattern of trusting men he had known before he achieved power.

This "crude" recruitment pattern has been taken by Browder as confirmation of the amateur status of the new Security Service: a professional espionage organization would have cast a wider and more carefully woven net. This is certainly true, and reveals a final characteristic of the new SD elite: almost none of them had experience in intelligence work. In this, as in their other traits, they were very much like their new chief.

Reinhard Heydrich had started from scratch, seeking the sort of peo-

Senior SD official Hermann Behrends (age thirty-six, circa 1943) joined the Nazi Party in 1932. As head of the SD office in Berlin starting in January 1934, Behrends helped oversee that summer's Night of the Long Knives, a purge that resulted in the murder of nearly four hundred Brown Shirts and consolidated Hitler's power.

ple with whom he felt most comfortable, and in the process stamping the SD with his own personal imprint. In doing so, he was acting as an "organizational statesman," a term coined by the sociologist Phillip Selznick to describe a relatively rare phenomenon—the leader who not only heads an organization but also defines its essential character, creating not merely a set of rules and offices but a guiding spirit as well.

Not surprisingly, this spirit is usually similar to the leader's own. Thus "the Service," as its members soon came to call Heydrich's creation, was also a sort of mirror reflecting various aspects of his political persona.

As the Sicherheitsdienst continued to grow, however, the picture it presented fragmented into a variety of parts, like a receptacle into which divisive elements have too frequently been thrown. In fact, it was never really a single entity at all, but a constantly evolving, unsteady mixture of people defined by different roles and projects. Its aims expanded drastically through the years, and its forms changed according to need. At the heart of this flux—and usually responsible for it—stood Heydrich himself, surrounded by a changing guard of carefully chosen subordinates, seizing every opportunity to maximize his power, and theirs.

A look at the way three of his closest collaborators got their start in the SD provides a good illustration of Heydrich in action, learning as he went along, creating his organization. They are Alfred Naujocks, who became a specialist at dirty tricks; Walter Schellenberg, a crafty charmer who specialized in foreign relations; and Otto Ohlendorf, an early and dedicated Nazi who thrived as an irritant to the system. A fourth and final example was a man who did not entirely fit in, although he became the best-known former SD individual of all, Adolf Eichmann.

In 1933, about a year and a half after he became its chief, Heydrich visited a beleaguered SD outpost at 16 Eichenallee, in the northwest outskirts of Berlin. At that time, this was only a token office in the heavily guarded labyrinth of power, where Heydrich was still struggling to find his bearings.

The Berlin SD was housed far from the center of political activity, in a villa where the members both worked and slept. Indeed, their domineering commanding officer, a former detective named Hans Kobelinsky, rarely let them off the grounds. His staff lived almost like monks, hedged in by regulations, allowed to have guests only one night a month, and rarely going into the city. The newest member of the team, Alfred Helmut Naujocks—the man who would play a key role in the staged incident that "justified" Germany's invasion of Poland—had never even seen downtown Berlin, having come straight from his home in Kiel and simply stayed on. As the days passed, he became increasingly bored and dissatisfied.

At fifteen, Naujocks had joined the Nazis through a combination of accident and impulse. Seeing a swastika in a store window in Kiel, he bought the unfamiliar symbol because it looked pretty to him, placed it on his motor scooter, and was promptly beaten up as he rode near the docks. This was during the so-called *Kampfzeit* before Hitler came to power, when radicals of the far right and far left often fought openly in the streets. Alfred yearned for immediate revenge on his assailants. With his head still bandaged, he returned to the docks, sought out a bar frequented by the local Nazi leader, and insisted on joining the party. But he looked much too young and vulnerable to be taken seriously. The party boss jokingly told the boy he would have to prove himself in fisticuffs with the leader of a group of Communists lurking outside. With adolescent bravado, Naujocks walked up to the Red leader and slugged him. A general melee ensued, after which Naujocks was awarded his Nazi badge.

A boxer by avocation, an adventurer by disposition, the newly recruited Nazi was working as a welder in Kiel when he heard about a new, top-secret organization within the party headed by "a brilliant

Alfred Naujocks (above, standing, with Heydrich in 1934, and at left, age nineteen, circa 1930) secured his position as a Sturmbannführer—assault unit leader—by exposing the indiscretions of his superior. In August 1939, with Nazis posing as Polish commandos, Naujocks staged the Gleiwitz incident to provide a pretext for the German invasion of Poland, thus provoking World War II.

young man who was a close friend of Himmler" (who was, of course, Heydrich). Naujocks went to Berlin to wangle a job interview with Kobelinsky, who told him "responsible jobs" would be waiting when the SD expanded.

Naujocks loved the threatening, exciting aura of the SD, and impulsively signed up. He enjoyed his new job compiling files on the work, families, backgrounds, and hobbies of many enemies of the SS and the party, but his flamboyant nature rebelled against the restrictions on his liberty. One evening he sneaked out for a night on the town, and as punishment was placed on strict disciplinary probation. Providentially for Naujocks, this was on the eve of a Heydrich visit. Naujocks had already been doing all the KP work—clearing up, waiting on tables at dinner—and now he was assigned the task of chauffeur. He was to meet Himmler's brilliant friend at the railroad station, while the rest of the staff prepared a welcome. Naujocks had never even seen Heydrich, though he had studied his likeness in the party newspapers and had heard he was once a naval officer.

At the station, he had no trouble recognizing the tall, blond service chief, and was impressed that "he looked as if he had just stepped off the parade ground, instead of having sat in a train all day." The elegant young leader of the SD handed his even younger driver a black leather briefcase and took a seat in the back of the car. Unaware if protocol called for conversation, Naujocks politely asked about his trip and received a chatty reply. Emboldened, he said he came from Kiel, where he believed Heydrich had also lived. Perhaps Naujocks was unaware that most people avoided even oblique references to the navy in Heydrich's presence. Luckily, Heydrich responded with polite interest, and for the next twenty minutes they discussed life in Kiel. Naujocks reported later that he felt they were talking like old friends.

On the other hand, Heydrich's relationship with Kobelinsky was decidedly strained, as Naujocks observed from his post as waiter at dinner. "You're working too hard; you look ill," Heydrich said to his obviously nervous host. Indeed, Kobelinsky probably was sick—with worry. For one thing, he was rumored to be homosexual. In 1933, this was still marginally acceptable within the SS, if only because of the flagrant homosexuality of Ernst Röhm, to whom Heinrich Himmler was still technically subordinated. Yet Himmler, obsessed with purifying German bloodlines through the begetting of many Aryan children, loathed homosexuality. (Following his custom, he had once read a book about it. "Awful pictures. Very depressed," he had written in his diary afterward.) Whenever possible Himmler expunged homosexuals from the SS.

Heydrich was concerned with security, not genetics, but Kobelinsky turned out to be vulnerable on that score, too. On the drive back to the station, Heydrich switched to the front seat. "How do you like working here?" he asked Naujocks. Sensing opportunity, Naujocks complained about the restrictive rules and the lack of trust they implied: "We're not criminals." Then he offered a bit of inside information: Kobelinsky had met with a leader of the Gestapo to discuss mutual collaboration. The

Gestapo and the SD were at that time bitter rivals, and Heydrich was bound to have considered this unforgivable treason. (Obviously worried, Kobelinsky had specifically asked his staff not to mention it.) Heydrich listened impassively as Naujocks betrayed his boss's confidence. Then he silently boarded the train, pausing only to shake his talkative chauffeur's hand.

For a week, nothing happened. Then suddenly, "without warning," a representative from Heydrich came to talk to Kobelinsky. One hour later, the two men left together. Kobelinsky never returned. The next day the SS official Hermann Behrends arrived as the new Berlin chief of the SD. Immediately, he called for Naujocks to tell him Heydrich sent his best wishes—and a promotion.

A year later, in 1934, Naujocks followed Heydrich into the spacious new SD central office in the heart of imperial Berlin—directly across from Gestapo headquarters, which that same year also passed into the hands of the SS. The two men were now working closely together, plotting the sort of strong-arm derring-do Naujocks so enjoyed. Soon Alfred Naujocks was promoted to head of the SD department of dirty tricks: "I had to burgle, steal, kidnap, and lie." He later wrote, "I suppose that is part of secret service work everywhere."

On his first big mission, Naujocks was sent to Czechoslovakia to kidnap Rudolf Formis, an anti-Nazi radio commentator whom Hitler wanted captured alive. Pretending to be on holiday, Naujocks took along an attractive young woman as "cover," though Heydrich warned him sarcastically, "Just try and remember you have some work to do." For whatever reason, this mission went badly. Naujocks wound up in a shoot-out in a hotel room, inadvertently killing Formis and barely surviving himself. Heydrich was furious.

Fortunately for Naujocks, he was much more successful at arranging forgeries of various kinds, from obscure passport stamps to 100 million pounds of counterfeit English banknotes. To assist in these efforts, Naujocks could call on the new SD Technical Bureau. Camouflaged to look like a holiday villa, it was filled with printing presses, darkroom equipment, and experimental laboratories in which passports were fabricated, tiny cameras manufactured, poisons inserted into sausages or hollow teeth, and photographs reduced to the size of pinheads. Naujocks worked directly for the SD chief, and was given a very free hand in matters of travel, personnel, and expenses. Yet never for a moment did

Heydrich loosen his reins on Naujocks. He was allowed to improvise within a given framework, but Heydrich generally came up with the ideas. Indeed, Naujocks sometimes thought Heydrich devised bizarre projects more to satisfy a "showman's ego" than to serve the Reich.

Their relationship was erratic. Heydrich offered rewards but was quicker to criticize. He wanted fast work that was "damn near perfection," but if things went well, he made little comment; he had already moved on to another scheme. Naujocks came to feel that Heydrich was happiest alone, planning his next move before others made theirs: "That was the guiding factor in his work: to keep one step ahead." By contrast, Naujocks judged Himmler to be a "far safer man. His mind was not subtle enough for this kind of intrigue."

Alfred Naujocks felt he and Heydrich respected each other as fellow adventurers and risk takers, and indeed they often went out socially together after work (generally to bars, where they talked about women). Eventually, however, Naujocks realized that Heydrich never really let down his guard. Even while flirting with ladies of the night, "there were no half measures." Every place, every time, in the office and out of it, Heydrich played to win. His naval comrades had noted this also, but the chief of the SD now moved in a very different world. What if he decided that Naujocks knew too much about too many high state secrets? Naujocks concluded apprehensively that Heydrich was too shrewd "to allow sentimentality . . . or old friendships to stand in the way of loyalty to the Führer."

For his part, Heydrich had no illusions about Naujocks's limitations: "You will always be a problem," Naujocks later wrote that Heydrich told him. "You're too much of an individual, you resent authority."

In contrast to Alfred Naujocks's somewhat impromptu, interactive career, the advance of Walter Friedrich Schellenberg, the future SD intelligence chief, seemed almost magically guided from afar, though his success depended a lot on his crafty opportunism and calculated ability to charm. (Indeed, Naujocks described Schellenberg as a "glib-tongued egoist" who represented "the new generation of party executives—well-bred intellectuals, political psychologists.") As Schellenberg himself confessed in his memoirs, "In the SS one found the 'better type of people,' and membership in it brought considerable prestige . . . I can-

Walter Schellenberg rose from
apprenticing under Heydrich to serving
as Hitler's chief of counterintelligence.
His office desk, Schellenberg boasted,
was "a small fortress. Two automatic guns
were built into it which could spray the
entire room with bullets."

not deny that at the age of twenty-three such things as social prestige
and . . . the glamour of the smart uniform played quite a large part in
my choice."

One of seven children of an impoverished piano manufacturer, Schellenberg built his career by making the most of apparently unpromising
opportunities. In order to study law, he joined the Nazi Party primarily
to gain scholarship help. Next, to get out of military drilling, which
bored him, he volunteered to deliver lectures on various subjects, which
in turn got him recruited by the SD.

He was advised to continue his legal studies and to participate in SD
activities only in an "honorary" way, without obligation on either side.
But he soon found himself acting as an informer, in exchange for which
he got assigned important cases in his legal training. Suddenly, "without
any warning," he was ordered to continue his training in Berlin. Once
there, he found doors opened to him by courteous bureaucrats, quite
as if someone were silently guiding him "through the complex channels
of this huge machine."

Then one day Schellenberg was ordered to report to Heinrich Müller, the operational chief of the Gestapo. He confronted a burly man
with "the squarish skull of a peasant" and hooded eyes. He also found
himself dealing for the first time with one of the bitter intraservice
rivalries that divided the SS throughout its history. Once the Nazis

seized power, Heydrich's protégés in the SD had been deprived of much of their raison d'être. Now that enemies of the party could be reclassified as enemies of the state, they could more easily be pursued by the Gestapo—particularly as the SD lacked the power to arrest.

Who could the SD spy on now? One solution to this organizational identity crisis was to insert SD members into the Secret Police as observers. Heydrich had already begun this process—which, of course, was why Schellenberg had been assigned to Müller—but he was encountering fierce resistance. Müller passionately resented the college graduates without police experience whom Heydrich was forcing him to work with. "One really ought to drive all the intellectuals into a coal mine and then blow it up," he told Schellenberg. The latter soon reached the unsurprising conclusion that no real conversation was possible with the brutish Müller. Yet at the end of their inauspicious first meeting Müller told Schellenberg he was to be assigned to the main office of the SD. "Heydrich likes your reports," he grudgingly added.

In this roundabout way, Walter Schellenberg at last discovered that "the dreaded chief of the SD himself had been the unseen force guiding me like a pawn on a chessboard."

The two men had still not met. Heydrich was now too busy and too powerful to spend much time dealing personally with neophyte SD men. The next day Schellenberg did receive a detailed explanation of the mission and structure of the organization. He was informed that every sphere of society—the administration, industry, the theater, the press, the party, the police—was watched by SD agents to determine opposition movements and forces hostile to the state. After the agents' reports reached Berlin, they were refined into a general summary, which twice a month was sent to the Führer. Meanwhile, "a file was prepared for each individual whose name appeared in these reports, and the reports cross-indexed against their subject matter."

Schellenberg was clever enough to recognize behind this bureaucratic jargon the "pedestal" of Heydrich's power:

> The decisive thing for him was always to know more than others, . . . whether it touched on the political, professional, or most intimate personal aspects of their lives, and to use this knowledge and the weaknesses of others to render them completely dependent on him, from the highest to the lowest. It was this

that enabled him to hold and manipulate the balance of power in a milieu full of intrigue and crosscurrents of personal ambition, rivalry, and animosity, while he himself stayed in the background.

Schellenberg is given to exaggeration; yet it is absolutely true that Heydrich's rise to influence was reflected in a paper trail. Files were a life-and-death issue: because of them, men disappeared into camps or fell from influence; through them, other men could sit at their desks, and commit murder in the name of the state. This is reflected in the portrait of Heydrich by Josef Vietze, in which Heydrich was painted holding a document. In a film of guests at Hitler's mountaintop retreat, Heydrich appeared striding across a stone balustrade with a sheaf of papers in his hand. During the great pogrom of Kristallnacht in 1938, policemen under Heydrich's orders stood by while synagogues burned to the ground, but first they removed important documents. Later, the commandos he sent in behind invading German armies were given standing orders to confiscate any interesting papers they found.

In 1934, when Schellenberg joined the SD, the filing system had just been organized and was still incomplete, extending only sketchily over Germany, and containing little information about foreign countries. Schellenberg described the state of the art at that time: "A huge, circular table was constructed on which the files were placed. This table was electrically driven and by pressing a button one man seated at the controls could bring any one of 500,000 cards within easy reach."

The man metaphorically sitting at the controls was Heydrich, for Hitler saw only what was presented to him, and Himmler, too, relied on Heydrich's information. In Schellenberg's excited prose: "He was a master at playing antagonists off one against the other, feeding each one . . . detrimental information about his rival, and getting still more damaging information in return. Heydrich was, in fact, the puppet master of the Third Reich."

By the time Schellenberg finally met his formidable service chief, he was in a fever of apprehension. Indeed, his description of their first encounter is roughly what one might expect from a defenseless little creature that has just wandered into the lair of a much larger carnivore: "When I entered his office Heydrich was sitting behind his desk. He was a tall, impressive figure with a broad unusually high forehead, small restless eyes as crafty as an animal's and of uncanny power, a long predatory nose, and a wide full-lipped mouth. His hands were slender and rather too long—they made me think of the legs of a spider."

Having the advantage of his files, Heydrich already knew a great deal about his new subordinate. He began by chatting about Schellenberg's family, and then about music, in which he knew the piano manufacturer's son to be well versed. Then he asked the young man many questions, especially about his legal training. (He knew everything about it, including the details of a job Schellenberg had just been offered.) Finally, Heydrich began to declaim, saying that a new generation of lawyers, less "fossilized" than the old and with open minds toward the New Order, should play an important role in public life. He spoke in an urgent, staccato style, rarely pausing even to finish a sentence, though Schellenberg understood his meaning: he was preparing to thrust his Security Service beyond its role of secret party watchdog and openly into the area of foreign intelligence. This involved deliberate encroachment on the territory of the military's intelligence (or Abwehr). It also required adroit maneuvering, clever words, capacity for swift, flexible action—all skills possessed by both Heydrich and Schellenberg—as well as diplomatic ability, which Heydrich often lacked and was now seeking in others.

The two men conversed for an hour and a half, and Schellenberg walked out of Heydrich's office "overwhelmed by the strength of his personality to an extent I have never experienced before or since." Even after the war, he still maintained: "This man was the hidden pivot around which the Nazi regime revolved . . . He was far superior to all his political colleagues and controlled them as he controlled the vast intelligence machine of the SD."

Schellenberg's characteristically hyperbolic language and intense sense of drama infuse his memoirs, and have helped to make them one of the best-known personal accounts of Nazism. Yet even for the more down-to-earth Alfred Naujocks, drama and Heydrich's presence went hand in hand. He had a gift for stirring up the people around him. His sudden moves, resulting in orders issued "without warning," created a feeling of excitement, of being caught up in important things. Heydrich's conduct also made them feel constantly on edge. But it wasn't that simple: Heydrich won the allegiance of his bright young vassals by a compelling mixture of traits, differently revealed on different occasions.

· · ·

To a few of his SD men—to Otto Ohlendorf, for example, who as an SS Obergruppenführer would become responsible for intelligence and security within Germany—Heydrich even served in the unlikely role of rescuer.

On the face of it, Ohlendorf should hardly have needed help. He was everything a young Nazi should be; indeed, it was his very dedication as such that got him into difficulty—that and the self-righteousness that went with it.

Ohlendorf's Nazi credentials were better than Himmler's, and much better than Heydrich's. Unlike them, he had actually been born on a farm (in Prussia), which made him a candidate for restoring what the Nazis—and Himmler especially—talked endlessly about, the nobility of "the soil." Ohlendorf had excelled in law and economics at the prestigious universities of Marburg and Göttingen, but unlike Walter Schellenberg he was no late-arriving political opportunist. He joined the Nazi Party at eighteen, in 1925, when only true believers like Himmler were in the fold. He was pure Aryan, with no stain on his family name.

As an intelligent young man from the right background who got his foot in the door early, Ohlendorf should have had a glorious career in the New Order. He did rise high in the SD, but in spite of, not with the help of, the Nazi Party. As he later said, his entire career within the party was nothing but a miserable series of rejections and reversals.

Otto Ohlendorf (age thirty-two, in 1939) was appointed by Heydrich to command the Einsatzgruppe D death squad, which was responsible for the murder of ninety thousand victims, most of them Jews.

In his confession at Nuremberg, Ohlendorf said, "To me it is inconceivable that a subordinate leader should not carry out orders given by the leaders of the state."

Ohlendorf's troubles started in February 1934, when he was arrested by the Gestapo. In his job at the Institute for Economics in Kiel he had objected so strenuously to "Bolshevistic" tendencies in the local party leadership that its members had denounced him for causing political unrest. He was swiftly released, and moved to Berlin, where he once again began to attack "National Bolshevism." This time his efforts were criticized in the party newspaper by the official party philosopher, Alfred Rosenberg. Ohlendorf was devastated: "Something within me has been shaken," he wrote to his wife. "I don't any longer have the same carefree certainty with which I struggled for our National Socialism."

In 1935, Ohlendorf was moldering in a minor job at the Censorship Bureau when he was approached by Professor Reinhard Höhn, director of the SD Central Office. Heydrich, always looking for ways to expand his organization, had accepted the advice of Professor Höhn: in the absence of public criticism, the Security Service ought to step in to inform the party leaders of "wrong tendencies" and "mistaken developments." Höhn actually praised Ohlendorf for "his very critical political opinions." These were "just what the SD was looking for," he said.

Like Heydrich before him, Ohlendorf lacked a clear model for what the SD should be. But also, like Heydrich, he had been desperate before joining the SD, and was not going to be deterred by the SD's disorganization or inexperience.

Enthusiastically, Ohlendorf and Höhn laid plans for a new Department of Domestic Intelligence. They organized networks of "V-men" (short for *vertrauen*, "to trust"), who were asked to report objectively on popular reactions to Nazi policies. As commentators have often noted, these surveys were similar to public opinion polling, except that informers were used instead of stratified random sample takers. Obviously, the V-men had to be strategically placed. They also had to be completely reliable. Inland-SD agents caught submitting false reports were severely punished by Ohlendorf, who wanted nothing less than "the best intelligence service in the world." He praised the integrity of his V-men in words that recall Heydrich's original notion of an honor service: "Of course, we've got our confidential agents everywhere . . . ; they report to us how the situation stands in every field and they don't take a penny for it."

Such models of probity were assumed to have little in common with the motley band of spies, saboteurs, and double agents, often motivated by greed or revenge, who operated in the fields of foreign intelligence. Nor were they like high-level operatives such as Naujocks, who worked directly for Heydrich, performing "special tasks" on the thin edge between adventure and crime.

The recruiting of Otto Ohlendorf marked the official recognition of a division of labor within the SD that had imperceptibly been occurring for some time. The organization was constantly expanding and subdividing, and was finally splitting into two major divisions, the Inland-SD (domestic intelligence) under Ohlendorf and the Ausland-SD (foreign intelligence) under Schellenberg and his boss, SS Brigadeführer Heinz Jost.

But while foreign intelligence continued to expand wildly, pushed by both Heydrich and Himmler, the Inland-SD had to struggle for survival. The plain truth of the matter was that Nazi leaders (except Heydrich) were not interested in the plain truth. Ohlendorf's careful, often critical, reports of what Germans' attitudes actually were toward, say, the rampant corruption within the party (hostile), the prospect of war (negative), and, later, the chances of winning one (low), were less than welcome.

The fate of his first opinion survey was typical: Himmler found it too controversial, and Heydrich had to hide it in his safe. The party Gauleiters had never liked the sneaky, prying SD. They hated Otto Ohlendorf. Finally, Julius Streicher, publisher of *Der Stürmer* and publicist of anti-Semitism, became so enraged at the unvarnished way his corruption and sadism were presented in SD reports that he complained to Hitler.

Himmler felt obligated to reprimand Ohlendorf personally. Heydrich was forced to instruct V-men to avoid criticizing party potentates. Even his old party ties failed to protect Ohlendorf from the growing animosity of the Reichsführer SS. Himmler derided him as "dull," "intellectual," even "defeatist." Himmler—himself regarded by many SS men as dull and intellectual—complained also that Ohlendorf had no sense of humor. "He's like a schoolmaster watching over me to see that I do things properly."

For the SS leader, confronting Otto Ohlendorf must have been like watching an irritating impersonation of his own schoolmasterly mannerisms. Once, Himmler even accused the head of the Inland-SD of acting like "a second Reichsführer."

Heydrich, by contrast, was careful never to disagree with Himmler in public. Some observers thought he was even obsequious, always saying, "Yes, Herr Reichsführer." Privately, they had furious arguments that could be heard through closed office doors. I once asked Frau Heydrich what they were about. She couldn't remember. I asked her how her husband could behave so politely afterward. She replied that he visualized Himmler in his underwear.

Nor could Heydrich's leadership style ever be confused with Himmler's. One of their many differences, in fact, was Heydrich's pragmatic awareness of how useful a man like Ohlendorf might be. Even if his reports failed to correct Nazi abuses, they contributed to Heydrich's secret hoard of information. Himmler's differences with Ohlendorf also enhanced Heydrich's power, letting him moderate their disputes, while providing leverage over the obstreperous upstart. During the Streicher debacle, Ohlendorf offered to resign. Heydrich wouldn't let him go: he was useful, and one didn't *resign* from the SD.

Heydrich's bright young men were unusually individualistic and disputatious, and his relationships with them were rife with flare-ups, as he sought both to exploit and control their various "weaknesses." Naujocks's daring irreverence, Schellenberg's crafty opportunism, Ohlendorf's stubborn willfulness: none were considered desirable for Nazi subordinates, and all led to murderous rows with Heydrich, who, having shown these qualities himself, also knew their dangers.

There was one SD man, however, who was never too opinionated or devious, one with whom Heydrich never quarreled. He was not really the SD type, either. By his own admission, Adolf Eichmann was no student, and lacked ambition in his youth. After a dismal record in school, he worked briefly for an unsuccessful mining company owned by his father. Then he spent two years selling radios until Eichmann *père* concluded that his son wasn't getting anywhere and decided he should work for the Vacuum Oil Company. Eichmann spent a pleasant, "dreamy" interval in a remote mountain area before he was transferred to Salzburg, whose hectic pace he found uncongenial: "I didn't enjoy my work anymore; I lost interest in selling." He also got fired.

Back home in Linz, Austria, he sometimes attended Nazi rallies. One day in 1932, Eichmann happened to meet one of his father's business associates, Ernst Kaltenbrunner, a future Obergruppenführer in the SS, who was also a leader in the Austrian SS. "You're going to join us!" Kaltenbrunner announced to him. Later Eichmann told his interrogators in Israel, "That's how it was done in those days, all very free and easy, no fuss. I said, 'All right.' So I joined the SS."

Shortly thereafter, the SS was declared illegal in Austria; Eichmann decided to move to Germany to look for work. At first, Eichmann helped the SS patrol the border between Austria and Germany. He was happy there; it was, he said, "a dead, lazy sort of existence." Then, however, the young drifter was sent for training to the concentration camp at Dachau, where he received regular military instruction from imported Prussian commanders. He was ambivalent about his hard new life. On the one hand, he began to think of himself as someone who

Adolf Eichmann (age twenty-six, circa 1932) was assigned at the Wannsee Conference, which he had organized for January 20, 1942, to coordinate what was being called the "evacuation to the East," the mass extermination of occupied Europe's Jews.

Eichmann was captured by Israeli agents in Argentina in 1960 and tried in Tel Aviv for his war crimes. "There is a need to draw a line between the leaders responsible and the people like me forced to serve as mere instruments in the hands of the leaders," Eichmann argued in his unsuccessful bid to seek clemency. "I was not a responsible leader, and as such do not feel myself guilty."

could endure harsh discipline; on the other, he wondered, "How am I going to get out of here?"

When he heard that the "Reichsführer's SD" was recruiting among his peers, he signed up at once. Unfortunately, he had misunderstood the nature of the SD, guessing that it comprised the men who stood nobly in front of buildings and cars, guarding the Nazi leaders. Instead, Eichmann was ordered to report to the main SD office, at 102 Wilhelm-strasse in Berlin. Soon he found himself behind a desk, transcribing the names of members of the Freemasons onto the ubiquitous SD file cards. The work didn't make much sense to him (he had never heard of the Freemasons) and he was appalled that all the cards had to be in alpha-betical order: "It gave me the creeps . . . we sorted and sorted." After a while, he was asked to sort Masonic seals and medallions. He liked this work even less; once again, Adolf Eichmann lost interest in his job.

And once again, he was taken in hand by someone else. This time it was Untersturmführer Leopold von Mildenstein, a fellow Austrian who had just opened up a Jewish desk in the SD and wondered if Eichmann would be interested in working for him.

This occurred in 1935, the year of the anti-Semitic Nuremberg Laws. This new Nazi legislation abruptly lowered all Jews into the position of second-class citizens, and then surrounded them with a fence of cruel regulations curtailing their freedom of action. Politically sensitive careers, such as journalism or military service, were now closed to Jews, and marriage (or sexual relations) between them and "Aryan" Germans was made a criminal offense.

As far as the SD was concerned, the new laws meant that with a single stroke every Jew in the land became eligible for surveillance. Of course, the Jews would be discontented; of course they would be automatic suspects as potential critics of the regime. Heydrich had good reason to know how they must feel: had he remained in the navy, he would probably have been denounced as Jewish to some leader like him in some organization like the SD.

Until von Mildenstein appeared on the scene, however, the SD had paid scant attention to Jews—unless they were involved in politically hostile activity, in which case they wound up in a special "poison" file dedicated to people with more than one blemish against their records. Nor had Heydrich played a major role in Nazi racial policies, which were determined by more powerful men, such as Himmler, Joseph Goebbels, and, of course, Adolf Hitler. Now, however, Heydrich's "shock troops" would be expected to help supervise a racially segregated society.

Most of the clever and well-informed SD men knew perfectly well that the Jews, less than 1 percent of the German population, were generally harder working and more law abiding than, say, the Nazi Storm Troopers. Von Mildenstein told Eichmann he despised the radical party fanatics and was looking for a new "political solution" to the Jewish problem. Eichmann agreed to join him: "I'd have gone in with the devil himself just to get away from that business with the seals."

Von Mildenstein set his new subordinate to work reading books about Judaism, especially the efforts of the Zionist movement to resettle Jews in British-occupied Palestine. Eichmann was fascinated: "Before going into the SD, I didn't read at all—much to the dismay of my father, who often pointed out to me that he had an excellent library in the house . . . evidently to no purpose."

Soon Eichmann was preparing summaries of the materials he had read and sometimes even dared to venture an opinion: he began to admire the Zionists and then to hope that the Jews of Germany might be induced (or forced) to imitate them. Like most members of both the Inland- and Ausland-SD, he made reports of his observations. Von Mildenstein certainly read them, and so, eventually, did Heydrich, as

Naujocks had done when the SD was smaller and Heydrich far less powerful.

Still, one day in 1938 Eichmann submitted a report on Jewish resettlement, which Heydrich returned with "good" written in the margin. If he wanted to bind Eichmann to him for life, the SD chief could hardly have done better than write this single word, a judgment Eichmann had heard so rarely, and never from someone so highly placed.

Adventurers and idealists, bureaucrats and brawny specialists in dirty work coexisted warily in the SD, each convinced he represented the true mission of an increasingly heterogeneous vanguard once described as suffering from multiple schizophrenia. Robert Gellately, the Canadian historian, has written, "The role of the SD was so complicated and confused that many members themselves were uncertain about their tasks and their place" in the Nazi scheme. The organization most closely identified with Heydrich is perennially viewed as suffering from an identity crisis.

Certainly, Heydrich's SD reflected his restless, volatile nature, but the men who worked with him epitomized various strategies he learned to employ as he fought his way to multifaceted power. Like Naujocks, he used intrigue, backed up with violence; like Schellenberg, he used cleverness, allied to opportunism; like Ohlendorf, he used knowledge, leavened with moralistic criticism; like Eichmann, he did everything as the agent of another leader's will (but also under that leader's protective aegis).

If Reinhard Heydrich may be regarded as the "face of National Socialism," then it is worth remembering that Nazism was a social movement whose image and methods underwent a variety of sea changes. One member of the especially protean SD acknowledged this when he recalled Heydrich's leadership style as a series of ongoing "experiments."

All of the four SD leaders followed very different paths into the SD, and rose along with Heydrich to great power. Yet their ambitions, like Ohlendorf's "Gallup polling," often foundered against the opposition of the party they were supposed to serve. There were definite limits set on how far Heydrich's brain trust might go without the aid of such basic necessities as consistent encouragement from Hitler and the power to lock up their enemies. The most famous among their number, Adolf

Eichmann, only achieved real influence after he was transferred out of the SD and into an organization that possessed the power to arrest—and much more. Yet it, too, was eventually to be led by Reinhard Heydrich. This time, however, Heydrich was acting as Himmler's deputy, and for this new role, he himself acquired a special assistant, the same Heinrich Müller who had told Walter Schellenberg how much he hated the bright young men.

8

THE EVIL TWINS

"[Reinhard] was a police perfectionist."

—LINA HEYDRICH

T HE GESTAPO, an acronym for Geheime Staatspolizei, Secret State Police, has sunk so deep into our consciousness as the ultimate symbol of torture and terror that it is sometimes hard to remember it existed for only twelve years. Even Lina Heydrich once called her husband's job as deputy chief of the Gestapo the "most terrible of all terrible careers," as if it were a timeless sort of role, like that of an executioner, grimly enduring from generation to generation.

Yet she knew perfectly well that Heydrich had not merely stepped into a preexisting position. Instead, he and Heinrich Himmler, the eventual Gestapo chief, gradually created new roles out of a confused amalgam of traditional bureaucracy and revolutionary ideology. Until 1933, when Hermann Göring formed the unit, the Gestapo hadn't even existed; Himmler and Heydrich had to struggle for fifteen months even to get their hands on its parts, so to speak, and after that, they had to fight to hold on to them. Himmler had long dreamed of a "State Protection Corps" with himself as the head, but if you had told any Nazi in 1933 that he might actually achieve this goal, you would have been laughed right out of the beer hall.

The obstacles were immense. For one thing, Himmler would have to win control of the existing German police departments, yet policemen were forbidden to join political organizations like the SS, which was

"Himmlers Hirn heisst Heydrich"—Himmler's brain is called Heydrich—became a common alliterative quip, although both men individually clung to the identical myth that Germany had not suffered a military defeat in the Great War but was being weakened by degenerate forces from within.

strictly the Nazi Party's security corps. Himmler also had to contend with the feudal nature of the public police system. There was no real central authority: each of the eighteen German provinces had its own police president, who worked under the local interior minister, who was himself subordinated to the region's political leaders. (The national minister of the interior had only intermittent control over local police affairs.) In addition, every region had its own political police department to fight enemies of the state. This generally operated separately from both the detectives who pursued regular criminals and the policemen who maintained public order. In this bureaucratic bramble patch, an independent national police force like the American FBI had never existed. To create something comparable, Himmler would therefore have to stalk through the underbrush step by step, province by province.

Most of the provincial leaders were far from welcoming. True, Wilhelm Frick, an old friend of Hitler's, was already entrenched in the state of Thuringia. But in Himmler's native Bavaria, the police were openly, sometimes violently, anti-Nazi. "Let them come, we'll settle their hash for them!" snarled Heinrich Müller, who was leader of the Munich Political Police (and a long way from his eventual role as chief of the Gestapo). In Prussia, Hermann Göring resisted any encroachment in his special domain. "Himmler and Heydrich will never come to Berlin!" Göring liked to proclaim.

Nevertheless, in the spring of 1934, Himmler and Heydrich did arrive in Berlin, where (with Göring's help) they presided over the establishment of a national police force, while still retaining control of the SS. This feat is perhaps the greatest success story of Nazi internal politics. Yet it is also so confusing that historians still don't know quite how it happened. Some don't even *want* to know. According to Edward Crankshaw, author of a famous history of the Gestapo, "Nothing could be more tedious" than "the arid, repetitive moves in any struggle for power . . . old and dreary as the desert hills, but still in the hands of the master, infallible in their effect."

In fact, the outcome was not as inevitable as Crankshaw suggests, and Himmler's and Heydrich's struggles for police power were hardly repetitive. They actually fought on three different fronts (first Bavaria, then the smaller provinces, and finally, Prussia); and, each time, rather than repeated brute force they used varying tactics, winning through flexibility, psychological acuity, diplomacy, and duplicity—though they were perfectly willing to use brute force as well. It is an incredible tale, not arid but frighteningly, prophetically, instructive—how they took over a countrywide system of independent public police departments responsible for upholding national laws, and transformed it in a mere six years into a secret security system independent of judicial review and ultimately responsible only to Hitler. In short, it is the story of how they turned their nation from a system of state police into an all-devouring single police state. And in the end, Himmler and Heydrich emerged not just as separate victors but also as a recognized team—one of the few among the high Nazi leadership, and, indeed, one of the most fatally effective partnerships in modern history.

On January 30, 1933, the ailing octogenarian president of Germany, Hindenburg—or, more formally, Field Marshal Paul Ludwig Hans Anton von Beneckendorff und von Hindenburg—reluctantly appointed the Austrian upstart Adolf Hitler as chancellor.

Three days earlier, Reinhard Heydrich had officially resigned as chief

On January 30, 1933, Weimar president Paul von Hindenburg bowed to pressure and appointed Adolf Hitler as chancellor. That April 4, the elder statesman wrote the new leader: "Recently, a whole series of cases has been reported to me in which judges, lawyers, and officials of the judiciary who are disabled war veterans and whose record in office is flawless have been forcibly sent on leave and are later to be dismissed for the sole reason that they are of Jewish descent. It is quite intolerable for me personally." Hitler replied that when it came to the judiciary, "Jewish parties . . . are of little use in these positions but can do limitless harm."

of the SD and joined Himmler's staff as an officer for special duties. "Faithful Heinrich" was obviously anticipating a major appointment from his old comrade Hitler, and was likely putting Heydrich in a spot to replace him in his old position.

The appointment never came. Weeks went by, while other Nazis grabbed their share of the spoils. Hermann Göring became minister president of Prussia, also assuming control of the police in that huge province that covered almost two-thirds of Germany. Even Himmler's representative in Berlin, Kurt Dalüge, was appointed police controller in the Prussian Ministry of the Interior. But Himmler himself received nothing.

While the disappointed Reichsführer waited sullenly in Munich, Heydrich set off to Berlin to plead their case. For several humiliating weeks, he loitered around the capital, eliciting only rebuffs. Göring wouldn't talk to him, and Dalüge, supposedly Himmler's subordinate, wouldn't either. On March 5, Heydrich returned to Munich, leaving behind a letter to Dalüge bemoaning his failure to penetrate Dalüge's "protective screen": "I have telephoned no less than six times . . . I beg you to recognize this as a token of my visit and hope that the opportunity for a personal visit will present itself . . . I remain your most humble and obedient servant."

Aligned with Himmler since 1928, Kurt Dalüge (age forty-three, in 1940) took control of the police force in the Prussian Ministry of the Interior after Hitler's ascension. Under Nazi totalitarianism, freedoms offered under the Weimar constitution were substituted with laws that forbade opposition to the new regime.

In the end, however, it was not personal visits but events in Berlin that gave the outsiders from Munich their opening. On February 27, the Reichstag building burned to the ground. Although absolute proof of the Nazis' complicity in setting fire to the house of the German Parliament has never been established, they certainly made maximum use of the event by blaming the Communists. With the fire as provocation and pretext, the Reichstag voted to suspend civil liberties throughout the country. This "Enabling Act" in fact allowed Adolf Hitler to seize power. Declaring martial law, Chancellor Hitler empowered members of the SA and SS to act as auxiliary police while "order" was "restored." Thirty thousand armed Nazis were thus able to add search and seizure, confiscation, and arrest to their long roster of intimidation techniques.

Against this background of disorder and "legal" illegality, the last election campaign in the history of Nazi Germany took place. On March 5, the Nazis emerged as the strongest party, with 43 percent of the popular vote. Popular they may have been, but not overwhelmingly so, since more than 50 percent of the voters had rejected them.

Nevertheless, Adolf Hitler now felt strong enough to incorporate Bavaria into his new order. Until then, Bavarian prime minister Heinrich Held had successfully fortified himself with ancient separatist traditions. But now Hitler decided to appoint a Nazi Freikorps general, Franz Ritter von Epp, as the governor of Bavaria.

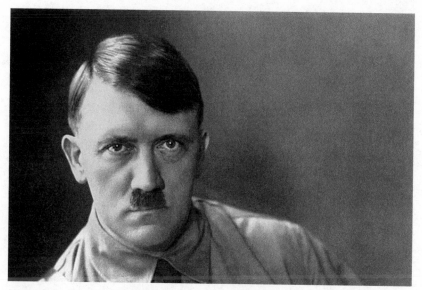

Adolf Hitler (in his early thirties, circa early 1920s) was appointed Germany's chancellor on January 30, 1933. "You have handed over our sacred German Fatherland to one of the greatest demagogues of all time," former general Erich Ludendorff telegrammed Hindenburg on the day of the announcement. Ludendorff predicted that "this evil man . . . will inflict immeasurable woe on our nation. Future generations will curse you in your grave for this action."

Hermann Göring (age forty, circa 1933) was named Prussian minister of the interior, commander in chief of the Prussian Police and Gestapo, and commissioner for aviation. With Himmler and Heydrich, Göring early on established concentration camps for political rivals and set the precedent for intimidating both real and perceived enemies of the state.

On the 9th of March, Reinhard Heydrich appeared at the telegraph office in Munich, Bavaria's capital, with gun in hand. He had not left his home that morning bearing arms—he had to phone home to ask Lina to fetch his gun—but the Nazis were expecting a telegram from Hitler announcing von Epp's appointment, and it had not, apparently, arrived. Heydrich decided to use the threat of force to prevent anyone from destroying the Führer's message. He brandished his revolver, the telegram was swiftly handed over, and the change of power occurred— literally at the point of a gun, an ingredient in a mixture of ordinary politics and violent theatrics that the Nazis had made their own. It was no accident that Heydrich was the one to star in this little dramatic production. In the Nazi theater of power, Bruno Heydrich's introverted son suddenly revealed a flair for drama as great as his father's, and no less effective for being displayed largely behind the scenes.

Ritter von Epp immediately appointed Himmler commissar of the Munich police. (Heydrich was rewarded for his contribution with the leadership of Department VI, the Political Section.) These were regarded as minor appointments, but their implications were major, though it seems to have taken Heydrich, at least, a while to see them. Unlike Himmler, whose grandfather had served in the border patrol, Heydrich sneered at the job of policeman. At the time, he told his wife he couldn't endure too many weeks of police work, which he compared to sifting through piles of garbage. (The SD, of course, had been doing similar sifting for two years, though its leaders glorified the activity as part of the great, gentlemanly game of intelligence.)

As chief of the political division, Heydrich's first task was to screen his own staff for political reliability. Many of the policemen whose files he reviewed expected to be sacked—or worse. Mass arrests were already under way throughout Germany; and on March 21, Himmler opened the first Bavarian concentration camp, Dachau, to hold the thousands of new political prisoners.

Yet once in his new office, Heydrich did not behave as violently as expected. Quickly, he put away the gun of the revolutionary agitator, and slipped back bureaucratically behind his desk, where he was actually far more dangerous.

With his high regard for expertise, Heydrich soon realized he needed experienced men to run the machinery of state. Whatever their politics, the detectives he found in Department VI were members of the vener-

Franz Ritter von Epp (age fifty-one, circa 1919) was appointed by Hitler on March 9, 1933, to serve as governor of Bavaria. Under Nazi command, the Bayerische Politische Polizei grew into the Gestapo, whose duties included the marginalization and deportation of Jews, as well as brutal acts against foreign forced laborers and concentration camp prisoners.

able German civil service, who had undergone professional training and passed exams on police procedure. Few SS men could meet these qualifications, and in any case, there weren't enough of them to go around. Heydrich had to find a way to turn former enemies into obedient subordinates.

Of course, this was not his problem alone. Everywhere in Germany, battle had been joined between the Nazi *arrivistes* and the entrenched state bureaucrats referred to as *Beamte* ("officials") with a tone of reverence and authority close to that accorded hereditary aristocrats. As the American historian Edward N. Peterson writes, "The institution the NS party set out to conquer in 1933 had been the pride of Germany for two centuries, a professional career elite with the status of a caste. It was a group difficult to enter and governed by its own code, which commanded obedience to the state but also to the law." Such officials generally served for life, immune to the vicissitudes of politics (which most Germans considered both transitory and "dirty"), and guided instead by the enduring norms of law and custom.

Most *Beamte* were deeply conservative, and therefore opposed to both the Communists and the Nazis. In Nuremberg, for example, Benno Martin, a clever and charming man from a family whose members had been *Beamte* for three hundred years, made the highest grade in the civil service exams and, with a full range of choice, decided on police work. The author of a textbook on police procedures, he was already securely in place when the Nazis came to power. In 1934, Himmler appointed him police president, a position allowing Martin secretly to undermine many Nazi policies, including more than a few of Himmler's own.

The great German sociologist Max Weber argued that it is almost impossible for a political leader to co-opt unwilling bureaucratic officials, since the latter have too many ways of undermining their boss. They can, for instance, fail to inform him of pertinent information so that he makes stupid decisions. They can manipulate documents to justify their own points of view, interpret rules to suit themselves, fashion hidden traps from the red tape that is always available, and use the magic of methodical procedures to make crucial deadlines vanish.

Nazi archives are full of complaints from party members about *Beamte* acting either too slowly or not slowly enough. Munich Gauleiter Adolf Wagner thought his plan to remove crucifixes from the schools was deliberately wrecked by "immediate and flagrant" action, rather than the "gradual and disguised implementation" he had ordered. Another Nazi who was inexperienced at his new job of engineering inspector felt "raped" by his fellow officials.

Heydrich, however, had several advantages as he confronted the anti-Nazi police of Munich. For one thing, he too didn't yet admire the Nazi Party. Many of its early adherents (who called themselves "Old Fighters") felt entitled to carouse and plunder now that Hitler was in power. Heydrich made up satirical nicknames for these party profiteers, calling them "lacquered monkeys" and "golden pheasants." In Prussia, Hermann Göring was amassing a fortune and spending it on jewels, fancy uniforms, and palatial dwellings. Heydrich dubbed him *Herr Reichspompführer* (roughly, "Sir Stuffed Shirt"). He also detested Adolf Wagner, the beer-swilling Gauleiter of Munich, with whom Himmler was gladly cooperating. Wagner's staff expected a full-scale purge at police headquarters, and were particularly hostile to Heinrich Müller, the detective captain who had sworn to fight the SS. To Wagner's surprise, however, Heydrich not only failed to purge Müller, he gave him a promotion.

Even members of Heydrich's entourage were confused, by both his behavior and Müller's. In one interview I conducted during my visits to Germany, a former high-ranking Gestapo officer, Bruno Streckenbach, told me he had discussed Müller's peculiar change of loyalty with a psychologist. ("He was not a National Socialist; he didn't even *like* National

Socialists.") They decided that Müller's ultimate motive was his love for his son and his consequent desire to protect him from the Communists. Müller must have felt that working for the National Socialists would be "his guarantee that Communism would be kept in check in Germany." They concluded: "His other assignments, the suppression of other enemies of the Reich, they were of secondary importance to him. They were just part of the job."

The "job" eventually engrossed Müller to such an extent that he became known simply as "Gestapo" Müller. Yet even before he met his new boss, Heinrich Müller had been preparing the ground for a meeting of opportunistic minds. Shrewdly, he greeted Heydrich's arrival with a series of memos describing everything he had learned about the origin, goals, and methods of Communism. Heydrich read them all and was impressed; Himmler read a summary and accepted Heydrich's judgment. Soon, Heydrich and Müller struck a deal advantageous to them both: Müller was given more money, power, and independence from civilian control than the Weimar democrats could ever have offered, and Heydrich obtained a devoted underling who owed him his job and perhaps even his life. In the wolf-eat-wolf world of Nazism, sheer physical protection was one of the best guarantees of loyal service—particularly since one could always threaten to withdraw it.

Heydrich allowed Müller to retain most of his colleagues, men who

Bruno Streckenbach (age forty, circa 1942) assumed leadership of the Gestapo in Hamburg once the Nazis took power. As commander of Einsatzgruppe 1 in Poland during the May 1940 "Aktion AB," he ordered that 3,500 intellectuals, the majority being professors from the University of Kraków, be arrested and killed.

Chief of the Gestapo Heinrich
Müller (age thirty-six, circa 1937) was
Heydrich's closest associate, despite
lingering questions about Müller's
commitment to the Nazi Party.
As Adolf Eichmann's immediate
superior, "Gestapo" Müller, as he was
nicknamed, signed the circulating order
that condemned forty-five thousand
Jews to their deaths in Auschwitz by
January 31, 1943.

already knew the system well. At one stroke, he had thus obtained a
cadre of proven experts, desperate to ingratiate themselves: "Müller
was irreplaceable," Bruno Streckenbach told me. "Without people like
them, Heydrich could not have handled all the details."

Yet Streckenbach thought Heydrich was very good at details as well.

"How he achieved his enormous knowledge," Streckenbach added,
"that I don't know. Whenever you entered his office, there was never
anything on his desk at all.

"Just an example. I don't like to say yes if I am not really convinced.
And so in Heydrich's office, I took on Heydrich. The meeting turned
into a dispute. I was totally convinced I was right. Müller, who had an
excellent memory, and complete mastery of his field, said, 'Bruno, keep
still. Don't take on the boss, you know he will turn out to be right.' But
I was sure; I was the one familiar with the file. I was convinced that
Heydrich had never even looked at the papers. And yet, he did turn out
to be right! (Also, you see that he did not object to opposition.)"

Frau Heydrich told me her husband never had to look up a phone
number after he had used it once; Heinrich Himmler called him "a
walking file cabinet." It is difficult to dispute a man with a photographic
memory: even the cleverest officials were rarely able to manipulate data
to Heydrich's disadvantage.

However tractable his new police minions seemed to have become,
however, Heydrich never relied entirely on their goodwill. They were

also monitored by trusted SD functionaries, generally given titles like "coordinator of communications" to mask their watchdog roles. The shadowy presence of the SD men was a constant reminder too that, unlike other Nazi leaders, Heydrich did not have to call in the SD to check out unreliable subordinates: he *was* the SD, incarnate. Heydrich encouraged unusually ambitious (or anxious) police officials to join him in the SS or the SD, bypassing the Nazi Party if they wished.

Frau Heydrich insisted this was not mere cynicism. Above all, she said, he valued "the perfect functioning of the shop . . . He was a 'police perfectionist.'"

He had to be, if only to keep "the shop" in business. Particularly during this early period, the SS stewardship of the police was constantly under attack by the *Beamte*. For instance, in 1934 a Bavarian bureaucrat proposed that Himmler be replaced by a "fully qualified lawyer." In response, Heydrich reasoned that if Himmler could persuade lawyers and experienced policemen to work for him—and do so efficiently—such sallies would be blunted. The trouble was, the bespectacled Reichsführer SS, who seemed the perfect school administrator, had nevertheless learned from Hitler to despise bureaucrats, particularly lawyers. So the commandingly flamboyant Heydrich hired them in droves, even naming a former lawyer his stand-in as official chief of the SD.

In 1933, after completing the preliminary screening of the police, Heydrich was ready for his second major task in Bavaria: to use the newly cleansed police to strike down the Nazis' major political opponents. The Enabling Act had authorized "protective custody" of enemies of the state. Theoretically, this prevented them from disrupting civil order, while also offering them protection from the "wrath of the people." In fact, protective custody offered an easy way for Nazis to vent their own wrath under the cover of legality.

In March, Himmler and Heydrich began to order mass arrests, starting with Müller's favorite target, the Communists, and soon moving on to the leaders of the largest opposition party, the Socialists. Before the end of the month, Himmler was promoted to police chief for all of Bavaria. He appointed Heydrich chief of the political police network, and they continued their systematic attacks on opposing sources of political influence.

On May 5, the Bavarian police joined a nationwide "action" (the Nazi euphemism for police roundups) against the trade unions, taking their officials into protective custody and confiscating their property. On June 26, it was the turn of the Bavarian People's Party, the huge organization to which Himmler had once belonged. (This was considered a "large action," involving the arrest of several thousand leaders.)

On the 2nd of July, the political police began to arrest clergymen whose actions were deemed suspicious; this was the first thrust in a continuing campaign to prevent religious officials from "interfering" in politics. The smallest offenses served as pretext. Thus, a cleric was arrested for simple possession of Marxist books, although his job as a teacher required access to such materials. When church officials complained to Heydrich, he initially expressed "warm sympathy," then later insisted, "I regret . . . that I have found no objective reason to change my reports."

Regret was hardly an apt word: Heydrich had carefully publicized the case as a deterrent to other clergymen. Shlomo Aronson writes that such deceitful arrogance was "typical of the gangsterdom of the Himmler-school," but it also reveals the unwillingness of either Himmler or Heydrich publicly to admit responsibility for their actions. Unlike many gangsters, the two SS leaders did not openly place themselves above the normal laws of human decency. Whatever they may have thought—or done—in private, Himmler and Heydrich adopted the public pose of exemplars of benevolent order. Himmler, in particular, was an expert hypocrite, adept at expressing appalled surprise when people complained about SS violence; Heydrich, perhaps because he looked so much more threatening, was never as convincing in his protestations of innocence.

In July 1933, the State Ministry for Instruction and Culture rejected Heydrich's expressions of "sympathy," and issued a decree requiring the police to consult church authorities in protective custody cases involving members of the clergy. Temporarily stymied, Heydrich instructed his policemen, "The decree is to be unconditionally obeyed." As he thus acknowledged, the elaboration of the police state was a gradual and uneven process based on trial and error, sometimes requiring a tactical step backward.

On July 19, Heydrich and Müller moved against their fifth target— the Jews. All Jewish organizations that were not "purely religious" or "purely charitable" were dissolved and their property confiscated. The aim of this "action" was similar to the others—to prevent political activity by a group regarded as hostile. Individuals were arrested only if they openly opposed the New Order or violated its norms of "folk justice." A Jewish doctor, for example, was taken into custody because he was supposed to have underpaid his cleaning lady and overcharged his patients. The Bavarian Political Police also arrested an Aryan industrialist named Strassner who had refused to pay his employees the minimum wage, and had boasted "he was the lord of his factory." Furious, Heydrich denounced Strassner as "more than an exploiter of the worker, . . . he lacks any kind of social understanding. In his inner being, he is a bitter enemy of the state form of the present day."

As this example shows, the category of "enemy" encompassed everyone who seemed unwilling to be "coordinated"—as the Nazi phrase so gracelessly put it—with National Socialism. It also demonstrates that, two years after he had been thrown out of the navy for immoral conduct, Reinhard Heydrich had become an arbiter of the new Nazi morality.

More highly placed leaders, such as Hitler and Himmler, determined the various criteria of criminality, but it was Heydrich who placed actual people within the categories. The Führer and the Reichsführer may have proposed, but it was Heydrich who disposed. Or, as T. S. Eliot observed in his verse play *Murder in the Cathedral,* "King commands; Chancellor richly rules. That is a lesson not taught in your schools." Hitler, of course, was the actual chancellor, but there were dozens of newly created feudal lords, each ruling richly in his own domain. Heydrich may have been a political amateur, an inexperienced administrator, and a man with no police training, but he was learning fast.

As SD chief he had long been empowered to peer into men's minds and hearts; now, as a police leader, Heydrich could arrest them too. Then, he could send them to a state prison, or, more likely, to a concentration camp, there to undergo political "reeducation" at the hands of the Storm Troopers and the SS. The logical next step was to gain influence within the camps themselves.

But Heinrich Himmler had been learning too. Warily, he refused to share this control with his energetic young assistant. Instead, he turned to Theodore Eicke, an older Nazi who had been hospitalized for mental illness, who owed his salvation to Himmler, who didn't get along with

Heydrich, and who also outranked him. "Divide and conquer," Hitler often said, and Himmler was a good listener.

In April 1933, Heydrich countered by establishing a political department within each camp. His agents determined when a prisoner could leave—often a life-or-death decision. But Eicke created and trained the Death's Head Battalions (Totenkopfverbände) who guarded the prisoners, and he was responsible only to Himmler. Eicke's minions called him "Papa." The prisoners knew him better as a personification of the devil, for he used group complicity in violence to unify his men, tolerating excesses of cruelty but punishing "misplaced humanity."

In a world where, as one Nazi said, "everyone arrests everyone; everyone threatens everyone with arrest; everyone threatens everyone with Dachau," Himmler considered the concentration camps a "pillar" of SS power equal to the police. According to a report signed by Heydrich, 2,097 people had been taken into protective custody during the month of July 1933 alone. On the other hand, 1,820 were released during that same period. Beneath these dry figures the outlines emerge of a sinister plan to get human juices flowing. Soon, "in every place, in every town, someone could be found who had disappeared and then returned, downcast and full of fear . . . Thus a legend of terror originated that often surpassed the reality."

Himmler is viewed by Shlomo Aronson as the originator of this fearful use of protective custody: as the good son of bourgeois parents he realized that the very idea of being arrested was almost unendurably humiliating to the German middle classes, hampering their will to resist.

There were camps and terror throughout the rest of Germany, of course, but no one was as skilled in using them as polite, inoffensive Heinrich Himmler, who had read books on the Soviet Cheka, immersed himself in fantasies of vindictive triumph, and enjoyed telling the "weaker" members of his family what to do.

And no one else had such an able assistant. A few months after they had taken over control of the Bavarian police, the fundamental, stupendously successful division of labor between Heydrich and Himmler was already emerging. Heydrich chose the prisoners; Himmler controlled the camps. Heydrich supervised the investigatory work; Himmler reported the results to Hitler. Heydrich acted as the organization's "political" facilitator; Himmler devised its ideological guidelines and attempted to persuade the other Nazi leaders to follow them.

. . .

In the Heydrich household too, a basic differentiation of roles was in process. Reinhard Heydrich had found and prepared the couple's first apartment, a cheap little flat on the outskirts of Munich, but soon Lina took over their domestic arrangements. Either by accident or clever sabotage, when it came to serving his wife, Heydrich secured an indefinite furlough.

As his wife described the situation, "I would want to hang a picture on the wall, and would say to him, 'Why don't you give me a hand? This is where the picture should go.' And he would say, 'Where is the hammer?' I would get the hammer. 'Where do you have the nail or picture hanger?' I would get the hanger. 'And now I need the measuring tape.' I would get him the tape. 'And now, please hold the picture. I will have to measure. How high should I hang it?' And then: 'Please hold it for me.'

"Really! You try this once, then you leave such a husband be. It is quicker to do it yourself!"

In a letter Heydrich wrote to his mother-in-law in 1932, he was already describing their flat as a separate realm, far from the city's clamor, where they could find "relaxation and peace" and where "Lina directs and administers in her Reich."

Heydrich obviously welcomed this emergent division of labor, but his wife was evidently ambivalent. Repeatedly she told me how much she treasured their earliest days together, before Hitler came to power and their lives began to split apart. "This time was the most beautiful time in my life. So what if we also starved? It was all so precious, every little thing! My husband bought a dress for me, for three marks fifty. What an event that was! In a sale, no? The dress was certainly not beautiful, but *he* bought it for me; to buy a dress for three marks and fifty without being asked—that unites. That always held us together. The real thing wasn't important at all. It was the *idea*!"

Reinhard and Lina Heydrich had married for love, against the wishes of both their families, in the face of scandal and without financial security. In the first days of their marriage they stayed, romantically, at home. During the *Kampfzeit* in Munich, it wasn't easy to enjoy an unpolitical evening out. But the young couple devised elaborate means to keep the turbulent outside world at bay. Before Heydrich left work at the end of the day, he often phoned his wife to tell her he would like to go out that evening: "That meant I had to cook something pretty, to decorate the table in a festive way, with candles and everything, and then we played nightclub! We put on music and we dined and then we went 'out' dancing. That was our game! We were entirely by ourselves!"

When she spoke of this more than forty years later, Lina's voice took on a fluttery, whispery tone. In her memoirs she wrote, "He always knew how to excite me."

But the precious solitude was not to last. In 1933, the Heydrichs moved to a large two-story house on a tree-shaded corner lot near the elegant gardens of Nymphenburg Palace (the main summer residence of the former rulers of Bavaria). The newlyweds had a living room and bedroom on the second floor, but they were no longer truly alone: Reinhard's SD offices occupied the first floor, and the poverty-stricken members of his staff arrived early and stayed late, sharing the food, heat, and companionship.

Although Hitler had come to power in January, the SD staff was seldom paid. Heydrich constantly begged Himmler and Röhm for funds, but meanwhile, everyone had to pitch in. At first, Lina Heydrich enjoyed the transformation: "The best years of my life were when we had nothing and I worked with my husband. I received no money for it; that was not at all essential."

Part of the fun for her were the weekly beer evenings in which she joined all of the men. "In the neighborhood there was an inn where one could buy a great massive tankard of beer very cheaply—a liter, that today costs, I believe, four marks seventy, cost fifty pfennigs then. Herr Strohmeyer was an unemployed laborer who always dined with us. Because he was so strong, he would carry back eight tankards. We ate bread with that—naturally without butter—and also herring salad (though in this herring salad was everything—except herring! Herring was too expensive!). But we had everything possible in the way of vegetables, little pieces boiled and sliced, and mixed with some vinegar and some sugar and perhaps a little oil, and placed in the middle of the table. And we had this mass of beer with it. And for once, we had a proper meal!

"For a long time, I cooked for everyone. It was cheaper, and truly, they had nothing!"

It was the *idea* of things that counted to Lina Heydrich, and so for her this was obviously a time of great abundance. She loved to confer titles on her multifarious activities: the "general maid," the "general factotum," the "housemaster," the "mother of the company."

She was also "guardian" of the gates of the house; from her post in the kitchen, Lina Heydrich commanded the best view of the path leading to the front door. Until Himmler got control of the police, the SD was sometimes the target of surprise raids. Lina was expected to warn the men whenever the police appeared, and on such occasions, she also had temporary custody of the secret files. Pretending to be grievously ill, she would take to her bed and hide the files under her bedclothes where no respectable German police officer would dare to pry.

In fact, the struggle between the Nazis and their opponents in Munich once got so tense that Himmler ordered the evacuation of SS wives to a secluded spot up north. Lina remembered the trip as a time of joyous camaraderie—as one of her best stories illustrates: "Do you know, we had three ovens, but each was in a different room. In the mornings, I always had to light the ovens at six o'clock, so when the men came at eight, the rooms were warm. I was the factotum for everything.

"And there was a little shelf above one oven, and I always put the matches on it, but every time when the men came, my matches were gone! Obviously, one of the eight men picked them up, although they weren't really valuable. Still, it was a *crime*, and I wanted to find out who was stealing the matches.

"I went to the *Stockhaus* in Munich—they had all kinds of magic things for *Fasching* [Carnival] and for family celebrations—and I got a little box of special matches. One strikes these matches and after a short time, they explode! I put them in the place above the oven, and on the very day I put them there, we got a call in the morning. Himmler! And he said he was coming with Herr Röhm for an inspection!

"Naturally, I forgot about the matches. I was thinking about whether everything was clean. I had to make a little breakfast somehow, something with salad perhaps, something that didn't cost much but tasted good.

"And then they came and it was terribly festive, and I thought everything was going well, and then my husband, because he knew that Röhm used cigars—at the end of the inspection of the little rooms he offered Röhm a cigar. But he had no matches, and so here comes Herr Strohmeyer, pulling matches out of his pocket—he was *fearfully* devoted—and of course, *PENG*!

Ernst Röhm (age thirty-eight, circa 1925) was arrested along with Hitler for his participation in the Beer Hall Putsch. As chief organizer of the Brown Shirt paramilitary, Röhm later sought to combine the Reichswehr with the SA, establishing him in a position of power that threatened both Himmler and Heydrich.

"Naturally Himmler thought it was the beginning of an assassination! And my husband said, 'My God, what happened!'

"And I said, 'Come, just allow me,' for now I knew who had picked up the matches, and I said, 'Listen to me, it was nothing more than this,' and then I explained it, and they were *so* amused at me. Yes! It had become a *comedy*!

"Ha, ha, ha, ha, ha, ha," she laughed, in a series of tiny explosions. "When I think of that, I can *still* amuse myself!"

Rough-and-ready Ernst Röhm obviously shared Frau Heydrich's sense of humor: after the unexpectedly exciting visit, he authorized increased funds for the SD, opening the way to further expansion.

When I asked Frau Heydrich what her husband thought of the matches episode, she said he found it all very funny. In his early days in the party, Heydrich sometimes tried to get SS men to display a better sense of humor. He himself occasionally revealed flashes of irreverent wit—though his style was more sardonic and far coarser than Lina's. (The jokes of the Nazi leaders tended toward deflating denigration with political overtones, as, for example, Heydrich's derisive reference to a group of homosexual German diplomats as the "backwards-service in the Foreign Service," a jape that probably loses something in translation.)

Frau Heydrich told me that Himmler too enjoyed her jokes, and that she could sometimes render him "helpless" with laughter. Could she recall an example? I wondered. She looked surprised: "Oh . . . not really . . . When I am asked to perform, I can do nothing . . . Humor must arise spontaneously from one's situation, *nicht wahr*? Perhaps I will think of something later."

Lina and I returned to the subject of Bavaria, where the new masters of the Bavarian police were looking for other fields to conquer. At some point in 1933, Reinhard Heydrich changed his mind about the value of garbage collecting. His wife told Aronson he had concluded, "Now we do not need the party anymore. It has done its job and has opened up the road to power. Now the SS should penetrate the police and form a new organization with it." To me she was more evasive. Perhaps her husband thought up these things, perhaps Himmler. "Who knows where such large concepts come from?" she said, placing the blame on "the flow of history," which develops slowly, and then becomes inevitable.

Inevitable too, though she didn't say so, was their movement away from provincial politics and toward a collision course with other leaders of Hitler's new regime. As Himmler and Heydrich turned their attention beyond Bavaria, the Nazi Party began to devour itself from within, and threats of assassination were no longer a joking matter, even to Lina Heydrich.

9

THE ROAD TO BERLIN

"I wasn't on the scene . . . and I make it a policy never to discuss
things I have not experienced for myself."

—LINA HEYDRICH

I N THE AUTUMN AND WINTER of 1933, both Himmler and Heydrich
periodically abandoned their desks in Munich to travel throughout
Germany. On the face of it, Heydrich was expanding his SD network, Himmler gaining converts for the SS, the growing paramilitary
group that had begun as a Nazi security force. But their familiar roles
as second-rank Nazi leaders masked an ambitious private agenda: to
create a unified national police force controlled by the SS, the final
piece in the structure of which would be Berlin and Hermann Göring's
Gestapo.

Adolf Hitler did not know about this plan, and wouldn't have
endorsed it if he had. At the time, the Nazis were still consolidating
their power. Hitler felt he faced enough trouble trying to balance the
claims of party radicals like Ernst Röhm, the apostle of violent "permanent revolution," against the demands for social peace by the army and
bureaucracy.

An awareness of the pervasive conflict between politicians and
bureaucrats—between men who owed their careers to politics versus
those who derived authority from serving the state—is absolutely essential to any understanding of the continued rise of Himmler and Heydrich; for they built the foundations of their SS empire across what
had always been a vast and unbridgeable gulf in German life. Actually,

their challenge was compounded by another, similarly deep, conflict that Hitler's rise to power superimposed on German society. Added to the timeless friction between politicians and career bureaucrats (both civilian, or the *Beamte,* and military) was a new source of tension—that between the government and the Nazi Party (and their respective heads). So great were the entanglements that these pervasive yet over-lapping conflicts created that it would be a near-impossible challenge all by itself to track where one began and the other left off.

As Reichsführer SS, Himmler commanded thousands of men pledged to obey him to the death, but this awesome power belonged to him only insofar as he was a personal vassal of the charismatic leader of the Nazi Party. While Hitler lived, Himmler reported directly to him; if Hitler died, Himmler's powers (theoretically) vanished.

On the other hand, Adolf Hitler had just become chancellor of Germany, and could exercise state authority independent of his political role. When Chancellor Hitler gave Himmler the job of police president of Bavaria, he was also assigning him a place in the governmental hierarchy—far below that of fellow Nazi Wilhelm Frick, who was now minister of the interior. Even the Bavarian ministers of the interior and justice felt entitled to interest themselves in Himmler's state activities, and (theoretically) could force him to follow the traditional, tedious, time-consuming rules of bureaucratic procedure.

Himmler was thus doubly subordinate to Hitler, but in almost every other respect there was a world of difference between the SS and the police bureaucracy. The pay varied substantially (SS salaries were usually far lower); membership requirements were very different (the SS demanded loyalty above all, while the police stressed technical training); and the aims of the two groups were totally at odds (policemen were supposed to uphold the laws of the land while SS men were encouraged to break them if the Führer ordered it).

Nevertheless, when Himmler was sworn in as police president, he did not cease to function as Reichsführer SS. Nor did Heydrich, his new deputy, give up his role as chief of SS Intelligence. The Nazis gave the name "personal union" (*persönliche Vereinigung*) to the odd, oxy-moronic phenomenon they exemplified—that of one person occupying two basically incompatible roles at the same time.

Originally, Hitler had thought of this as a good thing. The man serv-ing simultaneously as agent of the government and of the party was supposed to provide a "clamp" between them. This "Nazification at the top" was one way the new rulers hoped to control the administrators they inherited from the old regime. As it turned out, however, "personal union" was often a prescription for psychological confusion. Men whose main experience had been in street fighting found it hard to switch gears to office infighting, often vacillating erratically between them. In the end, though, the office behavior tended to prevail.

It wasn't merely that German tradition, unlike that of Western democracies, reveres bureaucrats. All charismatic authority tends to become routinized finally, if only because revolutionary enthusiasm fades, especially when confronted by the results of successful revolution, such as lists of grievances, committee meetings, and surging tides of paperwork. Eventually, Hitler turned against his own idea of merging state and party roles in single men, concluding that it turned good Nazis into petty bureaucrats who had lost touch with "the people."

Among Hitler's underlings, only Himmler and Heydrich managed fully to exploit the Machiavellian possibilities of "personal union." As intelligent sons of successful, upper-middle-class teachers with professional connections among the German nobility, they were neither one of them typical Nazis. Himmler truly loved paperwork, having once chosen to spend his free time perusing the files of his college fencing society. Heydrich had spent his naval holidays actually fencing, as well as both playing the violin and playing around, and had come as late to bureaucracy as he had to Nazism. His subordinates believed that to him, the famous SD files represented a huge musical instrument, on whose keys he could play infinite variations of influence and intrigue. The dossiers of which the keys were made did not have to stand the test of legal scrutiny. They composed exactly the sort of "facts" that had been used so effectively against his family in Saxony and himself in the navy, to identify them all as "Jewish." More than most people, Heydrich understood their potentially devastating power.

However skilled they were at manipulating bureaucratic files, however, Heydrich and Himmler were also political rebels in the classic Nazi mode. Because both had been misfits in their youth, they didn't want the old order back, they wanted a new order, in which they could at last dominate.

Heydrich and Himmler were thus both bureaucrats and revolutionaries. Far from being undone by the confusion of dual roles, they welcomed the many chances of expanding their power under confusion's helpful cloak.

Viewing their campaign geographically, they can be seen to have gradually advanced on their ultimate objective, the capital city of Berlin, with its most recalcitrant police force, the Gestapo. Their first victory occurred in the northern city of Hamburg, a locale that Heydrich knew well. Obviously expecting great things, he appointed Karl Oberg, one of the SD men from the early days in Munich, as his representative. But Oberg fell afoul of the local Gauleiter, Erik Kaufmann, when he tried to set up a cell of secret informants in Hamburg. Kaufmann was outraged at this invasion of "his" domain. Heydrich had to recall Oberg.

Meanwhile, the political police in Hamburg were proceeding with the usual purge. Members of the Storm Troopers were rendering predictably harsh service as police auxiliaries, their "excesses" provoking lawsuits and anti-Nazi propaganda. At this point Himmler appeared on the scene, testing out a new role as peacemaker.

Unlike Oberg, Himmler enjoyed a fine relationship with Kaufmann: they had been using the familiar *du* (the informal form of "you") since 1927. Himmler dismissed Kaufmann's troubles with the SD as mere reflections of the general lack of discipline in Hamburg. He offered him honorary membership in the SS, and even provided a little financial help. In October, Kaufmann reciprocated by appointing a local businessman who was also a member of the SS to the post of governmental counselor.

This man, Bruno Streckenbach, worked with Heydrich from 1933 until the latter's death nine years later. "Did you know I was Heydrich's boss for a few weeks?" Streckenbach asked me during one of our interviews. Then he laughed. "Not for long, of course; *that* situation soon reversed itself!

"I have had a number of superiors in my life," he told me. "Smart people, some of them. And I always learned from my bosses, but I never had a boss who could think as fast and as clearly as Heydrich. When *I* wanted to learn something, I had to work for it. I had to start over from point zero twice in my life, and so in earlier years the books I read were Alpha and Omega to me. I had hundreds of books . . . yet I never saw Heydrich read anything."

Bruno Streckenbach was seventy-four when we met in 1976, and had a serious heart condition; his hands sometimes trembled when he lifted his teacup. Still, his conversation was tough-minded, complicated, and ironic. He loved wry jokes at his own expense—and mine. "Are you sure you're not a Soviet commissar?" he asked me once, when he didn't like a question. He had already spent thirty postwar years—more than ten of them in Moscow's notorious Lubyanka prison—being interrogated by the victors. He was used to hostility, and good at surviving it. One could see how his fellow Nazis might have thought him a good compromise candidate to restore order to Hamburg in 1933.

Bruno Streckenbach did so well in Hamburg that he was soon appointed chief of police, from which position he managed to bring about a reconciliation between the SD and Gauleiter Kaufmann. After traveling to Munich to "study the Bavarian system under Heydrich," he returned to Hamburg to launch a second purge against the worst offenders in the police auxiliaries. Through him, the SD had suddenly become a major force in Hamburg, but until then it had been less than helpful, having alienated the very leaders Himmler was trying to cultivate.

Negative stories about the intrigues of Heydrich's secret intelligence service swiftly spread among the party chieftains, who felt they should be immune from surveillance. In the free state of Brunswick, the Lower Saxon city to the south of Hamburg, no figure like Bruno Streckenbach was present to promote the SD's interests with its leaders. There, a clash between Heydrich's bright young men and the local Gauleiter ended up on Himmler's doorstep. Himmler, instead of defending the SD's leaders in Brunswick, disavowed them, did nothing when they were arrested, and invited the Gauleiter's men to join the SS.

This was neither the first nor the last time that Himmler's self-protective instincts overwhelmed his loyalty to those taking risks on his behalf. As many SS men have testified, he was notorious for not backing up his subordinates. ("Faithful Heinrich" was loyal primarily to himself and to Adolf Hitler—until the end, when he betrayed his Führer too. For one thing, late in the war, he attempted to open peace talks with the Western Allies, and, for another, he countermanded Hitler's orders to exterminate all the Jews remaining in death camps throughout Europe, a cynical and self-serving act that did save the lives of a few thousand, but came far too late for millions of others.)

On the other hand, the situation may have been desperate: Hitler had apparently considered even disbanding the SD entirely. In October 1933, by contrast, he concluded it was "not to be disturbed" and might even expand its operations, but it must have been a close call. Both in Hamburg and Brunswick, Heydrich's little Security Service had behaved with foolish bravado, moving both too fast and too aggressively. Yet the SD had also succeeded in making a name for itself, attracting Hitler's attention for just the sort of revolutionary recklessness he secretly admired and increasingly had to subordinate to the demands of political prudence.

In addition, the SS as a whole may actually have profited from what appeared to be dissension in its ranks. The self-righteous arrogance of the young SD leaders made Himmler seem almost tolerant by comparison. It was as if in Brunswick, Himmler and Heydrich were experimenting with a good cop/bad cop routine, reversing the roles they had played in Bavaria. Heydrich, who had treated with open-minded pragmatism the hostile policemen of Munich, the capital city of the southernmost state of Bavaria, now acted the role of bogeyman, whose sinister SD minions seemed to be everywhere, stealthily creeping into hidden recesses of power. Meanwhile Himmler, the exponent of terror who had created the hellish concentration camp at Dachau, was gradually transformed into a quietly reasonable man with whom one might openly talk and easily compromise.

We do not know whether these differences in behavior reflected a clever two-pronged strategy, mere inexperience, or the beginnings of the rivalry of later days. In any case, Himmler's small elite corps, the SS, was dwarfed by the Storm Troopers, or SA, from which the SS had by this time split off, and Heydrich's tiny SD, although the SS's intelligence wing was only one of many competing spy organizations. Both Himmler and Heydrich knew that all roads to power led to Berlin, their ultimate objective lying to the east of the tier formed by Hamburg, Brunswick, and Munich; before anything else, they had to get there themselves. They could not use open violence against other Nazi officials: they had to negotiate and connive their way to the capital, using every form of influence they possessed.

Himmler was willing to promise almost anything to win allies. If a party official could not get along with the obstreperous Storm Troopers, Himmler took his side; if a Gauleiter couldn't afford to maintain his own concentration camp, Himmler offered the services of the SS.

In exchange, all he asked was control of the resulting police entity. He wasn't ashamed to cover it with a gloss of official subservience: again and again, he "recognized each Reichsstatthalter [provincial governor] as his personal superior" in the bureaucratic hierarchy. Again and again, the provincial leaders took the bait, forgetting that personal union offered Himmler a fine way to get around these obligations. As leader of the SS, he had easier access to Hitler than they did—and Hitler was the final arbiter of all disputes.

Eventually a bandwagon effect was created: no one wanted to be left out of a profitable deal or left alone to face the growing power of the SS. Himmler offered a solution to this problem as well—the comforting security of an SS uniform. (The obligations that came with it could be left to another day.)

While Himmler was busy on so many fronts, Heydrich's SD managed to play an uncontroversial public role only in the southeastern state of Baden, where Carl Rudolf Werner Best, a legally trained deputy of Heydrich's and the new Southwest SD leader, in December 1930 convinced the governor to give police power to Himmler.

However, there was another category of SD leaders who were not as visible as Best or Streckenbach. Quite the contrary. Heydrich used a technique he called the "Trojan horse," in which state officials joined the SD or SS but kept their allegiance secret, thus providing him an excellent source of inside information.

Heydrich's best "horse" in Prussia, one Günther Patchowski, also helped open the door to SS infiltration. Patchowski was a counterespionage expert for the police in Breslau, the capital of Silesia (which was taken over by Prussia after its defeat of Austria in the eighteenth century's Silesian Wars). Hearing from an informer that the main office in Berlin was recruiting new personnel, Heydrich arranged to get Patchowski's name on the list of candidates. Then the SS Führer Southeast helped to get Patchowski appointed Berlin's chief of the Division of Treason and Espionage. By November he was in Berlin, a sleeper agent in a pivotal position long before Heydrich, his real boss, arrived on the scene.

As David Crankshaw has commented, "The fifth column did not begin in Spain; it began in Germany." This is the case with almost every major strategy—and atrocity—identified with Nazism. Invariably, these were tested at home before being exported abroad: the leaders of the Third Reich took literally their famous adage "First Germany, tomorrow the world."

By January 1934, Himmler and Heydrich had acquired all but one of the provincial offices of the political police, and were now free to turn their full attention toward the last holdout, the Secret State Police—otherwise known as the Gestapo—the dungeon stronghold of the great Prussian empire of Hitler's heir apparent, Hermann Göring.

Göring held a portfolio of offices (minister of state, president of the Reichstag, Prussian minister of the interior, commissioner of aviation, police president of Prussia) that made him the second most powerful man in Nazi Germany. A former ace fighter pilot now inclined to fat and drug addiction, Göring had perfected a swashbuckling joviality that made him extremely popular with the masses. Alone among the highest Nazi leaders, Hermann Göring dispensed with a protective escort, driving in his open convertible through the streets of Berlin, exchanging quips with passersby. But "Fat Hermann" didn't just tell jokes; he also dared to utter the starkest truths of the new regime.

After taking control of the newly christened Gestapo—the dreaded acronym for Geheime Staatspolizei, or Secret State Police, was created by accident, when his men began fiddling with the fragmented rubber stamps in the police building, and liked the sound of the syllables that fell together—Göring made a series of speeches in which he spelled out proper police etiquette, Nazi-style.

He began on an elevated note, a few hours after Hitler came to power: "A new chapter opens today, and in this chapter, liberty and honor will constitute the very basis of the new state." In the new *police* state, however, honor became identified with blind obedience and liberty with limitless violence. "Every policeman must grasp the fact that inaction is a more serious crime than an error committed in the execution of orders," Göring advised. "I may shoot a little wildly, one way or the other. But at least I shoot."

Tirelessly, the police president of Prussia encouraged mindless mayhem: "When a man lies dead, it is I who have shot him, even if I happen to be sitting up there in my office in the Ministry." In February 1933, he elaborated: "If you call that a murder, it is I who am the murderer . . . I assume the responsibility and I am not afraid."

In a speech in early March honoring the construction of the first official concentration camp, Oranienburg, Göring carried Nazi nihilism to its logical conclusion: "Fellow Germans, my measures will not be crippled by any bureaucracy. Here I don't have to worry about justice; my mission is only to destroy and exterminate; nothing more."

Himmler and Heydrich of course knew what Göring was saying, and may even have been influenced by it. But Göring's egotistic, swaggering bluster was incompatible with the SS posture as oath-bound servant of the leader's will. Never did Himmler presume to call his actions "murder." Indeed, the closer he came to Prussia, the more self-righteously he acted, condemning "all excesses, lies, or infringements of the law."

Yet in the arena into which Himmler and Heydrich now moved, open gang warfare had become the norm. All of the competing factions in the brand-new Reich seem to have achieved a tenuous foothold within the Gestapo, yet none was able to secure it. Inevitably, the shooting Göring glorified soon began to occur inside Gestapo headquarters, where it didn't seem half so grand or noble: as one of the participants admitted, "We were living in a den of murderers."

The atmosphere was so tense it verged on hysteria. In 1933, Hans Bernd Gisevius was a young lawyer assigned to the Gestapo by the Prussian Interior Ministry (though eventually he would become a covert opponent of the Nazi regime). When he visited his friend Arthur Nebe, chief executive of the Criminal Police (Kripo), he was advised to walk up the inner side of the staircase, next to the wall, as this would make it more difficult to shoot him from above. "Everyone feared everybody else," and Nebe wouldn't even go to the toilet without giving his destination to friendly colleagues who might be called on to rescue him.

To describe situations of such complexity, sociologists often draw a "sociogram," a chart in which each member of a group is represented by a dot. These are then arranged in a circle and the interrelationships between them are shown by lines connecting the dots. If we tried such a thing in this instance, everyone would be interconnected in so many ways that the lines would become hopelessly snarled, like a web spun by a cluster of inebriated spiders.

One can, however, distinguish several competing factions. On the truly conservative side were a few career officials who wanted to eliminate the Nazis entirely; Gisevius, a member of the resistance, represented this doomed point of view. In a more obscure corner were Nazi officials, like Interior Minister Wilhelm Frick, who owed their power to the new regime but had not totally abandoned the old German ideal of the *Rechtsstaat*, or a state in which force was restrained by the rule of law.

Gisevius's friend Arthur Nebe represented yet another faction, one that seems very peculiar today. Nebe was an SS "Trojan horse," having joined the organization secretly in 1931. A figure so shadowy his views vanish when exposed to the light of reasoned analysis, Nebe tried desperately to function as both an independent professional and a loyal SS man, sometimes leaking information to the SS, and sometimes to its bitterest opponents. Arthur Nebe thus epitomized an unhappy transitional figure—of which there were many—caught between the restraints of the old order and the unfettered dynamism (and criminality) of the new.

Nebe had a sometime ally in Kurt Dalüge, a tall, handsome, empty-faced SS man who had been appointed by Göring as controller of the (nonpolitical) police, perhaps because as leader of the Northern SS he was regarded as a rival of Himmler's, as head of the Southern SS. A few months earlier, as it will be recalled, Dalüge had ignored Heydrich when he came to Berlin as Himmler's emissary. But now Himmler and Heydrich were advancing on Berlin more aggressively. Like the others, Dalüge wanted to secure a place among the winners; like them, he therefore jumped constantly from ally to ally and side to side.

All of these men—Frick, Nebe, Dalüge, Himmler, and Heydrich—were after control of the Gestapo. But two others happened actually to be in command of it, and they were determined to remain. In Prussia, Himmler and Heydrich finally confronted this pair: Hermann Göring and his deputy chief of the Gestapo, Rudolf Diels.

Diels had been the expert on anti-Communism for the Weimar Secret Police in Berlin. He and Göring soon forged an alliance, with Diels functioning as Göring's "personal combination of spy, blackmailer, and bulldog"—much the same tasks that Heydrich had originally performed for Himmler.

There were other similarities between the two. Like Heydrich, Diels was intelligent, ambitious, and opportunistic. In his personal life, Diels shared with Heydrich an inclination to recklessness, and was known as a great womanizer. One of the women with whom Diels kept company was Martha Eccles Dodd, daughter of William Edward Dodd, the American ambassador to Germany appointed by President Franklin D. Roosevelt. Martha estimated that twelve people a day were killed while Diels was chief of the Secret Police. In one of her memoirs, she described his persona exactly the way others would soon describe Heydrich: "When he walked into a room, or rather, crept on cat's feet, he

Rudolf Diels (age thirty-three, in 1933), Hermann Göring's young and ambitious deputy chief of the Gestapo, was targeted for death on the Night of the Long Knives, after Himmler and Heydrich had perceived him as a threat to their authority. In the end, Göring served as Diels's protector.

created a nervousness and tension that no other man possibly could . . . Suddenly, late in the evening (he always came late), you would almost feel a chill in the room, and Diels would appear at your elbow in all his dark and horrible glamour!"

Martha Dodd once visited Frau Diels, whom she thought a "pathetic, passive-looking creature who must have gone through hell living with Diels." A short time later, Lina Heydrich too met Frau Diels and described her as a sinister, aggressive woman who kept telling her husband what to do. Beyond that observation, Lina would say to me absolutely nothing about her own husband's progress to Berlin or the people against whom he was waging something very like war: "I wasn't on the scene. I was at home in Munich expecting our first child. And I make it a policy never to discuss things I have not experienced for myself."

Beyond her ken, in the autumn of 1933, the battle was escalating between the SS and the Gestapo. One day Frau Diels opened the door of her apartment to find a squad of SS men, sent by Daluge to root through her husband's personal effects for evidence of secret links to Communism. Nothing was found, but Diels was so infuriated that he personally led an assault party to arrest the SS squad leader. He thought he had disarmed his opponent, but at police headquarters his prisoner suddenly pulled out a concealed gun. Before he could fire, a guard dog jumped at him, saving Diels's life.

Hans Bernd Gisevius later wrote, "It was so usual for members of the Gestapo to arrest one another that we scarcely took notice of such incidents." In the larger picture, however, these "incidents" provide the most graphic illustration of the circumstances that allowed Himmler and Heydrich to prevail over the other contenders.

Rudolf Diels had made so many enemies that he had become inconvenient, and Göring decided to replace him with a less feisty official. He chose a confirmed alcoholic, who soon proved inadequate to the demands of a job that would drive almost anyone to drink. Meanwhile, Diels was making a desperate bid to return. Finally, the Gestapo made a night raid on the home of their own leader, arrested the drunken man, and reinstated Diels.

Police President Göring cleverly coupled the return of Diels with the announcement of a famous decree of November 30, 1933, in which he declared that the Gestapo was now independent of the Ministry of the Interior and subordinate only to him. Such a move seemed disastrous to the anti-Nazi Gisevius. He and Dalüge called a secret meeting to plan ways to cripple Göring by getting rid of Diels (again). The only idea that seemed practical to them was to ask Diels to come to their office and then throw him out of the window. As they discussed this incredible tactic, emissaries from Diels did in fact appear—with the aim of arresting them all. The terrified Gisevius escaped through an emergency exit.

These attempted "arrests" exemplify a climate of action in which the preferred solution was always violence, usually involving a misuse of police authority. ("Arrest them! Arrest them! Arrest them!" Göring used to shout, whenever he heard someone had defied his orders.) They also reveal a group of groping bumblers, lost in a thicket of personal rivalries and unable to find a consistent strategy. As the historian George C. Browder has put it, "What emerges clearly from the contradictory sources about the developments and deals that brought Himmler to Berlin is a healthy leaven to stereotyped images of the Nazi leaders as Machiavellian draftsmen of a blueprint for totalitarianism. Their Third Reich grew less from design than as an awkward assemblage of pragmatic compromises."

In this den of inept conspirators only Himmler and Heydrich possessed the ideal combination of attributes: flexibility of means coupled with single-mindedness of aim. In a war of all against all, two determined men who stick together are apt to win. The bitter struggles and cross-cutting rivalries eventually strengthened the SS hand, as the other groups came to realize that control of the police had to be centralized before whirlpools of conflict engulfed the country. Although he was not by any stretch of thought a moderate, Heinrich Himmler gradually slipped into the role of moderator—the man most likely to control the excesses of Nazi violence without selling out the Nazi revolution.

One by one, Himmler's competitors were neutralized by the growing magnetic force of the SS. This was coupled with additional forms of pressure. Heydrich's official SD representative, his old friend from his navy days Hermann Behrends, secured an unmonitored phone connection to Munich, at last clearing the way for unhampered intrigue. Himmler began gradually stripping Dalüge of his independent SS offices, thus making himself less valuable as an ally to others, and forcing him back toward obedience.

With Dalüge more or less in line, Himmler and Heydrich went to work on Nebe and Gisevius. Later Gisevius described his "first encounter with Heydrich." An SS leader merely appeared at his door inviting him in Heydrich's name to an important conference. Gisevius asked Nebe along for protection.

To their amazement, they were treated as guests of honor, and congratulated for "leading the fight against corruption." Their host, SS General (and Hitler's former bodyguard) Josef "Sepp" Dietrich, told them, "Himmler detested the excesses of the SA," and "could no longer put up with the rampant sins of the Gestapo." He asked them to write down all their grievances.

"Naturally everything would be held in the strictest confidence. Himmler wanted the material as the basis for a personal appeal to Hitler." Carefully, the two men listed "any number of instances of extortion, torture, and killing." It was a year before they realized Himmler had no intention of remedying the abuses, and by then it was too late.

The SS's Dachau camp was generally reputed to be worse than the SA's Oranienburg, and Heydrich had ordered protective custody more often than Diels. Stories about the violence in Bavaria had preceded Himmler and Heydrich, disquieting even the Prussian potentate himself. "My God," Göring blurted one day to Frick, "if Himmler takes over the police, he will kill us all!"

Rudolf Diels was equally afraid of Heydrich's vengeance. When Göring told him he was considering making a deal just with Himmler, but would arrest Heydrich first, Diels worried that two hours after

Josef "Sepp" Dietrich (age fifty-two, circa 1942) was promoted to SS Obergruppenführer thanks to his key role in the Night of the Long Knives. Likened to a gladiator for his aggressive spirit, Dietrich held a position in Hitler's inner circle—even if his commanding officer at the Battle of the Bulge, German army field marshal Gerd von Rundstedt, found him "decent, but stupid."

Himmler arrived, he would set Heydrich free—and then what? According to Martha Dodd, "Diels became more neurotic and full of obsessions than anyone I knew in Germany—even those whom he persecuted."

One of the great advantages enjoyed by the men Gisevius had come to call "the evil twins" was precisely that they did not have "Himmler-and-Heydrich" to fight. They exploited other kinds of fears as well. Heydrich is said to have paid a friendly visit to Göring to show him evidence of an assassination plot against Göring himself—one that his own police had missed. Thus he illustrated Himmler's perennial proposal: If the SS wore police uniforms in addition to their own, might it not be to everyone's benefit?

In fact, the Führer was pondering this very question. Torn between the desire for a strong, centralized police force and the fear of augmenting SS power, he told Diels, "With Röhm and his friends I have enough lice under my skin at the moment. If Göring thinks he can involve me with Himmler and Heydrich as well, he is mistaken. Himmler can go on running his SS and you shall stay in your post as head of the Gestapo."

Göring, Diels, and Frick were now the only rivals to the SS who were still in the running. Had they been able to maintain a common front, they might have held on to the Gestapo, but this was beyond their abilities. Frick was too bureaucratic and colorless to appeal to most other Nazis, and Göring too voracious and egocentric to make a trustworthy ally. In any case, both of them were more worried about the openly vicious Röhm than about pliable, "faithful" Heinrich Himmler.

One day in March Göring told Diels that he had decided to let Himmler take over as chief of the political police.

"You mean: Heydrich is going to come and take the whole police in hand," Diels replied.

"What's that supposed to mean?" asked Göring.

"I suggest you get a reliable bodyguard," Diels responded.

Yet in spite of his fears, Rudolf Diels, the perennial opportunist, eventually decided to accept the preferred SS uniform and see what would happen next.

What happened next was a nightmare of bloody fratricide that altered the course of Nazism and changed the lives of everyone involved. The necessary prelude occurred on April 20, 1934, the day Heinrich Himmler moved up from Munich and into 8 Prinz Albrechtstrasse, Berlin SW. His formal title was soon to become "Reichsführer SS and Chief of the German Police." Reinhard Heydrich moved in as his deputy, without a clear title; it was supposedly temporary, everyone said. Göring had insisted that Himmler remain subordinate to him as prime minister of Prussia and to Frick as Reich minister of the interior. Himmler of course agreed. He was always amenable to what appeared to be a compromise.

10

THE RULES OF THE GAME

"My husband never read *Mein Kampf*!"
—LINA HEYDRICH

T HE WORLD IN WHICH Reinhard and Lina Heydrich now moved
was dominated by the character and political tactics of Adolf Hitler. Heinrich Himmler had opened the gates of possible power to
his young assistant, but it was the Führer who provided the directional
signposts that set him on his way.

Small wonder that the politically inexperienced Heydrich found
the chaos within the party headquarters "indescribable" at first: power
relationships in Nazi Germany did not at all resemble the efficient,
disciplined community of ideological comrades pictured in their own
propaganda. The Third Reich was not a monolith, but a mess, and
Adolf Hitler designed it that way.

Many books have been written about Hitler, one of the reasons being
the difficulty of knowing what he "really" thought. Reputable historians
still cannot agree on such basic issues as the nature of his sexual orientation, the extent of his personal maladjustment, the precise reasons for
his extreme anti-Semitism, the degree of either fanaticism or opportunism he displayed—or even whether he was best described as a reactionary or a revolutionary.

The lack of consensus about der Führer is the ur-symptom of the
fundamental disease of life in Nazi Germany: it was an inherently
unsettled society, perpetually in transition, never hardening into coher-

ence. One may argue that this is true of any country at any time, yet a regime described by its creator as "motion itself" obviously presents special problems of historical interpretation. For the moment, we shall consider only two of these: the confused nature of Nazi philosophy, and the extreme pragmatism of Hitler's political orientation.

The Führer was not an original thinker: a self-taught man and an unsystematically voracious reader of books on science, history, art, and philosophy, he has often been described as a great borrower and simplifier of other people's ideas. Hitler acquired the essentials of his worldview during a long period of bohemian shiftlessness in Vienna before the outbreak of the First World War; later, he boasted, "I have had but to learn a little beyond what I then created, there was nothing I had to change."

Distilled to its absolute essence, his *Weltanschauung* may be summarized in a sentence from *Mein Kampf,* whose title translates as "My Struggle": "He who would live must fight, and he who will not do battle in this world of eternal struggle does not deserve to live."

Originating within his troubled childhood, where he was the muchbeaten rebellious son of an intolerant and inflexible father, Hitler's intuitive notion of eternal struggle found confirmation in the "new" philosophy of Social Darwinism, in which the survival of the fittest was held to be the basic law not only of nature but also of human relations. As he simplified this scheme: "The world is given to the best nation, and the best minds in the nation must lead it."

In 1914, young Adolf Hitler had gone off to fight in a ghastly war of attrition in which a generation of brave men bled to death in a noman's-land created by military deadlock, where the opposing trenches lay so close together that the enemies could hear each other's military anthems and dying screams. The horror ended only when the arrival of American soldiers resolved the stalemate, and the German generals realized they were certain to lose.

But Hitler interpreted the situation differently: returning from the front he blamed his country's defeat on the Social Democratic Party, to whom the generals had given the awful task of accepting the peace terms dictated by the victorious and vindictive enemy powers. To Hitler, it was the Democrats who had negated the bravery and sacrifices of the frontline soldiers, sapped their will to fight, and ultimately lost the war. He cursed democracy as a "pestilence" and a "poison gas."

Then came the Red Republic in Munich (1918–19) and the Communist uprising in Berlin (1919). Hitler blamed all of Germany's post-war turbulence on a few extremist leaders, like Rosa Luxemburg and Karl Liebknecht—outsiders, Jews, not "true" Germans at all. An "alien people" had taken over; he wrote: "Only a knowledge of Jewry offers the key to a grasp of the universal, that is, the real intentions of Social Democracy." Behind both Democrats *and* Communists, Hitler discovered a Jewish common denominator. He saw no contradiction in this, accusing both groups of repudiating "the aristocratic principle of nature," and favoring "the eternal privilege of force and energy, numerical mass and dead weight."

Adolf Hitler decided it was his mission to restore the natural order to Germany, after which he would revise the country's shattered boundaries and position in Europe, in the process destroying both Marxism and democracy.

In roughest outline, all of this is clear enough, though it certainly isn't based on a reasonable account of German military or political history. The confusion arises with Hitler's attempts to "search for and discover the forces that are the causes of those results which appear before our eyes as historical events." Like many self-taught men, he despised intellectuals. He avoided rigorous analysis of ideas that appealed to him—but he was willing to borrow from anyone, even his enemies.

In *Mein Kampf,* for example, he admires the Americans for restrictive immigration policies, the British prime minister, Lloyd George, for his stirring oratory, the German Communists for the use of violence in politics, the Jews for lack of compromise in philosophical struggles, and the French for their tough occupation policies in Alsace-Lorraine.

The result of this haphazard eclecticism was a great seething cauldron of badly integrated, often conflicting ideas. In Martin Bormann's record of his "table talks," Hitler puts forth two antithetical principles within two consecutive paragraphs (and this was not unusual): "The social state must be maintained by a rule of iron," he says in one sentence, and then, in what follows, he lists exceptions to the rule, and a few words later remarks that "circumstances alter cases." When asked by a French diplomat why he had never altered passages in *Mein Kampf* that were no longer consistent with his current policies, Hitler replied, "I'm a politician, not a writer . . . my corrections are made in the great book of history."

Despite his apparently disarming frankness, the Führer did not see himself as a mere politician at all, but as a rare and magnificent combination of many additional roles, including statesman, orator, military commander, and theoretician. The theoretician, he argued (or "programmatist," as he referred to it), "is invariably misunderstood because he works for the future. And whereas it is he who lays down the aims of a movement, it is the politician who brings them to fruition. The one must think in terms of eternal truths while the other concentrates on present reality."

Hitler, as "a politician and statesman rolled into one," was constantly performing on several levels at the same time. It was hard even for insiders to know what governed his choices. After Hitler told him that written words cramped his freedom of action, Albert Speer decided he needn't bother to finish *Mein Kampf.* (Lina Heydrich told me her husband hadn't read it either.)

The inherent confusion of Hitler's ideas, coupled with his unwillingness to be tied down, has meant that Nazi life is often described in paradoxical terms—words like "permanent improvisation," "conservative revolution," "charismatic bureaucracy"—in which concepts usually opposed to each other are merged together.

Nevertheless, Hitler was remarkably consistent about the strategy and tactics of dictatorial political leadership. He gave his ideas the catch-all title "thinking in party terms" and presented them as a series of principles, adages, and stratagems, announced casually (but repeatedly) to the members of his inner circle. So well did these axioms relate to one another that we can justifiably call them the rules of a game whose stakes were personal political gain and whose players were the inner circle of Nazi potentates. Such games have been played by tyrants and courtiers since despotism was invented. Of course, Hitler's Third Reich was also a totalitarian state utilizing modern methods of persuasion and coercion, but it rested on a sturdy, unchanging base of factional rivalries and clashing individual ambitions. "What is your program?" a Nazi leader was once asked. "We're going to get power," he answered. "And then what will you do?" said the persistent questioner. "We will keep it!" the Nazi replied.

Politics is a game, in which every sort of trick is possible, and in which the rules are constantly being changed by the players to suit themselves.

The "rules" of this daily struggle were the realities that confronted Heydrich when he joined the SS, and he followed them the rest of his life, becoming one of the great masters of a sinister martial art. Without a knowledge of what one participant called "the National Socialist war

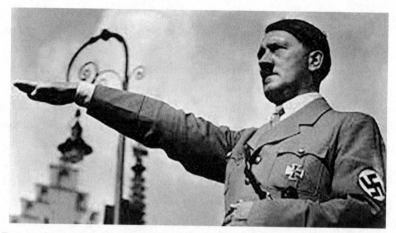

Despite the aggressive nature of the "Hitler Salute," its genesis was both banal and benign, according to the U.S. Office of Strategic Services. "In 1923," said the OSS, Adolf Hitler "adored American football marches and college songs. The 'Sieg Heil!' [roughly meaning, 'Hail Victory!'] used in all political rallies is a direct copy of the technique used by American football cheerleaders."

games," it is impossible to understand his rise to power, his professional relationships, or, even, his married life. Lina Heydrich sometimes participated in the endemic conflict, and did astonishingly well—for a woman.

Frau Heydrich often told me that both her actions and those of her husband were conditioned by the "framework of the situation." Heydrich himself spoke of the need to adapt to the "political reality of the present time." As a step toward clarifying these amorphous terms, I offer here a brief description of ten fundamental rules of the power game under Hitler, taken from the leader's conversations and writings, as recorded or remembered by contemporaries of Reinhard and Lina Heydrich. It is meant to be suggestive rather than definitive: another observer might well alter the elements or combine them in different ways.

1. "OUR PROGRAM IS EXPRESSED IN TWO WORDS—ADOLF HITLER."

The longing for a single powerful ruler who can unite his subjects under the banner of a God-given mission is an ancient theme of German history. A typical Teutonic legend tells of the great eleventh-century emperor Frederick Barbarossa, whose spirit sleeps beneath a high mountain peak, ready to return in the hour of Germany's greatest peril. (In his mountain retreat, the Berghof, Hitler designed a wall of windows to look out on Barbarossa's reputed resting place.)

Even during the Weimar Republic, seedbed of abstract expressionism in painting, Brechtian theatrical techniques, and Bauhaus architecture, many ultramodern youth still longed to throw themselves at the feet of a new savior. This yearning was shared even by older, successful members of the establishment. Albert Speer's first mentor, the noted (and anti-Nazi) architect Heinrich Tessenow, told him in 1931, "Someone will have to come along who thinks very simply; . . . an uncultured man . . . would solve everything much more easily merely because he would still be unspoiled. He would also have the strength to carry out his simple ideas."

Simple ideas were the Führer's intellectual meat and drink, and he gave his followers even less to feed on: "You have . . . no longer to do your best, according to your lights, but to obey orders. What may seem to you advantageous may, from a higher point of view, be injurious. My first demand from you, therefore, is blind obedience."

But the famous "Leadership Principle" did not mean that Hitler made all the decisions. Indeed, he often said his greatest problem was finding gifted subordinates: "What would happen to me if I didn't have around me men . . . to do the work for which I can't find time? For me the best man is the man who removes the most from my shoulders, the man who can take 95 percent of the decisions in my place." Hitler compared the "courage" needed for this responsibility to that of a soldier, and occasionally boasted that he didn't really know what his Gauleiters did, such was his trust in their abilities.

The Führer's insistence that his closest associates display initiative in the name of obedience placed them in a constant position of uncertainty. Caught between competing demands, they had to turn to him for validation. Luftwaffe chief Hermann Göring once summarized the vulnerability of Hitler's paladins: "We each possess just so much power as the Führer wishes to give. And only with the Führer and standing behind him is one really powerful, only then does one hold the strong powers of the state in one's hands; but against his will, or even just without his wish, one would instantly become totally powerless. A word from the Führer and anyone he wishes to be rid of falls."

2. "THERE MAY BE ONLY ONE SINGLE RULE: THAT IS CORRECT WHICH IS USEFUL IN ITSELF."

Whatever his fanaticism about Germany's racial and historical destiny, Hitler regarded the politics necessary to achieve it in a brutally opportunistic light. He liked to say that the only "real conviction" of politicians "is lack of conviction." In the daily language used by the Führer and his cronies, people were described as being "programmed" in various ways, and even the bravest Aryans were considered merely "human material," to be used—or used up—when necessary. During the war, a German general complained that poor logistics were causing soldiers to die needlessly in Russia. Hitler told him not to worry, that was what soldiers were for.

Hitler was proud of his "hardness," and felt that it derived from a scientific approach to life. "I look at everything with an immense, ice-cold lack of bias," he boasted to his intimates, extolling the "logic" and "reason" which enabled him to see through conventional bourgeois illusions. "Why doesn't God protect churches from lightning?" he asked contemptuously. In place of the irrational "magic" of religion, Hitler substituted "the principle that nature herself gives all the necessary indications, and that therefore one must follow the rules that she has laid down." He was constantly advising his military tacticians to invent new machines mimicking natural forms, and he himself designed the Volkswagen in explicit homage to the beetle. He urged his subordinates to be as swift as greyhounds, or faithful as hunting dogs, but it was analogies to a bloodier nature, red in tooth and claw, that Hitler liked best. "Who is to blame when the cat eats the mouse?" he once remarked, in a famous rationalization of the extermination of his enemies.

Beneath Hitler's mock-*Volks*y style glinted a steely view of life as an eternal fight with knives, whose brutal force could be checked only by greater force. Small wonder he admired associates like Göring, who shared his gelid cynicism: "I have always observed that when it comes to the breaking point, he is ruthless, hard as iron; . . . he becomes ice-cold," he said of his presumed successor, Göring (who went out of his way to express disdain for "ideological junk").

3. "THE NATIONAL SOCIALIST THEORY IS TO MAKE USE OF ALL FORCES, WHEREVER THEY MAY COME FROM."

The natural corollary of Hitler's opportunism was his insistence that "all imaginable means" could be used in the struggle for power. (He said he kept a copy of Machiavelli's *The Prince* on his bedside table.) His flagrant amorality gave Hitler a formidable advantage over more conventional opponents, yet he was consistently underestimated in his early struggles, and misunderstood later, because of another tactic he used with consummate skill. As Albert Speer remarked, Hitler liked "to show different selves to different people." He was a marvelous actor: "Never in the whole history of Western Europe had politics been so theatrically stage-managed."

Hitler did not always try to meet his visitors' expectations; frequently he tried to throw them off base. Diplomats anticipating a monster were often surprised to meet a mild petite-bourgeois offering them cream puffs and tea. On the other hand, Hitler staged such a fearful rage for the benefit of the Czech leader Emil Hácha that ever afterward, his entourage referred to this treatment as being "Hácha-ized."

Hitler's great dramaturgical gifts were used in the service of a general strategy that has been aptly summarized as "advancing on several fronts at once." In these "dual tactics," he particularly favored a combination of surprise blows and reassuring talk. In 1933, for example, he combined the "liberating deed" of tearing Germany out of the League of Nations with talk of the need for peace in Europe, supported by the enactment of a national plebiscite "proving" that over 99 percent of the German population was opposed to war. Mesmerized, his opponents were lulled into inaction, setting the pattern for six more years of successful Hitlerian double-talk.

4. "CLARIFICATION WOULD MEAN DIVISION."

Hitler also pursued dual tactics on the domestic front, refusing to formulate clear policy guidelines and insisting on keeping all "doors open." Deliberately, he made incompatible promises to different groups whose support he needed. To the farmers he promised price supports, to the urban workers, cheap food. One day he would threaten to socialize German industry; that same night, he might meet with a group of industrialists and swear to hold private property sacred. Nor did he neglect the ladies: although he constantly pledged that women would no longer have to work outside the home, by 1939, more were employed in factories than ever before.

Ordinarily Hitler handled foreign enemies by playing them off against one another; on the home front, he often gave overlapping grants of power to two competing institutions or men and let them fight it out. Thus, the Abwehr, an information-gathering organization, and Heydrich's new political intelligence service exercised functions so similar that no one knew the boundaries between them. Heydrich and his opposite number, Admiral Canaris, had to determine these for themselves, in a series of clandestine battles that lasted until Heydrich's death.

Hitler also liked to test the second in command of an organization, by "spontaneously" giving a job to an untried leader to see what he would make of it—and in the process preventing the two top leaders from forming a strong alliance. In the latter half of his career, Heydrich received much of his authority from Führer orders, as Hitler bypassed Himmler to brake the growing power of the SS.

The surface of the supposedly granite Reich was rent with such fissures between competing leaders and institutions, gaps in power which were never closed. Hitler, one of the great experts in the old art of divide and conquer, didn't mind this at all. "Friction produces warmth," he said, "and warmth is energy."

5. "THE STRONGEST ALWAYS DOES THE JOB."

The Führer believed that the natural leader will always have enough authority. Through the "warmth" of the continual struggle for internal power, the most courageous, resolute, and competent leaders would gradually emerge.

Most of the Nazi leaders, however, didn't want to take the heat all by themselves. Instead, they encouraged an almost medieval emphasis on loyalty. Lesser officials (like Heydrich at the beginning of his career) were assumed to be their bosses' "man"; offenders were regularly purged, as each local satrap tried to create a little bastion of certainty to protect his own exposed position.

Their desperate search for security also inspired multitudes of secret alliances. A clandestine network of relationships grew up parallel to the public institutions and often in opposition to them. These "bridges of cooperation" were usually temporary, since they tended to involve trade-offs between two chieftains that might bring them into conflict with a third. Thus, for example, Göring sometimes put pressure on the police to arrest writers who made jokes about him in newspaper columns. Himmler, as police chief, might agree, if he owed Göring a favor; but this could then provoke a quarrel with Goebbels, who controlled the press, and often used it to ridicule his enemies. As the historian Joachim Fest has remarked, these secret deals created a "confusion of intrigues . . . cabals, accusations, and embittered rivalries. This was the other face of the party based entirely on the Führer idea and the principle of loyalty. In the absence of any firm ideology or objective principles, every issue was decided on purely personal grounds."

6. "ONE MUST ALWAYS CHOOSE A WEAKER OPPONENT. THAT IS THE SECRET OF SUCCESS."

The atmosphere of subjectivity and uncertainty within which the fight for power took place induced a compensatory reliance on a macabre pseudoscience of human fallibility. The Führer believed he could achieve a "mathematical certainty of success" through the "exact calculation of all human weaknesses."

Albert Speer said that the Führer consciously selected minions who had "a flaw in the weave," since this made them easier to manipulate. Yet there was more to it than that. Hitler realized that the men who followed him in his early days were largely failures in ordinary life—they had to be, or they would not have wanted to serve a leader with his dubious social credentials and dim prospects.

In exchange for their loyalty, he was willing to excuse personal peccadilloes. The alcoholic sprees of Robert Ley, the wild spending of Hermann Göring, even Julius Streicher's admitted sexual pleasure in whipping defenseless victims—all things that gave many ardent Nazis pause for thought—were cheerfully dismissed as the necessary concomitants of a warrior's life. "Misdemeanors are natural to a Nazi," Hitler argued. "We are brawling our way to greatness."

In 1931, five Nazi thugs broke into the apartment of an opposition leader, dragged him from bed, and beat and kicked him to death while his wife watched. After they were condemned by a Weimar court, Hitler wrote a letter publicly claiming "solidarity" with the perpetrators. As he privately instructed, "There are two things which unite men—common ideals, and common scoundrelism."

Hitler's tolerance was not unlimited, however. He relished gossip that placed others in an unflattering light. Propaganda Minister Goebbels often dined out at Hitler's chancellery on the strength of humorous stories in which his competitors were made to appear stupid, greedy, warped, or incompetent. Party Secretary Martin Bormann also built much of his career on defaming his rivals, occasionally whispering innuendoes into Hitler's ear just as the unfortunate subject approached.

Hitler prided himself on his skills as a "detective," and rejoiced in "tearing the masks off the mugs" of vassals who seemed disloyal or deceitful. He might then banish the offender forever, often without speaking to him first. Albert Speer has described the inhibiting effect thus produced: "Among rivals an honest word was rarely spoken for fear it would be carried back to Hitler in a distorted version. Everyone conspired, took Hitler's capriciousness into his reckoning, and won or lost in the course of this cryptic game."

Speer does not dwell on one inevitable component of a game in which human weaknesses were used as tokens: "Under Hitler's system of government it was practically impossible to attain office or remain in office without using blackmail." Himmler and Heydrich were not the only Nazis to keep a little file on the faults of their enemies; one never knew when a well-timed comment, a secret threat, or a self-righteous denunciation might come in handy.

7. "THE VICTOR IS NOT ASKED AFTERWARD WHETHER OR NOT HE HAS TOLD THE TRUTH."

Blackmail flourishes within an atmosphere of conscious deception and duplicity. In *Mein Kampf* Hitler argued that if one tells a "big lie" frequently enough, it will eventually be believed. The important thing was not veracity, but the need to sway the masses with simple slogans of unity, patriotism—and hate. "If there were no Jew, we would have to invent him," he is reported to have joked to his aides. Whether he actually said it, the plausibility of his having done so makes the point sufficiently.

Hitler's blithe prevarication engendered a pervasive fear among his cronies that they might have slipped, unknowing, into the ranks of the simpletons who believed him. Perhaps the sense of being in the inner group, of sharing the Führer's confidence, was just a "trick," designed to make it easier to control his subordinates? Doubts like these scurried like cockroaches across the minds of men who had scrambled for the precarious privilege of belonging to Hitler's court.

Nor was it easy to argue the doubts away. Hitler disliked free and easy discussion, preferring to give vent to his own opinions. His intolerance of real conversation, and pride at being "immune to advice," once reduced the head of arms production, the tough Fritz Todt, to tears. "Criticism would be the worst kind of democracy," Hitler intoned, leaving those who wished to clarify a troubling point with no redress.

Almost no one dared to disagree openly with the leader. Most dissent tended to be oblique, emerging in the form of casual "historical" references, jokes, lists of technical requirements in which more substantive remarks could be inserted—even fake astrological charts. Sometimes, too, Hitler would accept a fait accompli if it were skillfully accomplished and satisfactorily explained. (This, after all, was what he himself had been doing for years: "It is the age of faits accomplis!" he told his underlings.)

In the end, Hitler became cut off from independent sources of information, as the tactics he advocated in the struggle with others were inevitably turned against him. Albert Speer was convinced that everyone lied to Hitler. Like a con man victimized by one of his own ruses, the great liar was often unable to see through "clever chess moves" and "methodical deceit." Both Canaris and Himmler, reporting information from Heydrich's SD, routinely avoided telling Hitler unpleasant or "disturbing" facts, even though that was supposed to be their job. Lesser fry, like Speer, did the same. "I was condemned to either impotence or cunning," Speer wrote after the war, whose disastrous ending for Germany was caused in part by the time-consuming, energy-draining, goal-distorting politics of lying.

8. "THE WORLD CAN ONLY BE RULED BY FEAR."

"The rabble has to be scared shitless!" was a favorite maxim of Dietrich Eckhardt, a crony of Hitler's earliest Munich days and a founder of the

Nazi Party. A much older man and experienced freebooter, he served as a political inspiration to the young agitator, who did not exempt his own countrymen from his deep contempt for human frailty.

Almost no one lived up to Hitler's standards: the hereditary aristocracy had proved "degenerate," the bourgeoisie lacked imagination and nerve, and the industrial workers had grown too soft for revolution. Women were often praised by Hitler because he thought they acted on healthy feelings, rather than reason. (On the other hand, they were therefore more easily swayed.)

"I hate the masses," wrote an early adherent of Nazism. The New Order was to belong only to the hard, virile, and stalwart. Elitism was as important to Hitler's thinking as racism—and indeed, he considered them natural companions. According to the American social historian David Schoenbaum, Hitler envisioned a postwar world in which even victorious Germany was to be divided into a permanent servant class, a group of faithful party workers, and then into a higher group of leaders who had distinguished themselves through achievement. Germans who did not "fit in" would be kicked out, no matter what their previous position or degree of wealth.

Part of what Hitler called his "revolutionary process" consisted of a reactionary revival of the "insurmountable" caste system of "ancient great civilizations." As he saw it, "True aristocracy existed only where there was also true subjection." Initially, the mere decision to follow Hitler was taken as an indicator of real nobility, but after a few years, the leader began to winnow through his courtiers, not all of whom survived the encounter. Fear of falling from a tenuous grace, sheer physical fear, crept along the marble hallways of the party potentates as surely as it stalked the tenements of the powerless workers. Even Himmler occasionally confided to trusted subordinates his fear that he "might be hanged" if he openly disagreed with Hitler. Inevitably, anxiety rose to the highest level: one day the Führer himself gestured toward his SS bodyguard and remarked, "These are the men who will kill me some day."

9. "THE IMPOSSIBLE ALWAYS SUCCEEDS."

In his dinner table conversations, Hitler presented himself as a model of cunning, courage, ruthlessness, and audacity—coupled with the usual "iron" control over stray humanitarian impulses. Legions of demi-Hitlers, determined to hide their inner fears and reservations, vied with each other in attempting to enter the psyche of their leader. Nowhere else in the Third Reich was empathy so valued as when Himmler tried to determine "the correct psychological moment" to approach Hitler with bad news or Albert Speer tried to induce him to make a difficult decision about armaments production.

Their problems were enhanced by Hitler's erratic methods of decision-making: believing himself a creative genius, he neverthe-less wanted to move with the "certainty of a sleepwalker." When this oddly passive form of inspiration failed him, he tended to improvise impulsively—and often aggressively. "Attack! Attack! Always attack!" he advised his subordinates. Nothing was impossible to the true Nordic hero, he argued, sometimes going so far as to counsel, "What is unlikeli-est is surest."

The pressure toward impossible performance produced a mindset once described as "the categorical imperative of the Third Reich." The best way to resolve doubts was to "always act as if you were the Füh-rer, himself." Since the Führer most admired "hard men who act as energetically as I would do myself," the categorical imperative generally operated to push the Nazi leaders in the direction of fanaticism, and into Hitler's zero-sum game of radical solutions to problems and swift, brutal, cruelly competitive action.

10. "WE MUST NEVER ALLOW OUR DIFFERENCES TO BE BARED TO OUTSIDERS."

The Führer was convinced that "people will not follow with blind faith if we destroy their trust in the leaders." In the midst of their cutthroat competition, the Nazi potentates were still expected to raise their voices in a chorus of comradely solidarity. "The masses have a simple system of thinking and feeling," Hitler said, "and anything that cannot be fit-ted into it disturbs them. It is only because I take their vital laws into consideration that I can rule them."

One of the laws concerned the inspirational power of violence: "Why babble about brutality and be indignant about tortures? The masses want that. They need something that will give them a thrill of horror . . . The plain man in the street respects nothing but brutal strength . . . women, too, for that matter, women and children."

Nevertheless, Hitler also insisted that "public decorum" be maintained, and explicitly advocated "a screen of legality" to cover acts the bourgeois world would otherwise regard as crimes. "Moral commonplaces are indispensable for the masses," he claimed. "Nothing is more mistaken than for a politician to pose as a nonmoral superman. That is a fool's game." However vicious the game of power became, it had to be conducted behind an intentionally donned "mask" of propriety. Hitler's concern for appearances was a great boon for the SS, for Himmler had always justified his vindictiveness as necessary for the common good and hidden his unacceptable impulses behind a bland persona.

Sometimes love, as well as war, was affected by Hitler's theatrical concern with how things looked. At various times both Joseph and Magda Goebbels wanted to dissolve their troubled union and marry others. But they had entertained too lavishly and reigned too publicly as one of the few glamorous couples of Nazidom, and the beautiful, blond Magda had long been regarded as a model of Aryan womanhood. Hitler forbade them to divorce, though he had no particular objection to discreet affairs. "Goebbels is a cynic where women are concerned," he remarked tolerantly, perhaps because the same could be said of him.

Returning once again to Hitler's pervasive cynicism, one comes back to the second rule of the game—that, essentially, it had no rules save success. Nazi Germany offered its citizens a rhetoric of discipline and of continuity with hallowed Germanic traditions, but underneath this facade, nihilism festered.

Hitler gloated over the dualistic universe he had created: "It gives us also a special, secret pleasure to see how the people about us are not aware of what is really happening to them. They gaze fascinated at one or two familiar superficialities . . . As long as these are kept intact, they are quite satisfied. But in the meantime, they have entered a new relationship: a powerful social force has caught them up. They themselves are changed."

Yet Hitler, the sorcerer who exhorted his entourage to give up "the degrading, bourgeois chimera called conscience," seems to have thought he himself could remain unchanged—and untainted. He spoke of "doing the Lord's work" and of his brutalities as a temporary expediency of the period of political transition. Someday, he said, he would cease the necessary "negative" work of destruction and begin his "positive" task of building a harmonious new world. In his table talks, he sometimes spoke eloquently of a future in which jobs, social justice, education, and beautiful physical surroundings would be granted to all of his followers.

On the other hand, he also looked forward to the day when he could remove the masks of the diplomat and statesman and let his enemies see the "barbarian" underneath. Hitler's ambivalence, as he vacillated between longing for the bravado of aggressive opportunism and the grandeur of peaceful construction, pervaded his entire entourage.

In 1934, for the first time, the Führer had to choose between them. In that year, Hitler's mask slipped for a long, traumatic moment. Never have the murderous amorality of the rules of the game been more starkly and painfully revealed than in the bloody events that were collectively described in Nazi mythology as the Night of the Long Knives.

11

A LESSON IN LIFE

"This [first mass murder] brought my husband a deep spiritual sorrow."

—LINA HEYDRICH

O N THE FIRST ANNIVERSARY of his accession to power, the Führer wrote a letter to his most powerful ally, "my dear Ernst Röhm," thanking him "for your unforgettable services." He concluded with gratitude "to destiny for having given me the right to call a man like you my friend and comrade-in-arms."

Less than six months later, on June 30, 1934, Hitler arrived at dawn at the Bavarian lake resort of Bad Wiessee, where Röhm was on holiday with a few of his SA men. Bursting into his old friend's room, Hitler yelled, "You are under arrest!" and stormed out. Even before he left the room, squads of SS began dragging off Röhm's subordinates, starting with his chief of staff, Edmund Heines, whom they had surprised in bed with a young boy. "Exterminate this pestilential tumor!" Hitler shouted as he left. In the three days that followed, hundreds of people (no one has ever known the precise number) were murdered in a wave of violence spreading throughout Germany and engulfing generals, diplomats, Catholic priests, and one former chancellor, in addition to Röhm and his cohorts.

The Blood Purge has been called the Nazis' "first mass murder." It stunned the nation. Even following the war and its attendant geno-cide, Gerald Reitlinger, the author of a famous book on the Holocaust, *The Final Solution: The Attempt to Murder the Jews of Europe, 1939–1945*

Ernst Röhm (center) was the highest-ranking openly homosexual official in Nazi Germany. Given his opposition to Paragraph 175 of the German penal code—introduced when the empire was founded in 1871, and which called for "unnatural sexual offenses" between men to result in prison sentences of up to six months—it was thought that he might use his influence to temper the Nazi stance on homosexuality. Instead, the party intensified crackdowns and punishments for same-sex acts between men. (Lesbianism was largely overlooked.)

(1953), described the Nazi 1934 bloodletting as "the great drama of the mid-twentieth century."

It was certainly a crucial turning point in the history of the Third Reich, particularly in the lives of its leaders, and at a time when Hitler was presenting himself abroad as a misunderstood moderate. Although the bloody remains of the victims were speedily removed, the trauma endured. For those most closely involved, the purge seems to have marked a moment of personal commitment, and, for many, a spiritual point of no return. Impaled on the knives of June 30 were precious ideals and illusions: even many "winners" felt pierced by dilemmas that at that time still seemed unnatural. Everyone felt driven to try to learn from the experience; and though the assessments varied, they all boded very ill indeed. Lina Heydrich told me that for her husband, the Röhm purge was "a lesson in life." In fact, the lessons were all about death—and the Nazi game of power that made it inevitable.

Complicating the judgments was the character of the major victim. A beefy man, reminiscent of a warthog, with a puffy, scarred face out of which small eyes peered warily, he looked as disreputable as he was.

In his autobiography, Röhm had written: "Since I am an immature and wicked man, war and unrest appeal to me more than the good bourgeois order." Scarcely bothering to disguise his homosexuality, he spent his free time carousing with numerous lovers. Many of them wound up in high positions in his SA, which under Hitler's new emergency legislation was now empowered to act as auxiliary police. SA men staffed numerous concentration camps, among them Oranienburg—and in Berlin alone, more than fifty detention centers in garages, cellars, and warehouses—where they improvised such swinish punishments as tossing prisoners into cement mixers or drowning them in excrement.

Even those who seemed to support the new regime were not immune: one balmy May night some SA men had invaded a formal ball at the home of an aristocrat, knocking bejeweled and titled ladies to the ground, then playing catch with the ceremonial helmets of the gentlemen. "Many complaints are being lodged concerning the alleged excesses of SA men," Röhm admitted, adding brazenly that it would require "a skyscraper erected over the Brown House" (the party headquarters in Munich) to hold them all.

Ernst Röhm felt he could afford such insouciance, secure in the Führer's protection. If he had spoken out openly and honestly about what he knew, his testimony would have been devastating. The prototype of the anti-democratic outlaws who fought in the war, then in the Freikorps, then in the civil war, and then in the streets, Röhm had provided Hitler with weapons, influential contacts with the military, and, according to the German historian Hermann Mau, a powerful role model: "Under Röhm's influence Hitler . . . acquired the exaggerated esteem for soldierly bearing that ultimately led to his stylized 'Führer' personality."

When they met, Hitler had merely been a political agitator and part-time informer for the German Army. Impressed by his nationalistic fervor, Röhm organized the Storm Troopers to protect him, quarreled with Hitler when he turned toward legal tactics in 1923, then returned to the fold in 1931 to help the Nazis in their final struggle for power. He built the SA into an immense, loutish political army, using violence to impress and intimidate the opposition—exactly as demanded by the rules of the game. In the elections of 1933, Hitler secured 40 percent of the vote (he was never legally supported by majority opinion) and became chancellor of a coalition cabinet under von Hindenburg.

As his reward, Röhm expected to be given command of the German Army, which he hoped to use as the foundation of a radical new form of military-socialist state. But the game had changed: with Hitler in power at last, Röhm's freebooter behavior was going out of style. "I can't seriously be expected to draw the material for my military elite from the bow-legged and knock-kneed SA!" Hitler said to his intimates. Publicly, however, he staunchly defended his roughneck militia, as "an association of men for a political purpose . . . not an ethical institution of the education of gentlewomen."

Yet this was not enough for Röhm. "I demand the primacy of the soldier over the politician," he wrote. The two old friends began to drift apart, their tactical differences fanned by newly clashing temperaments. Röhm treated Hitler as an equal, refusing to share the latter's growing infatuation with his own role as Führer: "What he wants is to sit on the hilltop and pretend he's God. And the rest of us, who are itching to do something, have got to sit around doing nothing . . . Are we revolutionaries or not?"

Of course, Röhm had hardly been doing nothing: indeed, his outrageous behavior and demands for greater power were making him increasingly unpopular with the other players in the game. Joseph Goebbels and Rudolf Hess, like other Nazi Party administrators, felt threatened. Now his military ambitions alarmed Göring, who wanted control of the army himself. And Himmler, once an ardent disciple, was having his usual second thoughts. Röhm was still the boss, but his lifestyle had always offended his puritanical subordinate. In 1931, moreover, Hitler had called on SS troops to put down the revolt of a rebellious SA warlord in Berlin. Himmler's history-loving mind could hardly have missed the importance of this precedent. With Röhm out of the way, his own power would inevitably increase.

Outside the Nazi Party, the members of the old establishment—the nobility, conservative businessmen, and, especially, the military—saw in the SA the embodiment of every new trend they loathed: social revolution, anarchic violence, and proletarian manners. Nothing would compel them to accept Röhm as a peer, much less a commander.

In early June, Franz von Papen, an aristocrat who had helped Hitler to power, expressed these feelings in a speech denouncing the "selfishness, lack of character, mendacity, beastliness, and arrogance that are spreading under the guise of the German revolution." If we continue to confuse vitality with brutality, von Papen argued, the resulting chaos would destroy Germany.

Röhm, in the meantime, had joined Gregor Strasser, Himmler's former mentor, in calling for a "second revolution" against capitalism and bourgeois morality. The Führer was caught between the revolutionaries in his own party and the conservative reaction outside it; and the conflict was heightened by his knowledge that President von Hindenburg was dying, and could last only a few more weeks. Hitler feared his conservatives would see von Hindenburg's death as the signal for demanding the return of the Kaiser monarchy.

In terms of the "game of protecting his own rule," as the historian Joachim Fest has put it, Hitler had to find the "simultaneous solution of no less than five problems." He had to quash Röhm, placate the army, "dispel public dissatisfaction with the rule of the streets and visible terrorism," and stymie the conservatives. And, "all this had to be done without becoming the prisoner of one side or the other."

But Hitler hesitated, waiting for inspiration. Meanwhile, the National Socialist war games went on without him. Although Röhm controlled approximately 4 million men in arms, the other Nazi leaders gradually realized that his isolation from all other sectors of influence had made him vulnerable. They began to establish rickety bridges of clandestine cooperation. In April 1934, after Göring transferred the Gestapo into Himmler's hands, it was clear that he and the Reichsführer SS were now allied. There were foreshadowings aplenty. The strains of the official Nazi anthem, the "Horst-Wessel-Lied," hurled death into the air. One of its most famous stanzas was horribly prophetic: "Sharpen the long knives on the sidewalks . . . When the hour of reckoning comes, we stand ready for any mass murder."

This was widely regarded as hyperbole; yet murder had long been an acceptable instrument of Nazi policy. In 1933, Röhm sent an SA squad to kill a renegade comrade, the engineer and spy Georg Bell. In earlier days, Bell had clarified the "procedure": "We call it self-defense . . . On moral grounds, I find nothing extraordinary in doing away with a man if it is in the interests of the party."

"Thinking in party terms," as the leadership was evidently doing, it was clear that Röhm could not merely be dismissed; he must die. For one thing, the millions of SA men had to be "scared shitless" to prevent rebellion. For another, Röhm, alive, was the obvious rallying point for those who wanted a "second revolution" against Hitler's policies.

At the time that Hitler began to contemplate the problems that

Röhm presented, Heydrich's Security Service had suddenly surfaced as a player in the game. In April, he had finally moved to Berlin, becoming second in command of the Secret Police, as well as chief of the SD. Until then, almost no one knew what Heydrich had been doing. We don't know either exactly what he did during the event called the Night of the Long Knives: it has all been constructed afterward from the anecdotal testimony of conflicting sources. (There are almost no written documents; Göring and Himmler ordered them burned.)

Historians agree that there were two major centers of conspiratorial activity, Munich (where Hess and, ultimately, Hitler himself were in charge) and Berlin (where Göring and Himmler shared the dishonor). But the situation was even more complicated than that. If one asks the simple question, who murdered Ernst Röhm, the best answer is the one so favored by American radicals of the 1960s: the "system" killed him—the cold "logic" of the vicious game of competitive opportunism that Hitler had long taught.

The Night of the Long Knives consisted of a series of murders, authorized and performed by different men in different parts of Germany. Generally, the killers were acting according to Hans Frank's "categorical imperative": they did what they thought Hitler would do (or ought to do), pushing toward radical, violent actions that in the end he endorsed as his own.

Hitler had once advised a young disciple, "We must become a single family of conspirators." For a few weeks, that is exactly what happened. Even the reactionary Reichswehr and the radical SS agreed to a temporary rapprochement. The army, limited to 100,000 men by the Treaty of Versailles, had been dwarfed by the millions of unruly Storm Troopers. Werner von Blomberg, the handsome and amiable new minister of defense, was ambivalent about the new Führer, and his wait-and-see attitude expressed the position of most of his class. But serving under von Blomberg was a man with no such reservations. Nicknamed "the Nazi General," Walter von Reichenau has been described as a more "modern" sort of officer—"ambitious, brutal, politically gifted, and more intelligent than his minister."

This is exactly the way Heydrich is often viewed in relation to Himmler. Von Reichenau began to appear at SS offices in Berlin in the spring of 1934, and some historians say he met with Heydrich and found him "congenial." (Heydrich's subordinates testified after the war that von

Reichenau usually saw Himmler, while Heydrich relayed their instructions to the various local SS leaders.)

At any rate, an accord was soon achieved: weaponry began to find its way from army warehouses to various SS barracks, while information flowed in the other direction, as secret SD reports circulated among the military leaders, fanning their fears that the brown-shirted rabble army was about to attack. Today one would call this disinformation: Heydrich was deliberately exaggerating—sometimes falsifying—the SA menace.

Hitler had long ago ordered the SD to investigate Röhm's activities. Informers reported many intemperate remarks ("If only we could get rid of that limp rag," Röhm once said of Hitler) but no true proof of conspiracy. Röhm was more loyal than he sounded; yet the game was supposed to be played the other way around. In fact, he had never really learned all the rules, not bothering to hide his beliefs or his feelings: of cunning, duplicity, and methodical betrayal, the disreputable old warrior knew almost nothing. It was from these new strategies of "cold, silent revolution . . . operating below a surface of seeming normality" that the net was woven to bring him down.

Directives, "signed" by Röhm, ordering preparations for a putsch, were conveniently unearthed. Local SD commanders spread tales of secret SA gatherings; agents provocateurs took to the streets, pretending to be Storm Troopers advocating revolution. At Hitler's headquarters, Göring and Himmler repeated the rumors of incipient civil war. Soon the country was ablaze with hysterical talk, but the Führer still waited. Even now, no one is sure what he actually believed.

In the meantime, Röhm, like a dim-sighted mastodon failing to observe the presence of hunters, continued to behave with fatal arrogance. At a reception in early June, he chatted jovially with Gregor Strasser, the French ambassador, and a former chancellor, General von Schleicher. Hitler hated France, distrusted von Schleicher, and had already broken with Strasser. Now there was a "real" incident for SS Intelligence to report to their Führer. In Berlin, Göring and Himmler began to draw up lists of enemies they had always wanted to eliminate. (There was ample precedent; Hitler himself had kept such lists for years.) Still hesitating, Hitler ordered Röhm to assemble his SA leaders for a conference at Bad Wiessee. Röhm obeyed, allowing the rumormongers to hint the SA was gathering to plan a coup.

Meanwhile, in the province of Silesia, the regional army commander, Ewald von Kleist, began to suspect that the SS was inciting the SA and the Reichswehr against each other. He sped to Berlin to warn his superior officer, General Werner von Fritsch. But von Fritsch called in von Reichenau, who coolly belittled his fears with the cavalier remark, "That may be true, but it's too late now."

Von Reichenau knew what he was talking about: on June 22, Himmler had placed the SS on "unobtrusive alert," and on June 27, he had ordered local SD commanders to shadow their Storm Trooper bosses and report suspicious moves.

Hitler had been out of the center of power for a few days, attending a wedding in Essen, and conveniently leaving the field open to the stage managers of death. When he returned, he once again listened to the rumors, read the dossiers, and suddenly decided to act. "We must make an example of them!" he said, using a characteristic rationale for the removal of an opponent. During the night of June 29, he stormed off to Bad Wiessee.

In all of these preliminaries, the SD had proved its special value. Independent of Röhm's supervision, it possessed a national network of cells that Heydrich had carefully built up since 1931. No other Nazi organization was so well placed in the very center of conspiratorial activity, yet so shielded from public observation. Though the other Nazi leaders might conspire, make lists, and give orders, only the Sicherheitsdienst possessed the secrecy, coordinative ability, and paramilitary discipline to carry them out. On June 9, three weeks before the beginning of the purge, Hitler signed a decree making the SD the sole intelligence agency for the Nazi Party. Having also proven itself an able department of dirty tricks in the smear campaign against Röhm, it was now wielded like a knife to finish him off.

Only at this point can Heydrich be documented as a full participant in the proceedings, emerging at last from the protective shell of the SD. The German historian Heinz Höhne describes him as the power behind the scenes, the man who convinced Himmler to act and then orchestrated the conspiracy, which he calls "Reinhard Heydrich's deadly game." Max Gallo, the French historian, too, calls it "Heydrich's plan." Frau Heydrich, on the other hand, said he had little to do with it: "He was too small, too unimportant."

This time, the truth seems to lie in that familiar historical territory called somewhere in the middle. Heydrich's behavior throughout seems much more that of a man scheming his way to the top than one who has already arrived there. Once the violence began, he was relegated to the role of glorified errand boy, a Nazi Hermes delivering deadly messages.

Most of his actions were a series of variations on the role of executioner by remote control. In Silesia, he launched the purge by telephone: voice to voice, Heydrich ordered a subordinate to take over the police and communications centers, and also to deliver a sealed letter to the SS leadership. If you fail, Heydrich cautioned, we will have your head. The letter (written on Hermann Göring's office stationery) spoke of an attempted coup by Röhm, declared a state of emergency, gave executive power in Silesia to an SS Oberabschnitt named Udo von Woyrsch, and enclosed a list of SA leaders "to be eliminated." With nervous tenacity, Heydrich followed up the order, repeatedly calling on June 30 to make sure the executions had been carried out.

In this case, his anxieties were misplaced. Von Woyrsch in fact widened the purge to include dozens of his personal enemies. Yet in other places, SS leaders were reluctant to strike down their former comrades. Heydrich's old friend from Halle, Karl von Eberstein, refused to obey the verbal orders until Heydrich personally signed a letter saying the instructions had come from Hitler. Werner Best, a newly appointed police assistant, tried to persuade Heydrich to remove the name of a friend from the Berlin death list. "He is just as dangerous as the rest!" Heydrich snapped, ending the discussion.

Discussion was not the order of the day. Heydrich was tersely, icily efficient, rapping out commands with sleekly militarized precision. Executioners were ordered in groups to his office in Berlin, where all were given the same laconic explanation: "Putsch by Röhm—state of emergency—order from the Führer—immediate action." Then, they were called one by one into his inner sanctum to receive their individual orders.

We know the most about the instructions given to Hauptsturmführer Kurt Gildisch, the commander of Hitler's personal bodyguards, who arrived at the head of an action group of eighteen men. Heydrich told him to take special responsibility for "the Klausener case." "You will shoot him personally," he said. "Go at once to the Reich Ministry of Transport."

As Gildisch prepared to depart, the SD chief called him back. Did he happen to know Erich Klausener personally? he asked. No, said Gildisch. Heydrich seemed relieved. "Heil Hitler!" he replied, and sent him on his way.

Arriving at his victim's office on the early afternoon of June 30, Gildisch told him he was under arrest, and when Klausener turned to get his coat and hat, he shot him in the back of the head. After the murder, Gildisch, following instructions, called Heydrich, using the phone on Klausener's desk. "Fake a suicide!" the SD chief said, whereupon Gildisch placed a gun by the dead man's hand and went back to Heydrich's office. There he was at last given a token justification of the crime already committed: Klausener was "a dangerous Catholic leader."

Long afterward, Göring testified at Nuremberg that the murder of Klausener had been a totally "mad" action on Heydrich's part. Like others (including Göring), Heydrich was obviously weaving a personal vendetta into the fabric of the purge. Himmler and Göring had long ago marked Gregor Strasser for death: in addition to his rivalry with Hitler, he made much-repeated jokes about their obsequious behavior toward Hitler. Generals von Bredow and von Schleicher were also killed—and von Schleicher's wife, who accidentally "stepped into" the line of fire. When reproached for atrocities not remotely justifiable by fear of an SA revolt, Göring blandly replied, "I expanded my mandate."

Heydrich, too, had seen an opportunity to eliminate an enemy, and seized it. The leader of a powerful political group called Catholic Action, Klausener had recently given a speech criticizing the regime. He had also served on the Police Presidium in Berlin, and may simply have been too well informed, independent, and influential to please the new deputy chief of the Gestapo.

The lists of enemies that had been piling up for years represented an accumulation of "stored violence" that exploded with unexpected ferocity. The pretense of efficient order could not hide the fact that the participants were inexperienced in mass murder, which in any case is singularly lacking in etiquette. In Bavaria, former minister president Gustav Ritter von Kahr, an old man of seventy, was hacked to death with an ax. In Prussia, two SS men calmly shot another SS officer in his smoking room. Leaving, they encountered his young son, and paused to tell him they had just shot his father.

The mixture of swift action, amateurism, and blood lust produced unfortunate mistakes. The death squads murdered a drama critic named Schmidt before bothering to check if his first name matched the one on their list; it didn't. There was of course no trial by jury, and the teams of killers usually had no idea why their victims had been chosen.

When victim and executioner knew each other, hysterical scenes occurred. A former comrade of Göring's from the First World War received word to put on his splendid uniform and go at once to Göring's office. Sure that his old friend would save him, he found instead that Göring merely wanted the theatrical pleasure of ripping off his war medals. The man suffered a nervous collapse and had to be dragged to the execution block.

On the other hand, Ernst Udet, chief of the SA air force, was in Hitler's presence when the SS came to get him. He shouted a question at his Führer: How could he punish soldiers for obeying the orders of their superiors? It was an all-purpose defense, one the Nazis would use again and again. Udet survived to become a famous fighter ace in the next world war.

Heydrich's use of the pretext of suicide in the "Klausener case" may have shown his Secret Service background, with its predilection for "indirect" methods—or his insecurity as a new leader. Many of the other conspirators, like von Woyrsch or Göring (who shouted, "Just shoot them down . . . shoot!" from his doorway), didn't bother with such elaborate subterfuge, for hadn't they merely followed the rules of the game?

The cool calculation of one's own advantage, the opportunistic use of any means at hand, the willingness to "trample on friends," the reliance on force to settle disputes, the sudden "spontaneous" move that has actually been well prepared in advance, the simultaneous attack on several fronts at once, and the unwillingness of Hitler to clarify guidelines or to commit himself until the last possible moment—all are classic tactics of "thinking in party terms." Yet until 1934, Hitler's power game had never been carried so far. For years the Nazi leaders had practiced the cruel theatrical gestures that accompanied the moves of the game and made them seem part of a glamorous historical drama—but that had been dress rehearsal, and this was life, with all its messy acts and unwelcome consequences. On the first day of the purge, however, the killing seems to have been treated with an almost adolescent glee by its leaders, as if the actions they authorized were not quite real. A witness has described the scene at Göring's office in Berlin on the morning of June 30:

> Now and then couriers from the Gestapo rushed into and out of this room, slips of white paper in their hands. Through the door we could see Göring, Himmler, Heydrich . . . We could see them conferring, but naturally we could not hear what was being said. Occasionally, however, we could hear a muffled sound: "Away!" or "Aha!" or "Shoot him!" For the most part we heard nothing but raucous laughter.

But after this followed two more days of mayhem, and it seems to have gotten harder as time went on. Many people had been killed, but many more now languished in prisons all over Germany. What was to happen to them? What about Röhm, stuck in a cell in Munich, who kept asking to see Hitler and straighten everything out? While the Führer once again paused for thought, the other conspirators fell to wrangling, sometimes snatching victims out of each other's clutches. When two SS guards tried to arrest Vice Chancellor von Papen (whose administrative assistant had already been murdered on Himmler's orders), one of Göring's aides stopped them, shouting, "We shall see who gives orders here, the prime minister or the SS!"

No single group was really in charge, however, and most disputed cases slipped into the jaws of death. One by one the arrested officers of the formerly dreaded Sturmabteilung were brought out of basement cells into closed courtyards, where they faced squads of SS executioners, formerly their subordinates. Many of these men held guns loaded with blank cartridges, to ensure that no one would ever know who had fired the killing shot; the others used bullets so powerful they passed through the bodies, splattering gore everywhere. In Berlin, late-arriving victims stood against a wall thickly coated with blood and chunks of flesh. The teams of killers sighted accurately for their first round of shots; after that their aim faltered badly, and they had to be replaced.

Röhm meanwhile remained in Stadelheim prison, in Munich. At last, Hitler ordered that his old mentor be given a gun, providing a way out for both of them. But Röhm refused to connive in his own murder, shouting, "Adolf himself should do the dirty work!"

Heydrich has sometimes been cast in the role of ultimate executioner,

General Theodor Eicke (age fifty, in 1942) personally executed Ernest Röhm, exactly a year after Himmler had appointed Eicke the SS leader of Dachau. He was soon placed in command of all concentration camps, where he replaced their guards with Totenkopfverbaende (death's-head formations).

but in fact, the nasty job fell to General Theodor Eicke, commander of the death camp guards. Walking into Röhm's cell, Eicke shot him at close range. Still, his aim was bad, and Röhm lived awhile longer. "My Führer, my Führer," he said, dying. "You should have thought of that earlier," Eicke replied. "It's too late now."

After the death of Röhm, the purge slowly ran down, and then the time for second thoughts began in earnest. As skillfully as he had played the game of power, Hitler had nevertheless broken its final rule—he had been forced to "bare his disputes" to outsiders.

Unused to accounting for his actions, the leader gave a series of contradictory explanations. On June 30, he summoned his loyal party officials and talked primarily of his loathing for Röhm's homosexuality (which he had actually tolerated for a decade). On July 3, he told the Cabinet of Ministers that the massacres had been emergency measures to put down a treasonable conspiracy. Two weeks after the bloodletting, he finally appeared before the Reichstag, "justifying" the seventy-seven deaths to which he would admit in a speech full of shameless lies, coupled with efforts to take a more philosophical tack. Röhm and his SA leaders were denounced as victims, not of the purge but of the political collapse of 1918, which had made them "incapable of any real cooperation, ready to oppose any order . . . appeased only by constant intellectual and conspiratory preoccupation with the destruction of existing institutions."

In his new role of conservator of order, Hitler's acting was, as always, first-rate, which is more than can be said of the shabby behavior of his audience. From President von Hindenburg downward, members of the conservative classes sounded a chorus of approval for what they desperately wanted to see as the triumph of the "good" Nazis over the bad. Von Hindenburg is said to have told Hitler that all births require the shedding of blood; even the future resistance hero Klaus von Stauffenberg, then a young cavalry officer, passed off the carnage as the "lancing of a boil." And the army chief of staff General von Fritsch ignored a prophetic warning from his friend, retired army captain Erwin Planck: "If you look on without lifting a finger, you will meet the same fate sooner or later."

Attacking on two fronts at once, Hitler had cleverly let two of his enemies neutralize each other, for the Reichswehr was swiftly relegated to "unpolitical" status, warned to stay there by the murder of General von Schleicher, and morally compromised by its acquiescence in the annihilation of its rivals.

Yet General von Reichenau still reveled in his folly, boasting that the army had succeeded in giving the purge "the surface appearance" of a purely party matter. Even many Germans who were thoroughly disenchanted with the New Order failed to grasp the deadly import of the slaughter. "The entire Röhm Putsch is strange, full of unfathomable ramifications," wrote the anti-Nazi Count Friedrich Reck-Malleczewen, in his *Diary of a Man in Despair*.

It was left to the Nazis themselves to fathom the "ramifications."

The benumbed and embittered members of the SA accepted the destruction of their officer corps without external resistance. An SA leader, Victor Lutze, who had secretly connived against Röhm, now replaced him as new chief of the Storm Troopers, but he remained a powerless puppet. (An ur-Quisling, or collaborator with the occupying enemy, had thus appeared—in what Himmler called the "war theater of inner Germany.") The turncoat Lutze was also involved in the most prophetic dialogue of this Nazi passion play. When Hitler dashed off at dawn to revile Röhm to his face, Lutze went along, and was sent to search for weapons in the room of the arrested SA leader Edmund Heines. "Lutze, I have done nothing. Can't you help me?" Heines begged him. "I can do nothing . . . I can do nothing," was Lutze's reply. Again and again in the future, innocent victims were dragged away; again and again, dismayed onlookers found they could do "nothing."

With Röhm's organization in ruins, the SS, which had burst from its SA chrysalis in a shower of blood, now faced an unobstructed road to power. On July 20, 1934, it collected the wages of sin: Hitler officially recognized the Schutzstaffel as a fully independent organization. This powerful new status was coupled with thanks for "services rendered" during the purge. Heydrich, planning an immediate expansion of the SD, discovered that men now vied to join an organization seen as "saving the new Germany from anarchy."

Too late, the other Nazi leaders realized that Hitler could never dispense with the need for political soldiers to enforce his will. His reliance on terror had not lessened; it had merely taken a more disciplined— ultimately far more insidious—form.

As early as June 30, the minister of the interior, Wilhelm Frick, worried that Hitler had "called in Beelzebub to drive out the devil." Göring, too, was disappointed: Hitler did not make him chief of the armed services, and he had gambled away his greatest bastion of power, the Gestapo, when he transferred it to the SS. The alliance between Göring and Himmler began to unravel under the strain.

But there were victims among the SS, too. The anti-Nazi journalist Bella Fromm wrote in her diary on July 8, 1934,

In my office works a young photographer. He is tall, blond— a perfectly cast "Aryan." After Hitler seized power, this young man was seen only in the black SS uniform. After June 30th . . . he was absent from the office for several days. Finally, this morning, he came in—a changed man. He was jittery and uneasy and was constantly watching the door. When questioned as to his strange behavior, he broke into tears and stammered: "I had to shoot in the Gestapo cellar. Thirty-seven times I shot . . . Thirty-seven are haunting me . . . I can't escape from those thirty-seven ghosts."

He could not escape the consequences of his rash honesty, either. A few days later he disappeared, and another SS man told Frau Fromm that he had "talked too much" and was now dead.

In his prison cell, Röhm had quoted to a visitor Robespierre's remark that all revolutions devour their children. The real children of Nazism, however, were not the Storm Troopers, but those who had gained most from the purge—Hitler, Himmler, and Heydrich. After Röhm's death, hypocrisy, cruel calculation, and most of all, duplicity entered the arena to stay. Even Hitler's cunning and contempt for his fellows increased, as did his conception of himself as the omnipotent leader who stood above all criticism.

Yet for a month or so, he was troubled by dreadful nightmares, and sometimes spent the small hours of night pacing the corridors of Munich's Hall of Heroes, gazing mutely at the rows of Nazi battle flags. Occasionally, he talked fondly of the men he had labeled traitors, and his voice shook when he tried to draw a lesson from the mayhem: "They, too, have died for the greatness of our movement." The purge had scrawled his conclusion in blood: "*My* will is the final one. Whoever fails to obey my orders will be destroyed."

In private conversations, Hitler argued that SS recruits should be warned not to sign up unless they were prepared "to pay the butcher's bill." In October 1934, Himmler acknowledged this, giving a self-pitying description of the work of the SS executioners: "To have to shoot one's own comrades . . . is the bitterest thing which can happen to a man." By the time the war broke out, Himmler had taken Hitler's maxim to heart, or, literally, stomach, for he was increasingly immobilized by cramping attacks of intense pain, which sprang from no clearly physiological cause. In 1943 (approximately one year after the construction of Auschwitz) he gave a secret speech to his highest SS leaders in which he spelled out exactly what he had learned in 1934. If at that time we "had to" kill our own comrades, men of our own race and party, how, Himmler asked, could we later hesitate to kill our racial enemies, strangers of a different culture, with whom we are locked in a total war of annihilation? After that early baptism of blood, he argued, the SS was never again in a position to shrink back from murder. Throughout his career Himmler labored to link the idea of killing and self-sacrifice, destroying his own health and sanity in this ghastly fool's errand.

Heydrich's initial reaction was similar, at least if we can believe the testimony of his wife. She told me "the Röhm revolt" immediately "brought" to her husband "a deep spiritual sorrow.

"He had to go against a man before him in the service, the godfather of his son . . . Truly, it left very deep marks on my husband. He said, 'I cannot let a friendship deepen; I cannot do something like that again . . .'"

Her voice faded in and out, in the irresolute rhythms of emotional distress.

"Was Röhm a good friend?"

"Röhm was a mercenary, and he was guilty of treason . . . Some meeting with the French ambassador. But yes, at that time we were always comrades . . ."

But not exactly friends: "My husband was . . . so unimportant . . . And thus one cannot speak of a relationship to us . . . at all."

"You say that Röhm was the godfather of your first son, but I have heard also that Himmler was the godfather."

"Himmler *and* Röhm . . ."

"Did you know Röhm better by then?"

"No . . . Once we rented a house, my husband and I . . . And Röhm visited us there once. And after that we were closer . . . I met his sister once. She was very nice. And he was also very nice. But the Röhm story had little to do with us."

Still, she could not deny the impact of the "Röhm story" on her husband: "Afterward, he said many times, 'I don't want to get entangled if I may have to imprison someone.' All that very much distanced him from people. He had, I must say again, a fear of friendship. Because he, so to say, didn't want to become spiritually divided."

"So, you would say that your husband became depressed?"

"Yes. Very much. Very much. Not depressed alone; rather, it was a shock. It was not so entirely simple. This is something that gave him a lesson in life . . ."

Part of the lesson took some time to become apparent. Though all the participants in the Night of the Long Knives had behaved with callous brutality, Heydrich began to acquire a uniquely ferocious aura. Stories about his infamous actions began to circulate, many of them untrue (such as the claim that he himself had shot Röhm) or impossible to verify. The most widely repeated rumor involved the death of Himmler's old boss Gregor Strasser, who had been kept in Gestapo custody in Berlin. According to Gisevius, a prisoner in the cell next to Strasser heard the "crack of a pistol," followed by sounds of a man thrashing on his cot, then loud footsteps in the corridor and the barking of orders: "The guards clicked their heels. And the prisoner recognized Heydrich's voice saying, 'Isn't he dead yet? Let the swine bleed to death.'"

This is hearsay evidence in the most literal sense, and several times over, for Gisevius was repeating an oft-told tale. Yet it *could* have been true. Heydrich had his distinctive high-pitched voice, and he was in Berlin at the time. Later, the Nazis claimed Strasser committed suicide—the same lie Heydrich had used to explain the death of Klausener.

On the other hand, the young SD leader didn't have sufficient power to order the murder of one of the founding fathers of Nazism. That had to come, at the very least, from Himmler. The problem of Strasser's death is in fact one of the early examples of a continuing phenomenon: when we try to assign responsibility for an event, a policy, or a decision, the two men often merge together. We know one or both had to be involved, but cannot easily separate the one from the other. This drives some historians to heights of creative nomenclature: the "dreadful duo," the "Dioscuri of the SS," "Castor and Pollux."

That so much of the blame would be attributed to the junior partner, however, suggests that already in 1934, Heydrich was beginning to take on a demonic aspect as representative of SS evil, particularly the kind that reaches out to attack others from a shadowy, protected position.

A few weeks before the purge, Himmler had met with Röhm to urge him to change his unsavory friends. Röhm had cried tears of gratitude for the kindly warning, though he did not change. Himmler didn't either. He had been skillfully turning Hitler's mind toward destroying Röhm before the meeting, and he continued to do so afterward.

As we have seen, Hitler also seemed to hesitate, but Heydrich had always pressed forward, relentlessly drawing together the strands of information and conspiracy, the very embodiment of SD cunning and pitiless police "action." During the murders, he had urged his men on with the implacability of a General Staff officer on maneuvers. Beforehand, he expressed no ambivalence; afterward, he offered no public confessions of sorrow. It was easy to see him, as Schellenberg did, as a calculating "puppet master" manipulating his partners in crime for his own ends. Perhaps this was more comfortable than to accept the fact that emotional Hitler, jovial Göring, idealistic Himmler had betrayed and destroyed one of their oldest friends. Unlike them, the newcomer Heydrich offered the world the hard face of Nazi malevolence, unsweetened by platitudes, unsoftened by conciliation. It was unsettling to contemplate.

The waves of reaction to the purge carried in their wake Heydrich's increasingly fearsome reputation. On February 10, 1935, seven months after the Night of the Long Knives, he attended a gala formal reception at the home of Foreign Minister von Neurath. There, he happened to meet Bella Fromm, who described her impressions:

> Heydrich is known as Himmler's bloodiest man. He is six feet tall, lean, trim, yellow haired . . . His appearance is ascetic, and he rarely, if ever, smiles. They say he is the brains of the Gestapo, merciless, brutal, despotic, and has more power than his master, Himmler . . . He was one of the executioners during the June purge, and is also known as the hangman of Gregor Strasser.
>
> I shivered when he clicked his heels politely in front of me. Not for all the gold in all the world would I have touched the hand of that murderer-in-chief.

Since joining the SS, Heydrich had known that, in Lina's phrase, he had to "show people he was there." In helping destroy his son's godfather, he had succeeded all too well. Though he most certainly knew that the Jewish Frau Fromm was an opponent of the Nazis, Heydrich had behaved courteously—and had not received the same treatment in return. He had been absolutely correct when he told his wife that his job required a "fear of friendship." Yet, until the very end of his life he would resist the obvious conclusion that the fear inevitably traveled both ways.

PART III

EXERCISING POWER

12

TRANSFORMATIONS OF OUR STRUGGLE:
THE INVISIBLE APPARAT

"It happens so easily that a man who has to watch over such criminal things believes in the end that everyone steals, everyone is evil. That is so easy. And it simply belongs, so to say, to the lot of every policeman to be mistrustful. If he weren't, he wouldn't be a good policeman."

—LINA HEYDRICH

REINHARD HEYDRICH's primary function, from the beginning to the end of his career, lay in defining the enemy. This process proceeded in stages, growing ever more expansive, like the unfolding of a huge, poisonous flower. This burgeoning demanded the construction of a hothouse to contain it as exotic and dangerous as the flower itself. Thus was formed nothing less than the Reichssicherheitshauptamt, or Reich Security Main Office, called RSHA for short. It was this organization that embodied the SS's successful creation of its long-envisioned police state.

When Heydrich was initially hired by Himmler, his attention was concentrated on opponents of the SS, including many inside the Nazi Party itself. When the SD became the official Nazi intelligence organization, primarily enemies of the party (such as Ernst Röhm) were included; then, when the SS took over the police, enemies of the state were added. Finally, when the Germans began to take over Europe, enemies of the "Greater German Reich" were embraced. And, at every stage, Heydrich kept a close watch on his numerous personal opponents, ranging from "dangerous leaders" such as Erich Klausener, the director of the Reich Ministry of Transport, who was murdered for being a "dangerous Catholic," to some of his own closest associates, among them (at various times) Alfred Naujocks, the trickster; Walter

Schellenberg, the diplomat; and Werner Best, the supremely articulate lawyer.

Heydrich was not alone in the preoccupations generally described as "paranoid": Nazi propagandists spoke incessantly of rings of hostile forces surrounding Germany and penetrating to its very heart. But his fellow Nazis also called Heydrich "the hyper-suspicious," implying that he exceeded the normal boundaries of self-protective vigilance. He had a precedent for this as well: it was said of his Gestapo predecessor Rudolf Diels that he "liked and trusted no one . . . and no one liked and trusted him. No matter how fine and innocent a character might originally be . . . a job of the nature of his would invariably and inevitably corrode the character."

During the approximately fourteen months prefacing Himmler's and Heydrich's takeover of the Gestapo, the entire German nation had been placed on the rack of "coordination" with the new despotism. There were local variations, but the process everywhere was similar: the Secret Police arrested the most obvious, visible enemies, with special emphasis on articulate leaders—intellectuals, opposition party spokesmen, writers, teachers—anyone who might be able to rally the forces of dissent—such as Communists, socialists, trade union members, clergymen, and Jews.

Often arrests were not even necessary: it was easy enough to make life so miserable that most opponents would ultimately have to knuckle under, or retreat into an "inner immigration" that rendered them equally powerless. The plethora of new laws spreading like brambles over the old legal pathways merely made the going easier for the Nazis.

The method of Nazi harassment rarely varied. It was always a one-two punch: first, isolate the victims; second, maneuver them into some perilous corner where they could be dispatched at leisure—if they didn't save the police the trouble by running away on their own.

By the time of Himmler's and Heydrich's arrival at Gestapo headquarters, in Berlin, after years of "emergency" programs, followed by the Night of the Long Knives, open opposition to the New Order had been effectively eliminated. Indeed, the crushing success of Nazi intimidation techniques soon gave rise to a new problem, one of central importance to Heydrich: what to do now with the shiny new instruments of political supervision? He was especially concerned about "his" SD, whose internal security functions were steadily being usurped by the far richer and better organized Gestapo. He pondered a variety of solutions, all involving an inevitable expansion of the enemies lists. His subordinates were already at work. Otto Ohlendorf's information service was just beginning to plant its agents in every sphere of German life, and Walter Schellenberg had started pondering ways to strengthen SD intelligence gathering abroad. Alfred Naujocks's operatives already worked outside German borders at various forms of violence and skullduggery, including kidnapping enemy agents. But Heydrich, always restless, always wanted more. Lina told me that he never wasted time contemplating his successes; the only thing that made him happy was to push onward, creating something new.

In 1935, Heydrich wrote a prophetic pamphlet accurately titled "Transformations of Our Struggle," based mainly on preliminary work by the SS main office, in which he blew the clarion of an ominous new theme.

Unlike Himmler, he was no speculator about philosophical matters. At work, Heydrich liked to divide complicated issues into neatly ordered categories, transforming them into a series of problems to be solved logically, sequentially, systematically, pragmatically. The Nazi terror system has often been described by both observers and participants as a huge machine—of observation, of coercion, and finally of destruction. Heydrich was the de facto lord of this machine: his specialty was that mixture of manipulation and intimidation now called "social engineering." While Himmler paraded in the foreground, making grand speeches and setting the broadest guidelines of SS policy, Heydrich was busy in the background tinkering with the machinery.

He hated making speeches, and was, Lina affirmed, shy in large groups. Nevertheless, his associates remarked on his great powers of lucid exposition in direct, face-to-face situations. Himmler, among many others, sometimes found it more than *he* could face. In gatherings of his subordinates, the Reichsführer SS liked to give rambling lectures about history or philosophy, evading both precision and decision, and self-importantly keeping the focus on himself. ("With him, no *true* discussion was possible!" Frau Heydrich fumed to me.) Behind closed office doors, however, Heydrich's persuasive powers often prevailed, prompting the observation by Felix Kersten, the physical therapist who used his influence with Himmler to save many Jews, that Himmler sometimes emerged from such an encounter looking as if he had been "raped mentally."

Now, in 1935, Heydrich had something to tell the Nazi masses. It wasn't good news. Like the sanctimonious guest who arrives just in time to ruin a wild party, he told his comrades their victory celebration was premature. In the early *Kampfzeit*, he lectured, the major opponent was German Communism, but in "the current situation," the opposition had been driven underground. Though the "visible enemies" had been vanquished, the "disguised enemy" still remained.

Already, Heydrich warned, far too many Nazis had "let themselves be fooled by appearances" and "unable to find the enemy in his new positions . . . dissipate their strength in meaningless, limitless, personal illegalities." Heydrich did not say he disapproved of illegality. (By inference, ideologically meaningful, limited, impersonal illegalities—that is, those in the basic SS style—might be tolerable.)

Still, the comrades should know better. Did they quit fighting when it appeared they would never win? Of course not: they believed in the Nazi idea and carried on regardless. The enemy, Heydrich argued, is now doing the same thing, and as a result, "the form of the struggle has changed." Combat between political parties was over; "the battle of the spirit" had begun.

"Every organization is nothing without the ideological strength which animates it," Heydrich said. Aware of this, the enemy was now attempting "systematically to hollow out the German people characterologically and spiritually, in order to poison them and to leave them with nothing but their Nordic appearance."

What were the poor Aryans to do? Not surprisingly, Heydrich knew the answer. Two things were necessary: "the correct recognition of the enemies in their deepest nature . . . but also of our own mistakes, with all their reasons and consequences."

Relentlessly, Heydrich pounded away at his thick-headed comrades in arms, trying to get them to see things his way: "It is necessary to recognize that the struggle has become deeper, . . . to recognize the enemy from the history of the last thousand years . . . recognize that this enemy isn't finished merely when we take over the apparatus of state, for they sit with their cross-connections in all branches of our folk life."

Having fixed the simple idea of a new enemy in his readers' minds, Heydrich could proceed on to what he did best: tracing "cross-connections" and describing malign influences.

The "more or less visible enemies" were already familiar from the writings of other Nazis. Nineteen thirty-five was the year in which the Nuremberg Laws had been promulgated, and Heydrich jumped on the rolling bandwagon, listing the Jews as the major problem. They were divided into two groups: "Zionists," who openly represented a "strong racial standpoint," and "Assimilated" Jews, who pretended to have become German but were merely feigning patriotism to serve their aim of destroying Nazism, and then dominating the world.

Aiding them were Heydrich's special bugaboos of the moment, the "political clergy," especially the Jesuits, and the Masonic lodges. And, aiding *them* were a group of "bad bureaucrats," and "even some folk-comrades . . . who don't want to grasp the racial principles." There were also bad teachers who taught soulless "pure science" or sought to undermine Aryan unity by emphasizing the "culturelessness" of the ancient Germans. (This was undoubtedly a sop to Himmler, who was obsessed with early Teutonic rites and artifacts.)

Gradually the old political enemies became transformed into "the Great Enemy," a shadowy evil much worse than the sum of its myriad parts. Heydrich followed Hitler in equating good character with "sound racial instincts"—which, alas, were so fragile that they might easily be destroyed by "alien" influences. When Heydrich began to delineate the second manifestation of evil influence, the "Disguised Enemy," he became more original, attempting to take his readers behind the scenes of the theater of power he knew so well. The man often described as secretly "pulling the strings" of influence now delighted in pointing out the hidden machinations of others.

To eyes accustomed to the imagery of modern psychology, much of what he saw seems the purest projection. Heydrich excoriates the Masons for glorifying "blind submission" to their superiors, a character-less obedience "strengthened by the performance of an oath." He reviles his enemies for "underhanded" behavior like exploiting the weaknesses of others, seeking illicit "back doors" to power, and using social events as a cover for spreading propaganda. The SS, of course, did all of these things as well.

Some of Heydrich's concerns, however, seem peculiar to his own experience. He speaks with revealing fervor of the problems of children of marriages between "non-Germans" and Aryans, of the resulting internal divisions that "poison the German," diluting his purity of will and mind, leaving only an Aryan facade behind. He describes a variety of duplicitous methods allegedly used by Jews to worm their way into influential German circles: in addition to intermarriage with Christians, they give generously to charities, offer their services as advisers or teachers, and even demean themselves at social gatherings, playing the "house fool." Heydrich's father, who used to amuse his fellow lodge members by pretending to be a Jew, had played all of these roles in his quest for social advancement.

Bruno Heydrich's son also argued passionately against the enemy technique of spreading lie-packed rumors about the Nazi leaders. Even as he wrote, the rumors about his father's presumed Jewish origins were spreading, as relieved rivals speculated that perhaps Reinhard Heydrich only "looked" German. "We must see this work and tactic of the enemy in order to be able to meet it," Heydrich wrote. Again and again, he implored the reader to learn to see differently, see clearly, see through the enemies' lies.

Finally, he reached his crescendo: above all, we must learn to recognize the existence of "an invisible apparat," spreading venom through thousands of hidden channels, all connected to one another through their creator, the ubiquitous Great Enemy. What had begun as a set of "hints to sharpen the view of the enemy" ended as a sort of quasi-religious vision, an exercise in learning to see the invisible. An early Christian writer once wrote, "The glory of God is spread across the earth, and the people see it not." Now Heydrich offered his own negative vision: the evil of the enemy is spread across the Fatherland, and the comrades see it not.

Five years earlier, in 1930, Heydrich had professed to be an unpolitical naval officer; three years earlier, in 1932, he had told a friend he had doubts about Nazism. Now, in 1935, he announced the acquisition of amazing grace. "Transformations of Our Struggle" thus has a double meaning, as a record of personal as well as political change. It is no accident that it ends with a statement of his own lifelong credo of personal achievement:

The work on ourselves . . . must take place. We must deepen the good elements of our German heritage . . . We must be just, we must be faithful . . . In order to prove the correctness of the principles of our community and our selection, we must gradually become the best in all spheres. We must be the best recruits in the ranks of the . . . weapon carriers of the nation; in sports, we must always be the best. In our profession also, it must be the rule that the intentionally political SS man is also the best expert, in examinations, and, yes, also in practice . . .

And we, the SS, want through this to be the ideological shock troops of the Führer idea and simultaneously through the achievement of the tasks of the State Police to be an internal political protection corps of the National Socialist state.

The renunciation of his father's cosmopolitanism that had begun when Heydrich left the music conservatory to join the navy thirteen years earlier was now officially complete. And the man who had originally thought he could endure police work only for a few weeks now sometimes answered criticism with this question: "Don't you know who I am? I am Heydrich of the Gestapo!"

As always in Heydrich's case, we cannot completely disentangle the pragmatically useful from the personally meaningful. His claim that the invisible apparat had its tentacles everywhere also served to augment his own power. If his comrades did not use his helpful "hints" to learn to see what he told them was there, they would "be forced to recognize" the reality dictated by the one true faith. It was a time of inquisition, and Heydrich was poised to become the Grand Inquisitor.

Heydrich had created a mandate for coercive organizations as diverse as the varied forms and manifold ramifications of the Great Enemy. Not accidentally, his views accorded well with Hitler's. The Führer intended to reclaim German territory lost in the war, thus smashing the Treaty of Versailles and possibly provoking Allied intervention. Heydrich knew he would feel the need for a powerful security force to maintain order at home.

A few months after the publication of Heydrich's article, the State Ministry of Prussia decreed: "The duty of the Gestapo is to investigate and suppress all anti-State tendencies, . . . to assemble and evaluate the results of any unrest, to keep the state government informed, to keep other authorities abreast of any conclusions of importance to them and to put forward suggestions." The Secret State Police had received sweeping powers: it could investigate, suppress, evaluate, inform, and suggest—everything except make law, and as we shall see, Heydrich was now regarded by virtually all of his peers as the very embodiment of the will to power. According to his nephew, Thomas, even his own brother thought him guilty of "murderous ambition." By 1942, Reinhard Heydrich openly admitted to the inevitable goal of a chief of security responsible for complete ideological conformity: "the total and permanent police coverage of all men within the Reich and the resulting possibility of keeping a permanent check on the situation of each individual."

As time went on, the lists of possible enemies became ever broader and more ornate. A member of Heydrich's staff reconstructed the major categories "to be combated" by the Gestapo—and the means for doing so—on the eve of the Second World War:

Right- and left-wing opposition.
Antisocial, work-shy, and contract-breaking elements.
Foreign Legionnaires, foreign workers.
Resistance groups in occupied territory.
Religion, sects, Freemasons, Jews.
Emigrants, conscientious objectors.
Deserters (Wehrmacht).
Listeners to foreign broadcasts.
Protection of industry against sabotage and espionage.
Supervision of the [Nazi] Party and affiliations.
Homosexuality.
Protection of high personalities, and at meetings.
Political card indices.
Protective custody department.
Telephone and post supervision.
Mail censorship.
Frontier police and later Zollgrenzpolizei
    [Border Customs Police].

In pursuing these legions of enemies, the policemen were aided by code letters indicating appropriate action: A meant "arrest," B, "arrest if no fixed address," C, "report place of residence," D, "for deportation," E, "search for missing persons," F, "recover lost papers," G, "unobtrusive observation," and V, "professional criminal—arrest." The "A" cards were further subdivided to take into account the possibility of war. Red tabs indicated people to be arrested as soon as preparations for mobilization began. Blue tabs were apprehended only after mobilization was publicly announced, and green tabs were to be closely supervised in "times of stress."

In their restless vigilance, the police behaved rather like a wolf that has categorized all the rabbits according to color, then makes appointments for convenient times to catch them. This orderly scheme was menaced, however, by constant squabbling with other wolves, like the rivalry between the Gestapo, the Criminal Police (Kripo), and the SD. Heydrich controlled them all, and often played them off against one another, encouraging the "friction" favored by Hitler.

Himmler, now police chief of all Germany as well as Reich leader of the SS, both gave Heydrich instructions and played him off against the other high SS leaders. Himmler needed such rivalries to hold Heydrich's dynamism in check, but he also worried—with good reason—that the SS was in danger of splitting up into fragmented, feuding groups. Occasionally he even tried to clear things up within Heydrich's own domain.

In 1937, Himmler gave a lecture at the Wehrmacht school of political instruction, in which he tried to build conceptual fences to separate the predators of the police and the SD. Both were interested in "Communism, political activity by religious groups and reaction," but the SD should deal only with "major ideological questions."

Heydrich seems to have taken such statements as encouraging the SD to compete in foreign intelligence and counterespionage with the part of the Defense Ministry called Abwehr headed up as of January 1, 1935, by Heydrich's former mentor Admiral Wilhelm Canaris. But the SD experts were also more than willing to take on long-term research projects. Hitler, for example, once wanted to know the exact amount of property owned by the Catholic Church in Germany. Heydrich asked his subordinate Albert Hartl to look into it, and he, in turn, created a small department for this question alone. Hartl was still trying to answer it when the war ended.

Heydrich, meanwhile, had more concrete worries. There were now so many wildly competing, explosively expanding agencies of surveillance that the fabled German efficiency was endangered. The journalist Heinz Höhne has documented a series of mistakes made in the late 1930s by the security agencies under Heydrich's control. The Kripo failed for years to catch a serial killer murdering scores of women in Düsseldorf, and in another city, a group of con artists pretending to be SD men operated a highly successful extortion ring for months before anyone in the real SD found out.

Finally, in 1938, the Gestapo badly mishandled secret information in the scandalous von Fritsch affair, in which General Werner von Fritsch was forced to resign his command over false accusations of homosexuality (so that Hitler could strengthen his hold on the Wehrmacht). The consequence was that for a few weeks the police state itself trembled on the brink of collapse; every remaining dissident in Germany began laying hopeful new plans for the fall of Adolf Hitler. Something had to be done.

Having learned a hard lesson, Heydrich and Walter Schellenberg began to plan a restructuring of the SS security agencies. For over a year, memos flew back and forth, competing sub-leaders tried to eliminate each other's offices, and careers were made or broken as Heydrich pondered how to create a workable balance of power. Schellenberg said that Gestapo representatives almost convinced Heydrich to get rid both of him and the SD itself—but he changed his mind at the last moment, and promoted him instead.

After a year of acrimony, Heydrich finally completed a hybrid organization that reflected a myriad of compromises. Himmler announced its existence on September 27, 1939. To be called the Reich Security Main Office, or RSHA (for Reichssicherheitshauptamt), it comprised seven main divisions, or *Amten* (offices), and managed somehow to mingle the bright young bureaucrats of Heydrich's SD with the detectives (and thugs) of the Security Police (Sicherheitspolizei, or Sipo). In a daring step, Heydrich had merged their personnel offices to form Amt I, Administration. Never mind that the members of the two groups often distrusted and disliked one another. Now they reported to one man, the former lawyer and judge Werner Best. Amt II was headed by another lawyer, Dr. Hans Nockemann; it dealt with legal issues.

Both of these offices were agencies of the German state. Amt III, Domestic Intelligence, was a Nazi Party formation. It represented one half of the SD, and it was still headed by the stubbornly willful economist Otto Ohlendorf, one of Heydrich's bright young men. Many Nazi leaders had complained about his doggedly factual reports on what

Heydrich had called "our own mistakes." Heydrich refused to bow to their pressure, but Ohlendorf felt he had settled for "the solution of the external facade" with no real power behind it. As he had before, he told Heydrich he wanted to quit. Heydrich, as usual, refused him.

Amt IV belonged, once again, to the German government. This was the Gestapo, still headed by Heinrich Müller, who by 1939 had become so powerful that much of the time he really ran the Secret Police in Heydrich's name (and behind it, Himmler's as well). But he was Heydrich's man, feared and disliked by most of the others—which didn't bother him, and was exactly what Heydrich wanted.

Amt V was the old Criminal Police, or Kripo, a venerable state formation headed by Arthur Nebe, who had run it in the old days, too. Heydrich had little time to waste supervising the experienced Kripo professionals, though he and Nebe occasionally had minor disagreements. "I may be just an amateur, but . . ." would be the way Heydrich began his criticism of, say, the correct behavior for a detective in a crime film produced by the Kripo in one of its more daring projects. Arthur Nebe usually gave in. But then, because he occasionally helped the resistance, he very much did not want to call undue attention to himself.

Amt VI was the other half of the SD, Foreign Intelligence, nominally headed by a lawyer named Heinz Jost, who was widely regarded as lazy and passive. For years this had suited Heydrich, who had personally supervised many of the SD's foreign adventures himself. Now, however, he appointed his new protégé, Walter Schellenberg, as Jost's primary assistant, though his task was really to help Heydrich reorganize and strengthen the SD. Jost was clearly being shoved aside. He was expected to resign, but instead obstinately clung to his position. Heydrich could, of course, have fired him, but he rarely chose such obvious moves. Rumors, as usual, abounded. Some people thought Heydrich might be having an affair with Jost's wife, and was holding back for that reason. On the other hand, some thought he was rejecting Jost because of his wife's lower-class origins. Or perhaps Jost's health wasn't good? (Gestapo officials had recently suggested he should take sick leave.) Eventually Heydrich began to "forget" to invite him to meetings of divisional directors. Finally, Jost did submit his resignation, but Heydrich told him to wait, as he hadn't decided on his successor. In late 1940, Walter Schellenberg finally got the job that Heydrich himself had obviously hesitated to relinquish.

Under its section chief Heinz Jost (age thirty-seven, in 1941), Foreign Intelligence (Amt VI) aimed to reshape the Gestapo's counterintelligence department. The effort failed to impress Heydrich, who criticized Jost's files as "a poor combination of newspaper and radio news of foreign senders." Eventually, Jost resigned the post, only to leave his imprint elsewhere; as commander of Einsatzgruppe A, he oversaw the genocide in the Baltic States and in Belarus.

By then, Heydrich and the articulate jurist Werner Best had quarreled, and Bruno Streckenbach had taken over Amt I, now called Personnel. Heydrich dissolved the legal department and moved the last of the original seven divisions, Amt VII, a party organization dealing with ideological research, into the vacated slot at Amt II. This unit, headed by Franz Six, a former chair of the political science department at the University of Berlin, wasn't very important: Heydrich wasn't very interested in ideology. Almost always, he left that to Himmler.

The RSHA now consisted of six divisions, and remained that way until the end of the war, when the Gestapo building in which it was located was bombed out of existence. For five years it had been constantly mentioned in intra-SS correspondence, and Heydrich had been known to his peers as its creator and chief. (Or "Der C," as he was called in RSHA shorthand.) It looked as if he had finally straightened out the muddled lines of authority and communication, as well as enhancing his own reputation and power.

Yet nothing in Nazi Germany was ever that straightforward. Hitler could never quite bring himself to accord the RSHA official status. For one thing, it combined party and state organizations, something of which the Führer didn't really approve. And then of course there was the vexed problem of his ethnic origins. If Hitler and Himmler were really using Heydrich as "the force we can always control," then it is likely that neither wanted to give him so much open recognition. He had already risen further, faster than any other Nazi leader. (The few people who outranked him had all been in the party far longer.) Hitler and Himmler seemed to have paused for a few more years of thought.

In the meantime, "the RSHA . . . led a shadowy existence; officially no one was supposed to know of it. It remained an organization valid for internal purposes only." Within the organization, Der C used RSHA letterhead stationery. But to the outside world, he was still "only" chief of the Security Police and the SD. It was as if the RSHA didn't exist, though everyone who mattered knew that it did, and feared the total, streamlined subordination to one chief that it represented.

Nevertheless, the RSHA always remained officially invisible. Heydrich had created the ultimate counterpart to the "invisible apparat" he had conjured into existence in 1935—an invisible apparat of his own. But unlike the Great Enemy's alleged organization, with its thousands of channels of influence and control that existed only in paranoid fantasy, the RSHA was real, immense, and deadly—as the rest of the world was soon to discover. Two years later, Adolf Eichmann was to begin directing the Final Solution of the Jewish Question from a sub-sub-division of the RSHA, Amt IV (Gestapo), B (Ideological Enemies), 4 (Jews).

13

THE EXPERT ON THE FORMS OF WORDS

"My husband always had trouble with Dr. Best. He was an autocrat . . . He was a jurist . . . And he was a paragraph person; he placed law higher than living men . . . They were so different in their feelings and their mentality."

—LINA HEYDRICH

I N THEIR EARLY DAYS at the helm of the Gestapo, Himmler and Heydrich faced stiff opposition from old-line bureaucrats horrified by SS violence. Yet when these opponents presented their grievances, many were surprised by their encounters with Dr. Carl Rudolf Werner Best. He had been trained as a lawyer and a judge and seemed to speak their language. Almost unknown outside of a small circle of historians, Best was, after Himmler and Heydrich themselves, perhaps the most crucial figure in the development of the Nazi police apparat. The history of his tenure with the Gestapo defines Heydrich's evolution from a power-

Werner Best (age thirty-nine, in 1942) served as chief legal adviser to the Gestapo. Amoral and ambitious, he argued that because the Gestapo was carrying out the will of the state, the brutal force was "acting legally."

Werner Best represented the Reich in Denmark from November 1942 to 1945. Evidence points to his purposely ignoring Himmler's orders, thereby forbidding German forces from raiding Jewish residences. As a result, out of seven thousand Jews listed for rounding up, fewer than five hundred were arrested.

seeker with restraints into an instrument of violence, lawlessness, and, finally, outright warfare.

Prior to the creation of the RSHA, Best as an SS Brigadeführer had been a deputy to Heydrich. After September 1939, he became head of Amt I in the RSHA, overseeing legal and personnel issues for the SS and SD. But his real job was to placate worried officials. As one of them, the future anti-Nazi Hans Bernd Gisevius, later recalled,

> One day [Best] would claim that Himmler was at last going to take care of Heydrich. Another time Heydrich's overstrained conscience could no longer endure the brutal character of his superior. Or else Himmler and Heydrich together were going to send all of their roughnecks to the gallows. In short, everything would undoubtedly be cleared up once and for all, provided that . . . you, Herr So-and-So, withdraw that troublesome complaint. When on such occasions Best quite incidentally broke into one of his radiant smiles, no ministerial councilor or army colonel was able to resist such sincerity and goodness of heart.

The bureaucrats who encountered Werner Best were often shocked by his good manners, condemnation of brutality, and intellectual credentials. Indeed, throughout the twelve years of their "Third Reich," the Nazis were always surprising each other with their own variety and complexity.

Werner Best was certainly unusual. Polished, sophisticated, well read, well spoken—and good-looking with dark hair combed straight back above bright, only slightly arrogant eyes—the suave Dr. Best was still regarded by many officials as a profound thinker, even after they realized he had duped them into acquiescence. The complexities and ambiguities of Nazi leadership could have no better illustration than his uncomfortable, unpredictable, and ultimately unsuccessful career as Reinhard Heydrich's right-hand man.

In a questionnaire completed long after the end of the Second World War, Werner Best described the two "decisive events" of his early life: the death of his father in the First World War, and the collapse of the German Reich in 1918.

In addition to his father, Best also lost his home in the Rhineland, when it was requisitioned by the French army. His family's money vanished in the postwar inflation, and when the young man won a university fellowship, the French took it away again, on the grounds that his father had fought against them.

Like many who joined the SS, Best's earliest personal battles were against the humiliating role of victim. Arriving penniless at the university, he could not afford to join a fraternity, so he created a new one for all those who shared his problem. Werner Best—a member of what the historian Claudia Koontz has called a "fatherless generation"—had replaced the masculine authority missing at home with the camaraderie of young men debating the great problems of the time: "When we young nationalists met groups of young socialists or religious fundamentalists somewhere in the countryside, we didn't beat each other up, but instead sat all night around the campfire, talking about God and the world."

In the end, Best concluded he could accept neither the old-fashioned monarchical "values of his elders" nor the new Weimar ideals of individualism, liberalism, egotism—and "selfish" competition. He decided the transitory individual was important merely as a link in an endless chain connecting the past with the future. What really mattered was the survival of some larger entity, such as the family—or *das Volk*, grandly defined as a "suprapersonal, supratemporal totality of unified blood and spirit."

Best later claimed to have reached these airy conclusions without ever having heard the Nazi proclamation of a mystical Aryan *Volksgemeinschaft* (folk community). But when he finally did hear Hitler speak, he immediately accepted him as a "prophet."

This is exactly the way the very differently educated Lina von Osten had reacted to the Führer: "He was not important as this or that kind of individual, but because he could put into words what the people felt and could not express. The workingman in Hamburg, the farmer on Fehmarn, they never met Hitler, but he became a sort of idol to them. It was only the ideas that counted, not the man."

The ideas that appealed to Lina had to do with ending unemployment and putting food on the table, but these were no longer Best's problems. In 1928, he passed the legal exams required for a prestigious career in the German governmental bureaucracy. After the Nazis won 107 seats in the parliamentary elections of September 1930, he decided to join them. Too self-consciously intellectual to enjoy "mass agitation," he hoped to maintain an "inner distance" from the vulgar party leadership. Soon, he was asked to become legal adviser to the Nazi Gauleiter of Hesse-Darmstadt.

While thus employed, he wrote the so-called Boxheim Documents (named after the estate in Hesse where they were drawn up), a set of starkly radical proposals for countering any future Communist uprising. Best wanted to abolish unearned incomes, create a national labor service, and distribute food only to members of this service. Anyone attempting to sabotage his plan would be shot at once: "Basically, resistance will be punished with death."

The Nazis felt obliged to denounce this unpractical mixture of authoritarianism and socialism, but their leader always enjoyed an appeal for radical, violent action, even if he felt unable to act on it. Adolf Hitler happened to cross Best's path one day in Munich and came over to shake his hand. "Ah, you are the prophet of evil," the Führer said, smiling. Then they discussed their political differences. Best was enthralled: he thought Hitler had behaved "not like a leader giving orders, but like an older comrade."

Having been smiled on by Hitler, Werner Best was offered another job. By then he had decided that the duties of a good Nazi included observing and criticizing the party leadership. Soon, he was fired again.

Like Heydrich before him, Best was rescued from unemployment by Heinrich Himmler, who wisely assigned him to Heydrich's SD, the one part of Himmler's empire where criticism of the party officials was perfectly acceptable.

Frau Heydrich told me her husband was "firmly convinced that the party should definitely have been dissolved in 1933: 'Why not give each of them a castle, if necessary,' my husband used to say, 'But get rid of them!' . . . The party was nothing. *Nothing!* By then the ones who carried the responsibilities for the state were totally different people. The Organization [i.e., the SS], the Hitler Youth, the League of German Girls, even the Women's Association had their area of responsibility. But not the party bosses . . . They were my husband's natural enemies . . . We simply did not need them. They were just drones. They were totally unnecessary people."

By 1934, Werner Best had become so necessary to the SD that he was conferring daily with its chief. Heydrich seems always to have maintained a niche for a legally trained adviser—flexible and quick thinking—with whom he might plan strategies and exchange ideas. (After the war, his special protégés spoke of how nerve-wracking their job had been; at the time, however, they vied to obtain it.)

Himmler's higher position might have made him a more appealing mentor, but he often alienated his most able officers. The feeling was often mutual: Himmler had such "negative charisma" that almost none of his early staff stayed with him.

Heydrich, by contrast, was almost terrifyingly seductive. As Best announced with typical grandiloquence: "If we eliminate the mystical, fantastical connotations of that often-used catchword, *demonic,* and use it instead in its basic sense of suggesting the extraordinary effect of an elementary strength, then one can call Heydrich the most demonic personality among the National Socialist leaders."

Men like Werner Best—bright sons of ruined families, struggling to find a place in the world—were particularly vulnerable to the special combination of cunning, intelligence, and aggressive, almost feral energy that now made up Heydrich's persona. As Best perceived his new boss:

> Heydrich was very tall, taller than most of his subordinates . . . The long, narrow face under the blond crown of hair was dominated by the strong noble nose and the close-set blue eyes. These eyes usually looked cold, searching, and mistrustful, and were often irritated by a flickering restlessness. I had the impression that Heydrich's appearance and his glance already made many people—not merely his subordinates—feel insecure and anxious.
>
> Heydrich's speech and his gestures were usually hasty, choppy,

and restless . . . With an urgent surprise attack, he immediately suggested his conceptions and intentions, thus forcing the other into the position of either agreeing with them or of launching an opposing attack—for which very few had the courage.

As Best reported, Heydrich's "law of behavior" was to force others immediately to reveal whether they were friends or enemies. Many people were simply overwhelmed into submission. Many others were reduced to a state of "fear mixed with admiration, admiration mixed with fear."

Far from being repelled by Heydrich's domineering leadership style, many of his associates were mesmerized. Frau Heydrich said young men often told her he was their ideal of the "New Man" of Nazism: a "political soldier," who excelled in both sports and military "hardness," both administration and politics.

Werner Best's intellectual bent did not prevent him from succumbing to Heydrich's vision of an elite-within-the-elite, commanded by a supremely clever and forceful chief. In 1930, Best had written an essay calling for "a new moral code" suited to a world in which there was no true peace, and struggle was the only enduring reality. This was the very model of the Germany in which he had grown up, but Best thought it also represented the cosmic order—or lack of it. In a chaotic universe, the only philosophical position he found acceptable was the "refusal to contemplate a definitive solution" to any problem.

He gave to this endless, unresolved struggle the glowing name "heroic realism," and argued, "The yardstick of the new code of morality is not its content . . . The important point is not what we fight for but how we fight. The fight itself is essential and permanent; the aims of that fight are temporary and changeable."

By glorifying a "continuous high-tension existence," Werner Best was mixing an early form of existentialism with ancient chivalric notions of the noble fighter for lost causes, and in the process perverting them both. The self-proclaimed "realist" who lets others set the goals for which he fights is in fact preparing himself to be used.

In Best, Reinhard Heydrich's predatory willfulness had found the perfect foil. Heydrich was glad to set the primary goal—the augmentation of his own power and that of the organizations he led. Beyond that, Hitler would decide, for the SS existed to serve his will. Their iron commitment to the "leadership principle" turned Himmler and Heydrich into heroic realists as well, though they expressed it less grandly. Himmler trumpeted endless variations of the SS motto, "Our honor is loyalty." Heydrich's more vigorous ethos of unrelenting achievement was more classically heroic: "We must work on ourselves. With unprecedented self-discipline . . . we must be generally the best in all spheres."

One day, after donning his new SS uniform, Werner Best paid an unexpected visit to an old friend. They fell to discussing philosophical matters just as they had done in their student days; only Best's philosophy had changed. Explicitly rejecting his former *völkisch* idealism, he now proclaimed, "Expediency is the thing . . . power . . . The three or four among us who are going to remain in the end will throw dice to see who is the strongest. The rest don't count."

Best dismissed even his fellow Germans as "the chaff of history." "But we are the masters," he said. "Doesn't that tempt you?" When his friend began a counterargument, Best rebuked him: "Now it's not a question of logic, but of facts. And we are creating the facts. You, however, are going to sit in the corner and think, while we make history."

When Heydrich took over as deputy director of the Gestapo, Best came along as his legal adviser. Until the outbreak of the war in 1939, Reinhard Heydrich and Werner Best made hideous history together, working in tandem to replace the rule of law with the rules of Hitler's game of power.

In 1935, Best and Heydrich attempted to reform conditions in the dozens of concentration camps that had proliferated throughout Germany since Hitler became chancellor in 1933. Undeterred by any need for consistency, the same men involved in deflecting criticism of the Gestapo began compiling their own files of SS abuses. On August 10, 1935, Theodore Eicke, commander of the Death's Head Legions of camp guards, complained to Himmler that "Heydrich's deputy, Dr. Best," had said that "disgusting things went on in the concentration camps and that the time had come to place them under control of the Gestapo."

SD investigators found such devastating proof of atrocities in the camps that Eicke was temporarily forced to ameliorate the treatment of the prisoners. Nevertheless, Heydrich failed in his bid to take them over: Himmler, like Hitler, knew the value of encouraging a balance of power among his subordinates. Heydrich could still send people to the camps with a stroke of his pen, and if they were still alive, he might get them out again, but otherwise, he had to content himself with a tiny, strictly monitored enclave of "political officers."

In February 1936, after Hitler accorded to the SS official control of the police, Werner Best could turn a harsher face to the world. He began to dispense terse authoritarian maxims in addition to honeyed charm.

"The goal of each individual authority within the state is to assure its dominance over the others," he wrote, putting Hitler's private dog-eat-dog philosophy into public words. Even the state itself competed for power: "The more complete its predominance, the more perfect the state." And the more important became the police. Best suggested Heinrich Himmler as the logical person to run things in Hitler's name: "Under the leadership of the Reichsführer SS the German police has become the focus of the movement and of the state."

These three assertions—that all authorities fight for power, that the most power is the best, and that the political police were therefore the legitimate "focus" of political power—reveal the essential assumptions on which a police state must inevitably be based.

Werner Best's great skill, however, lay not in describing these primitive fundamentals, but in elaborating their implications in high-flown, academic language. What is law? Best asked rhetorically. His answer: It was merely a "codification of the outcome of a preceding phase of struggle—accession of power on one side, loss of power on the other."

Of course, such a struggle could not be governed by binding rules: "It is no more possible to lay down legal norms for the means to be used by a political police than it is possible to anticipate for all time to come every form of subversive attack or every other threat to the state." Or, as Himmler said, the police had to be protected against bureaucratic measures that would imprison them in a "network of paragraphs." He added, "We fought lawyers with lawyers. This was a matter of necessity."

As the lawyer charged with giving the police a free hand, Werner Best had to argue against the free play of intellect in which he had once believed: "Any attempt to gain recognition for or even to uphold different political ideas will be ruthlessly dealt with as the symptom of an illness . . . regardless of the subjective wishes of its supporters." Or, as Heydrich said, "Who will care in a hundred years if a certain Fräulein X was happy or not?"

"The political executive," as Himmler and Heydrich called their conglomerate of police organizations, began to encroach further and further into the realm of law. Years before the creation of the RSHA, an administrative court had ruled that the actions of the Gestapo were not subject to judicial review. This meant that a person protesting unjust arrest now had no recourse except the Gestapo itself.

In 1937, Heydrich felt sufficiently emboldened to attempt a widening of the concept of "preventive detention." Since the Röhm purge, the Nazis had considered the prevention of political crimes to be as important as punishing the offenders afterward. Hitherto, precautionary arrests were ordered by a judge for use against specific individuals. Now Heydrich and Best extended the idea to entire categories of people and began to arrest "social undesirables" and "habitual criminals"— with no traditional legal authority at all.

The Nazi regime had been built on the *appearance* of legality, and these blatant tactics were not well received. Many conservative Germans could endure the viciousness and violence of the Third Reich only if they could be rationalized as "momentary exaggerations" within an essentially legal order.

Enter Werner Best, master of the smooth sophism, to argue that preventive arrests suited the "folk law" of the new national community. After all, the courts knew a criminal merely on the basis of one case, but the political police knew everything about him, and could therefore render a fairer judgment. Thus, when a detective arrested a criminal the two were really working together for the good of society, with the policeman serving as the "active partner" and the criminal as the "passive" participant.

Not every official accepted such tortuous reasoning, but most were glad enough to clutch at any alternative to the awful risks of dissent. As Himmler gleefully noted, "It always particularly amused me to see what a sigh of relief came from some poor pudding-head, . . . how he would puff himself out and juggle with the legal paragraphs to make our measures legally unobjectionable."

Yet however clever they were, Best's words could not really obscure the gradual dissolution of the famous German *Rechtsstaat* (rule of law). Theoretically, Hitler ruled as dictator only through his constitutional right to declare "temporary" martial law. The suspension of civil liberties was buttressed by the Enabling Act passed by the Reichstag in February 1933, by the Nuremberg Laws of 1935, and by occasional plebiscites where the use of marked ballots guaranteed the desired outcome. The old parliamentary procedures and the revolutionary New Order thus existed side by side.

One contemporary described the resulting situation as a "dual state," but that makes it all too simple. Nazi Germany more accurately resembled Freud's image of the subconscious as a ruined city within which new buildings were constantly being built before the remains of the old had been cleared away.

Within a confusing world of ever-shifting perspectives, Werner Best now turned his attention to finding order amid the chaos he had helped produce. In keeping with Hitler's predilection for either/or alternatives, Best divided the sphere of government into two distinct parts. "Normal" administration, he argued, "works on general and regularly legalized rules," while new organizations like the Gestapo operated according to "special principles and requirements."

These special principles rested on Hitler's revolutionary politics and personal charisma. His "Führer orders" were deemed "ideological" or "political" in contrast to merely "legal." Ideological orders still had to be justified, however. Himmler sometimes referred to the "sound judgment of the people," or "what our consciences tell us is right." Heydrich and Himmler both spoke of "our historic mission" and the "requirements of the situation." As time went on, the commonest justification—and the one that Heydrich usually used—was simply the Führer's will. By 1940, Werner Best had found the right words: a Hitler decree both "creates law and alters existing law . . . Providing the police are carrying out the will of the leadership, they are acting legally."

According to the German historian Hans Buchheim, this meant that "whenever it was necessary to switch over to irregular procedures, the normal could be turned off like an electric current." Werner Best thought that Heydrich's "vitality and over-average intelligence" were particularly well adapted to this "non-normal" atmosphere:

> It was the intelligence of the hunter, the fencer, the conqueror. Heydrich surveyed and understood situations and problems from the first go. But, whereas others turned their attention to the thing itself or to its factual context, Heydrich "switched gears"—this was his own expression—immediately to the significance of the thing for his own goals . . . He was interested only in . . . how he could

win an advantage or ward off disadvantage. These considerations, in combination with his quick grasp of things, meant that he almost always got a head start in his decisions over everybody else.

In this world of totally pragmatic action, Heydrich's legal adviser was increasingly relegated to providing a veneer of correct style for acts no longer requiring clever legal rationalizations:

The acceptance of the stateless person into the concentration camp designated by me will take place under . . . the provisions of Gestapo Form No. 240. On acceptance of the deportee, the concentration camp will forward to me the top copy of Gestapo Form No. 240, together with the index card Gestapo No. 98 carrying a photograph of the deportee.

Nevertheless, despite his role as a facilitator, Werner Best had achieved the kind of power he once boasted about to his friend. When Heydrich appointed Best chief of the huge Division I in the RSHA, including personnel, administration, and law, he was thus enabled to manipulate the fate of thousands of officials, as well as hundreds of thousands of German citizens—"the chaff of history," as he had called them.

The ideas Werner Best had advocated in earlier days were also becoming reality. After the German invasion of Poland on September 1, 1939, police officers responsible for security behind the lines began summary executions of civilians accused of sabotage. This was approximately the strategy Best had advocated in the Boxheim Documents, and when the minister of justice objected, he defended it strongly, arguing that the SS had the right to use "every means" to safeguard the state. Justice Minister Franz Gürtner then complained to Heydrich, who laconically advised him to "go directly to Hitler about the shootings." He did, and was told that Heydrich and Best were right—the civil and military courts had proved unequal to the "special conditions" of war. The Gestapo independence for which Best had struggled so long was about to be extended to the newly occupied territories, where the "perfect" police state with perfectly omnipotent power could now arise on foreign soil.

If logic were all, Werner Best should have been perfectly happy, joining Heydrich and the privileged few playing with the dice of history. Instead, he made a startling about-face: at the end of 1939, he asked Heydrich for permission to resign from his job and retire from "the service." Suddenly the masterful Heydrich-Best partnership had blown apart in a bitter quarrel, exposing the inner feelings behind the masks of arrogant self-control the two men usually wore.

Their rift was a cause célèbre in its day, and provides a rare glimpse behind the scenes of the ultra-secret "SS state." As usual, nothing occurring behind that apparently monolithic facade was quite what it appeared to "civilians."

Despite his years of apprenticeship in despotism, Werner Best was still regarded as suspiciously intellectual by SS old-timers like former Gruppenführer Bruno Streckenbach: "To have studied law meant to possess logic, perceptiveness, and intelligence to a degree that would qualify you for a leading position in any field of management. And Herr Best was the prototype of such a person—fussy, neat, orderly, correct."

At first, these characteristics had been just what Heydrich wanted. If he had exerted a certain demonic power over the young jurist, the attraction seems initially to have gone both ways. Heinrich Himmler, himself fussy, neat, orderly, and correct, nevertheless hated lawyers—those annoying hindrances to the free flow of mystic fantasy. But Reinhard Heydrich (never described as fussy or correct) had left his family's bohemian household in search of order. He placed a high value on "logic, perceptiveness, and intelligence." Frau Heydrich told me that her husband would often accost Himmler (behind closed doors) and try to talk him out of some of his most irrational "whims." She wouldn't say what these were—only that Reinhard would sometimes come home so furious she thought he should consider resigning. For his part, Himmler once flew into a rage and shouted at Heydrich, "I am sick to death of you and your goddamned logic!"

According to Best, in the heady days when they were attacking Eicke's concentration camps, Heydrich flirted with the study of law, engaging a famous professor to tutor him on the sly. It had to be secret, given the nature of his position as enforcer of the Nazi ideology, and the way his boss felt about lawyers. Best saw the whole project as ridiculous, and said that Heydrich soon reached the same conclusion: it was the only logical one, after all.

By this time, Best himself had thrown off some of his infatuation, and begun to oppose the domineering ways of his boss. It seemed to him that Heydrich made decisions in an unsystematic manner, basing them far too much on ephemeral tactical considerations. He decided to speak out on behalf of impersonal objectivity. Heydrich derided Best as a "wet blanket"; Best began to think of Heydrich as a "dilettante."

They had stormy disagreements about personnel. Heydrich chose subordinates intuitively, seeking Nordic features and military demeanor in addition to intelligence. Best rejected this "soldier play," preferring factual preparation: "As leaders of the main Gestapo offices, I demanded jurists!" In turn, Heydrich jeered, "Oh, you and your assessor's kindergarten!"

Heydrich was forced by his own hatred of the inept party hacks to tolerate Best's obstinate behavior, but he hoped someday to "make the pure, unpolitical mere expert superfluous."

Best resisted this with all his might, and later claimed that his success in appointing "morally irreproachable expert officials" was the immediate cause of his break with Heydrich. For one thing, the men he had chosen and trained turned naturally to him for advice. After years of cultivating charm, he was also much more pleasant than his volatile boss. Then too, Heydrich was often out of the office: conferring with other Nazi leaders, advising Himmler, briefing Hitler, traveling to the front, fencing on the SS team, leading the annual route march, learning to pilot his own plane, entertaining guests on Fehmarn—the list of what Best called his "many interests and tasks" was endless. Best, by contrast, was "always" on hand.

All of this aroused in the ever-vigilant Heydrich a growing suspicion that he was forfeiting control of his staff to a scheming subordinate. Soon the insecure chief of security was giving vent to periodic fits of jealousy, exercising, as Best said, "absolutely no restraint." Word got around that Heydrich considered Best his *Gegenspieler*, or "counterplayer," a typically graphic German expression that is inadequately translated as "opponent."

This was a dangerous label to receive, and Best tried desperately to remove it, repeatedly asserting he had already achieved all his ambitions. But Heydrich assumed there had to be an ulterior motive beneath such an assertion of modesty.

As it turned out, he may have been right. In 1939, Werner Best wrote an article in which he claimed a special function for the lawyer as "a monitor within the structure of society . . . who possesses such knowledge of the tasks both of the leadership and of the community that he is in a position to carry out his monitoring function in every sphere."

"In every sphere" sounds very much like Heydrich's ideal of a "permanent check" on every individual. For years Best had been Heydrich's official mouthpiece, yet he now seemed to be competing with his service chief. Enraged, Heydrich ordered Walter Schellenberg—himself a lawyer—to write an article disavowing Best's point of view. Snidely condescending, Schellenberg belittled the "arrogance of the expert on forms of words."

A few months later, Bruno Streckenbach suddenly replaced Best as chief of security personnel. (The legal department, in Amt II, was dissolved and replaced by Franz Six's organization dealing with ideology.)

According to Streckenbach, Best asked him to stop by. "So I came and he said, 'Are you willing to do it?' At first I said no, because I was starting my furlough, but on the way back I thought it over and said yes."

Streckenbach described the Heydrich-Best altercation: "A big fight can usually be settled by negotiation. What is much more difficult to settle is the sum of many small differences. What you could not call fights but rather points of friction. And such friction between Heydrich and Best existed for a long time. It centered on a certain principle. Himmler had a hard and firm rule: No deputy for anyone.

"Well, there *were* substitutes when someone had to be away from his job temporarily . . . But there is a position called *Vertreter im Amt* [representative in office] whose function is to be his boss's deputy, and that is something we did not have in the Security Police.

"But then one day someone tried to call Heydrich and Best answered the phone. The person calling asked to speak to Heydrich, and Best said that Heydrich was not there, 'but you may speak to me, I am his deputy.' That did it! Best was reprimanded severely.

"And then a few weeks later, a publication came out that Best had written. He described the organization chart of the police . . . just at the moment when Himmler was working on reorganizing the entire structure.

"Now Herr Best not only had Heydrich against him, but Himmler as well. And so when he asked for a leave of absence to participate in the western campaign in memory of his father, they agreed to it very quickly. And I was—very suddenly—within days—I was here in this job. Best handed over his office and disappeared."

Before he left, Best and Heydrich had a confrontation later described by Best as "frank." Heydrich accused his would-be deputy of being a "brake" and a "hindrance": "Whenever I had a good idea," Heydrich said, "I risked that you would cross me up and prove with your juristical arguments that it wouldn't work or that it had to be done differently."

Best replied he had deliberately intended to play the role of brake, that he saw it as his duty. Indeed, he had hoped his boss might actually want such a "complementary relationship." A person of your "temperament, dynamism, and one-sidedness" needs a brake, he told Heydrich, "in order to avoid disaster for itself and others."

Best seems to have hoped to re-create the camaraderie of his student days. But Heydrich, who had endured ridicule and discrimination for nine long years as a naval cadet, had no such frame of reference. Moreover, he had learned most of what he knew of politics from Himmler and Hitler. Like them, he regarded the struggle for power as a zero-sum game. He was happy to hire argumentative, clever subordinates (which his mentors were not), but he never forgot or forgave a direct challenge to his authority. In the end, Heydrich and Best concluded that their separation—treated by Best almost like the ending of a romance—was necessary if they did not want to "wind up fighting against each other as enemies."

Best seemed under the impression they had parted friends, but both he and Heydrich continued to brood about their ruined relationship. They weren't alone: the rupture unleashed a wave of gossip. People began to assume the two had been serious rivals; some discreetly hoped Best might someday prevail. Even a less suspicious man than Heydrich might have worried.

Heydrich began to ponder ways to solve "the Best problem." Best's colleagues in Berlin warned him Heydrich was saying it would be a good thing if he died in the war. When he returned unscathed, Best discovered his former boss was blocking his efforts to find an influential administrative position. Fearing his life might be in danger, he found a job farther from harm's way, in occupied France.

But Heydrich had apparently decided to kill the very idea of a legal brake. Later, he summarized his position in a letter to Kurt Dalüge of October 30, 1941:

The most important point is to change the relationship between the police and the legal profession . . . I . . . have confined the lawyers in my office to the duties which are properly theirs, namely those of officials employed to advise on the forms of words. In my office the lawyer is . . . merely an adviser and an assistant . . . ; he has no power of decision. This, as you know, was in essence the reason for my disagreement with Dr. Best.

Like Bruno Streckenbach, Heydrich viewed the rift with his former protégé primarily as a struggle for power. Best, by contrast, saw it as more personal: "I promised your wife, who has always been very sensitive to atmosphere, that I would be a friend to you, but you don't want a friend, you want a subordinate."

The two former partners-in-legalized-crime were to meet only once again, in Paris in 1942, shortly before Heydrich's death. By then, they were truly "counter-players," for Best now worked for the Wehrmacht, with which the SS was constantly feuding. Best's record as head of staff for civilian administration was as complicated as he was. Sometimes he seemed to work too closely with his old associates in the SD; sometimes he "amazed" his colleagues by helping a Jew or signing an order forbidding the police to rearrest a man who had already served his time. (In Germany, the latter procedure was common.)

In Paris, Heydrich treated his old comrade with the icy courtesy he reserved for enemies, but Best thought he "let his emotions break through" on one occasion: "You have . . . certainly enforced this regulation with pigheaded tenacity!" Heydrich snarled before "recovering himself."

In that same year, Werner Best showed tenacity of another sort, continuing his independent intellectual development in his last published article, in which he discussed the "inevitable consequence of a short-term master race hallucination":

It must be remembered that in the long term no people has been able to exercise leadership without or against the consent of the led. People seem to think that it is possible to destroy the personality of a subject people but still preserve them as effective human beings to be used in the service of our own people who will be the master caste; the Roman Empire and numerous other examples are proof of the result of such a concept.

All during the 1930s, Best had helped Heydrich coerce and dupe his way to supreme police power. Yet at some point, Best seems to have changed his mind and reverted to his old rejection of permanent solutions. (In 1939 Hitler had announced that the conflict in the East would be bound by no rules of war: the solutions there would be "final.")

Werner Best quarreled with Heydrich about many things—power, friendship, hiring practices, personality differences—but also about something more disruptive than any of those: the danger to police supremacy that Best had labeled "different political ideas." One of them was the very concept of limits itself. Best was, of course, correct in perceiving that his boss—and *his* bosses—needed a brake. Unfortunately, Heydrich had long ago been forced by the nature of his job and by his own headlong way of performing it into the role of accelerator of the deadly political programs of Nazism. Unlike Werner Best, he was prepared to make the "hard" choices necessitated by the Nazi version of total war.

The horrors of war and of "the master race hallucination" made many Nazis question their previous fanaticism. But by the time most of them thought again—like Werner Best—it was already too late. As those who experienced it have frequently pointed out, the momentum of Nazism was immense. Once pointed in a certain direction, the machinery of violence, lawlessness, and, eventually, war, was almost impossible to stop. The vague "catastrophe" about which Best had warned Heydrich was about to assume myriad forms. And this time, they weren't mere words.

14

"GARBAGE CAN OF THE THIRD REICH"

"The only people who had to live in fear had cause to be afraid. No one else! Otherwise everyone would have left. But it was only the ones who during the Weimar Republic had set themselves against National Socialism, knowingly, purposely, and honestly. They *were* enemies . . . They emigrated."

—LINA HEYDRICH

ONE THURSDAY NIGHT shortly after the outbreak of the Second World War, Reinhard Heydrich dropped by the *Stammtisch*, or "regulars' table," of a weekly gathering of foreign correspondents stationed in Berlin. He came as their guest for an evening of beer and informal questions about life in the Third Reich. Such mutual interchange between the press and the powers was regarded as useful by both sides—at least until Heydrich arrived on the scene. This evening's exchange reflects Heydrich's demeanor when he no longer felt he had to answer to mere words.

The journalists noted that their tall young visitor spoke in "the clipped sentences of a man accustomed to dealing with people who can only listen and take orders." For a while, they sat silently while he tried to convince them there were fewer prisoners in the concentration camps than they had been told by other sources. A Swiss writer finally commented ironically, "I suppose you never shoot anybody without first thoroughly investigating the case from all angles."

Heydrich stared at the foreign upstart before replying: "There is no great trick in finding the guilty in big subversive plots . . . once you have the key to the situation and know the ringleaders. All you have to do after that is to follow their tracks and pick up the facts one by one. It is like unrolling a ball of yarn. The rest takes care of itself."

Unpersuaded, the correspondents wanted to ask about "shadow arrests," mass shootings, and "the direct-method procedure of the Gestapo and the SS." Icily, Heydrich dismissed such talk as vicious slander designed to "terrorize . . . the German people's peace of mind." The Gestapo could not arrest anybody, he said, without prior action by the "usual machinery and process of justice."

The journalists continued to display an initiative long since forbidden to Germans. A Swedish correspondent wanted information about the rumors of anti-Christian "godlessness" within the SS. Heydrich denied them. When the questioner persisted, Heydrich launched a tirade: "We do not consider it necessary to march into church every Sunday or to listen to sermons which mean nothing. The SS is trained to believe in God, but we do not intend to be handicapped by superstitious rules and regulations . . . If a bishop or a priest . . . agitates in his community against his government . . . then I see no reason why I should not justifiably interfere . . . But that doesn't mean that we are godless."

When the foreign correspondents asked for details of "tribal" religious rites and practices within the SS, Heydrich got up from his seat and strode furiously from the room. Later the journalists heard he had complained of their insolence. They began to worry about the "dossiers against us."

The author of this account, the American war correspondent Pierre J. Huss, commented that Heydrich's violent reaction to the writers' unseemly curiosity was merely a reflection, "cold-blooded and vengeful," of the very police methods he had refused to discuss. But there was more to it than that. For many years no one had dared to challenge him in such a manner, much less publicly to doubt his earthly godliness. Among the new Nazi demigods, such *lèse-majesté* invited retaliation rather than reflection: challenging thoughts had to be warded off like any other threat to security. Heydrich was now used to getting away with murder but he didn't like to be reminded of it.

Even when trying to relax and socialize, he could not drop his guard. In Vienna, after an evening spent discussing music and the theater with a young woman (who did not know his official identity), he asked her opinion of *Anschluss*, the recent merger of Austria and Germany. "You may be a perfectly nice man," she answered, "but I think the Nazis are bandits . . . and your Brown Shirts are disgusting brutes." He replied with a burst of laughter, but also felt compelled to add, "Well, we'll have to change your mind about that, won't we?"

Even in the privacy of the family, he was forced to act defensively. After his mother, the devoutly Catholic Elisabeth Heydrich, questioned his judgment in ordering the arrest of Bishop Galen of Münster (which Hitler countermanded), she and Heydrich barely spoke to each other again. Of course, Heydrich couldn't walk out on his own mother (whom he was supporting financially), but he could certainly "act out" against that favorite SS target—a gang of hostile journalists.

Such behavior was the product of Germany's new culture. Totalitarianism demands the complete mobilization of all those under its sway. The majority of people represents not only ignorance but also cowardice, ready to bow to a superior will. In Nazi Germany, nobody was allowed to stand on the sidelines or take the role of uncommitted observer.

Deprived of free access to the real facts, constantly watched and prodded by various agencies of surveillance, Germans of all kinds, from fanatic Nazis to members of the resistance, learned to hide their second thoughts beneath the appearance of conformity to the party line. (As a prudent father might counsel his teenage son: "What you read in the papers isn't true, but you mustn't say so. Outside, you must always act as if you believe everything.")

Such duplicity required an adroit sense of timing, since the rules of the game permitted Hitler to change policy constantly. Even Himmler and Heydrich occasionally had to scramble to straddle the perpetually moving party line, hiding their own views behind the mask of SS obedience, while trying to unmask the pretensions and intentions of others.

By 1941, no one was above suspicion. All Germans were now routinely watched in their work, and even their homes provided little refuge. As a Gestapo defector writing under the pen name Hans-Jürgen Köhler later reported,

> I used to know a Berlin family . . . They had three children, fair-haired little angels, two girls and a boy. They were Aryans—not even the most painstaking research could find a single drop of Jewish blood in their veins. They had expected much of Nazism; a new consciousness, sweeping economic reforms, a higher standard of living. They were disappointed—at least the father was.

One night, in the privacy of their dining room, he voiced his opinions. Two days later he was arrested and taken to a concentration camp . . . His fair-haired little daughter, his pet and spoiled darling, had denounced him.

Many Nazi elite even felt free to order the Gestapo into action to further their own greed. Foreign Minister Joachim von Ribbentrop acquired a fine luxury villa after he had its owner arrested. The Gestapo could also furnish a home for themselves or others simply by stealing the furniture from apartments sealed off by the police.

Sexual favors were even easier to achieve: a woman in Berlin whose family was denounced on six different occasions secured her freedom by enduring the brutish sexual advances of her Gestapo interrogator— a man who also had the power to remove her Jewish mother's name from a deportation list, casually sparing her life as part of the illicit exchange. (Such departures from SS orthodoxy were bitterly condemned by the strait-laced Himmler—if he ever found out.)

Perhaps the greatest benefit of all, however, was the ability to settle personal scores under the cover of *raison d'état*. Hermann Göring, still technically in charge of the Gestapo, liked to use it to get rid of his enemies. So did Admiral Canaris, who commanded no police of his own. Even the punctilious Werner Best was said to have arranged to send difficult people to Dachau as a favor to a Gauleiter whose influence he was cultivating.

Gradually, as a consequence of this corruption, a dualistic universe arose, in which the apparent surface of things and the actual realities were often drastically at odds. "If I had to describe Hitler's Reich in one figure," wrote the journalist Howard K. Smith in 1941, "I would compare it with a fine-looking fat apple with a tight, red, shiny skin, which was rotten in the core. The strong, polished hull is the army and the Gestapo, which has become the main constituent of the Nazi Party . . . The rotten inside is the whole of the fabric of Nazi society."

Increasingly, the Gestapo was what mattered. As the Gestapo defector Köhler wrote,

The Gestapo has its voluntary or involuntary agents in every household. Sometimes it is a trusted servant, grown gray with the family service; the janitor of the block of flats; the tram conductor or the attendant in the park. Germany has become a country of suspicious glances, of whispers and surreptitious movements. Even those who are high up in the governing machine are afraid . . . Nobody is safe from slander or intrigue. And the spiritual effects of such a system may be worse than its physical ones.

Visibly on the Gestapo throne, of course, sat Heinrich Himmler. But, in Köhler's view, Himmler would have been "just a senseless dummy" without Heydrich, who let his boss take all the honors in public: "Although he is hot-blooded and impetuous himself, [Heydrich] remains soberly, coldly calculating in the background . . . Together they represent a symbol of unscrupulous terrorism, horrible for all real or alleged opponents, whether personal or political."

Heydrich was aware that the security conglomerate he now headed bore little relation to the "honor service" he had envisioned when he joined the SS. As he himself commented in a speech to his officers on German Police Day in 1941: "Secret State Police, Criminal Police, and the SD are still described with a mixture of fear and shuddering, . . . bordering on the sadist." Heydrich and his security professionals did not like to think of themselves as sadists. "Bordering on the sadistic" was as close as the Nazis could come to accurately describing their abominable acts of cruelty. Most were only too glad to blame others for Nazi "excesses." On the surface, even Heydrich liked to behave as if he were still accommodating his former assistant Werner Best. It was the defector writing under the name of Hans-Jürgen Köhler who became the first of Heydrich's former subordinates to describe him as "the all-powerful police executive of the Third Reich . . . the man who moves everything . . . the Power Behind the Throne."

Köhler's disillusionment came about as follows. Like Best, he had once been a trusted member of the Gestapo, who spent many hours with Heydrich, talking "like friends." But one day, after they had worked together for five years, Heydrich called his friend into his office and announced, "I am sending you to a concentration camp."

Desperately, Köhler tried to remember what he had said or done to warrant such punishment. After a moment, Heydrich interrupted his thoughts. He was smiling in amusement. "Don't be afraid," he said. "You haven't deserved to be sent there."

Köhler was sent, nevertheless, to Buchenwald. On a secret mission for Heydrich, he had been ordered to locate a man who had stolen some vital documents and was now believed to be in one of the camps under an assumed identity. Since Heydrich could not openly intervene in Theodore Eicke's jealously guarded domain, he decided to disguise his investigator as a regular prisoner. The secret policeman endured slave labor, exhaustion, starvation, and a brutal flogging, during which he fainted and had to be sent to the hospital, before he found his man—in the cot next to his. His quarry was mortally ill. Before dying, he told his new comrade in misery where the documents were.

Köhler was released and richly praised for his brave work. But it was too late. He had been stunned by the brutality of camp life: "We of the Gestapo had seldom such 'dirty' work to do; few of us were sadists. But all Eicke's men seemed to be just that."

Heinrich Himmler also realized his notoriety: "We know some people become sick when they see our . . . black tunic; we recognize this and do not expect to be beloved by too many people." On the contrary: "All those . . . whose conscience toward the Führer and the nation is not clear in any way or at any time *should* fear us. We have built up an organization to deal with such people and it is called the Sicherheitsdienst." (Heydrich, by contrast, ignored his own SD and said it was "Himmler and the Gestapo" that were seen "in a bad light.")

Himmler and Heydrich had long specialized in eliminating the rotten elements, the people Himmler called political "trash." In his speech on Police Day, Heydrich summarized the situation: "There is no problem down to the smallest egotistic longing that the Gestapo cannot solve. Regarded in this way, we are, if a joke is permitted, looked on as a cross between a general maid and the garbage can of the Reich."

Despite Heydrich's joking about it, the heart—or at least the fangs—of the terror system lay in its deliberate use as a deterrent. Future crimes against the New Order were to be prevented by fear of swift detection and ghastly punishment. For deterrence to work effectively, however, fear must be spread as far throughout the system as possible.

The resulting webs of fear and fakery, deception and self-deception, make it difficult to fully appreciate the immensely complicated texture of life in the Third Reich. Only through examining firsthand personal accounts can we begin to understand the way systematic police terror became woven into the patterns of "normal" experience—as well as what happened when the veil was removed and people came face-to-face with the reality of the Gestapo.

. . .

Like everything else in Nazi Germany fear began at the top, where the Führer's moods of euphoria alternated with premonitions of doom. Hitler dreaded both assassination and binding decisions. His resulting penchant for sudden last-minute changes of plan saved his life at least once, when "providence" guided him away from a bomb-laden plane. Other times, it inspired sudden attacks on presumed enemies, ultimately embroiling him in the actual multi-front war that ended up destroying his empire.

The atmosphere resulting from such attacks led not only to a sense of fear, conformity, suspicion, and denunciation, but also to the Gestapo exercising its newly unlicensed powers. Victims had to undergo interrogation at a Gestapo office, enduring, at the very least, a humiliating brush with an authority both overwhelming and arrogant. Minor offenses (such as remarks mildly critical of the regime) by people regarded as basically harmless (such as most women) received only a "minor" punishment. A woman who said that life was not getting any better under the Nazis had to appear every day at her local police headquarters, there to proclaim loudly and repeatedly that everything had gotten better after all. Other female offenders were ordered to scrub the floors.

Generally, however, most Gestapo detainees were men, facing other men across a desk, answering some charge written on a piece of paper they were usually not allowed to see. From then on, the procedures varied greatly, according to the position and the personality of both interrogator and prisoner.

Once, for example, Heydrich summoned an old friend of his father's, the composer Hans Pfitzner, whom Heydrich himself had known from boyhood. Pfitzner had been attempting to protect "non-Aryan" musicians, and had even written an article in which he praised Mendelssohn, whose works, because of the composer's Jewish background, were no longer performed in Germany. "I can risk more than others; the fellows would not dare to threaten me," Pfitzner speculated. But Bruno Heydrich's son received him coldly, "as though he were a complete stranger," then reprimanded him for ignoring the racial laws. "Herr Pfitzner, you have been denounced to us. I warn you!" he said, by way of dismissal.

Pfitzner was stunned by Heydrich's offensive impersonality. But Reinhard Heydrich may have thought he had done the old man a favor:

a special warning from the chief of the Gestapo was the best treatment that could be expected.

The worst was reserved for known enemies of the regime. They would often be arrested suddenly, in the middle of the night—the famous knocking on the door appearing in so many movies and spy stories. Rarely did the police break the door down, preferring to wait until their apprehensive victim opened it for them. He would then be taken, often in whatever clothes he had on, to a Gestapo prison, where he might be left in a cold cell, often handcuffed or chained to the wall, for many days before anyone but the lowliest guard bothered to speak to him. By then, the prisoner was eager to be interviewed officially, to find out the charges, to end the uncertainty. Often, he waited awhile longer. Then one day, usually without warning, he would be ordered to report to someone's office, and marched double-time, almost running, down long corridors, for what seemed an even longer time.

Most suspects were treated more bureaucratically, however, receiving a letter in the mail requesting them to appear at a certain Gestapo build- ing at a certain hour a few days away. Once they arrived, a courteous SS guard would direct them to the proper office, where they usually had to wait.

Here, the atmosphere became cooler in more ways than one. Often the anteroom was unheated; frequently, it was filled with other people, some of them prisoners in chains, a few perhaps in the act of signing confessions. Christabel Bielenberg, in her memoir of an Englishwom- an's experience living in Nazi Germany, describes observing a female secretary at Gestapo headquarters in Berlin slapping a man who wanted to read his confession before signing it. Such treatment would be a shocking reminder that the usual hierarchy of status and power was no longer in effect, however important the prisoner might have been in ordinary life.

Sooner or later the wait ended with the appearance of a guard or two, come to usher the unhappy visitor into a warmer room invariably containing an uncomfortable chair, a portrait of a Nazi dignitary on the wall, and an immense desk. Behind the desk, the prisoner might encounter anyone, who might do almost anything. That was part of the mystique.

Prisoners of a certain stature might even come up against the dreaded Heinrich Müller, the Munich detective whom Heydrich had brought to Berlin to supervise daily operations.

Often Heydrich pointed Müller toward the arena of deadly conflict, calling him in when he needed to intimidate his opponents. In 1941, while conducting sensitive negotiations with the army, Müller behaved so abrasively that Heydrich had to replace him in the midst of the discussions. "He gets very stubborn about unimportant details," Heydrich complained. "Well, he's nothing more than a petty police official, after all," he commented on another occasion.

Müller's eyes seem to have been his dominant feature, remembered by everyone. General Walter Dornberger, head of the V-2 rocket program, was once called to Müller's office. The latter sat with his back to the window, an old Gestapo technique that forced the suspect to squint into the light. In the course of their meeting Müller used another classic method of intimidation—the claim to omnipotent knowledge: "Do you know what a fat file of evidence we have against you here?"

Dornberger wondered aloud if he was about to be arrested. Müller replied it would be "pointless as yet," articulating a third common strategy, that of waiting to see how the situation developed and what else could be made out of it. After the war, the general recalled his interrogator primarily as "a pair of piercing gray-blue eyes, fixed on me with an unwavering scrutiny."

An English spy also had cause to remember Müller's peculiar gaze. In the autumn of 1939, shortly after the outbreak of the Second World War, Schellenberg's Ausland-SD managed to kidnap the two British intelligence officers responsible for Holland and Belgium, spiriting them across the frontier into Germany. One of them, Captain Sigismund Payne Best, wound up in police headquarters in Berlin, confronted by "Gestapo" Müller: "He had rather funny eyes which he could flicker from side to side with the greatest rapidity and I suppose that this was supposed to strike terror into the heart of the beholder."

Payne Best, however, behaved with that British imperturbability that so infuriated the Nazis: "I have something the matter with my eyes, too," he said. "Could I perhaps have my glasses?" Müller jumped up. "Don't you worry about glasses or anything else. You will probably be dead before morning . . . You don't seem to realize your position. It is war . . . Don't you know where you are? At the headquarters of the Gestapo. Don't you know what *that* means? We can do anything we like with you, *anything*."

Payne Best replied that although he had read about so-called Gestapo methods, he had "paid no greater attention to such stories than I did to

On November 9, 1939, British MI6 agent Sigismund Payne Best (age fifty-four, in 1939) was taken into German custody in the tiny Dutch border town of Venlo at the authorization of Hitler. Repercussions from Best's arrest included the effective crippling of the British spy network on the continent.

other reports published in the press." He had said the right thing: both Himmler and Heydrich complained bitterly about the "atrocity stories" in foreign newspapers. "Ah! I am glad to find an Englishman who is so sensible," Müller said. "Give Mr. Best what he wants," he instructed an aide.

Payne Best's policy was to appear quite willing to talk, while actually saying nothing of value. Eventually realizing he had not provided any real information, his interrogators threatened to kill him immediately unless he told all. He ignored the threats, considering them badly staged "theatricals." After he had been resisting such pressure for about a month, the English spy was brought upstairs to a suite of rooms:

> Almost as soon as I entered, a young and very resplendent officer whom I recognized as Heydrich (his enlarged photograph hung in every room) jumped up and started shouting at me in a most threatening manner.
>
> "So far you have been treated as an officer and a gentleman, but don't think that this will go on if you don't behave better than you have done. You have two hours left in which to confess everything. If you don't, I shall hand you over to the Gestapo who are used to dealing with such gangsters and criminals—you won't enjoy their methods a bit."

Technically Payne Best was still a prisoner of Schellenberg's Ausland-SD. Ignoring the "personal union" that made him chief of both that organization and the Gestapo, Heydrich acted as if he had only minimal connection to the police. For his part, Best pretended he hadn't seen Heydrich's picture. "Who is this excitable young officer?" he asked Müller:

> At this Heydrich really went off the deep end and literally foamed at the mouth; at all events he sprayed me most liberally with his saliva. Müller quickly pushed me out of the room and into my own. Later on, he came in again and told me that I must not take the matter too seriously, soup is never eaten as hot as it is cooked.

Müller's homely maxim proved true. Soon afterward, Payne Best was transferred to the concentration camp at Sachsenhausen, where he spent the rest of the war as a VIP prisoner, listening to beatings occurring in nearby rooms, but never touched himself. (After the war, Frau Heydrich said her husband told her he had a "guilty conscience" about Best, toward whom, as an officer and intelligence professional, he had a certain "fellow feeling." Perhaps this was enhanced by Schellenberg's discovery that Best—like Heydrich—was a skilled violinist.)

One day in 1942, a little man with an "absolutely expressionless face" appeared at the door of Payne Best's cell. Heinrich Himmler greeted him politely. "Well, Mr. Best," Himmler replied, "you have certainly been able to ascertain for yourself that all the stories of atrocities in the British White Book were nothing but lies, Jewish inventions." After this, Best couldn't restrain himself from voicing his actual opinion—that conditions were worse in the camp than he had expected. Himmler stormed out of the building, yet once again, nothing happened to this special British prisoner whom the Nazis had decided must be kept reasonably comfortable.

Another prisoner, Berthold Jacob, was also kidnapped on foreign soil and survived to tell of it. Jacob, a German-Jewish émigré, had been writing detailed articles about conditions in his former homeland. Having concluded Jacob must have had an informant on the German General Staff, the Gestapo abducted him in Basel and took him back to Germany for questioning.

The following account appears in various books based on evidence from the Nuremberg trials: One morning, Jacob heard a voice outside his door. "Here sits the pig!" the voice said. A very tall man entered the room along with three companions. Coolly, Jacob considered the "owner of the voice," who was dressed in the blue civilian clothes favored by military men.

Jacob had once seen a photo of Heydrich, and guessed his identity, though he seemed younger than in his picture: "This man could hardly be over thirty. [Yet] it was entirely clear that he was the lord of this prison."

In a youthfully boisterous manner, Heydrich expressed his satisfaction at having Jacob in custody. He advised him "amiably" not to make any trouble: "Don't try to impress us with a hunger strike or anything like that. It would go badly for you." Then he left, followed by his entourage, whose laughter echoed down the corridor.

The next day, Jacob was taken upstairs, where he found Heydrich sitting behind a huge diplomat's desk. This time he was wearing the uniform of an SS group leader. Two other men were present, and Heydrich spoke first to them: "Jacob has spread the dirty slander that the Gestapo beats its prisoners." He turned to face his captive: "You are much too filthy for me to bother punishing you for that."

Heydrich asked his men if they had any questions for the prisoner. They said no. In a few months, the Gestapo bowed to international pressure, and released Jacob.

To borrow Captain Payne Best's phrase, there was much of the "badly staged theatrical" in Heydrich's manner. Whether coolly insulting, explosively threatening, boyishly jubilant, or rudely contemptuous, his behavior toward his various prisoners seems excessively dramaturgical, like an actor experimenting with a difficult role. There were in fact almost no models for the police position Heydrich now occupied. The Reichsführer seems often to have copied the behavior of his schoolmaster father; perhaps Heydrich was imitating the operatic braggadocio of his own father, the professional master of mime.

Melodramatic theatrics were in any case a favorite tactic of police interrogators, who often tried to unnerve their political prisoners by alternating appeals to "reason" with the direst threats. Yet both times Heydrich mentioned Gestapo punishments to his foreign prisoners, he implied a personal distancing from the methods used by his men. The word he used for "filthy" derives from *Dreck*, the German term for "refuse." Heydrich may have joked about being the Reich's garbage collector but, like Himmler, he lacked immoral courage when face-to-face with his victims.

Of course, he very rarely was. Most prisoners did not receive such elaborate personal attention from high SS leaders. More typical was the case of an "unpolitical" young man, Horst Krüger, whose best friend had lured him into the resistance. They were both arrested, and Krüger was interrogated by the Gestapo.

"They said please and thank you and addressed me as Mister," he later wrote. They had also been intercepting his mail for a year and already knew he was not the stuff of which true resistance is made. Though not physically molested, Krüger was interrogated for months, until he felt worn down, a "leftover," a "victim." Finally, he was awakened in the middle of the night. Two guards led him through a labyrinth of passages to a room in the basement. It contained an "examining magistrate," sitting behind a desk on which were piled two stacks of paper, one red and one green. The red pile contained forms on which were written the word *PROSECUTE!* The green forms said *DISMISS!*

The magistrate, who seemed surprisingly small and old, berated Krüger for his poor choice of comrades. Then he said, "Do you know the opinion our colleagues formed about you?" He read aloud from a file: "With proper treatment, may possibly still be salvaged for the people's state." He paused. "Well, Krüger, what do you have to say about that? Is it true, do you think?"

Krüger sat mute, paralyzed with anxiety. Only after he saw the old man begin to extend a hand toward the red pile did he speak: "Let me out of here, sir—for the love of God!" The man looked meditatively at his young visitor. Suddenly he reached for a green form and, wordlessly, began to write. Soon thereafter, Krüger was set free. Most prisoners of the Gestapo were released in the end, adding their own exhalations of angst to the fog of fear enshrouding the political landscape.

Not everyone, however, was allowed to go, particularly after the war began, and particularly if they were Jews or members of the resistance. A Jewish hero of the resistance, Dr. Albert Haas, has written of his encounters with several Gestapo officers. Having been called for interrogation in occupied France, he first met the regional leader responsible for the area around Nice:

Hauptsturmführer Recsek was wearing elegantly tailored civilian clothes. He jumped from his desk to greet me with a warm and open geniality. I was totally unprepared for the immediate and mutual sense of rapport I experienced. He behaved like a warm-hearted, intelligent English aristocrat . . . He was always extremely polite and well spoken, a quick-witted and well-educated man who had taught history at Breslau University before the war . . . Hauptsturmführer Recsek actually became one of my close friends.

Recsek claimed to be able to "smell" Jews; nevertheless, he took Dr. Haas to be a friendly Aryan collaborator. Haas was released. He continued his resistance activities, and was eventually denounced, imprisoned, and this time, tortured, to force him to reveal the names of his contacts. He saw Recsek only once after that, when he walked into the interrogation room and slapped his face. The two men had a bitter argument. Finally, Haas appealed to the Gestapo leader's sense of honor. "As a fellow officer [you] should appreciate the fact that if I really were a spy I would never confess and betray my country." Apparently moved, Recsek ordered his men to stop the torture, and left the room.

Dr. Haas was sent to Dachau, escaped from there, and was recaptured. Once again, he faced Gestapo questioning. His new interrogator asked him politely to sit down and offered him a cigarette: "As he leaned over the desk toward me his hand suddenly jerked forward and the flame from his lighter burned my lips. 'Oh, how clumsy, please forgive me,' he said."

For a while the policeman asked simple questions and Haas provided simple, evasive answers. Then:

> I started to put out my cigarette in the ashtray. I was suddenly speechless with excruciating pain on the back of my right hand. I looked at it. My interrogator had crushed out his cigarette in my flesh.
>
> Again the sarcastic apology: "I'm so sorry. Pardon my clumsiness. I was so absorbed in your fairy tale I didn't notice your hand in the ashtray." The disarmingly casual manner of my interrogator and the deadly cat-and-mouse game he was playing with me disrupted my ability to think quickly.

Haas decided to try the moral appeal he had used with Recsek, explaining he "could not knowingly put someone's life in jeopardy." This time it failed utterly: "My Gestapo interrogator looked at me with what seemed a kindly expression, and replied, 'Look, we're not in the Middle Ages. Why should you want to suffer for the sake of your honor? You won't be allowed to leave this room until I have your confession.'"

The courageous doctor eventually survived with his honor intact, but not before enduring more agony at the hands of men who had long ago placed their own honor at the disposal of the state.

We know all too much about the details of their bestial acts, but not enough about the thoughts and feelings of the men who performed and ordered them. Individual attitudes were not supposed to be relevant. "Our men must be ready to sacrifice all pride, all outward honor, all that is personally near and dear to them," Heinrich Himmler once wrote; "they must never hesitate but must comply unconditionally with any order issued by the Führer or their official superiors." But did the Führer sanction torture?

In a general way, he certainly did. The leader seems to have felt that violence served the welfare of the body politic, much as a parent might argue, "Spare the rod and spoil the child." In his table talks, the father of the Third Reich criticized Minister of Justice Franz Gürtner for hesitating to apply the rod to a suspected killer:

> I suggested that he should allow the Gestapo to try their hand, adding that nothing would happen to the fellow, that at the most he would get a good hiding, that had I myself received in one fell swoop all the thrashings I deserved (and had had) in my life, I should be dead. The net result was that the blackguard confessed to one hundred and seven murders of which Gürtner would have remained in ignorance but for the Gestapo . . . I quote this example to prove that there are cases in which severity is essential.

Before the Röhm purge, the Storm Troopers had reveled in "severity," beating and torturing their prisoners. Himmler had even sanctioned this when he announced, "In certain cases the Reichsführer SS and chief of the German Police will order flogging in addition to detention in a concentration camp . . . In this case, too, there is no objection to spreading the rumor of this increased punishment . . . to add to the deterrent effect."

The camps that Himmler refers to were run by the Nazi Party, however, whereas the police, and their violence, were supposed to be subjected to bureaucratic controls. Werner Best testified at Nuremberg that he had questioned Heydrich in 1937 about a new decree legitimizing "third-degree interrogation methods." (Best was careful to say he "was not called in on such matters.") Heydrich replied to Best that the measure was necessary to prevent conspiracies by organizations hostile to the state. He said, Best testified, "foreign police agencies widely applied such methods. He emphasized, however, that he had reserved for himself the right of approval on every individual case in the German Reich; thus he considered any abuses quite out of the question."

Heydrich seemed unaware that torture, itself, is an abuse.

Efforts to codify "intensive interrogation" (the bald word "torture" was never employed) passed through the bureaucratic channels: a standardized type of cane was to be used, no more than twenty-five blows were permitted, after ten blows a doctor should be called. (But if "abuses" occurred, who would be likely to tell of it?) No record can be found of Heydrich's presence during such an interrogation, though in 1939 Himmler appeared at the questioning of Johann Georg Elser, the carpenter who had just attempted to assassinate Hitler. In a rare display of unfettered emotion, Himmler kicked the manacled man several times and ordered that he be whipped.

Elser had readily admitted his guilt, but claimed he had acted alone. The Gestapo had used its most skilled investigators to question him— even Best had tried his hand—and they were convinced he was telling the truth. But Hitler wanted very much to believe British Intelligence was behind the attempt. "What idiot conducted this interrogation?" he asked. Himmler was furious: the SS was never supposed to disappoint the Führer.

As time wore on, particularly after the war turned against Germany, occasions of torture increased, methods multiplied, a pestilence of medieval devices proliferated throughout occupied Europe, and far-flung individual Gestapo offices often exercised their own "initiative." In theory victims were not tortured to make them confess, but "only" if they knew something about others still at large. Klaus Barbie, the Gestapo leader of Lyons, was presumably trying to find out additional names when in a meeting in his office in 1943 he beat to death the leader of the French resistance.

Such things came to be known almost exclusively from the reports of victims and from scattered German documents. SS men who survived the war tended, like Sturmbannführer Albert Hartl, Heydrich's expert on religion, to evade such uncomfortable knowledge:

> When I went to visit . . . SS Stubaf Plath, he received me while still interrogating a prisoner. Apparently not satisfied with one of the answers he struck him a number of times with a heavy stick . . . This was the one case of mistreatment of a prisoner being interrogated which I experienced in eleven years of working with the RSHA and SD.
>
> I often *heard* officials state a slap in the face was the best method of interrogation. I also knew that the Gestapo had a second degree, which was only used with the personal permission of Office Chief Müller. I also noticed that Müller was frequently in the company of a doctor, who always smelled of fresh medicine.

Sturmbannführer Plath confided to Hartl that in addition to his interrogation duties "for a long time he had shot two to three thousand persons a week." Hartl himself witnessed a mass execution and was able to describe it in some detail. Like Hartl, SS men typically spoke more freely of mass murder than of torture. Mass murders are crimes performed by a group, into which the individual may attempt to merge both identity and responsibility. Torture, by contrast, is man to man, hand to bloody hand. No one wants to talk about it. Klaus Barbie refused to take the stand at his own later trial in Paris.

I asked Bruno Streckenbach, former chief of security personnel under Heydrich, about his leader's apparent approval of torture. He didn't, apparently, understand my question.

I asked him whether he had been afraid of Heydrich.

"There were always rumors about a man in his position," he said. "But that those who worked closely with him stiffened in fear when they as much as saw him, that was not true . . . If anyone was afraid, it was because he had done something wrong. And in that case he had reason to be afraid.

"Because the outcome was always uncertain. It could happen that Heydrich would shrug it off, but it could also happen that he would punish harshly . . . In this respect he had a rather fickle temperament.

He might make a fantastic speech . . . but what he really did depended on his mood at the moment and on the special circumstances. He was impulsive.

"And because not everyone was willing to oppose him, it was dangerous to oppose him. Well, not dangerous, but it was difficult to oppose him. And most people didn't. So gradually the rumor developed that he had been a fearful man, a frightening man. In reality, he was a person just like we are."

"Did you ever argue with Heydrich?" I asked.

"Argue with him? Yes and no—there are always disputes when you work with someone. But as his subordinate I did not actually argue with him. The subordinate always loses. I used a different method. I sulked. I pouted . . . Like little children do. That's what I did to Heydrich. Then we would not speak for a week or so; he would send me memos—'I am going to be in Hamburg tomorrow evening.'

"I must say, I was not very argumentative. I laughed easily. I couldn't work well if I was not cheerful. It contributed to an easy cooperation with my colleagues, and it kept me from taking many things too seriously. So I always tried to cheer up quickly, even when I had been seriously annoyed. It helped me to get over it quicker. And Heydrich knew that, and mentioned it occasionally . . . Let's say we were discussing something and I was of a different opinion, and he would say, 'We are going to do it this way.' And then he would say, 'Go on, do your grinning outside the office. Go outside before you start to laugh.'"

Such levity may seem to indicate that members of the Gestapo had no reason for fear during the Third Reich, yet even this apparent exception proves illusory. Himmler and Heydrich were said to fear each other, according to office gossips, most of whom expected an eventual showdown. ("Many people were scared out of their skins when they met my husband—even sometimes, Heinrich Himmler," Frau Heydrich once remarked to me, refusing however to elaborate.)

In fact, both the chief of the German Police and the SS and the chief of the Security Police and the SD (to use their official titles) knew their uneasy but highly successful partnership could not be dissolved—at least until after the war. During the war, they had other fears, of the special kind reserved for the men who did the dirty work, men who called themselves "bearers of secrets." The psychological disposition to play "hide and seek" with the sordid realities of Nazism intensified year by year as the regime grew steadily more brutal. Just as "normal" citizens feared knowing the real truth (because then they might have to act), so Himmler's elite vanguard feared acknowledging the horrors they knew well (because then they might be unable to act). According to a woman whose father commanded a police murder squad, "When there were shootings and one of the men had trouble pulling the trigger, my father would laugh and say, 'Oh, he's thinking about his kids back home.'" When independent thinking is forbidden, laughter, however mirthless, may be socially useful as a way to "get over it quicker."

In his memoir, *Timebends: A Life*, the playwright Arthur Miller, writing about America and the Vietnam War, described the "culture of denial," speculating that perhaps "we all tended to deaden our connections, and hence our psyches, to those actions we found it difficult to justify." To the Nazis, confronting their connections to the rest of humankind could be immobilizing. In a world where morality had been inverted, and it was politically correct for the strong to attack the weak, salvation lay in maintaining emotional distance from the objects of persecution. This required rigid defenses, rigidly maintained. When the defenses broke down, however temporarily, so too did the shaky new standards of right and wrong.

Heydrich was said to have given standing orders that no woman related to a police prisoner be admitted to Himmler's presence, in case she broke into tears, which might move him to mercy. Heydrich himself was reputed to be much tougher, rarely pardoning anyone. When he did bend, it was usually to avoid an unpleasant confrontation with the tiny segment of humanity to whom he acknowledged a connection. Thomas Heydrich, the son of Heydrich's younger brother, Heinz, remembers that his father used "rather frequently" to call "the palace" and make an appointment with his brother:

> To go to my uncle and say, "Look, you've got someone in custody . . . You've arrested so-and-so, how could you, have you gone insane? He's a really nice fellow; she's a really nice woman. So release the person." And this was taken care of immediately. As far as we know, my uncle never once refused my father what he wanted when it was a matter of letting someone out of a concentration camp . . .
>
> My aunt told my mother later that when my uncle would come

home in the evening or whenever and say, "Heinz came by again today," she would respond, "Well, I guess someone had to be let free again, right?" It was obviously a Heydrich family joke.

"I want to say one more thing, and then we can close this out," Bruno Streckenbach told me. "I give the impression of a pleasant, cheerful atmosphere. And we did not always weep, but always in the background there was our work. Our work, which depressed all of us—at least all of the ones I observed. You cannot just forget such things. Problems that would arise in the course of a war—especially this, the greatest war of ideologies the world had ever known. They would eventually come across our desks at the Security Police and had to be handled. And these were not things you could just shrug off. Nebe's instability, Müller's short temper, all of it you have to consider against that background."

Perhaps the "background" offers additional explanation of Heydrich's short temper during his encounter with the hostile journalists of the *Stammtisch*. Like Bruno Streckenbach and almost all of the rest of his Gestapo companions—men who spent their days deciding the fate of others—Heydrich believed that "you should not judge yourself." He must have thought he would be damned before he let *foreigners* judge him.

Heydrich felt himself to be an "ideological soldier," an elite knight of Nazism, bound by an oath of obedience to Hitler that absolved him from all ordinary standards. "You'll see," he told one of his subordinates. "The day will come when Adolf Hitler is regarded as greater than Jesus Christ!" "Someday," he told a visiting dignitary, "people will thank us for what we have taken on ourselves." Yet what Heydrich expected most Germans to look up to in admiration, they turned away from in fear. In the end, the lords of the Secret Police were themselves imprisoned by the terror they created. As the great war of ideologies continued, the leaders of the SS turned east to play the roles for which they are best known to us. Thomas Heydrich himself thinks of them today as "devils in human form."

15

THE HOUSE ACROSS THE WAY

"[Canaris] was always his own spy."

—LINA HEYDRICH

ONE DAY BACK IN JANUARY 1935, Reinhard and Lina Heydrich had taken their new baby out from their Berlin home for a stroll in his pram, and happened to run into Heydrich's former commander on the training ship *Berlin*, Captain Wilhelm Canaris, whose wife, Erika, Heydrich had impressed with his musical skills. Lina Heydrich used to insist that this meeting was the purest surprise: the two men had not met for twelve years, and had totally lost track of each other.

Well, it makes a nice story, but it cannot possibly be true. Their lives were already deeply entangled, and they were destined to be bitter rivals. Lina's report of their dialogue may be accurate enough; but if so, these were the opening lines of a mutual charade: "Why hello, Heydrich," Canaris is alleged to have said. "Fancy running into you!"

"Herr Kapitän!" Heydrich replied, clicking his heels as if he were still aboard ship. "Do you live in Berlin?"

"Sometimes. I hope we shall see something of each other. Are you still so interested in music?"

Heydrich would probably have spurned such an overture from any other naval officer he had loved and lost. But Wilhelm Canaris had treated him with extraordinary kindness. It wasn't just that he had invited a miserably lonely boy home to join his wife's string quartet, thus transforming his musical skill from a curse into a social asset;

Erika and Wilhelm Canaris pictured in 1944 at their home in Berlin, where they socialized with their neighbors, the Heydrichs. Walter Schellenberg recalled that in 1941, Canaris tried in vain to convince Heydrich that a German invasion of Russia would be detrimental to Germany.

Canaris had also entertained his young guest with stories of his exploits as a spy—and a spymaster. Some of these bits of espionage lore had no doubt even adorned the fanciful plan for an SS Secret Service that Heydrich employed to bedazzle Himmler into giving him a job. Clever, daring Captain Canaris may have been the closest thing to a role model that Reinhard Heydrich ever had.

And so at their chance meeting the dreaded young chief of the Security Service apparently smiled at the much older man before him and said he certainly was still interested in music. Once again Canaris offered an invitation: "Splendid! We can have a musical evening. And there's a croquet lawn in our garden."

From that day on, until Heydrich's death eight years later, the two men and their families met often in an intimate relationship that included musical evenings, informal dinners, croquet afternoons, Sunday brunches, and shared celebrations of all kinds. These would have been easy to arrange: since 1936, they had also been the nearest of neighbors in the Berlin district of Schlachtensee. Their houses sat on adjoining streets, with an easy way between them through their back gardens.

And yet given the opposing career objectives of the two men, and the striking differences in the way their lives came to an end—the one by assassination while a rising Nazi leader, the other by execution for high treason against the Nazis—their ambiguous friendship must be counted as unique among their cohorts.

Intercourse between the two households was so casual that Canaris's two daughters, who sometimes took messages back and forth, were allowed to remain unsupervised in Heydrich's home. One day the chief of the SD discovered Canaris's thirteen-year-old riffling through the drawers of his desk. Heydrich told the girl, "One doesn't do that!" and sent her home. Afterward he marveled to his wife that the Canaris children were "snooping already!"

As Nazis were wont to do, Heydrich was dabbling in conversational eugenics, for Canaris was regarded as an insatiably curious man, a natural-born snoop. As a child, he had been nicknamed *der Kieker* ("the peeper"); in the First World War, he deliberately chose "Herr Kika" as a nom de guerre.

When the war broke out, Canaris had been an ordinary naval officer. Then his ship was captured by the British off the coast of Argentina. The German officers were all interned, but Canaris managed to escape. Speaking Spanish and using a fake passport, he traveled by land and sea all the way back to Germany. After that, he was asked to organize a secret U-boat command post in Spain, where he built up such a solid network of contacts that much of it was still available for use twenty-three years later when the next war broke out.

In 1916, however, he was exposed as a spy and had to flee. Attempting to sneak through Italy disguised as a Chilean invalid, he was arrested in Genoa, but managed to slip away, narrowly avoiding execution. He returned to Spain, and finally escaped from Cartagena harbor at night in a submarine vainly pursued by British and French gunboats.

When the war ended, Canaris found it hard to settle down. Like almost all of his fellow officers, he was a conservative monarchist, and despised the new Weimar democracy. Nevertheless, at that time he began to play the political double games that occupied him for the rest of his life. On the one hand, he served as adjutant to Gustave Noske,

Wilhelm Canaris and Heydrich engaged in a power play once Canaris was named chief of the Abwehr. The rivalry was believed to have fueled Canaris's deepest doubts about Nazism, which would culminate in his involvement in the failed July 1944 attempt on Hitler's life that would result in Canaris's own execution.

the Socialist minister of defense in the Weimar Republic. On the other, he lent his talent for intrigue to various right-wing conspiracies.

Canaris personally abhorred violence, but he defended those who used it. Appointed one of the judges in the trial of the naval officers responsible for the brutal bludgeoning murders of the Communist leaders Rosa Luxemburg and Karl Liebknecht, Canaris manipulated behind the scenes to get them acquitted. Only when his escapades were denounced in a liberal newspaper did Captain Canaris consent to presumably hazardless duty aboard the tiny fleet of training ships permitted by the Treaty of Versailles. It was at this juncture that cadet Heydrich appeared on the scene, and Canaris invited him home for dinner and a little house music.

Thirteen years later, in January 1936, Wilhelm Canaris and Reinhard Heydrich would sit down together at an elegant Berlin restaurant and formally inaugurate one of the most controversial partnerships in the history of espionage. It has vexed historians ever since, as they attempt to trace a relationship so complicated that no one has clearly established whether the two men were close friends or bitter rivals—or, more likely, both at the same time.

Such ambivalent associations flourished within the warped confines of Hitler's game of power, which forced all the Nazi leaders into vicious competition, while insisting they were also blood brothers of the *Volk* community. Canaris and Heydrich—particularly Heydrich—seemed to have become entangled in the affectional bond most encouraged by Nazism: the love-hate relationship.

So, on that freezing January day when the two men met, they did so for the first time as professional equals: Canaris had just been named chief of the Abwehr, a post that placed him on a collision course with Heydrich in his SD role of head of political intelligence for the Nazi Party.

In fact, Canaris and Heydrich were meeting on terrain contested throughout centuries of German history. The German Secret Service had been founded in the eighteenth century by Frederick the Great, who authorized a former diplomat and soldier, Baron Colmar von der Goltz, to gather information about his numerous foes. After Frederick, however, the Secret Service was split into two parts—political (usually handled by the Secret Police) and military (under the aegis of the Army General Staff).

This separation created a troubled heritage of constant disputes. As far back as 1809, a Westphalian police commissioner demanded sole jurisdiction over all aspects of national security, thereby giving Himmler a precedent. The General Staff successfully resisted this encroachment, and during the First World War managed to get the intelligence function assigned to their own Colonel Walter Nicolai. "The Father of the Lie," as Nicolai was dubbed by his stifled opponents, nevertheless thought of himself as saving the country from reckless behavior by upstart politicians. "The intelligence service is the domain of gentlemen," he argued. "If it is left to others, it will collapse."

His words fell on receptive ears: during the war, Wilhelm Canaris had attended an intelligence course given by Colonel Nicolai. On arriving at the War Ministry as Abwehr chief, Canaris told his staff, "We must have a high idea of the rights of man, of international law and morality. I need gentlemen in the Abwehr and not unscrupulous gangsters."

Canaris certainly knew that Heydrich was already being reviled in some military circles as a "political gangster," yet he also knew that he owed his important new job to Heydrich's machinations.

Canaris's predecessor was another naval officer, Conrad Patzig. Hitler had ordered Heydrich's security network and the Abwehr to pool their information, but Patzig, an open foe of the SS since the murders of military officers during the Röhm purge, often refused to cooperate. When Heydrich wanted to know the names of all the Abwehr agents in Germany, Patzig turned him down. When Heydrich wanted a list of clandestine munitions factories, Patzig said he didn't have one. Finally, both sides turned to Werner von Blomberg, army minister in Hitler's new cabinet, but he vacillated, first telling Patzig to try to get along with the SS, then asking Himmler to dismiss Heydrich instead. Himmler refused.

Matters came to a head in the autumn of 1934 when the Abwehr was caught taking clandestine aerial photographs of the French Maginot Line, an action prohibited by the Versailles Treaty. Heydrich complained that such recklessness endangered German security, and von Blomberg agreed. Patzig was forced to resign.

As his last act in office, Patzig resolved to recommend a successor who might be able to check Heydrich's growing power. In Canaris he chose an old friend who had once been able to give Heydrich orders, and established amicable relations with Himmler and Hitler. The trouble was that Admiral Erich Raeder, commander in chief of the navy, distrusted Canaris's chameleon nature. "I can't work with that man!" he said. (He hadn't been able to work with Heydrich, either: it had been Raeder's decision that sealed his dishonorable discharge from the navy.) Yet no other candidate had Canaris's credentials, and in the end, Raeder consented. Before he left, Patzig warned Canaris to be careful of Heydrich and his bright young men. Canaris shrugged it off. "I am well disposed toward those youngsters," he said.

At first, the good feelings were mutual. Heydrich told his wife he was surprised by Canaris's appointment, but "personally very pleased. I hope we'll be able to understand each other."

Heydrich may have been surprised that the military had actually chosen Canaris, but it is inconceivable that he would not have checked up on Patzig's friends, particularly since the SD was responsible for reviewing the political reliability of Abwehr personnel. And of course, the perennially curious Canaris would also have followed his former subordinate's new career with interest. If each thought it prudent to ignore all this when they met in the park, it was because such a duplicitous style suited them both. The hypocrisy and intense theatricality of public life in Nazi Germany favored those, like Heydrich and Canaris, who never told a simple truth if they could play a double game instead. They understood each other very well indeed.

For the first few years after Canaris took over the Abwehr, it was the amiable side of the understanding that predominated. The two men were now neighbors twice over. The War Ministry was just a block away from Heydrich's SD headquarters, and members of both the SD and the Abwehr referred to each other as "the house across the way."

To ensure neighborly cooperation, Canaris appointed an ardent Nazi, Colonel Rudolf Bamler, as his organizational liaison to Heydrich. (Bamler was a frequent guest in the Heydrich household; "He was our best agent inside the Abwehr," Frau Heydrich told me.) Heydrich, in turn, chose as liaison his smoothest diplomat, Dr. Werner Best. Best spoke Spanish and shared Canaris's intense interest in Spain. They exchanged books on history and philosophy, and sometimes met each other for early-morning horseback rides in the Tiergarten. Soon Heydrich joined them, stabling his horse in the stall next to Canaris's.

Lower down in the hierarchy, convivial "beer evenings" were fostered between SD and Abwehr staff members. The formerly feuding participants were dubious, waiting for the inevitable explosion to drive Heydrich and Canaris apart. Instead, they arranged a weeklong conference between their two organizations. Both leaders gave inspirational speeches, and then their underlings adjourned for a series of workshops on the mechanics of collaboration. An Abwehr officer kept a copy of the agenda, which covered an immense range of topics from security in military barracks, defense plans, and airports to supervision of foreign officers, to defense against spies during Reich Party Day. The Abwehr seems to have served as host (Canaris launched the proceedings with a friendly greeting to all), but one long day—9 a.m. to 8 p.m.—was spent at Gestapo headquarters, where Heydrich spoke about the goals of the SD and the need for cooperation with both the military and the police. Every day, time was allotted for "subsequent discussion," and "regulation of closer cooperation"—all in addition to joint lunches, group outings, and "comradely gatherings."

Yet despite these feats of forced friendship, Canaris and Heydrich, like rulers of small, related principalities, were constantly negotiating their respective spheres of influence. On January 17, 1935 (soon after their "surprise" street encounter), they finally signed a formal treaty. Immediately christened the "Ten Commandments," it listed five areas of expertise assigned to the Abwehr and five allotted to the SD. They could not agree on the exact apportioning of counterespionage tasks, so they left them vague—just as Hitler had done with their deliberately overlapping responsibilities.

At first, the SD and Abwehr avoided the "friction" so valued by the

Führer. SD officers relied heavily on the older and better-developed Abwehr files, and Abwehr personnel used the SS-controlled police when they needed to take someone into custody. (The Abwehr, like the SD, had no formal powers of arrest.)

An example from those early days shows both the extent and the limitation of their mutual cooperation. Shortly before Canaris took over, Patzig's counterespionage section had been on the trail of a spy ring operating among the highest social circles in Berlin. The ringleader was a handsome Polish officer, Jurik von Sosnowski, who carefully courted the secretaries at the War Ministry. These were often unhappy young women from military families reduced to penury by the German defeat. Relying on his personal magnetism, Sosnowski lured them into compromising situations—including orgies at his elegant apartment—and then blackmailed them into copying the documents that passed across their desks. Sometimes he also paid their bills, enabling a few of his better agents to return to their grand, prewar lifestyle.

This intricate romantic edifice was obviously too fragile to endure. Eventually Sosnowski was denounced to the SS by one of his paramours at approximately the same time that the Abwehr had began to investigate another woman's sudden wealth. The organizations pooled their resources, finally staging a joint raid on Sosnowski's flat—cleverly timing their arrival to coincide with a wild party featuring an exotic dancer. At the sensational trial that followed, the SD and Abwehr cooperated again, passing the relevant files back and forth until Sosnowski was convicted.

Canaris had been appalled that Poland would stoop to utilizing female spies: it wasn't a gentlemanly thing to do. Scornfully, an Abwehr agent wrote across the top of Sosnowski's file: "Rotten through and through with no political ideals. Money, women, horses, and social life with him take the place of ethics."

That ended it for Canaris, but not for Heydrich, who phoned Walter Schellenberg, his Foreign Intelligence chief, to order him to determine if any of Sosnowski's agents were "recoverable for our Secret Service. You've got ten days to send me your report."

This was a great opportunity for the ambitious young man. Schellenberg himself loved money, women, horses, and social life. He threw himself into his research, methodically characterizing the qualities of Sosnowski's lady friends. He rejected one woman for "political infantilism," but another won higher marks. Schellenberg asked Heydrich for permission to visit her in prison. Afterward he concluded she could be "salvaged," whereupon Heydrich asked the Ministry of Justice to suspend prosecution in her case. The unfortunate woman was taken directly from jail to Schellenberg's office, where he told her that judicial proceedings could always be reinstated if she didn't cooperate. She went back to work for the Poles, while simultaneously denouncing her fellow agents to the SD. (Schellenberg also claimed, with typical immodesty, that she had fallen in love with him.)

In espionage jargon, he had "turned" an agent. The word gives an innocuous gloss to the cruel life-and-death decisions entrusted to a young man in his twenties. Yet the venerable Abwehr also turned agents, manipulating the instincts of fear and affection just as Schellenberg had done. In truth, the techniques of penetrating another country's defenses in order to uncover damaging information are generally unsavory, whoever is in charge. The "game of foxes" involves deceit, treachery, and every kind of double dealing; it assumes a willingness to exploit others for one's own advantage and demands constant vigilance in return.

Canaris and Heydrich shared a profession in which paranoia, mendacity, and cynicism are often essential to survival. Canaris sometimes joked that only his dachshunds were certain not to betray him.

Heydrich constantly worried that his associates were scheming against him. He once rebuked Werner Best for displaying a sign with the motto "In the end, truth always gets the better of any enemy." In "real life that principle is nonsense!" Heydrich snarled. In his gentler style, Canaris told a subordinate, "You are the ideal intelligence man. You always tell the truth, and in our service no one believes that."

Old-fashioned heroism among members of both services was not impossible: in August 1941, after the Allied invasion of Iran, the SD sent two men to assist an Abwehr agent fleeing from Teheran. The vastly outnumbered trio fought off various attackers until they were surrounded, and taken prisoner.

Generally, however, the two organizations met on more problematic moral ground. Canaris dearly loved a *ruse de guerre*, and for a few years SD men revered him as the grand old man of stratagems. Even Himmler sometimes bypassed Heydrich to go to Canaris with exotic projects, such as his own idea that the Abwehr should arrange to doctor the wine rations of the French troops with an undetectable purgative in order to render them temporarily helpless. As Schellenberg remarked, the Reichsführer did not understand much about the limitations of Secret Service work. Still, Abwehr experts did manage to produce explosives cleverly disguised as lumps of coal or oranges, designed detonators that could be set to go off after a delay of forty days, and claimed to have discovered the microdot, or secret message reduced to the size of a printed period.

Alfred Naujocks, Heydrich's master of dirty tricks, who was frantically trying to build up a comparable technical section for the SD, claimed the same thing. The debilitating confusion of Hitler's system of *divide et impera* is epitomized in this tiny example of wasteful competition and unnecessary duplication of function. Nazi Germany did not need two microdots; it needed one unified intelligence service, and more important, one definition of correct behavior acceptable to all. In the end, it was their differing conceptions of honor at least as much as competitive ambition that finally destroyed the alliance between Heydrich and his former mentor.

It had long been apparent to every observer that Canaris and Heydrich made an especially unlikely pair of collaborators. If one considers only the obvious evidence of appearances and surroundings, the two men would seem to have inhabited entirely incompatible worlds. Heydrich's headquarters were in an airy baroque palace filled with grand stairways, marble floors, saluting sentries. By contrast, to reach Canaris's office in the old War Ministry building required a lonely trek through dimly lit passages resembling a labyrinth.

On arriving at the lair of the Abwehr chief, the visitor was ushered into a shabby room, barely furnished with standard-issue military desks and chairs. Canaris was only five feet three inches tall, usually dressed in rumpled uniforms, and unassuming in manner. Some say he lisped. His hair had been snow white for years; he was seventeen years older than Heydrich, and appeared ancient. (His SS rivals sometimes referred to him derisively as "Father Christmas.") An aide would warn first-time visitors, "The admiral doesn't look like much, but he's as sharp as they come." (In contrast, Heydrich's adjutants assumed everyone knew that their splendidly attired boss was lethally sharp; what they spoke sotto voce about was the sort of mood he might be in.)

Heydrich, who of course was no longer a naval officer, usually acted like one anyway, clipping his words and speaking tersely. But Admiral Canaris (he had been promoted when he took over the Abwehr) cultivated an eccentric style. He professed never to trust tall men or people with big ears, left meetings at ten o'clock in the evening no matter what was happening, and in a stoic society of would-be warriors, talked openly of his insomnia and minor illnesses. He doted on his two pet dachshunds and brought them to the office, where he played with them behind closed doors. He also took his pets on official journeys. Allied cipher experts occasionally intercepted "important" radio messages about the bowel movements of his dogs, and were dumbfounded to discover these were not in code after all.

People liked to describe Canaris as mysterious and inscrutable, an attitude he encouraged. Among the scarce personal mementos on his desk was a trio of brass monkeys said to illustrate the Abwehr adage, "See all, hear all, say nothing." On Heydrich's desk stood his model of an SS fencer, ready for open combat. A picture of Hitler graced his office as well. In Canaris's rooms, pride of place was given instead to a rendering of an alleged ancestor, a Greek brigand also named Canaris.

Lina Heydrich told me she remembered the picture: "I can still see it—an etching. It showed a man in a fantasy costume, and he had a flag and it was fluttering, and this was Canaris the freedom fighter. But it wasn't true. It was all dramatics."

Canaris's whimsical streak often placed him at odds with the grim, gray norms of Nazi etiquette, yet oddly, his peers seem to have found this endearing. Gossips loved to repeat his double-edged remarks. Once, for instance, Canaris and a few of his aides were driving in an open car through a rural part of Spain when the admiral suddenly stood up in his seat and offered a solemn salute to a nearby herd of sheep. "You never know," he said. "One of them might be a superior officer."

There was more to Canaris, however, than mere iconoclastic charm: sometimes a steeliness flashed up from beneath the surface play of whimsy. At staff conferences, he would take out a cigar, wait through the inevitable moment when all present leaned forward to offer him a light, then suddenly whip out his own match after theirs had burned out. Like Heydrich, he often interrupted the reports of his subordinates to offer cutting comments, to tell them to hurry up, or to challenge their point of view. Sometimes he pushed them so far that they were forced to admit they were no longer certain of any of their premises— which Canaris said would teach them the elusive nature of truth.

Eventually, his young SD rivals also discovered Canaris's wily refusal to be confined by fixed notions of either reality or proper behavior. Sometimes he made strange requests to have people arrested without any evidence. Perhaps he was using the police to further his own personal intrigues? The Heydrichs, too, began to wonder how far they could trust him. Frau Heydrich told of a "dark-skinned man, a Negro" named Mohammed that Canaris brought back from Marseilles to wait on his guests. He reassured them, "You may speak freely; Mohammed does not speak a word of German." His guests believed him, but later someone discovered that Mohammed spoke German "fluently."

Heydrich began to caution his men against "that old fox you can't be too careful about." Canaris started to describe Heydrich as "that most clever beast." Their choice of language was one more sign of the "peculiar affinity" between foxy, eccentric Canaris and wolfish, aggressive Heydrich. In 1937, a photographer took a picture of them seated side by side at a formal banquet, both wearing identical expressions of feral wariness.

The wolf, however, usually hunts in packs; the fox alone. Heydrich exerted tight control over both SD policy and individual operations. Since he had carefully chosen men capable of independent action, his supervision was sporadic but carefully timed. Having given a definite assignment (e.g., "report in ten days"), he usually left people alone, but his restless spirit hovered over their activities. Directing, requesting constant reportage, occasionally intervening, Heydrich played across the structures of the SD like a man sitting at an organ. He himself sometimes boasted that it was his musical instincts that told him which keys to press.

Canaris, by contrast, played most skillfully on men, not organizations. Many people found Heydrich terrifying, but almost everyone— including Hitler and Himmler—had a soft spot for the foxy "little admiral." For years, this gave him a great advantage over Heydrich, particularly when coupled with his right of "first report" to Hitler. As head of the Abwehr, Canaris could communicate directly with the Führer whenever he wished; Heydrich had to go through Himmler.

On the other hand, not even his greatest apologists argue that Canaris was a clear thinker or skilled leader of a large organization. He hated paperwork; sitting in an office made him fidget. Going out in the field to gather information firsthand was his deepest pleasure. His constant journeying throughout Europe contributed to Canaris's legendary image as a "wily Odysseus," but it also meant he was frequently out of the office, unable to lead or consult.

Unlike Heydrich, Canaris was not regarded by his staff as a good judge of character. He was too impulsive in his judgments, too tolerant of failure, and too easily swayed by deceit and flattery. Debilitating rivalries sprang up as his sectional leaders connived and maneuvered to catch his wavering attention.

Even his finesse as a master spy was questionable. Once, while traveling incognito during a top-secret trip, Canaris sent his shirts to the laundry but forgot to remove the name labels sewn inside the collars. Soon he was being paged by his real name over the hotel loudspeaker system.

"Canaris was a complicated individual," one of his subordinates observed, and this was one of the simplest things anyone ever said about him. William Shirer has described the resulting muddle: "Canaris was so shadowy a figure that no two writers agree as to what kind of man he was or what he believed in, if anything, much." This is actually an understatement: forty years after one of the bitterest wars in history, many historians are not sure what side he was on.

Soon after the war, the British Intelligence leader, Sir Stewart Graham Menzies, chief of MI6, hinted that Canaris had played "an extraordinary game." A British undersecretary of state went even further: "Well, our intelligence was not badly equipped. As you know, we had Admiral Canaris."

The man who during the war had been characterized in the enemy press as "the trainer of Heydrich and Himmler in the arts of murder" now appeared one of their most determined foes. The story beneath the story of the long rivalry between the chief of military intelligence and the chief of political intelligence began to emerge.

Reinhard Heydrich and Wilhelm Canaris were not just friends, not just organizational rivals: a very few years after their cozy familial visit over the baby carriage, they also became engaged in a duel to the death involving nothing less than their lives and the future of their country. What makes the story really interesting is that they were performing all three roles simultaneously. That is an extraordinary game, indeed. But for it to happen, Heydrich had to press much further along Hitler's Via

Barbarossa than Canaris could bear to go. His next step would involve a disastrous redefinition of the nature of the enemy they both, allegedly, faced. And once he had completed that step, he had one last series of projects to undertake before he could begin the actual destruction of the enemy.

16

DRAWING THE LINE: THE ABWEHR RESISTANCE

"[Canaris] was a minor spy, nothing else! He only had a certain importance because he had been a traitor!"

—LINA HEYDRICH

T HE PECULIAR LOVE-HATE relationship between Reinhard Hey-drich and Wilhelm Canaris runs threadlike—or, better, tripwire-like—through the sometimes seismic, sometimes absurd, events that led Nazi Germany finally into World War II, at times reflecting them, at times affecting them, but always there, threatening to trip up or blow up those who stumbled across it.

Take for instance the contest between Himmler's and Heydrich's SS and Canaris's Abwehr. It was inevitable that those Germans who resisted the Nazis would have cast hopeful eyes on the one organization viewed as both strong and secure, namely the Abwehr, originally, in 1920, set up as a spy agency within the Defense Ministry, and in 1938 made part of Hitler's Supreme Command of the Armed Forces, or OKW (for Oberkommando der Wehrmacht), under Admiral Wilhelm Canaris. According to Hans Bernd Gisevius, who became an anti-Nazi historian, only the Abwehr had "the capacity for finding out practically everything worth knowing in a 'legal' fashion," and for assembling "evidence without arousing suspicion."

Soon after Canaris moved into his new office at the Defense Ministry, Gisevius came to present evidence of Gestapo abuses before the man he thought "was craftier than Himmler and Heydrich put together." Unfortunately, an informer of Heydrich's in the Abwehr, Lieutenant

Police official Hans Bernd Gisevius (age forty-two, in 1946) belonged to a small circle of German counterintelligence agents aligned with Canaris against the Nazis. "To Gisevius," said a colleague, "a victory for Hitler meant the end of Christian civilization, and of Western culture, and possibly in the world."

General Rudolf Bamler, was also present. The very next day, Heydrich himself phoned Gisevius in a rage, berating him for trying to "sway" Canaris against the Gestapo at a time when all were working to bring about a reconciliation. "Please take note of the fact that I can see my deadly enemies to the grave!" Heydrich snarled before both men slammed down their receivers. They never spoke to each other again.

For a long time after that, Canaris avoided Gisevius. Heydrich's fit of rage had evoked a compensating reaction in the Abwehr chief without the two men ever having to speak directly about the matter. In any case, Gestapo abuses did not much bother the authoritarian Canaris. Only when the SD turned against his beloved military did the little admiral begin the peculiar metamorphosis that turned him into legend.

His path toward a martyr's death emerged gradually out of the underbrush of service rivalries. One day during the winter of 1936, Heydrich asked Canaris to lunch, and requested a briefing on the contacts between the Russian and German armies since the First World War. (Both outcasts at the war's end, the two countries had launched a policy of military cooperation; some of the participating officers had even become friends.) After lunch Heydrich asked to see the Abwehr files containing the officers' correspondence. By now puzzled and wary, Canaris said he would be happy to comply if the Führer ordered it. Heydrich wondered if Canaris might just let him look at the files on an unofficial basis. Canaris regretted that he could not disobey regulations, and Heydrich apparently dropped the matter.

In fact, he merely moved outside the realm of regulations. What the SD could not receive legally, it was willing to steal. Heydrich had heard from an informer that Marshal Mikhail Tukhachevsky, the former commander in chief of the Red Army and now an important military theorist, might be plotting with German officers to overthrow Stalin, and he hoped to use this information to engineer a purge in Russia, so as to weaken Russia militarily. When a mysterious fire broke out in the Abwehr file room, SD agents borrowed a few documents. Finding no evidence of a plot, they were told to fabricate one. Heydrich's trickster Alfred Naujocks ordered his forgers to go to work copying the signatures of various Soviet generals, including Mikhail Tukhachevsky. These were attached to fake letters discussing Stalin's imminent demise, then sold via a double agent to Stalin's Secret Police. The agent was instructed to ask a high price, in German money, cash only—the final touch in a plan Naujocks felt was, as one commentator describes it, "a typical Heydrich brain-child, grandiose, dashing, murderously subtle."

Stalin paid the cost. In due course, Tukhachevsky was executed, along with many Soviet generals, in a great purge that decimated the officer corps and weakened their combat readiness. Heydrich boasted of his great espionage coup. Only after the war did historians discover Stalin had been planning to purge the marshal anyway, and had paid for the SD forgeries with forged banknotes of his own.

In 1936, however, Canaris thought Heydrich had helped the Communists murder Russian officers, behavior he thought incompatible with a German officer's code of honor. He was shocked, even after Heydrich told him it had been the Führer's idea. A year later, during a lunch with his predecessor, Captain Conrad Patzig, Canaris was discussing Himmler and Heydrich, and suddenly exclaimed, "Those men are criminals!" Patzig advised him to resign. "No, I cannot do that," Canaris replied, "because Heydrich would succeed me."

Canaris often gave vent to transitory doubts or fears about other Nazis, and then later changed his mind, but he was absolutely single-minded about a long-held conviction: another war would destroy Germany. Hitler's desire to harm the Soviet army suggested that war was on his mind, and after what became known as the notorious "Blomberg-Fritsch affair," in February 1938, Hitler's plans could no longer be doubted. The resulting scandal might have ended Heydrich's career and could conceivably even have brought down the Nazi regime. For a few

General Werner von Blomberg (age fifty-six, in 1934), commander in chief of the German Army, suffered as a result of Hermann Göring's envy. Employing the Gestapo to investigate von Blomberg's new bride, Erna Gruhn (thirty-five years Blomberg's junior), after the couple's 1938 wedding, Göring discovered she had been a prostitute who also posed for pornographic photos. Göring used the information to blackmail von Blomberg into tendering his resignation.

days in March 1938 the Secret Police itself was on trial, undergoing the pitiless scrutiny usually reserved for others.

It all started with the disastrous second marriage of Field Marshal Werner von Blomberg. This handsome, elderly man who served as war minister in Hitler's cabinet had been a widower for several years. When he announced his desire to marry again, all Berlin was agog at his choice: one Fräulein Erna Gruhn, a pretty young typist at the Reich Egg Marketing Board. Even in the New Order it was shocking for a general to marry so far beneath his class. Indeed, von Blomberg had been worried enough to seek advice beforehand from Hermann Göring, who told him to relax, the Nazis welcomed an alliance with a woman of the people.

A few days after the small wedding ceremony on January 12, 1938 (attended by both Göring and Hitler), a member of the Berlin Vice Squad was perusing some obscene photographs when he recognized one of the women depicted. She was the new Frau von Blomberg, who, he discovered, had a criminal record of ill repute.

In his pungent English, the former SS journalist Gunter d'Alquen described the policeman's reaction: "Good gracious, I found something that can't be possible!" As d'Alquen put it, "She had been entangled in an affair with dirty pictures . . . The wife of the highest German Army officer, who had been married under the testimony of Göring and Hitler, was mixed up in an affair impossible to think about."

As d'Alquen tells it, the news traveled "in a normal way" to Himmler, who "was shocked" as if he had suffered "a stroke." He discussed the problem with Heydrich and they decided Himmler had to tell Göring. Other sources hold that Count Wolf von Helldorf, the police president of Berlin, had bypassed Himmler and given the politically explosive information to von Blomberg's son-in-law, General Wilhelm Keitel, supreme commander of the armed forces, and Keitel, always irresolute in a crisis, had turned for advice to Hermann Göring.

In any case, Göring had long wanted to replace Keitel and be war minister himself. Now he grabbed the opportunity to strike against a troublesome competitor—or two. The timing was perfect, for Hitler was growing impatient with his chief military advisers. In November 1937, he had told his highest generals he was considering war against Czechoslovakia or Poland. Von Blomberg had opposed the idea, and so had Werner von Fritsch, commander in chief of the Wehrmacht.

Seizing the moment, Göring presented his Führer with the file on Frau von Blomberg. As expected, Hitler demanded her husband's resignation. Few of his fellow officers stood by the field marshal (nicknamed "the rubber lion") in his hour of need. Indeed, one of them, possibly encouraged by Heydrich's old nemesis Admiral Raeder, counseled suicide as the only way to restore von Blomberg's lost honor. (Instead, he went on holiday to Rome with his wife.)

On the heels of his announcement that the war minister had married a prostitute, Göring found another bombshell to detonate before Hitler: the commander in chief of the army, Colonel General Werner Thomas Ludwig Freiherr (Baron) von Fritsch, was a homosexual with a fondness for sleazy young men, one of whom had been blackmailing him for years.

This high-ranking officer was no rubber lion. A brilliant officer revered by his troops, he was regarded as the spokesman of the conservative military establishment, so opposed to the upstart Nazis. With his pinched aristocratic features, monocle, and trim little mustache, von Fritsch seemed the very embodiment of hallowed tradition.

Colonel General Werner von Fritsch (age sixty-five, circa 1935) was another official framed by Göring—falsely accused, in a case of mistaken identity, of being homosexual. Coming in rapid succession, the Blomberg and von Fritsch scandals triggered a shakeup of the German military that also saw sixteen senior generals retired and forty-four others demoted.

All the same, Göring insisted there was ample evidence against him. Von Fritsch had never married. He had once taken a member of the Hitler Youth into his home as a temporary resident. And the blackmailer had identified him, both by picture and by name, to the Secret Police.

In 1936, during a Gestapo campaign against homosexuality (declared a felony after the purge of Röhm), a petty criminal named Otto Schmidt had listed General von Fritsch as one of his lovers. Himmler, who considered homosexuality a "Jewish crime" that sapped Nordic warriors of their fighting will, was stunned, and hastened with the news to Hitler, who was then trying to placate the military, and thus refused to listen to such "filth." He ordered Himmler to tear up the file on von Fritsch. According to office legend, Heydrich destroyed the dossier "after his fashion"—that is, he preserved selected excerpts first.

Two years later, after von Fritsch's opposition to war became known, Gestapo agents shadowed the general during a trip to Egypt, hoping to catch him visiting its fleshpots. The Abwehr complained to Heydrich, who said the surveillance was not his idea, but Göring's. In January, Gestapo first lieutenant Josef Albert Meisinger, director of the Reich Coordinating Office for the Suppression of Homosexuality, launched a second investigation of von Fritsch; later he said Göring had ordered him to reassemble the "destroyed" file.

Hitler had always behaved respectfully toward the great gods of the General Staff, but after Göring's second disclosure, he flew into a monstrous rage at the moral abyss into which the army had fallen, and ordered von Fritsch to report to him at once.

When he heard the charges, von Fritsch answered Hitler in the appropriate military style: he gave his word of honor that they weren't true. "I do not accept your notion of honor!" Hitler stormed. The hitherto unassailable commander in chief had no behavior in his repertoire to counter such inconceivable behavior. Stunned into numbed silence, he left the chancellery, with the scandal spreading in waves before him.

Meanwhile, back at police headquarters, an inspector had been reviewing Schmidt's testimony when he suddenly realized the blackmailer had confused Baron von Fritsch with a retired cavalry officer named Achim von Frisch. Quick research confirmed the egregious error: von Frisch looked like his commander and even wore the same kind of coat. Moreover, he admitted to indiscretions with Schmidt. But it was too late. According to Walter Schellenberg's written account, "By the time Heydrich found out about the mistake, the file already lay on Hitler's desk."

If Himmler and Heydrich were to admit error now, Göring's machinations would be forgotten; it would look to all the world as if the SS had fabricated a coup to discredit the Wehrmacht, and gotten caught in the act. Heydrich therefore ordered a vast cover-up operation. Frantic detectives intensified their investigations of von Fritsch's associates, quite as if they were perfecting a faultless case against him. Meanwhile, the real homosexual officer disappeared into darkest protective custody, along with his blackmailer, Schmidt, who was bluntly informed that if he confessed his mistake now, he would die for it.

The leaders of the anti-Wehrmacht police must have expected to be unmasked at any moment. And then, they were struck with incredible luck. Though army officers were not subject to police jurisdiction, the illustrious General von Fritsch consented to questioning by the Gestapo. The interview was conducted by the same Meisinger whose department had made the mistaken identification—a man whose career was thus at stake—and he treated the baron with the insolent contempt usually reserved for criminals.

Witnesses were appalled (one even said that if the troops knew, they would have mutinied) but von Fritsch's behavior was the most shocking of all, for he endured the ignominy without storming out. The Gestapo had providentially arranged to record the scene on phonograph records.

Arthur Nebe (age forty-eight, in 1942) was head of the Reichskriminalpolizeiamt and reported directly to Heydrich. Discreetly harboring personal doubts about Nazism ever since Röhm was assassinated, Nebe turned whistleblower.

Presenting them to Hitler, Himmler interpreted the general's passivity as a sign of guilt.

On February 4, the Führer used the Blomberg-Fritsch scandal as a pretext for a purge of the army. Sixteen generals were dismissed, and the aristocratic antiwar diplomat Konstantin von Neurath was replaced as foreign minister by party stalwart Joachim von Ribbentrop, a former champagne salesman whose noble title was the fizziest ersatz. Bypassing Göring, Hitler announced that he himself would take the roles of war minister and commander in chief from the tainted hands of the men who had been the two most powerful officers in Germany. The way was now cleared for war.

It began to look as if Heydrich's bold effrontery had succeeded; the mud thrown at von Fritsch was obscuring the mistakes of his accusers. In February, however, the duplicitous Kripo chief, Arthur Nebe, leaked the real facts of the von Fritsch affair to his friends in the Abwehr resistance. Canaris was shocked into drastic action. Now it no longer mattered whether von Fritsch was homosexual or not: the issue had become the Gestapo's incompetence and mendacity. Canaris called for a military court of honor to assess the evidence in the case.

Once again Berlin roiled with rumors, as it had in 1934 before the murder of Röhm. Perhaps the army would at last take action against the SS, or even the Nazi Party. Large meetings requiring party potentates to gather in one place were canceled out of respect for the anxieties of the participants. Finally bowing to the pressure, Hitler agreed to convene a court of honor, jointly chaired by Göring (for the party) and lawyers appointed by the military. Himmler and Heydrich were not scheduled to testify, but they were most definitely on trial.

Lina Heydrich had told a German interviewer that her husband had been under immense nervous strain during this period. When I asked her about it, she decided, typically, to fix lunch. I could not induce her even to recognize the names von Fritsch and von Blomberg. We were discussing something else when she suddenly blurted out, "My husband had to go against the generals for immoral conduct—he, who had been thrown out of the navy for impropriety . . ."

I tried to hold her to the topic of her husband's embarrassment. "He didn't want to do it then?"

"No, when he himself . . . I think it is time for coffee . . ."

The alliance between Himmler and Heydrich shook as they braced for the expected storm of protest. Himmler began to talk about "bad staff work," distancing himself as usual from the errors of his subordinates. Heydrich, left alone far out on a breaking limb, seems to have succumbed momentarily to the terror he usually planned for others. Late one evening he ordered Walter Schellenberg to report at once to Gestapo headquarters—and to bring along his gun and a lot of ammunition. When he arrived, the young man found Heydrich in a "state of extreme tension. After dinner, he took a large number of aspirins. Then suddenly he said, without any preamble, 'If they don't march from Potsdam during the next hour and a half, the greatest danger will have passed.'"

Heydrich had heard through his informers that the army might move that very night against the SS. He and Schellenberg waited long hours, presumably ready to go down fighting, for an attack that never came. The military leaders had evidently decided to await the judgment of the tribunal.

The court convened in early March 1938, and heard one day of testimony. Providentially for those on trial, on the second day, German troops marched into Austria, incorporating it into the Reich. From a certain narrow perspective, a historian might be tempted to argue that Hitler decided on *Anschluss* to save the Gestapo. In any case, the trial ceased while Göring, Himmler, and Heydrich dashed to Vienna to fight for possession of spoils, files, and power.

Despite all his other problems, Heydrich still remained responsible for Hitler's security in Austria. During this turbulent period, Frau Heydrich also moved to Vienna, staying not with Reinhard in his headquarters in the Imperial Hotel, but with the family of Ernst Kaltenbrunner (who would one day take her husband's place as security chief). Her memoirs offer a glowing description of the Kaltenbrunners' ancient house, where odors of medieval spices still filled the air, and she felt "immediately at home" in the presence of "real tradition, true patricianhood."

Beyond the fragrant house, however, things were less satisfying. To the union of Austria and Germany, she admitted only the dimmest, most ambivalent connection. One night, Lina and her husband attended a theatrical evening featuring Austrian performers in native costumes, singing traditional songs of the Tirol. She felt the atmosphere was sad, and noticed people crying. At the end of the performance, the swastika flag was raised over the footlights and everyone stood to sing the "Horst-Wessel-Lied." "I felt like vomiting," she wrote in her memoirs. And then she added, "I found the time had come to persuade Reinhard to go back to Berlin."

In the capital of the Reich, meanwhile, the atmosphere at the court of honor had changed radically. Most members of the military were euphoric over the Führer's bloodless victory in Austria. Bismarck's old dream of a united German-speaking realm in central Europe had finally been achieved. What did von Fritsch's honor really weigh in such a balance?

Only Hermann Göring, who had started the whole sordid mess, seemed to be having second thoughts. Thwarted in his own military ambitions, he now turned in fury on the organization he had created and then handed over to the SS. Relentlessly he began to probe, exposing the Gestapo's cover-up, and eventually forcing Otto Schmidt to admit he had been ordered to lie in court. Von Fritsch was resoundingly acquitted, but his victory came too late: Hitler had taken von Fritsch's job and didn't intend to give it back. The army's leaders would have had to force him, and they couldn't bring themselves to do it.

A grim national tragedy subsided into the futile gestures of farce. Friends persuaded von Fritsch to challenge Himmler to a duel—an intriguing notion, for the leader of the Black Order of "chivalry" could hardly refuse, and would no doubt have lost. But General Gerd von Rundstedt, entrusted with the delivery of the letter of challenge, decided instead to keep it as a souvenir. Von Fritsch waited in vain for Himmler's reply. When the war he had opposed broke out a year later, the broken-spirited old general went off to fight, deliberately taking risks to draw the enemy's fire, and dying by virtual suicide during the early days of the Polish campaign. In his last letter, he listed three "battles" Germany must win—against the working class, the Catholic Church, and the Jews. No better symbol of the impotence of the old ruling class could be found than this fool's testament from a general who refused to fight when it really mattered and died without ever recognizing his true enemies.

At police headquarters, a few underlings were dismissed, Chief Inspector Meisinger was transferred to Tokyo, and the blackmailer, Schmidt, was "eliminated," just as Meisinger had threatened. Hitler, who now needed security experts more than ever, noted that, after all, everyone makes mistakes.

Most observers felt the SS had won a great victory, pulling the Wehrmacht down from its previous Olympian heights, but police insiders thought Heydrich's position had been badly damaged in the process. His policemen had appeared stupid, vicious, and dishonest, some had shown divided loyalties, and he himself had lost any pretense to soldierly solidarity with the military, becoming indelibly identified with the "dirty business" of politics. Even today some people believe that the whole Blomberg-Fritsch affair was a machination by Heydrich to help Hitler eliminate his opponents. "Anyone could see that Himmler and Heydrich were pulling the strings," the former French ambassador to Berlin told the Yugoslav journalist Eduard Čalić in 1960.

In the past, however, Heydrich had boasted when he won a round against the stuffy officers who had snubbed him in the navy and then decreed his dishonorable discharge from the military. This time, like his wife, he seems to have fallen into an embarrassed silence. It wasn't enough to preserve his uneasy friendship with his former mentor. Unlike General von Fritsch, Admiral Canaris was learning to recognize his enemies. His comradely cooperation with Heydrich was headed toward its inevitable ending.

In the spring of 1938 it seemed as if war might break out in the Sudetenland, an ethnically mixed region of Czechoslovakia whose German majority was on the brink of rebellion. Hitler asked Canaris to organize disguised combat and sabotage teams to assist the Germans.

Abwehr II—the section committed to covert contact with and exploitation of discontented minority groups in foreign countries for intelligence purposes—began work, dividing Czechoslovakia into seven zones of action. Yet simultaneously, the leader of the Abwehr lent himself to efforts to depose Hitler.

Such schizophrenic tactics inspired a U.S. prosecutor at Nuremberg to describe Canaris as a Jekyll and Hyde character who "introduced the murderous weapons of sabotage and surreptitious infiltration, and who on the other hand, permitted individual officers to conspire against the regime."

Even Lina Heydrich, who knew him well, couldn't make up her mind about the meaning of his duplicity. In our first interview, she called him "my husband's only peer," and said he treated Reinhard like a son. In the last one, she had grown weary of my persistence. "He was a minor spy, nothing else!" she snapped. "He only had a certain importance because he had been a traitor!"

"But maybe he was not really—" I began.

"You know, Canaris was always Canaris, that's all. He was not a traitor, not a . . . he was simply Canaris. He never became part of anything. All he would do would be to stick his nose in, and that was his misfortune. If he had kept his nose out of things, he would still be alive today."

The obvious opponents of Nazism—liberal intellectuals or trade union leaders, for example—had been eliminated by Himmler and Heydrich during the first years after Hitler came to power. Those who remained, tended, like Canaris, to be more reactionary than democratic. They agreed only in longing for an end to Nazi militarism and brutality, not on what they wanted afterward.

They were also hampered by the very virtues that led them to resist in the first place. Old-fashioned men, they believed in chivalry, and hence felt bound by their oaths of loyalty to Hitler. Religious men, they shrank back from murder. Patriotic men, they could not endure the thought of another disastrous military defeat with its attendant woes of disorder, dismemberment, starvation, and humiliation.

After World War II, the anti-Nazi Hans Bernd Gisevius was asked where he drew the line to avoid feeling like a traitor. He relied on the classic German distinction between military and political action: "If I knew German troops were going over the Brenner Pass to Italy on a specific day, I wouldn't tell . . . but if I learned a piece of political news, for example that an invasion of Sweden was being planned, I might leak the news to the enemy because something might be done to put a stop to it."

For every nonviolent resister like the siblings Hans and Sophie Scholl—still memorialized in Germany today as members of the White Rose, a nonviolent student resistance group in Munich that defiantly preached the purest, most radical recalcitrance—there were ten other resisters who sat alone at night and wrestled with fear, not only of disgrace and agonizing death but also of picking the wrong moment or drawing the moral line incorrectly.

At the Abwehr, perhaps only a certain Major Hans Paul Oster seemed to have had no doubts and to stop at nothing. Like Heydrich he had been cashiered by a military court of honor for improprieties involving a woman; like him, he was both willful and reckless. Oster had long nurtured the idea of a coup against the SS. Now he concluded the only way to prevent war in Europe was to move against Hitler as well.

General Ludwig August Theodor Beck, the army chief of staff, agreed to support a military revolt. So did General Erwin von Witzleben, and the two thought they could win the support of the chief of the High Command, General Walther von Brauchitsch. One afternoon, several of the resisters made a clandestine tour of Berlin, viewing secret SS installations and trying to determine the minimum number of troops necessary for successful attack. Gisevius later admitted they "had to admire" the skill Heydrich had shown in artfully camouflaging the SS strongpoints protecting each police precinct.

But the conspirators themselves had camouflaged contacts within the police. Arthur Nebe, chief of the still barely Nazified Criminal Police, told the opposition where the secret installations were, helped them avoid surveillance, and blocked incriminating information from reaching the Gestapo. Himmler and Heydrich had no inkling of the approaching threat to their power—and lives.

In the house across the way from the Heydrichs, Canaris talked with the various generals, conferred daily with Hans Oster, and deliberately skewed inconclusive intelligence data, telling Hitler that Britain and France preferred war to a German-held Sudetenland.

Slowly the conspirators moved toward a coup d'état. There were many disagreements, mainly about whom to trust, whom to arrest, and what to do about Hitler. Canaris held aloof from the general planning, snapping impatiently, "Just get on with it!"

Yet that was exactly what they could not do. General von Brauchitsch still hesitated, saying he wanted better evidence of SS crimes to place before the people. Gisevius begged him to proceed anyway: once in control of SS headquarters, he would find plenty of incriminating documents in their own files. Only when war looked inevitable, however, did the chief of the High Command agree to act. Then, he decided to wait just one more day to ensure that nothing had changed. Unfortunately, something had. On September 30, 1938, England's prime minister, Neville Chamberlain, chose appeasement over war. He flew to Munich to hand Hitler the Sudetenland. "Chamberlain saved Hitler," wrote Gisevius bitterly.

With most of the military made euphoric by easy victory, the members of the conspiracy devoted themselves to frantic efforts to cover their tracks. Canaris had taken a dangerous risk in misrepresenting England's bellicosity. When, a few scant months after Chamberlain had exulted over his achievement of "peace in our time," Hitler decided to move against what remained of Czechoslovakia, he turned to Heydrich, not Canaris, for his insurrectionary bands. SD agents pushed Slovakia to the edge of civil war. On the Ides of March 1939, from the steps of Hradčany Castle in Prague, Hitler declared the new "Protectorate of Bohemia and Moravia," and incorporated it into the German Reich. Two and a half years later, Heydrich would move into the palace as the second Reich protector. Power is a volatile element that cannot stay constant; Heydrich's power was waxing; Canaris's was on the wane.

As Hitler continued his relentless "drive toward the East," Heydrich began to turn speculative eyes on Canaris, whose inclinations toward "defeatism" were becoming known. War was looming again on the near horizon, and Heydrich called on Walter Schellenberg to help plan methods of expanding SD foreign intelligence. Schellenberg was thrilled: secretly, he was already dreaming of creating a united German intelligence service with himself as the chief.

Following their established protocol, Heydrich invited Canaris to a sumptuous lunch in order officially to present his new assistant. Schellenberg was infatuated with spy lore, and venerated Canaris. But nothing was more important to Walter Schellenberg than his own ambitions. Now, two pairs of watchful eyes were turned in Canaris's direction. As

Werner Best warned friends in the Abwehr, Heydrich was gathering evidence against Canaris in order "to bring him down."

On September 1, Germany invaded Poland, touching off the Second World War. Shortly before the invasion, Hitler gave a secret speech to his military leaders in which he called his enemies "worms" and exhorted the generals, "Close your hearts to pity; proceed brutally."

On the day war was declared, Canaris broke into tears. "This means the end of Germany," he said, with genuine defeatism. A few weeks later, he visited Poland and was appalled by the devastation wrought by "lightning" warfare. There was worse to come. On the eve of the invasion, Hitler had ordered Heydrich to annihilate the ruling classes of Poland and other leading citizens. Once again, the SD sent out commandos, their mandate now widened into atrocity.

The operations of these Einsatzkommandos (Special Forces) were top secret, but as chief of military intelligence, Canaris both knew about them and was expected to render aid when necessary. In anguish, he rushed off to confer with Heydrich. We do not know exactly what they said to each other about this ghastly foreshadowing of the Final Solution. Heydrich would have had difficulty refusing the order, but nothing suggests he wanted to: the SS had for years been "eliminating" sources of potential resistance according to predetermined lists and categories. When Canaris emerged from the meeting, he was disturbed enough to quote disapprovingly some of Heydrich's words: "We'll spare the common folk, but the aristocrats, priests, and Jews must be killed. After moving into Warsaw, I shall arrange with the army how to squeeze them out."

Momentarily transformed into a decisive man, Canaris once again decided, *Hitler must go!* He confided to a fellow officer, "A war waged with no regard for moral principles can never be won. There's such a thing as divine justice on earth."

Canaris had taken his stand on a high moral level and in the face of the prevailing mood of triumph, but that did not mean he was skilled at direct confrontation. Diligently, the Abwehr gathered evidence of SS atrocities; bravely, Canaris set off to visit the leading generals—and could not command their attention. "What was that fellow driving at?" General Wilhelm Keitel, commander in chief of the Wehrmacht, asked his aide.

Meanwhile, the dissident Hans Oster was again reviving his plans for a coup. He drew up a list of victims—Hitler, Göring, Ribbentrop, Himmler, and Heydrich—and was determined they should all be shot. Canaris, however, was unable to resolve his ambivalent feelings about violence; he hoped General Franz Halder, who had replaced General Beck as army chief of staff, would do the dirty work. Halder finally told Canaris if he wanted to get rid of Hitler he should do it himself. Now it was the admiral's turn to fly into a rage. "Herr Halder is not going to turn me into an assassin," he railed.

Gisevius believed Canaris "would never go far enough." Another dissident, Major General Erwin von Lahousen (who after the war testified as a witness for the prosecution at the Nuremberg trials), said that "in the existing situation" Canaris had to play a double game, but couldn't guess "where the limits of that game lay." In 1940, after his quarrel with Halder, Canaris apparently reached one of his limits. From that point on, his major contribution to the resistance seems to have been to try to protect the other conspirators.

As the Abwehr opposition faltered, Hans Oster carried on alone, driven to desperation by the same unbearable tension that had immobilized Canaris. Finally, Oster crossed the thin line that in German tradition separates high treason (plotting against the national leaders) from a far worse offense called *Landesverrat* (betrayal of national secrets to the enemy). In May 1940, Oster warned the British of the impending German invasion. Later, he passed them the exact date of the Nazi attack on Holland and Belgium. "No German would do a thing like that!" said a high Allied official. For that reason, Oster's warnings were ignored—but only outside of Germany.

Hermann Göring had long maintained a special communications bureau to monitor diplomatic messages all over Europe. In May, his office intercepted a telegram from the Belgian ambassador to the Vatican in which he remarked that a German officer had leaked the invasion plans. When Hitler heard the army had been betrayed from within, he was so furious that he called in both Canaris and Heydrich, ordering them to cooperate fully in tracking down the man responsible. An Abwehr counterespionage expert, Joachim Rohleder, was appointed to lead the investigation.

Before Rohleder even began, both Canaris and Heydrich knew his investigation would lead straight back to the Abwehr itself. "That is like making the goat your gardener!" Heydrich joked when he told his staff that "the Canaris group" was in charge of the detective work.

Oster's Abwehr agents seemed only dimly aware that loose talk costs lives. In Rome, a priest involved in secret plans to negotiate peace with England got drunk one day and told all to a cohort who also doubled as an informant for the SD. In a few days, his report lay on Heydrich's desk.

Heydrich recalled this double agent to Berlin to confirm the information; then he talked to Josef Müller, a "civilian" whose name had been mentioned in the report. (The SS was not permitted to arrest or question military officers.) In fact, Müller, a devout Catholic and leading figure in the Catholic resistance to Hitler, had been in charge of the negotiations with England, though he had prudently concocted a makeshift alibi placing him in Switzerland at the time. Heydrich merely listened attentively, and sent him on his way. But no one could imagine that "Herr Suspicion" would rest content with that. The Abwehr's defensive shield had been penetrated in several places at once; now, it was Canaris and not Heydrich who was in mortal danger.

For the next several years, the two men would engage in a battle of wits, while the future of the Abwehr hung in the balance. Nothing reveals the nature of the hidden warfare beneath the Nazi mask of unity better than the thrusts and ripostes used by Canaris to fight Heydrich to a temporary draw.

To counter Heydrich's move on Josef Müller, the "old fox" acted with speed and audacity. First, he went to Heydrich and blandly told him the Abwehr was negotiating with the British—a "fact-gathering expedition" quite within the range of normal intelligence practice. Perhaps, Canaris asked, Heydrich might give him some political data to feed to MI5? Heydrich replied that the SD refused "on principle" even to pretend to treason, but he was lying. (Schellenberg had recently beguiled British agents into believing he was a traitorous military officer.)

Having made his point, Canaris sent Josef Müller to Rome to "investigate" the leak—thus allowing him to erase his own tracks.

Yet despite all of Canaris's crafty maneuvering, he never succeeded in allaying Heydrich's suspicions of him. In the autumn of 1940, the chief of Reich security told Schellenberg he "felt certain Canaris had betrayed the date of the attack in the West."

"Why don't you act?" Schellenberg reports having asked.

In response, Schellenberg writes, Heydrich said he wanted to gather more evidence. "The day would come, however," Schellenberg con-cludes, "when Canaris would be made to pay for all the damage he had caused the regime."

But why hadn't that day come already? What additional evidence did Heydrich really need? After all, he had suspected the Oster group from the beginning, had personally talked to the double agent, and had long maintained informers at Abwehr headquarters.

Hans Oster made no secret of his hatred of the Nazis. How hard would it have been to find proof against him? And Oster stood so high in the Abwehr and so close to the admiral that the two might well fall together, taking the Abwehr with them, delivering it into Heydrich's hands. Heydrich could have put pressure on Rohleder to share his find-ings, could have determined the weakest nonmilitary link in Oster's network and found some pretext to "intensively interrogate" that per-son. He could conduct surprise searches, steal or forge documents, intimidate, blackmail, kidnap, drug, torture, kill.

Instead, he merely criticized the technical competence of the Abwehr—a stale old ploy. What game was Heydrich really playing?

Perhaps he had concluded with his famous icy rationality that the SD, still in the process of reorganization, was not yet able to absorb the Abwehr. Perhaps he thought neither Hitler nor Himmler was ready for such a drastic step. But Reinhard Heydrich was also famous for reckless action, raging ambition, and ruthlessness. Ambitious Schellen-berg never understood why he "seemed to have some inhibitions" about attacking the admiral's political reliability.

At least he didn't until much later when Canaris hinted that black-mail might have been involved. Just as every Nazi leader seemed to have wondered if Heydrich were on his trail, so they all tended to think that somebody had to be blackmailing Heydrich. Canaris certainly had a file on Heydrich: an Abwehr officer claimed to have seen it in the late 1930s and remembered that it contained records of three slander trials Heydrich instigated against people who had supposedly spread word of his rumored Jewish background, as well as an old story about his having removed the gravestone of his grandmother Sarah Heydrich and replac-ing it with a new stone with the more harmless inscription S. Heydrich. Yet scholarship has established that this was threadbare, useless stuff. Canaris should have had something better if he was going to play the Jewish card against Heydrich.

In any case, this blackmail theory has another, graver, weakness: just who, exactly, could Canaris threaten to tell? Only two people—Hitler and Himmler—had authority over Heydrich, and if Himmler's masseur, Felix Kersten, is correct, they themselves were already blackmailing him. Two seemingly contradictory facts must be repeated: (1) no archival source of any kind, anywhere, supports the thesis that Heydrich had Jewish blood, and (2) nevertheless, almost all of his contemporaries were sure that he did. In Fortress Europe, as the Nazis sometimes called their realm, actual truth was almost always secondary to what people could be made to believe. Any time they chose, Himmler and Hitler could have pretended the rumors were true and treated Heydrich accordingly.

Provided, that is, he was not in turn blackmailing them. No one else in Germany possessed the key to Heydrich's private armed file cabinet, not even Himmler—indeed, particularly not Himmler. Heydrich's aides assumed it contained information about blots on the backgrounds of both the Führer and the Reichsführer SS, as well as various scandals from Hitler's early days. (In *Inside the Gestapo*, Hans-Jürgen Köhler claims he had seen a file on Hitler that by itself could have brought down the Nazi regime.)

Blackmail rests on a receptive state of mind. Perhaps Canaris was merely telling Schellenberg what he was disposed to hear. (Both Canaris and Heydrich liked to hint that some hidden political agenda lay behind their frequent socializing.)

It is also possible that Canaris was exerting on Heydrich a subtler form of influence, rarer than actual blackmail among the Nazi leaders and therefore even more effective: the seductive power of an intimacy that seemed almost illicit to the members of their organizations—and not merely to them.

Both Heydrich and Canaris used to call each other "friend," although Frau Heydrich refused to acknowledge that meaning of the term: "When you use the expression 'friend' in that sense, then you must never use this expression in connection with my husband . . . You see, Canaris was a naval officer. And there are always ties between brother officers; these ties have more to do with shared training and background than with personality. You have to accept a brother naval officer as a comrade in arms. That was part of their unwritten code. This strict military discipline is unknown nowadays."

"But," I said, "they also had personal things; they played croquet, for example."

"Yes, we did that. They were neighbors, and wanted to have good neighborly relations. This had nothing to do with their work. It is not so easy for a foreigner to understand this distinction. I don't think this is something you have in America . . . You cannot separate comradeship and friendship; for you, it is the same."

"But the two men had similar interests."

"Of course. Very similar interests, even . . . Of course it would not do that a man who is in the position my husband is in—my husband *was* in—to make distinctions in dealing with persons who appealed to him, and those he did not particularly like. The man might be a colleague with whom he had to discuss this or that . . ."

"I have heard Canaris was very . . . entertaining."

"No. No. He was anything but charming . . . He always walked around with a mournful expression on his face. I mean he had excellent manners. He was always polite, and very courteous . . . but not gallant. I cannot imagine that he related well to women. Erika, his wife, was not very pretty either . . ."

"Didn't your husband play the violin with Erika Canaris?"

"After all, we were living next to each other in the same suburb . . . This making music, this was . . . simply a hobby, you might say, like students do these days. And I think Canaris was gone a lot, and Frau Canaris was very glad when she could come over to us in the evening . . . It would be once a week—usually on a Wednesday."

"I have also read that Canaris and your husband would go riding in the morning."

"Yes, that was going on for a while, too. That was—" Lina Heydrich paused for a moment before she went on. "You know, if people would always know in advance what to think of another person, then they would save themselves a lot of grief."

Frau Heydrich had been perceptive when she called Canaris her husband's only peer. Both were by nature solitary, introverted men, though they moved through their days in a swirl of adjutants, underlings, messengers, petitioners, and obligatory social gatherings. Both stood at the pinnacles of their respective intelligence organizations, they were the two best-informed people in Germany, sharing the lonely burden of knowledge and the common problems of pursuing it in a regime essentially hostile to intelligence in any form.

But there was more to their similarities than that. Heydrich and Canaris aroused very different emotions in those who met them, yet they seem to have been equal in their powers of fascination. Each generated a powerful personal aura that attracted attention, and held it: everyone aware of them has a little story, a quotation, or a speculation. It is no wonder that they seem also to have mesmerized each other.

The flavor of the sensibility they shared can be illustrated by a little contretemps into which Heydrich once fell while walking his dog. At home in Schlachtensee, a quiet, elegant suburb favored by writers and artists, both Heydrich and Canaris usually wore "mufti," and remained in deep cover. They avoided publicity, were rarely photographed, and shunned the gaudy vulgarities favored by "golden pheasants" like Göring and Goebbels.

One morning Heydrich's dog suddenly charged toward a pianist named Helmut Maurer, who was hastening to catch his train. Heydrich called the animal back and nothing came of it, except for a shouted threat from Maurer: next time, he would shoot both the dog and its owner. It says something about the degeneration of civility in Nazi Germany that he would say such a thing without hesitation to a stranger. (Obviously, Maurer did not know who Heydrich was.)

A few days later, the two men ran into each other again at a social occasion presided over by Canaris. As the admiral began to introduce them, Heydrich explained he had already met Maurer, and that the man wanted to shoot him.

"Yes?" Canaris exclaimed. "How soon?" This last presumably in tones of pleasurable anticipation.

Both Heydrich and Canaris seem to have found the situation amusing. Both were highly intelligent, highly intuitive men, who loved a swift give-and-take, a dramatic moment, a chance to explore new roles and possibilities. They both went out of their way to seek adventure, and found conventional Nazi society boring. It is possible that when they were together, they had fun.

Yet, all this time the admiral was still collecting evidence of SS war crimes and Heydrich was still adding material to his Canaris file, even though Schellenberg thought he would already be able "to bring about his downfall at any time."

I asked Frau Heydrich whether her husband had been in some way protecting Canaris.

"Who should he have protected him against?" she said. "Canaris had full access to Hitler. My husband did not."

"There was a lot of criticism of the Abwehr, and your husband might have said, 'Oh, Canaris is all right.'"

"Canaris had a nickname: '*Der schräge Fürst.*' My husband gave him that name. 'The crooked prince.' That means, trust him if you dare; you cannot really trust him. But my husband never discovered that he had been a double agent and that he had been a traitor. He never suspected this. This is something that events revealed later on. What linked them was the uniform they had both worn . . . He was the older one. He was an admiral when my husband was nothing . . .

"My husband was suspicious of him, that is something he had told me. But that he did not then follow these thoughts to their logical conclusion in his own mind was because it was so far from his own mind: an officer is simply incapable of such a thing. It is impossible."

Just as Canaris drew back from actual assassination, so Heydrich too seemed unable to reach the "logical conclusion" that would lead to his destroying the man known to some as "Father Christmas."

It wouldn't have been easy. Heydrich would have had to go to the Führer with iron evidence of Canaris's treason—or persuade Himmler to do so—and then take an energetic, irrevocable, stand against him. Hitler and Himmler still believed in the old Canaris myth; they might have been hard to convince, and once they were, the resulting scandal would further strain the precarious cooperation between the military and the SS. At best, Heydrich would have taken over a shattered organization whose members despised him. They would not be the only ones. Heydrich's reputation was bad enough already; among his former colleagues in the navy, it would now be anathema. And the one man who really understood him, perhaps even liked him, would be gone.

There was simply no way to replace Canaris. Gunter d'Alquen, Nazi editor of *Das schwarze Korps*, who worked closely enough with Heydrich to be invited to his home, told me, "I never had the desire to be on friendship terms" with him: "He was cold, always at a certain distance. Sometimes, if he pleased, he was very nice, a little bit joking, a little bit civil about this and that, but there was always a cool zone—for example, between myself and him."

To d'Alquen, Heydrich was the epitome of the "cool radical, a defender of some sort of extraordinary philosophy, perhaps." (Whereas

Heydrich's protégé Schellenberg reminded d'Alquen of a "very nice, very modern professor of gynecology.")

Yet how much easier in the case of Canaris it would have been for Heydrich to ignore whether he needed more evidence or not, and to avoid breaking the last connection to the old order and to his old life. Canaris would in April 1945 be executed for high treason, along with his deputy General Hans Oster and the theologian Dietrich Bonhoeffer at Flossenbürg concentration camp in Bavaria. But for the time being, Heydrich seems to have turned away from the awful, amoral, pitiless "rationality" that was his hallmark. "I'm sick to death of you and your goddamned logic!" Himmler had once shouted at him. Perhaps, face-to-face with an unreasonable, unique affection, Reinhard Heydrich momentarily grew sick of it, too.

17

THE NIGHT OF BROKEN GLASS

"But we had nothing to do with it. We only locked them up, let them go, that was the end of it."

—LINA HEYDRICH

ON NOVEMBER 10, 1938, Hermann Göring had an argument with his wife, Emmy. They had been discussing an event of the previous evening, the monstrous riot that the Nazis called Reichskristallnacht. "The Night of Broken Glass" or "Crystal Night" are the usual English translations, but such poetically evasive terms hardly do justice to an orgy of smashing, burning, and mayhem in which at least thirty-five Jews were killed, hundreds of synagogues wrecked or burned, and many thousands of Jewish homes and businesses destroyed. The Night of Broken Glass was the most infamous pogrom of the twentieth century.

Nazi propaganda minister Joseph Goebbels, instigator of the whole bloody mess, had described it differently—as fair retribution for murder. On November 7, in Paris, a Jewish teenager, Herschel Grynszpan, had shot and grievously wounded the third attaché of the German embassy, Ernst vom Rath. On November 9, vom Rath died. Unhappily, this date coincided with the anniversary of Hitler's Beer Hall Putsch, a sacred day in the Nazi calendar. That evening in Munich, Goebbels gave an inflammatory speech, hysterically attacking the Jews and touching off a wave of violence that stunned many Germans, even after almost six years of Nazi rule.

Emmy Göring, formerly an actress, had been given her first big break by a Jewish director. She was so shaken that she broke with her usual custom and began to criticize her husband's politics: "Your party has brought this fate on us!"

"'Your party,' you always say 'your party'! You are my wife! It is *our* party!" Göring replied.

"No, Hermann, when something like this happens in the name of the party, then it is no longer *my* party."

Hermann Göring covered his face with both hands. "Do you think I wanted something like this to happen?" he said.

Emmy Göring recounts this story in her autobiography, *At My Husband's Side*. Lina Heydrich tells a startlingly similar tale in *her* memoirs, *Life with a War Criminal*. Her husband, too, professed to be appalled by Crystal Night. Lina often didn't know what to make of such things until Reinhard explained them to her. But when she asked him about Kristallnacht, he was so upset—with a "snow-white face and empty expression in his eyes"—that at first he told her just to leave him alone. After a while, he said a few words: "They have knocked everything to pieces . . . businesses destroyed and plundered . . . And the worst thing is . . . it's supposed to appear spontaneous. But no one believes that about us anymore. From now on, we won't be able to talk about a decline in aggressive acts against the Jews."

Neither Emmy Göring nor Lina Heydrich may remotely be regarded as objective witnesses, yet it seems possible that scenes similar to what they describe may really have occurred. For years, both Hermann Göring and Reinhard Heydrich had opposed open violence against the Jews.

Until late 1938, the Nazis had no single or consistent Jewish policy—aside from virulent official animosity—toward the tiny minority representing less than 1 percent of the German population. After the Nuremberg Laws reduced the Jews to second-class citizens in 1935, Hitler had turned his attention to efforts to bring Germany economic and political independence. Left without real guidance, the Nazi leaders began to compete in creating policies that Hitler might later endorse. They agreed on only two things: there *was* a "Jewish problem" and it had to be solved somehow.

As the official in charge of a current Four-Year Plan, Göring was trying to finance rearmament, and hoped to transfer as much Jewish money as possible into German hands. His preferred method was "Aryanization," the Nazi catchword for a process of forced expropriation in which Jews were manipulated or coerced into selling their property at a fraction of its real value (usually around 10 percent). For Aryanization to proceed smoothly, however, it had to appear legal in the eyes of the international financial community. Göring was worried that violence might provoke foreign creditors to boycott German goods.

Heydrich, as usual, was more interested in power than money. In 1935, he had expressed scorn for "senseless" acts of illegality, and the SS newspaper, *Das schwarze Korps*, had spoken out against "an anti-Semitism which harms us." Open violence in the streets had rarely been the Sicherheitsdienst style. The intellectuals in the SD positively sneered at the "medieval" ranting of radicals like *Der Stürmer* editor Julius Streicher. His lurid tales of evil Jews poisoning village wells and deflowering German maidens tended to appeal to ill-educated, small-fry Nazis. Though Adolf Hitler was also a loyal *Stürmer* reader, Heydrich and his bright young men rejected such "unrealistic fool's wisdom."

Even after the publication of his "Transformations of Our Struggle," Heydrich was still searching for his own solution to the "problem." One day he came across an article by the economist Leopold von Mildenstein suggesting the deportation of European Jews to Palestine. Immediately, he appointed von Mildenstein chief of the Jewish desk in the SD.

The latter soon found his own deputy in the new recruit Adolf Eichmann. Mildenstein's relaxed demeanor was the opposite of Heydrich's: "He didn't have that brusque, clipped way of speaking that overawed you so much that you didn't dare to say a word," said Eichmann. Under von Mildenstein's tutelage, Eichmann read *The Jewish State* by Theodore Herzl, the founder of Zionism, who advocated Jewish resettlement in the Middle East. This was one of the few books that Eichmann had ever read. ("At that time, I belonged to the category of people who form no opinions of their own," he later admitted.) Eichmann was overwhelmed, becoming an instant apostle of Zionism. He began to make contacts with Zionist leaders in the German-Jewish community and even learned a little Yiddish. Soon he was passing as a "Jewish expert."

According to Lina Heydrich, her husband too sometimes referred to himself at this time as "a Zionist." In "Transformations," Heydrich had distinguished between Jews who were proud of their Jewishness and those who cravenly tried to "disguise" it. (To Heydrich and Himmler, obsessed as they both were with "de-camouflaging," the disguised enemy was always the worst.) The SD began to support Zionist efforts to train Jewish youth for an agrarian future as pioneers of the desert.

All of this reached an ironic crescendo when Eichmann encountered an article about the Haganah, presented as "a military Zionist organization" willing to use force to persuade the British High Commission in Palestine to raise Jewish immigration quotas. When a representative of the Haganah came to Berlin, Eichmann took him to lunch. (After the war, some members of the organization said they would have met with the devil himself to get more Jews out of Germany.) A second lunch followed, during which the Haganah invited Eichmann to visit Palestine to see Zionism in action. "And something I hadn't thought possible: Heydrich authorized me to accept the invitation."

This was the first time Adolf Eichmann could be certain Heydrich knew he existed. Every year the SD chief had grown more powerful, more inaccessible, with more and more men under his command. But now Eichmann had attracted his interest. He went to Palestine—or at least to its borders: the British Secret Service had found out about his mission and blocked his entrance. In any case, Hitler was definitely not a Zionist, and opposed concentrating Jewish refugees in a single area where they might unite to work against German interests.

Though Eichmann's efforts had come to naught, they helped inspire the SD's next Jewish policy—emigration, no matter where, on a massive scale, with official bureaucratic support.

When German troops marched into Austria in March 1938, the SD had the chance to put this program into action. Heydrich sent Eichmann to Vienna to head a new Office of Jewish Emigration. With an efficiency and creativity he had never before shown in his life, Eichmann conceived of the idea of a bureaucratic "conveyor belt," a row of officials in one room processing the mess of required documents until "the passport falls off at the other end." In Berlin, emigration applications took months to process; in Vienna it was now possible to arrange for departure in a single day.

Would-be emigrants faced another problem, however: under Göring's Aryanization program, they could take no more than 10 marks out of the Reich. Not surprisingly, most people willing to emigrate tended to have money or connections abroad. Eichmann began to formulate plans to force rich Jews wishing to leave Germany to finance the passage of their poorer brethren as well.

Himmler and Heydrich were willing to authorize "harsh pressure" to force the pace of emigration. In the spring of 1938, Himmler ordered the arrest of stateless Russian Jews who had fled to Germany after the Soviet revolution. Heydrich offered them a way out of the concentration camp: "As soon as the Jew is prepared to leave Germany, the arrest is to be terminated."

Like Göring, the SS leaders considered mob violence detrimental to their efforts. Both Göring's and Heydrich's policies relied on government-sponsored compulsion, wearing the mask of legality. By June 1938, when Storm Troopers began to plaster city walls with posters depicting Jews being assaulted or mutilated, Heydrich was opposing both them and Göring in a three-way struggle over control of Jewish policy.

It is easy enough to see the SA as "radical," but this does not mean that Heydrich and Göring were moderate. By 1938 there were no true moderates left among the ruling class of Germany: the survivors had committed themselves to Hitler and Hitler's power game however they might evolve. According to the American historian Karl A. Schleunes, Heydrich and Göring did at least represent "a certain professional rationality." This was now the best the Jews might hope for—and it was precious little.

In October, the brutal nature of the SS policy of forced emigration suddenly became the object of world attention. The Nazis felt it was all Poland's fault. In the chaos after the First World War, many Polish Jews had fled to Germany to escape pogroms in Poland. This sudden influx of "eastern Jews" had alarmed many Germans, and helped fuel the fires of Nazism. In her memoirs, Lina Heydrich mentions a family of *Ostjüden* who had moved into her neighborhood, and explicitly notes how "foreign" they seemed to her and her schoolmates. (Hitler had said much the same thing in *Mein Kampf.*)

In October 1938, the government of Poland announced plans to block the reentry of Jewish citizens living abroad. Himmler ordered the police immediately to transport Polish Jews living in Germany back "home." The next day, the Gestapo began a swift, surprise roundup of approximately twenty thousand people and hurtled them by train toward the border. The Polish government refused to let them enter. While the two nations negotiated, the miserable refugees waited in the no-man's-land between the frontiers, where housing and food were minimal and the weather had turned bitterly cold.

Herschel Grynszpan's parents had been among the unfortunate evacuees, whose plight had made headlines everywhere. In retaliation, the

Nazi Minister for Public Enlightenment and Propaganda Joseph Goebbels (age thirty-seven, in 1934) seized on a November 7, 1938, incident in which a young German Jew, in protest of the treatment of his parents, assassinated a German diplomat in Paris. Two nights later, Kristallnacht took place throughout Germany.

distraught seventeen-year-old boy decided to shoot an official of the German embassy in Paris. His choice fell on vom Rath, who was in fact an opponent of the Nazis, under observation by the Gestapo.

Undeterred, Goebbels tried to exploit the assassination to seize control of Jewish policy and push it in the violent direction he believed reflected Hitler's real preferences.

Thus, it might well be true that on the evening of Crystal Night Reinhard Heydrich complained bitterly to his wife about the destruction Goebbels had unleashed. Nevertheless, even as he spoke, policemen under his command had also taken to the streets, participating in their own peculiar way in the Night of Broken Glass.

They were strangely reluctant bullies, arriving very late on the scene. Yet after the war, it seemed to some historians that Heydrich had implicated himself as the real author of the pogrom through a directive he issued to the police shortly after 1 p.m. In it, he announced that "demonstrations against the Jews are to be expected throughout the Reich," and issued a set of guidelines:

(1) Synagogues could be burned only if there was no danger of the fire spreading to nearby buildings.

(2) Jewish stores and apartments could be destroyed but not plundered. Looters were to be arrested.
(3) Foreign citizens, even if Jewish, were not to be harmed.
(4) "Historically important" Jewish archives were to be confiscated by the police to prevent their being burned.

As soon as the course of events permitted it, police officials in each district were also to arrest as many well-to-do Jewish men as existing prison facilities could accommodate. They were to be in good health and "not too great an age." After arrest, they were to be sent to concentration camps where "it is especially to be noted" that they were "not to be mistreated."

These were the orders dealing specifically with Jews. The rest advised the police to prevent any destruction of German life or property, and otherwise "not to hinder the ongoing demonstrations."

It has been endlessly debated whether these instructions represent efforts at containment or incitement. Yet it seems obvious that they are really two types of orders, combined. Most of the instructions are about what *not* to do, and that is clearly containment, but the mass arrests are something else altogether. The "night" of broken glass was actually several nights (and days) during which the Gestapo gained increasing tactical ascendancy over the proceedings.

On November 9, according to three eyewitness accounts, Heydrich was sitting with some of his cronies in a luxury hotel room in Munich when "Gestapo" Müller called to ask for instructions in dealing with the pogrom in Berlin. Heydrich was so surprised, he had no answer to give. Finally, he sent someone to ask Himmler what to do. Himmler allegedly checked with Hitler, who told him not to interfere. (According to Heydrich's old family friend Karl von Eberstein, who was now serving as police president of Munich, Himmler also met with his high SS leaders to decide on "acceptable" behavior.) Only after all this was the directive sent in Heydrich's name to police stations throughout the Reich.

The actual beatings and burnings and smashing of glass shop windows were carried out primarily by the SA, supplemented by passersby and members of the Allgemeine (General) SS or the Nazi Party. Hitler was overheard describing the pogrom as a "last fling" of gleeful lawlessness, a deliberate sop to the little men who had been bypassed for power and prestige.

After the war, ten people in the small town of Kronenberg were interviewed about their activities on Kristallnacht. A local Storm Trooper testified that at midnight, he was sitting in the public room of the Huntsman's Rest when an SA Standartenführer entered and said, "The synagogue will be burned tonight." Their local commandant asked for volunteers and about half of the Troopers went along. No policemen were involved.

The next day, Willy Hofmeister, a fifty-seven-year-old inspector of the Criminal Police, set out to undertake the second part of Heydrich's orders by arresting Salo Marowitz, a Jewish tailor whom he knew personally. (Marowitz was the last on a list of Jews whose names began with *F* through *M* handed to him by the police chief.) Walking along familiar streets and carrying no gun, he arrived at the tailor's around nine in the evening. Marowitz had heard about the roundup and had already packed a suitcase. Hofmeister said that he suggested:

"Why don't you take a blanket, just to have one, and maybe some bread and sausage or something, Herr Marowitz?"

"Thank you, Herr Kriminalinspektor . . . Mama, come in and say good evening to Kriminalinspektor Hofmeister."

"No," from the other room.

"I'm sorry, Herr Kriminalinspektor. Frau Marowitz isn't so well this evening . . . A glass of wine, Herr Kriminalinspektor?"

"No, thank you, Herr Marowitz, not on duty, you know."

Slowly the two men set out, accompanied by Marowitz's teenage son, who carried his father's suitcase. "If you don't mind, Herr Marowitz, I'm tired tonight. If you and Samuel care to walk on ahead, I'll catch up with you," the inspector finally told his companions.

None of the participants in this heartbreakingly polite scene—except, probably, Frau Marowitz—seem to have realized that a turning point in Nazi Jewish policies had occurred. Jews had often been called to the police station for registration or various forms of harassment, but they had not been arrested en masse. Until 1938, most people in concentration camps were German Aryans, being "reeducated" after committing various crimes against the state. But the Jews were guilty of no crimes, and therefore no expiation was possible. Instead, the Nazis regarded them as a sort of poison within the body politic, an "alien element" that had to be neutralized—or expelled.

It seems clear that Heydrich, with his characteristic swiftness of thought and action, had improvised quickly to extract some advantage from a chaotic situation. The Jewish prisoners were essentially hostages, held for ransom until they agreed to buy their way out of the country. The policemen were rarely as polite as Herr Hofmeister had been. Often, they insulted or robbed their victims. In Düsseldorf, Rabbi Max Eschelbacher lost everything he had on him, and had to ask for his suspenders back. "I assure you that I shall not try to hang myself," he told his persecutors. "You want to live," one of them jeered, "but you Jews have nothing to live or die for." Dr. Eschelbacher replied, "You haven't the slightest notion what a Jew is."

Despite his efforts to contain the violence and then to profit from it, Heydrich was not in complete control of events. Armed mobs moved from place to place, fanning local animosities, particularly in the countryside where the Jews were more visible. In one village, a group of children killed a Jewish woman who was trying to prevent valuables from being burned. Everywhere malcontents used the occasion to get back at presumed enemies, both Jews and those considered "Jew friendly." In Vienna, Adolf Eichmann was furious at the "senseless destruction" of the Jewish Community offices. When an Allgemeine (General) SS man came in and tossed a typewriter on the floor, Eichmann told him he would be reported to "my superior officer, the head of the Security Police and the SD" (i.e., Heydrich). The intruder hurled an obscene word at Eichmann and threw him out.

Neither the General SS nor the camp guards were under Heydrich's authority, and his instructions to avoid mistreatment of the prisoners were not obeyed. The daughter of two of the victims described their experiences, which were not unusual: "In November 1938, when my parents' apartment was completely smashed up in the Night of Broken Glass, my mother suffered a heart attack . . . My sixty-three-year-old father was dragged off to Sachsenhausen, where he lost his life. They beat him with dog whips because he had refused to say, 'I am a filthy Jew who has no right to be in Germany.'"

Conditions in the suddenly crowded camps were deplorable, and the guards often took special pleasure in attacking or humiliating Jews. Many of the prisoners suffered terribly, and many died. Martin Gilbert, the English historian, has estimated that the death count was more than a thousand. Far more victims died in the camps than through the violence of the mobs, and the survivors were more than willing to leave the country.

Meanwhile, both Himmler and Heydrich privately denounced Kristallnacht and refused to accept any responsibility for the destruction or the deaths.

More than forty years later, Lina Heydrich continued this tradition: "They were arrested and then the next day, they let them go," she told me. "It was a propaganda thing of Goebbels. But we had nothing to do with it. We only locked them up, let them go, that was the end of it."

"I have heard that many people were killed."

"*Ach!* That's all a fairy tale! There were no dead. That belongs to the atrocity stories; there are still many such stories, many!"

Frau Heydrich knew that Crystal Night had not been well received in Germany. Indeed, it was probably the single most unpopular act of the Nazi regime before the outbreak of the war. Many Germans worried about the insult to public order and the wanton destruction of property. Some rallied to the defense of Jewish neighbors, helping them clean up or giving them furniture or food. A few had the courage to voice their doubts. One of these was Benno Martin, the police president of Nuremberg, who said that "he was ashamed to go out on the streets or to belong to a people who could do such things."

The prevailing attitude, however, was that of Reinhard Heydrich's brother, Heinz, as recalled by his son, Thomas:

A synagogue was directly next to us. We often played there, because it had such nice steps. And it was on fire and I raced home and yelled: "Mutti, that big house (I did not know what it was called) is burning and there are no firemen." And my mother said, "That can't be true." She came outside with me. And she said, "That's strange, the Fire Department is way over there."

They let the synagogue burn, did not try to extinguish it, but protected the house behind it, an apartment building. And my mother said, "I have never seen anything like it." Then, the same day my father, who was a journalist, came home and told my mother—and I listened to him with my eyes and ears wide open, because it was so interesting—that he had been in a part of Berlin where Jews (and I had no idea who they were) had been brought out of a house and had been taken away. I don't remember exactly what he said but what was worse was that SS men had thrown a piano from the third-floor apartment. That was much worse! How could anyone—for my father played the piano very well himself—how could anyone throw a piano out of a third-floor window? It was hardly noted that down below, on the street, Jews had been loaded into trucks and taken away.

Behind the scenes, both Himmler and Göring criticized Goebbels savagely in Hitler's presence, hoping the Führer might remove him from office. Goebbels was kept on, but Hitler realized that street violence had been discredited. He turned to Hermann Göring, his heir apparent and old personal friend, and asked him to take the situation in hand.

On November 12, three days after Kristallnacht, Göring convened a conference to which he invited one hundred high officials of the Reich, including Heydrich. The meeting lasted several hours, and consumed many words, ten thousand of which have survived in the form of incomplete minutes.

Even from this truncated version we can observe that Heydrich entered the conference in the minor capacity of "walking file cabinet," full of facts and figures about the effects of the rioting, but departed a major leader in the planning of Jewish policy. The raw material of history is frequently also the stuff of raw drama: reading the conference minutes, we see Heydrich's role change before our eyes.

There is no way to tell from the protocol that both Heydrich and Göring were furious at Goebbels. Instead, the minutes reveal tension between Göring and Heydrich. It is a pity Emmy Göring and Lina Heydrich were not present to hear their husbands at work in the political arena, after the distress they had allegedly shown privately a few nights before. Göring, like Heydrich, prided himself on the lightning swiftness of his decisions. Having recovered from their shock, both men now attempted to seize the initiative.

At the beginning of the meeting, Heydrich said very little, speaking in incomplete sentences, and offering only statistics on such things as how many businesses were wrecked (7,500) or synagogues destroyed by fire (101).

"What do you mean 'destroyed by fire'?" Göring asked him, in what the reader imagines as a sort of snarl.

"Burned down, burned out," Heydrich snapped back.

The central issue of discussion, however, was not the extent of the wreckage, but who would pay the huge insurance costs, estimated at 5 billion German marks. The destruction of Jewish property had also affected many Germans: the bankers who had lent Jews money, land-owners who collected rent from them, insurance brokers who had to pay the immense costs of replacing the shattered shop windows that gave Crystal Night its name. "You don't harm the Jews, you harm *me*!" Göring thundered, in his role of chief of economic planning.

Still, he was happy to borrow Goebbels's rhetoric of vengeance to propel the members of the conference toward the program he favored—driving the Jews from the German economy.

The participants easily agreed that the Jews—blamed by Nazi pro-pagandists for "causing" Crystal Night—should not be indemnified for their losses. If the insurance companies simply defaulted on their pay-ments, however, it would make the Nazis look unreliable at a time when they wanted desperately to attract foreign currency.

At this point, Heydrich adopted another of his several roles, that of brash and unscrupulous expert in the use of underhanded force. He suggested a way to "save face": "One may peacefully pay the Jews if the money is confiscated again afterward."

Göring worried that such chicanery might be criticized by the min-isterial bureaucrats. Heydrich then suggested "as a matter of principle" that the confiscation not be included in an official decree. "I would do it secretly," he advised.

But Göring was adamant; everything had to be "legal." Instead, he wanted to extend Aryanization (already acceptable under Nazi law) to all Jewish businesses. Notorious for his greed, he was also concerned about valuables stolen from looted Jewish stores. "Dalüge and Hey-drich, you must get these jewels back through enormous raids!" Göring instructed the two rival SS chieftains who between them supervised all the police forces of Germany.

Heydrich replied that hundreds of people had already been arrested for plundering. Still, it was difficult to recover furs and jewelry once they had been thrown out into the street. "Even children have stuffed their pockets for the fun of it," he complained, adding that the Hitler Youth should not be allowed to participate in "things" that so easily get out of hand.

Gradually, Heydrich was shifting away from the illegalities of his

Secret Service job and toward his newer role, that of chief of police, presumed instrument of justice. (Moving from information gatherer to SD chief to Gestapo deputy, it was almost as if he were recapitulating his progression up the SS organizational ladder.)

"I wish you had slain two hundred Jews and not annihilated so much property!" Göring remarked, in his customary blustering style.

We do not know to whom Göring had addressed this aside, but Heydrich was the one who answered. "Thirty-five were killed," he said in his customary style of military brevity, and we can't tell whether he sounded disapproving, approving, or, as some have guessed, "defensive." At any rate, he waited some time before launching his own "solution." It was not enough to eliminate the Jews from the economy, Heydrich said; they should also be driven out of Germany itself. "May I make some proposals about that?" he asked politely. As a model of future action, he described his own Central Office of Jewish Emigration in Vienna, which had already succeeded in sending fifty thousand Jews abroad, whereas in Germany during the same period, "only nineteen thousand Jews were brought out."

Perhaps taken by surprise, Göring employed the natural reflex of Nazi leaders—he attacked. "Most of the time you have had to collaborate with local commanders at the frontiers to arrange illegal crossings," he said.

"In only a tiny fraction of cases," Heydrich replied. "At least forty-

The Nazi second in command, Reichsmarschall Hermann Göring (age forty-two, circa 1935), had met Hitler in 1921, when he joined the emerging National Socialist German Workers' Party. Of Göring's many voracious appetites, perhaps his strongest was that for amassing art from Jews.

five thousand Jews were brought out through *legal* measures," he added, now squarely on the side of law and order.

"How was that possible?" Göring asked. Heydrich described Eichmann's new scheme of requiring wealthy emigrant Jews to help finance the departure of poor Jews as well. Some money would also be raised from Jewish charities abroad. "The problem was not to get rid of the rich Jews, but rather the Jewish mob," Eichmann's boss summarized, as if the idea had been his own.

Göring was in no mood to be easily won over by the young man who had succeeded him as chief of the Gestapo. "But, children, have you ever thought this through?" he admonished. (His addressing them as "children" is likely the equivalent of calling them "fellows" or "guys.") "Have you considered whether this method may not in the end cost us so much foreign currency that it isn't practical for the duration?"

Heydrich argued that financing Jewish emigration would not cost Germany very much money. (After all, the Jews' assets would all be left behind.) "May I propose that we erect a similar Central Office in the Reich, with the participation of the responsible Reich authorities, and that on the basis of this experience—with rectification of the mistakes which the Herr General Field Marshall has correctly criticized—we find a solution for the Reich?"

(Heydrich's language now mimicked the unctuous and convoluted tones of the conservative officials he despised.)

"Agreed," Göring replied.

Heydrich estimated it would take ten years to arrange the emigration of every Jew in the Reich, and noted a further difficulty: Aryanization would inevitably force all the Jews into the ranks of the proletariat. Therefore, he summarized, he must take measures that on the one hand will isolate the Jews from the normal life of Germany, and on the other, ensure that they have a limited range of economic activity.

"For purely political reasons," Heydrich also proposed that the Jews be required to wear some mark of identification.

"A uniform!" said Göring. (He himself loved uniforms, and possessed many, including a snowy white one, richly bedecked with medals.)

Heydrich rejected this idea. A badge would be enough: "Through this we can avoid the harm that could arise if the foreign Jews, who cannot be differentiated by appearance from the native Jews, had to share their suffering."

"But, my dear Heydrich, you are not going to avoid the creation of ghettos on a very large scale, in all cities. They shall have to be created." (At last, Göring had addressed Heydrich with the politely formal form of "you," *Sie*.)

But Heydrich rejected his ghetto idea too. From a police point of view ghettos could not be adequately supervised. They were also breeding grounds for crime and epidemics. "The control of Jews through the watchful eye of the German population is better. I don't want to take up this question right now." (The word *I* was creeping increasingly into his sentences.)

Heydrich proposed that instead, a restricted area—

"Stop!" Göring interrupted. He didn't care whether the Jews could "hide someplace where I don't have them." He only wanted them to make all their purchases from Aryan businesses.

"No," Heydrich replied. "I would say, that for the little things of daily life, Germans should not wait on Jews."

"One moment! . . . If you say that then some Jews are back in business again . . . We must decide that only Germans remain in business and the Jew must buy there."

"It must be decided whether we want that or not."

"I want to decide that right now . . . that the Jew has nothing more to seek in the German economy."

"I wouldn't want to decide that—there are still some things of psychological importance to consider."

Heydrich and Göring were now arguing as if they were equals, but in fact, they were not. In 1938, Göring was the second most powerful man in Nazi Germany; and this was *his* meeting. Economic decisions rested ultimately with him as well. As Göring continued to discuss universal Aryanization, Heydrich had to back down—but he was never a good loser.

"I must say," he ended, "one shouldn't want to build a ghetto today. But through these measures the Jews are automatically going to be forced into a ghetto . . ."

Göring hastened on to consider a suggestion that the Jews be socially isolated from the rest of the German population. Heydrich seemed to follow Göring's lead, though he was actually pursuing his old practice of "switching on" to anything serving his own interests. Quickly, he proposed a series of measures excluding Jews from sacred Nazi shrines like the Königsplatz in Munich, as well as health resorts (not even all *Germans* could afford them, he noted) and hospitals patronized by Germans.

Like sharks, the other Nazis tore into what remained of the Jews' freedom of action, debating banning them from public conveyances, theaters, movies . . .

Heydrich no doubt saw these measures as a way of convincing the Jews that only emigration could "safeguard their existence"—as well as his own power as the enforcer of the law. His last comment was designed to get it all in writing: "I want merely to ask for a basic agreement that we should introduce these things." No one disagreed.

Göring raised a final point: "Just one question, gentlemen: How would you react if I announced today that the Jews as punishment had to deliver a billion marks?" No one objected.

The man Emmy Göring describes as consistently kindhearted summarized the sense of the meeting: "Those pigs will think twice before they commit another murder. Once again I am forced to admit that I should not like to be a Jew in Germany." He also had a message from Hitler for "the rest of the world: Why are you always talking about the Jews? You take them." The kindly Reichsmarschall proposed that rich Jews might buy "a large territory" in North America or Canada. Or all German Jews might be evacuated to the island of Madagascar. "No other solution is left," Göring stated flatly.

At 2:40 in the afternoon, Hermann Göring adjourned the meeting. It had lasted three hours and resulted in official approval both of his policy of Aryanization and Heydrich's strategy of forced emigration. For the Jews of Germany, however, the November conference marked the end of their participation in the life of their homeland, even as second-class citizens. All were about to be forced, like Herschel Grynszpan's parents, into a fatal no-man's-land from which many would never emerge.

Göring, Heydrich, and Eichmann, the apparent victors, were also stepping over a momentous threshold. From that point on, their names would be linked with the various "solutions" of the Jewish Question. They were now in charge of increasing degrees of atrocity, culminating several years later in the Holocaust the Nazis called the "Final Solution."

On January 24, 1939, Göring ordered Heydrich to create and direct a Reich Central Office for Jewish Emigration. He was entrusted with making "all preparations for stepping up the emigration of the Jews, including the establishment of a suitable Jewish organization," arranging for funds, locating destination countries, and anything else necessary for a "fast and smooth" operation. It was a virtual carte blanche.

Heydrich sprang into action, duplicating Eichmann's model in Vienna, and sending Eichmann himself to Prague to set up a branch office there. On February 11, Heydrich held a conference of his own, describing his efforts and requesting the cooperation of other Reich ministries. He also reopened negotiations with underground Zionist organizations, arranging to smuggle thousands of Jews into Palestine in the summer of 1939. Those who did not volunteer were dragooned: the Berlin emigration office insisted the local Jewish community provide, every day, a list of seventy families who had agreed to leave.

As a result of this forced exodus, approximately 500,000 people, or more than half the entire Jewish population of Germany, Austria, and the annexed Czech provinces of Bohemia and Moravia, had left by the time emigration was officially discontinued in 1941.

Günther Deschner, the conservative journalist and historian, has argued that Heydrich's emigration policy may be seen as "a sort of large-scale rescue operation . . . even if the objective facts of the case certainly bore no relation to the subjective motives of the leadership of the SS."

Frau Heydrich and Frau Göring believed that their husbands' "subjective motives" were compassionate, yet *they* did not speak, even to their wives, of "rescue." Instead, they dwelt on their own personal anguish—and apprehension. Observers noted that Göring had begun to lose weight, and seemed fatigued.

Himmler took a month's leave from work the day after Kristallnacht and disappeared into a spa in the south of Germany. And Frau Heydrich thought her husband was "depressed." Only once before did she admit to seeing him so downcast: in 1934, after the murder of Ernst Röhm in which he had played such a pivotal role.

At that time, Heydrich allegedly told his wife that more opponents should have been killed, to get the bloodletting over once and for all by eliminating the remaining enemies of Nazism. Yet in the end, Heydrich built his security empire on the perennial pursuit of increasing numbers of "enemies."

Did he once again foresee an inevitable escalation in Nazi violence? Certainly, some of his minions were reaching this conclusion. One month after Kristallnacht, the SS journal published an editorial drawing the "logical" consequence of the new policy of isolating and pauperizing the Jews: they would probably be reduced to starvation, and then to overtly criminal acts. If that happened, the SS would itself be "forced" to act toward them as toward all other "criminals"—that is, to eliminate them "with fire and sword."

Reinhard Heydrich had good reason to be "depressed." But if he felt any moral qualms (something he usually ridiculed in others), it would have been in character for him to have pushed them aside, quickly moving on to the next task and the next opportunity for self-aggrandizement. The primitive emotional energy released by propagandistic incitement was about to be replaced by a far deadlier force—a great bureaucratic apparatus controlled by men whose brutality and ruthlessness were increasing every day.

"The roar of the machine running at full speed was to them an assertion of their power and security and they were quite unaware, in the intoxication of that power, of how far they had drifted into evil," Walter Schellenberg later wrote.

When Adolf Eichmann returned to Vienna in February 1939, the Jewish community leaders to whom he had previously used the polite form of address and offered seats as if to guests, were shocked by his behavior. One of them reported, "I immediately told my friends I did not know whether I was meeting the same man. So terrible was the change . . . Here I met a man who comported himself as a master of life and death. He received us with insolence and rudeness. He did not let us come near his desk."

The distance between Eichmann and his victims was about to widen into an abyss, as the machinery of terror accelerated in response to the demon of war. On September 1, 1939, German troops invaded Poland, touching off the bloodiest conflict in history.

Sometimes after supper, Frau Heydrich would start to tell me her views about the war. But she never finished. "The war," she would say, "the war changed everything." And then, *she* would get depressed. And the evening would be over.

18

INSIDE THE SPIDER'S WEB

"My husband did not want people who only said '*Ja!*'"

—LINA HEYDRICH

F RAU HEYDRICH WAS CORRECT: the war would change everything. However, the Reich Main Security Office (RSHA), that great, complicated organizational "machine"—comprising mainly a network of people working together under Heydrich's control—retained its essential outlines, even as its functions expanded and its momentum continued to accelerate.

Nazism, however, cannot be encompassed by any single metaphor or theory. Thus, Walter Schellenberg, who often described Heydrich as the lord of the machine, also characterized him as a black-garbed spider spinning threads of influence and intrigue from his lair in Berlin. This graphic depiction has some validity, for multiple lines of communication ended in the chair where Heydrich (sometimes) sat, and where he constructed his web of organizational connections from the inside out.

For years Frau Heydrich blocked my efforts to draw a general picture of the way her husband, allegedly the grandmaster of SS tactical planning, organized his own days. She viewed such questions as frivolously journalistic. ("Imagine! Someone asked me once what my husband ate for breakfast. As if that had any world-historical significance!")

She did reluctantly contribute a few bits and pieces of information about his professional life, but only about things observed firsthand. Referring to the German editor of her memoirs, she commented tartly, "The Herr Professor, he was always saying you surely must have information about this or that event. But I didn't, and cannot talk about what I do not know."

I did learn that her husband got up early, ate his historically insignificant (and therefore undescribed) breakfast at home, and then read newspapers while his personal barber gave him a shave. (Subordinates recall Heydrich as both exquisitely groomed and vain about his appearance; one noted that he had frequent massages and sometimes took diet pills—amphetamines, as they were beginning to be called at about that time—to keep his weight down.)

After breakfast, the chief of the Security Police and Security Service was driven in his limousine—but without an escort or bodyguard—from his home in the suburbs to the immense police-SD office complex in the center of Berlin. The drive took about half an hour. On the way, he looked through files in the briefcase he brought home every evening.

Heydrich rarely seems to have gone right upstairs to work, however. Instead, he usually met his fencing instructor in a gymnasium in one of the buildings, where he trained for both domestic and international fencing competitions. It wasn't just political power that gained him a place on the SS team. "My brother fenced against him in 1935," George R. Wolff, a German-Jewish refugee from the Nazis, told me. "He said he was very good, 'an elegant fencer.' By the way," Wolff said, "did you know that Heydrich was a Jew?"

"Actually," I said, "I think that was just a rumor. There are no facts to support it."

"Well, you had better check again. He was partly Jewish at least. My brother heard that from very good sources—not that he was happy to hear it."

"Did the other fencers think Heydrich was Jewish?"

"Everyone thought so. It was an open secret, if you know what I mean."

As Frau Heydrich recounted, on some mornings her husband joined Admiral Canaris in the Grunewald for a ride and an unmonitored chat about intelligence politics. Often, he brought a favored subordinate along, usually Schellenberg or Best. She wouldn't admit to any other knowledge of Heydrich's office routine—except to tell me with pride in her voice that she could always get through on the telephone when she called. Apparently, she called rather frequently. "What about?" I asked her. "Oh . . ." She waved a deprecating hand. "Who can remember now? Probably about what we were doing that evening, or something about the family . . ."

Lina Heydrich said she would never have presumed to visit her husband's office without a definite invitation. That world was closed to "civilians," she insisted, and what she knew of it was the little her husband saw fit to impart.

The best information about Heydrich's work habits has in fact come from a number of interrogations of SS officers declassified in the 1990s (too late for Lina's viewing). Several members of Heydrich's staff were interviewed at length by Allied intelligence agents after the war, and from these new sources, as well as from my interviews with former SS Gruppenführer Bruno Streckenbach, we can piece together a picture of his office routine.

The people closest to Heydrich, and thus to the center of things, were his adjutants. Deliberately "unpolitical," they were gatekeeper figures entrusted with the maintenance of the web. This was a complex task, requiring considerable personnel. For example, one man (and his assistant) was responsible solely for Heydrich's anteroom. Hans-Hendrik Neumann, a successful postwar electrical engineer who served in this capacity from 1936 to 1939, described his duties:

> I was responsible for the timetable, for the entire technical course of the day, for receiving visitors, preparations for travel, inspection of car parks (we also had two airplanes), care of guests (there were always a lot of foreign visitors there), arrangements for food, and all entertainment . . . I was also responsible for sport. Heydrich was strongly interested in sports.

That was an understatement. Another adjutant summarized his boss's normal schedule:

> After horseriding early in the morning, he would work for an hour or two in the office, which was followed by an hour or two of sport

and then more office work. After lunch, which he usually ate in the office, he would go shooting or flying followed by more work in the office and then swimming, fencing, tennis, or rowing. The evenings were spent at the cinema, theater, nightclubs, parties, or at his desk in the office. Sometimes until the early-morning hours.

Adjutant Neumann was also a personal *Begleitsoffizier,* or escort officer, assigned to accompany his chief on social occasions. Lina Heydrich thought of him (and his wife) as close family friends. Neumann, like Heydrich, was from North Germany, and could understand his boss's abbreviated, staccato speaking style. Indeed, she said, he often imitated both it and his chief's jagged handwriting.

Beyond the *Begleitsoffizieren,* there were several other categories of adjutants. Herr Strohmeyer—the "simple" Bavarian who in earlier days had stolen Frau Heydrich's exploding matches—remained in Munich as special liaison officer to Heydrich until the latter's death. In Berlin, a special officer was entrusted with the secret correspondence of the adjutants' office, or Adjutantur, and Kurt Pomme, one of a group of "police adjutants," kept Heydrich informed on events over at Kurt Dalüge's Ordnungspolizei (Order Police), or Orpo.

Pomme also answered the telephone, took messages when the personal adjutants were out of the office, and administered Heydrich's private "benevolent fund" (approximately 25,000 to 30,000 marks a month drawn from the Gestapo administrative budget). This was used to pay confidential agents for special work, to help out when subordinates became ill or their wives had babies—and for anything else Heydrich wanted, since he himself decided how the money was allocated.

After 1937, Pomme had a new responsibility—looking after his boss's new hunting lodge in the western outskirts of Berlin. He was kept so busy constructing observation posts and fodder troughs that he was often out of the office. This he considered a "great relief," for he had been trying to get out of the office for years: he and Heydrich had never gotten along, and Pomme hadn't wanted the job in the first place. A veteran of the First World War, he had spent the next fifteen years working himself up the conventional police ladder, cooperating harmoniously with the leaders of the Weimar Republic. One day in 1934, Pomme had been ordered to report to Heydrich—a "surprise," because he didn't know him at all. On arrival, Pomme found he didn't like Heydrich's shifty-eyed gaze and ice-cold "mask." Intentionally, Pomme emphasized his previous democratic sympathies. Heydrich replied they would be "overlooked" and offered him the job anyway.

Pomme didn't try to explain why Heydrich accepted him. ("You soon learned in Heydrich's service never to question his motives nor try to fathom his hidden reasons," another subordinate once wrote.) Soon, the two men began to have serious "differences of opinion." In 1935, Party Secretary Rudolf Hess instructed the SD to investigate the political reliability of all Orpo officers being considered for major promotions. Pomme objected, on the grounds that this would exclude many good men who were strong Christians, had once belonged to democratic parties, or had friends in concentration camps. But Heydrich tended to approve any extension of the concept of political reliability, since for all practical purposes he was its final arbiter.

Pomme thereupon asked to be relieved of his duties. Heydrich agreed, but Orpo boss Dalüge did not. He told Pomme he had to remain, on the ill-demonstrated grounds that he could handle Heydrich's "ruthless, quick-tempered, and vigorous manner better than anyone else."

Kurt Pomme stayed on for five years after that, even though Heydrich reduced his political-reliability rating, excluding him from handling messages dealing with Gestapo or SD business. He also secretly enrolled him in the Nazi Party. (Pomme claimed he found out only when the party book appeared one day on his office desk.) The obstinate adjutant countered by refusing both promotions and SS membership, which he felt might make him "dependent" on Heydrich. And all this time, the two men saw each other every day, shielding their hostility behind their individual versions of the expressionless SS "mask."

Somewhat surprisingly, Heydrich often chose subordinates with "difficult" characters. ("My husband did not want people who only said 'Ja!'" Frau Heydrich said. "We were not in Russia, after all! We were not Communists!") His subordinates struggled constantly to find a proper balance between independence and obsequiousness. Anyone too outspoken, popular, or competent threatened Heydrich's supremacy; anyone too pliant could be hiding something. With Pomme, at least, he knew what he was getting.

Perhaps Heydrich also respected Pomme's stiff-necked rectitude—so useful in the manager of a "benevolent fund"—as part of the soldierly code of behavior he still admired, and still tried, when possible, to practice himself. According to Streckenbach, Heydrich stood at attention while talking on the phone to Himmler: "That was typical of him and his military training . . . All of us, oddly enough, used to speak on the telephone while standing, and dictated pacing back and forth."

As "political soldiers," SS men were supposed to embody the twin ideals of Nazi fanaticism and knightly honor. Never mind that every year these became harder to reconcile; every year they tried harder to believe that some men—Aryan supermen—can serve two masters. The seeds of confusion, compartmentalization, and duplicity were thus embedded in the very heart of the SS ethos.

It is also likely that Kurt Pomme was better at playing the Nazi power game than he wanted to admit in 1945. The exchange of gambits involving secret struggles for leverage and unacknowledged refusals of "dependence" was also a leitmotiv in the accounts later given by Walter Schellenberg, Bruno Streckenbach, Werner Best, and Alfred Naujocks, among many others. Heydrich's relationships with his closest associates resembled a never-ending series of clandestine simultaneous chess matches.

The Gestapo officer who later published a book under the name of Hans-Jürgen Köhler wrote in it that he joined "the Special Service" expecting to find "willing cooperation and a spirit of comradeship":

> I was gullible and trusting enough to forget the principle . . . valid among the big and small potentates of the Third Reich—the principle of the "survival of the fittest," of the fang and claw of the jungle. Everybody was willing to sacrifice the little finger of his left hand when he could cut off the right hand of the other man, his alleged friend. Of course, all this was done in the glorious name of the Führer.

Infighting and intrigue flourished everywhere in Nazidom. Heydrich, however, was commander not only of the Secret Police but also of a separate intelligence organization, specializing in the furtive twilight struggles of the Secret Service underworld. The man seen by outsiders as the stalking horse for every blood-drenched Nazi political "program" was known inside the SS ramparts as a master of manipulation, and a connoisseur of cunning stratagems. The threat of violence was implicit in every move he made; actual violence could be left to others.

In the end, it was not Heydrich but his wife who finally arranged Kurt Pomme's departure from the Adjutantur.

The precipitating events occurred far from the tense struggles at Reich security, in the very places where Heydrich sought relief from all that. From late spring until late autumn, Lina Heydrich moved with the children to her native island of Fehmarn. She told me she had never really liked Berlin, and during gardening season couldn't remain content with a small plot in a city backyard. So she went home to what she called a "simple little house" on the beach.

It was built in 1935, according to plans she herself designed. On his SS salary, Heydrich could not really afford such a luxury, so he had to borrow funds from friends—and from Himmler—to pay for it. Lina said her husband loved the house, commuting to Fehmarn every weekend from the city, usually in the small private airplane he was just learning to fly. Once on the island, he used a bicycle to get around, both to save money and to enjoy a rare time of quietude.

One day Frau Heydrich showed me a hazy photo of a long rectangular building with wood-framed windows, whitewashed walls, and a sloping thatched roof. It was the very opposite of "little," but it did have a certain folksy rusticity. Still, she wasn't roughing it. By Pomme's account, Frau Heydrich had the help of two gardeners supplied by the SS. One of them, Unterscharführer (junior squad leader) Neumeyer, was in Fehmarn so frequently that he decided to move his wife there. Naturally enough, he began to spend time with her in the evening, but (as Pomme told U.S. Intelligence) Frau Heydrich became so "annoyed" at this that she prevailed on her husband to order Frau Neumeyer to leave. Pomme refused to carry out the order since "there was no law against people living where they wanted."

Reinhard Heydrich then transferred Neumeyer to his hunting lodge outside Berlin. One night he "was seen by Frau Heydrich riding a motorcycle after 10 p.m., which was the time Heydrich had ordered that he should go to bed so as to be ready for a good day's work next day and every day." Once again Heydrich "followed his wife's wishes" and ordered Pomme to discipline Neumeyer. Once again, Pomme refused.

In October 1941, Frau Heydrich was invited to her husband's office to discuss the impasse with his police adjutant. At that time, Heydrich had just taken up residence in Prague Castle, leaving his wife in charge of their domestic arrangements in Germany. Yet he took time away from the packed agendas of his rare trips home to attempt to adjudicate her dispute with Pomme.

Bruno Streckenbach told me that Heydrich did not mind opposition "so long as it was presented in a very definite form." He continued: "The Prussian soldier could express an opposing view to his superior if he considered it necessary and nothing would happen to him so long as he followed the rules . . .

"But there was another side to him—the side where Heydrich made a decision and then insisted on the execution of this decision by any means whatever. (By the way, that was true of Himmler, too.) . . . At that moment, it was impossible to change his mind. If you could calmly discuss the matter with him it might work, but you had to know exactly by his tone of voice at what point the matter was closed—from then on, all arguments were futile."

Kurt Pomme did not follow the rules. Instead, he reprimanded his boss for wasting more gasoline flying each weekend to visit his wife than Neumeyer had spent on his motorcycle. The discussion ended in "a terrific argument" followed the next day by Pomme's resignation—even though he had been warned not to part with Heydrich "on unfriendly terms." To get out of his way, Pomme obtained a post far away in the East, at Winniza, in the Ukraine, near the Führer's new wartime headquarters. It wasn't far enough away. On Heydrich's advice, Himmler ordered Pomme's recall, since he was no longer considered "politically trustworthy enough" to remain in Hitler's vicinity.

In 1945 Kurt Pomme offered to tell the Americans everything he could remember about Reinhard Heydrich in exchange for their help in getting his wife and daughter out of the eastern zone. Unfortunately, his interrogations were not declassified soon enough for me to ask Lina Heydrich about them. She mentions Pomme only briefly in her memoirs—as a man who kindly offered to help out with the new hunting lodge.

Perhaps Frau Heydrich felt a woman's quarrel with her gardener had no "world-historical significance." But the former adjutant Pomme felt she had far too much influence on her husband—and that makes it a different story.

Everyone in Heydrich's entourage knew she was a spirited woman, constantly chafing against the limited role Himmler assigned to wives of SS men. Everyone knew that Heydrich allowed her far greater freedom than Himmler felt was appropriate. Everyone speculated about the balance of power in the Heydrich marriage, which—everyone guessed—was tempestuous. Beyond that, they could reach no agreement. Although he had never met Heydrich or his wife, Wilhelm Höttl, an Austrian SS officer who later became a witness for the prosecution at Nuremberg, said that he had heard that Lina was an ambitious goad, pushing her husband into competition with the Reichsführer SS. Walter Schellenberg, for a while a close confidant to both of the Heydrichs, felt she was under his thumb. Bruno Streckenbach, who often visited them at home, concluded they had attained a sort of equality of strong natures.

"I only remember she was very outspoken, fresh," Gunter d'Alquen, editor of *Das schwarze Korps*, told me. He recalled a dinner party that Frau Heydrich had attended without her husband. D'Alquen's deputy was also invited. He knew Frau Heydrich slightly because his wife had connections with one of Lina's sisters. "And all of a sudden, she made over the table an unbelievable remark to him: 'How are you caring, if I may ask, for your old father? I heard he is not quite well and nobody takes care of him.'

"Impossible!" d'Alquen exclaimed. "My good gracious; that was an insult . . . And my deputy wrote a letter to Heydrich . . . I saw it afterward. It was so impossible to try to convince somebody to more or less punish his wife."

D'Alquen didn't remember the content of that letter or of the one Heydrich allegedly wrote in reply, but he was sure Lina had been "very fresh with him. And I suppose she had a lot of reasons for this; I don't know. At that time, she was a very good-looking woman . . . Not so much beautiful as—like a horse: not an Arabian . . . a very good British fox-hunting horse."

I told d'Alquen his deputy sounded like a brave man to risk Heydrich's wrath.

"I wouldn't say so. Because that was a personal affair and then it had nothing to do with the rank or paycheck. That was the order of the SS. Anybody was a member of the club. And if it went to such lengths, there were no differences."

In any case, he thought, Heydrich "certainly believed she was wrong . . . I suppose behind the curtain he told her something, but he didn't admit it. He laughed about the whole thing. And that was easier than to make trouble for her." (Heydrich himself once allegedly confessed to his colleague Karl Wolff that he felt he had to tolerate some of his wife's more flamboyant escapades, because, after all, she tolerated his.)

In the case of the errant gardener, Heydrich probably thought the unpolitical Adjutantur was a relatively safe place for Lina to exercise a bit of influence. Beyond its boundaries was where the real spider's web began and the rules of permissible behavior narrowed. The further one moved away from Heydrich's elegant personal offices and the closer one got to whatever political disturbances activated the web of surveillance and suppression, the harder it became to oppose what he ordered. Even men who liked to think of themselves as Prussian officers thought long and hard before they dared voice a dissenting opinion.

Beyond the Adjutantur, the next filaments in Heydrich's web of official connections comprised departmental chiefs and their "authoritative assistants," usually specialists in some area of police or intelligence work. Much of Heydrich's time was spent conferring with these men. (There were, of course, no women.)

Kurt Pomme provided the Allies with a list of at least eighty-two people he believed had worked closely with Heydrich. They ranged from a "personal adviser" on espionage among prominent people abroad, all the way up to Heinrich "Gestapo" Müller, his most powerful subordinate. At first Müller spent "several hours daily with Heydrich giving his proposals and receiving Heydrich's decisions but later when he had accustomed himself to Heydrich's directives and opinions, he came about once a fortnight."

Müller was the chief of a main division. Heydrich informed Himmler about the activities of his seven RSHA section chiefs (Amtschefs), but they reported directly to him. They also had personal access to Heydrich whenever things had "piled up that really [couldn't] be handled in writing." As Bruno Streckenbach reported, "There was a rule that matters of special importance had to be submitted to Heydrich. But what occurrences were important enough? . . . You had to have a feel for it . . . It was not always easy to determine in advance whether something was important. We might end up being told, 'Why are you sending me all this junk? Can't you take care of it on your own?' . . . But woe to him who did not present something that later on developed into a major case; then there was the devil to pay."

Alfred Naujocks, the rambunctious SD specialist in dirty tricks, ended his long career in Heydrich's service with just such an "occurrence." Naujocks had long been a protégé of Heinz Jost, chief of SD Foreign Intelligence. But Walter Schellenberg wanted Jost's job for himself, and he and Naujocks had already been open enemies for years. After the war broke out, Jost arranged to send Naujocks on a mission to occupied Holland. He was to try to purchase a legitimate business, which the SD could use as a cover for intelligence activity. Jost apparently told Heydrich nothing of the plan: time enough for that after they could report success.

In Holland, Naujocks soon found a business to buy. It belonged to two desperate Jews who agreed to sell quickly if they could have the money in gold. On the day Naujocks was preparing to deliver the money, however, the German Secret Field Police knocked on his door. He was sent as a prisoner to Heydrich's office in Berlin, where his adjutants pretended they didn't know him. Heydrich kept him waiting for half an hour; then, when Naujocks was finally permitted to enter, merely glared and said nothing. As Naujocks later reconstructed their conversation, he himself broke the silence: "I should be grateful to know why I am here in this position."

"Once I used to admire you, but now there is nothing but contempt," Heydrich replied. "You are a traitor."

When Naujocks said that was "ridiculous," Heydrich flew into a rage. "Don't say that to me, you despicable traitor, you . . ." He crashed his fist down on his desk. Next, he accused his former "friend" of bargaining with enemy aliens for favors, illicit transactions in gold, and accepting bribes. The penalty for each was death.

Naujocks said he had been engaged in a legitimate business deal, authorized by the SD.

"Yes? I think it is more likely that you were blackmailing the two Jews—their life for their business—and that you were planning to escape with the gold which you had bought with official funds . . . You cannot talk or shoot your way out of this one."

Alfred Naujocks always claimed he was framed. Both Himmler and Heydrich were said to use people until they were used up; then they got rid of them. But it was Heydrich who bore the nickname "Herr Suspicion." Just as he was forever "proving himself" best in everything, so his subordinates felt they constantly had to prove their competence and loyalty. "Once he got his knife into someone, for any reason," Naujocks said, "friendship was never resumed."

Despite his reputation as the archetype of hardness, Heydrich's subordinates thought of him as volatile, unpredictable, and more emotionally expressive than they would have liked. Often, the emotion was explosive disappointment at the "failures" of others. Almost every close associate remembered at least one angry scene in which Heydrich attacked him savagely for mistakes or disloyalty. Bruno Streckenbach, however, had different memories:

> In a situation like that Heydrich had a cold and curt way of dealing with you . . . Himmler was obstinate. He became disputatious . . . Heydrich was much smoother, more polished. He did not engage in arguments. When Heydrich was displeased he might make a pointed comment; that was enough. If that had not been enough, he would have thrown me out for stupidity. "I gave you a hint. Didn't you get it? Out!"
>
> He usually kept his temperament in check, but his occasional bursts of temper could be dangerous. And the things he could be called guilty of—his occasional feats of cruelty—those happened during these rare fits of temper. When he did not really take the time to think things through.
>
> As far as his being suspicious; well, he probably did not trust me either. He probably did not trust anyone, as a matter of principle. And I guess his experience of life proved him right.

Heydrich may have been right in Naujocks's case. After the war, Schellenberg claimed Naujocks and Jost had been involved in a variety of shady financial schemes that had seriously embarrassed the SD. (There is rarely a final word where Nazi sources are concerned. The era that spawned the "big lie" does not offer historians much in the way of simple truth.)

For his part, Naujocks said he refused to confess to something he hadn't done. Finally, he was called again to Heydrich's office. There he found his boss scrutinizing a map of Russia, which the Germans had just invaded. Heydrich told his prisoner that in spite of his "unpardonable" actions he was still going to be allowed to fight for the Reich—as an SS private. Naujocks had been dismissed from the SD. "I do not expect to see you again," Heydrich said coldly.

Alfred Naujocks felt he had been given a death sentence: "Colonel to private in ten seconds. Hero to criminal, and if the Russians didn't get him he would certainly be shot in the back by his own people." But chance intervened. Naujocks was sent to a unit commanded by Sepp Dietrich, Hitler's former chauffeur and bodyguard and an old friend of Naujocks's—and an enemy of Heydrich's. Protected by Dietrich, Naujocks was wounded in combat, but survived to return to further adventures in Berlin.

As this example shows, the official network of relationships was interwoven with another set of informal ties based on friendship, shared interests, or shared antagonism. These ex officio contacts helped to ameliorate the unrelenting demands for compliance with rules so dizzyingly multifarious that no one could remember them all. As the political scientist Hans Buchheim has pointed out, the Nazi leaders tacitly accepted this second web of contacts as necessary for sanity, and often survival. Within the SS, the concept of "camaraderie" softened the rigors of political knighthood: the "strict copybook SS requirements could be met by no mentally or morally normal man . . . In the name of camaraderie increasingly serious failings become acceptable, offences can be covered up, communal dereliction of duty can be concealed both from the authorities and the outside world."

When the Nazis moved against their enemies, the first step was to cut away their protective bonds of social support, exposing them to the chilling winds of isolation, and allowing them to be picked off at leisure. This was the plan used against Ernst Röhm and it was repeated endlessly.

Inside the RSHA, Heydrich tried to keep the various members of his brain trust from forming separate alliances that might dilute their dependence on him. The "bearers of secrets" who provided their own defensive shields were supposed to be confined to their own spheres of activity. He usually met with his Amtschefs individually, except when the interests of several different offices were involved, as might happen in a political emergency, such as the sudden flight of Rudolf Hess to Scotland in 1941. Hess, who was then serving as Hitler's deputy, proclaimed his desire for a separate peace with England. Both the British and Nazi leaders doubted his sanity, and a few days after Hess's flight Heydrich chaired a meeting to debate the issue.

Ten people were invited, among them Hitler's personal physician, Dr. Karl Brandt; Germany's leading psychiatrist, Professor Max de Crinis; Amtschefs representing the Gestapo, the Criminal Police, and SD intelligence; and the RSHA religious expert, Albert Hartl. The doctors argued that Hess had previously shown signs of schizophrenic tendencies. Domestic Intelligence reported that the German people, though stirred by Hess's flight, remained loyal to Hitler. Hartl stated that Hess showed mystic tendencies and was very interested in astrology. Heydrich wondered if the British Secret Service had used astrologers to influence Hess's behavior, but the group decided there was no way to prove such a theory. In the end, they concluded that Hess had sincerely believed he could somehow end the war in the West.

Generally, however, such open discussion was avoided. As Streckenbach reports, an atmosphere of cloak-and-dagger intrigue prevailed:

Heydrich had double doors and walls in his room to make the place soundproof, a telephone switchboard of his own so that he could contact his officials, ministers, etc. without fear of being overheard (his own private line came direct from the telephone exchange in Berlin and he constantly changed his telephone number as a further security measure), and a direct secret teleprinter in the Adjutantur. All secret and personal correspondence to and from his chief officials was signed and sealed and carried in locked briefcases or folders by those appointed for the duty. All waste paper and carbon paper used in the course of the day's work had to be destroyed daily in a paper shredder in the cellar.

(Heydrich and the Adjutantur also had miniature shredders.)

Hans-Hendrik Neumann described Heydrich as "a master of organization and of secrecy"; Pomme said his boss handled all important matters personally so that no subordinate would ever know "everything"; Schellenberg claimed that Heydrich didn't even like his Amtschefs to meet socially without him, lest they compare notes. Streckenbach told me that it was unlikely anyway: "Each of us worked thirteen to fourteen hours a day, regularly. We really had neither the desire nor the energy to get together after work and discuss our official secrets!" Moreover, he said, "there was a strict order that everyone was to be informed strictly on a need-to-know basis":

> This came about after an accident concerning some secret plans. An officer from the General Staff had taken some secret documents along on a trip. The plane got lost and ended up landing in Belgium. And before the officer had a chance to burn the documents, the Belgian police were there and confiscated them . . . Ever since then the absolute rule was—and this regulation was posted on the front of every filing cabinet—that everyone was allowed to know only what he absolutely needed to know to perform his duties. Not even among friends. And we really adhered to this order. Totally. We had to!

Heydrich forced separation on his divisional leaders because of the fundamental Nazi policy of divide and conquer as well as because of the wartime imperatives of efficiency and secrecy. Traditional German respect for hierarchy seems also to have played a role. According to Streckenbach, the powers of decision in his own personnel division were "carefully echeloned." Adolf Hitler had to be consulted about promotions and transfers for "all officials from Riegierungsdirektor [civil service director] on up." All questions from there down to Regierungsrat (civil servant) were submitted to Himmler, Heydrich decided about other officials down to the Inspektor level, and Streckenbach himself handled Obersekretäres (upper secretaries) and their subordinates.

Every promotion required at least six signatures, and the pertinent documents were filed in sextuplicate, with copies for the archives, the administration, the personnel file, and on and on. Streckenbach estimated he "executed two thousand signatures a day. So, do you want to ask me again what I did in my job?"

I did ask him for a concrete example.

"Nothing easier than that. Let's say Poland has been occupied. The Security Police has to open an office in Warsaw. Two hundred fifty people are required: seventy Criminal Police, sixty Gestapo officials, twenty SD men, twenty men for general administration, ten girls for typing.

"Now where to find seventy Criminal Police officials. According to my records, I know that the largest bureau is in Berlin . . . So I would send an order to Berlin, to immediately submit the names of ten men who were available for transfer. They had to be healthy, should not be older than such and such an age, should not be subject to military service . . . Another order would go to Frankfurt for eight names . . . And then the people who had been chosen would receive a letter advising them when they were to present themselves, along with their luggage, how much luggage was allowed, and what was required to be in their luggage, where they had to report, et cetera.

"And the decision on who to put in the top spot; that was made by Himmler. I would have to make a presentation for Heydrich . . . Usually I did not even have to suggest anyone, because Heydrich usually had already . . . made a recommendation to Himmler . . . That's how these things are handled—everywhere."

Nazis often claimed—after the war—that they made choices no differently from "people everywhere," but this was not always the case: like many of their victims, the agents of the police state were simply told what they might bring along and where they had to report. (Of course, their destination was often a fine office in which to play the "heroic" role of political soldier.)

Twice a year, Bruno Streckenbach said, Heydrich bowed to the ideal of folk community and chaired a departmental conference. It was always the same: "Heydrich would give a speech, Werner Best would give a speech, and there would be presentations by specialists in various fields."

Some of these specialists might occasionally be drawn from the third tier of Heydrich's organizational web: fellow SS men who were not members of Reich security. Heydrich certainly knew all of the other SS leaders of any importance, but his relationships with most of them were not particularly cordial. Unlike Heydrich, Himmler liked to pretend his various vassals were all part of one big SS family, but this did not prevent him from playing them off against one another, as he had Heydrich and Theodor Eicke.

These cross-pressures tended to induce an unstable condition of alternating cooperation and enmity, in which each SS leader tried to block the rise of his major competitors, while still appearing willing to work with them if necessary. Meanwhile, Himmler was renovating a medieval castle to use as a retreat for himself and his twelve highest underlings, where he hoped philosophical discussion and meditation might help forge communal bonds. Frau Heydrich dismissed this as one of Himmler's peculiar "whims": "That my husband or the others would want to sit around in such a place and think—impossible!"

By the time war broke out, Heydrich was emerging as the first among these twelve presumed equals, but this did not make him more congenial. He had always been an upstart, a go-getter, a loner, using his position as arbiter of politically correct behavior to enhance his own power. Increasingly, his posture was hardening into that of a Grand Inquisitor, all-knowing, arrogant critic of the morals of others.

Yet, like everyone else, Heydrich needed allies, and—like everyone else—he stooped to expediency to get them. Traditional sources have always claimed that he was a bitter rival of Karl Wolff, chief of Himmler's personal staff, whose wife, it will be recalled, played an ambivalent role in the Himmler intrigue to end the Heydrichs' marriage. Schellenberg said that Heydrich "hated" Wolff; Frau Heydrich told me her husband and "Wolfie" were in constant competition. Yet Wolff later claimed they had actually cooperated frequently, while agreeing to keep the alliance a secret.

In the early days, Wolff admitted, they had clashed often: as Himmler's closest advisers, "both had their offices next to Himmler's, both reported directly to him, both wanted to advance." After Heydrich did advance to chief of the SD, he began to treat Wolff as a subordinate. But Wolff controlled Himmler's appointment book and telephone access, and he enjoyed keeping Heydrich waiting. Finally, after a "high-volume disagreement," Karl Wolff felt things had gone too far, and invited Heydrich to a peace conference, "officer style." The two rivals sat down together one evening at a Berlin wine bar. After a few glasses, they moved on to a nightclub. Soon each met a girl and invited her to their table; in this giddy company, they agreed to try to work harmoniously together.

According to Wolff, the new allies met from time to time to renew their camaraderie—and to enjoy a bit of dalliance on the side. Heydrich graciously gave Wolff the key to a "conspiratorial refuge" owned by the Gestapo in Munich that he himself used on visits there. Wolff claimed that "the mutual knowledge of such manly sins strengthened the friendship."

In general, however, awareness that a man was pursuing his own "personal" benefit made a useful charge for Heydrich to level against someone who was otherwise unassailable. As Werner Best once noted,

Heydrich tended to attribute to opponents qualities he possessed himself.

One day, for example, Bruno Streckenbach met an important official at the Finance Ministry, who told him, "I have tried several times to get in to see Heydrich. Would you please ask him if he could not spare half an hour for me? I would like to talk to him."

When Streckenbach relayed the request, Heydrich replied, "But I don't want to see him! If he's not able to say what he wants in ten minutes, I don't want to talk to him at all."

"That was typical of him," Streckenbach said. "Anyone who was not able to express himself clearly and precisely in ten minutes was a *Trödmudel* to him. That is a North German expression for a slow person, who walks slowly, eats slowly, works slowly. Heydrich had to have people around him who were quick on the uptake."

Heydrich's enormous physical vitality, like his photographic memory, was the stuff of which office legends—and personal authority—is made. Many members of his staff seem to have run themselves into the ground trying to keep up with him. Pomme was ill for months after he left the Security Office in 1941, and Schellenberg had a nervous breakdown in 1939, something he admitted casually in passing to his postwar interrogators. His memoirs have the hysterical tone of someone pushed to the brink of endurance. Albert Hartl, the religious expert, also had a nervous breakdown, as did Heydrich's personal adjutant in Prague during the first weeks after Heydrich became Reichsprotektor, in 1941. According to Frau Heydrich, this man told his boss, "I am exhausted; I can't stand it anymore!" SS men were not supposed to give up, or even to know the meaning of the word *impossible*, but "my husband just wore this man out!"

Breakdowns—or at least serious illness often followed by recuperation in a sanatorium—seem to have been commonplace within Heydrich's entourage. Bruno Streckenbach and Werner Best both received extended treatment from Himmler's personal physician, Dr. Gebhardt; other exhausted security personnel were examined by Professor Doctor Maximinus Friedrich Alexander de Crinis, the influential Nazi psychiatrist and a sponsor of euthanasia, who had become an honorary member of the SS.

Heydrich himself apparently never wore out, even when forced by his official duties to leave his own domain, where he could choose the people around him. According to Pomme, "Heydrich had little to do with the higher-ups, his equals . . . because in that case he wouldn't be the center of attraction." The record suggests that Pomme is wrong about the facts, though he is right in viewing Heydrich as a man for whom the reciprocity of true friendship did not come easily. Still, the SD chief's frequent presence in various accounts of the period suggests that he got around: he met the outspoken journalist Bella Fromm at a formal reception at the home of Foreign Minister von Neurath, and Unity Mitford at a brunch in a bivouac tent during a Party Day exercise. He impressed a foreign journalist at the 1936 Olympics with his good manners, went sailing with Gauleiter Josef Terboven in Norway in 1940, gave a champagne reception at the Ritz in Paris in 1941.

Since Heydrich did not keep normal working hours, he maintained an apartment at Berlin police headquarters in case he worked too late to go home. This was not a simple bachelor flat. It was sufficiently spacious for Lina Heydrich to stay there with the children for a few days during her move, in 1934, from Munich to Berlin. And it was elegantly furnished, with fine mirrors to reflect the luxury, at least if we believe a story SS men delighted in telling foreign visitors. Apparently, Heydrich returned to the apartment late one wine-filled evening and caught sight of his reflection in a full-length mirror. He was dressed in his ceremonial SS uniform. Whipping out his service revolver, he fired several shots into the glass. "At last I've got you, scum," he shouted at his own image.

Though the story may be apocryphal, its point is clear: You cannot run away forever from your own shadow. Gruppenführer Heydrich had glimpsed a hateful manifestation of himself, the man his victims had sometimes confronted, that the artist Joseph Vietze had captured in paint, that his wife had told me wasn't "really" him.

Generally, Heydrich "echeloned" off his roles as neatly as the RSHA personnel chart or the rows of peas he planted on Fehmarn. He rushed from role to role, from office to office, from job to home, deftly switching "gears" between them. Only when jolted by sudden, unexpected confrontations did the gears seem to lock, permitting a momentary vista of the deep contradictions between the New Order Heydrich personified and the old morality of his childhood.

Yet when Heydrich donned a different uniform, his standards subtly altered. When one considers the outermost ring of his SS contacts, his relationships with his fellows in the fencing arena, one sees that he tried to make a more benign impression.

Heydrich (at an SS fencing meet in 1939) excelled as a saber fencer, yet never managed to qualify for the German Olympic team. Resigned to his second-rate standing, he set his sights—with an equal lack of success—on ascending to the presidency of the German Fencing Association.

Heydrich was interested in many sports, but it was fencing that has become so associated with his image that it is almost his hallmark. The mixture of calculation and instinct, of cunning and aggression, of swiftly slashing attack and dogged, untiring persistence—all seem to epitomize his leadership style.

Heydrich's treatment of his Belgian fellow fencer Paul Anspach shows us these techniques in action within the very playing field in which he may have honed them. His path had already crossed Anspach's briefly at a tournament in Germany, in 1935, where a German fencer had warned the Belgian, "Watch out, that man is dangerous." Five years later, Anspach was elected president of the International Fencing Federation, the FIE. After Germany invaded Belgium in 1940, Anspach was called in for questioning by the Gestapo. "That will certainly interest our boss!" his interrogators said when they discovered he was a fencer. How right they were: in August, SS officers seized the archives of the FIE and transferred them to Heydrich's office in Berlin. Anspach complained to the German authorities, setting off a political contest with Heydrich that lasted over a year and provoked the latter to use every form of persuasion except the one most associated with his name—physical violence.

Already inspector of physical training for the SS, Heydrich now managed to get himself appointed director of fencing for the entire Reich.

His appointment became effective in January 1941. In February, Heydrich ordered Anspach to visit him in Berlin. He greeted his apprehensive guest effusively, calling him a typical Fleming, and thus conferring Nazidom's highest accolade: recognition of "mutual Germanic stock."

Brushing off Anspach's protests that in fact he was not a Fleming at all, Heydrich launched his attack: "for practical reasons" during wartime, the FIE files must remain in Germany, but he would be happy to help "revitalize" the organization if only his guest would transfer the presidency to him.

Anspach resisted. Heydrich suggested he think about it for twenty-four hours. In the meantime, he would appoint two distinguished German fencers to serve as liaison between them. No doubt Heydrich hoped another day spent in the capital of the empire that now ruled western Europe would have a softening effect. It usually did: in the spring of 1941, resistance to the Nazi juggernaut was both ineffectual and rare.

Nevertheless, Paul Anspach concluded that the presidency of the FIE should remain in Belgium and insisted that Heydrich give the archives back. Then he returned to occupied Brussels, across a border patrolled by Heydrich's frontier police, using documents that had to be stamped by Heydrich's Gestapo, to a city full of Heydrich's SD agents, who could have easily arranged a little accident or an unfortunately virulent disease.

On February 17, one of his liaison officers appeared in Brussels with a letter for Anspach. It was addressed to Heydrich, and purported to be from Anspach himself, praising Heydrich's "personal standing" and arguing that because of it, he should become president of the FIE. All he had to do was sign the letter, his German colleague advised. Outraged, Anspach instead wrote several missives of his own, complaining both to German fencing officials and the International Olympic Committee.

Heydrich backed off, but he didn't give up. He almost never did. On June 25, 1941, he sent a personal letter to "Dearest Herr Anspach," informing him of a recent triumph: Giulio Basletta, the fascist president of the Italian Fencing Association, had agreed that he should serve as president of the FIE until its "ultimate direction" could be settled after the war.

Anspach did not give up either. With stubborn courage, he wrote Heydrich several letters refusing to accept the fait accompli. He never received an answer: having finally managed to cast a veil of legitimacy over his annexation of the FIE, Heydrich was content to leave bad enough alone. (Paul Anspach survived the war to tell the story to Günther Deschner.)

As this incident suggests, Heydrich rarely practiced intimidation for its own sake: his driving obsession was success—being first, being best, achieving, winning.

Recognition, validation, and *confirmation* were the words Lina Heydrich used most often when she talked about her husband's motivation. For him, she said, sport was one way to ensure that others recognized his worth.

Confirmation, however, is both fragile and difficult to measure, and Heydrich never seemed to get enough of it. In his endless quest for validation, Reinhard Heydrich wore more official hats and engaged in more extracurricular activities than any other major Nazi leader. His energy, flexibility, and ambition propelled him toward assuming multiple, indeed frequently contradictory, roles. In this sense, he was the closest thing the Hitler era offered to a Renaissance man.

Again, the Anspach affair is instructive. During the winter of 1940, Adolf Hitler decided to invade the Soviet Union, a momentous event that threw the Nazi leaders into a frenzy of anticipation and preparation. All during the spring of 1941, Heydrich was desperately busy providing intelligence data, increasing police surveillance, conferring with other Nazi leaders, and organizing SS commandos for murderous use in Russia. Yet sometime during this period, he also managed to make his little deal with Dr. Basletta. His letter to Anspach announcing this coup was written three days after the invasion of Russia, at a time one might have thought Heydrich's mind would have been on other things. Small wonder that his subordinates never felt they acquired an overview of the whole spectrum of his activities and wondered darkly whether his left hand even knew what his right one was doing. His behavior—like that of a good fencer—was often described as unpredictable.

Yet, however much Heydrich's fencing skills may have epitomized his style of leadership, he also behaved a little differently in his favorite sporting arena from the way he did anywhere else. Freud might have said his interest in fencing was "overdetermined." It was, for one thing, a rare familial link connecting him both to his father (who had also fenced, though not as well) and to his young sons, already taking lessons at his insistence.

Then, too, games of all sorts were very popular in the Heydrich household. Tennis, bridge, croquet, fencing—Reinhard Heydrich found time for them all. Frau Heydrich told me that games, especially fencing, were one of the very few "connections" to others that her husband embraced without suspicion or reluctance. (Each, of course, although it is a playful imitation of war, also has rules containing competition within precise spheres and limited spans of time.)

Fencing, in particular, may also have offered a therapeutic escape from the incessant and utterly serious "war games" of the Nazi political bureaucrats. "Don't you see, I have to get out; I can't just sit in the office all day!" Heydrich told his wife. When the chief of Reich security walked up the marble staircase of his RSHA stronghold after his daily hour of fencing practice, perhaps he felt a glow of transcendent well-being. "When you are fencing well, it's a feeling of being in control, a feeling of extending yourself as far as you can, a one-pointedness," an American fencer, Frederic Torzs, has observed. "And you forget everything else."

The Nazi emphasis on producing stalwart warriors gave Heydrich's physical activities official sanction. His example was cited as proof that "even the heaviest claims of one's official duties do not prevent one from being purposefully and systematically active in sport at the same time." Moreover, Himmler noted, fencing was an "intellectual exercise, as it demands an instant reaction to every move of your opponent."

Gradually Heydrich's escape from the office circled back to become integrated into service routines. Members of SS fencing teams got jobs in the RSHA personnel division, and his division chiefs were encouraged to take up the sport. Ernst Kaltenbrunner, facing certain death at Nuremberg, still complained jealously that Walter Schellenberg had used his skill with épée and saber to beat him out with Heydrich. "I had to fence with him," Schellenberg countered in his own testimony. "Everybody did."

"Did Himmler ever fence with your husband?" I asked Frau Heydrich. She found this shriekingly funny. "Oh, no, no, no. It would have been too ridiculous! Himmler was not that stupid!"

Heydrich could easily have defeated his boss: indeed, by 1939, he had become one of the best fencers in Germany, often joining the SS teams to compete in international tournaments. He seems to have gotten along atypically well with his teammates, some of whom visited him and Lina on Fehmarn—and, more indicative, even came to see her after the war. ("They told me all sorts of pretty stories about the old days," she said.) His relationships with "civilian" fencers, however, were always difficult. "He couldn't lose, only complain," Bruno Streckenbach told Günther Deschner. Kurt Pomme said Heydrich would insult the gamekeeper if others surpassed him in hunting; when he lost in fencing he still tended to blame the referee, just as he had during his navy days. Frau Heydrich disagreed with these assessments, insisting she never saw such a thing, and "I was always with him . . . He wanted someone to talk about it with afterward." When he lost, she said, "he blamed himself," becoming white and silent, and withdrawing to brood alone.

His colleagues did recall dreadful "white rages" in addition to embarrassing public scenes in which Heydrich sometimes threatened to investigate the political attitudes of the judges. This was boorish behavior, of course, but also rather commonplace in a country where people routinely accused one another of being "overdue for a concentration camp." Still, Heydrich was the one who sent them there. This power and his willingness to use it to get more power had poisoned his relationships with all but a few family members and political associates.

Hitler's rules offered few rewards for old-fashioned courtesy. Heydrich generally seemed indifferent to the wildly escalating brutalization of German life, which, indeed, the SS had helped to create and then capitalized on. On the fencing field, however, he seems sometimes to have tried to resist his own worst impulses. On at least three occasions, members of the German fencing establishment offered him sharp rebukes. Heydrich not only accepted them, but also attempted to modify his bullying, abrasive behavior.

During one particularly acrimonious argument, an official whom Heydrich had tried to intimidate with the power of his office responded with a lecture on the shabbiness of such tactics. (After that, they got along much better.) Another time, one of Heydrich's coaches told him that he couldn't serve as a model for other SS fencers if he continued to question the decisions of the judges. Chastened, Heydrich asked the man to warn him if in the future his actions seemed unsportsmanlike. Nevertheless, his behavior was so unbecoming during a 1940 saber competition that the referee publicly admonished him over the loudspeaker system: "On the fencing strip the laws of sporting fairness apply and nothing else." Listening in astonishment, Heydrich exclaimed, "My God, I never dreamed there was anyone left like that!"

Sometimes he even bowed to the type of resolute resistance he spent most of his days trying to destroy. Günther Deschner argued that this was because Heydrich encountered firmness "so seldom in those around him." Yet he did not hire yes-men; more likely Heydrich was responding to rare encounters with ghosts of civilities past.

His infatuation with the romantic, gentlemanly sport of fencing seems to have strengthened Heydrich's faint capacity for sympathetic empathy. He was always excellent at understanding others' weaknesses and fears ("hostile empathy" might be an appropriate description) but recognition of their struggles and strengths seems to have been activated primarily by his own troubled efforts to abide by the normal rules of decency. These were rare occasions. Pierre J. Huss, the International News Service war correspondent, said Heydrich gave no one a break. This was not true: a very, very small group of people got a break—and a disproportionate number of these were fencers. He is said to have protected the Polish Olympic team (including its Jewish members) during the war, and to have helped a German-Jewish fencer who had once been national champion emigrate to America. This man was only a Jew "in the sense of the Nuremberg Laws," a catch term for someone whose "Jewishness" might be mitigated by an Aryan ancestor or two. A competitor who was best in his field, a winner deprived of just recognition by the unfair, unalterable factor of "mixed blood"—Heydrich had perhaps found that rare person with whom he could, briefly, identify.

19

THE SECOND SEX AND THE THIRD REICH

"If a man wants to go out dancing after work, if he is tired and needs to relax and have a drink, well, how does that harm me?"

—LINA HEYDRICH

WHATEVER SYMBOLISM one gives to Heydrich's complicated attitudes toward fencing, however, his wife took a homelier approach: her husband's sporting activities interfered with the dwindling amount of time she shared with him, and fencing was merely the last straw.

It didn't really matter, she told me, that she had to live with state secrets, that she could no longer work together with her husband, that she was excluded from parties, receptions, and trips abroad: "I didn't care! That might have been a problem for you, but not for me. But the fencing—that was a problem. To be practicing all week and at tournaments on the weekends! To not even be sure of Sunday dinner with the family! A man must know that he has children! So that is when I rebelled."

To understand fully the form Lina's rebellion took, it is necessary to consider her position as a female in Nazi Germany. As always, the Nazi leaders found it easier to agree on a fundamental point of power—that they would decide what the role of women in the New Order should be—than on the concrete details of policy. They were much better at knowing what they *didn't* want, which was anything resembling life in the ultra-democratic Weimar Republic. After the end of the First World War, monarchical, conservative, prosperous Germany had been turned

Lina and Reinhard Heydrich in 1931 (right), the
year they married; and with son Klaus, in 1934
(above). Lina, demonstrating an independent spirit
despite her status as a Nazi wife, continued an
ongoing rivalry with Margarete Himmler, wife of her
husband's boss, Heinrich Himmler.

almost overnight into a place where freedom of religious and political
expression was rampant, women could vote and hold seats in Parliament, foreigners occupied the Rhineland, and inflation had wiped out
the savings of all but the very rich or ingenious.

Many women sought work outside the home, either to help feed
their families or because they had none. (So many men had died in the
war that young women knew it would be hard to find a husband, and
older women often gave up hope.) In 1938, the American sociologist
Clifford Kirkpatrick found that more women worked in factories in
Germany than in the vastly larger United States.

To many conservatives, women as well as men, it seemed as if the family were disintegrating, along with almost every other traditional institution. At the same time that a brilliant group of writers, artists, architects, and musicians were creating the modern culture of Weimar, many Germans were worried about what came to be known as the *Frauenfrage*, the "woman question." Kirkpatrick found a bibliography of eight hundred pages devoted almost entirely to the problem of whether a woman could have a job and also have babies—and do them both adequately.

The *Frauenfrage* became a symbol of the chaotic personal and social dislocations produced by radical social change. Everything seemed hopelessly mixed up, the victor's laws and the victor's liberalism having unleashed a confusion of sexes and roles that seemed to some observers a veritable war of worlds.

As Hitler wrote,

> [A woman's] world is her husband, her family, her children, and her home . . . How could the larger world exist if there were no one to take as a life task the care of the smaller world? . . . To the one belongs the power of feeling, the power of the soul . . . to the other belongs the strength of vision, the strength of hardness, the decision and willingness to act.

The viewpoint expressed in these words of Adolf Hitler was shared by many people who thought themselves enlightened, rather than radical or revolutionary, and who hoped to spare the women the "double burden" of outside work in addition to housework. Some wanted to infuse the "feminine" ideals of compassion and nurturing into a society wracked by conflict, while others thought the New Woman was to be the custodian, not only of the moral soul of the nation, but of the cupboards—and by implication, the finances—of her house. Whatever happened outside, she was to reign supreme there, possessing the legal right of "the power of the key" within her own home.

It was during the liberal Weimar Republic that the concept of a feminine *Lebensraum* (living space) came into wide usage—as a place removed from the competitiveness and harshness presumed to be masculine, where women and "women's values" might prevail. (Soon, Hitler would monopolize the term, using it to mean territory German men must conquer in the name of national destiny.) It was also during this period that Lina Heydrich, at fourteen, in 1925, made her decision to reject political feminism. Her family, she told me, knew many "liberal" women who had successful careers outside the home. Nevertheless, she claimed to have made up her mind "absolutely" not to be a career woman. "I totally rejected all that!" she told me vehemently. "Must everything important have to do with *business?*"

Nevertheless, she also determined to go away to school to learn a trade. In 1929, while she was making plans to attend a business course for genteel young ladies, the Great Depression arrived in Germany. It has been estimated that between 6 and 7 million men—almost half the workforce—were thrown out of work, adding massive unemployment to the list of problems facing the country's inexperienced political leaders.

The Communists were ready with a solution to everything, but it involved class struggle and violent revolution, which they had already attempted in 1918. Alone among the other scrambling statesmen, Adolf Hitler offered easy answers. He attacked "double earners" (families in which both wife and husband earned salaries) while other families starved. To the unemployed men, he promised jobs—the socialism part of National Socialism—but in speeches to women he often said simply, "I give you man!" Depending on how one interpreted it, that could mean anything from a guaranteed husband, to the protection of a strong provider, through economic and political disfranchisement.

To both sexes he offered a vision of a great national folk community, a *Volksgemeinschaft* cleansed of class divisions, with every group allotted its special sphere and unselfishly working for the benefit of all. "*Gemeinnutz vor Eigennutz!*" shouted the Nazi agitators, meaning, "The common good before that of the individual!"

In 1930, Adolf Hitler's party, so neatly combining appeals to both radicals and reactionaries, had won its first major electoral victory. In 1933, a group of conservative politicians had offered him the position of chancellor, assuming they could control him and exploit his popularity, and his position would be only a temporary phase until they figured out what to do next. Before the year came to an end, however, Hitler had declared himself dictator and pushed through a series of decrees removing women from the Reichstag, the civil service, and positions of authority in teaching and the law. Rigid quotas restricted women's access to university education. Married women in all spheres were laid off by the thousands, and "marriage loans" were offered to poor couples, allowing them to wed—provided the female partner agreed to resign.

Meanwhile, the party leaders vied to determine women's proper role. In 1933, it was still possible for a writer in the Nazi journal *Die Frau* to claim, "We unconditionally recognize, of course, the woman as a companion of man with perfectly equal rights in political life."

But what did "equal" mean? The Führer preferred to give himself the widest possible latitude, remarking vaguely, "Equal rights for women means that they experience the esteem that they deserve in the areas for which nature has intended them."

Some Nazi men lumped Jews and women together, claiming they were both inferior species destined by nature to play a subordinate role. In 1935, Gottfried Feder, the Nazi economist, represented the view of the old-guard militants when he wrote, "The Jew has stolen women from us through the forms of sex democracy. We . . . must march out to kill the dragon so that we may again attain the most holy thing in the world, the woman as maid and servant."

That same year, however, the new SS journal *Das schwarze Korps* disagreed: "Woman is sacred to us . . . She is not the servant of the German male, but his comrade and companion in life."

Curt Rosten, the author of the pamphlet "The ABC of National Socialism," would not have concurred: "German women wish in the main to be wives and mothers. They do not wish to be comrades as the Red philanthropists try to convince themselves and women."

Even these few quotations reveal that the woman question had not been definitively answered. In theory, all differences were to be resolved by the panacea of motherhood—seen as necessary both to enhance women's well-being and to produce more members of the master race. While women were fighting "the battle of the birthrate," they were effectively removed from competition with men. What Lina Heydrich called the "castle of the family" was thus to replace the ruined fortress of feminism. Women were to be segregated within their "natural" domain, much as the Jews were gradually being relegated to the ghetto by a parallel—though much more comprehensive—series of restrictive laws.

The Nazis not only offered dowries to poor couples, but also payments for each child they produced, as well as pre- and postnatal care subsidized by the state. The Nazi "mother care" programs won high praise, even from outsiders. Lina Heydrich also admired them, particu-

Heinrich and Margarete Himmler (in background) on a family
outing in the Bavarian town of Valeep in 1935. Margarete,
born 1893, was seven years older than her husband. Their one
biological child, daughter Gudrun (center foreground, age
seven), was born August 8, 1929, a year after her parents' July 3,
1928, wedding. The Himmlers also adopted a son, Gerhard von
der Ahé (far right), also born 1928. The son of a deceased SS
officer, Gerhard never took the Himmler name. The child on the
far left is one of Gudrun's playmates.

larly Himmler's controversial Lebensborn homes for unwed mothers.
"That is the best you can do for a woman!" she told me.

Members of Nazi leadership tried to go along with the party consensus, but all too often they ran into practical difficulties. Reichsführer
SS Himmler struggled endlessly to reconcile his ideological outlook on
women with the difficulties of his marriage, which seems to have been
a social as well as personal disaster from the start. A year after their
wedding in 1929, Marga Himmler was already complaining that her

husband spent too much time away from home. The Reich Youth leader Baldur von Schirach understood his absence: "I never met a man so henpecked . . . He oozed amiability, but the more amiably he behaved the worse he was treated. At home the head of the police and the SS was a zero."

Reich citizens knew that unfavorable comment about party officials or their families had become a criminal offense, but nothing kept them from laughing secretly among themselves. Von Schirach's wife, Henrietta, dismissed Frau Himmler as "a small, bad-tempered woman who seemed born to be unhappy." Bella Fromm insisted she was not small, but far too large: "The pleasures of the table are apparently about all the pleasures she gets."

In 1936, Hedwig Potthast—youthful, cheerful, and charming—joined Himmler's secretarial staff; by 1939, at the latest, she had become his mistress. Long before that, Himmler had begun to tinker with the customs of matrimony within the SS, simultaneously tightening the marriage regulations to prevent unsuitable matches and tacitly legitimizing extramarital flings. In 1936, he founded the infamous Lebensborn homes for women who had been impregnated by SS men. Himmler ordered that no distinctions be drawn between married and unmarried mothers.

"If a man has an affair with his pretty secretary, at most she will exert some influence over him, but she won't affect his ability to work," Himmler mused aloud to his masseur, Felix Kersten. "In certain circumstances there will be a child." By the outbreak of the war in 1939 he was openly urging each SS man, whether married or not, to father a child before he went off to fight.

The war made anything possible. One day in 1941, Kersten was kept waiting for an hour while Himmler shared with Heydrich his plans for a new marriage law. It featured institutes for the training of "chosen women" (only the blond and blue-eyed need apply) to be taught such diverse subjects as history, languages, diplomacy, chess, fencing, equitation, driving, and how to shoot a pistol, as well as the traditional feminine skills of cookery and housekeeping.

"Just look at many of our National Socialist leaders' wives!" Himmler later exhorted Kersten. "They are good and worthy housewives, adequate during the struggle for power, but being unable to rise in the world, they're no longer suited to their husbands. They quarrel all the time. The husbands find other women . . . We must find a way to separate men from their wives honorably."

Himmler's fanciful solution was to give unsuitable wives a pension and force their former husbands to select a new bride from among the chosen few: "Imagine what that will be like, when in the future our leading men will only marry women who are both gifted and charming, noble in soul and body!"

Real life, however, proved remarkably resistant to fantasy. Himmler never summoned the nerve to divorce Marga, though he did set up housekeeping with Hedwig Potthast, who bore him two illegitimate children. By 1943, Himmler had decided that one woman—even a chosen one—was no longer enough. Bigamy was Himmler's new plan: it would produce more babies for the Reich, and "each wife would act as a stimulus to the other so that both would try to be their husband's dream woman—no more untidy hair, no more slovenliness."

By this time Heydrich was dead, and the Reichsführer was confiding his quest for feminine perfection to Felix Kersten (who was secretly taking notes on their intimate conversations). It isn't known whether Heydrich had applauded his boss's ideas, but he certainly didn't share his finicky orientation. Heydrich was not a perfectionist about women; he took them as he found them—and he tried to find them often.

Lina Heydrich told me emphatically and repeatedly that her husband did not believe in reforming human nature. In fact, he was a consummate opportunist: if people seemed threatening to Heydrich, he attacked them; if they got in his way, he pushed them aside; if they were pliable, he used them.

Whereas Himmler, the idealist, clothed his appetites in extravagantly colored, high-sounding words, Heydrich, the pragmatist, alternated between the language of bourgeois morality and of the gutter.

On March 17, 1942, little more than two months before his death, Reinhard Heydrich gave a speech to members of the League of German Girls who were helping with war work in Prague. He thanked his entirely female audience for their support of the Führer and the German people, adding, "Many spoiled little dolls have in your company learned to understand . . . the meaning of work." In earlier times, he said, youth was "superficial and pleasure seeking," but now it embodied the virtues of the New Order: self-discipline, self-knowledge, clarity of character, love of truth, healthy ambition, and the drive for high achievement. Encouraging his young listeners to serve as "models of National Socialism"—which was what he told his male subordinates, too—the protector added a special bit of advice:

> You should not, through all of your self-discipline and self-control, become at the same time militarized and hardened. The most beautiful thing about a woman—and especially a German woman—is her womanliness, her femininity, which in itself makes a woman beautiful.
>
> In the midst of all your work, and all your activity, guard your womanliness.

Heydrich did not define femininity for his audience. Perhaps he assumed everyone already knew, for the requisite traits were presumed to be genetically encoded, only needing to be brought out by the "right" environment. The Nazi leaders believed emphatically that anatomy was destiny.

Like Himmler, Heydrich also led a double life, maintaining a second sexual existence beyond the confines of conventional marriage, but he represented a different tradition, that of an habitué of the demi-monde—"a nightclub king in politics." On his twilight expeditions, he liked to be accompanied by members of his SD staff, and to choose companions of widely diverse character, as if having company were all that mattered. Eichmann, Naujocks, and Schellenberg all talked of long, tedious nights drifting in and out of bars and cabarets, competing for the favors of women of dubious distinction. The next morning Heydrich would act as if the whole thing had never happened.

Of course, his sexual proclivities aroused intense interest among Heydrich's associates in "the Service." Everyone in his entourage knew the general story of his expulsion from the navy for sexual impropriety. Insiders pondered whether Gruppenführer Max Thomas got his powerful job as police commander in the Ukraine because his daughter was rumored to have been Heydrich's mistress. Conversely, a man who was sent to unpleasant duty in Russia wondered if this was retaliation for the night his wife slapped Heydrich's face after he made improper advances. SS men joked that the golden angel crowning the dome of the new Reichstag building was the only virgin in Berlin he hadn't ravished.

Werner Best said that Heydrich's sexual promiscuity sprang from a compulsive need to conquer in every sphere. Schellenberg, by contrast, insisted his boss's amorous evenings were a sort of antidote to the poisons of perpetual political maneuvering. He considered them his "only weakness," and claimed he surrendered to Eros "without inhibition or caution," completely losing the "calculated control which characterized him in everything else he did." Other sources told of passionate long-term liaisons.

The wave of speculation inevitably spread to include Heydrich's wife. Everyone agreed that *his* blond and blue-eyed *Frau*—in contrast to Himmler's—was both spirited and beautiful. (Although Lina Heydrich told me she always dressed austerely and wore her hair in a bun.) Some people thought the peculiarly enduring bond between the Heydrichs was primarily sexual in nature. On the other hand, one SD officer expressed the belief that Heydrich's amorous excesses—as well as his urge to excel as a fencer, a pilot, a horseman—were derived from "sexual-pathological complexes" brought on by a cold wife's fanatic ambition.

In totalitarian societies, gossip replaces the free press, and it is all too tempting to *cherchez la Frau*. The important thing, however, is not this or that transitory rumor but one hard fact: the vast power that both Himmler and Heydrich possessed enabled them to carry out vendettas, indulge fantasies, even commit follies, all in the name of the *Volk*, for were they not its designated agents and arbiters? There can be no revolution without experimentation, no political reconstruction without licensed social engineers.

If Himmler was allowed his little hobby of nurturing unwed mothers in Lebensborn homes, Heydrich's inclinations took him in another direction—to 11 Giesebrechtstrasse, Berlin. This was the address of "Salon Kitty," said to have been the most elegant bordello in Germany. Its clients came from the highest social circles in the Reich, and included artists and diplomats as well as the leader of Hitler's bodyguard, Sepp Dietrich; German Foreign Minister Joachim von Ribbentrop; Reich Press Chief Otto Dietrich; Labor Front leader Robert Ley, and Foreign Ministers Galeazzo Ciano of Italy and Ramón Serrano Suñer of Spain.

Salon Kitty was small but choice. It had only nine rooms for the clients, in addition to a drawing room furnished in the best taste of the time. The elegant decor featured velvet draperies, Persian rugs, crystal chandeliers, plushly upholstered armchairs, and a grand piano, all complemented by a luxurious scattering of fine artwork and cut glass. Those were the features known to the patrons. In addition, there were hidden microphones in every bedroom and secret tape recorders in the basement, running twenty-four hours a day, making a record of even the most intimate utterances. The madam of this unusual establishment was a middle-aged prostitute, Kitty Schmidt; the girls it employed were amateur Secret Service agents; the procurer who had found them in the Vice Squad files was the chief of the Reich Criminal Police, Arthur Nebe; the man who supervised the furnishings was Walter Schellenberg; and the patron of the whole elaborate arrangement was Reinhard Heydrich. All of them worked for him.

Salon Kitty was in no way necessary to the survival of the Nazi state, and has been dismissed as little more than a "whim" of Heydrich's. Certainly, it *was* a fine plaything for a man obsessed with both security and sex. Lina Heydrich once advised me that the best time for a woman to confide in her husband is at night, in bed. Heydrich, too, had considerable respect for "bed whispers" as the blurted-out repositories of real truth. Perhaps he was extrapolating from his own behavior.

Even if no interesting political information turned up, there were still rich opportunities for blackmail—and besides, the company was bound to be congenial. Periodically, Heydrich indulged in personal "inspections" of the premises, during which the microphones were presumably turned off.

Nevertheless, both Schellenberg and Naujocks have told a similar, peculiar tale in which they are summoned to Heydrich's office and blamed for failing to silence the recorders during one of his visits. ("If you think you can make fun of me . . . you'd better think again. Get out!") Each professed innocence, and concluded that Heydrich had staged the whole scene to catch him in a "mistake" and thus weaken his position.

Like much of Nazi life, Salon Kitty was a theater in disguise, with much more going on behind the scenes than the chosen audience was allowed to know. If the two witnesses are accurate, it is interesting that Heydrich, who had often been jeered at in his childhood, chose this method of reversing the story and making himself the hidden master of the situation.

The real truth about Salon Kitty was top secret in its day, and little is known about it now, the shrouds of official secrecy having been replaced by the ornamentation of postwar fantasy. Conflicting memoirs, reconstructed historical dialogue, even a movie that managed to show Heydrich naked in his Gestapo office, holding a fencing foil and discussing Salon Kitty, have blurred almost everything but the basic facts of its existence and purpose. One does not really know, for instance, how Heydrich ever came up with the plan in the first place; in fact, everyone who talks of it has a different theory.

Walter Schellenberg said that after the Blomberg-Fritsch debacle (leading to Hitler's takeover of the army), Heydrich was clutching at any new source of information about his competitors in the Reich; whereas Albert Naujocks says that he simply wanted to grasp female flesh. Naujocks claims he was present in a bar one evening when his boss, a little the worse for drink, encountered a blond tart who pleased him: "You know who I am? I'm Heydrich, you know? Like to work for me, Heydrich? I've got an idea, haven't I, Alfred? We could use our friend here, couldn't we, Alfred?"

Kitty's "salon" brought out the dramatist in everyone—except perhaps for Lina Heydrich.

"Do you know how Salon Kitty originated?" I asked her.

"I know exactly, quite precisely. My husband and Herr Nebe, who was the chief of the Criminal Police, opened up a criminal museum to explore the possibility of discovering the nature of the criminal intellect . . . And the result was that all the criminal officials of Europe and beyond Europe traveled to this museum to orient themselves."

There was indeed a criminal museum, though most of the visitors may have been disoriented by it. Heydrich himself offered a tour of it one day to a Swiss representative of the Red Cross. The museum consisted of four or five rooms full of amateurish exhibits on favorite Nazi bugaboos like the Jesuit menace and the worldwide conspiracy of Freemasons. One room was almost entirely dark and contained a human skeleton whose bony hand brushed the visitors as they passed.

"But," Frau Heydrich continued, "there was a negative side to this criminal museum—that these people, whether they were from Japan or China or America—in the evenings, they wanted to amuse themselves in Berlin. And so, Salon Kitty originated. And then, naturally, many people who came on the pretext of seeing this museum had something else in mind—to conduct espionage, no? And in order to separate these . . . this chaff from the wheat, and also to find out what kind of people they were—that's how it originated."

"It was not your husband's idea?" I asked.

"No! It was the *young* people! I believe it was Schellenberg—I don't know exactly—but, in any case the wives of the married men would have made trouble . . . So it was the young people.

"My husband told me about it in full detail and we were very amused by it. But I was never there . . ."

Frau Heydrich seemed to falter, then veered away in a more promising direction. "An erotic experience . . . young men in foreign offices, boasting . . . it is the same everywhere . . . I believe that is *international*!" She laughed. Kitty had been gracefully declawed; Reinhard Heydrich's wife had turned her into a joke.

Lina's speculation that Walter Schellenberg dreamed up Salon Kitty is nowhere confirmed, or even referred to, in his memoirs. But then other details go unmentioned here, among them his wife's, Käthe's, extreme jealousy, how it would have been provoked by Schellenberg's involvement in a project such as Salon Kitty, or particularly his and Käthe's perfectly dreadful, archetypically messy divorce. In reality, as events would prove, Schellenberg's wife was, emphatically, the jealous kind, as was Lina's husband, Reinhard himself, as the disintegration of Schellenberg's marriage, which involved all four of them, would prove.

Lina's own attitude toward the status of women in Nazi Germany was difficult to pin down. On the one hand, she supported in principle the Nazi ideal of the domesticated woman; on the other hand, she often expressed admiration for spontaneously ambitious and accomplished women such as the filmmaker Leni Riefenstahl, the pilot Hannah Reitsch, and Hitler's admirer Winifred Wagner, the daughter of the composer.

Initially, Lina and I rarely discussed the lives of women during the Third Reich. I had come to ask her about her husband, his colleagues, his work. Questions about men were obviously what she had expected, her too-swift answers and abrupt pauses suggesting that we were proceeding down a well-worn path. But as she attempted to guide me over skillfully constructed hurdles and along artfully camouflaged byways, we sometimes wandered into the uncharted terrain of female experience.

One of Frau Heydrich's favorite evasions was suddenly to remember that she had left something cooking in the small kitchen adjoining the living room in which we always sat. Such tactics might have deflected the male interviewers who had preceded me, but I offered to help. Soon I was standing at the borderline of her sanctuary, handing her a dish or two when she emerged. Eventually, we moved from dishes to recipes. I told her about broiling marinated fish outdoors on a grill, and she described the local tradition of baking it with fresh horseradish sauce.

Gradually, our camaraderie of the kitchen extended into other areas. In the dark, cool living room, it was easy to become disoriented. It sometimes seemed we could have been anywhere, conducting age-old feminine business. One evening Lina Heydrich told me she thought she had become stronger as she grew older. "The best years in the life of a woman are between forty and fifty," she said earnestly. Then she began to laugh. "Remember that on your thirty-ninth birthday!"

But in her rebellion against her husband's "fencing" (and perhaps against his extramarital exercises) she abandoned any sort of theory on women's status, and moved onto that far more dangerous playing field where the battle of the sexes takes place. As her unwitting partner, she daringly chose Heydrich's closest professional associate, the rising young star of SD Intelligence, Walter Schellenberg.

Schellenberg, slim and dark, with delicate features and a look of courteous alertness on his heart-shaped face, was widely regarded as a handsome man. Schellenberg was also considered one of the cleverest schemers in the Reich, yet he almost lost his life in Lina Heydrich's little domestic uprising. (Loving a good drama as she did, she sometimes called her own reports of him the "Schellenberg Theater.")

Despite his reputation as a calculating schemer, Schellenberg had made a bridal choice that for sheer ineptitude was worse even than Himmler's—which it also somewhat resembled. Like his Reichsführer, Schellenberg had married a woman who neither aged nor "presented" well: her grammar was bad, her manners imperfect, and her class too low to complement a "striver" who admitted he joined the SS for its social prestige. The Schellenbergs had met in 1931 when he was twenty-one, and just beginning six years of graduate study in Bonn, where she

Walter Schellenberg (pictured at age thirty-six, in 1946) provided the technical support to allow Nazi Intelligence to record activities in the Berlin brothel known as Salon Kitty, whose clientele included both German and foreign officials.

was employed as a seamstress. Like Marga Himmler, Käthe Schellenberg was eight years older than her husband.

Unlike the prudish Himmler, however, young Walter Schellenberg defied his family by persisting in a passionate liaison "based on a sexual relationship," as he later put it.

The couple did not marry until 1938. By then Schellenberg's passion had cooled, but he convinced himself that matrimony was a "moral duty." He made a careful list of his reasons: Käthe had broken an engagement to someone else when they met, and now she was dependent on him financially and psychologically. Moreover, Schellenberg's immediate superior in the SD had made it clear that any other outcome would signify the end of his "career development."

Until the very last moment, Schellenberg hoped something would happen to prevent the nuptials. Perhaps the SS doctors would conclude that Käthe, at thirty-five, was too old to bear children? Alas, while they thought it difficult, they concluded that it was possible. Though he was breaking one of the Nazi "Ten Commandments" of proper marital choice (Number 8: "Marry for Love!"), Schellenberg resolved to keep his wife from realizing he now saw his marital duties as "work."

Back at the office, Heydrich's career was accelerating. He needed a polished speechwriter, an agent for delicate tasks in foreign espionage, a skilled lawyer to help him reorganize the whole department. And it didn't hurt if that person could make charming conversation at dinner, participate in the planning of Salon Kitty, yet also be presentable to Lina Heydrich.

Schellenberg, in his memoirs so evasive about his own wife, was voluble about Frau Heydrich: "A cool Nordic beauty not without pride and ambition of her own, yet completely enslaved by Heydrich, was glad to find in me someone who could satisfy her . . . longing for more intelligent and cultivated society in the world of literature and art."

Schellenberg presents himself as a sort of knight of higher culture, and even claims to have opened doors for Heydrich into "the very best circles in Berlin society." Like so many things in Schellenberg's memoirs, this claim is difficult to substantiate. Whatever doors in the best circles may once have been open to Heydrich, they were subsequently closed, even to his memory.

On the other hand, Lina Heydrich's recollections of her husband's handsome subordinate seemed passionately vivid. Her voice, so often subsiding into flat singsong when uncongenial matters like the Jewish Question were mentioned, sprang to life at the mention of his name: "Ah, Walter Schellenberg! I have known this man so well! He was a man who thought only of his career . . . I knew him as a very unimportant man, and then he came to power and was deformed as a person."

"Have you read his book?"

"*Ach!* I have never read anything so bad! Unbelievably exaggerated."

Lina Heydrich recalled Schellenberg with approval only during "that completely unspoiled time" (as she called it) before the "Schellenberg Theater" began. At that time, early in 1939, Walter Schellenberg had become Heydrich's new protégé, a constant guest in his home and a frequent companion in his evenings on the town.

Meanwhile, his marriage of less than a year was already disintegrating. Part of the problem may have been the bridegroom's efforts to instruct Käthe in the "little things," like clothing, hairdo, and fingernails, "over which a man stumbles many times when he is so overloaded at the office that what he truly wants is to find another world in a woman."

It didn't seem to Schellenberg that he had succeeded at all. Sometimes his heart would leap up when he saw her dressed tastefully. But generally, she either let herself go entirely or went the opposite direction and appeared "rigged out like a target practice figure."

For her part, Käthe Schellenberg wasn't sure that her husband really spent as much time working as he said. If he even talked to another woman at a party, she fell into a jealous rage. Was this, Schellenberg wondered, the kind of marriage he was going to have—leaving for the office at seven and not coming back until nine or ten o'clock at night, often with a loaded briefcase, and in the meantime, having received one or two hysterical phone calls from his wife—was *this* supposed to be fulfillment? He imagined himself in the future: "an ossified married man . . . living with an out-and-out shrew."

Then one night, he came home late and hungry and had just removed some tomatoes from the refrigerator, when Käthe attacked him from behind, hurling insults and blows. Suddenly, Walter Schellenberg couldn't stand it anymore. He decided to leave, but it wasn't easy. First Käthe blocked the door, and wouldn't let him out. Then he brandished his service revolver and said he might do something "stupid" unless she gave him his freedom. Later, she grabbed the weapon and threatened to kill herself. Finally, Käthe agreed to a trial separation.

Schellenberg sent Käthe to his parents for a rest cure, but she returned even more upset than before. His best friend, Heydrich's adjutant Hans-Hendrik Neumann, tried to serve as a discreet go-between, but Käthe preferred public confrontations. In a railroad waiting room, she shouted loudly; in a restaurant, she burst into tears; and when Hans and Walter took her to the sports stadium for lunch, she suddenly sprang up and tried to hurl herself over a barricade. An interested crowd watched her husband's frantic efforts to calm her and take her back to the table.

Something had to be done. What if Heydrich found out? Or Himmler? Schellenberg's powerful boss barely succeeded in moderating the intense hostility between his own wife, Lina, and the Reichsführer SS. Hadn't Himmler once shouted at Heydrich, "How can you run an organization when you cannot even control your own wife?"

Desperately, Schellenberg arranged for Käthe to be examined by several doctors specializing in nervous disorders. It seemed to them that she was feigning illness: the wild scenes, threats of suicide, and similar "theater" were just the efforts of a hysterical woman to regain her man's interest.

As the doctors may have known, Eva Braun had tried suicide attempts with great success vis-à-vis Adolf Hitler. Pitiful outbreaks were one of the traditional options for a neglected woman in this flagrantly male-dominated society.

But there were others. Women were steadily losing their legal rights, but this did not mean that they had no power at all. On the afternoon of April 16, 1939, Käthe Schellenberg interrupted a consultation at a private sanatorium, raced to the cupboard, pulled a coat on over her nightdress, and attempted to "run to the wife" of her husband's "highest chief."

Enter Lina and Reinhard Heydrich . . .

From this point on, the action in the Schellenberg Theater shows some of the hallmarks of French bedroom farce: not one of the participants seems to have known all the facts, and in any case, none is disposed to tell the whole truth. Yet oddly enough, there is a superabundance of source material: Schellenberg's memoirs, Frau Heydrich's memoirs, my interviews with her. There is also an extraordinary file now stored at the National Archives in Washington, D.C. We know Schellenberg's marital woes so well primarily because he wrote a long, intimate letter pouring out his feelings to a person identified only as "X." That letter formed the first entry in a twenty-page portfolio of notes, legal opinions, and interview transcriptions, all pertaining to his marriage and prepared in the surprisingly casual style of secret intra-office memos within the SS bureaucracy. This file was intended for the eyes of Heydrich and Himmler alone. Yet even this top-secret portfolio doesn't contain the whole story. The SD was not as omniscient as most Germans thought: none of the men involved apparently ever suspected that Lina Heydrich was anything but a bit player in the drama.

Desperately, Käthe Schellenberg continued her efforts to make contact with Frau Heydrich. Finally, she wrote her a letter, which arrived inauspiciously on the eve of the birth of the Heydrichs' third child.

Since childbirth was assumed to be the defining feminine experience, it had become, inevitably, politicized. As Minister of Propaganda Joseph Goebbels put it, "We must develop organizations in which an individual's entire life can take place. Then every activity and every need of every individual will be regulated by the collectivity represented by the party. There is no longer any arbitrary will, there are no longer any free realms in which the individual belongs to himself . . . The time of personal happiness is over."

Women were exhorted to give at least four racially and physically correct children to the Fatherland. (The government helped out by making the Nazi mother care facilities among the best in the world.) Sexual intercourse with non-Aryans was a criminal offense, Aryan Germans with genetically transmitted diseases were forced to undergo compulsory sterilization, abortion was forbidden, and homosexuality was regarded as a "crime against the race."

All of these Nazi practices had as their aim the generation of an abundance of babies destined to serve as soldiers and administrators of a new German empire. Only the act of childbirth itself was relatively sacrosanct: there a woman had at least a chance of exercising her own preferences, particularly if she were the wife of a powerful man.

When their first child was born in 1934, Lina Heydrich decided to remain in her own home for the birth. Reinhard Heydrich limited his influence to insisting that a doctor also be in attendance—as he was, himself. Lina told me it was unusual in those days for a husband to participate, and that such a thing would not have been permitted in a hospital: "It was only for our own satisfaction that we did it that way." She admitted, "Today there would be more modern methods, but we didn't have them at all. When I had the feeling that I had to squeeze someone, my husband said, 'Yes, come, here is my arm. Hold on to me.'

"But he had the jacket of his uniform on. I thought he shouldn't dress so correctly. And I said, 'Take your jacket off!' And he told me the next day that his arm was blue all over! All over! Yes, I can still remember that!

"And then the birth process quickened, and then—with the first child it often happens that you tear. And this tear has to be sutured. And the doctor said my husband had to gather his strength together and serve as an apprentice. I was under anesthesia and my husband must have been afraid, but he couldn't just sit there, he had to hold me down and so forth. After all, there was no operating room—I was at home.

"Well, afterward, he didn't say anything at all about it, so later I asked him, 'How was it, then?' And he said, 'Thank God I was always there for us!' But, he said, 'if you want a comparison it was just like with a Christmas goose, that is first cleaned out and then sewn up again!' "

When her third child, and first daughter, was born in 1939, Lina Heydrich was at home again. This time Reinhard was not constantly in attendance—"although he visited me a great deal." However, many friends managed to stop by even before Silke was born: "The house was full of visitors, and it was joyfully celebrated."

Meanwhile, however, since Lina Heydrich was temporarily absent from many of the festivities, her husband intercepted Käthe Schellenberg's letter to his wife.

On April 26, he requested a meeting with Frau Schellenberg at his magnificent office at police headquarters. Heydrich sent a limousine to pick her up, and assigned one of his trusted officers, Walter Rauff, as her escort. Sturmbahnführer Rauff also took extensive notes during the meeting. It lasted for fifty minutes—five times longer than the norm in Heydrich's office.

Some moments were necessarily spent on courtly protocol: Käthe Schellenberg apologized for intruding on Heydrich's time; he replied it was his duty as Schellenberg's commanding officer to help clarify the situation. Then he suggested that the unhappy couple might try living apart for a trial year.

Rauff noted that Frau Schellenberg did not respond "objectively," but instead asked whether Heydrich realized how happy her marriage had always been.

Heydrich responded, "I have never had reason to concern myself with the happiness of the marriage, although I did notice that Schellenberg was not working with his usual efficiency. Then your letter to my wife arrived and I asked him, '*Was ist los* between you?'"

In a manner Rauff describes as "peaceful, objective, and very human," Heydrich advised her that when a love between two people has been broken, it cannot always be put together again. If one or both parties to a marriage have the impression that they no longer suit each other, is it not fairer to dissolve it rather than let it endure in some contorted form?

"I cannot find my way without my husband," Frau Schellenberg replied.

Time heals all wounds, Heydrich counseled. Above all, he said, work helps lift depression. "Did you once have a career, and could you go back to it?" (Perhaps he already knew Schellenberg's new plan, which was to find her some little newly Aryanized business far away from Berlin.)

"I don't think at all anymore; my husband has brought me to that," she said. "I'm not capable of doing anything."

For a rather long while, the two seem to have become stalemated. Finally, Heydrich asked her, "How do you conceive of your future relationship to your husband?" Käthe suggested that anything would be all right so long as she wound up with an apartment of her own in Berlin.

But the new capital of the Greater German Reich was undergoing an acute housing shortage, and anyway Schellenberg couldn't afford to maintain two apartments on his low SD salary. (As it was, he was struggling to pay off the installments on their furniture.)

"The point," Heydrich said at last, "is not the apartment; it is that you have apparently not shaped your life in such a way as to retain your husband's love and now we must all deal with this situation as responsible people. So, if you will not agree to leave Berlin, then I will be forced to transfer Schellenberg somewhere else."

With that, he picked up the phone, and ordered his chief of personnel to come right up for a talk.

This had to be nothing more than a bit of dramatic business, for Heydrich was not likely to sacrifice the man he was grooming as his SD deputy. As Käthe knew perfectly well, such a move would have meant the end of Schellenberg's brilliant career.

She gave in, and offered to pack her bags that very night. "I have sacrificed everything for my husband and will do this too," she said. "But you don't know him! He is an egotist! He can't take a stand on anything!"

"I cannot take either one side or the other," Heydrich concluded. "With the best will in the world, I cannot do anything more for you."

For most Germans, the trip to Heydrich's office would have been enough. Yet Käthe Schellenberg refused to be intimidated. Rauff had been instructed to escort her home again but after they had gone part of the way, she "took her leave in such a form that further accompaniment became impossible." Then she added, "I have no one to help me, now I'm going to handle it myself . . . I am going to get revenge."

There is a gap of four months between Rauff's protocol and the last three entries in Schellenberg's file, and it can be assumed that in the interval—the long, hot summer of 1939—things were almost as busy on the little sexual battlefront as they were in the larger theater of European politics.

When Frau Schellenberg said she had no one to help her, she wasn't being quite accurate: Lina Heydrich told me she had served as confidante to both Käthe and Walter. "I went through this entire *tragedy* with the wife!"

As she spoke of tragedy—a word she rarely used—Frau Heydrich began to stammer. "Terrible!" (Another word I almost never heard her say.) "Terrible . . . Terrible . . . Terrible . . .

"She was jealous, with good grounds, I assume. It came naturally from this: she was older than he and wasn't beautiful any longer. Walter Schellenberg was a young man with a career, with prospects. I think it was a marriage with a certain dual intention. She financed his studies and he felt obligated to marry her. And he blamed himself a little when she couldn't converse with him. Whether she was right to be jealous or not, he found it unpleasant, that is clear. I tried to explain it to her one day in the woods, but it didn't work."

As Lina described her role: "I always had to regulate things with fellow workers of Reinhard's. When the marriage didn't work, I had to take care of the women, to regulate things. There were no men to take care of it."

No men? Hadn't Reinhard told her about his chat with Käthe? One senses that the Heydrichs weren't communicating too well at the time. In fact, it wasn't only the Schellenberg marriage that was falling apart.

"Schellenberg wrote that your husband neglected his family. Would you say that's correct?" I asked her.

"*Ach*, Schellenberg. Yes. He always believed that. Yes. He sympathized with me."

"But what is *your* opinion?"

"*Ach*, I've already told you of Schellenberg with his first wife. And then my husband had a tournament. You know he had begun to fly, and he was always fencing, always going to tournaments, always away. And I had not complained to him, and then Schellenberg came and I gave him advice again about his wife, and then I said to him, 'You come every day . . . and my husband works the whole day and otherwise, he is somewhere in some town with his fencing and I don't see him at all anymore.' That was just during this time . . . Schellenberg was with us at the house a lot—at a really unhappy time, I must say.

"But," she continued, "soon my husband achieved the title of German master of fencing. He didn't practice so much after that, and I was happy. Then it was over."

I realized I had been waiting for Lina Heydrich to provide a bridge between events, the transitional arc of meaningful sequence that she often failed to construct. This time, she was being even more elliptically evasive than usual.

"I suppose you have heard about the rumors of an affair between you and Walter Schellenberg?"

"I took an interest in Walter Schellenberg. Bridge with him and his friend Hans Neumann: that was the theme of that time . . . Walter Schellenberg was always at the house."

"Wasn't your husband jealous? Didn't he hear the rumors?"

"My husband was jealous by nature. But not so it became bothersome to me. It was somewhat flattering. A man must be a little jealous."

That was clearly intended to be her last word on a subject that has excited considerable speculation, particularly among readers of Schellenberg's memoirs.

In them—though only in the English version—he tells a chilling story that begins at an SS and police conference on Fehmarn, sometime in the summer of 1939:

> Heydrich's wife came from the island, where they owned a lovely summer villa. After the conference, Heydrich . . . flew back to Berlin in his own plane. I, still having one free day, remained there. In the afternoon, Frau Heydrich asked me to drive her to Plöner Lake. It was a harmless excursion. We had coffee and talked about art, literature, and concerts . . . Before it grew dark, we drove back.

Four days later, Schellenberg writes, "Gestapo" Müller invited Schellenberg to join him and Heydrich for an evening out in civilian clothes. The young man, thinking it was one of "the usual escapades," accepted without a thought. True, he did have an uncomfortable premonition about the evening, but dismissed it as an occupational hazard of "people who continually feel their lives to be in danger." He found Heydrich "at his most charming," and the three men had a pleasant dinner and then decided to visit an out-of-the-way bar near the Alexanderplatz. Schellenberg was enjoying the drink Müller had fetched for him, until the Gestapo leader suddenly asked, "Well, how was it at the Plöner Lake? Did you have a good time?"

Schellenberg looked at Heydrich and saw his face had gone very pale. He asked his boss if there was anything he might like to know about the excursion with his wife. It is no wonder that many years later, he could still quote Heydrich's reply: "You have just drunk some poison. It could kill you within six hours. If you tell me the complete and absolute truth, I'll give you an antidote—but I want the truth."

Schellenberg considered Heydrich "quite capable of making just such a grisly joke with a perfectly straight face." His heart pounding, he tried to remain calm as he described the innocent lakeside expedition.

The area of gravest difficulty concerned a fifteen-minute walk that Walter and Lina enjoyed after their picnic. "Why did you hide that?" Müller wanted to know. "You must realize surely that you were being watched all the time?"

With his six hours ticking by, Schellenberg described the walk in minute detail, including the conversations that had taken place. After he finished: "Heydrich sat motionless and withdrawn for several minutes. At last he looked at me with glittering eyes, and said, 'Well, I suppose I must believe you, but you will give me your word of honor that you won't attempt this sort of escapade again.'"

"A word of honor secured in this sort of way is just an extortion," Schellenberg replied. "First, I must ask you to let me have the antidote . . . then I'll give you my word of honor. As a former naval officer, would you have it any other way?"

For a few moments, the SD chief glared at his subordinate. Perhaps he was reviewing whether Schellenberg was truly "indispensable" (as the young man liked to describe himself). Both of them felt a deep, almost obsessive love for the Ausland-SD, and that, as much as Schellenberg's protestations of innocence, may have saved his life.

Eventually, Heydrich nodded his head, and Schellenberg was given a dry martini:

> Was it my imagination, or did it taste peculiar? Certainly, it seemed to have an added dash of bitters. I gave Heydrich my word of honor, then in view of what had passed between us I begged to be excused. But he wouldn't hear of it, and we had to continue the evening's merrymaking. Once more, he had failed to entrap me.

Schellenberg's difficult wife was not the only trial he had undergone in that last year before the beginning of the Second World War. For some time, he had felt his predatory boss was trying to get something on him. Perhaps Heydrich had used "this new relationship between his wife and me to set a trap."

A lonely lake—complete with an unseen Gestapo surveillance team—might seem to have provided the ideal opportunity. But why was Heydrich so upset? (Was he a good enough actor to have turned pale at will?) And if Schellenberg had nothing to hide, as he claimed, what was the point? It seems far more likely that Herr Suspicion was not motivated merely by office politics: this time, Schellenberg was not the only one who had unwittingly fallen into a trap.

In her memoirs, the same woman who told me she rarely complained to her husband ("We didn't have time for that!") admits she repeatedly reproached him for not spending more time with the family. Afterward, things would improve for a while, until he once again began to find excuses for his repeated absences from home. Finally, she began to ponder a daring course: "whether it paid to jeopardize our marriage through my behavior. For I had no talent for being the housewife who only waits, always, through everything."

Then an incident occurred that gave her an idea. Walter Schellenberg had told her of his marital troubles: "He trusted me and asked me to help him." Lina agreed to invite Käthe Schellenberg to her hunting lodge for a woman-to-woman chat. As they walked through the woods, she suggested that Käthe try to be more broad-minded about Walter's behavior.

A few days later, Lina Heydrich asked Schellenberg to come hear her report of the visit. As they talked, she concluded that his marriage was being destroyed by his wife's unusual jealousy: "Jealousy? A light went on in my head. Reinhard is also very jealous. I could do something with that. I decided to invite . . . Schellenberg to come and 'discuss his marriage' frequently—and very ostentatiously."

In other words, she deliberately turned her husband's ever-suspicious mind in the direction of the man who—she has just told us—"trusted me."

Did it work? In the very next sentence of her book, Frau Heydrich offers this conclusion: "Schellenberg's marriage could not be saved; ours, however, survived and became good again."

I tried to find out more details on my next visit, after I had read her newly published memoirs.

"Weren't you worried about what might happen to Schellenberg? The poison story—"

"Idle gossip, that's all," she interrupted swiftly.

In her version of events, the controversial expedition to Plöner Lake never took place. However, she *did* once ask Schellenberg to drive her to Fehmarn, since she had too much luggage for the train. And then they decided to take a detour to Oldenburg, because Lina wanted to show him where she had gone to school. Unfortunately, this caused them to be late, and Heydrich, who was meeting her at the station, waited and waited, becoming increasingly upset as time went on.

Frau Heydrich still wouldn't tell me what happened next, though she wrote that after the Schellenberg Theater her husband stayed home more, and "for the first time had a normal relationship to our sons, and now for the first time recognized the difficulties that he had left for me alone to resolve. "

Now, too, she finally convinced Heydrich that he needed some measure of regular private contact with his subordinates and their families. "I proposed to take in hand the wives, who, like me, must lead a lonely life."

I asked her what happened to Käthe Schellenberg, but Lina said she didn't know: "I went to Fehmarn for the summer with the children, and when I came back he had married Irene."

It seems clear that the last few scenes of the theater occurred when Walter and Reinhard were left alone in the city for a few months, and the obstreperous Käthe Schellenberg had once again returned to Berlin. This time, her estranged husband found rooms for her in a pension. (By now, he must already have met Irene.)

Frau Schellenberg soon realized that her husband was avoiding her, and began to call various colleagues and their wives to complain about his ungentlemanly behavior. (Some of them thought she had a point, and even Schellenberg's parents wavered occasionally in their loyalties.) The unstable, unpleasant situation continued until the day Käthe phoned Schellenberg's adjutant and told him to get her husband on the phone in five minutes or she would kill herself immediately. "My death will be on your conscience!" she shouted into the receiver.

The adjutant raced off to fetch his boss. The next time Käthe called, however, Schellenberg's friend, Hans Neumann, answered the phone and threatened her with arrest by the Gestapo. Neumann was Heydrich's personal adjutant, and Käthe Schellenberg had been around the SS long enough to know he had no technical right to invoke police powers that only his master possessed. She wrote to Himmler, complaining of this and requesting a personal audience.

Käthe had played a plucky, daring game, but writing Himmler was a fatal mistake. Heydrich had already seen her, and now she was trying to go around him to involve *his* boss. Whatever the strain in his feeling for Schellenberg, this was worse—it was an attack on the entire leadership principle, the sort of affront he didn't tolerate from *men*. On Heydrich's orders, Schellenberg assembled a file that granted his jealous and ruthless superior officer access to deeply intimate letters and humiliating accounts by lawyers and doctors of a situation of which he had completely lost control. Schellenberg also included a covering letter bemoaning "the feeling of struggling against an invisible enemy, who is spreading to all my friends all kinds of rumors about me." He was regaining some of his customary astuteness, for he knew that Heydrich had struggled against defamatory rumors all of his life.

In August, Heydrich wrote his own covering letter to Himmler, warmly defending Schellenberg. Heydrich's oral reports to the Reichsführer SS were famous in their day as models of logical exposition inexorably leading to a single overwhelming conclusion. They are gone now—but his letter designed for his boss's eyes only offers a reasonable approximation.

If Schellenberg had been clever, Heydrich was masterly. His young subordinate had been "enthralled" into a foolish marriage that had become a "tragedy" for him, even a "martyrdom," Heydrich summarized, knowing this was approximately what Himmler felt about his own relationship with Marga. Frau Schellenberg complains too much, Heydrich went on, playing on all of Himmler's prejudices, and has "little feminine pride, inner responsibility, and consciousness of duty." Whereas, he wrote, Schellenberg "is characteristically one of my best and hardest-working, most reliable supports."

Ignoring his own recent fit of jealousy, Heydrich said he had no reason to doubt any of Schellenberg's assertions about his marriage: "Having inserted myself into the situation, I had the misfortune of speaking to Frau Schellenberg personally. Frau Schellenberg did not leave a good impression behind."

Even Neumann's threats against her were "understandable," Heydrich argued, "as a defense against the continuing, daily, frequently repeated (by telephone and in person) intrusions, burdens, and insolences which Frau Schellenberg has systematically undertaken."

Heydrich's language has a scathing, scornful, pounding rhythm that plunges forward like the route marches he led for SS recruits. "To get a well-grounded picture of the Schellenberg marriage, it is necessary to read his report of 11 August with *all* enclosures," he advises his Reichsführer sternly, before concluding smartly, "This picture can be completed through a personal conversation with Frau Schellenberg only to her disadvantage."

Heydrich's letter was written less than three weeks before the German invasion of Poland that touched off the Second World War. There is no indication that Himmler ever saw the unfortunate Käthe Schellenberg, who at this point disappears from the records.

At the end of the summer of 1939, Schellenberg finally received a divorce—on the grounds that his wife's behavior had made "the exercise of his career impossible." This reason for marital dissolution had just been written into a new Reich Divorce Act. A special Nazi variant of the mental cruelty justification, it facilitated a wave of divorces, 80 percent of them requested by men.

It seems, in fact, that the Schellenberg Theater ended happily for everyone except Käthe, who had waged a brave frontal battle against hopeless odds and opponents skilled in the more effective strategies of duplicity and intrigue. Reinhard Heydrich, too, got something he desired. As Schellenberg says, he finally achieved "a hold over me, and by a strange twist of fate, it was I who had given him the means."

Apparently Schellenberg's new mother-in-law had a sister who was married to a Jew. Schellenberg's enemies at the Gestapo gathered this information into a file, classified it with the highest top-secret rating available, and let it slide across his desk before it disappeared into Heydrich's safe (*Panzerschrank*). "After that he was satisfied and stopped all other efforts to entrap me," Schellenberg wrote.

But that doesn't mean Schellenberg's life was easy: "Heydrich, always extremely suspicious and with a personal aversion toward me, closely checked every phase of my work—and put every difficulty in my way . . . There were times when I felt more like a hunted beast than the head of a department."

Nevertheless, one could hardly say that Heydrich blocked his advancement. When the Reich Security Main Office was formally unveiled in September 1939, Walter Schellenberg moved into Division VI (Foreign Intelligence) as Heydrich's de facto deputy. That same month Salon Kitty also opened for business, and the secret written reports made by the girls, as well as the clandestinely recorded tapes, were all routed through Schellenberg's office. Salon Kitty enjoyed three exciting years—with both Heydrich and Schellenberg occasionally in attendance—until Allied bombing attacks put an end to such frivolity.

(In June 1941, on the eve of the German invasion of Russia, Heydrich promoted Schellenberg to actual leadership of the Ausland-SD, making him, at thirty-one, the youngest head of a major SS division.)

Lina Heydrich was one year younger than Schellenberg—and seven years younger than Heydrich—yet she had successfully pulled the strings for the puppet master, almost gotten the secret agent poisoned, managed to make fools of them both.

I continued to ask her about the whole dramatic story, hoping to provoke an admission of guilt at such crass manipulation—or perhaps an assertion that all's fair in love and war.

"You know Schellenberg wrote that there was tension between him and your husband, and I wonder why that was . . ."

"He was a fellow worker, but my husband always had a . . . distant personal relationship to him."

"I read somewhere that it was a love-hate relationship."

"Love? Hate? Many human things came to play in it." And then she paused, her voice fading away. "Yes . . . No . . . Walter . . ."

On September 1, 1939, before he went off to war, Reinhard Heydrich wrote his wife a letter. "Dearest Lina," he said, "I think that however difficult for both of us the last weeks have been . . . they have nevertheless brought a deepening and strengthening of our sense of belonging to each other . . . I may have made mistakes, I *have* made mistakes, professional, personal, of thought and of action, [but] I have loved you without end."

Heydrich's enduring bond to his wife was not incompatible in his mind with extramarital dalliance (as it had not been to his father before him). Perhaps Lina Heydrich shared something of this orientation. She told an interviewer shortly after the war, "There were always other women," though she would not admit this to me. One day, however, she speculated, "My husband did not have time to have affairs. He was always too busy. He worked so hard, and then there had to be time for the fencing and the flying. No, no, when could he have done it?"

I thought of Heydrich's apartments in Berlin and Munich, the long summers when Lina was with the children on Fehmarn. And there was always Salon Kitty.

She interrupted my thoughts: "Besides, if a man wants to go out dancing after work, if he is tired and needs to relax and have a drink, well, how does that harm me?"

She shrugged, and smiled. "But, then, perhaps I am not the jealous kind," she said, and exited, laughing.

20

A DISGRACE—FOR GERMANY

"Who knows what causes wars?"

—LINA HEYDRICH

I N THE EARLY EVENING of August 31, 1939, six armed men wearing Polish military uniforms crept silently toward the small radio station at Gleiwitz, Upper Silesia, on the German side of the disputed frontier with Poland. On a signal, the squad attacked the German installation, overpowering its staff and then using the station radio to broadcast, in Polish, a message of defiance toward its purported Nazi neighbor. Departing swiftly into the twilight, the group even left behind the body of one of its members, evidently killed during the raid.

The next morning, the German Army invaded Poland, touching off the most devastating war in history. In a speech to the Reichstag, Adolf Hitler cited the incident at Gleiwitz as one of several "attacks on German territory" justifying his aggression.

As usual, Hitler was lying: the "Polish commandos" had actually been Germans in disguise. The unprovoked assault on Gleiwitz has been called the "first Nazi war crime." Like the first "mass murder"—of Röhm and his colleagues in 1934—the operation had been authorized by Hitler, given to the Reichsführer SS, and orchestrated in large part by Reinhard Heydrich. As Heydrich later described Hitler's idea: "It has been decided to partition Poland between Russia and Germany, and for purely optical reasons vis-à-vis foreign and German opinion, we must shift the blame."

This elaborate coup de theatre involved the coordinated effort of several governmental divisions, not all of them equally enthusiastic. Authentic Polish uniforms were furnished by Military Intelligence, although Canaris objected and only complied when Hitler ordered him to cooperate. Dr. Herbert Mehlhorn, a longtime SD man who ran many errands for Heydrich, also balked at this one: "Heydrich has given me this assignment to get rid of me," he complained to Walter Schellenberg. "He wants my death! What can I do?" Schellenberg claimed to have advised him, "Try to talk your way out—make some excuse . . . Whatever happens through your refusing that kind of order, it'll be preferable to the consequences of your carrying it out."

At the very last moment, Mehlhorn did back out, and in retaliation, Heydrich sent him to a dangerous post in the East. The role of attack leader then fell to Heydrich's expert on clandestine violence, Albert Naujocks. Yet even Naujocks didn't like this project, reasoning that if he failed, it would be fatal, and if he succeeded, he might know too much to live.

According to testimony by Naujocks after the war, Heydrich had some misgivings, too: "The risk of being found out seems too high, and that, of course, is the worst crime we can commit." Later Heydrich elaborated, "If you fail, you will be dead, though I have no wish to be dramatic. Maybe I will be dead, too, and many others besides . . . That, however, would not matter a fig beside the larger issues. It would undo the planning and effort of thousands over many years; failure would be a disgrace for Germany." To himself, Naujocks added the thought, "In the eyes of the world, it would be a disgrace, anyway."

The only participant who seemed untroubled was Heinrich "Gestapo" Müller. His task was to furnish dead "Poles"—in actuality concentration camp prisoners, who were to be given a near-fatal injection, then shot on the spot to add verisimilitude. As usual, Müller professed no scruples, cavalierly referring to the doomed men as "canned goods" (*Konserven*) to be delivered on demand.

Recorded details of the raid are confused, largely because Naujocks gave differing accounts on two different occasions, saying variously that Heydrich provided him with a commando team and also wrote its provocative speech, or, alternatively, that he himself did. At any rate, Heydrich thought up the code phrase used to launch the operation: "Grandmother is dead."

This phrase was sometimes used to touch off Nazi violence in the early *Kampfzeit*, yet it is tempting to imagine that for Heydrich it had also a deeper meaning. "Woe to anyone who has a Jewish grandmother!" Nazis liked to say after passage of the Nuremburg Laws. Perhaps as he launched the first salvo of a massive attack on Poland's national identity, Heydrich also was affirming his own—that is, attempting, finally, to put the ghost of his tainted grandmother "Sarah" to rest.

The actual attack lasted about fifteen minutes, and was not a total success. The radio expert couldn't locate the master switch and had to use a local wavelength, which was too weak to reach Berlin or much of anywhere else. The Gestapo did *its* job, however, shoving a moribund German prisoner out of the back of a large dark car, which immediately drove away again, leaving what looked like a victim of the skirmish. (At any rate, this is Naujocks's version; the station staff thought the man was killed by a mysterious SD man who appeared only after the others had left.) Perhaps Heydrich, who liked to reserve total knowledge for himself alone, had ordered some secret SD backup. (Earlier, he had told Naujocks, "I am in your hands and I hate it.")

After the raid was over, Naujocks called Heydrich to announce that all had gone well. "You're lying!" Heydrich retorted. He had waited the whole day and heard no broadcast. Naujocks, in a panic, returned immediately to Berlin, traveling all night and arriving about seven in the morning. He went straight to Heydrich, who was in a surprisingly good mood: Hitler had called at five o'clock to say he was pleased with the operation. "I must say I was shaken last night when nothing came through," Heydrich added, smiling.

Suddenly, Naujocks's deadly charade became a great success. Later, a member of Heydrich's staff ordered the building of a scale model of the Gleiwitz station, which he used to illustrate a speech to visitors about the "Polish attack." Heydrich would often listen in, occasionally murmuring, as if to reinforce the truth of his aide's misinformation, "Yes, yes, that is how the war started."

I wondered if Lina Heydrich would share his willingness to propagandize. She had told a German interviewer that the Gleiwitz deception was "very amusing" at the time. She told *me*, however, that it was legitimate as "a cover story": if the Germans had not attacked, war would have come sooner or later anyway, since Poland and Germany were totally at odds over disputed territory. "Who knows what causes wars?"

she mused, wondering if the best defense is often an attack. Then, she remembered a "pessimistic" remark of her husband's: "*Ach*, the people don't understand what they are getting into!"

Though Heydrich considered failure to be the "worst crime," his pessimistic aside foreshadowed far grimmer events. The wooden replica in the SD headquarters was not the only legacy of the brutal theatrics at Gleiwitz. The treatment of human beings as expendable objects, the deliberate camouflage of atrocity under a veil of lies, the separation of command from execution, the use of specially chosen men from various SS agencies held together by nothing but the "personal union" of Heydrich's leadership, the reluctant, tangential cooperation of the military, even the forebodings and reservations of otherwise "good" Nazis—all were portents of sinister things to come. In all these respects the attack at Gleiwitz was an early model, in design and spirit, of the commando operations that would become infamous under the name Einsatzgruppen.

Einsatz means "action" (among other things) in German; Einsatzgruppen were mobile, armed units of the SS, following in the wake of the advancing German troops during the Second World War. They have been called "the Reich Security Main Office on wheels" because they were largely Reinhard Heydrich's creation, and were led by men chosen by him and deployed according to his orders.

Heydrich's Einsatzgruppen had diverse functions, all allegedly related to safeguarding German security in recently pacified lands. They also murdered approximately 100,000 people every month between June 21, 1941, when Germany invaded Soviet Russia, and December of that same year.

The action groups were monstrous, bastard children of modern war, borne of the unholy marriage of so-called political necessity with more classical military strategy. They were thus a transitional stage of great historical significance between the "normal" atrocities of war and the radical species of killing we now call genocide. To study Heydrich's Einsatzgruppen is to observe the Nazi system sliding over the abyss into unprecedented evil.

Yet that descent was not perceived by most of its participants as a headlong fall. Instead, it followed the customary Nazi pattern of gradual, exploratory steps toward a shadowy brink that was often recognized only afterward, if at all. Lina Heydrich always insisted on viewing the action commandos as soldiers, brave men taking risks to defend their fellow German troops—that is, in the few times she would speak of them at all. "I cannot talk of this with *the laity!*" she snapped the first time I mentioned them.

The earliest Einsatzgruppen were, in fact, composed of real soldiers. Wilhelm Canaris, Heydrich's great role model and rival, had created special teams for subversion and sabotage in the Balkans during the recurrent crises preceding the outbreak of war. Quickly the SD began to use them, too. In an office memorandum of 1940, Heydrich claimed that police Einsatzgruppen had been deployed in Austria, the Sudetenland, and Bohemia and Moravia, entering "with the advancing troops in accordance with a special order from the Führer . . . They were able through arrests, confiscations, and safeguarding of important political material systematically to deal heavy blows to those world movements hostile to the Reich."

Until the war, their actions retained some flavor of classical intelligence skullduggery. War, however, was linked in Hitler's mind with the complete destruction of any opposition to his plans for a thousand years of Aryan hegemony in Europe. After a month of bitter siege, Poland was defeated, and that desolated country became the laboratory for Nazi experiments in the politics of racial cleansing.

In October, the Führer appointed Heinrich Himmler "Reich Commissioner for the Strengthening of Germandom." Himmler's mandate was threefold: to arrange for the repatriation of Germans who had been living abroad, to form new German settlements in the conquered territories, and to eliminate the "injurious influence" of recalcitrant sections of the native population.

This required the screening and subsequent resettlement of approximately 14 million people. The result was predictable: warring Nazi authorities created a chaos of administrative confusion and human misery that lasted for the duration of German rule.

Some people, however, were denied even the opportunity to be judged on the basis of whether they were recalcitrant or not. In sum, they were considered to be an "injurious influence" simply by virtue of who they were. Even before the outbreak of the war, Heydrich had begun to form Einsatzgruppen for temporary service in Poland. Special units of approximately 450 men each, led by high officers of the SD, were assigned to each of the invading German armies. These were ad hoc formations, performing a variety of security and administrative tasks. They also had one top-secret mandate ordered by Hitler: "Whatever we can find in the shape of an upper class in Poland is to be liquidated."

According to the Führer principle, the only serious enemies were potential leaders: the more tractable masses could always be dealt with later. During the first month of the war, Heydrich's commando units moved swiftly through the desolated countryside, hunting down a diverse quarry of government officials, intellectuals, clergymen, members of nobility, and Jewish leaders. Sometimes they arrested their foes, but more often they simply killed them where they were found. By the end of September, Heydrich could report in the antiseptic SS style: "Of the Polish upper classes, in the occupied territories only a maximum of 3 percent is still present."

Yet despite the grisly success of the Einsatzgruppen, no one was satisfied with their performance. In 1940, Heydrich wrote a memo in which, following his usual custom, he tried to appraise "the situation clearly." He was particularly troubled by the many army commanders who did not seem to understand "the basic problems of suppression of enemies of the State."

This of course was not the first instance of friction between the military and the SS. But, Heydrich noted, previous problems were dealt with "by personal contact and explanation." In the Polish case, however, this had not been possible. He wrote,

> The reason was that the directives governing police activity were exceptionally far reaching—for instance, the liquidation of numerous Polish leading circles running into the thousands of persons was ordered; such an order could not be divulged to the general run of military headquarters, still less to members of the staffs; to the uninitiated therefore the action of the police and SS appeared arbitrary, brutal, and unauthorized.

"In addition," Heydrich added, "in understandable anger at Polish atrocities, the self-defense organizations took somewhat unacceptable and uncontrolled reprisals which were then laid at the door of the SS and police."

The situation had to have been bad for Heydrich to use words like *arbitrary*, *brutal*, *unauthorized*, *unacceptable*, and *uncontrolled*, even if these were carefully hedged with softening disclaimers. (The "self-defense organizations" he mentioned consisted of German settlers and groups of SS men organized by Himmler, and encouraged to launch pogroms against Jews, sometimes losing control of their rampaging followers.) The same military leaders who had applauded the Night of the Long Knives in 1934 were appalled at massacres that violated the rules of war, and this time their criticism was both vocal and damning. The commander in chief in the East condemned the executions as illegal; the commander of Frontier Section South wanted the SS units disbanded before they sullied "the honor of the entire German people"; authors of section reports expressed anger that "instead of fighting at the front, young men should be demonstrating their courage against defenseless civilians."

Even General Walter von Reichenau, who had collaborated with Heydrich to eliminate Röhm, joined the general condemnation. Some officers went further: it was during this period that Admiral Canaris and his circle launched their secret campaign to break the power of the SS, and remove Hitler, Himmler, and Heydrich from office.

As subsequent history has borne witness, their efforts were foiled by the irresolution of even the best military leaders, coupled with the fanaticism of the worst. With the concurrence of army chief of staff General Wilhelm Keitel, Hitler announced on October 17, 1940, that there could be no legal restriction of the racial struggle: "Jews, Poles, and similar trash were to be cleared from the old and new Reich territories."

From that point on, Germany fought what amounted to two wars—a conventional military campaign against the enemy armies, and a half-clandestine political "war against the Jews" and other so-called alien groups. True, for the first year and a half of World War II, both organizations concentrated primarily on conquering the nations of western Europe, and assimilating a vast new Reich, stretching from Poland to the islands of Guernsey and Jersey, just a few miles from the imperiled English shores. And the Wehrmacht kept tight control over this western empire, heavily restricting the autonomy of the SS. Racial politics, though not forgotten, at least occupied a secondary role—until Hitler made his fatal decision to attack Soviet Russia. He saw this "drive to the East" as a holy war against Communism and the Jews he regarded as its source.

When the German leadership concluded that the only way to solve the Jewish Question was to exterminate the Jews is not exactly known; nor is there any written document that links Adolf Hitler irrevocably with this decision. Following the strategy he had used since the Röhm purge, he signed nothing, relying on verbal orders.

Heinrich Himmler, who occasionally admitted responsibility (under Hitler) for the attempted genocide, also produced no written blueprint of a general plan. And Heydrich concerned himself with "short-term" directives—at least until the Wannsee Conference, in January 1942.

In the absence of definitive data, most historians agree that by the summer of 1941 the terrible choice had been made. On March 3, Hitler told General Alfred Jodl that "the Bolshevist/Jewish intelligentsia must be eliminated" in Russia. On March 13, General Keitel issued his famous "Barbarossa" directive, announcing that Hitler had ordered Himmler to undertake "special duties" in the East. (Keitel later tried to dissociate the Wehrmacht from "any dishonorable breach of international law" arising from a war that "deviated from the normal rules" by claiming Hitler had told him, "Such dirty work was the province of the police.")

On that same date, Heydrich began negotiations with the general quartermaster of the army, Eduard Wagner, to arrange for the creation of another round of armed SS Einsatzgruppen. Army cooperation was essential, for the action commandos, moving in behind the advancing troops, would be dependent on them for provisions, communications, fuel supplies, and accommodations. Having learned from his experience in Poland, Heydrich was determined that the military would be forced into complicity from the very beginning.

He knew that much had changed since 1939. The German General Staff now faced the awful prospect of fighting the Soviet army, and had little time to worry about enemy civilians. In his Orders of the Day for October 10, 1941, Field Marshal von Reichenau expressed the new attitude: "In the eastern region the soldier is not merely a fighter according to the rules of the art of war, but also the bearer of an inexorable national idea . . . Therefore the soldier must have full understanding for the necessity of a severe but just atonement on Jewish subhumanity."

On April 4, General Wagner sent Heydrich a draft proposal conceding that SS commandos could carry out "executive measures" against the civilian population, "on their own responsibility." Then the discussions reached an impasse. Heydrich, who was deputizing for Himmler, had appointed the unsavory "Gestapo" Müller as his own personal representative. Realizing his error, he now turned to the suave Walter Schellenberg, saying, "Müller's terribly clumsy over this sort of thing. He's incapable of finding the right words . . . Wagner was quite right when he complained to me."

Heydrich told his young assistant that the Führer had requested mobile SS formations to protect against sabotage, guard archives, and maintain "general security of the rear areas." Heydrich also wanted to employ them directly on the front line, again citing Hitler as his authority: "The Führer has had a further thought, too, which also occurred to me." Every member of an action group serving at the front would have a chance "to prove himself and to earn a decoration. This should finally dispel the false impression that the staff of the executive departments are cowards who have got themselves safe posts out of the fighting line."

In early May, Wagner agreed to Heydrich's terms. As before, Himmler passed on to Heydrich the "functional direction" of the Einsatzgruppen. Calling a meeting of the important leaders of the RSHA, Heydrich began by asking for volunteers. Witnesses say Heydrich was vague about the duties of the commandos, admitting only that they would perform "hard tasks" in the East. "I need real men," he said, "and hope that my heads of division will place themselves unreservedly at my disposal."

"Real men": Nazis had been spouting theories about this particular species for years. Often the term implied sexual behavior, as when Himmler listed the three ways a "real man" might properly behave toward a woman. SS General Jürgen Stroop articulated another requirement: "Anyone attempting to be a true man—that is, a strong one"— had to become "hard."

To many young SS recruits, Reinhard Heydrich already stood as the shining exemplar of this strange new virtue, combining willingness to take on "heavy" tasks and apparent imperviousness to the pain they caused either themselves or others. (In their study *The Genocidal Mentality*, Robert Lifton and Eric Marcusen have argued that hardness really meant "the capacity to maintain extreme psychic numbing," a necessary part of the genocidal imperative of learning to kill without feeling like a murderer.)

"Abroad they take us for bloodhounds, don't they?" Heydrich once asked a Swiss diplomat. "It is almost too hard for some people," he continued, "but we must be as hard as granite or the work of the Führer will surely perish. Someday people will thank us for what we have taken on ourselves."

It was notoriously difficult to say no to Heydrich, as subordinates like Werner Best had discovered. Yet of all those present at that first meeting, only one "real man" stepped forward—and that one, Arthur Nebe, chief of the Criminal Police, was a secret member of the resistance. His motive for volunteering was later said by his friends to have been the need to *show* loyalty and thus evade suspicion. In the end, the rest of the highest SD and police leaders had to be forced to participate. Heydrich and the RSHA personnel chief, Bruno Streckenbach, seem to have chosen most of the commanders themselves. Only after they had departed for pre-invasion training were they told what they would have to do.

This led to a terrible irony: the men who were to direct perhaps the most ghastly atrocities of the twentieth century were also among the *least* fanatically conformist of Nazi leaders. The brutal thugs of the early Storm Trooper days had never found a niche among the bureaucrats and intellectuals in the RSHA, and concentration camp commanders had always reported to Himmler. Indeed, even as Heydrich was forming his special troops, Himmler was creating his own "Higher Police and SS Leaders" and groups of "anti-partisan" fighters. According to Gerald Reitlinger, the English art critic and Holocaust historian, these groups were conceived in part as a way of combating the "excessively powerful position of Heydrich within the SS." Himmler wanted to ensure that the East should belong not only to the SS, but also to him. While they continued to collaborate on various "police tasks," the two leaders were also increasingly in competition, and "Heydrich's bright young men" were expected to do everything possible in his support.

Relentlessly, he combed through the top leaders of the Reich Security Office. Bruno Streckenbach (Amt, or Office, I) had already commanded an action group in 1939 and was indispensable for organizing the new ones; "Gestapo" Müller (Amt IV) had to stay home and direct the police, but all the other divisional commanders were expected to "prove themselves." Nebe, of Amt III, had already volunteered, and Professor Franz Six, of Amt VII (Ideological Research), was summoned to command a special unit near Moscow. Schellenberg, of Amt VI (Foreign Intelligence), managed to avoid service by appealing over Heydrich's head to Himmler, whose life he had once saved by grabbing his arm, preventing him from being sucked out of an airplane door. Himmler had grown fond of Schellenberg, whose charm and obvious opportunism disqualified him from the extremes of competition in hardness (and who had secretly resolved not to "lay down my life as an offering on the altar of the totalitarian state").

Stubborn Otto Ohlendorf, Schellenberg's opposite number at Domestic Intelligence, was neither so lucky, nor so clever. For one thing, the Reichsführer still sensed (correctly) that "there were always critical thoughts lurking behind his forehead." In 1939, Ohlendorf had objected to SS excesses in Poland, and Heydrich, who sometimes defended his outspoken subordinate, stood aside, giving Himmler's animosity free rein. Finally, in 1941, Heydrich demanded that Ohlendorf take command of an Einsatzgruppe. Ohlendorf protested that he was not a soldier, not even a policeman. (His heroism lay solely in attacking the corruption of important Gauleiters.) Heydrich called him a "coward." In the end, after repeated scenes with Heydrich, he complied.

By the end of May, the chief of Reich security had formed four major groups, each led by a high official from his RSHA. The largest, containing 940 men, was headed by SS Brigadeführer Franz Walter Stahlecker, once chief of the Security Police in Prague until ill-advised office intrigues aroused Heydrich's wrath. Arthur Nebe, the secret resister, commanded Group B. Group C was headed by Otto Rasch, a veteran of the Einsatzgruppen in Poland, who had been passed over for promotion and was trying to get back in Heydrich's good graces. (Later Rasch claimed he intended to argue with Heydrich but couldn't summon the nerve.) Group D, the smallest at approximately five hundred men, was led by the reluctant Ohlendorf.

These large groups were then subdivided into four or five smaller units called Kommandos, also led by officials from the SD and the Security Police. It has been suggested that these people were mostly social and organizational "misfits." Certainly, they were a diverse lot, including men who had once been opera singers, Lutheran ministers, dentists, and architects, as well as eight with legal training. One of them, Heinz Jost, had been the chief of Foreign Intelligence until Schellenberg edged him out. Their real common denominator seems to have been that they had fallen out with their demanding, unpredictable, and abrasive boss.

Observers thought Heydrich showed an uncharacteristic lack of

SS Brigadeführer Otto Rasch (age fifty-four, circa 1945, at the Nuremberg Trial case no. 9) was named commander of Einsatzgruppe C in northern and central Ukraine by Heydrich in May 1941. In late September of that year, during a two-day period in Kiev's Babi Yar ravine, Rasch's Einsatzgruppe executed more than thirty-three thousand Jews. It was the largest such massacre up until that time.

pragmatism in sending his highest-ranking administrators off to head groups of armed marauders doing butcher's work. As Bruno Strecken-bach said of Ohlendorf's fate, "Rationally speaking, this assignment was nonsense. He was needed much more at home in Berlin."

Of course, there are many kinds of rationality—or at least rational-izations. The infamous chief of Reich security seemed determined to share his fearful burden of responsibility. As Streckenbach said, "Hey-drich took a malicious pleasure in picking out intellectual, desk-bound SS men . . . so that they became as fully tainted with mass murder as himself." Certainly, he pursued his closest associates with the same implacability he showed his foes. One of them has given a detailed description of the harsh pressure he was willing to exert on his own "knightly" companions. According to Walter Hänsch, a lawyer who dealt with disciplinary infractions among SS personnel, and also served as leader of Sonderkommando 4b:

> I only got an opportunity to talk to Heydrich when . . . I received my marching orders . . . In his usual brief manner he told me very explicitly that the life of every German soldier needed special pro-tection, and that I was always to remain conscious of the fact that in such a situation the lives of fathers of German families and the lives of the German men were at stake . . .

He told me he did not want to receive any complaint. "If you do not obey orders," he said, "I need not tell you . . . since you are an expert on disciplinary matters that you, just like every soldier at the front, are subject to the laws of war, and that any dereliction of duty is subject to heavy penalty."

That Heydrich would resort to open threats suggests how much difficulty he must have been experiencing. Yet one must not imagine that the considerable opposition to action group service took the form of forthright moral attacks on Nazi programs or philosophy. In the opinion of the Holocaust historians Raul Hilberg and Hannah Arendt, that was the one form it could not take. Open defiance was openly punished, and in any case, people with the capacity for such action had usually been purged long ago. Those who survived usually acted as if they had to appear unassailable before launching sporadic objections couched in suitably "tactful" language.

By 1941, even Admiral Canaris seemed afraid to show "too negative an attitude," counseling General Erwin von Lahousen to raise only tactical objections to Einsatzgruppen atrocities; that is, that mass killings would be bad for army morale or might detract from the achievement of military objectives.

Arthur Nebe's young assistant at the Criminal Police managed to evade service in the East by using a similarly circuitous style. When Heydrich asked him to take the place of his boss as leader of Group B, he replied, "I am happy, Group Leader, to have your confidence. But I will need a little time in which to brief Nebe. So much has happened in these last few months. I believe Nebe is also very sick. But perhaps someone else can brief him. Whatever you order, Group Leader."

Reminded of the assistant's irreplaceability, Heydrich gave way, but such irresolution on his part was rare: by the autumn of 1941, he had decided that "*every* member of the Security Police and the SD has to prove his worth, once, in foreign action." He had extracted from the Wehrmacht the enormous concession that action group membership qualified as military service; yet even with the powerful incentive of evading the draft, he was unable to find enough Sipo men to complete each group. Finally, he widened the net to include his rivals over at Dalüge's Order Police, as well as members of SS military units who had fallen afoul of the system. A Waffen SS commander described these latter who had joined the army of death: "They are late or they fall asleep on sentry duty. They are court-martialed, but are told that they can escape punishment by volunteering for special commandos." If the soldiers objected to mass murder, they found they hadn't evaded punishment after all: "They are told that the orders that have been given them are a form of punishment. Either they can obey and take that punishment or they can disobey and be shot."

Einsatzgruppen leaders also made use of local ethnic groups who were willing to collaborate, sometimes employing them to incite pogroms that could then be blamed on the local inhabitants: "without any visible indication to the outside world of a German order or of any German suggestion." (By the end of 1941, Himmler had created units of native collaborators totaling thirty-three thousand men, more than ten times the size of the original Einsatzgruppen.)

The evasiveness, deception, and strong-arm tactics to be practiced against the victims were already foreshadowed in the treatment of the future perpetrators, who were callously manipulated by a regime that viewed people of all races primarily as "human material." For both groups, the horrible agenda of Einsatzgruppen activity was revealed only gradually, step by step. But there the similarity ends: the SS leaders had joined the organization voluntarily, and had both a rough idea of the ferocity of their task and some possibility of evading their orders. The Jews of Russia, by contrast, were largely cut off from accurate information by the chaos of rapid warfare. At first, most had no warning of what was about to happen.

In late May, the members of the Einsatzgruppen were assembled at the SS training camp at Pretzsch, Saxony-Anhalt, on the Elbe River, and subjected to a combination of intense ideological indoctrination, lectures by "experts" on Russian geography and history, military drill, and target practice.

I would get to talk to Bruno Streckenbach about this, especially the fact that in early June he is said to have visited Pretzsch, apparently to exhort the troops to "behave ruthlessly." But at the end of my interview with him, I asked what he remembered about this speech. Up to this point, he had struck me as a mild-mannered old man, remarkably straightforward in his answers, who served cookies and tea and apologized about the heart condition restricting the time he could give to interviews. Suddenly, his face became red, and he leapt up from his cozy armchair and strode into another room. "I wasn't there!" he shouted at me. He picked up a book whose title I couldn't manage to see, opened it, and gestured at several passages underlined in yellow. "It says Streckenbach wasn't there. How can I be clearer than that?"

"But, three witnesses testified at Nuremberg that you were—"

"Nuremberg! Everybody lied! I tell you, Streckenbach wasn't there!"

At that moment, Frau Streckenbach, a small woman, dressed in a blue dress with a pattern of small flowers, entered the room. She looked worried. "Is anything wrong?" she said. While he and I sat silent, she lectured her husband about the importance of not straining himself. Then, shortly after that, she saw me to the door. (Years later, I read in a German study of the Einsatzgruppen that three former comrades who claimed to have seen Streckenbach at Pretzsch recanted their testimony after they learned he had not been killed in Russia. His whereabouts on that day, like the identity of the book he quoted, remain uncertain.)

Only in June, after the troops had reached the departure point, in Pretzsch, did Heydrich finally appear and address the hundreds of men now assembled in the barracks square. He spoke only of a task involving "unparalleled hardness." Later he made a speech to a smaller group of officers. According to notes made secretly by one of the participants, he offered one of his customarily terse explanations: "The Jews in the East are the intellectual reservoir of Bolshevism and therefore, according to the Führer, must be wiped out." He gave some individual briefings, also verbal, and then he sent the commandos on their way, three thousand men, off to hunt down millions of people, in a vast territory of many thousands of square miles, encompassing all of European Russia from the gates of Moscow to the Black Sea.

The Einsatzgruppen were also heading toward a terrible place in the bloody annals of annihilation: the record of their actions is so appalling that in the words of a Nuremberg prosecutor, "the mind rebels against its own thought image."

Otto Ohlendorf, whose subsequent execution for war crimes was ensured by his behavior in Russia, later said that in naming him as chief of an Einsatzgruppe, Heydrich had wanted "to morally annihilate" him. Whatever Heydrich intended, Ohlendorf is correct about the result: the remaining "idealism" of the SS, as well as many of its members, was to perish in the East, their fate inextricably entangled with that of people they despised, from whom they had hoped to separate themselves forever.

PART IV

GOING TO WAR

21

"PERFECTLY NORMAL MEN"

"[My husband] always felt like a soldier, never like an administrative official."

—LINA HEYDRICH

H AVING USED his organizational skills to create in the Einsatzgruppen a machine of destruction and to send it hurtling across the last frontiers of civilized decency, Heydrich retreated to his command post in Berlin. From there, he tampered periodically with the machine's workings, issuing special instructions when necessary, as, for example, a memo advising his leaders that Russians of Turkish extraction were often circumcised and should not be confused with Jews.

More often, however, he *received* information. The group leaders were required to write descriptions of their daily activities, summarized into weekly reports and forwarded to Heydrich's office, where they were combined into a longer "Activity and Situation Report of the Einsatzgruppen of the Secret Police and the SD in the USSR," and sent biweekly to approximately one hundred high Nazi officials.

There was no purely rational reason why so many people had to be informed of such a top-secret program. In fact, some didn't want to know. Foreign Minister von Ribbentrop said he wished for no more reports, but, implacably, Heydrich sent them anyway.

Ribbentrop's feelings are understandable: the terse summaries have a chilling air of steely precision, as if they had been cut from metal and spewed out by a machine. Two aspects are particularly striking: First, the figures concerning liquidations are peculiarly, even ridiculously, precise, given later admissions by group leaders that they exaggerated or misestimated the body counts, and Heydrich knew it. Second, careful justifications are nevertheless provided in every case.

Here, for example, are some typical comments from Situation Report 6, sent by Heydrich to Ribbentrop on November 25, 1941, with the request "Please take note":

> 222 Jews were shot in Talca [Russia] because of anti-German propaganda and 996 in Marina Gorka [Belarus] because they sabotaged decrees of the German occupation authorities . . . Since they had participated in sabotage actions, another 627 Jews were shot near Schklow [Russia] . . . Because of a great danger of plague, the liquidation of the Jews of the ghetto in Witebsk [Belarus] was begun . . . In Gorodnis [Ukraine] 165 Jewish terrorists and in Chernigow [Ukraine] 19 Jewish Communists . . . In Bobrik [Ukraine] 380 Jews were shot, who had carried on agitation and atrocity propaganda against the German authorities.

Significantly, the figures on "liquidations" are buried within a mass of information on the "Situation in Leningrad, Arrests and Shootings of Communists and Criminals, Confiscated Materials, Economics and Business, Agriculture, Culture, Behavior of the Natives vis-à-vis the Germans." By emphasizing the diverse security tasks of the commandos, Heydrich was deliberately masking indiscriminate murder with a gloss of soldierly necessity.

These reports are our primary source of documentary information about the Einsatzgruppen, and their awful precision has helped to further two misconceptions about their activities. First—perhaps because they were so few and their prey so many—a legend has arisen of demonic Einsatzgruppen "efficiency." This is no doubt the way the hard-faced, relentless, merciless executioners appeared to their victims, but from the viewpoint of those responsible, the situation looked much more problematic. Their leaders knew that the mobile commandos were not particularly efficient at all, either in choosing their victims or in killing them.

Though the group commanders had been ordered by Heydrich immediately to kill all Jews holding positions in the state or Communist Party, they had received neither a general operational blueprint

Joachim von Ribbentrop (age forty-seven, circa 1940) served as Germany's ambassador to Britain before his 1938 appointment as foreign minister of Nazi Germany. Although his power within the Reich hierarchy diminished over time, Ribbentrop played a key role in diplomatic efforts that pressed Germany's Axis partners into rounding up and deporting those countries' Jews to Nazi concentration camps.

nor master lists of victims. Like huntsmen, they had to search out their quarry, varying their methods according to circumstances and personal style. Commonly, they asked local collaborators where the Jews were, then descended for surprise roundups. Sometimes they simply took everyone who looked to them Jewish. Often, the Jewish elders of each village or town were told to provide lists of all members of their religious community, or were ordered to assemble them for "resettlement."

The group leaders usually tried to catch their prey unaware. As the German journalist Heinz Höhne has observed, "No brutality was too base, no trick too mean." Sick people were told they would be taken to "a better place," intellectuals were promised office jobs, officials were assured that identity cards or work permits would be issued to all who came forward. (Those who tried to hide or were too frail to move were frequently killed on the spot.)

The hunters, moving quickly, necessarily cast a loose net: people who did not report, who managed to escape the searchers, and who were not denounced by others had a chance to slip through the holes. They had only a limited respite, however: in May 1942, a second sweep began. (By then, units organized by Himmler's regional leaders had largely replaced Heydrich's temporary troops.)

During the first several weeks, most of the people shot were Jewish male leaders. According to Christopher Browning, an American historian of the Holocaust, "only in August did killing of women and children become common." Some leaders objected to the widening of the boundaries of death: "They [the killers] are all young men," one Kommando leader argued. "How are we going to answer to them if we make them shoot small children?" After several days' delay, he finally ordered Ukrainian auxiliaries to shoot a group of homeless, starving infants and children whose parents had already been killed. Later an Abwehr officer criticized such "atrocities"—while simultaneously concluding that the children should have been killed immediately to avoid "this inhuman agony." Obviously, the boundaries of acceptably human behavior were also widening every day, an inexorable process described by observers as "moral drift."

After the victims had been gathered together, they were brought by foot or vehicle to an isolated spot—such as the large ravine at Babi Yar, near Kiev, where in an unusually big "action" in September 1941, 33,771 Jews were massacred in two days.

Like the strategies of the hunt, the methods of execution varied. Almost always, the people were divided into lines, stripped of valuables and often of their clothes, and made to move in small groups up to the edge of a trench where they stood or knelt until they were mowed down by men with guns. Sometimes the killers used pistols—shooting their targets individually in the back of the neck—but they preferred repeating rifles or machine guns, which allowed several shots to be fired in swift succession and from a greater distance. The executioners usually worked in squads, occasionally shooting for an hour and murdering as many as a thousand people before they took a break. They fired simultaneously to blur individual responsibility.

Heydrich had commanded that "avoidable unkindnesses were to be avoided," yet what could this mean under such barbaric circumstances? Death was supposed to be mercifully swift, but not all the killers were expert marksmen and more than a few were drunk. "Such a life was quite intolerable sober," a member of one action group later told a German court.

No doctors were present at the scene. Often only cursory efforts were made to ensure that the victims were dead before they were thrown into mass trenches and covered with other bodies, sometimes piled six deep before they received a shallow blanket of earth. Many people bled to death slowly, or suffocated, or choked on their own blood and that of others, their limbs entwined so closely together that they could not afterward be pried apart. The mass of entangled bodies reminded observers of sardines in a tin.

Onlookers, however, were not welcome. After a few notoriously public executions, Heydrich reaffirmed, "Spectators may not be admitted as a matter of principle." The group leaders liked to believe the people they slaughtered were unaware of their fate until the last moment. Yet most could hear the shots, and many waited hours, even overnight, for their turn to die.

Active resistance was rare—and, in any case, was immediately and viciously suppressed. The victims had no weapons, were surrounded by heavily armed men, and had not yet viewed the actual circumstances of their doom. "We saw people naked lined up. But we were still hoping that this was only torture. Maybe there is hope—hope of living," one survivor testified later.

As Heydrich's reports indicated, the vast majority of the victims were Jews, joined by varying numbers of partisans, Communists, Romani, criminals," and others selected by the Kommando leaders. All tended to behave similarly, frequently impressing the bemused, sometimes reluctantly impressed executioners with their dignity and stoicism. Many helped their weaker brethren into the trenches before their own time came.

Since Wehrmacht cooperation was essential, army observers could not be totally excluded, and both they and the killers themselves were so mesmerized by the hideous spectacle that they sometimes felt driven to photograph it. The Wehrmacht declared this "beneath the honor of a German officer"; Himmler forbade it (except pictures allegedly made to show to Hitler); Heydrich ordered existing photographs confiscated—all to no avail.

The phenomenon of the photos leads us to a second myth about the SS commandos: that they performed their repulsive duties with no more personal concern than a hired photographer might have toward his subject. Lucy Dawidowicz, the Holocaust historian, has argued that these men must have internalized the hate-filled Nazi racist philosophy—or how else could they have acted at all? Yet this is comparable to the Nazi trick of deducing mental state from physical acts or appearance, as, for example, when Lina Heydrich argued that her husband's constant squabbles with Himmler showed that he "couldn't have had" an "inferiority complex" about his clouded racial origins. In the absence of other evidence, we must know people through their actions. In this case, we cannot ignore the testimony of the perpetrators themselves. Self-serving and self-justifying though they often were, their accounts reveal moments of profound clarity or unease breaking through the mists of denial and moral obfuscation. Many of Heydrich's political soldiers could not evade anguish and anxiety—sometimes of hysterical proportions—about the atrocities they were committing.

Indeed, that was what they were supposed to feel. According to Otto Ohlendorf, "At the moment when it was noted that a man had experienced joy in carrying out these executions, it was ordered that this man should never participate in any more executions." The killers were expected to rise above normal human decency rather than to lack it entirely—to become, as Himmler put it, "hard but not hardened."

It is not surprising that many could scarcely achieve this paradoxical goal. It has been estimated that approximately 20 percent of the group members became toughened killers, another 20 percent had severe mental difficulties, and the rest occupied an ambivalent gray zone in the middle. Realizing this, the unit commanders devoted considerable time to alleviating "psychological strain" among their group of killers.

Of course, some men perceived no strain, appreciating the frequent furloughs and exemption from combat. (It is true, Frau Heydrich told me tearfully, that one Einsatzgruppe commander, Franz Walter Stahlecker, was killed in Russia, but this turned out to be during a real battle with armed partisans.) Execution duty was not hazardous, and in addition offered opportunities for illicit profits from the valuables from the victims. In theory, looting was strictly forbidden. Confiscated property was supposed to be given away to local groups or Germanic charities, according to Himmler's dictum that the SS had "the moral right . . . to destroy this people who wanted to destroy us. But we have not the right to enrich ourselves with so much as a fur, a watch, a mark, or a cigarette, or anything else." Himmler, however, was far away, and a sly man might pocket money or gold without any living witnesses. This profiteering attitude was embodied in such heartless slogans as, "In the morning we shoot, in the evening, we feast."

One presumably carefree executioner described his attitude:

The death candidates assembled with shovels to dig their own graves. Two of them were weeping. The others certainly have incredible courage. What on earth is running through their minds during those moments? . . . Strange, I am completely unmoved. No pity, nothing. That's the way it is and then it's all over. My heart beats just a little faster when involuntarily I recall the feelings and thoughts I had when I was in a similar situation . . . And here I am today, a survivor standing in front of others in order to shoot them.

Meanwhile, Heydrich's SD leaders were hearing reports of "psychic collapse." In one case, "an active participant in one of the mass executions suddenly shot and killed a number of his comrades." In another, a man "who was carrying on a normal conversation with his best friend suddenly stood up and shot him dead. An interesting medical phenomenon . . . was the fact that the men, who had frequently taken part in the execution of women and girls, became sexually impotent for a certain period of time." Other observers noted that "terrible nightmares" were almost universal.

Otto Ohlendorf described his own efforts to "make it as easy as possible for the unfortunate victim and to prevent inevitable excesses": "The Einsatzkommandos shot in a military manner only on orders. It was strictly ordered to avoid any maltreatment, undressing was not permitted. The taking of any personal possessions was not permitted. Publicity was not permitted. The men could not report voluntarily, they were ordered."

Ohlendorf made "unexpected inspections" to ensure his men followed his guidelines, and tried to lift their "psychic burden" in other ways. In particular, he insisted they perform additional security tasks aside from murder. (Heydrich had asked the groups to find "reliable individuals" as well as "suspicious elements," italicizing his next comment: "*I point out again that both duties are of equal importance.*") By contrast, Ohlendorf said, Himmler's police units performed "nothing but executions, and it is understandable that this would ruin these people spiritually, or make them completely brutal."

To relieve the distress his men felt directly after the killing, Ohlendorf ordered them to cover the bodies immediately. When his incredulous interrogator asked him, "You believe that it's a relief to shovel sand on top of corpses?" he replied that physical exertion was the best way to maintain one's psychic balance. He also dispensed alcohol when all else failed, though he preferred to arrange evening diversions such as movies, theatrical events, or speeches.

Of course, the commanders worried about their own "balance" too. In July 1969, Emanuel Schäffer, the leader of Kommando 9, a subdivision of Arthur Nebe's Group B, bared his inner conflicts to the British psychoanalyst Henry Dicks. Trained as a lawyer, Schäffer had been a high officer in SD Foreign Intelligence until 1939, when Himmler ordered his brother's arrest for making hostile remarks about Hitler. To escape this "impossible situation," Schäffer requested a soldier's posting in the front line. But his timing could not have been worse. Heydrich pounced, sending him at once to an Einsatz command.

After the war, Schäffer was sentenced to life imprisonment for the murder of eleven thousand people. The presiding judge noted he had gone beyond Heydrich's instructions in his zeal to track down victims. Nevertheless, Schäffer told Dicks how.

"I have looked after so many criminals, and now I have become one myself," his superior officer, Arthur Nebe, told Schäffer, while simultaneously warning, "Don't give your family any more trouble than it is in already." Schäffer went back to work, exhorting his men to be ruthless. He also began to allow peculiar lapses.

When a young lawyer confessed he couldn't bring himself to perform the executions, Schäffer blurted, "Don't say that aloud!," then found him an office job. Four months after he arrived, Emanuel Schäffer suffered a nervous breakdown, succumbing to fits of weeping: "To be degraded into a hangman and murderer—nobody believes I felt it." Dicks asked him how others managed to carry on. Schäffer guessed they used a "defensive posture of bravado against a feeling of despair."

Testimony like this led Dr. Dicks to conclude that guilt over SS atrocities, if it occurred at all, was a gradual process involving three stages of development. Before they set out, the men often fortified themselves against doubt through affirming their ideological commitment to the Nazi cause. Once in the bloody field, they attempted to evade their rising anxiety by losing themselves in the camaraderie of the trenches. Only if these methods proved ineffective did their defenses collapse, allowing revulsion and anxiety to break through.

Christopher Browning, on the other hand, found in his 1992 case

Paul Blobel (age forty-eight, circa 1942), as commanding officer of Sonderkommando 4a of Einsatzgruppen C, also bore responsibility for the Babi Yar massacre of 1941. A year later, on orders from Heydrich and reinforced by Himmler, Blobel took charge of Aktion 1005, which called for destroying all evidence of Nazi mass murders in the German-occupied Soviet Union.

study of Reserve Police Battalion 101 that its members became "increasingly efficient and caloused executioners" as time went on. The extreme case of Paul Blobel illustrates an uneasy merging of these two lines of development.

Blobel, commander of the Einsatz units at Babi Yar, could hardly be called a man of refined sensibilities. An alcoholic who had failed in his chosen career of architect, he had joined the SD only when "down to his last shirt." In his postwar court appearances, his periodic epileptic seizures were eclipsed by the breathtaking callousness of his testimony. Among other things, he observed that human life was not as important to the victims "as it was with us. They did not care so much. They did not know their own human value . . . I must say that our men who took part in these executions suffered more from nervous exhaustion than those who had to be shot."

In March 1942, Paul Blobel happened to be passing the Babi Yar ravine. "Here my Jews are buried," he remarked coolly to a companion. But the gases produced by the decaying bodies caused noticeable eruptions in the earth, making a mockery of the burial. In May, Heydrich ordered Blobel to take on a new assignment: the elimination of all traces of the mass executions through exhuming and then cremating the bodies. Faced with this ghastly task, even Blobel lost his sangfroid. Heydrich might have been expected to show a little tolerance toward one of his most effective executioners, but instead he said, "Well, you have developed a stomach. You are just a sissy, only fit to be employed

Kurt Gerstein (age thirty-seven, circa 1942), as head of the Technical Disinfection Services of the SS, oversaw the delivery of the cyanide-based Zyklon-B gas to Auschwitz, Treblinka, and other camps. He later would record that Jews were delivered by the trainload, robbed of their possessions, shorn of their hair, then packed so tightly into what resembled a giant shower room that their naked bodies could not fall to the chamber's floor as they were blinded, suffocated, and killed by the fumes.

as a porcelain manufacturer—but I will push your nose much deeper into it." He sent Blobel back to his new work—from which he was not relieved when Heydrich died a month later. Himmler, through "Gestapo" Müller, ordered him to continue.

This incident reveals why everyone feared Heydrich's whiplike tongue, even though the softer-spoken Himmler was almost as intransigent where resistance to his orders was concerned. Otto Ohlendorf claimed to have had only two private talks with his Reichsführer during his nine years of SS service, but in one of them, "I pointed out the inhuman burden which was being imposed on the men in killing all these civilians. I didn't even get an answer." Later, when a subordinate expressed the timid hope that the executions would soon be over, Himmler snarled, "If you don't keep your nose out of the Jewish business, you'll see what'll happen to you!" Kurt Gerstein, one of the (very few) SS men who repeatedly tried to sabotage the extermination process, avoided open opposition because, as he later said, "I would certainly have been subjected to terrible torture and put to death."

The mental linkage between disobedience and death was widespread among even the highest SS officers. The commandant of Treblinka, Franz Stangl, said he agreed with a friend that "what we were doing was a crime. We considered deserting . . . But how? Where could we go? What about our families?" After the war, Stangl concluded he should have committed suicide. (Ohlendorf also thought suicide was the only

Franz Stangl (age forty-one, circa 1945) supervised the Euthanasia Institute at Schloss Hartheim, where the mentally and physically disabled were put to death. Ultimately, he was sent to Poland to serve as commandant of the death camps of Sobibor and Treblinka. "I rarely saw them as individuals. It was always a huge mass," he said of the approximately ninety thousand people he put to death.

escape, but condemned it as "a senseless martyrdom that would not have changed anything.")

The pervasive fatalism and fear shared by many SS officers meant that their moral qualms almost never worked to help their victims. Almost universally, they followed the rule of correctly "hard" behavior in public, while waiting for a private opportunity to plead with their bosses. This meant, in turn, that Himmler and Heydrich were constantly faced with some new case of an officer who at last had had too much. In October 1943, Himmler, in a speech he gave at Posen (Poland), finally attempted to articulate an official policy for dealing with reluctant murderers:

> If a man believes he cannot take on the responsibility for obeying an order, he must candidly state: "I cannot take the responsibility; I beg to be excused." Probably in most cases, an order will then come through, saying, "You must carry it out anyway." Alternately, one may think, "His nerves are shot, he's weak." In that case, one can say, "Very well, retire on a pension. But orders must be sacred."

Himmler was tacitly admitting something his cleverer officers had long ago realized: the most reliable way to get back to Berlin was to appear too "weak" to carry on. SS men were, as the commandant of Auschwitz put it, "not supposed to think," but they *were* expected to

Franz Six (age thirty-one, circa 1940) was appointed by Heydrich to lead Amt VII, Written Records of the Reichssicherheitshauptamt (RSHA). Its purpose was the creation of anti-Semitic, anti-Masonic propaganda. In 1940, Six was promoted to director of state police operations to handle what Hitler foresaw as an occupied Great Britain.

push themselves to the limit. In an organization of ferociously "hard" men, the nervous breakdown became surprisingly acceptable, perhaps because of its honorable similarity to battle fatigue. In addition to Schäffer, Arthur Nebe, Blobel, and other group leaders also had breakdowns, and many more were hospitalized for various types of physical illness.

Rarer were the commanders who deliberately evaded their orders. Emil Otto Rasch moved Group B away from Riga in an effort to avoid murdering women and children. Both SD commanders Franz Six and Heinz Jost managed to leave their Einsatz groups after only a few weeks. After the war, Jost claimed that he had placed an execution order from Heydrich in a desk drawer and never acted on it. (The Allied prosecutors were disposed to believe him, since his record revealed he had been broken in rank and sent into combat as punishment for a disciplinary infraction.)

Browning found no evidence that anyone was ever shot for requesting a transfer, and Franz Six testified, "I was not demoted as a result . . . and not disadvantaged apart from remaining on very bad terms with Heydrich until his death."

Despite their threatening rhetoric, Himmler and Heydrich seem to have been surprisingly lenient to men who did not openly defy their authority or question their morality. It was almost as if the SS leaders were more concerned with forcing their subordinates to participate in the exterminations than in making sure they did a really wholehearted job of it. The psychiatrist Leo Alexander has likened this behavior to that of mafia chieftains who deliberately force their minions to commit "sufficient criminal activity to cut off their return to normal society"— creating a bond of complicity that induces continued obedience.

The society they were forced to keep, however, retained more familiar characteristics than we may find comfortable. Recent research has repeatedly confirmed that conformity to group pressures far outranked blood lust, criminal impulses, or even intense racism in explaining the behavior of the men who stayed in Russia in the last half of 1942. Christopher Browning speculated that the siege mentality of war, the lack of personal responsibility caused by giving the dirtiest tasks to civilian volunteers and splitting the others up among differing groups, and fear of being thought cowardly by their commanders or peers were more potent inducements to obedience than hatred of the victim.

Many were motivated by flagrant careerism. An SS Scharführer from another unit epitomized this attitude when he candidly admitted,

> I was worried that I would be affected adversely in some way in the future if I allowed myself to be seen as too weak . . . not as hard as an SS man ought to have been . . . I carried out orders not because I was afraid I would be punished by death if I didn't but because I did not want to be seen in a bad light . . . my chances of promotion would be spoilt.

Group Commander Ohlendorf, whom Heydrich had accused of cowardice, put a selfless gloss on his own compliance:

> As long as I thought in political terms, I no longer considered myself as an individual person who only could think and act responsibly for himself . . . Despite everything, I considered this my duty and I shall consider it today as much more valuable than the cheap applause which I could have won if I had at that time betrayed my men by simulating illness.

If, as we have seen, Ohlendorf, Schäffer, Nebe, Rasch, Blobel, et al. were more troubled than they allowed their men to see, one might well ask where this process ended. Did the high leaders who sent such commanders out into the killing fields—Bruno Streckenbach, Heydrich, and Himmler—ever admit to secret doubts?

I asked Streckenbach if he had ever talked to Heydrich about the Holocaust. "Yes, of course; of course. As soon as I heard of it. (In the beginning, not a soul knew of it.) When I did hear, I talked with him about it. Those were the occasions—I talked with Himmler about it too—those were the occasions when I got to know both of them well enough to be able to compare them with each other. I spoke to Heydrich about it as soon as I heard of it, and Heydrich stopped what he was doing—something he usually did not do—and quietly and very seriously sat on the corner of his desk and talked to me: 'Streckenbach, this is an order by Hitler. Neither you nor I have the right to criticize it. You had better keep quiet. I am helpless against it and you are even more helpless.'

"Then he died and Himmler took over temporarily as head of the Sicherheitspolizei . . . I talked with Himmler about it—and . . . Himmler got so enraged that he screamed at me as I have never been screamed at in my life. I don't take well to something like that, because I am pigheaded myself. If someone treats me unjustly, I don't react in a biblical way at all, I don't turn the other cheek; I defend myself. But I was too shaken. Because only someone who actually agreed with what I said could have lost his composure so completely. Because I told him that for us the SS uniform had been a mark of honor, but now it no longer was. And that was his fault. I also said that in my opinion—and in the opinion of many of my comrades—it was wrong to shoot a few thousand Jews (no one thought of those much larger numbers. No one, including me, could have imagined those)—to shoot a few thousand Jews, as long as there were millions of Jews all over the world who would influence world opinion against us. That's when he exploded! . . . I left the police department and never returned."

At the time his conversation with Himmler took place, Bruno Streckenbach certainly knew about the "larger numbers" of Jews—the memory of SS men often fails when these are considered—but in other respects his assertions may well be accurate. It was widely believed within the SS that Heydrich was not especially enthusiastic about his duties as organizer of the Einsatzgruppen, but simply performed them coldly and efficiently as he would any other job that enhanced his power.

Streckenbach's remarks also offer a tenuous additional confirmation of the famous, highly controversial claim by Himmler's masseur, Felix Kersten, that Hitler and Himmler felt Heydrich's reputed Jewish blood had delivered him helplessly into their power, making him "a force we can always control," especially in matters of racial policy.

Even Heydrich's confidant, Schellenberg, claimed he never knew "what was really in his mind." He explained: "Thus, one day in the summer of 1941, when we were together at his hunting lodge, he remarked to me, apropos of the direction the war was taking, 'The way things are being handled by us there must be a sticky end. Also, it's sheer madness to have created this Jewish Question.'"

Madness and *created* are strong words to use about a "problem" presumed so serious that its solution became the holy writ of Nazi ideology. Schellenberg's surprise at this off-the-cuff remark is one more testimonial to the success of Heydrich's usual persona—a posture of soldierly disdain for ideological wobbling, tempered with the usual Nazi malice toward men who could be successfully intimidated. His contemptuous treatment of Paul Blobel has already been examined. Blobel, of course, was a subordinate, yet even when writing to a peer of his realm, Heydrich took the tone of someone so far above the fray he can barely condescend to notice it.

In 1942, the Gauleiter of White Ruthenia, Wilhelm Kube, launched a series of protests against the mass killings of German Jews evacuated

Wilhelm Kube (age forty-seven, in 1934), the governor of White Ruthenia (that portion of Ostland that was eastern Poland and Soviet Belorussia before 1939), argued with both Heydrich and Himmler over the mass murdering of Jews being carried out in his territory.

into his district. "I am certainly hard, and ready to solve the Jewish Question," he wrote to Heydrich. Still, he objected to treating "people from our own cultural milieu" the same way as "the animalized native hordes." He also enclosed a list of Jews to be exempted from execution.

Heydrich wrote Kube a reply with the blistering frigidity of dry ice: "You will agree that in the third year of the war, there are matters of more importance for the war effort, and for the Security Police and the Security Service as well, than worrying about the wailing of Jews." Time-wasting investigations had reaffirmed that the people on the lists had made "repeated attempts to deny their Jewishness." It was especially "natural" for half-castes to try this; Heydrich added, before ending, "I regret having to write such a justification six and a half years after the Nuremberg Laws were issued."

In fact, Heydrich had offered no real justification at all. As both he and Kube knew, the Final Solution was based, not on the Nuremberg Laws or any others, but on a secret Führer order superseding all ordinary law.

By focusing on things "of more importance," Heydrich was distancing himself from any further discussion of the Einsatzgruppen. But he also practiced a more physical form of separation, deserting the political front to engage in a more conventionally honorable form of war.

Flying with the Luftwaffe in his own Me-109, secretly defying Hitler's edict forbidding members of the SD from engaging in activities where they might be captured, Heydrich performed countless, clandestine reconnaissance missions over enemy territory. (On one of them, his plane crashed behind enemy lines, though he managed to get back after a day or two. No one knows if he even brought the poison pill that a cautious man like Schellenberg always took on his own missions.)

This was foolishly risky behavior, for Heydrich knew all the secrets of the Third Reich—everything about the rumors of Hitler's failing health that had begun to circulate around 1940, the security arrangements for the Nazi leaders, the morale of the German people, the instruction of SD agents, the state of research on the atomic bomb and the V-2 rocket—the list was endless and he had a photographic memory. "What a feast that would have made for the Russians, to have Reinhard Hey-

Heydrich in his Luftwaffe uniform, circa 1940. The previous summer, he took flying lessons at the aviation school in Werneuchen, near Berlin. By September 1939, Heydrich carried out his first combat mission as a turret gunner over Poland.

drich fall from the sky into their laps!" his wife told me. Adolf Hitler felt the same way, flying into a rage when he heard of Heydrich's illicit flights, and ordering him to stop.

I asked Frau Heydrich why her husband undertook such dangerous missions, which other high officials did not find necessary—

"Naturally they were not necessary," she interrupted. "It was much more to prove himself as a man. His comrades from the navy were all in action. They were all soldiers, and he wanted to remain a soldier. He always *felt* like a soldier, never like an administrative official. He didn't want to be in the papers, to be a boss in the official sense. He wanted always to continue being a man. Not a *Mensch* but a man."

"What is the difference?"

"A *Mensch* can be womanly, or manly—or even selfly." (This latter was a made-up term, her play on words.) "But to be a man," she went on, "has something to do with discipline, and determination, and being a model of correct behavior. But he didn't want to impress people; if he had wanted to impress, then he would have told everyone. Probably my husband knew that no one would find it correct."

Probably he also knew that word would leak out, and everyone would find aerial combat more manly than mass murder. Despite his insistence on the courage required to command an Einsatzgruppe service, Heydrich tried to prove his own bravery in the clouds, leaving his political soldiers mired in the gory mud below. (He received the Iron Cross, an award conferred for "special action.")

Unlike his high-flying subordinate, Heinrich Himmler frequently inspected the mobile commando units in the field, often favoring them with a long-winded speech. In yet another variant of the intricate division of labor necessary for systemic, wide-scale "atrocity by policy," Himmler and Heydrich thus tacitly acknowledged the classic distinction between instrumental and expressive leadership.

Sociologists have found that almost no one is equally gifted at acting effectively and at explaining why action was necessary in the first place. Since both arts are essential to the smooth running of an organization, they are usually performed by different leaders. Heydrich, the junior partner and former staff officer, had built his career on getting things done: aggressive, decisive, fast-moving, brusque, he never pretended to be a philosopher. It was Himmler who represented the SS on Party Day or Hitler's birthday and he who felt compelled to teach his minions the New Order's new version of the knightly virtues.

Although the two men had collaborated to create the complicated machinery of murder, they behaved very differently when called on to justify it. While Heydrich evaded the whole problem, Himmler walked straight toward it, embracing the hopeless task of speaking the unspeakable.

The lectures he gave to SS leaders and field commanders have become, justifiably, infamous. It is surreal to hear him speak of "having to" hold down hostile populations, "to shoot, cart people about, and drag howling women around," or to remark that "most of you know what it means to see a hundred, five hundred, a thousand bodies lying there. It is this that has made us hard . . . yet in our own selves—in our souls and in our character, we have suffered no damage therefrom."

Perhaps the disdain felt by many lower-ranking SS men for their

Reichsführer stemmed in part from his vociferous, *expressive* presence. While Himmler talked, his men had to think about what they were doing, when what they wanted was to soar away from it like Heydrich. Many deeply resented "phenomenon Eichmann," the desk bureaucrat who gave orders without having to do the dirty work himself. But Himmler was particularly disliked, not only because he bore the most responsibility, but also because he didn't behave enough like the "real man" he extolled. According to one camp guard, "Himmler was hated in the SS, but feared because he was such a mean-minded pedant. He could bawl you out for a comma in the wrong place; he acted like a petty tyrant . . . Even Heydrich knew men and had a certain gentlemanly way of dealing with subordinates."

What the guard probably really meant was that Heydrich knew when not to behave like a gentleman: his reputation for reckless bravado, enthusiastic womanizing, and late-night drinking bouts with his underlings made more sense to men desperate to forget themselves than Himmler's incessant moralizing.

Even some officers in Himmler's personal entourage shared the general malaise he came to symbolize. One day in Minsk, he asked Arthur Nebe to let him observe an actual execution. The disastrous results were described by two witnesses. As Himmler's chief of personnel later testified,

> Himmler had never seen dead people before and in his curiosity, he stood right up at the edge of this open grave . . . While he was looking in, Himmler had the deserved bad luck that from one or other of the people who had been shot in the head he got a splash of brains on his coat, and I think it also splashed into his face, and he went very green and pale . . . and then I led him away from the grave.

The second witness, Erich von dem Bach-Zelewski, chief of antipartisan warfare for the Eastern Front, noted that Himmler was also disturbed when two women did not die immediately, and "yelled to the police sergeant not to torture them."

Von dem Bach seized the moment of Himmler's weakness to give him a little lecture: "Look at the eyes of the men in this Kommando, how deeply shaken they are! These men are finished for the rest of their lives. What kind of followers are we training here? Either neurotics or savages!"

Pulling himself together, Himmler made a speech of bluntly horrible honesty: "I hate this bloody business." This was the man who had once issued a reprisal order instructing, "Even the brood in the cradle must be crushed like a swollen toad . . . Everybody has therefore to do his duty without asking his conscience first." Now he admitted that the duties of the Einsatzgruppen were repulsive. If Germans did such things gladly, he agreed, it would be a very bad thing. But we are all soldiers here, he went on, "and we must obey both our orders and the laws of nature. We are locked in a battle to the death . . . A man has to defend ourselves against vermin."

Wolff was not impressed: "He appealed to their sense of patriotism and their readiness to make sacrifices. Well yes—and then he drove off, 'leaving the unit' to sort out the future for themselves, to see if and how far they could come to terms with this."

In 1944, Karl Wolff began to negotiate secretly with the Allies behind Himmler's back. Far less adroit than Wolff, Bach-Zelewski went through many stages of gradual collapse, beginning with the recurrent nightmares experienced by almost everyone, on to stomach trouble (which he shared with Himmler), through the not uncommon nervous breakdown, to an extremely rare postwar admission of moral guilt in which he accused himself of mass murder when the Allied tribunals neglected to do so.

But even Himmler couldn't quite "come to terms" with the barbarities of the Einsatzgruppen. After his speech, he ordered Nebe to find more humane methods of killing. The result was the portable gas van, a specially rigged truck into which victims could be herded, and then killed with the carbon monoxide from the gasoline engine. Unfortunately, this procedure took far longer than was desirable—approximately fifteen minutes, during which everyone could hear the screaming—and the killers were still faced with the awful task of disposing of the soiled, contorted bodies. Otto Ohlendorf thought the vans were "morally" unsound, since they required the intimate contact with the victims that mass firing in front of trenches had been designed explicitly to avoid. In any case, the vans were soon superseded by the stationary gas chambers of Auschwitz, and the subsequent innovation of using camp inmates to dispose of the bodies.

. . .

The commandant of Auschwitz, Rudolf Höss, summarized the reaction, inside the SS, to the new murder factories which to the outside world became the byword for absolute evil: "I must admit that the gassing process had a calming effect on me. I always had a horror of the shooting, thinking of the number of people, the women and children. I was relieved we were to be spared these bloodbaths."

The transitional experiment of using amateurs at atrocity and forcing them directly to confront their victims was not repeated, and the death camps that began operations in the winter of 1941 were primarily staffed by experienced camp guards and headed by more seasoned killers. (Stangl, for example, had been involved in the euthanasia program; Höss had been indicted for murder.) Yet even many of them had to suppress vestigial feelings of pity and revulsion. According to Höss, nothing was more difficult than remaining visibly unmoved: "I had to exercise intense self-control in order to prevent my innermost doubts and feelings from becoming apparent. I had to appear cold and indif-

Rudolf Höss (age thirty-nine, circa 1940) served as commandant of Auschwitz, where the facilities could annihilate two thousand people per hour. Höss lived in a two-story gray stucco villa on the outskirts of the camp with his wife, Hedwig, and their five children, and, with the use of a gas mask, he would watch the killings himself. "I must even admit that this gassing set my mind at rest," he recalled, because "at that time neither [Adolf] Eichmann nor I was certain as to how these mass killings were to be carried out." Once they had the gas, he said, "We had established a procedure."

ferent to events that must have wrung the heart of anyone possessed of human feelings. I might not even look away when afraid lest my natural emotions get the upper hand."

A Jewish survivor of the camp he ran offered a further assessment with which Höss might have agreed: "I know hardly a single SS man who could not say that he had saved someone's life . . . No more than 5 or 10 percent were criminals by nature. The others were perfectly normal men, fully alive to good and evil."

Phillip Zimbardo—the author of a psychological experiment in which randomly chosen American college students role-played camp-guards so vividly that they had to be stopped before people actually got hurt—came to a similar conclusion: "Perfectly normal people will, in certain circumstances, treat others in a brutal, inhumane way, even though they know that their victims are ordinary people much like themselves, even though they know . . . that there but for chance would they be."

Lina Heydrich used to forestall questions about the Einsatzgruppen by asserting that although their members were just "ordinary soldiers," the sphere in which they had moved was one that "normal people could not understand"—including herself.

I think she was saying that no one who participated in such incomprehensibly ghastly events, not even her "soldierly" husband, could emerge undamaged—and that this (like the portrait of him looking "primitive" in his SS uniform) was a reality she could not bear to accept.

It is also very likely to have been a major reason for both the intense focus of the executioners on their own psychological strain and their equally striking lack of empathy for their victims.

When Emmanuel Schäffer had his nervous breakdown, he wept for himself and not his victims. The man with the gun who stood at the edge of the trench—steeling himself to do his job or already so defensively hardened that he had no difficulty in contemplating it—was already in such deep trouble that the victims were the last thing on his (conscious) mind. His eyes—which looked so cold to observers—were already turned inward toward his own problems, or sideways to see how his comrades were behaving. The direct frontal view, the one encompassing the humanity of his victims, was simply something he did not have the courage to face.

22

THE ROAD TO WANNSEE

"My husband never thought of death! He thought of resettlement."

—LINA HEYDRICH

O N THE COLD MORNING of January 20, 1942, fifteen high-ranking German officials gathered at a secluded villa in the lush Berlin suburb of Wannsee, named for the lake whose silver water shimmered beyond the tree-shrouded lawn. They had come at Reinhard Heydrich's invitation, for a meeting he called a "Conference of State Secretaries." It is known today as the Wannsee Conference, and it is probably the most famous official gathering ever held in Nazi Germany.

Like their host, the guests must have been more than a little apprehensive; certainly, they expected the proceedings to be difficult: Heydrich had informed them in advance that their stated purpose was to "coordinate" the planning of a "total solution to the Jewish Question in Europe." Under his leadership, the esteemed gentlemen—eight of whom had PhDs—met for the first (and last) time to discuss the coolly systematic murder of 11 million people.

The meeting was top secret, and none of its participants are alive today. What is known about it rests largely on two sources: a single copy of the conference minutes (or *Das Protokoll*), and the man who wrote the *Protokoll*, Adolf Eichmann, who also survived to testify about it at his trial in Jerusalem in 1961.

At Wannsee, Heydrich gave a speech briefly summarizing the history of the Jewish Emigration Bureau he had created two years before.

Eichmann had written it. Heydrich also gave detailed estimates of the remaining Jewish population of every country in Europe from Ireland (4,000) to Turkey (55,500). He even included a chart on "the occupational distribution of Jewry in the European area of the USSR." As his Jewish expert, Eichmann had provided all of this information too. He is thus the closest thing to Heydrich's alter ego—in questions relating to the Wannsee Conference—that has been available to date.

Eichmann, of course, was an imperfect source, just as he had been a radically imperfect man. He made a better witness: though he tended to mix up historical dates, underestimate his own influence, and overestimate his good intentions, he also tried hard to present the facts as he had experienced them. He didn't often attempt to deny what he had done, and differed from his interlocutors primarily on its meaning. As Hannah Arendt has said, "What for Eichmann was a job, with its daily routine, its ups and downs, was for the Jews quite literally the end of the world."

The Wannsee Conference—which marked the formal beginning of the end—was also the beginning of the "job" that would one day make Adolf Eichmann a worldwide symbol of infamy. For Heydrich, by contrast, the meeting marked the conclusion of his contribution to the evolution of the Holocaust. He intended to go on to more "positive" tasks, not of course realizing that he himself would die much sooner than many of his intended victims. The Wannsee Conference marked a fatal turning point for everyone involved. Like Eichmann, all had traveled down a long and winding road to reach this point of no return.

By his own account, Adolf Eichmann had been having a miserable time since the invasion of Russia on June 22, 1941. Indeed, nothing had really gone his way since the end of 1939. This period roughly coincided with the demise of the program of forced emigration he had supervised—first in Vienna, then in Prague, and finally, in Berlin. Eichmann frequently said that this period, when he experienced his first important contact with luminaries like Heydrich and his assistant "Gestapo" Müller, was the happiest time of his life. And it wasn't just interaction with powerful Nazis that he enjoyed: Eichmann also met frequently with the leaders of various Jewish organizations as they worked "together" (as he saw it) on the common aim of facilitating Jewish emigration from the Reich.

Eichmann was in most respects a disastrously stupid man, but he had the sense to admire the cultivation and determination of many of the Jews he met, and some of them he regarded as "friends." He had come to believe fervently in the nobility of giving the Jews "soil" of their own, and he went to his death convinced that he had saved hundreds of thousands of Jews from annihilation. Forced emigration had been Heydrich's policy, and Eichmann believed sincerely—both in this policy, and in the power he got from working out the administrative details.

The German conquest of Poland, however, presented the Nazis with a new set of Jewish "problems." The Jewish population in Poland was far greater than that in the entire Reich, and now there was almost nowhere for them to go. Hundreds of thousands of the remaining German Jews had already applied for exit visas, and found few countries willing to absorb an influx of penniless emigrants.

Beyond that, Adolf Hitler had announced as early as January 1939 that the outbreak of war in Europe would mean the "annihilation" of the Jews. Hitler was given both to wild hyperbole and actual acts of destructive bloodletting. It was therefore hard to know his real intentions, but easy to guess these would become more radical now that he had finally attained some *Lebensraum* in the East.

To Hitler and to his eugenically obsessed acolyte, Heinrich Himmler, Poland quickly became a great, grim laboratory of racial experimentation. On October 7, 1939, the Führer appointed Himmler to the newly created position of Reich commissar for the protection of Germandom. They agreed that "good blood" was to be "Germanized," "bad" blood was to be banished to the East. It was a mandate for massive social upheaval.

Germany and the Soviet Union had divided prostrate Poland into three major regions. One was incorporated into the Reich, one became part of Russia, and the area in the middle, called by the Germans the Generalgouvernement (General Government), became an occupied territory under Nazi control. Hans Frank, a crony from Hitler's early days, moved to Kraków as governor general. Soon he became known as "King Stanislas the Last," presiding over a regime so corrupt that it attracted the dregs of Nazidom from all over Europe.

If they didn't come on their own, they were sent. Himmler, with his great gift for finding the "right" man for a given job, appointed Odilo Lotario Globocnik, an Austrian thug who had recently been disgraced

As his power eroded after 1942, Hans Frank (age thirty-nine, in 1939), governor general of Poland, believed the road to redeeming himself in Hitler's eyes was by inflicting greater acts of terrorism and murder.

for violent behavior and financial corruption, as his SS and police leader in Lublin.

"The wild East" also attracted Eichmann and Dr. Franz Stahlecker, one of the many lawyers who worked for Heydrich. Stahlecker had recently been appointed head of the Security Police and SD in Prague, and he and Eichmann often met on Sunday mornings to exchange ideas about advancing SD influence. One day they decided on an ideal "political solution" to the Jewish problem: "Give the Jews an autonomous territory."

Eichmann and Stahlecker traveled to the Generalgouvernement to look around. They were impressed with the area around Nisko, on the San River near Lublin. As Eichmann put it, "This is perfect. Why not resettle the Poles, seeing there's so much resettling being done in any case, and then move Jews into this big territory?" Stahlecker presented the idea to Heydrich, who gave it his approval.

Since September 21, Heydrich had been working on plans to move all Jews out of German Poland and into a few large ghettos farther east. This was part of Himmler's grand scheme of transferring vast populations of people, and Heydrich's operational directives sounded both vague and sinister. Indeed, they clanged with evil portent.

"Distinction must be made," he said, between

(1) the final aim (which will require extended periods of time), and
(2) the stages leading to the fulfillment of this final aim (which will be carried out in short terms).

The planned measures demand the most thorough preparation in their technical as well as economic aspects . . . It is obvious that the tasks that lie ahead cannot be laid down in full detail from here . . . For the time being the first prerequisite for the final aim is the concentration of the Jews from the countryside into the largest cities. This is to be carried out with all speed.

The "final aim" was to remain "strictly secret," and to this day, no one is sure exactly what it was. It is possible that Heydrich himself knew only that it involved first concentrating Jews in certain locations, before moving them somewhere else, somewhere permanent. Heydrich generally proceeded "with all speed," sometimes before having planned his next step—though always assuming "thorough preparations" would be made somewhere along the way.

At this time, the Nazi leaders were *all* improvising, grasping wildly at promising ideas, discarding them if they proved unfeasible—and always, always, trying to anticipate Hitler's next move. In 1939, however, the Jewish Question was temporarily subsumed in the struggle to assimilate the newly conquered territories in the East. If Hitler had a clear "final aim," he did not articulate it. (As the historian Raul Hilberg has noted, however, concentration of the victims is always the first step in a process of mass destruction.)

In any case, Stahlecker's proposal suited Heydrich's short-term aim of "evacuation." Eichmann had enthusiastically envisioned communities of self-sufficient farmers, but in fact the Nisko "protectorate" was located on inhospitable, boggy terrain. (SD intelligence experts antici-

Franz Walter Stahlecker (age thirty, in 1930), commander of Einsatzgruppe A, the bloodiest of the four death squads, was eventually made police leader of Reichskommissariat Ostland, which encompassed Estonia, Latvia, Lithuania, and Belorussia.

pated considerable "wastage" of the population.) But the SS was not interested in helping Jews to live long or well. In the autumn of 1939, Eichmann ordered the Jewish community of Vienna to select several thousand able-bodied artisans for involuntary resettlement in Nisko. A few weeks later, he welcomed the earliest settlers to a grim "new homeland": "There are no apartments and no houses—if you will build homes you will have a roof over your heads . . . The wells are full of epidemics, there's cholera, dysentery, and typhus. If you dig for water, you'll have water."

Meanwhile, Heydrich was encountering obstacles on the highest level. (The outbreak of real war had done nothing to lessen the "war games" between competing Nazi potentates.) Hans Frank objected to his kingdom being used as a "dumping ground" for Jews, and he won Göring's support. Soon afterward, Hitler told an associate that "a Jewish state around Lublin would never signify a solution."

In April, the Nisko project was dropped, and Eichmann transferred his attention to the so-called Madagascar plan. The idea had already surfaced in Göring's conference of November 12, 1938, following the Night of Broken Glass, when he spoke of sending Germany's Jews to the French island colony of Madagascar. This was a common idea in anti-Semitic circles. (Heydrich first heard of it in 1934.)

In May 1940, Heinrich Himmler sent the Führer a memo describing his ideas for the treatment of the "foreign peoples" of occupied Poland. In brief, they were to be reduced to abject servitude. "I don't think reading should be required," Himmler wrote. Education would be confined to simple arithmetic and to learning it is divine law to obey the Germans. Polish culture—like the Polish nation itself—would cease to exist.

"As inhuman and tragic as each individual case might be," Himmler argued, this was milder and better than "the Bolshevist method of the physical destruction of a people," which "on grounds of conscience" he rejected as "un-Germanic and impossible." Himmler barely mentioned the Jews, commenting as an aside that perhaps they could be sent to Africa.

In June 1940, after the German Foreign Office had also begun to investigate the Madagascar plan, Heydrich wrote to Foreign Minister von Ribbentrop, reminding him that his RSHA had long been in charge of Jewish emigration. As Heydrich argued,

The whole problem—there are already about three and a half million Jews in the territories at present under German sovereignty—can . . . no longer be solved by emigration. A final territorial solution is therefore necessary. I request to be allowed to take part in the forthcoming discussion dealing with the Final Solution of the Jewish Question, should such discussion be planned.

Two weeks later, the Foreign Office more than let him take part: they suggested that SS leadership would be the logical choice to organize deportations to Madagascar, since only they had the necessary police experience.

On Heydrich's orders, Eichmann began to draw up detailed plans, even sending emissaries to occupied France to examine the archives there. SD officers studied tropical conditions, transport possibilities, and probable sequences of departure and arrival. (They guessed it would take ten years to move 4 million people from Europe to Madagascar.)

In August 1940, Eichmann presented Heydrich with a comprehensive report. Heydrich, however, did not take any action. He couldn't. First, Germany had to gain freedom of the seas, either through diplomatic alliance or victory in war. The Madagascar plan was also time-consuming and cumbersome, involving great expenditures of money and manpower.

Some historians have concluded it was never really feasible, and was actually just a "cloak" for murder. Others have argued that Heydrich had good reason to take the project seriously, since supervisory control was to remain in his hands, giving him his own island empire, and, of course, more power. Most likely, Heydrich was pursuing the time-honored Nazi policy of exploring all possible options while waiting for Hitler to make a decision. Whatever the leader decided, the Madagascar plan assumed that the Jews would be shipped off somewhere and that Heydrich, as before, would be in charge. It thus served as what the German historian Hans Mommsen has called a "psychological link" between the old policy of emigration and the deadly "evacuations" to come.

With every day of war and of waiting, with every territorial "solution" that could not be realized, the Jews' chances of survival lessened. Already, more than a million Jews from Poland and the eastern parts of the Reich had been "resettled" into overcrowded, walled ghettos in the

Generalgouvernement, where, as Heydrich had predicted in November 1938, they began to fall prey to disease and starvation. Now, however, he no longer objected. In fact, he suggested to an SS doctor that it might be wise to "start an epidemic" in the Warsaw Ghetto and reduce the numbers that way.

Himmler had decided that only the Jews of western Europe should be sent to Madagascar. The eastern Jews were too dangerous: the many rabbis and scholars among these less assimilated peoples could provide the nucleus of a new Jewish revival. Better that women be driven into the swamps to die, men be gradually eliminated through slave labor, leaders executed in reprisal for partisan activity. At various times and varying places, all of these things were ordered by Himmler as he experimented with ways to make the Jews "disappear from European territory and consciousness."

The use of murder to "solve" problems had long been a part of Hitler's power game, and it was already clear that many Jews would not survive the harsh conditions of ghetto life. Even without a coordinated plan, the Nazis were moving step by grisly step toward wholesale annihilation. (Some SS officers serving in the East had already proposed that it was more "logical" or "humane" to kill the Jews than watch them slowly dwindle away. Sometimes they took matters into their own hands. Usually no one objected.)

In December 1940, Adolf Hitler finally brought this unholy experimentation to an end when he ordered his armies to begin preparations for the invasion of Russia. "Operation Barbarossa" was to be an ideological crusade—the final battle to the death between West and East, between Aryan Nazism and Jewish Bolshevism, between good and evil. It was to be yet another version of the war to end war: the expected Nazi victory would usher in a thousand years of "peace."

The German Reich would also acquire an estimated 5 million more Jewish inhabitants, all of them seen as mortal enemies. For them—the presumed source of Communism—there would be no second-class citizenship, no emigration, no "territorial solution."

When precisely the term *Final Solution* became synonymous with mass murder has never been established. Most experts agree that by March 1941, when Himmler ordered Heydrich to organize special SS troops to operate directly behind the advancing armies, "defending" them against Jews, Communists, and other "partisans," the dreadful decision had been made. The primary task of the Einsatzgruppen was murder, impure and simple.

This, however, was only one of the tracks along which the Nazi political machine now hurtled toward genocide. The Einsatzgruppen were quasi-military in conception and action—they killed with guns, working closely with the armed forces, under the command of a man who had once been a staff officer in the navy. But Heydrich was also—and primarily—a bureaucrat, and this was the form of power he understood best. On July 31, 1941, Hermann Göring sent Heydrich a second mandate:

> As supplement to the task which was entrusted to you in the decree dated January 24, 1939, to solve the Jewish Question by emigration and evacuation in the most favorable way possible, given present conditions, I herewith commission you to carry out all necessary preparations with regard to organizational, substantive, and financial viewpoints for a total solution of the Jewish Question in the German sphere of influence in Europe.
>
> Insofar as the competencies of other central organizations are hereby affected, these are to be involved.
>
> I further commission you to submit to me promptly an overall plan showing the preliminary organizational, substantive, and financial measures for the execution of the intended Final Solution of the Jewish Question.

The "solution" of the Jewish Question was now both "final" and "total," including the Jews of western Europe as well as those of the alien East. It had now also become, at last, the official, irrevocable, Nazi policy. Many would say this was inevitable. In 1939, the Nazis had experimented with gassing Germans who were mentally ill; they had slaughtered the Polish upper classes, and resettled a million Jews into eastern ghettos. Like the Madagascar plan, these were additional "psychological links" in a chain of ghastly "logic" leading to the Holocaust.

Hitler had always had the motive of destroying his enemies, in the SS bureaucracy he had the means, and the cover of war provided the long-awaited opportunity. He could even make use of the same people who had previously worked to organize the earlier, provisional, incomplete efforts toward a solution. The chain of command running from

Himmler to Heydrich to Müller to Eichmann was already in place. All the Führer had to do was change their orders.

Sometime in the fateful summer of 1941, Reinhard Heydrich called Adolf Eichmann to his office. As Eichmann remembered it,

> I reported. He said to me: "The Führer, well, emigration is . . ."
>
> He began with a little speech. And then, "The Führer has ordered physical extermination." These were his words. And as though wanting to test their effect on me, he made a long pause, which was not at all his way. I can still remember that. In the first moment, I didn't grasp the implications because he chose his words so carefully. But then I understood. I didn't say anything, what could I say? Because I'd never thought of a . . . of such a thing, of that sort of violent solution.

It would be interesting to know what the two men thought and felt as they sat in silence in Heydrich's palatial office.

Heydrich spoke very rarely of his personal reaction to the Final Solution. When members of an Einsatzkommando resisted their assignment, he did not give ideological justifications. Instead, he said they were under military discipline and would be treated as deserters if they didn't comply, or he accused them of cowardice, or he said he wanted "real men" to prove themselves by undertaking a "very heavy task." To Bruno Streckenbach, he said not to resist the orders for mass murder, that they were both "helpless" against them. And, in the summer of 1941, he confided to Walter Schellenberg, "The way things are being handled by us, there must be a sticky end. Also, it's sheer madness to have created this Jewish Question." All of these remarks, however, are unsubstantiated by written documents.

The public record, by contrast, reveals a man totally committed to the madness, restlessly working to clear away the obstacles to SS domination of the East and to keeping control of Jewish policy in SS hands. Heydrich is even said to have written the order of July 31 that Göring then sent back to him as his own. It seems likely that he was already planning the conference that would take place in Wannsee the following January, and wanted to control the precise wording of his mandate.

But was the mandate what he had wanted all along, whatever he occasionally said in private? Similar discrepancies exist between people's behavior in public and in private—part of a pattern of striking disjunction between the facade of public order and the actuality of hidden disagreements; between the ideal of SS chivalry and the reality of SS deeds; between the game of power as actually played and as propagandistically described; and between the glowing official ideal of a stable, unified folk community and the endemic rivalry, ideological fragmentation, and personal disorientation that festered underneath.

The SS leaders, representing the vanguard of Nazism, also tended to embody its contradictions, and are routinely described as having "split personalities." Psychologists have labeled this phenomenon "dual-track thinking," "doubling," or even "institutionalized schizophrenia." Some Nazis recognized it in themselves: "I have a good side and a bad side," Heinrich Himmler often said. Others talked of the conflict between their "official" and "private" selves, or between what they wanted "personally" and what was required by "the framework of the situation." Heydrich never talked about such things at all. Instead, he kept maniacally busy and worked at such a breakneck pace that it often seemed as if he was running away from something. Perhaps that something was the sense of honor he used to talk about, that had apparently gotten lost somewhere along the way.

Unlike Heydrich, Adolf Eichmann spoke very clearly about the process through which he learned to "overcome" his better nature. Of course, he was relying on fickle memory, at a time when he was a prisoner among people who despised him and were going to kill him afterward. Still, he seemed often to welcome the death awaiting him. We have no reason to assume that he lied.

In 1941, after Heydrich and Eichmann had sat for a while in silence, Heydrich gave Eichmann his new orders: "Go and see Globocnik in Lublin . . . The Führer has already given him instructions. Take a look and see how he's getting on with his program. I believe he's using Russian anti-tank trenches for exterminating the Jews."

In the next several months, Adolf Eichmann toured various killing centers in Poland. "I was horrified," he said. In Lublin, Odilo Globocnik was now using a Russian submarine engine to pipe carbon monoxide into sealed houses where Jews were imprisoned. "I visualized the scene and began to tremble," Eichmann remembered, "as if I'd been

Odilo Globocnik (age thirty-four, in 1938) proposed to Heinrich Himmler in October 1939 that a gas chamber be built at Bełżec, exclusively for the murder of non-able-bodied Polish Jews. Construction began November 1, and the *Aktion*, secretly named Operation Reinhard (after Heydrich), expanded to other camps and the list of victims to as many Jews as possible. In all, Globocnik was responsible for the deaths of more than 1.5 million.

through something, some terrible experience." A little later, "Gestapo" Müller sent him to Chelmno, where "an action against the Jews" was under way. He didn't put it as "crassly" as Heydrich had, Eichmann noted. Already the official euphemisms used to camouflage the Final Solution were going into effect—even in private conversations between the major perpetrators.

At Chelmno, where the Nazis had been experimenting with mobile gas vans, Eichmann "saw the most horrible sight I had seen in all my life." He witnessed only the end of the "action," in which a truck was unloaded of its corpses, which were then thrown into a trench: "Just thrown in. I can still see a civilian with pliers pulling out teeth. And then I beat it. I got into my car and drove off . . . I sat there for hours without saying a word to my driver. I'd had enough. I was through." Back in Berlin, he told Müller that Chelmno was "terrible, an inferno," and that he couldn't bring himself to watch what happened there.

"What did Müller say?" an Israeli interrogator later asked.

"Müller never said anything. Never! Not about these things and not about other things. He was always very terse and unemotional," Eichmann replied. Müller did ask how long it took to kill the people in the van, but Eichmann hadn't stayed long enough to find out.

Eichmann's next visit was to Minsk, where the executioners were still using guns in the old-fashioned manner. (The experiments with gas were designed as a response to Himmler's order to find something "more humane.") Eichmann arrived late in Minsk, when the "work" was ending for the day. He watched SS riflemen shooting at Jews in a pit: "I can still see a woman with her arms behind her back, and then her knees crumpled, and I cleared out."

This time, Eichmann told Müller that what the SS was doing was "horrible . . . They're training young men to be sadists . . . How can they stand there firing at a woman and children? How is it possible? . . . This is no solution to the Jewish Question." He also begged Müller to assign him some other task: "There are plenty of other men who can bear to see such things, who won't keel over; I can't stand it, I can't sleep at night, I have nightmares."

Eichmann's request was denied. He could not have known that Himmler felt "maintenance of secrecy" compelled him never to release those heavily involved in the atrocities from their wearisome duties. As the Reichsführer SS wrote,

> I can well imagine that we shall be denounced and blackened by powers that see only the deed, but not the compelling necessity behind this action . . . I cannot allow the small circle of SS leaders who have been implicated in these things, and who therefore have to bear this burden entirely for themselves, to be widened and varied through constant transfers to the front and relief replacements.

In the early autumn of 1941, Heydrich told a group of subordinates that Hitler wished the Reich to be *Judenrein* ("Jew free") by the end of 1941. Therefore, all of the Jews inside German territory were to be shipped out. The fact that we have no place to send them is not to be considered an excuse for inaction, Heydrich told his men.

On October 17, the first trains of Jews left Germany for Minsk and Riga. Though the transports were still listed under the code name of "resettlement," the passengers, packed together in unheated cars with no sanitary facilities, no food, and no water, were now being sent to their deaths.

At the beginning, the first mass executions were even messier than the ghastly Einsatz norm, and serious mistakes were made. Himmler and Heydrich had decided to exempt from execution elderly Jews and those with high military decorations. But by some error, a thousand of these exempted Jews were sent on a death convoy to Riga. Discovering this, Himmler called Heydrich to ask him to stop their execution, but it was already too late. Neither of the two top SS leaders had been on the scene—or even in Berlin. Himmler was traveling on the special train that enabled him to stay close to Hitler; and Heydrich was in Prague, where he had moved on September 27 to take up the additional role of Reich protector of Bohemia and Moravia. Distracted by their other duties, they were absentee leaders of an operation on the brink of chaos.

To make matters worse, the Riga executions were held in the Rumbuli Forest, which was so close to town that passersby could hear the shots; some of them observed the killings as well. Secrecy proved impossible to maintain. An outraged Abwehr officer sent a detailed report to Admiral Canaris, who apparently went to Hitler and read the horrible details out loud. This took great courage, for Heydrich already knew that Canaris was implicated in treason. But Canaris's extraordinary act of bravery was of no avail. "You're getting soft," the Führer told him. "I have to do it. After me, no one else will."

It was around this time that, according to Hannah Arendt, Eichmann disobeyed Heydrich's orders for the first and only time. Asked to arrange the transportation of ten thousand Jews and Romani to Riga, where they were to be met by armed SS troops and immediately executed, Eichmann sent them instead to the ghetto at Łódź, where no such "actions" had been planned. Immediately he got into trouble. The Nazi authorities at Łódź felt the ghetto was already too crowded, and complained to Heydrich and Himmler. Eichmann wasn't punished for his mild display of compassion, but it was the last time he dared to reveal it. Hiding his misgivings, he "coordinated" himself with the "framework of the situation" as he had done several times before.

In the meantime, Himmler had ordered the swift expansion of the concentration camp at Auschwitz. Its location would make what happened there easy to "camouflage," the Reichsführer SS said. The camp—along with five others in Poland—was to be converted into a factory of death. A few weeks before, the Nazis had discovered that the poison gas Zyklon-B, previously used to exterminate vermin, was also extremely effective against humans. Himmler ordered that gassing rooms (disguised as showers) be installed at the camps in Poland. Eichmann was once again assigned the job of "inspecting" the work in progress.

The first gassing facilities actually began to operate in December at a small installation at Chelmno, but Eichmann was sent most often to talk to Rudolf Höss, the commandant of Auschwitz. The immense machinery of death there would not be fully operational until July 1942, but the personnel were happy to demonstrate its workings.

"Herr Hauptmann," Eichmann later told the Israeli police interrogator Avner Less, "those fellows were very cruel, describing those things as gruesomely as possible to a man accustomed to desk work . . . Naturally, they laughed their heads off when my nerves broke down and I couldn't keep up my military dignity—that's what they called it—the way they did."

Eichmann wrote that "Höss himself was thoroughly hardened," but that is not how the latter presented himself in his memoirs. Instead, he wrote about his great difficulties in hiding his emotional distress—his weak and therefore unmanly side—from his companions in crime.

In any case, Eichmann was not privy to Höss's "private self." He looked at his peers, and saw reflected back the bland face of obedience, the blind stare of conviction, the iron "mask" of orthodoxy. Like them, he kept his doubts to himself.

And all of this time, Eichmann had never seen a written order or given a report in writing: "I couldn't do that. I was expressly forbidden to; by Heydrich, I believe."

At the Wannsee Conference, however, Heydrich himself broke the SS secrecy regulations and put in writing hidden policies of almost unbelievable horror—enough to damn everyone who attended as well as the millions of people whose fate they had come to discuss.

But if Adolf Eichmann was damned, he didn't realize it at the time. On the contrary, for him the conference was a moment of moral revelation—and profound relief. Heydrich, too, was said to be almost euphoric afterward. At Wannsee, he had, among other things, forged a bond of blood that would force others to share the guilt of the SS and implicate themselves in writing. No doubt he felt it was worth almost any risk.

23

THE WANNSEE CONFERENCE

"My husband was no stranger to death."

—LINA HEYDRICH

FOR MANY YEARS, the Wannsee Conference was regarded as the place where the Nazis "decided" to exterminate the Jews of Europe. Yet nothing was actually decided at the elegant suburban villa, at 56–58 Am Grossen Wannsee: that was not the point. The guests were really little more than an audience for an elaborately planned theatrical piece, with Reinhard Heydrich at center stage.

If he ever played the role of "puppet master of the Third Reich," it was at Wannsee, where for one and a half hours the chief of the SD and the Security Police pulled together the diverse and deadly strands of Nazi policy toward the Jews.

The Wannsee Conference is mainly important for what Heydrich said there—and also for what he did *not* say. Allegedly convened to clarify policy, the proceedings he orchestrated have caused enough confusion among historians to inspire much scholarly debate on its true purpose and significance.

"My husband was no stranger to death," Frau Heydrich had announced, without apology, on the evening we first met. Heydrich's fellow Nazis apparently felt similarly, calling him "the blond beast," likening him to Cesare Borgia, joking that he was "king of the underworld," or echoing the Swiss diplomat Carl J. Burckhardt's vision of Heydrich as a "young, evil god of death." "My husband's evil Satan,"

Marga Himmler said of him, though it was also her husband who exhorted the commanders of his knightly order, "You must be super-humanly inhuman."

When Reinhard Heydrich strode into the conference room at the Wannsee villa, he brought death and the devil in with him. Yet once there, he did everything in his power to make them disappear. He used some of the most potent weapons at his disposal: words.

Throughout the Third Reich, but particularly within the SS, elaborate "language rules" had grown up like thick underbrush, surrounding the most sensitive areas of conduct and preventing clear-eyed perception of the grimmest realities. We have already seen them sprouting through the reports of the Einsatzgruppen leaders, as the uncomfortable word *shot* was gradually replaced by an endless efflorescence of euphemisms: *removed, resettled, rendered harmless.*

Bloodless code words not only shielded top-secret Führer orders from prying eyes, but also protected the bearers of those orders from explicitly confronting their own guilt. As Robert J. Lifton discovered in his study of Nazi doctors, bland bureaucratic terminology provided "a discourse in which killing was no longer killing; and need not be experienced, or even perceived, as killing." Instead, they could talk as if it were just one more imperative of the relentless administrative machine, another in an endless series of "tasks." At Wannsee, Heydrich performed a prodigious feat of sleight of hand, veiling murderous intentions behind a curtain of evasive verbiage. Like all good theatrical producers, he had worked everything out beforehand. This time, he was totally in control of the situation—and of the protocol, which he revised three or four times before sending it out to thirty Reich dignitaries entitled to "bear secrets."

To read this document is to become lost in the language of a bureaucratic "rationality" so insidious it can make mass murder seem ordinary, even a bit dull. Afterward, one always feels a little ill. Yet Heydrich had arranged the whole show in the hopes that his guests would *feel* nothing.

Heydrich, himself split into so many incompatible parts, perfectly embodied a hopelessly confused amalgam: a man of action with a photographic memory for organizational details, an athlete of Spartan stamina who worked behind a desk, a *Draufgänger* (daredevil) famous for speed and decisiveness, who also possessed the malevolent patience of a master of intrigue. And perhaps most disarming to his Nazi peers, a leader who looked like a Wagnerian warrior but thought "like an adding machine," all pragmatism, precision, and icy "logic."

At Wannsee, Heydrich spoke more than once of the need to learn from experience. He practiced what he preached. The entire protocol—including its deliberately misleading language—can be regarded as a summation of what he had learned from nine years as a technologist of "applied terror." Indeed, some of the mysteries of the conference can only be understood in that chill and brutal light. Five of them are briefly noted here.

I. THE GHOST OF ADOLF HITLER

The first words Heydrich said were a stark justification of his own power: Reich Marshal Göring had appointed him "Plenipotentiary for the Preparation of the Final Solution of the European Jewish Question." Göring had also requested a summary of relevant issues, Heydrich said, thus necessitating "prior joint consideration by all central agencies directly concerned with these questions, with a view to keeping policy lines parallel."

In the first thirty seconds, Heydrich had used Göring's name twice. But in Nazi Germany, it was always necessary to read between the lines of what Adolf Eichmann called "office-speak." Thus, when the participants heard Heydrich say "Göring," they were supposed to think "Hitler."

Everyone knew that Hermann Göring and Reinhard Heydrich were not on good terms; everyone knew Göring wouldn't lend his name to an undertaking by Heydrich unless the Führer had agreed. Göring—widely regarded as Hitler's official heir apparent—was thus a sort of proxy for the man who had consistently required that his name never be linked to the murders he ordered.

In 1939, Heydrich had lamented that many complaints about the Einsatzgruppen could have been avoided if he were free to say his orders had come from Adolf Hitler himself. In 1942, one minute after the beginning of the Wannsee Conference, Heydrich had already called forth Hitler's empowering presence. This time, he was covering himself with a cloak of official approval.

2. THE RESPONSIBILITY OF HEINRICH HIMMLER

In the second paragraph, Heydrich invokes Himmler's authority: "Primary responsibility for the handling of the Final Solution . . . is to lie centrally, regardless of geographic boundaries, with the Reichsführer SS and the chief of the German police (chief of the Security Police and the SD)."

The odd elision of Himmler's title as police chief with Heydrich's own as chief of the Security Police has been the subject of some speculation. The German historian Eberhard Jäckel has argued that Heydrich convened the conference to grab power away from Himmler, and included his boss's name first only out of "consideration."

Yet Heydrich had always stood in Himmler's shadow—"Himmler, with Heydrich behind him" was the way Gerald Reitlinger put it. Heydrich's merging of their official roles reflected harsh reality. The "terrible twins" who had been so effective in snatching the Gestapo out of Göring's hands still functioned as a team for the devil's work of mass murder.

By 1942, Himmler and Heydrich had evolved a complicated division of labor. While Heydrich hammered out a series of "near-term" and "final" operational directives, Himmler was busy on what he would have considered a more exalted level. It was the Reichsführer SS who traveled to Hitler's side for the confidential one-on-one meetings in which the Führer made his secret wishes known. It was Himmler who then relayed these wishes, orally, to the various SS chieftains whose offices would implement them. And it was usually Himmler who met privately with the highest Nazi officials—men like Hans Frank, Joachim von Ribbentrop, and Göring himself—to discuss the Führer's objectives.

Like Heydrich, the guests at Wannsee were one step below this level. They were not heads of governmental ministries, but the most powerful deputies of these men. If Göring's orders seemed to bypass Himmler, Heydrich was careful at Wannsee to place his service chief in the center of the carnage, where he belonged.

In the winter of 1941, five death camps were constructed along the Bug River in Poland. Himmler was in charge, as he was of every other camp. His inoffensive manner masked an iron will to this form of power as well as a streak of sadism enhanced by his frequent visits to inspect his secret empire of permanent death camps and temporary encampments of roving executioners.

Himmler, though sickened by the sight of blood, nevertheless ordered women prisoners at Ravensbrück beaten merely to "observe the effect." In Lublin, when Odilo Globocnik suggested the experiment of blowing up a group of Jews with dynamite, Himmler agreed, over the objections of the rest of his staff. Another day, he pondered putting out the eyes of partisans as a warning to others. His presumably hardened companions were stunned.

Heydrich's thinking, by contrast, reflected a greater physical, and perhaps emotional, distance from the macabre "front" he rarely visited. His staff was more apt to be stunned by the remote Olympian ease with which he pulled the strings of others' lives.

This is chillingly apparent in Part III of the conference protocol, when Heydrich moves on to the subject at hand.

3. EVACUATION OF THE JEWS TO THE EAST

Heydrich began—just as he had when he told Eichmann about the Final Solution—with a short summary of the emigration he had supervised since January 1939. He sounded a little defensive, admitting the scheme had "disadvantages":

Financial difficulties—such as increases decreed by the various foreign governments in the moneys which immigrants were required to have and in landing fees . . . lack of steamship berths . . . bans on immigration hampered the emigration efforts exceedingly. Despite these difficulties, a total of approximately 537,000 Jews was processed into emigration between the assumption of power and the date of October 31, 1941 . . .

Since then, in view of the dangers of emigration during wartime and in view of the possibilities in the East, the Reichsführer SS . . . has forbidden the emigration of Jews.

Emigration has now been replaced by evacuation of the Jews to the East as a further possible solution, in accordance with previous authorization by the Führer.

However, these actions are to be regarded only as provisional options; even now practical experience is being gathered that is of major significance in view of the coming Final Solution of the Jewish Question.

Heydrich did not define what he meant by "practical experience" or "possibilities in the East." (However, the inclusion of Sturmbannführer Dr. Rudolf Lange—the SS commander in charge of the executions in Latvia—among the illustrious guests might have suggested what kind of experience was going to prove relevant.) The term *evacuation* was also left dangling. (People of all races were being evacuated to all sorts of places; certainly Hitler could be mentioned as approving such a commonplace action.)

Gliding over these amorphous words, Heydrich paused to offer a detailed accounting of the Jewish population of Europe, methodically subdivided into thirty-two different countries.

Then he sketched the outlines of the new operational plan:

Under appropriate direction, in the course of the Final Solution, the Jews are now to be suitably assigned to labor in the East. In big labor gangs, with the sexes separated, Jews capable of work will be brought to these areas, employed in road building, in which task a large part will undoubtedly disappear through natural diminution.

The remnant that may eventually remain, being undoubtedly the part most capable of resistance, will have to be appropriately dealt with, since it represents a natural selection and in the event of release is to be regarded as the germ cell of a new Jewish renewal. (Witness the experience of history.)

In the course of the practical implementation of the Final Solution, Europe is to be combed through from west to east . . .

The evacuated Jews will first be brought, group by group, into so-called transit ghettos, to be transported from there farther to the east.

An important prerequisite for the implementation of the evacuation as a whole . . . is the exact determination of the category of persons that may be affected.

The intent is not to evacuate Jews over sixty-five years of age, but to assign them to a ghetto for the aged. Theresienstadt is under consideration.

Along with these age groups . . . Jews with serious wartime disabilities and Jews with war decorations (Iron Cross, First Class) will be taken into the Jewish old-age ghettos. With this efficient solution, the many interventions [requests for exceptions] will be eliminated at one stroke.

It is not surprising that these are the best-known paragraphs of the protocol. They are a stunning example of coolly Machiavellian cynicism and deliberate bureaucratic obfuscation. Once again, Heydrich does not define his terms: "natural diminution," "appropriately dealt with," "lessons of history": these are left to the reader's imagination.

In Heydrich's place Himmler might have offered a long "inspirational" discourse converting piles of corpses into an unwritten "page of glory" in our history. Heydrich, however, confined himself to "practical experience." The use he intended to make of the so-called model ghetto he had just created near Prague is a revealing example.

4. "THERESIENSTADT IS UNDER CONSIDERATION."

The only concentration camp initiated under Heydrich's auspices, it was also the only one that the Red Cross was allowed to visit. Like the protocol itself, Theresienstadt was a monument to the stage-managing of grim realities.

From a distance, the heavily walled old town looked charmingly picturesque. Inside, one could find a bank, theaters, shops, and a park. Men and women generally lived in separate barracks, but were allowed to make dates for social or sexual assignations. A few prisoners had tiny rooms of their own (some of them artfully arranged by inmate architects) containing amenities like rugs, bookshelves, and potted plants. Visitors could also observe several hospital areas, containing clean beds and real medicine. There were no extermination chambers.

For a year or so, Theresienstadt functioned as a sort of refuge for Jews in especially privileged categories, but as a former inmate has put it, it was also "a colossal hoax," part of a systematic effort to disguise the real nature of the Final Solution. By 1943, space in the camp was filled up. After that, the SS relieved the crowding by alternating trains into Theresienstadt with trains from there to Auschwitz.

In any case, the main point, as far as Heydrich was concerned, was to eliminate "interventions." Practical experience had taught him that most efforts to save Jews were made on behalf of the prominent or the wealthy. If these groups could be sent to a camp open to Red Cross inspection, criticism would be blunted and (justified) fears allayed.

With the framework of discourse—a ferociously cold-blooded perversion of conventional bureaucratic "rationality"—now firmly established, the participants moved on to a brief discussion of the ways the "problem" might be solved in each European country.

Though the Foreign Office would obviously have to participate, it was clear that the SS was in charge. Slovakia and Croatia had already been taken care of; France, as well as "the Southeast and West of Europe," would probably pose few difficulties; Heydrich himself would handle negotiations in Italy and would "take things in hand" in Hungary. (Only the "Nordic states" were seen as offering any possible resistance; Heydrich "postponed these countries for the time being.")

State Secretary Erich Neumann worried about evacuating Jews working in essential war industries. Heydrich said he had already exempted them in the "current evacuation actions."

State Secretary Josef Bühler, representing the once reluctant Hans Frank, now urged Heydrich to begin in the Generalgouvernement, or that part of Poland that had not been devoured by either Germany or Russia. Perhaps politely, the latter didn't point out that the Final Solution had already been initiated there in October. Bühler also asked Heydrich to act "as quickly as possible." This, too, was superfluous: Heydrich had hustled the proceedings along like a train going at full speed. Only once—in the matter of the *Mischlinge* ("mixtures," although literally "mongrels" or "hybrids")—did he slow the breakneck pace.

5. THE *MISCHLING* PROBLEM

A disproportionate amount of the protocol is devoted to the *Mischlinge*, those vexing mixtures of German and Jewish blood whose every existence defied clear categories and prevented a perfectly "complete solution."

The area of decision actually open to the guests at Wannsee was confined to this small group of perhaps fifty thousand people, a tiny percentage of the projected 11 million victims—and even here, Heydrich said their conclusions would be "only theoretical."

But should the *Mischlinge* really be victims if they were partially Aryan? Exhaustively, sometimes passionately, the men debated a variety of alternatives, which varied according to the "degree" of racial mixing. They produced pages of hairsplitting distinctions. Even the first one is hard to follow:

(1) As far as the Final Solution of the Jewish Question is
concerned, first-degree *Mischlinge* are deemed equal to Jews.
The following will be exempt from this treatment:

(a) First-degree *Mischlinge* married to persons of German blood
from whose marriages children (second-degree *Mischlinge*)
have been born. These second-degree *Mischlinge* are deemed
essentially equal to Germans.

(b) First-degree *Mischlinge* for whom exceptions with respect to
any area of life have been granted prior to the present time by
the highest authorities of the party and the state.

As the wearying talk ground on, the discussants came perilously close
to admitting a feeble empathy with their prey. SS General Otto Hofmann guessed the *Mischlinge*, "faced with the choice of being evacuated
or sterilized, would rather submit to sterilization." Heydrich pondered
the effect that evacuating Jewish spouses might have "on the German
relatives." State Secretary of Justice William Stuckart argued strongly in
favor of compulsory sterilization for first-degree *Mischlinge*, thus freeing
the partners in a mixed marriage from further restrictions.

After considerable discussion, the *Mischling* problem was left unresolved. (Hitler was known to be hostile to the *Mischlinge* and to feel
they should be eliminated unless they had "proved themselves" through
extraordinary service to the party.) Heydrich had displayed fortitude
under what must have been trying circumstances, for of course he knew
that his guests were likely to assume he himself was a *Mischling*. (Even
Lina Heydrich admitted that most people attributed her husband's ruthlessness toward the Jews to a presumed "inferiority complex," resulting
from "tainted blood" and "Jewish self-hatred.")

What must the other participants have thought as they heard Heydrich recommend that every individual case should be examined separately in terms of the police and political record of the *Mischling* in
question—his "appearance in racial terms," and whether he "feels and
conducts himself like a Jew."

Their tall, blond, blue-eyed host looked like a textbook model of the
Superman, and his police record was, of course, perfect. It is hard to do
a better job of proving oneself a Nazi than Heydrich did at Wannsee.
Perhaps this prompted his guests to recall he had recently been promoted to Obergrüppenführer in the SS, risen to ministerial rank as the

new Reichsprotektor in Prague, and lived in a castle from which he had just commuted in his own private plane. And he was still chief of Reich security, charged with judging their own political reliability. Apparently, Heydrich's guests also felt the need to prove themselves. That, too, had not been left to chance.

In the autumn before the conference, Heydrich and Himmler had methodically either courted or intimidated the Nazi leaders most resistant to a "total" solution. Hans Frank had preferred the "solution" of ghettos, but the SD had finally gathered enough evidence of corruption to make him vulnerable to blackmail. Foreign Minister Ribbentrop had also been uncooperative—until Heydrich managed to establish a good working relationship with his most powerful assistant, ironically named Martin Luther.* In December, Heydrich had also met with Wilhelm Stuckart of the Ministry of Justice. For years, Stuckart had tried to thwart the rise of Himmler and Heydrich. After Wannsee, however, he began to advise his subordinates that the "highest authority" had authorized the Final Solution—another way of saying that Adolf Hitler's will must be obeyed.

Adolf Eichmann had said Heydrich wanted at Wannsee to "nail down" the invited leaders, to "catch them by their words." In fact, he had already nailed them to the swastika before they ever arrived at the conference. Once there, they caught themselves, scurrying to ratify a fait accompli.

The spectacle of so many powerful "gentlemen" discussing murder as if it were perfectly normal and acceptable had a dramatic impact on Adolf Eichmann, who sat mutely at a table in the corner, taking notes. When he was asked at his trial why he had not played more of a leading role, Eichmann professed shock. The guests were all so much more powerful than he: "I was not authorized to open my mouth." Instead, he observed, as one by one the participants acquiesced to genocide.

Eichmann was particularly affected by the behavior of Wilhelm Stuckart:

---

* It was Luther's copy of the hitherto secret *Protokoll*, copy number 16 of 30, all thought to have been destroyed, that was discovered by a prosecutor at the International Military Tribunal at Nuremberg and first revealed that the Wannsee Conference had taken place. (Scott Christianson, *100 Documents That Changed the World: From Magna Carta to Wikileaks.* Milford, CT: Universe, 2015.)

Gauleiter
Dr. Meyer

Reichsamtsleiter
Dr. Leibbrandt

Staatssekretär
Dr. Stuckart

Staatssekretär
Dr. Bühler

Unterstaatssekretär
Luther

SS-Oberführer
Klopfer

SS-Gruppenführer
Müller

SS-Obersturmbannführer
Eichmann

SS-Oberführer
Dr. Schöngarth

On January 20, 1942, fifteen top-ranking Nazi Party, Schutzstaffel (SS), and government officials, numerous PhDs among them, attended a not-quite-two-hour meeting at the lakeside guesthouse of the Security Police in Berlin's Villa Minoux. The topic was the deportation and murder of the more than 11 million Jews who inhabited Nazi-occupied Europe. Chaired by Reinhard Heydrich and known as the Wannsee Conference, the gathering framed the concept of genocide as a general bureaucratic policy, rather than the obligation of any one individual, and allowed those present to coordinate their efforts to carry out the mission.

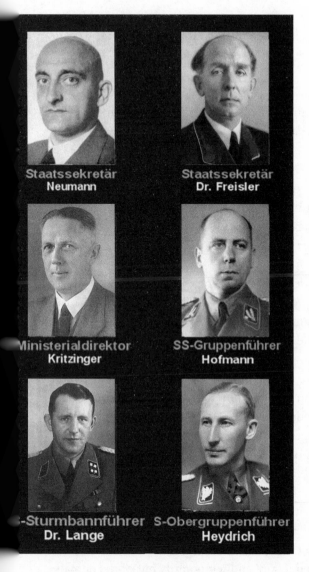

**Staatssekretär
Neumann**

**Staatssekretär
Dr. Freisler**

**Ministerialdirektor
Kritzinger**

**SS-Gruppenführer
Hofmann**

**-Sturmbannführer
Dr. Lange**

**S-Obergruppenführer
Heydrich**

THE PARTICIPANTS:
(Top row, from left)
Dr. Alfred Meyer, regional party leader, state secretary, and deputy Reich minister, Reich Ministry for the Occupied Eastern Territories; Dr. Georg Leibbrandt, Reich Head Office, Reich Ministry for the Occupied Eastern Territories; SS Brigadeführer Dr. Wilhelm Stuckart, state secretary, Reich Interior Ministry; SS Oberführer Erich Neumann, state secretary, Office of the Plenipotentiary for the Four-Year Plan; and Dr. Roland Freisler, state secretary, Reich Ministry of Justice.
(Middle row, from left)
Dr. Josef Bühler, state secretary, Polish Occupation Authority; Martin Luther, undersecretary, Reich Foreign Ministry; SS Oberführer Dr. Gerhard Klopfer, permanent secretary, Nazi Party chancellery; Friedrich Wilhelm Kritzinger, permanent secretary, Reich chancellery; and SS Gruppenführer Otto Hofmann, head of the SS Race and Settlement Main Office (RHSA).

(Bottom row, from left) SS Gruppenführer Heinrich Müller, chief of Amt IV, RHSA, SS; Obersturmbannführer Adolf Eichmann, head of Referat IV B4 of the Gestapo Recording secretary, Gestapo, RSHA, SS; SS Oberführer Dr. Karl Eberhard Schöngarth, commander of the Einsatzgruppen in the general government of Poland; Dr. Rudolf Lange, commander of the Sicherheitspolizei (Sipo) and the Sicherheitsdienst des Reichsführers (SD) for Latvia; deputy commander of the Sipo and the SD for the RKO Head of Einsatzkommando 2, Sipo and SD, RSHA, SS; and, presiding, SS Obergruppenführer Reinhard Heydrich, chief of the RSHA and deputy Reich protector of Bohemia and Moravia, SS.

He was usually hesitating and reserved, reticent and furtive, but all of a sudden he gave expression to boundless enthusiasm, with which he joined the others with regard to the Final Solution of the Jewish Question . . .

Look here, I told myself, even this guy Stuckart, who was known as one of these uncles who was a great stickler for legalities, he too uses language which is not at all in accordance with paragraphs of the law.

As he listened, Adolf Eichmann experienced a revelation that changed his life. When he saw that none of the men he called "the popes of the Third Reich" seemed to share his inner doubts, the doubts melted away: "At that moment, I sensed a kind of Pontius Pilate feeling, for I felt free of all guilt."

Eichmann could relapse once again into his natural posture of unquestioned conformity to the values of his betters. As he shed the burden of conscience, his ambition was also liberated, and he turned to his work with a boundless enthusiasm that lasted at least as long as the Reich itself.

Heydrich concluded the official part of the meeting with a request that his guests "afford him the appropriate support." (By that time, of course, they already had.) After that, the gathering broke up into small groups for informal private discussions. Over food and wine, they reviewed various methods of eliminating the Jews. Eichmann remembered they talked "quite bluntly, quite differently from the language which I had to use later in the record."

"Well, I don't want to say there was an atmosphere of drunkardness there," Eichmann said, but apparently the guests lost some of their stiff formality and "just talked at cross-vertices." They had passed behind the scenes of the theatrical production, and temporarily out of the domain of the language rules. By the time they read the protocol, they would have reverted back once more into their "official" selves. As Eichmann told the Israeli court, only the "important part" of the deliberations appeared in the minutes.

After the other men had left, Heydrich, Müller, and Eichmann enjoyed a cognac and a cigarette. It was the first time Eichmann had ever seen his boss drink or smoke. He never forgot this rare moment of relaxed equality with his fearsome service chief, who seemed in very high spirits. Heydrich had "expected considerable stumbling blocks and difficulties." Instead, he, like Eichmann, seemed surprised by the total capitulation of his guests.

Indeed, at that moment the two men were very likely sharing more than a glass of excellent brandy. Lina Heydrich claimed that after the Röhm purge her husband told her he regarded his hangman's work as "something like a great personal sacrifice": "When in moments of doubt, I begged him to give it up, he said that he neither wanted to nor could. 'I feel myself free of all guilt. I can place myself at the disposal of our leaders; everybody else just pursues egotistic goals.'"

It is highly unlikely that Heydrich and Eichmann collaborated on the coining of the term they both used. More likely, "free of all guilt" was a common verbal formula, expressing a widespread yearning among SS men to merge their responsibility with that of the larger community. That way, they could see themselves as mere agents of the whole, absolved from personal connection to the orders they executed.

Werner Best once claimed that he had never known a member of the Gestapo who broke the law on his own, "as an individual." The psychologist Leo Alexander put it another way: "War crimes are crimes committed by a group."

One of the paradoxes of Nazism was the much-observed fact that its adherents seem to have vacillated between seeing themselves as omnipotent dictators, entitled to choose who lived and died, and impotent cogs in a vast machine, helpless before its awesome magnitude. Yet, even as they swung back and forth between these poles, they never lost a sense of immersion in their protective organization, nation, and race. Eichmann and Heydrich were very different kinds of men—one a natural follower, the other a natural leader—but they both took refuge in the "agentic state," the comforting sense that whatever happened they were never really alone, and never truly at fault.

No wonder Heydrich felt euphoric after Wannsee: he had performed a marvelous feat of mental sorcery, arranging simultaneously to confirm his power as plenipotentiary for the Jewish Question and to diffuse the terrible responsibility that accompanied it. In the same magical way, he had momentarily lifted the thick veil of secrecy around the Final Solution, then covered it back up again, both forcing his colleagues to acknowledge the ghastly truth and allowing them to ignore it at their convenience. It was as if a crack had opened at the feet of the guests, swallowed up the Jews, then closed, leaving no trace of blood on the polished villa floors. In the bloodless language of the protocol, murder openly discussed was transformed into murder in disguise, murder that need not speak its name. Never has what George Orwell called "double-think" and Adolf Eichmann dubbed "office-speak" been used with such devastating effect. Murder without guilt, death at a comfortable distance—have there ever been illusions more dangerous than these?

The Wannsee Conference remained top secret until years after Germany's defeat. In 1947, the Allies discovered a copy of the protocol in an obsolete archive overlooked by fleeing Nazi officials. A document never intended for public scrutiny became, year by year, the object of increasing historical fascination.

Lina Heydrich was obsessed with the Wannsee *Protokoll*, painfully aware that her husband—like his guests—is bound by this chain of words, held by them before the judgment of history. In her talks with me, she tried desperately to set him free. Early in my initial visit, she said bluntly, "Over the *Endlösung* [Final Solution] I am of an entirely different mind from what's usually said. My husband never thought of death! He thought of resettlement!"

But she could not let the matter lie; "I am pursued by nightmares," she said, but would not tell me what they were about. Instead she led the conversation back again and again to Wannsee: "I never heard a thing about it in my husband's lifetime. Never! He never mentioned it."

Like her husband, Lina Heydrich tried to use verbal sleight of hand to transform a moment of ultimate damnation into what she called "a routine meeting." Frau Heydrich said, "For example, the Wannsee Conference, *nicht wahr*? My husband had been given this meeting to lead, by Göring, entirely normally. But he didn't do it entirely by himself. How the others would have complained if he had done that! But rather, he just sent out invitations in Hermann Göring's name . . . He only conducted it . . . I want to compare it to something normal . . . as if your husband led a meeting in some industry.

"Göring was the executive; my husband only carried it out. But . . . because the Jewish people were affected, naturally they only saw him, *nicht wahr*? And they said, 'Heydrich did it.' But as God is my witness, he didn't do it at all!

"My son brought me these microfilms from America, and we have an entire list of invitations to this Wannsee Conference, and there is also an invitation to Herr von Ribbentrop, and there stands this one word that is for me, very correct. It is not 'Final Solution of the Jewish Question'; there stands the word *territorial* Final Solution.

"And this invitation to Ribbentrop: it is not in any protocol, and I find that interesting.

"And Herr Doktor Maser [the German historian Werner Maser, who provided footnotes and commentary for her autobiography] said, 'If that is how you analyze it, take a position in your book.'

"But I can only give my private thoughts over it. It is naturally entirely inappropriate to write something in my book that has nothing to do with the wife.

"But this is a photocopy, a read document—and the theme is the *territorial* Final Solution of the Jewish Question."

Perhaps Lina Heydrich was thinking of a letter Heydrich wrote to Ribbentrop in 1940, proposing a "territorial solution." Magical memory may have changed it into an invitation from the winter of 1942 in order to prove that her husband "always strove for resettlement, *always* for removal but not killing."

For a while, I assumed Heydrich had simply avoided discussing with his wife the brutal evolution of Nazi Jewish policy. It could be dangerous: SS officer Kurt Gerstein noted that several of his fellow officers "who couldn't keep their mouths shut" about their death camp duties were shot on the spot. Himmler didn't approve of talking to *anyone* about the Final Solution, least of all women, who were not "bearers of secrets." Besides, Frau Heydrich was known to have "a loose tongue."

"No," she said, "he *did* speak about it. But not killing, only resettlement. He had first tried Madagascar. It was once a French punishment community, but he knew that it was a very rich land. That was a solution. The Jewish people had striven for so long for their own state form. It would support this if they settled them in Madagascar.

"I believe the French rejected it. And then he had the idea of Russia. That is a large land; one might give them a possibility of life there, where they could truly live. My husband told me that very precisely. He said they had reserved a great area east of the Urals, and all the Jews from Germany and the German-occupied spheres were gathered there, and resettled. But a Final Solution in the meaning of today—that's just an assumption."

In her book, Frau Heydrich repeats a similar story. This time her husband points to the designated zone on a map, and tells her that the parents of his own adjutant came from a very cold land not so far away from Russia. It was a place where the Jews might prosper, he said.

What is one to make of this ghastly fairy tale? A resettlement in Russia could not have even been considered until after the German invasion in 1941, and by that time, the Nazis had decided on the "total solution" discussed at Wannsee. Trying to defend her vision of Heydrich, Lina sought to use words as a shield, just as he had. "Where does it say murder? Where does it *say* kill?" she repeated like a magical incantation. She told me she had even discussed Heydrich's cleverly ambiguous words with the Israeli historian Shlomo Aronson: "I asked him, Herr Aronson, 'Can you tell me, was there any time in any sentence in the Wannsee Conference where it said that the Final Solution is equivalent to murder?' And he answered, 'No, that wasn't said.'"

In the end, I had to give the same answer, not finding adequate words to convince her that her husband may have *said* one thing, but he *meant* another.

During Adolf Eichmann's interrogation in Israel in 1961, similar questions also arose, but Eichmann, who had never tried to be clever, gave recklessly unequivocal answers.

"What is meant by 'natural diminution?'" the interrogator asked him.

"That's perfectly normal dying. Of a heart attack or pneumonia, for instance. If I were to drop dead just now, that would be natural diminution."

The interrogator persisted: "If a man is forced to perform heavy physical labor and not given enough to eat—he grows weaker, he gets so weak that he had a heart attack . . ."

"That would undoubtedly have been reported as natural diminution."

Interrogator: "Heydrich [says]: 'Since the ultimate survivors will undoubtedly constitute the most resistant group, they must be treated accordingly' . . . What does 'treated accordingly' mean?"

"That . . . that . . . that comes from Himmler. Natural selection— that's . . . that was his hobby."

"Yes, but what does it mean here?"

"Killed, killed. Undoubtedly."

Finally, Eichmann was goaded into providing a succinct summary: "Heydrich did not at the time of the Wannsee Conference speak of killing. He spoke of putting Jews to work in the East. That was his way of camouflaging it."

But Frau Heydrich did not wish to strip away the camouflage. During our first visit, however, she still knew how the story really ended, though she had removed Reinhard Heydrich from participation in it: "And that was what he saw as the Final Solution, a *territorial* Final Solution. After his death, then the Final Solution was changed to death. And I believe this was an act of revenge by the Reich for his assassination. That's *my* version."

When I returned four years later, however, her version had changed, perhaps in response to the great interest aroused in Germany by the American TV movie *Holocaust*, in which her husband is portrayed as the scheming organizer of various atrocities as well as an evil influence on more idealistic SS recruits. The message having become unbearable, she now attacked those who bore it: "There were people who were witnesses as a career. Someone says, 'Yes, yes, that's true, I was there.' But no one can *prove* that the *Endlösung* is the same as killing! But you can't stir it up, because I don't know how many millions were paid. On the basis of these 6 million [Jewish victims] the Israeli state and the Israeli citizens have received reparations. Many billions from Germany!"

"So you believe that all of these [reports of] mass murders are not true?"

"That it never in life was the truth! Never! That it is technically not at all possible! It was once technically calculated how long it takes a person to be burnt up. Ask someone who is employed in a crematorium. At least one and a half hours. And according to the calculation, a person must be burned up in ten minutes for the numbers to be accurate. There are books about it that prove that!"

(On her shelf as we spoke, I could see a book called *The Myth of Auschwitz*. On my own shelf, I have Michael Marrus's *The Holocaust in History*. In it, he says that the crematoria at Auschwitz could destroy ten thousand bodies a day.)

Lina Heydrich continued, "You see, even *Holocaust*, this is a story, it is no document. The people are made-up people. It is not at all possible, because it is not true. But in America, no one cares whether it is true or not. The Americans were not in Germany during this period."

"Many Germans also say it is true."

"No, only German *emigrants*!"

"Joachim Fest and Günther Deschner are not emigrants—"

"Fest is also speaking only from hearsay! He just began to fantasize how it probably had to be. And he earned great money with this, one shouldn't forget that! It is always a matter of money! In Germany, we are satiated with all of these lying reports! And the people who lived through it, the simple people who know how it was . . ."

"Haven't they written anything?"

"They are *damned* if they do it!"

(As Lina Heydrich often mentioned, books considered "propaganda" favorable to National Socialism may not be legally published in Germany.)

"All of these books, like the one of Fest's, they have oriented themselves according to the utterances of the emigrants. And that is the *catastrophe! O*ne person brings it into the world, and everyone departs from him; so we can never get something correct . . . You see, Egon Kogon, who wrote *The SS State*. Today he is a great man! He can write what he wants! He doesn't need any documents! No one has asked him to prove it!"

Earlier I had asked Lina who, in her opinion, had written the best book on Nazism. Now, she replied, "I say, no one! They have all taken off from each other . . . from one who is allegedly an eyewitness. He can assert anything!"

Absolute truth.

Reinhard Heydrich had been very clever at Wannsee, but he cavalierly ignored a "lesson of history" that haunts the rest of us more with each passing year. No matter how superior you think you are, no matter how many opponents you destroy, no matter how adroitly you camouflage your tracks afterward; you can never permanently establish your own truth as absolute for everyone. On earth at least, and among mortals, there are no total solutions.

PART V

REICHSPROTEKTOR: BOHEMIA AND MORAVIA

24

THE CASTLE

"[Reinhard] was only happy when he was creating something."

—LINA HEYDRICH

T HE WANNSEE CONFERENCE was Reinhard Heydrich's last major contribution to the organization of the Holocaust. From Berlin, he returned to his new home in Prague, and to quite a different role in history—that of victim. Even as he planned the murder of 11 million people, Heydrich himself was a marked man.

He had come to "golden Prague" in September 1941, to play the part of all-powerful conqueror. As the new acting Reich protector of Bohemia and Moravia, he lived in the fabled Hradčany Castle, part of a great, ancient pile of structures known collectively as Prague Castle. Erected high on a bluff, the earliest buildings have loomed over the city for at least a thousand years, slowly evolving into the immense, labyrinthine fortress evoked by Franz Kafka in his novel *The Castle*. In Lina Heydrich's view, the eight months that Heydrich spent there were the happiest of his life. "It was his high time," she told me.

Yet the blow from an assassin's weapon that killed him on June 4, 1942, was not the only cause of his death. In a certain sense, Heydrich had gone out of his way to meet this fate. The sorcerer's apprentice had himself become enchanted by two perilous influences—the seductive lure of the limelight and the capricious muse of history.

No SS leader, not even Reichsführer Himmler, had ever achieved a position of ministerial rank comparable to that bestowed on Protektor

Heydrich. Himmler had dreamed for years of establishing a separate SS kingdom on the margins of Hitler's empire. Now, it looked as if the long-rumored SS state might rise within the heart of the "Old Reich" itself, in the ancient capital of the Holy Roman Empire, only a few hundred miles from both Dresden and Vienna. Himmler had evidently long been besotted by the grand sweep of history, the migrations of entire peoples, the legends of Teutonic knights risking all for a daring cause. But Heydrich had kept a cynical distance from this romantic rigmarole, indulging instead in brutally deflating remarks like his "joke" that the Gestapo was the "garbage can of the Third Reich."

Cynicism is often worn as a mantle of disguise by those secretly mourning the loss of an ideal. In Prague, Heydrich made a last desperate grasp for the honor he had left behind in the navy; but, in reaching out, he also let down his guard. He had built his machinery of terror on a foundation of perennial suspicion, of "de-camouflaging" and disillusion. Only in the very last moments of his life was he to discover that illusions can be equally deadly.

It was a time and a place rich in illusions, and Heydrich was not the only one who succumbed to them. The former president of the former nation of Czechoslovakia, Dr. Edvard Beneš, had fled to London in 1939 to form a government in exile. His group of émigrés braced themselves for "murder on a total scale, wildly, evilly, bestially," from the man they called the "vile agent of Himmler's wishes." Yet, though at first only his wife knew it, Heydrich intended to break free of what she called "the Himmler empire," to act for the first time in his career as his own man.

Walter Schellenberg had long felt that his boss was "yearning" to be

Edvard Beneš (age fifty-eight, circa 1942) was Czechoslovakia's president in exile, following his resignation in 1938. From his London base, he contrived a plot to assassinate a prominent Nazi within the German protectorate. The Nazi he chose was Reich Protector of Bohemia and Moravia Reinhard Heydrich.

František Moravec, as Edvard Beneš's chief intelligence adviser in London, worked in tandem with the British Secret Operations Executive. It was Moravec's decision not to disclose the plan to assassinate Heydrich—in a mission code-named Operation Anthropoid—to make the act look like a surprise act of resistance.

"building up something new again." For once, Frau Heydrich agreed with him: "Just to go to an office and be an administrator and do the same thing all the time, he had no joy in that. He was only happy when he was creating something."

There was also the delicate matter of what Heydrich did at the office. "Deportations, death marches, mass killings . . . were his daily occupation," wrote František Moravec, chief of intelligence for the Czech government in exile. We know the range of Heydrich's duties actually spanned a wider gamut, from producing sociological reports on civilian morale to supervising sports training for the SS. But it is true also that he was by now a murderer hundreds of thousands of times over. In every way but literally, Reinhard Heydrich was wading in blood. Yet, for men like him, who had rarely if ever fired an actual gun at a human being—his combat experience was in aerial reconnaissance—and whose boots were always meticulously clean; this reality could be suppressed from moment to busy, glittering moment. Suppression of one's emotions, however, is notoriously difficult. Heydrich had sometimes in the past expressed doubts to his colleagues about the value of his mission. One of his childhood confidants later provided a formidable understatement of the problem: "The radical measures against partisans and subversive elements, against agitators and saboteurs—Reinhard felt all that was necessitated by the war—but to 'bump off' all the Jews in the bargain, that got him down."

Heinrich Himmler also spoke of the "great efforts it cost this man to maintain his pose of hardness." This was Himmler's version of the old "white man's burden" of colonial times: the double load of having to arbitrate the destiny of "inferior" races while also maintaining a masterly posture of perfect self-control. Small wonder that many Nazi leaders led double lives of public obedience and wild, secret debauchery, and that the gossip about them always seemed designed to emphasize the discontinuities in their characters. One need only recall the story of a drunken Heydrich's glimpsing his own reflection in a mirror, then shooting at it, shouting, "At last I've got you, scum!"

Secretly troubled though he may have been, Heydrich was also overtly, overwhelmingly ambitious. Yet he was still Himmler's subordinate, and as insiders have reported, Heydrich likely was getting restless with his role of perfect staff officer, discreet adviser, perennial second in command.

But where was a true top job to be found? In 1931, at Reinhard's low point, the Heydrichs' family friend, the elegant Freiherr Karl von Eberstein, had stepped in to offer Heydrich an unexpected job with the SS; now, a second agent of fate appeared in the stocky, brown-shirted form of Nazi party secretary Martin Bormann.

Like Heydrich, Bormann was a skilled behind-the-scenes conniver and collector of interesting gossip; but unlike Heydrich, he also excelled at the flattery required of Hitler's intimates. Bormann had risen through the Nazi ranks to become the Führer's gatekeeper: he supervised his appointment books, ran his errands, and passed along the requests of others—or let them drop unheeded at the anteroom door.

"The Brown Eminence," as Bormann was nicknamed, thus joined Heinrich Himmler in the small circle of Old Fighters who were still at the top of the heap. The two men were even friends of sorts. (Bormann's nine children referred to the Reichsführer SS as "Uncle Heinrich.") Yet the party and the SS were constantly fighting for supremacy, and everyone expected open warfare to break out sooner or later. Bormann was universally dismissed as a crude man (*vulgar* and *gross* were the terms used by Lina Heydrich), but he was shrewd enough to know that the best method of weakening the SS was to drive a wedge between its leaders.

By custom, Heydrich had routed his intelligence reports to Hitler through Bormann's office. Now, the two experts at intrigue began to draw together. It was trouble in Bohemia that gave them their mutual opportunity.

Martin Bormann (age thirty-nine, in 1939), head of the party chancellery and private secretary to Adolf Hitler, controlled the party machine through which Nazi Germany was ruled. In effect, he ruled Hitler, too—owning and operating the Führer's properties at Berchtesgaden and on the Obersalzberg.

From the German point of view, a thousand years of trouble had already been stirred up by the small but difficult neighbors to the east. A look at the geographic placement of Czechoslovakia reveals the essence of the "problem." Shaped like a long and lumpy loaf of bread—or to those of a more melodramatic case of mind, like an irregularly hewn blade of a dagger—the country jutted both westward into the heart of Germany and eastward to the borders of the Soviet Union. Constantly fought over, constantly changing hands, this wedge of land between the great empires of the East and the West had also changed form through ages of strife.

The country that became the first in Europe to be occupied by the Nazis had only recently emerged from the great reshuffling of the cards of nationality that occurred after the First World War. It was actually composed of three entities, two parts Czech (Bohemia, with its capital of Prague, and neighboring Moravia) and one part Slovak. (The wild, rural terrain of Slovakia had frequently been ruled by Hungary.)

In addition to this rich ethnic stew, Czechoslovakia also contained some lumps of indigestible citizenry—the many thousands of Germans who lived in the so-called Sudetenland along the Czech-German border. Hitler felt the Sudetenland should be incorporated into his "Greater German Reich," which since March 1938 had also included Austria. At the Munich Conference in September of that same year, the leaders of the major Western powers tried to avoid war by granting the Führer what he wanted. This was the beginning of that oft-repeated, disgraceful activity, the dismemberment of Czechoslovakia.

At first Hitler promised that his grabbing up of the Sudeten Germans marked the end of his territorial claims. "We want no Czechs," he had sneered, and many believed him. Everyone knew the Führer despised the Czechs almost as much as the Jews, and for similar reasons. He thought them clever as well as sneaky—just as he was himself. As he had with the Jews, Hitler concluded that the only way to deal with such formidable enemies was to be "pitiless and brutal . . . There's no room both for them and for us."

If Hitler did not want Czechs, however, he most certainly wanted Czechoslovakia. The beautiful city of Prague, the armaments works at Skoda, the prosperous farmland of Moravia, the Slovakian gateway to Poland and Russia—his "drive to the East" required devouring them all, the more so because they belonged to one of the richest, most successful democracies in Europe. By December, Hitler had decided to smash it to bits.

Since the Czechs had a first-rate army as well as a defensive alliance with France, "diplomacy" seemed the best strategy. In Nazi thinking, this meant an intense propaganda campaign, often coupled with sabotage and subversion inside the target area. This was Heydrich's entryway into Czechoslovakian politics. After the Munich Conference, a separatist movement led by a priest, Father Josef Tiso, had flared up in Slovakia. Heydrich sent special SS units into the area, to "stir the Slovaks from their lethargy by a series of acts of terrorism," and also to urge Tiso to seek German assistance. In March 1939, Father Tiso was finally persuaded to proclaim a separate Slovak state; Hitler then announced his intention to intervene on his behalf. The aging president of Czechoslovakia, Emil Hácha, feared a bloodbath and therefore ordered his armies not to resist a German invasion. On the Ides of March 1939, SS troops paraded through the streets of Prague. That evening, Hitler arrived at Hradčany Castle to proclaim the Protectorate of Bohemia and Moravia. (Slovakia was granted a separate arrangement, but all parts of Czechoslovakia, as Goebbels expressed it, "belonged to the Reich.")

For the few remaining months before World War II, the Nazi leaders indulged their wildest personal and political inclinations in the newly "protected" territory. Himmler began plans to remove Czechs and import German settler farmers. Eichmann went to Prague to set up his assembly line for forced emigration of Jews. Heydrich and an SS confederate hoped to confiscate church land, thus finally taking a

Emil Hácha (age seventy, circa 1940s) succeeded Edvard Beneš as president of Czechoslovakia on November 30, 1938. On March 14, 1939, Hácha surrendered Czech lands, saying, "I have entrusted our country to the Führer."

public stand against a hated rival. Hermann Göring launched his usual self-enrichment program. Thousands of German officials and speculators moved into the area. German tourists came in droves and gobbled up savory foodstuffs long unavailable in the Reich. All public signs were changed into both Czech and German, with the German at the top.

The new masters agreed that the entire population would eventually have to be "Germanized." This meant different things to different people—*all* of the measures they considered came under the rough heading of Germanization—but most Nazi leaders envisioned a time when almost everyone who was not Aryan would be evacuated elsewhere. In the meantime, however, war broke out, and Hitler was forced to temporize. For the moment, he decided to create a model satellite demonstrating the virtues of Nazi domination. Göring began to placate the leaders of Czech industry; and the SS halted its radical resettlement and confiscation policies. Diligent efforts were made to create a fiction of Czech autonomy. Reich legal experts devised an intricate governmental structure in which the sixty-six-year-old Hácha stayed on as a puppet state president, supported by his abler, younger prime minister, Alois Eliáš. They chose their own cabinet and maintained the day-to-day operations of government. But they had to report to the newly created "Reich protector," a German official, appointed by Hitler, who set the general military, economic, and political guidelines. In addition, a special, intentionally vague provision gave the protector virtual carte blanche to "protest against measures calculated to harm the Reich, and . . . order measures necessary in the common interest."

It was as clear as German crystal whose interests the new overlord had come to protect.

Still, Hitler's choice of the first Reichsprotektor was designed to show good will. Baron Konstantin von Neurath, a career diplomat and old-fashioned aristocrat, was regarded by the Nazis as reactionary, lazy, and none too bright. (Lina Heydrich recalled Frau von Neurath as a frump-ish old dowager who perversely insisted on wearing too much youth-ful pink.) The von Neuraths' benign presence was intended to reassure the Czech leaders, implying they were not mere puppets after all. Von Neurath helped things along by conferring with Prime Minister Eliáš in French, which they had both used many years earlier when they met at the Geneva Disarmament Conference.

Hácha and Eliáš hoped that through collaboration they could avert the worse excesses of Nazi rule. There was little choice. Their former allies had betrayed them at Munich; without help, their situation was hopeless. Only the officer corps of the Czech army had wished to sol-dier on in a totally doomed cause. Some of these men had wept when ordered to lay down their arms without a fight; later many fled to En-gland, where they joined Czech legions preparing for armed combat.

Meanwhile, in the protectorate both the SS and the army maintained separate commands, bypassing the protector's office, and reporting directly to their own leaders in Germany. After a few months, the army withdrew, but the SS stayed on, earning a reputation as "the effective petty dictators in the protectorate." The Gestapo established its Prague headquarters in a palatial building, formerly a bank, with convenient, soundproofed vaults in the basement. Known opponents of Nazism were swiftly arrested in March, and after the war broke out in Septem-ber thousands more (who would have been listed in the files under the tag "arrest in case of hostilities") were picked up. These included for-mer officers, troublesome intellectuals, and unbending public officials. But a full-scale "cleaning up"—of the grisly kind that occurred a few months later in occupied Poland—would not have accorded well with the high-sounding concept of a protectorate. Heydrich appointed one of his most trusted subordinates, Dr. Franz Stahlecker, to the key role of chief of the Security Police in Prague, and left it at that.

In the meantime, Hitler had chosen a Sudeten German SS man, Karl Hermann Frank, as deputy Reich protector. Frank was a tall man, with staring eyes and a long head, peculiarly flattened in back as if he had lain

Obergruppenführer Karl Hermann Frank (age forty, 1938) was Reich minister for Bohemia and Moravia. While Frank never considered himself a friend of Heydrich's, he did, on the orders of Hitler, take charge of the retributive act of leveling Lidice.

too long in a hard place. He came to Prague as a scornful outsider, who just happened to have been a citizen of Czechoslovakia but actually represented the bitter extreme of German nationalism. Frank wanted to be Reichsprotektor himself, and von Neurath fed his hopes by frequently absenting himself from Prague. Hitler was playing his usual game of divide-and-rule: almost balanced in power, Frank and von Neurath governed tensely together, while the Czechs waited, uneasily.

Only once in the first two years was there any real trouble. October 28 had been Czech Independence Day. Shortly before that date in 1939, anonymous pamphlets began to appear in Prague urging the populace to gather in public to celebrate it. Many did so, and some were daring enough to wear boutonnieres adorned with the German abbreviation for National Socialist (NS) worn upside down, thus transforming it into the Czech initials for "Death to the Germans." Stahlecker had agreed to let the Czech police handle the situation, but Karl Hermann Frank impatiently called in some of his own SS troops to break up the mob, touching off a riot in which several Czechs were wounded and one was killed. On November 15, the day of the victim's funeral, many university students appeared, defiantly singing patriotic songs. This time, Czech police broke up the demonstration on their own, and Heydrich circulated an SD report minimizing the importance of the incident.

But Adolf Hitler had a different reaction. At a meeting in Berlin with

Frank and von Neurath, he flew into a rage, claiming that if anything else happened, he would evacuate all the Germans and blow up Prague. Frank immediately ordered the arrest of twelve hundred students and the closing of the university. The next day nine of the arrested students were shot, and the rest were sent to concentration camps, where they suffered terribly. The Czech government in exile published detailed accounts of sadistic sexual assaults on female students, and the mutilation and torture of prisoners of both sexes. The horrid news spread like flame through the protectorate, along with rumors that the Germans were about to poison the wells or deport the entire population. The SD reported a mood of intense anxiety and unrest.

Soon thereafter, a Czech journalist in London, Jiri Hronek, analyzed the altered situation: "The methods of fighting being used by the subjected nations of Europe today can be classified under the following headings: mass demonstrations, individual terrorism, passive and active resistance and sabotage. Only the two last named methods have any real chance of success."

Demonstrations—as well as the removal of "hated personalities" through terrorist acts—were dismissed as ineffective, except in inviting reprisals of "utmost brutality." "The liquidation of individuals does not destroy the system," Hronek wrote, prophetically.

Until Heydrich's arrival changed everything, however, passive resistance, supplemented by "scientific sabotage," was now the order of the day. The sabotage was primarily confined to the German railroad and transport system and to the armaments industry, where the phrase "a Czech bomb" came to apply to an intentionally created dud. Even more effective was the deliberate work slowdown. The government in exile estimated that efficiency in some iron, steel, and weapons factories had fallen at least 25 percent. Peasants, farmers, and butchers employed their own form of sabotage, selling young animals to their neighbors at a loss, rather than fatten them for German consumption. Often they lied, minimizing the real extent of the harvest.

This was risky business, however, and most people learned from sad experience to express "subtle contempt" in a "veiled manner." Czechs boycotted German concerts and festivals, mispronounced the occupier's language, gave deliberately misleading directions. They listened in silence during public gatherings featuring German radio propaganda, then went home and tuned in to the BBC, which carried messages from the government in exile. The Gestapo arrested dozens of illicit radio operators, but to little avail, for they sprang up again, encouraged tacitly by Hácha and overtly by Eliáš, who sent frequent messages abroad. (It has been estimated that from March 1939 to Heydrich's arrival in September 1941, fourteen thousand communications flew back and forth between the Czech governments in Prague and London.)

There was also a flourishing tradition (previously expressed in Jaroslav Hašek's famous novel, *The Good Soldier Schweik*) of "carrying out instructions with such blind obedience as to be obstructive." Jiri Hronek argued with stubborn optimism that such "seemingly harmless forms of anti-German resistance are not as ineffective as they may appear, because, being carried on night and day on a high scale, they make life almost unbearable for the Nazis."

Nothing could have been further from the truth. As the war worsened for the Germans, the rich, peaceful protectorate was the very opposite of a hardship post. It was safer even than Germany, Lina Heydrich told me: "It was a place where no bombs fell." Frau Heydrich also observed that the ladies of Prague were far better dressed than their peers in Berlin. For Germans of both sexes, the luxurious living almost rivaled occupied France: there were many servants to assist the women ("Even our servants had servants!" said Lina Heydrich to another interviewer) and the men could dabble in the black market and other lucrative ventures on the shadowy border between privilege and corruption.

Moreover, the Germans felt at home in Böhmen-Mähren in a way that eluded them in France. Most of the Sudeten Germans could speak Czech, and more important, most educated Czechs knew German. From 1526 to 1918, the Germanic Hapsburg dynasty, with its center in Vienna, had also ruled in Prague. Even Germans of minimal higher education—like Lina Heydrich, who had only gone to trade school—knew something of this tradition. "Czech history is our German history!" she told me emphatically.

The Czechs tried to counter such cultural imperialism with "spiritual resistance" based on veneration of heroes who had fought German domination. Pointedly, they commemorated the death of the famous fifteenth-century martyr Jan Huss, whose motto had been "Freedom prevails." Soon the letter *V*, symbolizing this slogan, was plastered in public places all over the protectorate.

At first the Germans arrested likely suspects; then they decided to appropriate the *V* sign for themselves. Claiming it really stood for the German name Viktoria, they emblazoned it on newspapers and cinema marquees. This mixture of force and devious doublethink came to characterize Nazi policy under the dual leadership of Frank and von Neurath. Both had concluded "the Czech problem" could not be solved "at one stroke." They agreed on a policy of "simultaneous application of the most diverse methods."

While the Nazis improvised, the Czechs could play a double game of their own. Vojtech Mastny, a Czech-born American historian, has observed that "the frontiers between collaboration and resistance were fluid, and often the same persons participated in both." Prime Minister Eliáš, for example, not only sent messages to London, he also helped transfer money to the resistance. In February 1940, the Gestapo uncovered evidence of Eliáš's underground connections. Frank urged his immediate arrest. Hitler, however, decided not to rock the boat and ordered the continuance of normal relationships. Until June 1941, "good" Czech servants continued to confront "good" Nazi masters in a dazzlingly hypocritical display of mutually harmonious role-playing.

On June 22, however, German troops invaded the Soviet Union, drastically widening the war and irrevocably altering Czechoslovakia's fate. Since August 1939, Russia and Germany had been joined in a non-aggression pact, and Communists all over Europe had therefore held back from opposing the Nazis. Now they actively joined the resistance, meeting Nazi violence with violence of their own, and forcing other resistance groups to reexamine their policies. In the protectorate, incidents of sabotage increased in both number and extent, culminating in a dynamite attack on a home for German refugee children.

In September, Hitler called for a meeting to evaluate the changed situation. Sturmbahnführer Horst Böhme, the Prague SD leader, began to brief Heydrich, who in turn would provide information for Himmler. Meanwhile, Frank urged von Neurath to authorize "draconian measures." Von Neurath refused. In the resulting crisis, the Führer decided to confer personally with his chief of political intelligence. This was Heydrich's big opportunity to impress Hitler face-to-face, and he rose to the occasion. Spouting the complicated facts and figures that Himmler could never quite master, Heydrich used his phenomenal memory and terse, emphatic style to best advantage. He argued that German policy in Bohemia and Moravia had been inconsistent, both needlessly offending Czech pride and overly permissive of Czech rebellion. As a solution, he offered a simple slogan: "Less provocation together with less tolerance."

An aide of Bormann's was impressed enough to suggest to his boss that Heydrich should replace von Neurath as Reich protector. Now Bormann had *his* opportunity, and went to Hitler to argue on Heydrich's behalf. Almost immediately, the Führer made one of his famous impulsive decisions and agreed. Heydrich was so elated that he called his wife from the Führer chancellery, right after he heard the news.

Lina Heydrich told me she was completely surprised. "What did you do when your husband told you?" I asked her. "I cried," she said. In her memoirs, she wrote that she had thrown a scene, reproaching him for not being home enough as it was. Now the children would *never* see him. "Do try and understand what it means to me," Heydrich replied.

"And so," she told me, "he tried to pacify me . . . And he said, 'Don't cry, calm down, I am taking you along.' I really forced that decision."

It had been a time for swift decisions. On September 24, Hitler approved Heydrich's appointment; by September 28, when the Czechs were informed of the choice, Heydrich had already arrived in Prague.

Hitler confronted the deposed von Neurath with a fait accompli, saying that the time for diplomacy was over, "sharp measures" now being necessary. Heydrich's appointment was only temporary, Hitler added, for of course he knew how shocked everyone would be. "Don't you know," one appalled Nazi official warned another, "the name Heydrich signifies a political program?"

What it did *not* signify was any sort of normal governing or the exercise of diplomatic experience. As he had when he named his court architect, Albert Speer, to be the new minister of armaments (a choice Heydrich had opposed), Hitler was replacing an expert with an amateur. Most Germans hadn't even heard of Heydrich, and those who had thought primarily of his fearful reputation as deputy chief of the Secret Police. The Czech government in exile put the general apprehension in strong words, railing against "monsters of the Gestapo" coming to brutalize their nation. What else, after all, did Heydrich know how to do?

On the sunny afternoon of September 27, 1941, the new Protektor arrived at Hradčany Castle (now called, in German, the Hradschin). He had left Lina behind in Berlin, telling her, "There are many things to do there that aren't good. If you want to rule a country, you have to grasp things very strictly at first and overcome all adversaries. Afterward, you can rule much, much more easily and happily."

In his first twenty-four hours in office, Heydrich declared a curfew, imposed martial law, arrested Prime Minister Eliáš, and put him on trial for treason—the highest official in any occupied land ever to be so treated. It looked as if the young police leader was determined to justify everyone's worst fears. In fact, he was improvising with furious haste.

On the evening of September 25, the day after his appointment as protector, Heydrich had appeared at the apartment of Dr. Otto Thierack, president of the People's Court. The court was a special Nazi institution created to deal with cases of unusual political importance. It had been handling the prosecution of Oberbürgermeister Josef Klapka of Prague, who had been accused of giving money to the Czech emigrant army. Ostensibly, Heydrich had come to inquire how the case was going, but what he really wanted was for Thierack to join him in a little palace intrigue. Heydrich intended to put both Klapka and Eliáš on trial at once—which meant he would need help in bypassing the cumbersome bureaucracy of the Ministry of Justice.

Heydrich played on Thierack's ill-disguised desire to be minister of justice himself. The two men concocted a daring plan. Quietly, they would prepare to indict Eliáš for treason, using the excuse of top-secret evidence to justify their conspiratorial silence. Only at the last minute would outsiders discover the sinister venue of the trial—the Gestapo headquarters in Prague—and the identity of the prosecutor, the Prague Gestapo leader, Obersturmbannführer Hans-Ulrich Geschke. This was without precedent even for the People's Court, which had always appointed one of its own members as prosecutor. But that would take time, and Heydrich argued that waiting was "politically" impossible. The Nazis had always tended to view legal proceedings symbolically, as pieces of propagandistic theater. The trial of Eliáš was really a show of force, and of Heydrich's own power. Above all, he wanted to demonstrate that no Czech, however important, was to be allowed to play a "double game" any longer.

Heydrich's own little game with Thierack went exactly as planned. Eliáš had been arrested on September 27. On Tuesday, Thierack flew to Prague to preside over the special sitting of the People's Court. By then the minister of justice had discovered what was afoot, and complained vehemently. But it was too late: Heydrich, like Hitler, was a master of the fait accompli.

At ten o'clock on Wednesday morning, the show went on as scheduled. Eliáš appeared neatly dressed and apparently in good health. He denied the general accusation that he had conspired against the Reich, but admitted he had permitted others to do so. When the prosecutor accused him of being a "fanatical Czech" who had accidentally let fall his mask of collaboration, Eliáš countered that he was loyal to friends he could not betray, and had therefore felt split between "the demands of humanity and the interests of the Reich."

Four hours after the trial had begun, Eliáš was convicted of high treason and sentenced to death. President Hácha appealed to Heydrich for clemency, and Heydrich grandly postponed the execution—temporarily. Hitler thought this very clever, since the former prime minister was now a hostage dependent on his nation's good behavior.

To Heydrich, the trial must have seemed almost fair, since Eliáš really was guilty of most of the charges brought against him. But the prime minister had also signed a document in which he said he hoped his death would "atone" for his crimes. Of course, everyone wondered just what sort of pressure the Gestapo had been able to exert during his three days in custody.

Meanwhile, the curfew remained in effect, keeping everyone at home, while the police conducted numerous house searches and raids on secret radio transmitters. Most of the suspects, like Eliáš himself, had been on police lists for a long time. Now, drumhead courts simply swept them away. Thousands of people were accused of treason, agitation, and various kinds of sabotage. There were only three possible verdicts: death, acquittal, or "remand to the Gestapo," which was another way of saying to a concentration camp, and a slower form of death.

Most of the accused wound up in this last category, but more than a few were immediately shot. Lists of the executed were announced in the Nazi-controlled press, together with a statement of their "crimes." By design, people of all classes, from generals to factory workers, appeared on the lists. Approximately 10 percent were Jews, many of them butchers, bakers, or greengrocers, accused of war profiteering. The largest single category among people of all groups were speculators on the black market. This was the beginning of what was to be Heydrich's own independent political line, a peculiar blend of force, economic paternalism, and "social welfare," Nazi style.

None of this was apparent under the barrage of arrests and the volleys of the firing squads. In the first week after Heydrich's arrival, 58 people were executed. By the end of December, this number had risen to 404, with approximately 5,000 people sent to concentration camps. Fewer than a hundred were acquitted.

To the Czechs, all of this seemed startlingly, excessively brutal, a true reign of terror. In Heydrich's scheme of things, however, the execution of a few hundred people, the arrest of a few thousand more, was so negligible as to be almost humane. Since 1939, the Nazi practice in every eastern territory they occupied had been to exterminate the leading classes, to uproot and remove entire communities, both Jewish and Slavic, and to butcher partisans and saboteurs, whenever they found them, without a trial. In the protectorate, by contrast, Heydrich's policy was to "render harmless" only the ringleaders of the opposition. As he explained it, "The rest I left in office and acted as if I hadn't noticed anything. I didn't think it suitable fully to sweep out this space, for there would hardly have been anyone left to work with here."

At the very beginning, at least, Heydrich had no illusions of ultimate popularity. "We shall not win the people over to our side," he said. "We do not want this and we shall not be successful in that either." Instead, he advised: "We shall only have to make it quite clear to everyone in a practical manner . . . that from the realistic point of view it will be best for the Czechs to work a good deal at the moment, even though they may think in their heart, if after all the Reich should go under then I should get my freedom back."

In the inner circles of the Reich, Heydrich was known not so much for brutality as for cunning, ice-cold analysis, and most of all, pragmatism. All of these qualities were apparent on October 2, six days after his arrival in Prague, when the new Protektor gave a speech at a reception for high officials of the government and the Nazi Party. It was his first meeting with these leaders, and his words were top secret. Afterward, the audience must have been tempted to gossip anyway, for it was an extraordinary address, the record of an intelligent, willful, totally amoral mind attempting to bring order to the chaos of history. It also hinted at the personal changes Heydrich was already experiencing, after less than a week on the job.

According to his wife, Heydrich dreaded public speaking. It is also likely that he had hardly slept since he arrived. Lina Heydrich told me he didn't go to bed at all during the first seven days of his stay in Prague Castle. Perhaps exhaustion and nervousness explained the unusual frankness and rambling character of his remarks. At first, Heydrich sounded like the expected man of steel. He spoke of "militant tasks," and said the Führer had ordered him to "ensure with all the severity at my command" that the Czechs could not evade "obedience to the Reich." He gave Karl Hermann Frank credit for advocating this position, promising it would provide "the natural, human, urgent, and friendly condition for collaboration between Colleague Frank and myself."

As Himmler's garbage collector, Heydrich had rarely bothered with such friendly flourishes. Now that he was out on his own, however, he would have to imitate the Reichsführer and swiftly weave a network of personal alliances. (A few days later, he went out of his way to praise Thierack, adding he hoped this would "help him in his future career development.")

In his speech, Heydrich also began to veer off in a new direction: "In me you see the chief of the Security Police and the SD. In this you generally see—in any case I have become accustomed to this being so in the administration—the man of the executive, who, if possible, intends to solve everything in an executive manner. This view is erroneous and false."

Explicitly rejecting the "executive, superficial view, fulfilling of things and carrying out of orders," on which he had built his career, Heydrich insisted his new task "presupposes deep feeling and thought given to the problems and action based on the understanding of problems: it requires not a superficial observation but a thorough treatment and comprehension of affairs."

Heydrich could hardly have expressed more clearly his desire to transcend the negative "executive" role. Deep feeling and thought? Action based on the understanding of problems? What did these have to do with the SS credo, "Believe! Obey! Fight!" What must his audience have thought?

As if to prove he had stayed up late doing his homework, Heydrich then launched an elaborate attempt to "place all the problems of this region into their frame." He asked, "From where did this space emerge, where do the people come from, where do they belong?"

Much of what he gave by way of answer was standard Nazi jargon:

the "fact" that there were "whole regions" in the East where "the Slav doesn't even want to be treated as an equal" and where "kindness is interpreted as weakness." Heydrich also praised Hitler's "fundamental line" in the protectorate: "The Czechs have no right to be here."

Sounding exactly like Himmler at his most school-teacherish, Heydrich also managed a little summary of centuries of racial strife, conveniently categorized in terms of bad *Volk*, or Slavic heroes who threatened Germanic tribes, and good *Volk*, like "King Ottokar [of Bohemia], Charles IV, Frederick the Great . . . the fateful power of the leadership of Adolf Hitler."

When he turned back to the disposition of the conquered space, he sounded like the old Heydrich again, hard, calculating, chillingly ruthless—the very man of the "executive" he had determined not to be. In his usual style, he distinguished "two spheres of action: One is the task of the near future linked with the war and the other is the preparation of the long-term final task."

Heydrich did not define this task, offering only "a few words on the Final Solution." He rejected what he called the "old method," that of trying "to Germanize this Czech rabble." Instead he wanted a complete screening of the national and racial background of the entire population. To avoid agitating the people, this would have to be done in a disguised form—perhaps "while pretending to form a national labor service."

Reaching an apogee of the bizarre "logic" for which he was famous, Heydrich then offered a little overview of the four categories under which this ill-gotten data would be classified. There were two main variables: the racial makeup of the individual and his "intentions" toward the Reich. "Well-intentioned" people of good race were no problem (they could easily be Germanized) and inferior races with hostile intentions were also easy to handle ("These people I have to get rid of. There is plenty of space in the East"). The "middle section," however, was to be thoroughly examined. Well-intentioned people of inferior race "must not be discouraged," but their opposites (good race, bad ideas) could not be treated in such a mild way. They had to be either educated "in keeping with our beliefs," or "put against the wall." As Heydrich explained the leadership principle: "I cannot expel them for the reason that over there in the East they would form a stratum of leaders which would be directed against us."

In any case, it would be up to Hitler himself to decide—later—
how to use the results of the national survey. "The first thing to do,"
Heydrich argued, "is to show the Czechs for once who is master in the
house." But the new protector barely mentioned the state of emergency,
the trials, or the executions, as if they were just a mere disciplinary slap
at unruly Czech servants. Instead, he emphasized the need for *Aryans* to
behave better: "We must not disclose weaknesses . . . The Czechs must
see that the German knows how to behave when on duty as well as in
his private life, and that he is the master from top to toe."

Heydrich had been attempting to live by this motto since at least
1935, when he called on his SS men to be the "best" at absolutely everything. Now, he announced that he had created a "Central German
Police Guard" to ensure proper decorum: "The German cannot afford
to booze in a pub," he intoned, apparently overlooking his own previous
behavior. "This is a battlefield," he said sternly, admitting that some of
the cause of the unrest "lies with us." "We must not cause the Czechs to
reach the point of explosion and self-destruction," he cautioned.

Gradually, Heydrich backed into a modest proposal of reform: "We
shall probably raise the fat rations of the Czech workers by about four
hundred grams per person. This is an amount that can make some
impression. It is after all to no avail to knock the Czechs about, . . . if
factually they do not get what they need to have the physical strength
to work."

The "essential point" was "to really see to things which are not in
order, notwithstanding all the hardness we are showing." Heydrich concluded with an almost pious hope that "during the short time I shall
probably be here, I shall be able to set many a foundation stone in the
affairs of the nation." This is the language of a statesman—or, at least,
of a man who would become one—rather than a police bully.

In fact, Heydrich had oscillated between various points of view. The
pragmatist, the fanatic "political soldier," the policeman, the historian,
the devious Machiavellian, and the benevolent despot had all made
their appearance during his speech. So also had that person we recognize in others (but so rarely in ourselves), the man who protests too
much: "I do not intend to stick to my task while holding this post here,
because this task is nice and pleasant and of a representative character,
but on the contrary I look on it as a militant task which I have to carry
out while representing someone else."

The task of "representing," which had previously been Himmler's job, now fell on an inexperienced man who took to it all too well. For the next eight months, he played this role so zealously it has aptly been called "Protector's Heydrich's one-man show." "I shall, of course, keep up pleasant social relations with these Czechs," Heydrich had said in his speech. "But I shall always have to watch out not to cross the barriers. I shall have to tell myself at every moment: 'Take care, they are Czechs.'"

In the end, however, the chief of Reich security forgot to take care.

25

THE FATAL CROWN

"But here [in Prague] for the first time, he saw the positive side
of things. And he was very happy about that. Now he had the
power to actually realize his thoughts and ideas, to put them into
action."

—LINA HEYDRICH

OF REINHARD HEYDRICH's assumption of power as Reich protector
of Bohemia and Moravia a story is told that transcends all ideologies, pulling him beyond history into myth. It seems that shortly
after his arrival, the new master of Prague Castle decided to visit the
coronation chamber, to see the famous crown of Wenceslas I, Duke of
Bohemia, who posthumously became King Wenceslas.

The crown, a sumptuous circular mound of gold studded with huge,
rough-cut gems in fiery colors, really dates from the fourteenth century, but it incorporates many "earlier elements," among them, a legend
arising from the untimely deaths of the Wenceslas era. Whoever is so
rash as to take the crown without being fully entitled to it—warns the
ancient lore—will die soon . . . and violently.

Reinhard Heydrich was of course told this cautionary tale. Whereupon, he picked up the crown and, smiling, placed it on his own head.
And just a few months later, he was dead.

Yet in spite of his arrogantly heedless behavior, Heydrich took the
memory of Wenceslas seriously—too much so for his own good. He
planned an elaborate propaganda campaign presenting Wenceslas as a
visionary who wished his people to live in harmony with Germany. "It
is this that can be exploited historically," Heydrich argued.

He decided to inaugurate the exploitation process with a little cer-

emony involving the crown jewels. To guard against theft, the coronation treasury had historically been protected by seven locks, entrusted
to seven different Czech officials. On November 19, Reich Protector
Heydrich arranged to meet President Hácha in the Wenceslas Chapel,
where they engaged in an elaborate ceremony to affirm the protectorate's trust in Germany. Hácha turned over the seven keys to Heydrich,
saying (as he had been coached to do) that they were "a symbol of
the loyalty of Bohemia and Moravia to the Reich . . . from whom the
dignity of the Czech kings once proceeded." To this Heydrich replied,
"You, Mr. President, are now the guarantor of the obligations and loyalty of the protectorate . . . Therefore, I hand back to your keeping three
of the seven keys I hold." Of course, that left him with a symbolic
advantage—the majority of the sacred keys.

　　"The robbery of the crown jewels" is the way the Czech government
in exile described the ceremony, but Heydrich, who a few months earlier would have laughed at the whole thing if, say, Himmler, had done
it, now viewed such ceremonies as effective symbols of genuine mutual
cooperation.

　　The Nazi leaders had long regarded propaganda and terror as the
"twin pillars" on which their regime rested, but Heydrich had little
experience with the former—except for his frequent speculations about
the "psychologically correct" way to evaluate an enemy. In an article
written in 1941, he described an aim of his police work: "perfectly to
understand one's adversary to the very foundations of his soul, perfectly
to get to know his forms of organization and leading personalities."

　　It is a short step from "perfect" understanding to using such knowledge to sway others. Less than twenty-four hours after his arrival,
Heydrich had already put into effect a policy in which he mixed the
customary intimidation with efforts at gentler forms of persuasion.

　　First, he paid a formal call to President Hácha, and began to work
on the Czech leader's weaknesses. Hácha was a tired old man, who had
let Hitler browbeat him into accepting German occupation in 1938. He
had fainted during his interview with the Führer and had to be revived
with an injection of drugs; now he was thinking of resigning to avoid
having to deal with Heydrich. To his surprise, the new Reich protector
emphasized the temporary nature of the martial law he had imposed,
saying that he had done so with a "bleeding heart." He stressed his confidence in Hácha himself—even though he was about to put his prime

minister, Alois Eliáš, on trial—and asked him to remain in office. The hope of escaping punishment and of ameliorating it for others persuaded Hácha to stay.

That afternoon, Heydrich met with the remaining members of the Czech cabinet, and with the president in his pocket was much less conciliatory. He told them he knew of their treasonous contacts with the government in exile, and warned against waiting for a German defeat in the war. Reluctantly, they swore unconditional obedience to the Reich.

But Hácha had gone further, asking the protector "to lend us your helping hand whenever I or my government address ourselves to you with suggestions." This had been a feeble effort to retain some autonomy, but Heydrich recognized it as another weakness to exploit. Bruno, his father, had delighted in acting and playing master of ceremonies at festivities; now his son arranged a series of amateur theatricals in which he took center stage, proffering his "helping hand" to groups whose cooperation he himself needed.

At first the hand seemed to hold little more than a club. Yet even as he acquired the nickname "the Butcher of Prague," Heydrich planned to moderate the terror. The worst point had actually been reached three days after he arrived, on September 30, when fifty-three people were executed. After that, the numbers had declined rapidly, as the Reich protector experimented with a new strategy—offers of "clemency" to anyone who turned over caches of forbidden weapons or secretly hoarded livestock.

According to Lina Heydrich, the Nazis were amazed at the thousands of pigs and cattle and piles of discarded weapons that suddenly appeared from nowhere. Whatever the cause of this excessive compliance, Heydrich reacted to it swiftly, declaring war on people judged guilty of "economic sabotage." What accounted for the livestock was that on some days, everyone on the execution list had been a butcher, grocer, or farmer accused of price gouging, hoarding, or speculating on the black market—acts described by the Nazis as "crimes committed against the workers and the socially or economically weak." Of the 404 people executed by January 1, 1942, 166 had been judged economic profiteers.

Secret Nazi reports reveal that the majority of the Czech population found themselves in reluctant agreement with the protector's violent assault on the black market. Following up this propaganda advantage,

Heydrich now began to promise better provisions to workers employed in heavy industry. During the month of October 1941 alone, some five hundred meetings were held inside Czech factories. Well-briefed collaborators explained the dangers of resistance and the material advantages of cooperation to captive audiences totaling over half a million people.

On October 24, Heydrich received a delegation from the factories that was allowed to convey "the wishes of the workmen." Heydrich called his visitors "fellow workers," and proclaimed that he "did not come to establish merely an order of iron, but also social justice." He chose this occasion to announce the substantial elevation in fat rations he had been planning since his speech of October 2, and also promised factory canteens that would dispense cheap food.

This carefully calculated encounter took place in the Emperor's Hall of the Hradschin, an opulent baroque space usually intended for folk of higher degree. This was a deliberate slap at the nobility and at von Neurath's habit of consorting primarily with people of his own elevated background.

After the war, Günther Deschner noted that many observers had been "loath to attribute to Heydrich alone . . . the amazing ability to put himself into the frame of mind of a social class to which he did not belong by upbringing, the staggering knowledge of the effect of words and token gestures."

The search for the "real" author of his policies has sometimes settled on the ubiquitous Deputy Reich Protector Karl Hermann Frank. Certainly Heydrich, who had been in Prague only once before he came to rule, relied heavily on Frank for advice. He also borrowed from other sources, including his old rival, the Wehrmacht, whose administrators had earlier proposed the introduction of workers' canteens. Lina Heydrich hints in her memoirs that her own hobby of gardening, as well as the family friendship with Herbert Backe, the minister of agriculture, had sparked her husband's interest in achieving a proper harvest. In his search for information, Heydrich also went out on his own, walking onto the floors of factories (where his security could not be guaranteed) to ask questions, visiting Czech historical sites, and even poring over history books in his spare time.

Frau Heydrich told a German interviewer that her husband had become fascinated by the story of Albrecht von Wallenstein, the Catholic nobleman who had fought for Bohemian independence and then switched sides to join the imperial forces during the Thirty Years' War. His interest was such that he even made pilgrimages to his grave on weekends. Allegedly, he pondered what Wallenstein, a great general, political schemer, and freebooting soldier of fortune, might do in his place. (Perhaps he forgot that, like Wenceslas, Wallenstein, too, was assassinated.)

With his vast power as chief of intelligence, Heydrich had access to many possible sources of information and inspiration. His policies reflected this, being eclectic in the extreme: he was not so much an originator as an organizer and orchestrator of the ideas of others. But as always, he kept the reins of control in his own hands. Unlike von Neurath, Heydrich wrote his own speeches, planned his own public extravaganzas, made his choices almost totally alone. Heydrich was also able to make more generous concessions than von Neurath ever had—precisely because he also controlled the instruments of terror. He was the ideal person to attempt to realize von Neurath's strategy of pacification through "diverse means."

On December 6, 1941, Heydrich made another grand gesture, entertaining a delegation of twenty-four Bohemian and Moravian farmers in the marble halls of the Hradschin. In Nazi films memorializing the event, everyone looks stiffly formal and self-conscious—as they do in paintings of medieval ceremonies, in which members of a social class swore fealty to the emperor in return for recognition of their importance to the regime.

There is no question that both Reinhard and Lina Heydrich thought such gatherings of pivotal importance. Frau Heydrich was still enthusiastic more than forty years later:

> We were very interested in actively involving the peasants to increase food production. And just as was being done in the Reich, we tried to appeal to the farmers' pride, to their patriotism, to make them feel special, to consider themselves a special caste, the ones being depended on to feed the nation.
>
> In Czechoslovakia farming and gardening had been held in the lowest esteem possible—lower even than the street sweepers. They were thought of as dumb. Everyone looked down on them.

And when someone was really hopeless he was called "You stupid peasant!"

And that was what had to be changed . . . And for that reason, all of the Czech farmers—or, rather, a delegation of them—were invited to a reception at the Hardčany.

And it was the right thing to do. Now the farmers enjoyed their work much more. They were finally given respect. Because we did not want them to come reluctantly, as if they had been commanded to come. We wanted them to come only if they wanted to, on their own. And that takes time.

Heydrich hoped to isolate the intelligentsia and the resistance by cutting them off from the lower classes, for which the luxury of political freedom was presumably less important than increased food and recognition. He was thus exporting the old tactic of divide and conquer that had served Hitler so well in Germany. The means were also similar: judicious applications of both the carrot and the stick, or as the Nazis liked to put it, the "whip and sugar."

Heydrich called this strategy "depoliticization." He had been heavily influenced by the ideas of the Austrian conservative Othmar Spann, a theorist of the Kaiser era, who advocated "the division of the population into unpolitical estates, where the interest of the small man would be completely absorbed in the material concerns of his occupation." If the Czechs would just renounce "empty political discussion," Heydrich was happy to dole out what his wife called "highly political fat." Most of the food extracted from the hoarders went to men employed in heavy labor and their families—approximately 30 percent of the population. In the factories, rates of production went up and sabotage declined, prompting some members of the Czech intelligentsia to denounce the workers for allowing themselves to be bribed into "Magen-Patriotism." (*Magen* is a not-too-delicate German word for "stomach." "All politics comes from the belly," Lina Heydrich liked to instruct me.)

In November, the Nazi-controlled press began to hint that the "hard lesson" Heydrich had come to teach had finally found responsive pupils. The "acting" Reich protector made no plans to go home to Berlin, however; instead he began to ponder his next step.

For some time, President Hácha had been trying to replace Prime Minister Eliáš and reestablish some order outside of martial law, but

Heydrich deliberately dragged his feet, writing to Bormann that it was too soon "to have an intact regime in the Czech sense." Now he began to reflect on the best way to create a model government—model, that is, from the German point of view. Heydrich told insiders that his aim was "to liquidate autonomy from within, without threatening the external facade."

Of course, the Czechs must not be allowed to see through this double game. The captive press spewed out a smokescreen of "realism," denouncing the "treacherous thoughts" of liberation fostered by Beneš and other émigrés: "It is the national duty of every one of us to render harmless the incurable dreamers . . . The future history of Europe will not be determined by foolish visionaries."

The simplistic, repetitious theme was trumpeted everywhere, coupled with its variation—that the Nazi colossus was simply too strong to resist. On the surface, this seemed true: active centers of resistance had either been destroyed or driven far underground.

Only in London was the will to retaliate still bitterly strong. Indeed, it was becoming stronger every day. The first week after Heydrich's arrival in Prague, members of the government in exile had met to ponder a more aggressive strategy. All agreed that something dramatic had to be done "to wipe out the stigma of passivity":

> In London, the resistance activities of the occupied countries were regularly reviewed. Their rating depended on the degree of damage they had succeeded in causing to the Nazis . . . In the second half of 1941, as a result of Heydrich's destruction of the military organization, Czechoslovakia was always at about the bottom of the list.

The author of this assessment, General František Moravec, chief of intelligence for the émigré government, claimed after the war that President Beneš had insisted on a "spectacular action against the Nazis" that would cause an "international stir." A dramatic assassination seemed the best course. The aim of the attack was twofold: to provide "a powerful manifestation of resistance," and to provoke the maximum German retaliation, thus forcing the Czech people into action to avenge their suffering.

Moravec was already preparing to drop paratroopers into the protectorate to restore the radio communications broken by Heydrich's terror. He says that late in 1941, Beneš ordered him to use some of these men to strike against Heydrich himself.

One hundred and sixty would-be commandos were already going through their paces in a secret training center maintained by the British Organisation of Secret Services. Now they would also be monitored by members of Czech intelligence, intent on finding that perfect mix of bravery and competence that made a man stand out from the pack.

Meanwhile, in faraway Prague, President Hácha had succumbed to the proffered philosophy of fatalistic "realism." On December 7, he launched a furious attack on his former colleague:

> Mr. Beneš . . . does not see, as I do, the tears of the mothers and wives who address their desperate pleas to me because their sons and husbands fell into disaster having been seduced by deceptive radio broadcasts. He is in a position to permit himself illusions, to build castles in the air, and to paint alluring pictures of the future . . . For us, there is no way but to face reality with resolution and to soberly act in accordance with bare facts.

Hácha's speech marked the final break between the Czech governments in Prague and London. For some time, Beneš had felt Hácha was becoming a "mere tool" of the Reich protector. (Hácha knew nothing of the assassination plans; only a handful of men did, and none of these had yet arrived in the protectorate.) As the two groups split apart amid a barrage of mutual denunciations, Nazi propagandists stepped in to exploit the gap, asserting that "the time of craftiness and ruses is definitely over."

Heydrich began to press for earnest cooperation rather than passive acceptance of Nazi rule. He had already tried this approach in framing a major charge against Eliáš—that of failing to inform on associates in the resistance. The philosophy was simple: "Every citizen who does not notify the police authorities of the criminal breaks the law and becomes a criminal himself."

Such attempts at totalitarian mobilization were more suitable for the Reich than for a hostile country only recently subdued. Yet Heydrich, as always, pressed relentlessly onward. Gradually, he was drifting away from the accepted policy of pacification toward a much more daring, innovative approach. He decided the time was now ripe for "a historically significant change of direction."

Heydrich intended nothing less than a complete reorganization of the government of Bohemia, in which the local bureaucracy would cease being "a supreme clearinghouse for Czech complaints against the Reich," and become instead "an extended arm of the Reich protector." This dramatic transformation was to occur in two stages, reflecting Heydrich's customary pattern of careful, sequential planning. The first priority, as always in Nazism, was the leadership class: the duplicitous Czech cabinet must be replaced by men acceptable to the Germans.

In practice, "to the Germans" meant to *Heydrich*, for he chose all the men himself. Avoiding the sleaziest sort of opportunistic collaborators, he selected men of considerable governing experience, some of it gained working against German interests. Dr. Jaroslav Krejčí, who replaced Eliáš as premier, was no lover of the Nazis, and only accepted the position to "salvage something for the Czech people." For his part, Heydrich believed Krejčí habitually "agreed with the last person he saw," and therefore posed no real threat.

The six other cabinet members also had to run the gauntlet of Heydrich's piercing cynicism. Two were factual experts in their fields, content to remain so, and acceptable for that reason. Another was considered pliable because the Gestapo had evidence that he had tried to bribe a German journalist. The one overt Quisling in the group, Emanuel Moravec, had been a high-ranking officer in the Czech army who had changed sides after Munich, feeling the Germans were sure to win. Heydrich judged him to have "a healthy degree of ambition," and appointed him minister of the newly created Office of Public Enlightenment.

Originally, Heydrich had also included one overt anti-Nazi in the cabinet, Josef Ježek, an old associate of Eliáš's whom Hácha wanted to keep on as minister of the interior. Heydrich agreed, with the proviso that Ježek must swear a pledge of loyalty to the protector and his Reich. Instead, Ježek indulged in what the Germans considered "outspokenly fresh and tactless remarks." Heydrich could have arrested him anytime he chose—tactless remarks were quite enough, even without prior treason—but he admired frankness and courage when it posed no threat to his own interests. Still, Heydrich replaced Ježek with an older man who had once fought Austrian domination but was now believed to have "cooled" enough to cooperate with a new German-speaking empire.

The German language was in fact an issue, for the cabinet now had to hold its meetings in that language, to accommodate its one German member, the minister of economics and labor, Party Comrade Walter Bertsch. This was the area of most concern to Heydrich, and he was taking no chances there, commenting in passing that the "other gentlemen cannot expect . . . Bertsch to learn Czech."

The appointment of Bertsch was the one forthright step in the direction of Germanization, but it was part of a less publicized policy of "systematic penetration" of key positions in the Czech bureaucracy. After careful scrutiny, politically pivotal roles were assigned to reliable Germans who set broad guidelines for action; the remaining humdrum or unpleasant tasks were then shunted toward Czechs who were to deal with them "responsibly" on their own. To the outside world, the desired "facade of autonomy" was maintained.

Indeed, Heydrich actually strengthened the power of these men within their circumscribed realm. Previously, contacts between the protector and Czech officials had been mediated by the prime minister's office, resulting in what Heydrich perceived as a tedious runaround, a barrier to swift execution of decisions. He informed his new cabinet they would be working "in close contact" with him to resolve problems in each of their departments. This was also how he preferred to work in Germany: his subordinates were kept apart, sharing difficulties and information primarily with him. Once when Krejčí attempted to call the cabinet into session, Heydrich intervened sharply, saying the prime minister could call for "conversations" but not "meetings."

Meetings—and real power—were reserved for the protector of Germany's interests, who intended to turn the Czechs away from decision-making and toward the "negative" work he knew so well. "You have the hard task," Heydrich told them, "of transforming the criminal development in the education and leadership of the Czech population from the ground up and to lead this population toward their best selves, often in the face of misunderstanding and rejection."

Heydrich's ambitions bore results. By the end of 1942, 738 Germans in the Protector's Office and 1,146 others scattered among various regional bureaus supervised more than 350,000 Czech employees. Before Heydrich's arrival, there had been over fourteen thousand German officials; his reforms thus reduced their number by approximately 700 percent, enabling the Germans to rule "with less effort, yet with undiminished effectiveness."

Heydrich's administrative innovations illustrate his characteristic combination of efficiency, Machiavellianism, and creativity. A good organizational leader is much the same in every culture, though neither the cause he serves nor the man himself may be "good" in our meaning of the word. The Nazis fancied themselves "technologists of power" in this amoral sense, but only a few of them really lived up to the billing, most being deflected by corruption, stupidity, inexperience, or ideological fanaticism. Heydrich's fanaticism, by contrast, had always been leavened by a love of tactical finesse and of the purity of clear, effective action. According to his wife, he had always prided himself on being above the petty little compromises of the corrupt party bosses, and would not even let her raise a few chickens at home for fear he would lose his right to criticize the profiteering and greed of others.

In the protectorate, Heydrich's lofty aim was to create an administration that fit in with those of the other countries of the Reich "without taking over their seamy side." He intended that his experiment in "mixed administration" be used as a model for other occupied countries in the postwar future. Hitler was apparently impressed, and had asked the young SS innovator to prepare a memo about it. He did not live to complete it.

While the protector was busy selecting the members of his new government in Prague, Czech Military Intelligence in London had finally settled on the right two men to execute their own plans, code-named Operation Anthropoid. Jan Kubiš and Jozef Gabčik met all the minimum requirements: they were young, unmarried, and had never lived in Prague, "which meant no relatives and old friends to jeopardize security." In addition, they were both considered "artists" with pistols, rifles, submachine guns, and hand grenades.

In other respects, they were very different from each other. Gabčik, a short, muscular man with alert blue eyes and light brown hair, was both outgoing and full of initiative, a natural leader. Jan Kubiš was taller, darker, soft-spoken, and a little shy, but also tenacious, disciplined, and discreet, a natural follower. The two men who were to pass together into Czech history had also, in England, become fast personal friends.

British-trained Czechoslovakian paratroopers Jan Kubiš (left), age twenty-seven, and Jozef Gabčik, twenty-nine, were selected to implement Operation Anthropoid, to rid the world of Reinhard Heydrich.

František Moravec, chief of the intelligence service for the Czech government in exile, thought their complementary personalities would make them an excellent team. Their fortitude reminded him of ancient Roman heroes. Both were resolved to complete their mission, no matter what, knowing they would "probably die with Heydrich." Now, all they needed was good weather in the vast landmass of Europe over which a British plane would have to fly to deliver them to their target.

On January 19, 1942, Heydrich presented his new cabinet to the people of Czechoslovakia. Now perennially mindful of propaganda effect, the protector chose that moment to end the remnants of martial law and release the university students who had been imprisoned by Frank two years earlier. The official proclamation—which Heydrich had helped to write—spoke grandly of "a government in which all positive and active forces are concentrated." It also announced "the final repudiation" of the emigrants, who had spurned their country to flee abroad "in a cowardly fashion."

The morning of the next day, January 20, Heydrich was in Berlin, presiding over the Wannsee Conference.

He had never given up his earlier positions as deputy police chief,

SD chief, and agent of the Final Solution, jobs far removed in spirit and practice from the major diplomatic and administrative role he was now playing in Prague. He returned from Wannsee to usher in the fourth stage of his short reign. After a week of terror, a few months of propaganda and pacification, and a month or so of governmental restructuring, Heydrich added the role of patron of the arts to the multiple functions he was already playing and, as usual, did not relinquish.

It is impossible to speak of an integrated personality within such a context. Heinrich Himmler had tried to solve the problem of wildly conflicting roles by maintaining that he had "a good side and a bad side."

Until he became Reich protector, however, Heydrich seldom knew the luxury of affirming to anyone but his wife that he longed to transcend his monstrous reputation. The schizophrenic pressures that were to lead Himmler to the brink of madness now began to overtake his deputy as well.

As Lina Heydrich reports, her husband experienced a great "human leap" during his time in Prague. As if to contain and exonerate some evil side of her husband, she told me, "I thought he seemed freer, he had much more insight into the overall situation, I might say. After all, his work with the Security Police and the SD was a single-track task, with very narrowly focused thoughts and actions. It was the negative side of life. But here for the first time, he saw the positive side of things. And he was very happy about that. Now he had the power to actually realize his thoughts and ideas, to put them into action. Especially his ideas concerning the attitude of the Germans toward the Czechs, which he considered very wrong . . . And he said, 'How can you expect a people to work for us and to stand by us, if we are not willing to give them the same advantages we have?' "

Frau Heydrich was not present during the grim early days in Prague; later she wrote of having learned how "hard and difficult" they were "more from newspapers than from Reinhard." But by the early winter of 1941, she had observed a change in him. His decisions became more considered, and also more independent. Instead of deferring to Hitler, Himmler, and Göring, Heydrich now enjoyed both "external recognition" and the company of "entirely different men." He told her he was "finding my way back to normal human relationships."

One of Heydrich's first visitors in Bohemia was Hitler's court architect, Albert Speer, whom Heydrich had summoned to advise him about a new project—making Prague into one of the grandest cities in Europe.

Speer told me he did not want to come, but felt he could not say no. "I had an image of Heydrich, which was I was afraid of him," Speer said in the English he learned in Spandau prison. "I thought he had a dossier where he is putting in one thing after another. I came because it was in my own interest to be on good terms with him. But he was astonishing to me, because he was not at all this man of steel concerning the Czech people." Seeming to succumb to Frau Heydrich's ethical myopia, he observed of Heydrich's treatment of the Czech people: "He tried to give them opportunities."

I asked Speer how Heydrich had behaved with him.

"Of course, he had good manners and I was his guest of honor . . . I don't want to disappoint you, but we talked about topics just the normal way . . . And then he showed me my suite in the castle, and we discussed the plans. And certainly," Speer concluded, with monstrously unintended irony, "he was trying to do no harm to the Czech people."

The "plans" concerned the construction of special quarters for the German residents of Prague, as well as new administration buildings and an autobahn to carry traffic around the edges of the city. Speer also wanted to "add something to the Hradschin," but Heydrich rejected this: "He said, no, Hradschin is a historic building that can't be changed."

"Would you say that he had an appreciation for beauty?"

"Yes, he did . . . But then he was on a higher level than normal Nazi leaders. He showed me through the Hradschin, showed me all the rooms . . . The general impression was he did care about these things, and that he was—'familiar' is too much to say, but he was not a man who was just coming from a very low level and was put on a high level now."

I asked the author of *Inside the Third Reich* how his description of Heydrich related to the latter's reputation as a war criminal.

"Well, the definition of being a criminal is a very difficult thing. Because a criminal can help other people and can have a wonderful family life . . . I think criminologists have their theories that the criminal is not really—as a whole he is not criminal, he is criminal in one part. In one segment of his life he is criminal and it comes through always when he is doing his crimes. But in the other segments of his life he is behaving very normally. Even in contradiction to his criminal side. He is trying to level it out."

The architect Albert Speer (left, age thirty-seven, circa 1938) shows Hitler blueprints for a project at Obsersalzburg, home to the Führer's Eagle's Nest retreat. Among Speer's other plans was a massively reimagined—and, ultimately, unrealized—Berlin, to be called World Capital Germania.

In his comprehensive study *The Nazi Doctors*, the psychologist Robert J. Lifton argues that SS physicians like Dr. Joseph Mengele, who, by experimenting on humans as if they were laboratory rats, destroyed lives at Auschwitz rather than saving them as medical ethics requires, defended themselves against acknowledging the inversion of their moral code by developing two separate selves. In Lifton's scheme, this "doubling" was essential to the doctors' survival in a poisonously abnormal milieu. Their two different personalities were adapted to the demands of two very different moral worlds. During the day, the new "Auschwitz self"—hard, brutal, murderous—would be (largely) in control. When the doctors performed acts of kindness, however, or went home to see their children, they reverted to what Lifton somehow manages to characterize as a "prior self" governed by traditional values of decency learned as children and later, in medical school.

The existence of the "prior," or previous, self, even if its appearance was relatively rare, enabled the Nazi exterminator to feel that he was something more than a mere killer. But, Lifton argues, it was not enough to feel that one was basically still a good person inside: others had to think so, too. Somewhere there had to be an affirming audience that recognized the old self, a mirror into which one might look without Heydrich's experience of encountering "scum."

On February 4, 1942, Reinhard Heydrich made a second secret speech to important subordinates and party officials. Unlike the first one, this was a progress report. Yet after describing his administrative reforms, Heydrich felt he had to "revert" to certain political problems, saying, "I should like to recall what actually is our inner purpose. Outwardly it looks at present as though we had formed a Czech government which would lead the entire Czech people into the Reich." In fact, he was still awaiting the results of the racial survey of the estimated 40 to 60 percent of the population eligible for Germanization. "We have now decided," Heydrich continued, "not to carry out the evacuation, or let us say, the removal of the elements unfit for Germanization in a brutal and violent manner." This meant, in turn, that the whole project would have to be "camouflaged," perhaps by including it in new plans for compulsory labor service.

As more and more German men fell on the battlefield, the Nazi authorities were dragooning civilians of occupied countries to assist in the war effort. Heydrich was considering this too, which was not extraordinary, but what he said next was:

> Those that cannot be Germanized *as yet* will *perhaps* be sent as soon as additional parts of the Arctic Ocean region are opened up—to areas where the concentration camps will be the ideal future homeland of the 11 million Jews from Europe . . . This region by the way is not so desolate as [it] is always considered to be. It just has a very long winter, but a markedly intensive and fine agriculture and an outstanding raw material basis. On the basis of knowledge which we have obtained through our security-political operational groups in the East, we have arrived at amazing results . . . We have quite terrific raw material bases.
>
> *These are things which are still not entirely clear*, but which are essential and can be considered. Because we must not chase the

Czech whom I consider unfit for Germanization to the East as an enemy, but must use him . . . so that in the East which is not colonized by us . . . he will stand as a European advance guard. *But these problems will still be discussed and clarified.*

Clarified indeed. Two weeks after the Wannsee Conference, Heydrich was speaking of a "homeland" for the Jews! Was he lying to camouflage the Final Solution? (The language used at Wannsee had, we remember, been carefully edited.) Yet this was a top-secret speech, in which he had earlier said that there would be "a revolution," if the Czechs found out they were not all to be Germanized. What, then, was the point of mentioning the Jews at all? Why talk at all about material bases and intensive agriculture? What did Heydrich mean by "as yet . . . perhaps . . . not entirely clear . . . still to be discussed and clarified"? For a man who had always insisted on correct details and lucid exposition, he sounds uncharacteristically wobbly.

In her memoirs, Lina Heydrich writes of a discussion with Reinhard about the "Final Solution of the Jewish Question." According to Frau Heydrich, her husband told her he had been charged with organizing the emigration of all the European Jews to Siberia. "It is only because of the Russian punishment camps that it has been made into an evil specter." It was actually "a wonderful land," he said, fruitful and full of minerals and coal.

When she asked him "skeptically" whether the Jews would be willing to undertake such a thing, he answered, "Certainly. They are intelligent and they need a new beginning." (He did add, however, that not all the Jews would survive the resettlement, especially the old people. Lina does not comment about that.)

Her husband's secret speech offers confirmation that Lina was not the only one to hear this peculiar fable of a Siberian wonderland. Perhaps Heydrich was trying on a gentler new persona, just as he experimented with the Czech governmental system, just as he had improvised a series of "positive" new "foundation stones" in the protectorate.

Lying to outsiders about the "bad side" of Nazi Germany was already second nature to him, as it was to all the leaders of that secrecy-shrouded state. For years, Heinrich Himmler had been pretending outrage when respectable acquaintances complained to him of the terrible conditions in the camps.

Like Himmler, Heydrich, too, may have come to need an audience for his presentation of the positive side of himself. For years, Lina Heydrich had listened as he practiced the speeches he hated to give. Afterward, she might offer a little critique. Generally, she concentrated on correcting his halting, inexperienced speaking style, but of course she would have heard the substance as well. Perhaps Heydrich could simply not bear that his wife, or his closest coworkers, or "his" Czechs, know the whole unimaginably "negative" truth.

At the time of her husband's second speech, February 1942, Frau Heydrich was relocating the family in Prague, and would have been available to help him rehearse. She told me she did not remember exactly when she arrived at the Hradschin. First, she said she had paid a brief visit in late autumn but had returned to Berlin by December 25: "We celebrated Christmas with the children; we were also still in Berlin for New Year's Eve." Somewhat later, she said disconcertingly, "The Christmas and New Year's Eve reception of 1941–42, I remember I was there . . . I remember the dress I wore. That was the only New Year's Eve I spent in Prague with my husband."

It is possible, of course, that she and Reinhard commuted back and forth, celebrating the holidays in both places. But it is more likely that after so many years, Frau Heydrich had rearranged things a bit in her mind, the way Heydrich rearranged them in his speech.

At any rate, she arrived in Prague at approximately the same time as the men sent to kill her husband.

Jozef Gabčik and Jan Kubiš were dropped into the protectorate by parachute from a British Halifax bomber on the evening of December 28, 1941. They did not land in Prague itself, but, as intended, in a remote rural area where a low-flying plane would not attract attention. That was almost the last thing that happened as intended.

The parachutists had been given elaborate instructions. After destroying all traces of their landing, they were to leave the area quickly and travel to Prague, where they were supposed to lie low, using the local money, the Czech-made clothing and personal products (including toothpaste and cigarettes), and the forged personal documents given to them before they left. The OSS and Czech intelligence had repeatedly told them not to reveal their true identity and purpose to anyone: "This last point was very important," František Moravec wrote later. "They

Lina Heydrich holds his one-year-old daughter Silke as sons Klaus, seven (right), and Heider, six, dote on the baby along with their father, Reinhard, in this 1940 family portrait. Daughter Marte was born on July 23, 1942, six weeks after her father's death. Klaus was killed on October 24, 1943, when he rode his bicycle into an oncoming vehicle.

were instructed to avoid all underground contacts." On the other hand, he wrote, "we made it clear that the final details of the plan would have to be determined on the spot. Heydrich's movements would have to be observed repeatedly, his timetable and habits studied. The timing of the operation could not be fixed in London. That decision was left to Gabčik."

It was also left in part to chance, and from the beginning the assassination team had peculiar luck, a capricious mixture of good and bad. Because of low-lying clouds in their dropoff destination, the paratroopers came to earth on strange terrain, where they were unable to hide their parachutes adequately; fleeing the site, they left marks in the

snow. Soon, well-meaning local hunters tracked them to their temporary hideout and offered food and aid. Kind souls like these, who were
also willing to take grave risks, tended either to be in the resistance or
sympathetic to it: within two days Gabčik and Kubiš were taken up by
the very underground they were supposed to avoid.

Nevertheless, while Heydrich was accelerating both the pace of his
reforms and his schizophrenic personal development, Kubiš and Gabčik
encountered one difficulty and delay after another. Almost six months
were to go by before they all came face-to-face.

26.

THE ROAD TO JUNGFERN-BRESCHAN

"I am a princess, and I live in a fairy-tale land."

—LINA HEYDRICH

WHEN SHE MOVED to the protectorate, Lina Heydrich was also coming, at last, into a share of the royal perquisites her husband had long enjoyed. For the first time in her life, she traveled first class on a train.

From the railroad station, a motorcade escorted her up the hill, along the winding medieval streets of the Old Town, through the scrolled iron gates of Hradschin Castle, into the ancient cobbled courtyard.

At first, she thought the gates had opened on a magnificent new world. In her memoirs, she described her sensations as she looked out on "shimmering golden-yellow Prague":

> I am dominated by elated feelings. I feel I am not just a "person" [*Mensch*] anymore. I am a princess, and I live in a fairy-tale land. There is no war, no enemies, no differences between people. I am standing in the midst of God's garden, and I can experience, behold, enjoy. Then I think of the history of this fateful city, in which for me all the threads of politics, nationality, and feeling have run together: Prague is Europe for me now.

The Frau Protektor moved into the castle with her husband—and into his world of princely power, though she soon found herself unable to share it.

During one of my earliest talks with Lina Heydrich, she revealed to me how much she had learned of the architecture—she called it "visible history"—of Prague. Suddenly pushing her chair aside, she went to a rickety shelf in a dark corner of the room and pulled out a large picture book with a battered but ornate cover.

She held forth:

"Here is the Palais Schwarzenberg. This the Wenzel Chapel . . . Here is the archbishop's palace . . . This is Georgskirche, the oldest church in Europe. And this ceiling—you see this kind of ceiling very rarely. Only the very earliest of churches had these ceilings. And these niches here: they are still in the Romanesque style . . ."

"Did you get to see the crown jewels?" I asked her finally.

She looked sad for a moment, then vaguely accusing. "No. In the Wenzel Chapel? No. That was not open to the public. I was never there. It was not possible for regular members to gain access. And they would not have made exceptions for us women."

"But you were a very important lady, weren't you?"

"I? I don't think so! See, here are the various tombs where several Austrian kings and emperors lie buried. See, here is the tomb of . . ."

In her memoirs, Lina Heydrich writes that the fast and difficult pace of her husband's life was more than some of his adjutants could endure. Some could simply not keep up. Then, with no further explanation, she describes the end of a process of intense disillusion: "So I grasped relatively quickly that I am not a princess, but only the teacher's daughter, Lina von Osten, from Fehmarn, whom nobody knows . . . Still I must fulfill my duty, and not only according to external appearances. I, the wife of Reinhard Heydrich, must grasp it internally and assent to it."

While Lina Heydrich struggled to adjust to occupied Prague, Jozef Gabčik and Jan Kubiš found their way to the city, moving from the fringes of the resistance movement into its very heart.

When, in October, Heydrich had designated former members of the Czech military and "the intelligentsia" as the most likely source of opposition, he had been right on target. Two former Czech officers, Lieutenant Colonel Josef Mašin and Major Václav Morávek, were in charge of sabotage. Major Morávek had given the Gestapo such trouble that a special investigator had been assigned to track him down. After that, Morávek added a Scarlet Pimpernel touch to his activities, sending derisive postcards to his police pursuer, and once leaving a pile of excrement on a table, with a note: "This is the only part of myself I leave to you . . . Give it to the [Nazi] Winter Relief [Fund]."

As early as 1939, the irrepressible Major Morávek had suggested that some high Reich official (preferably a Czech collaborator) be assassinated as an act of national defiance. By 1942, however, the major no longer pressed the issue. He was now fully occupied with the problems created by Heydrich's campaign to stamp out "troublemakers" in the underground, and sever radio connections to the exile government in London, which seemed to have been done successfully. One spy for the Czechs, the head of the Abwehr in Prague, Paul Thümmel (known in code as Agent A-54), had for many years been leaking information to the Allies. Thümmel was also an old friend of Heinrich Himmler's, but by 1942, Heydrich was on his trail. Major Morávek was Thümmel's contact man in Prague, and was desperate both to protect A-54 and to get the radio network back in operation.

Gabčik and Kubiš were not the only paratroopers thrown into the breach Heydrich had created. A team of radio operators had also been dropped into the protectorate, and by January they had succeeded in restoring liaison with London. In the next few months, the total of parachutists reached seventeen, each with a special mission, each in terrible danger, and spreading danger to everyone who helped them.

In Prague, two schoolteachers, Professors Ladislav Vanek and Jan Zelenka, were in charge of general organization for the plot—gathering information, obtaining provisions, and operating a network of safe houses and mutual support. Working with them were an extraordinary array of only apparently "ordinary" people, headed by a plump, middle-aged housewife, Marie Moravcova, known to everyone as "Auntie."

Women played a large role in the Prague resistance network, and were encouraged by the men to do so. The underground leaders reckoned that a woman could move about more freely, delivering the necessary supplies, clothes, and messages, without being subjected to the same intense scrutiny as men.

A few weeks after their arrival, Kubiš and Gabčik had met many of the members of the Prague network, and been given a relatively safe place to hide, and they asked their new comrades to help them move unnoticed around the city. They were attempting to trace Heydrich's movements, but no one in the protectorate knew the exact nature of their mission; people helped them out of patriotism, compassion, and faith in the government in exile.

In the last spring of his life, Reinhard Heydrich was continuing his program of calculated largesse, behaving more like a man fully entitled to wear the crown of Wenceslas than a Nazi usurper of others' land and rights.

Bowing to a request from President Hácha, he arranged to release some political prisoners from concentration camps. As the German historian Detlef Brandes has observed, in the old days such a request would have had to be transferred by von Neurath to the SS in Berlin and back again, but Heydrich needed to wait for nothing. He could also easily arrange a ban on the activity of a fascist Czech organization, the Vlajka (Flag), which had criticized Hácha for not being tough enough. (No one could say that of Heydrich, even when for pragmatic reasons, he acted against his own side.)

Generally, however, the protector's actions took a more "positive" form. Accelerating his policy of doling out incentives to industrial workers, he provided cheap lunches, vocational instruction, free clothes and shoes. From bread, Heydrich moved on to circuses, distributing hundreds of thousands of tickets to an enticing range of "unpolitical" entertainment—movies, musical plays, football games, concerts—all free.

In April, he announced an ambitious new social security program for workers: payments to the sick, the old, to widows and orphans were dramatically increased, sometimes as much as 75 percent. On the 1st of May, he declared a special "Day of Work" (actually a day of vacation) to announce the bestowal of free spa holidays for workers in need of physical recuperation. Immodestly, he called this program the "Prague Music Weeks," a festival in honor of Mozart's death, and scholarships for young students of music. He also supported the restoration of the Rudolfinum, an elegant little theater built by the Germans in the nineteenth century. Anton Bruckner had once played the organ there. Heydrich considered Bruckner "the best composer of his era," and was outraged that Czech parliamentarians had held meetings in the building, eliminating the organ entirely.

Lina Heydrich told me she often accompanied her husband to the theater, the only public events she admits attending with gusto. By then, she was expecting their fourth child:

> During the Music Weeks I attended a concert. You can see my big belly in the picture . . . but we just went there and came right back home afterward . . .
>
> I went along only when he went to the theater. It was a good place to meet friends. And besides, you see, by then we were in the third year of the war. Food was scarce, you could not entertain— but if you met at the theater you did not have to offer anyone any refreshments.

Frau Heydrich insisted that the Nazi leaders did not entertain lavishly once the war began—or at least, once the Germans began to sustain heavy casualties: "Many men died at the front. So many men were lost. No one felt much like partying. Stahlecker [commander of Einsatzgruppe A] was killed during that time and . . . so one attended funerals, but not parties."

"The only thing that was always rather festive was the opera," she added on another occasion. "One attended the opera every week. *Don Giovanni.* It was so festive. It was all so right for Prague."

The opera was attractive for other reasons, too: there was never any trouble getting tickets, and there were no air raid alerts like the ones in Berlin. "Here we could finally attend the opera truly relaxed and in peace. That meant a lot to us."

The theater was the closest thing to a war-free zone that Lina Heydrich ever found in Prague: "To have parties in official circles—you couldn't. After all, half the world was mad at us, so there weren't many people who could have attended a reception; there were just the few countries who were still with us in the war—the Italians and so forth. But no one else."

"And the Czechoslovakian government?" I asked her.

"The Czechoslovakian government, they came too. With their wives. After all, we had to shake hands with them occasionally; that we did. But only to the extent that was absolutely necessary. We worked, and we were at war. But as for living to the hilt and throwing big parties—it was 'zilch.'"

This may be an accurate depiction of Lina's life, but Heydrich, we know, lived to the hilt wherever he was. In Prague, as in Berlin, he had mistresses, including one who claimed he behaved freely and joyously with her, "like a child." In addition, Heydrich still enjoyed the pleasures of the capital of the Reich, where he tried to spend a few days every week. He had asked Schellenberg to be his SD liaison to Himmler and Canaris; and the Secret Police could be left, as always, in the cruelly capable hands of "Gestapo" Müller. But problems were constantly arising. Hitler had to be briefed, the Reichsführer advised, competitors squelched, personnel supervised, and the huge security network administered. And he was still the "political expert" of the SS. In January, he had gone to Berlin to chair the Wannsee Conference; in early May, he was in Paris, to preside over a reorganization of the French police. After the ceremonies were over, he hosted a conference at the Ritz. (And after that, he went to Montmartre for a little relaxation.)

When weather permitted, Heydrich commuted between Prague and Berlin in his own plane, often taking the controls himself. Generally, however, he used a train assigned to his special use, in which he could work and confer with associates.

Gabčík and Kubiš initially considered attacking the train, raking Heydrich's salon car with machine gun bullets as it went by. But they could not be sure of hitting their target, and the train traveled at top speed, making accuracy even more difficult. A friend who worked on the railroad thought he might be able to slow the engine long enough for a bomb to be thrown through the window. These plans were ruined, however, when the friend was suddenly transferred out of the area.

The two paratroopers realized they must find another way. Moving in and out of a series of temporary lodgings, they met more and more members of the resistance, including charming, brave, and desirable women. Gabčik and Kubiš had been in Prague long enough, by now, to fall in love.

In the palace, Frau Heydrich, too, was adapting to changed circumstances. She told me, "It was the first time that we lived well, that we had a real family life. But that had nothing to do with finances or such. Do you understand how I mean this?

"It was the nicest time of my marriage. The offices were downstairs, the private quarters were upstairs. If anything [happened] we could telephone, he could come up for a few minutes if I had visitors—one time my parents were visiting—he could stop by for tea for half an hour or so; we had really become a family.

"We had five rooms. It was furnished; those were not our things, it was an official apartment. Our predecessor, Herr von Neurath, did not live in the Hradschin . . . Because it really was not suitable for living there, I must say."

In the course of this one description, Frau Heydrich had moved swiftly toward a change of heart: "Yes, it was really very crowded up there. I almost had claustrophobia. That's when I said, 'Let's move to Breschan.' That meant, of course, that we could not have lunch together. But I was willing to forego that for the children's sake. So they could be uninhibited and free to play and move around, without having to be closely watched over by a bodyguard or taken for walks by the maid."

It is difficult to think of Prague Castle, actually a small village of clustered buildings and interconnecting courtyards, as too small. But when she talked about "space," Frau Heydrich, like any Nazi, really meant something a little more metaphorical, something to do with desirable conditions of life, rather than measurable distances: "One had to take the children by the hand and make them stay on the walkways. Everything was official. There was a small garden, but there were guards and there was no feeling of privacy."

I was sure Lina Heydrich was exaggerating until my Czech guide described memories of diapers hung up to dry, awkwardly draped on available battlements or even flag poles. "Nappies in the palace!" he said, in a voice heavy with scorn.

As time went on, even the intimate family lunches were invaded by members of Heydrich's staff or officials who happened to be passing through. And the huge palace kitchens were full of Czech servants. "I longed for my own kitchen again," Frau Heydrich later wrote.

She was also discovering that she, who had always loved to study history, was not as much at home amid the architectural trophies of Prague as her husband had turned out to be: "Always to have history before, behind, and around you didn't correspond to my nature. For Reinhard, everything was entirely different. He lived only in spaces that inspired him.

"I wanted to live a meaningful life," she told me, "and not just to be a showpiece for some political system. Of course, there were many who enjoyed it, to wear beautiful gowns, attend lavish parties, attend receptions, talk nonsense. But as for myself, I never thought much of it . . . I was rather disappointed when I had to live in the Hradschin as in a golden cage."

"A golden cage." This was exactly the phrase von Neurath had used two years earlier to describe his sense of confinement in Prague, shortly after his own arrival.

Lina Heydrich, who sometimes referred to herself as the "aristocrat from the village," soon followed in the aristocratic von Neurath's footsteps out of golden Prague: "And then I heard that the Reichsprotektor Herr von Neurath had a summer residence somewhere near Prague. I inquired further and was told, 'Yes, it is north of Prague, near Melnick; on the way to Dresden.' It was called Jungfern-Breschan. I went there one day with my husband to look at it and I told him, 'I will move here tomorrow. Here is room for the children to play.' I would be back in the country. There was space."

The private estate, named Panenské Břežany by its former owner, a Czechoslovakian Jew, is occasionally described as a castle, but was really an elegant villa in an almost Mediterranean country style, with wide, high windows opening to vistas of serenely rolling hills.

"Breschan," as the Heydrichs called their new home, was surrounded by large trees, green lawns, and gardens, of both the ornamental and kitchen variety. It was all quite grand.

"At first, I thought, *Thirty-two rooms! What can I do with that!*" Lina Heydrich said. "But"—she began to laugh—"it is amazing how quickly you learn!"

Of course, Frau Heydrich could not merely move in "tomorrow." Jungfern-Breschan was no place for a major Nazi leader suddenly to relocate his family in the dead of winter. Reinhard Heydrich may have been cavalier about his own security, but not about that of his children or his wife. Reconnoitering SS troops became a familiar sight in the area; finally, they took over the nearest village to provide space for a corps of armed bodyguards. Heydrich was, after all, the head of Bohemia and Moravia—the uncrowned king, and he could have requisitioned the crown, had he chosen to do so, instead of having merely borrowed it for a moment.

Jungfern-Breschan—in Czech, Panenské Břežany, roughly meaning "pristine clearing"—was the Heydrichs' home from early 1942 until 1945, three years after Heydrich's death. Hitler presented Lina with the property in recognition of her husband's service.

From the point of view of Kubiš and Gabčik, a direct attack on well-defended Jungfern-Breschan would have been both suicidal and fruitless. Earlier, they had considered waiting for Heydrich at the gates of the Hradschin, but abandoned that plan for similar reasons. Logic suggested that the Protektor must be caught in transit somewhere, preferably in a well-populated area, where the two assassins had a chance of escaping into the crowd. But Heydrich always drove, the way he did everything, fast. The two commandos asked their comrades to try to find them an automobile and on another occasion, some rope. Perhaps, their helpers surmised, the rope was for stretching across a road to stop a car.

Gabčik and Kubiš had still not openly divulged their mission, but by February, resistance leaders such as Professor Vanek and others had guessed their intent from the nature of the preparations involved. They were not pleased, for the Czech resistance was already facing enormous problems.

That same month, Heydrich had finally ordered the arrest of the spy Paul Thümmel, Agent A-54. By then the Gestapo had traced his link to Major Morávek, but Thümmel defended himself cleverly, arguing that it was all part of an elaborate Abwehr scheme to infiltrate the Czech underground. He was released, but all of his contacts were closely watched.

In March, the insouciant Major Morávek fell into a police trap and committed suicide to evade capture. His colleague in sabotage, Colonel Mašin, had recently been taken alive by the Gestapo, and one of the newly arrived paratroopers was also in police custody. At any moment, the Gestapo would be likely to succeed in penetrating the secret resistance network. If things were this bad now, what havoc would the Germans not wreak if one of their own were harmed?

Many of the remaining leaders thought a Czech target should be substituted—or none at all. But Gabčik and Kubiš held fast. They had been told in England that the war would end before the year was up. Just a few more months, they informed their dubious comrades. Meanwhile, they had a mission to perform. Whatever others thought, they intended to honor the oath of obedience they had sworn before leaving London.

Around Easter time, Lina Heydrich moved to Jungfern-Breschan with her young sons, Klaus and Heider, and two-year old daughter, Silke. By then, Frau Heydrich was six months pregnant. In Breschan, there was plenty of room for children to play. She told me, "We had an old gardener, he had a son who had been born to him late in his life—his name was Jarislaw, Jarislaw Picat. He was about the same age as my son Klaus. And these two, they became friends and playmates."

Frau Heydrich had at last found a place where she, like her husband, could indulge in "positive" illusions. Even long after the war, her talk of "Breschan" made it sound like a bucolic illustration of one of her favorite themes—that there were "no differences" between the various social classes under Nazi rule. It was in Jungfern-Breschan, rather than Prague, that she seems to have felt she was truly in "God's garden," the fairy-tale land where there was no war, where the child of the German Reich protector could play happily with the son of an allegedly inferior race.

Reinhard Heydrich now divided his time not only between Prague and Berlin, but between Prague and Breschan as well. He still maintained the official apartment in the Hradschin, but was increasingly drawn to his lovely country estate. By fleeing the Bohemian capital,

Reinhard and Lina Heydrich, at Jungfern-Breschan. On the morning of May 27, 1942, "Heydrich came out of the door with Lina and three-year-old Silke," household staff member Helena Vovsová remembered. "Heydrich got in the car, the soldiers at the gate honored him as usual." As this scene was playing out, Czech partisans Jozef Gabčík and Jan Kubiš were already positioned at V Holešovičkách Street, in preparation for the murder of Reinhard Heydrich.

Frau Heydrich had lured its protector out of his special masculine domain and back to her side, re-creating some of the camaraderie of the early *Kampfzeit*, when she was still the "mother of the company" of young activists. Heydrich began to bring his files home, sometimes sorting through papers on the living room sofa, in front of the fireplace, surrounded by his family.

Frau Heydrich insisted that Breschan was his "refuge" from the outside world, but some staff meetings were of necessity held there. Heydrich always interrupted them at his daughter's bedtime, so that he could wish her goodnight. Sometimes, he brought Silke downstairs. "They had to say how beautiful she was!" said Frau Heydrich, smiling. Lina Heydrich had at last been able to resolve the tension between her husband's view of the family as a sort of personal shield, behind which the only meaningful human relationships occurred; and her own view that it should be part of a vital, communal life.

In mid-May, Admiral Canaris and his wife, Erika, came for an informal visit growing out of an official conference the two men were holding in Prague. According to Schellenberg, Heydrich decided in the winter of 1941–42 that the time had finally come to strike against the Abwehr. Everyone had a different version of the reasons for the sudden animosity, but they all relate to new weaknesses in the faltering military organization.

On October 13, 1941, Gestapo agents had arrested Paul Thümmel, the senior Abwehr official, high Nazi Party member, and close friend of Himmler's, on suspicion of being a British agent. Canaris protested and Heydrich sent Schellenberg to invite the admiral to confer with him in Prague. After the war, Schellenberg described the resulting discussions in a manner that made them sound like a Teutonic version of the gunfight in the O.K. Corral.

"In proposing negotiations to you, Admiral, I knew very well that I would be wasting my time," Heydrich began. "If I persist in seeking compromise solutions with you, it is not in order to cajole you but solely because of the military situation. At the same time, I will not conceal from you that after the war the SS will take over everything still in the Abwehr's field."

"My dear Heydrich, I have never doubted your intentions, nor your ambition. I have known you for a long time, since our days in the navy. But you know me too, and you know very well that nobody will touch the Abwehr as long as I am alive."

"Nobody will touch the Abwehr, Admiral? Not even the Führer?"

"Do not imply what I have not said. The Führer is not concerned in this, as you know very well. It is you and I . . ."

Every day the two warring leaders of German intelligence stormed at each other amid the baroque opulence of the Hradshin. Yet every evening they drove back together to Jungfern-Breschan to join their wives for supper.

Lina Heydrich remembered this as a "lovely" time, and said politics were not discussed in her presence. Though Heydrich had already told her he suspected Canaris of treason, she seems to have felt that within the charmed circle of Breschan their longtime friendship might still prevail.

Heydrich's journeys back and forth with Canaris conformed to his new routine: into the palace around nine, back to Breschan around five. Sometimes he was accompanied on these daily trips by another car or a bodyguard, sometimes not. That was almost the only thing about his schedule now that varied.

. . .

Late that spring, Professor Zelenka, the resistance leader, asked a former student of his, who now repaired furniture at Prague Castle, to join him for a beer. The two men fell to discussing the bad times that had come to the land. After a while Zelenka announced his opinion that Heydrich "ought to be put out of the way." His student thought this was dangerous talk, but Zelenka finally persuaded him to meet with Gabčik and Kubiš:

> They always wanted to know when Heydrich reached the castle and at what time, and who went with him when he left in the evening. And I told those boys I didn't like it—the whole thing stank of the graveyard. But they calmed me down. The one from Moravia said, "Listen, Franta, don't say a word at home. All you have to do is tell us where Heydrich goes; and you only have to help before it happens. When we get him, you won't be in it at all."

On April 30, two of the steadily dwindling group of parachutists got trapped in a police ambush, and tried to shoot their way out, killing a Czech policeman and seriously wounding another before succumbing themselves. Heydrich, apparently unperturbed by the paratroopers' presence, concentrated on the propaganda effect. According to a newspaper of the time, "The acting Reichsprotektor has given orders that the widow of Sergeant Ometak, killed on active service, should be generously provided for. The acting Reichsprotektor has expressed his particular gratitude to the wounded policeman; and the SS Obergruppenführer Reinhard Heydrich has rewarded the carter who helped to find and catch the criminals."

No better illustration of the split state of Heydrich's mind can be found than this doubling of his roles of Reichsprotektor and SS Obergruppenführer—as if they were not held by the same person.

The resistance, too, was undergoing severe cleavage. In early May, Zelenka's colleague Professor Vanek sent an urgent message to London:

> From preparations made by Ota and Zdenek [code names for Gabčik and Kubiš] and from the place these preparations are made, we judge, despite their continuous silence on the matter,

that they intend to kill Heydrich. His assassination would probably not help the Allies in any way and would have the most far-reaching consequences for our nation. Not only would it endanger our hostages and political prisoners, but it would also cost thousands of additional lives, and the nation would be exposed to unheard-of-terror. At the same time, the last vestiges of organization would be destroyed. Thus it would be impossible for us to do anything useful for the Allies in the future. We ask you, therefore, to give orders to call off the assassination . . .

Delay is dangerous. Answer immediately.

Gabčik and Kubiš are said to have received a special communication in a code known only to them. Edvard Beneš also sent a normally encoded reply asserting that "an aggressive action" was indispensable: "In international politics this would mean salvation for the nation even at the cost of a large sacrifice."

Beneš was desperately worried that Germany and the Allies might yet make a separate peace, and feared that the Czech record of collaboration might lead to the country's being assigned permanently to the Nazi sphere of influence. As General Moravec later put it, the attack on Heydrich must look like "a spontaneous act of national desperation. We hoped that the spontaneity would become genuine when Heydrich was dead and the nation closed ranks and struck back against the Nazi terror." In other words, the government in exile decided to kill Heydrich, not because he was chief of the Sipo or agent of the Final Solution, but because his death would cause many other deaths, which might in turn provoke rebellion. To achieve this show of resistance, Beneš was willing to act even against the wishes of the resistance itself.

This movement's supremely brave people still existed by the thousands. Though opposition leaders were being picked off one by one, others had continued to replace them. Indeed, Nazi records showed that acts of sabotage were increasing from the low of the previous autumn. Heydrich, however, was far more concerned about the immediate effects of his success in Bohemia and Moravia than any problems that might yet occur there.

There is no question that the Nazis regarded his policy in the protectorate as "a truly model one." These were the words of Propaganda Minister Joseph Goebbels, who wrote in his diary in January 1942 that

Bohemia and Moravia was now "in the best of spirits, quite in contrast to other occupied or annexed areas."

A month later, Goebbels had "a long talk with Heydrich" in which the latter convinced him that the threat to German security was completely overcome: "He plays cat and mouse with the Czechs and they swallow everything he places before them. He has carried out a number of extremely popular measures."

Goebbels's approval was not matched by everyone in what Schellenberg called the "witches' cauldron" of Berlin. In the last months of his life, Heydrich had begun to worry that Bormann—and possibly also Himmler—had become so jealous of his unexpected success that they were now working to undermine his power.

One day when Heydrich arrived for a meeting with Hitler (probably in the so-called Führerbunker in Berlin), he thought he saw Bormann whisper something in the Führer's ear. Both men looked his way with "distaste," and shortly thereafter, Hitler canceled the appointment. How long would it be before they managed to turn the Führer against him? he wondered aloud to Schellenberg.

For the moment, however, Hitler was still disposed to accept Heydrich's innovations. In May, he endorsed Heydrich's approach: "Recklessly eliminating everything dangerous but otherwise treating them well is the right policy." Such a policy "will make the Czech population finally adopt Hácha's inner attitude . . . The Czechs could be made into fanatical supporters of the Reich now, if we give these gourmands double rations and don't send them to fight in the East. Then they will feel morally obliged to work twice as much in the armament industries and elsewhere."

Even the Führer was now talking of "inner attitudes," moral obligations, and securing the "fanatical support" of the population. Eight months earlier, both Hitler and Heydrich had scorned the idea of winning over the people; but as time passed, the "optical effect" of Heydrich's policies had become so intense that even their clever creator—and his usually cynical leader—were blinded. The talk should have been primarily of the recklessness of Heydrich's behavior—and not merely in terms of "eliminating everything dangerous." It is actually far more reckless to believe that everything dangerous *can* be eliminated.

A final tale told to me by a guide at Hradčany Castle reveals how much Heydrich had grown out of touch with the world around him. My

Czech source knew someone who had worked as a servant in the palace, in the private rooms used by the protector. This man had arranged to carve a little slogan on the underside of one of Heydrich's favorite chairs: "'Here sits the oppressor of the Czech people!' And he would be using it every day and thinking he was so wonderful, and he *never* knew!"

The chair's secret message was not the only thing that Heydrich had missed seeing, or else having seen, failed to really notice.

For weeks on end, Gabčik and Kubiš had loitered near Heydrich's country chateau, observing his movements. Openly, they picked grass by the roadside, for food was still scarce in Prague, and many Czechs grew rabbits to eat, fattening them up for the kill with free, country greenery. Bystanders often prudently retreated to their houses when the car of the Reich protector went by, but Kubiš and Gabčik "always greeted Heydrich politely and with respect."

The historian Günther Deschner has argued that "a really alert and suspicious German corps of bodyguards" should not have ignored two young men loafing together during working hours. Their frequent presence "ought instantly to have aroused suspicion."

But Reinhard Heydrich wasn't "Herr Suspicion" anymore. Others, more clearsighted, knew he was taking risks and warned him. Albert Speer said, "The thing which shocked me most" about his visit to Prague was not Heydrich's fabled hardness ("My impression that I was receiving was—this was not a ruthless man"), but the time he "invited me to have a ride with his car and with himself."

They drove in Heydrich's convertible, with the top down—in January—and without an escort. Speer was appalled. "I don't know if he drove or his chauffeur did, but, in any case, there were three or four people in the car and that was all. No machine guns—and this was his official car, people could have recognized it because in Prague there was only one."

"Why do you think he took such a chance?" I asked.

"I don't understand why, because he was the chief of the Secret Police and he should have learned to mistrust everything."

"Maybe he just thought he was so powerful that nobody would dare." ("The 'bourgeois Czechs' haven't enough guts to do anything," he is said to have remarked to one of the people who tried to warn him.)

"No, I wouldn't think so, because as Gestapo chief he should have known about all the possibilities of countermovements of the people who are resisting . . . No, he wanted to show his blood. He wanted to show, 'I'm a man and I don't care about those things.' "

Lina Heydrich said that her husband's dangerous missions in his fighter plane were intended to show he was a soldierly man, not just a desk-bound bureaucrat. Having demonstrated that, he was concerned to prove something else in Prague. "Why would anyone wish him harm?" she asked me. "The country was at peace, no bombs fell. He thought they would thank him."

Toward the end of May, a Czech servant at the Hradčany glanced at a schedule on Heydrich's desk and noted he was leaving Prague on the 27th to fly to Berlin for a conference with Hitler. The man had the impression that Heydrich might not be coming back. The resistance network at the castle had heard rumors that the Führer was about to appoint him Reichsprotektor of France, to re-create there his successful experiment in Bohemia and Moravia. Gabčik and Kubiš now determined that they must act at once, lest the moment be lost forever.

They had finally evolved a simple, seemingly efficient plan. On the daily drive between Jungfern-Breschan and Prague, Heydrich's car had to pass down a winding road toward the city. As it reached the suburbs, the road doubled back in a sharp, blind, hairpin turn, forcing all traffic to slow down rounding the curve. The two parachutists would wait around this bend, Gabčik with a Sten machine gun and Kubiš with a Mills grenade, weapons they had brought with them from England. The Sten gun was especially designed for close combat, and could fire 550 rounds of ammunition a minute, more than enough to riddle both Heydrich and his driver with bullets. If for some reason this proved insufficient, Kubiš would finish the job with his grenade. Then, with luck, the two men would still have time to melt into the crowd and ride away on bicycles before any alarm could reach German headquarters.

As an extra precaution, a third commando, Josef Valčík, would be stationed on the other side of the bend to signal Heydrich's approach with the flash of a mirror. Gabčik and Kubiš planned to disguise their bodies with raincoats and their faces with caps, worn low. Since they could not carry guns openly on the streets, they would hide the components in their briefcases. Both had been trained to assemble a gun with one hand, inside a briefcase, without looking down.

Because his Sten gun only worked effectively at very close range,

Gabčik would loiter on the curb as if waiting for the streetcars that continually passed the spot, then step into the road right next to Heydrich's car. Gabčik would be only two or three feet away, and would have the incalculable advantage of surprise. Heydrich would die instantly.

The weather on the warm, sunny spring morning of May 27, 1942, was magnificent. In the country, the fruit trees were in bloom; in the city, the smell of lilacs made the air sweet.

Reinhard Heydrich had spent the previous day on activities that seemed to have nothing to do with an imminent departure for France. According to his wife, he was preparing to explain to Hitler the many reasons why Hans Frank was too corrupt to remain in office as governor general of Poland. Heydrich also met with the Czech cabinet to announce the creation of a new organization for Czech youth from ten to eighteen. It was supposed to emphasize sporting activity, and culminate in a year of labor service. To the protector, it was also an experiment in "reeducation," pulling youth away from their previous academic training and encouraging development in a new direction— a process the Nazis called "national mutation."

That evening Heydrich attended a concert of his father's music, for which he himself had written a brief introduction. Bruno Heydrich had died a few years before, but this was a gesture of reconciliation on Heydrich's part toward the generous, flamboyantly theatrical, highly creative man whose style of life he had once so emphatically rejected. A picture of his father now stood on his desk in the Reich protector's office.

The next morning was so bright and clear that Heydrich delayed his departure to linger with his family, playing with his children on the fresh green lawn. Then he reassured his wife, "Frank will fall!," gave her a warm embrace, and joined his driver, Klein, in the front seat of the Mercedes convertible. Of course, the top was down; it almost always was. "It's the way we keep a cool head, Klein!" Heydrich liked to joke.

Unlike Heydrich, Jozef Gabčik and Jan Kubiš got an early start that morning. Gabčik told the young son of the couple with whom they were staying not to worry about the math exam he would have that day. "We will celebrate tonight!" he said.

At first, everything went according to plan—except that Heydrich's car was an hour and a half late. The two men with their weapons and their confederate with the mirror waited and waited, trying to appear inconspicuous in the busy suburban streets. Just as they had decided something had gone wrong, the Mercedes came into view. As planned, Gabčik threw away his raincoat and removed the newly assembled Sten gun from his briefcase.

Heydrich's car was still slowing down. Gabčik stepped out onto the road, raised his machine gun, and pulled the trigger.

He pulled it again and again, but the gun did not go off. (The Nazis later ascribed this to Gabčik's panic, but it is more likely that he had inadvertently caught some grass from the briefcase in the firing mechanism, jamming it.)

In the tiny dead space of time created by that failure, the Czech and the German stared at each other in shock. For a moment, the Nazi New Order lurched wildly out of orbit, the usual roles reversed, the Reich's young hunter of men now a perfect target for political soldiers from the other side. That moment lasted at most a minute of real time, long enough to make an incalculable alteration on the larger course of European history, and to smash many thousands of lives.

No one is quite sure what happened next. Heydrich may have said, "Step on it, man!" to his driver, which was the routine procedure in such circumstances. But instead, the protector's car slowed to a halt. Later, his driver said that Heydrich had ordered him to stop. In any case, somebody made the final, fatal mistake. Jan Kubiš had time to step out from behind a lamppost, run toward the car, and throw his grenade. It landed under the left rear fender, exploding on impact, throwing up a burst of yellow fire, sending shrapnel flying in all directions, wounding even Kubiš in the eye, and propelling bits of metal and upholstery material into Heydrich's back, spleen, and diaphragm.

Later, a Gestapo investigator concluded that such injuries "should not have been possible, as cars intended for personalities 'to be protected' should have had steel armor in the back of the front seat . . . This order . . . had not been carried out."

At the moment of impact, however, no one realized that Heydrich had been wounded. Nothing about the situation seems to have been quite real to anyone. As the pendulum swung back toward Nazi domination, the scene seemed to observers to resemble a film or a Wild West show rather than the normal life in the protectorate.

Everyone was brave; no one was particularly clever. Heydrich plucked

Heydrich's shattered open-roofed Mercedes following the ambush, after preliminary plans to kill him on a train or as he drove through a forest had been abandoned. Instead, Jan Kubiš and Jozef Gabčik stood at the tram stop in a bend of the road near Bulovka Hospital.

a gun from the side pocket of the car, jumped out of the vehicle, and began to fire at Kubiš, who ran toward his bicycle. Gabčik hurled his useless gun to the pavement, took a Colt revolver from his briefcase, and ran away up a hill, firing as he went. Heydrich's driver, Klein, dashed off in pursuit, trying to shoot him down. But he inadvertently released the magazine of his gun, and according to the Gestapo investigator, "he did not have the presence of mind to realize why the gun had failed to fire."

Klein continued to chase Gabčik, who ran inside a butcher's shop, looking for a back door. The butcher was a Nazi sympathizer and immediately gave the alarm. Gabčik and Klein collided at the door of the shop, where Gabčik managed to shoot the hapless driver in the knee and escape through the narrow streets.

Meanwhile, Heydrich suddenly began to feel the effect of his wounds. Clutching his back, he sank into the seat of the car, dazed by pain. He was completely alone.

Jan Kubiš, also alone, reached his bicycle and pedaled swiftly off. Covered with blood from his own injuries, he managed to reach the home of his friends, the Novaks, leaving his blood-stained vehicle several blocks away.

Shortly thereafter, the fourteen-year-old daughter of the household,

Jindriska, arrived home for lunch. "You've come at exactly the right moment," said her mother, who asked her to go at once to fetch the bicycle. Jindriska was stealthily quick, but others, watching out of their windows, saw her take it away.

At the turning of the road, a crowd had gathered around Heydrich's car. No one dared to approach him in either anger or friendship. Then a blond woman came running forward. "Oh, God, oh, God! Our Heydrich, our Heydrich!" she screamed.

The woman (who has never been identified) ran out into the street and forced a passing delivery truck to stop. A Czech policeman helped assist Heydrich into the truck. The reluctant driver, who would have preferred to toss the "bastard" into a ditch, noticed that he tried to walk upright: "He couldn't manage it, but proud to the bitter end, you know."

Heydrich reminded the driver of "a tiger that's just been wounded," but he clutched his briefcase in one hand like a bureaucrat. In the other, he still held his revolver. Afterward, the Gestapo discovered that the chief of Reich security had not bothered to load his gun.

27

THE TEMPLE OF FEAR

"It was as if he didn't care if he lived or died."
—LINA HEYDRICH

THE VAN RUSHED HEYDRICH to Bulovka Hospital, so nearby that the blast of the bomb had been heard in the operating room, provoking Dr. Vladimir Snajdr to cry out, "Murder!" by way of a joke, when he heard the explosion. Even when Dr. Snajdr got to the emergency room and encountered Heydrich sitting on an operating table, blood oozing from his back, alone except for two nurses applying ice compresses to his forehead, he wasn't sure he could believe his eyes: an apparent attack on the all-powerful Reich protector was more than most people could comprehend.

The startled doctor greeted his German ruler in Czech. Heydrich raised his arm but said nothing while Snajdr examined his wound. "He did not stir, did not flinch, although it must have hurt him," noted Dr. Snajdr, who was secretly wondering if patriotic duty required him to kill his patient. Before he could make up his mind, a German physician rushed in, came to attention, cried "Heil!," and clicked his heels.

"Herr Protector, we must operate!" the new doctor said, but Heydrich refused, demanding that a surgeon be sent from Berlin.

"But your condition requires an immediate operation!" the doctor insisted. Heydrich agreed to allow this doctor, Professor Josef A. Hohlbaum of the German surgical clinic of Prague, to cleanse the wounds and remove bits of metal and fabric embedded in his flesh.

This turned out to be Heydrich's last important decision, yet the Protektor, who was still talking, almost walking, and in command of his faculties, was not regarded as critically wounded. X-rays had disclosed a ruptured rib cage and splinters lodged in his spleen, but these were regarded as manageable problems. The operation itself seemed to go well, although Heydrich remained heavily sedated. Himmler's favorite physician, Dr. Karl Franz Gebhardt, arrived to supervise Heydrich's care, having been dispatched by the Reichsführer SS himself.

While Heydrich lay unconscious, the huge security machine he had built took up the task of avenging its leader. Like a mastodon, it lumbered gradually into pursuit, only slowly warming to the chase, then proceeding with crushing thoroughness.

When the local Gestapo chief was informed of the assassination attempt, he thought it was a joke. Valuable time passed before Karl Hermann Frank and a few police leaders arrived at the hospital. Now, when it no longer mattered, they ordered elaborate security precautions. The floor on which the Reichsprotektor rested was taken over entirely by the SS. German troops patrolled the corridors and outbuildings, guarding against a second attack.

Yet nothing was further from the minds of Jan Kubiš and Jozef Gabčik. As they fled from place to place in despair, the two men were certain they had failed. No one could yet imagine that both Heydrich and his attackers would soon be dead.

In the first confused hours, the shortsightedness of the assassins and their German enemies was mutual: Kubiš and Gabčik had no clear plan of escape, and the Germans had no plan to prevent their getaway. Then Hans Frank, who had been Heydrich's de facto deputy, took over, ordering the police to close all exits from Prague, block the roads, and search the railroad stations. He also instructed Criminal Commissioner Heinz Pannwitz, chief of Prague Gestapo Department G.II (Assassinations, Illegal Arms, and Sabotage), to organize an immediate, massive manhunt. "Sir, do you want investigation or retaliation?" Pannwitz inquired. "Investigation, of course," Frank replied.

At 12:30, he received a phone call from Adolf Hitler. As Frank later noted, "The Führer asked right away if Obergruppenführer Heydrich had driven without escort . . . This was sharply condemned by the Führer. Then he asked about the condition of the Obergruppenführer."

After he heard that Heydrich was expected to live, Hitler instructed

Frank to offer a reward of 1 million marks for information leading to the arrest of the assailants. Whoever helped the assassins, or even knew of their whereabouts without reporting it, was to be shot, along with his entire family. Ten thousand Czech "suspects" were to be arrested at once, and all political prisoners already in jail were to be shot— immediately. But Frank, long the voice of fanaticism in Prague, now assumed Heydrich's mantle of pragmatic calculation. He begged his Führer for a personal audience to discuss the "political implications." Hitler agreed, and Frank prepared to fly to Berlin that very afternoon.

Though no official announcement had yet been made, knowledge of the ambush was spreading among Nazi officials as fast as wireless, telephone, and gossip could carry it. In Berlin, a well-informed member of the German resistance politely telephoned Heydrich's brother-in-law to tell him the news. Lina Heydrich, however, did not hear even rumors of the attack, and was not informed of its reality until after the surgery, when her husband was considered out of danger.

At 3 p.m. the same day, Karl Hermann Frank summoned the local leaders of the SD and the Gestapo to a special meeting. "What a great mess!" Frank said. Then he told the men Hitler had ordered the deaths of ten thousand Czechs.

All assembled were "very negative" about this "monstrous" order, recalled Inspector Pannwitz after the war. "How do we know that the assassins were Czechs?" he argued. "It could just as well be the action of German refugees brought from England or English commandos."

By 5 p.m. Frank had left for the airport, determined to convince Hitler to rescind his decree. Later Pannwitz wrote, "If Hitler's senseless order had been carried out, the success of the assassination would have been complete . . . because the blood sacrifice of the Czech people would certainly have caused lasting unrest."

Before he left, Frank issued a brief announcement of the "assassination attempt" and declared martial law. People were forbidden to leave their homes after nine o'clock, and all restaurants and theaters were closed. Anyone who did not stop when challenged would be shot.

At 9:05 p.m., Heinrich Himmler, apparently thinking Frank was still in Prague, sent him a telegram, ordering the execution "this very night" of one hundred members of the Czech intelligentsia.

Both Hitler and Himmler had ordered the taking of hostages and the shooting of prisoners before they even knew the details of the assassination. On the surface, it looked as if the Nazi leaders—except Frank—

were behaving in their "normal" style, lashing out at available victims first, pausing to think later.

Yet behind their iron masks, the paladins of Nazidom were in a turmoil of confusion. In Berlin, Walter Schellenberg noticed that "instead of the hum of intensive activity, there was a hush of incredulity, almost of fear. How could such a thing have happened?" In Prague, on the other hand, SS and police officials dashed around frantically, almost crazed with anxiety.

No one knew who was behind the attack, but so many Germans might want Heydrich dead that the first culprit on most people's lists was certainly not the Czech government in exile. Schellenberg initially thought Himmler had done it—or Bormann. (Heydrich had recently told him that both men were now jealous of his success and might join together to bring him down.) An Irish doctor who had once met Heydrich also blamed Himmler. Some people suspected Alfred Naujocks, whom Heydrich had recently demoted and sent into hazardous combat. Others thought Admiral Canaris had planned the attack to save himself from ruin at Heydrich's hands.

In Paris, Werner Best worried that his past confrontations with Heydrich might make him suspect. Allen Dulles, when Swiss Director of the OSS, heard rumors implicating Himmler's deputy Karl Wolff. Only Himmler himself seemed utterly certain that the attack had originated in England.

In London, however, while newspaper columnists discussed the Nazis' penchant for murdering each other, the SOE (Special Operations Executive) remained prudently silent. Meanwhile, Beneš and Morávek ostentatiously praised local Bohemian patriots for the attack they themselves had planned. (Not until thirty years after the war did any of them admit the truth.)

While Beneš exulted in the demise of a "monster," Hitler was searching for a new protector who would be "much worse than Heydrich"—someone who would "have no scruples about wading through a sea of blood." If any further "grave acts" occurred, he told President Hácha, he might order the deportation of the whole Czech population: "As we had accomplished the migration of several million Germans, such an action would present no difficulties to us," the Führer boasted. The one voice missing from this cacophony of suspicion and threat was that of Reinhard Heydrich himself.

How conscious he was of the tension swirling around him is hard to know. Heydrich was in considerable pain, and receiving substantial doses of morphine and sulfonamide. His wounds were not healing well. (Allied doctors could have availed themselves of penicillin, but the Germans did not yet possess it.)

Lina visited him daily, and various underlings and attendants talked to him as well. What they discussed is not completely known. After the war, Hannah Arendt heard conflicting "legends," as she later reported: either the dying Heydrich repented of his crimes against the Jews ("his people") or he remained a defiant fanatic to the end. Neither of these claims can be substantiated. There is, however, no evidence that Heydrich ever advocated reprisals against the Czechs. Indeed, he did not seem to have talked about revenge at all. Lina Heydrich declared, "I no longer recognize my husband. This ambitious goal-striving man seemed to have lost his will to go on. It was as if he didn't care whether he lived or died."

On the 2nd of June, Heinrich Himmler visited the bedside of his fallen henchman. The two SS leaders avoided their usual business—torture, detection, deportation, death—and spoke instead of the tortuous ways of fate. Frau Heydrich reported that her husband quoted some lines from an opera his father had written:

> Yes, the world is just a barrel organ
> Played by God himself.
> We must all dance to the tune
> That just happens to be on the roll.

The English author Callum MacDonald calls this "a staggering evasion of personal responsibility. For Heydrich, who had murdered thousands in the pursuit of total power, to appeal to fate or predestination was hypocrisy on the grand scale."

The essence of the Führer principle, however, was precisely the evasion of personal responsibility. (It is much easier to murder thousands—not to mention millions—if you *don't* feel responsible.) Heydrich's reference to his father's strained simile was in fact disturbingly honest. An ambitious young man who came late to Nazism, Heydrich had never been deeply interested in its so-called philosophy. An outsider who was never part of the small circle around Hitler, he had wanted primarily to make dramatic progress along one of the few career paths open to him. Confronted by the rules of the game, he played by them, creating within their framework his own leadership style, based on energy, tenacity, ruthlessness, and calculation. He was not even an ideal of evil. He was, in a way, worse: a person devoid of ethical standards.

In this, he was truly the new man of Nazism—a rootless, restless *Draufgänger*, throwing himself totally into the action of the moment, letting the goals of the moment be set by others. The only time he had ever tried to create what the Nazis called the "framework" of his own action had been his short career as Reichsprotektor. And this had proved fatal. Heydrich's Machiavellian strategy of delaying the arrest of many resistance leaders, coupled with the lack of empathy of an arrogant man, certain his subjects *must* be grateful for such "protection," made the assassination possible.

For Reinhard Heydrich, as for most of the men he chose as subordinates, the joy of possessing power and of belonging to the master race far transcended his awareness of the real horror of SS rule in the East. Heydrich had always been more interested in perfecting his own swashbuckling version of the SS style than in examining the moral content of SS policies. In Prague, he seems to have believed he could don the elegant robe of princely rule and cast his previous reputation—and atrocious crimes—aside like a worn-out overcoat. He had long practiced divide and rule, division of the labor of "dirty work," and denial of threatening realities. He had lived by doubling, and in the end it also killed him.

Lina was convinced that Heydrich "considered himself a soldier, not a politician." Part of the credo of many soldiers is a certain blind faith in the fateful moment. The desperate assumption that only one (perhaps never to be fired) bullet truly has your name on it is honored in every foxhole everywhere. Frau Heydrich told Günther Deschner that her husband believed "destiny strikes whenever and wherever it will, and there is no defense against it." She told me he knew the dreaded "check" he had so often handed to others would someday be presented to him. He had never expected a long life, she said.

We do not know what Heinrich Himmler made of Heydrich's little discourse on fate, though he did tell his men a few days later, "As sons of Germania who, though no fatalists, are believers in destiny, we must say: When time runs out, well, then, it has run out. All the same we cannot leave everything to the good Lord and make him our personal security guard."

Himmler was obviously a little less fatalistic than the reckless, heedless Heydrich had been, but did the Reichsführer SS possibly have a hand in directing his assistant to an early death?

Himmler had burst into tears when he heard Heydrich was wounded, had called constantly to check on the condition of "our good Reinhard," and on the day of his death had torn the page out of his office calendar in a fit of strong emotion. He had also repeatedly advised the chief of Reich security to show more regard for his own safety. His surprise and anguish at the assassins' attack can hardly be doubted.

Yet Himmler had always been better at taking advantage of dangerous situations than at initiating them. What might he—or his agent, Dr. Gebhardt—have felt fated to do when his most ruthless rival lay helpless in the hospital? This tempting situation has provided the denouement of at least two mystery novels, as well as a great deal of real-life speculation.

Karl Gebhardt was the surgeon general of the Waffen SS. On the side, he ran a little private clinic to which various SS men exhausted by the psychic strain of knightly duty might repair for rest and rehabilitation. Heydrich had never trusted the unsavory Gebhardt, an opinion shared by Albert Speer. Speer told me he thought Gebhardt had attempted to murder him in 1943, during a time when Speer and Heinrich Himmler were constantly at odds.

I asked him whether Gebhardt could have killed Heydrich.

"*Ja, ja.* It's quite possible," Speer said. "I mistrusted him with Heydrich and I mistrusted him in another case. That [concerned] a minister of production, and I was careless. He wanted to be operated on in Gebhardt's hospital. He had quite a reputation and was a very well-known doctor . . . And so I thought [it was all right]. And my friend was dead afterward. Stupid!"

One Czech historian, Miroslav Honzík, shared Speer's suspicions, writing that one of the two German doctors who conducted the autopsy later claimed there were "no pathological changes found on Heydrich's body." The autopsy apparently did not include a toxicology examination. In any case, the autopsy report soon vanished. Like the missing records of Heydrich's racial ancestry, which clouded his birth, the evidence of his exact manner of dying seems lost to history.

In theory, Himmler had a lot to gain by getting rid of Heydrich. A man who knew all of Himmler's embarrassing foibles, who belittled him in private and pushed and prodded him at the office, who had at last gained private access to Hitler and might soon be Reichsprotektor of France—all of this made Heydrich a threat both to Himmler's vanity and to his power. Yet, in practice, Himmler had always relied on Heydrich's penetrating pragmatism, relentless "logic," and unstinting energy, while carefully distancing himself from his aggressive bravado and open disdain for party hacks. Heydrich was hampered by his unpopularity with the Nazi Old Fighters as well as by his murky racial background. In any direct trial of strength, Himmler would probably have won.

Probably, therefore, Himmler was guilty of nothing more than trusting Gebhardt's peculiar brand of medicine. As Gebhardt himself later testified,

> In the extraordinary excitement and nervous tension which prevailed, and was not diminished by daily personal telephone calls from Hitler and Himmler asking for information, very many suggestions were naturally made . . . I consider that if anything endangers a patient it is nervous tension at the bedside and the appearance of too many doctors. I refused, in reply to direct demands, to call in any [other] doctor.

After Himmler's visit, Heydrich's health rallied for a few days, then sharply, suddenly, declined. When Lina visited him, they tried to chat about family matters, as if nothing much had happened and he were certain to recover.

"Did he have some special last words for you?" I asked. She looked embarrassed. "Oh, no, we didn't believe in that sort of thing."

During their last meeting, however, Reinhard Heydrich gave his wife some terse, emphatic instructions: "Take the children and go back to Fehmarn." Obviously, he knew by then that he might die; he also knew the precise extent of Nazi atrocities in the East (including those for which he himself was responsible) and clearly wanted his family as far away from the war as it was possible to get.

"I'll see you tomorrow," Frau Heydrich said before she left that day, but she told me she was sure she wouldn't. (Even though others said he had sat up in bed and enjoyed a good dinner.) She was right. Shortly before dawn on June 4, at 4:30 a.m., Reinhard Heydrich breathed his last, allegedly succumbing to septicemia—infection of the blood— from his wounds.

Speculation has never ended that Heydrich might have been helped along to his destiny with a little something added to his last meal by Himmler's personal doctor. The question has never been resolved, simply because conclusive evidence pointing one way or the other appears unavailable. Still, there remains a cruel justice in the possibility that a man who arranged for the deaths of so many people may himself have been murdered twice.

Whether or not Himmler had a hand in hastening Heydrich's death, he certainly involved himself with both hands in Heydrich's funeral. As usual, there were discrepancies between the surface play of ritual and the tensions roiling beneath, between what Himmler intended to say and what he inadvertently revealed. In this sense, he created the perfect monument to the divided soul of Reinhard Heydrich.

Himmler's image as a priggish "schoolmaster" belied his great talent as a director of political spectacles. The man who had designed SS uniforms of sinister splendor was determined to transform his slain subordinate into the first great martyr of his knightly order.

On the evening of June 6, the ceremonies began on a muted note in Prague. Heydrich had died only two days before and the Nazis had as yet no clue as to the murderer's identity and motives. For once, the apprehension of the local population was balanced by an almost equal level of anxiety among its SS oppressors. The Reichsprotektor's body lay in state in the courtyard of Hradschin Castle, surrounded by a guard of honor and covered with an immense silver "rune of victory." Czech President Emil Hácha had ordered ostentatious displays of loyalty. While endless crowds of mourners filed past his bier, "Heydrich's" detectives were frantically searching for his killers. Meanwhile, the show had to go on.

Kurt Dalüge, a former rival who had just replaced Heydrich as acting Reichsprotektor, gave the oration. As chief of the Order Police, Dalüge controlled all constabularies not viewed as political. Himmler had tried to use him as a check on Heydrich's power. But since Heydrich had defined police work as "90 percent political," and usually prevailed, he left only the mouse's share of the spoils to Dalüge. (He also reveled in Dalüge's nickname, "Dummi-Dummi.")

In the main, Dalüge stayed in character, giving a speech that was stupidly fulsome and arrantly inaccurate. Heydrich (whom Dalüge had once tried to arrest) was depicted as a "faithful friend," mourned "with our hearts burning, our eyes wet, and our fists clenched." He was also a noble "prototype of the Aryan ideal," who nevertheless had deigned to march "shoulder to shoulder with simple, ordinary men."

Dalüge also claimed that Heydrich's solicitude for his staff surpassed that of the British Secret Service, whose "leaders as well as men are displaced, removed, or murdered as soon as they have ceased to suit the Jews and Communists who are the wire pullers in this field too." (In fact, more than a few of Heydrich's highest leaders had been convinced he intended to eliminate them at his earliest convenience.)

In some vital respects, however, "Dummi-Dummi" Dalüge displayed a fool's intelligence, rushing in to raise some truly frightening issues. He admitted that after the "infamous" attack, "hundreds of questions crowded into our minds . . . and were left without reply."

He conceded also that due to the nature of the tasks entrusted to the late Protektor, "nothing was said in the Reich about Heydrich and his work for years."

Perhaps this exercise in damning with ominous praise was also a warning to people not "our own" to behave themselves or else expect a "forceful" response. Whatever he meant, Dalüge reserved his greatest oratorical efforts not for Heydrich but for "the shining example of his dear wife":

> It is evidence of the common heartbeat and common soul of these two people that the farewell between him and his wife and also his children was on [the day of the ambush] longer and more hearty than usual, and it seemed as if he had felt that . . . he ought to stay with his wife and family. However, he had to go to Berlin . . . and he went out to meet his fate.

Dalüge had rushed to Prague immediately after Heydrich was wounded, and claimed to have witnessed some of "his last fateful hours":

His wife entered the room and although she knew that these were his last moments, she spoke to him in a normal manner. He did not know that his end was near. When he felt tired he bade her farewell, saying that he would see her again in the afternoon. Soon afterward, he closed his eyes forever. His wife's first words after his death were: "For me and for the children, he is not dead. For us, he will live forever."

Kurt Dalüge had the sense to recognize a good exit line. Praising his former enemy as a "great example of heroism," he swiftly took his leave: "Thy name, Reinhard Heydrich, will one day be carved in stone in the Hall of Memory of the SS."

After that, the SS itself took over. The SS band played the SS funeral march and the Reichsführer SS laid the first wreath on the coffin. Only then did Heydrich's two sons, Klaus and Heider, approach with their own two wreaths. The band played the traditional German Army anthem "Ich hatt' einen Kameraden" ("I had a comrade") while Dalüge put down his own offering. Then followed representatives of the Reich Security Office, the Wehrmacht, and the Luftwaffe. The collaborationist government of the protectorate, in the person of the gray, bent figure of President Hácha, was allowed to lay the last wreath.

Eight SS leaders stepped forward to lift the coffin and placed it on the carriage of a 10.5-centimeter howitzer. Slowly the funeral procession left the castle courtyard, led by Heinrich Himmler and Heydrich's family. Dalüge followed after them, then Nazi Gauleiters and SS leaders "according to rank," then the rest of the honored guests.

They made their way down the steep hill below the palace, through the narrow, winding streets, across the Charles Bridge, lined with stately old statues and stiff young men in glittering uniforms, toward the Square of St. Wenceslas, the medieval hero whose patriotic tradition Heydrich had claimed to represent. All traffic had been cordoned off, but the square was filled with thousands of people, standing in total silence. Gradually, other groups arrived to pack the space still further: boys and girls of the Hitler Youth, a battalion of Adolf Hitler's personal bodyguards, units of the Luftwaffe, the army, the Labour Force, a company of police, and, finally, Heydrich's closest associates at work. After them came a long column of cars carrying wreaths. "The many thousands on the square greet the coffin with raised arms," announced a Nazi commentator reporting live from Prague.

From Wenceslas Square, Heydrich's body was escorted to the nearby railroad station, preceded by wreaths and bands and men carrying two cushions bearing the medals he had received during his eleven years of service to Nazism. At the entrance to the station, the military battalions for the last time "presented arms for the deceased Obergruppenführer." Then the remains of Reinhard Heydrich were taken away by special train to Berlin, where three days later Heinrich Himmler would preside over the most magnificent state funeral in the short history of Nazi Germany.

On that day, June 9, 1942, Himmler gave a long oration, apparently reflecting both deep emotion and considerable thought. Dalüge had raised a series of rhetorical questions about Heydrich: "What was he in his work and activities? Who knows his work in all its detail? What do we know of him personally?" Now, the Reichsführer SS attempted to provide answers.

He had the most glittering—and probably the most attentive—audience of his life. The ceremony was held in the sumptuous Mosaic Hall of the vast new Reich chancellery, designed by Albert Speer as a grandiose monument to Hitler's dreams of imperial glory. The Führer himself sat in the first row of mourners, surrounded by row upon row of Nazi dignitaries, military officers, and bureaucratic potentates. President Hácha had come from Prague for the occasion. Everyone who could, wore a uniform and decorations. Squeezed in among them were various members of Heydrich's family, wearing black.

Once more Heydrich's body lay in state, enshrouded in SS regalia. Once more, the man who had been given a dishonorable discharge from the Weimar navy received an honor guard chosen from the new German military elite. Decorative elements ransacked from bygone eras gave totalitarianism a patina of barbarous antiquity: fires in Roman-style pylons, reflected from polished marble, glimmered beneath immense wall hangings. Most of the SS symbols, like the twin lightning flashes of the rune of victory, were derived from prehistoric Teutonic lore; the death's head insignia had more recently adorned the troops of Emperor Frederick the Great; the self-consciously tribal music was by that famous nineteenth-century individualist, Richard Wagner. Walter Schellenberg has written that he thought "the whole thing was like a Renaissance painting."

Around three o'clock in the afternoon, the ceremonies began. Reichsmarschall Hermann Göring strode into the great hall, and greeted his comrades. This was the signal for all to rise with right hands extended to salute the Führer's arrival. Himmler led Adolph Hitler to the place of honor. Then, muffled drums announced the beginning of Siegfried's funeral march from *Götterdämmerung*. Heydrich's father had played Siegfried onstage; his son was said by some to be Siegfried's living embodiment; it was inevitable that Reinhard Heydrich should be buried to music for a warrior hero murdered in a treacherous surprise attack. As the music faded, Heinrich Himmler rose, stood briefly in front of Heydrich's bier, then turned to face the assembled notables.

Surrounded by the detritus of vanished cultures, the Reichsführer SS used pompously elevated German to describe the character and work of a modern expert in police terror. Heydrich, he said, had had unique abilities allied with a nature of rare purity and a mind of penetrating clarity. He had been "radiant" and "glowing" and "shining" and "chivalric." His death was a "sacrificial contribution to our people's struggle for freedom."

It was as if Himmler were presiding over the ritual immolation of an ancient Greek aristocrat who had died fighting with sword and javelin against hordes of invading barbarians. Yet, of necessity, the Reichsführer's tone changed radically whenever he offered his version of the career of "this man, who was feared by the subhumans, hated and slandered by Jews and other criminals, and sometimes misunderstood even by many Germans."

Heydrich had gotten his start, Himmler said, brawling with the Communists and doing propaganda work in the streets of Hamburg. After that, he had reorganized the Munich Political Police, the Prussian Police, the Secret State Police, and finally the Criminal Police, providing them with "the most modern technical and scientific equipment."

As this is hardly the stuff of heroic legends, Himmler moved quickly back to the difficult new beginnings of the early 1930s, marked by "happy and unconcerned" struggles abroad against emigrants and traitors, and "hard, painful" duties inside Germany. Here, unintentionally perhaps, he had articulated the great inner divide within Nazism, the need not to destroy the obvious enemies of the Reich and then settle back to enjoy the New Order. No, everyone had to be watched all the time, even good Germans, to ensure they continued "purification, security, and protection."

All soldiers, we know, are trained to be professional killers. But the Reichsführer SS wanted his audience to feel the pathos of the "political soldiers"—himself included—whose "painful" duties often made them feared and shunned by their own countrymen:

> Heydrich correctly took the position that only the best of our people, the racially most select, gifted with excellent character and with good hearts and unbending will, were qualified for battling against negative things, and thus for working in what is actually a positive way for the good of the whole.

All Germans should be "thankful in their hearts to Reinhard Heydrich," Himmler said. Even during wartime blackouts, Germans could walk peacefully through the streets, unmolested and unrobbed. This was not the case in the "cordial, humane" democratic countries, he added, with howitzer-heavy irony. Again and again, Himmler returned to his basic theme of the unsung nobility of Heydrich and his kind. Modestly, Heydrich had sought no public recognition, preferring to let his acts speak for themselves. Heydrich had even sneaked off in 1941 to fly over the hazardous Russian front, getting shot down in the process, and having to make his way back on his own to the German lines.

Himmler knew that everyone was aware of the serious tensions in his relationship with his ambitious underling, widely considered his superior in the clandestine war games of the Nazi leaders. But who, now, could refute his claim that Heydrich was merely his daring, but loyal vassal?

Himmler described Heydrich's "last, great task," which was also the first "visible, positive, creative task" he had ever received. As Reich protector of Bohemia and Moravia, Heydrich had at last been allowed to display his brilliant governing abilities before all the world. And, as Himmler saw it, he had been generous. The Czech people had dreaded the arrival of the "feared Heydrich," only to discover he was willing to grant "the possibility of cooperation" to "everyone of good will."

On the 27th of May, however, an "underhanded bomb . . . thrown by a paid mercenary from the ranks of the worthless subhumans" brought him down. Himmler—still considered a leading suspect by many of those present—carefully noted that the explosive had been found to be of English origin. He also mentioned that Heydrich had taken few precautions: "Fear and overly great caution were foreign to a man who had been one of the best sportsmen in the SS."

Until this point, Himmler had at least been presenting a version of the truth as he knew it. Now, he waxed wildly hypocritical: "For long days, we hoped that the strength derived from [Heydrich's] sound ancestry and from the simple and disciplined life he led would hold off the worst danger." Himmler certainly knew that most of the mourners had been gossiping for years about Heydrich's possible Jewish ancestry, wild sexual escapades, and frenetically complicated schedule. It was Himmler who had tried to lead a simple life and advised his men to do likewise. "I told you so," he seemed to be saying, before rising to a loftier conclusion: "Fate, the Lord God, the Ancient One . . . in whom this great enemy of the misuse of religion for political ends deeply, unswervingly and submissively believed, brought his physical existence to an end."

Heinrich Himmler and Lina Heydrich had been feuding for years. To fall under his "loving care" was a dubious blessing, as those who knew them both would surely realize. As he came to the end of his oration, the contradictions in Himmler's nature were coming to the surface. His speech ended in an unsettling mixture of violent threats and vows of eternal affection. Heydrich, he concluded, would accompany his SS companions in spirit "when we . . . true to our law, fall in, attack, and hold out to the last . . . Ours, however, is the holy duty to expiate his death, to take over his tasks and, now more than ever, to annihilate the enemies of our people without pity or weakness."

Himmler announced he had only one thing left to say. Speaking directly to his dead comrade, he employed the familiar "you" that the living man had forbidden him to use: "*Du*, Reinhard Heydrich, were truly a good SS man! And personally I must thank you here for your unswerving loyalty and for the wonderful friendship that bound us together in life and that not even death can sever!"

In Zurich, Hans Bernd Gisevius advised Allen Dulles that the men he called the "terrible twins" must once have been lovers.* But no such elaborate (and ridiculous) explanations were necessary. Mutual associates claimed that Himmler, whatever his previous ambivalence about Heydrich, fell into a state of virtual paralysis after the loss of the forceful assistant who had hardened his constantly wavering resolve and accompanied him every step of the way to monstrous power. Before the memorial service, Himmler had twice assembled Heydrich's "bright

* Dulles wrote the foreword to Gisevius's *To the Bitter End: An Insider's Account of the Plot to Kill Hitler,* but found no evidence of this remark.

young men" in front of his coffin to ask them to honor his memory and to avoid rivalry and jealous animosity as he struggled to replace the man who had hired them all. Himmler knew that it had taken all of Heydrich's cunning and cleverness to hold their fractious ambitions in check. Later, when he addressed his departmental chiefs, the Reichsführer was still envying Heydrich's leadership ability. "*That* was Heydrich's greatness," he told them. "When one talked to his people in whatever forsaken corner of the world, in Poland or the Crimea, in Estonia or Serbia, they were all ideologically clear and correctly educated and took the right attitude to all problems. That was not merely guile . . . They aligned themselves correctly and always gave the right answer."

Even from beyond the grave, Heydrich was still giving advice. As Himmler and his chief of staff, Karl Wolff, were preparing to transport Heydrich's corpse from Prague to Berlin, his adjutant approached with a sealed letter for each of them. They were both from Heydrich, to be passed along only in the event of his death.

He advised Karl Wolff always to tell Himmler "bravely and unsparingly the truth." Wolff allowed Himmler to read his letter and waited for the Reichsführer to reciprocate, but he did not. Many years later, Wolff guessed Himmler's letter must have dealt with the "dirty handiwork" ordered by the two SS leaders—about which (he claimed) he himself was allowed to know nothing.

After Himmler had finished speaking, Adolf Hitler rose to place a wreath of orchids beside Heydrich's coffin. "I have only a few words to dedicate to the dead," the Führer said:

> He was one of the best National Socialists, one of the strongest defenders of the idea of the German Reich. He has fallen as a blood witness for the preservation and security of the Reich. As Führer of the party and as Führer of the German Reich, I give to you, my dear comrade Heydrich—after Party Comrade [Fritz] Todt, the second German—the highest honor that I have to bestow: the highest grade of the German Order.

Hitler placed the supreme decoration on a cushion near the rest of Heydrich's medals. It was never awarded to anyone again.

Adolf Hitler (center) and Heinrich Himmler (right) with Heydrich's sons, Klaus (left) and Heider, at their father's state funeral in Berlin, on June 9, 1942, five days after his death. As a prelude to the service, the State Orchestra performed Siegfried's Funeral March from *Götterdämmerung*.

An eyewitness later reported that Hitler had been so moved he could hardly speak. As he left the Mosaic Hall, the Führer reached down to brush the cheeks of Heydrich's two young sons. "Heydrich, he was the man with the iron heart," he murmured a few moments later. In Hitler's lexicon, there could be no higher praise. Nor did the bestowing of a medal that had been awarded before imply an invidious comparison. The coupling was actually flattering: as head of the armaments program and builder of the autobahn, Fritz Todt had been an "unpolitical" technologist respected by everyone. Heydrich had told his wife he admired Todt more than any other Nazi leader. Many years later, Frau Heydrich told me with unmistakable pride, "Hitler placed them on the same level!"

Todt had been a brilliant engineer, whereas Heydrich had excelled in "social engineering" of the grimmest kind. Todt had often worked outside in the sunlight; Heydrich had pulled strings from the shadows. He had not only arranged mass murders, but also made sure that records were kept to implicate the men who ordered them. He had known more secrets of Nazi life than any other German leader. Did Hitler and Himmler know that he had kept files even on them? Did the distinguished patrons of Salon Kitty know that he had taped records of their illicit sexual liaisons? Did Martin Bormann realize Heydrich thought he had been—and might still be—a Communist agent? Literally and figuratively, Reinhard Heydrich had been the one who knew where all the bodies were buried. Now Adolf Hitler was deliberately blurring his own distinctions between "clean" nonpolitical work and the dirty "security" work even Karl Wolff claimed to avoid; he was blending together the sunlight and the shadows.

After Hitler left, the orchestra played the German national anthem, and then the Nazi "Horst-Wessel-Lied." The many flags were lowered to half-mast. The funeral procession, once again led by Heinrich Himmler, walked slowly down Unter den Linden toward the Invaliden cemetery. On either side, Heydrich's little boys walked with him, their hands enfolded in his. Behind the family members, everyone else was arranged in the usual intricately graded hierarchical formations. In the cemetery, Heydrich was laid to rest near such military heroes as Gerhard von Scharnhorst, Manfred von Richthofen, and Walter von Reichenau—not to mention Fritz Todt. "Salvos of Honor" were fired over the grave, which "soon disappeared under a mountain of wreaths."

The British press called the elaborate ceremonies in Heydrich's honor a "gangster-style burial," but a more telling comparison may be found in the ancient world so beloved of Adolf Hitler. Observers of Nazi Germany sometimes called it the "modern Sparta." The analogy has its uses. Sparta was militaristic, imperialistic, and dictatorial. It is regarded by some as the first totalitarian state. Its small group of aristocratic leaders despised democracy, philosophy, and poetry; its citizens couldn't travel abroad without permission; most of its subjects were helots, with no legal rights, forced to live outside the city limits. The ruling class maintained both a small army of informers and armed vigilantes who roamed by night.

Next to their military barracks, Sparta's leaders erected a temple to fear. The Spartans had no illusion that the peoples they enslaved would love them; rather, they believed they could only be subdued through force and terror. In Nazi Germany, similar assumptions had long been part of the rules of Hitler's "game" of power.

Heydrich's assassination reinforced the Nazis' paranoia, brutality, and obsession with personal and national security. If the chief of Reich security—young, strong, brave, well informed, intelligent, and ruthless—could be taken by surprise, who was truly safe? Reinhard

Heydrich's entire funeral panoply could be considered a symbolic temple to fear.

Like Himmler's description of Heydrich's protective tasks, the fear was all encompassing, ranging from the Nazis' dread of Jews, foreign enemies, and domestic opponents to their secret distrust of one another and their own inner irresolution and disquietude.

The Mosaic Hall had been full of fellow Nazis who had feared Reinhard Heydrich. More than a few were relieved by his departure. ("Thank god that pig has gone to the butcher!" Sepp Dietrich, the head of Adolf Hitler's bodyguard, had exclaimed when he heard the news.) Still, almost everyone had something to lose by Heydrich's death. Admiral Canaris had fought Heydrich for years, but at his graveside, he wept. "After all, he was a great man. I have lost a friend in him," he said in a choked voice.

Most others mourned not the man himself, but the sense of invulnerability he had personified and sought to guarantee—the casual arrogance of the undisputed winner of the struggle of the fittest in Europe; the ruthless young lion they had all wanted to be. Now, the blond beast seemed for the first time to be an endangered species.

Shortly before his death, Heydrich had indicated that he himself had been afraid—of Himmler, of Bormann, and perhaps even of the Czechs. According to his nephew, Thomas Heydrich, he had told his brother, "I'm not going to get out of it in Prague . . . I won't make it out alive." Now the other Nazi leaders had good reason to share his anxiety. Never original thinkers, they fell back on their usual response to fear—creating more of the same. After the rituals, after Heydrich lay safe in the ground, Hitler and a few of his top associates, including Heinrich Himmler, met privately to choose another memorial to his memory—the complete destruction of the village and people of Lidice (erroneously thought to have provided aid to the resistance).

The plan was appropriately detailed, systematic, and ruthless. The village was burned to the ground. All of the male inhabitants over sixteen were immediately shot. All of the women and most of the children were sent to concentration camps, except for blond children judged capable of Aryanization, who were sent away to adoptive families in Germany. Even the burned bricks and timbers of Lidice were scattered over the ground and then buried by bulldozers beneath it. Finally, roads were obliterated and a river diverted to ensure that the location of the village would be lost forever.

To many Nazis, this was a rather mild reprisal, a mere beginning. But to the outside world, the annihilation of Lidice was a stunning revelation of the essential brutishness of Nazism. (The massacres of the roving action groups in the Soviet Union were not yet public knowledge; the slaughter in killing factories like Auschwitz was yet to come.)

Himmler's attempts to make Reinhard Heydrich a martyr with whom people might feel some sympathy were overwhelmed by the vicious policies Himmler also sanctioned. On his deathbed, Heydrich had not called for reprisals, preferring to talk instead about fate or his father's music or what his wife should do about the children. Yet his name first became widely known to history coupled with that of Lidice, a synonym for evil. Ironically, the atrocities there were the one form of political murder he had not endorsed.

PART VI

AFTERWARD

28

SURVIVING DEATH AND DEFEAT

"I do not let myself give in to fate, and remain firm as iron within its bonds. Only in this way can one master life."

—LINA HEYDRICH

SIX WEEKS AFTER Heydrich's death, his widow gave birth to a daughter, whom she christened Marte. "I held in my arms a child who had no father," she later wrote. Yet the memory of that father remained very much present. Heydrich's successor as Reichsprotektor of Bohemia and Moravia, Kurt Dalüge, had pledged that Reinhard Heydrich would never be forgotten, and for a while the various Nazi leaders vied in remembering him. An SS Gebirgsjäger (Mountain Hunter) Regiment was renamed "Reinhard Heydrich," and so was a "Comradeship Group" at the Nazi Party Leadership School in Nuremberg. "In our hearts he will continue to live," its members promised Lina Heydrich.

Heinrich Himmler asked her advice in helping to find a suitable marker for Heydrich's grave. (They decided on a huge piece of granite from Lina's native island of Fehmarn.) The site of the assassination was already decorated with a bust of Heydrich and was given an honor guard. A commemorative postage stamp was issued bearing his likeness.*

---

* The stamp, depicting Heydrich's death mask, was issued for the Protectorate of Bohemia and Moravia (Böhmen und Mähren) on May 28, 1943, with a face value of 60 heller and a surcharge (usually for charitable purposes) of 440 heller; the total of 500 heller equaled about half a Reichsmark. A limited-edition souvenir sheet was presented to all attendees of Heydrich's funeral. In 1947, a Czech stamp with a face value of 1.20 heller and depicting a shrouded, weeping woman was issued to commemorate "Lidice."

A few months after Heydrich's death, Martin Bormann wrote Lina to say that the Nazi Party still grieved for its "fallen friends": he hoped that it comforted her that the heavy loss "was necessary in the war for the future of our nation."

But Frau Heydrich did not think her husband's death had been necessary.

Later she wrote that as she suffered through the first days of mourning, two things particularly had preyed on her mind. The first was a constantly reiterated question: What did the government in exile gain from her husband's murder? As she saw it, the attack was totally irrational, nothing less than "national suicide" on the part of Czechs. (Significantly, she did not see Heydrich's planned obliteration of the independent state of Czechoslovakia as a national murder.)

I asked her, "Would you say your husband was popular with the Czech population?"

"No doubt about it. It is now generally accepted that the danger my husband represented consisted of his success in pacifying the Czech population . . . That was finally the reason he was murdered . . . All of a sudden the government in exile in London was losing its grip."

Frau Heydrich's views were not unique to her. Much later, the Czech intelligence leader who had planned the assassination gave a similar assessment of his motives—though not of Heydrich's popularity.

The second cause of Lina Heydrich's anguish was the realization that her husband's wider family responsibilities had not ended with his death. "Who will take care of our mother now?" his sister had made a point of asking. Frau Heydrich had not gotten along with either in-law; nevertheless, she felt obligated to try to help them. She had to provide also for her own children.

Once again (as so often in the past), Lina Heydrich saw herself facing poverty and the need to scrimp, save, and plan carefully—something, she emphasized, that Heydrich himself had never done. He never thought about money, she often told me, and had not even bothered to keep his SS insurance policy in order.

Reinhard Heydrich had lived a luxurious and privileged life, based primarily on official perquisites like limousines, airplanes, and opulent offices in both Berlin and Prague. Also at his disposal were the country estate at Jungfern-Breschan, private apartments in Prague Castle and Berlin Police Headquarters, and a hunting lodge near Berlin. Even on his low SS salary, Heydrich had managed to buy a house in Berlin, although he did have to borrow money to pay for his summer cottage on Fehmarn.

As a man to whom few could say no, the chief of the SD and Security Police also received multifarious unofficial favors and gifts—such as the cases of champagne someone sent him to celebrate the fall of Poland and the always-available fun and games at Salon Kitty.

Heinrich Himmler himself, though feverishly anxious to add to the power and wealth of his organization, disapproved of the personal graft openly enjoyed by many Nazi officials. In any case, the spoils of power and war flowed almost entirely into the hands of men; as a widow, Frau Heydrich would certainly be cut off from most of the largesse. In addition, Himmler's offer of legal "protection" ensured his puritanical scrutiny of her finances.

After a trip back to Germany spent trying to "draw the balance" of her new situation, Lina Heydrich decided to sell the house in Berlin. She herself would return to "Breschan," the only place, she told me, where her husband had been happy. It was also the only place where she might expect to earn a reasonable existence for herself and those under her care. Correspondence in the National Archives in Washington suggests that Frau Heydrich herself initiated the idea of staying on at Jungfern-Breschan, and in fact, went through protracted negotiations with Himmler over the issue.

This was not, however, what she told me. "I was like Jackie Kennedy," she said on the night we first met. "I was a sort of national monument." She claimed that the Nazis had wanted her to remain at the country estate as a symbol of the veneration accorded the memory of a great hero.

At that time, I did not know that her husband had asked her to take the children and return to Fehmarn. (The first thing he had said to her on the day he was attacked was, "Think about our children.")

Later in our talks, I asked Lina why she had dared to disobey Reinhard's last request. "Yes," she responded, "he said, '*In general* go back to Fehmarn.' But he didn't say, 'Go *immediately*.' That wasn't possible. The military were quartered there . . . The troops were remaining . . . Now I want to make something for you to eat . . .'"

In her agitation to escape to her refuge, the kitchen, Frau Heydrich had used the familiar "you" (*du*, as opposed to *Sie*). She must have been very shaken indeed; for she had often told me she never addressed anyone—even good acquaintances—with such dangerous familiarity.

Perhaps, I thought, the subject of her staying in Prague had brought the same sad subject to both of our minds: the death of her eldest son, Klaus, in a freak accident, at Jungfern-Breschan in 1943. She had written in her memoirs that Klaus was running to greet an arriving guest, Gruppenführer Richard Hildebrandt, whom he knew as "Uncle" Richard. Somehow the boy had been hit by a truck coming up the driveway, gotten run over, and died from his injuries.

Klaus's brother, Heider, remembered the event somewhat differently: "There was a big truck . . . It had no horn . . . It came down from the hill . . . My brother was on his bike . . . The truck hit him directly . . . It just brushed by me . . ."

Both Lina and Heider told me that no one was truly at fault. The only sinister hand that anyone could discern "behind" the misfortune was that of malevolent fate.

Lina Heydrich wrote in her memoirs that she went a little crazy afterward, and used to retreat to the woods to hide amid piles of brush. But otherwise, she was reluctant to discuss the early years of her widowhood. Even in her book she offers only a few scattered paragraphs.

She does remark that one person was particularly helpful in her recovery from what seems to have been an almost overwhelming despair. Both to help in the management of Breschan and to provide some distraction, Frau Heydrich began training for a certificate in forestry and animal husbandry normally required of all owners of farms of more than a few acres. To help her study, the Reichsführer SS sent his handsome young master of the hunt, Leopold von Zenetti. He was apparently a frequent visitor, who also functioned as a sort of liaison with Himmler.

Lina Heydrich was certainly in need of a friend in Himmler's court. The Reichsführer's main official contact with her now was as guardian of her children. As always, he was punctilious about ceremonial occasions. On the first anniversary of Heydrich's death he wrote to tell her that he had recently "visited Reinhard again," adding, "I will be with you and the children in my thoughts, above all at the still grave in the cemetery." On the first anniversary of Klaus's death, he sent flowers.

He also complied with Frau Heydrich's efforts to protect her family, especially her remaining son. When she received an anonymous threatening letter, he posted additional guards. When she asked him, on security grounds, to exempt Heider from the Labor Service and Hitler Youth, he agreed.

Just to mention Heinrich Himmler's name, Lina Heydrich told me, opened doors that would normally have been slammed shut in a woman's face. In the first year or so after Heydrich's death, the SS helped her locate rare porcelain for her personal collection and arranged for central heating in Jungfern-Breschan, as well as obtaining the property itself as her permanent dwelling place.

This did not mean that Himmler, the leader of "the knightly order of the SS," was consistently chivalric. Lina felt driven to complain to her husband's colleague Karl Hermann Frank that Himmler had promised to help her build a greenhouse and then said he couldn't find the materials. "In other words," Lina sneered, "it is, 'Yes, whatever you wish, but don't ask me for anything.'"

In the absence of Heydrich's moderating presence, his stubbornly outspoken wife and the domineering Reichsführer SS were free to fight for mastery. In one of our interviews, Frau Heydrich tried to convince me that "when my husband died, the old enmity was over," but this was by no means the case. The negotiations over the status of Jungfern-Breschan went on for years, largely because the Nazi leaders were initially willing to cede the estate to Frau Heydrich only if she promised never to remarry. (In refusing to do so, she was not defying her husband's wishes. In a short letter to her, dated 1939 but to be delivered only after his death, he had explicitly counseled her to "give the children a father again" someday.)

Himmler eventually helped Frau Heydrich to acquire Breschan on her own terms—but he wanted something in exchange. The pedantic Reichsführer had waited years for the opportunity to shove Frau Heydrich back into her proper (that is, subordinate) place. As she put it: "Reinhard had always . . . let me have as much freedom as I needed," but Himmler "was horrified when, as formerly, I did what I wanted." Now, shortly after her husband's death, she would have to use all of her formidable will and strength first to maintain Jungfern-Breschan—and then to leave it. Her SS "family" was about to fall to pieces, and Frau Heydrich would be left to her own devices where not even the bravest soldiers wanted to be—at the edge of the Eastern Front, awaiting the onslaught of the Soviet army.

.   .   .

Most men in high positions had several years to observe the specter of German defeat as it drew steadily, inexorably, nearer. As its inevitably became clearer, several of the Nazi leaders reacted in a variety of self-protective ways. Some, such as Walter Schellenberg, now sole chief of the Ausland-SD, was already plotting his own way out of what he called the Nazi "labyrinth." Slowly, he tried to draw the reluctant Reichsführer Himmler into his attempts to negotiate privately with the Allies. By 1944, a great deal of Schellenberg's energy was devoted to these danger-ously treasonous (but also conveniently self-serving) activities.

Yet many presumably clearheaded men who knew the Germans were losing continued to act like victors, while at the same time taking steps to ameliorate what victorious Allies would surely judge to be war crimes. In late 1944, Himmler assembled some of his experts in mass murder to announce the halting of convoys to Auschwitz. Many SS men were glad to cease their "resettlement" work, but Adolf Eichmann was both stunned and resistant, continuing to send thousands of Hun-garian Jews to their death. Eichmann simply could not believe that Hitler had decreed a halt to genocide. (In fact, he hadn't: pushed by Schellenberg, Himmler was negotiating behind Hitler's back, trying to trade the lives of the few remaining Jews for military supplies or Allied goodwill.)

By contrast, most wives of the Nazi leaders were not well placed to gain an overview of the dire situation. Shielded behind the "fortress of the family," protected from the "filth" of daily politics (as well as the intelligence reports circulating fitfully among the men), they could only snatch at whatever shreds of information blew haphazardly over the walls of their sanctuaries.

Perhaps this is one cause of the episodic quality of the few memoirs written by wives of high-ranking Nazis, women like Emmy Göring, Henriette von Schirach—and Lina Heydrich. All of them string together bits of personal experience like pearls in a row, apparently hoping to emerge with a complete necklace of facts, glowing with the luster of historical relevance. "I can only tell you how *we* lived," Frau Heydrich often said, looking both a little embarrassed and a little defiant.

Yet whatever excuses Nazi wives made for their menfolk, they did not hold themselves accountable to the same "soldierly" standards. By

1944, the Fraus Göring, von Schirach, and Heydrich had all experienced moments of open disagreement with Hitler's savage policies. Lina Heydrich, living far from Berlin and completely out of contact with Hitler, tells a story of a sudden awakening to Nazi cruelty. One day she asked Himmler what happened in the concentration camps. He replied that most of them were being converted into handicraft centers. Later on, after she had decided to remain at Breschan, Himmler sent a detachment of Jewish prisoners from the "model camp" of Theresienstadt to help install a new furnace.

They were commanded by SS guards, with "kapos" (privileged prisoners) as their assistants. One afternoon she saw a kapo beating another prisoner with a whip, while the guards stood watching. She asked the SS commander, "a man in the so-called best age of man—and a father of two children," to explain why he tolerated such brutality. He told her the prisoners were receiving relatively good treatment: Theresienstadt was much worse. This was a world, she claimed, "which until then I hadn't known about."

"So that's how the system is built!" she reported thinking. "Reinhard had never said even one word about it to me and had he done so, I would have opposed it. He knew that, and would have banished me to my cupboard, stressing that he would not tolerate any mixing in his service sphere."

This is all Frau Heydrich is willing to say about the camps to which her husband consigned millions of people, except to remark that when the Jewish prisoners were about to leave, she found an anonymous note on her desk begging her to let them stay longer. "I couldn't manage it," she wrote tersely.

Lina Heydrich neglected to mention postwar claims that she had mistreated the prisoners and should herself be tried for war crimes. Her dramatic little story, like those of other Nazi wives who told similar narratives of self-justification, is in fact more important as a statement of personal mythology than of historical truth. The real importance of the oft-told tale of clashing sensibilities between sequestered, "unpolitical" women and the defensive, equivocating husbands is precisely the lack of communication on which the story is based.

On the one hand, wives of powerful men like Göring and Heydrich led privileged lives. Not for them was the normal wartime round of endemic food shortages, long queues to purchase flimsy clothing of ersatz materials, and a lowered standard of living. On the other hand, the "party wives" were still women, barred from both political decision-making and reliable information about the consequences of their husbands' policies.

Men like Göring and Eichmann had made a fatal decision to turn their lives over to Adolf Hitler, and had publicly ratified this choice with an oath of unconditional obedience later used as evidence, either of their damnation (as the Allies thought) or of their exoneration (as they would have it).

The wives of such men had made an equivalent, even though largely implicit, Faustian bargain to give their fate over to their husbands' control. This too provided an easy, all-purpose defense, but it also contained considerable truth. The Nazi leaders, who spent their days conforming to a "framework" of increasing barbarity, needed to return home to a haven of a respectable, normal life within the family fortress. Heydrich had made this explicit when he urged a female audience not to become "hardened"—the word so often used in the SS to describe him.

The question remains: How much did such wives know of the realities of their husbands' official actions? And, specifically: What did Lina Heydrich *know*?

The question also remains without a clear answer. During the first months of the war, Reinhard Heydrich told his wife that he had ordered his Einsatzkommandos to kill the patients of a demolished Polish mental hospital, who had been wandering helplessly around the countryside. His troops were moving on. "What else could he have done?" Frau Heydrich later wrote.

One wonders if she had heard that before the war began, the SS had already granted a similar "mercy death" to hundreds of thousands of German inmates of mental hospitals. When I asked Lina Heydrich directly about specific Nazi racial policies, she usually refused to answer. In her book, however, she claimed to have discussed them, after Heydrich's death, with Bruno Streckenbach, who allegedly told her that his special SS security units were now being used to perform mass shootings in the East. She was appalled. "If he had only known!" she added, flying away, as Reinhard had, from dreadful reality.

Finally, Frau Heydrich herself certainly knew about the annihilation of the village of Lidice, in reprisal for her husband's murder. She had been told that some of the villagers had aided the assassins, and did not object to the massacre. "War has its own rules," she wrote in her memoirs.

Someone concerned to construct a realistic picture of Nazi violence against helpless civilians might have considered the foregoing incidents highly suggestive. But Frau Heydrich's interests lay elsewhere. Like Emmy Göring and Henriette von Schirach, she preferred to see her husband as a brave and obedient patriot, blaming Hitler alone for Nazism's moral and physical collapse.

Unlike such Holocaust survivors as Primo Levi, whose spare prose transmutes unimaginable agony into the clean bones of immutable truth, these three Nazi wives often seemed unable to assign meaning to their own macabre experiences. Amid archetypal scenes of destruction, despair, and folly, only Lina Heydrich seems, generally, to have kept her head. While she had characterized Joseph and Magda Goebbels's decision in the Berlin Führer Bunker to murder their children and then commit suicide as a superhuman act of courage, her own behavior under the stress of defeat reveals a very different attitude. At the beginning of 1945, she wrote to Heinrich Himmler, saying she had heard that a "sunset of the Eastern gods" mood dominated Hitler's headquarters. She asked "the guardian of my children" to explain what was happening:

> Supposedly all the leaders have been given poison capsules containing cyanide. They want to evade everything through death. I would like to know, Reichsführer, what we women are supposed to do. We have not borne our children in order to kill them. If no more protection can be given to us, I intend to migrate westward through the Bohemian woods and the Bavarian woods and to try to get back to my native island.

She told me Himmler never answered her letter.

"Didn't you feel angry at him?" I asked.

Instead, she got angry with *me:* "The men were fighting a war! They had other things to do besides worry about women!"

It was just as well that Lina Heydrich had already proved her ability to look after herself. As mistress of Jungfern-Breschan, she had enjoyed a relative freedom from constant masculine supervision, and indeed, had men of her own to supervise. In 1944, Himmler sent her some more prisoners from the camps. This time they were Jehovah's Witnesses.

Apparently, the prisoners behaved well enough to prompt Himmler himself to write a letter praising her handling of these new assistants and agreeing to release them into her custody.

Around the same time, she also reached an agreement with another SS man, Himmler's handsome master of the hunt, Leopold von Zenetti. In January 1945, they decided to get married. Frau Heydrich was thirty-one when Reinhard Heydrich died. Everyone agrees that she was an attractive, vivacious woman. "*Eine lustige Frau*," Bruno Streckenbach called her, a woman who likes to enjoy herself. In her memoirs, she describes Zenetti as helpful and patient; in the one time we talked about him, she spoke not of joys of love, but the need to provide security for her children.

January 1945 was not a propitious time for attaining such security. The once invulnerable German armies were now outnumbered, ill-provisioned, and in retreat. Leopold von Zenetti was transferred to the front. All around her, men were disappearing into the vortex of war, and women were fleeing back to Germany, but Frau Heydrich stood her ground.

According to Heider Heydrich,

> There were a lot of German families that left Prague very, very early and she said no, we came here, we have lived with the Czechs and we should not leave them alone before it is one minute to twelve, because they have accepted us, we have accepted them, we are living here with them and therefore she was not really very willing to leave.

Heider estimated that her little refugee community numbered around three hundred people: "Mostly women with nowhere else to go. It was not sponsored by the state, only by my mother."

In this emergency, Lina's family proved of little help. Her brother was fighting in Russia, her parents were far away on Fehmarn, and her in-laws had troubles of their own. The previous November, Reinhard Heydrich's younger brother, Heinz, had committed suicide while serving with his unit on the Eastern Front. To this day, no one in his family knows quite why he shot himself. His son, Peter Thomas, thinks his father had been "a broken man" after reading the hundred-page letter Heydrich left following his own death. Although Peter Thomas, himself never saw the letter, he speculated that it revealed either "that there really was Jewish blood in the family, or . . . what had really been going on in the Third Reich."

Momentarily overwhelmed by grief, Peter Thomas's mother sent him to stay for a few months with his aunt, Lina. "In January of 1945 I came back to Prague by myself," he wrote. "By then I was thirteen. By then all the fairy-tale part was gone."

As the oldest surviving male Heydrich, Peter Thomas was still treated with ludicrous deference by Himmler's black guard: "A tall SS man would always walk ahead of me, to protect me. We went to a movie theater to view the documentary of [Reinhard Heydrich's funeral]. A complete movie theater just for me . . . This was not real."

"I did not like my aunt," Peter Thomas told me. He admitted, "When my father killed himself, Tante Lina immediately came to my mother's assistance. And that was not something she had to do."

Still, he thought she was "not affectionate." If the children spoke out of turn at dinner, Frau Heydrich made them leave the table. Sometimes she also beat them. And the "worst memory" he had of her was once when she had gone on horseback to inspect some work that prison laborers had done in her garden, she had tried to beat several of them with her riding crop when they had "not immediately" jumped out of her way.

In March 1945, Heinrich Himmler passed through Jungfern-Breschan with some of his SS troops. On his way to take over the hopeless German defense in the East, he had achieved his lifelong dream of military command just at the moment when, in Lina's view, his mental and physical resources were collapsing. As the Reich disintegrated, Himmler vacillated between competing fantasies of fighting to the death or working with the Allies as police leader of a new Europe. Yet Frau Heydrich still thought this shattered man might help her and her children.

She told me he remembered the (unanswered) letter she had sent him two months earlier. Now, he praised her plan to trek home by herself through the Bohemian woods. He advised her to look for edible mushrooms in the forests, and to pack her belongings with hay instead of straw.

"What did he mean?" I asked her. Frau Heydrich retorted bitterly, "For the horses to eat!" For all his power, the dreaded empire leader of the SS could offer nothing else. For Lina, this was "the moment of total capitulation": "I knew then that we had to be ready for everything entirely alone."

Nevertheless, she assembled the women of Jungfern-Breschan so that Himmler might bid them farewell. Afterward, she told them prophetically, "We have seen this man for the last time in our lives."

From then on, the stories she tells are of friends, acquaintances, and servants—almost all female—banding together to help one another. She told me that thirty thousand German women had been left defenseless in Prague. In Lina's view, most of them were content to wait passively for the arrival of a new set of uniformed men to tell them what to do, comforting themselves with the thought that they had "done nothing evil." Enraged, she lectured them, "It's enough, now, just to be German!"

Frau Heydrich began to plan her escape, but many of her charges still refused to realize the seriousness of their situation. In the face of this "resistance in my house," she finally told them they had to leave: "If you won't listen to reason, I will not be responsible for your deaths!"

By then, Prague was teeming with desperate refugees, a mixture of civilians and ragtag German troops, retreating westward before the Soviet army. The railroad stations were jammed; people fought for every seat and clung to the sides of the trains trying to get a handhold. The roads were choked with military vehicles and lines of refugees. All the while, Allied planes attacked at will.

In April 1945, Lina Heydrich finally left Jungfern-Breschan. She departed, not in a horse-drawn wagon as Himmler had assumed, and not, as she had implied, without the aid of "men and institutions," but in an elaborate caravan that she had helped to organize—in secret.

Heider Heydrich told me his mother had not informed the children until the day of departure, and the Czech people didn't know, "because she did not want to show them that we wanted to leave." Only Heider's teacher, a Frau Schilling, was in on the plans. These must have been quite elaborate since three different groups of people were involved, each with some form of transport. One was a group of cars to carry food and medical supplies for the Czechs who were leaving their country. Another involved transport for the Germans who had lived in Breschan. The third was a vehicle for Lina's family.

This "car" was actually a trailer built on the body of a truck requisitioned from the police. It had beds and an area for cooking. (Stored in a secret compartment was Vietze's immense picture of Heydrich in his SS uniform.)

The little convoy was helped along by members of a German Army unit protecting the border between Bohemia-Moravia and Bavaria. On April 20, the frontier post passed into American hands. Frau Heydrich's group had just made it through. "We were really the last ones who left without being attacked by the Czechs or by the Russians," Heider said.

This does not mean that they weren't attacked at all. Traveling in close proximity to a military convoy, they were pursued by British fighter planes. One day during an air attack, Frau Heydrich and her children hid in another vehicle. Only after an afternoon spent listening to the muffled sound of falling bombs did they learn their hiding place had been filled with explosives.

After a few days, the little convoy arrived at Lake Tegernsee, in Bavaria, where Frau Heydrich's group was interned by the American army, in a special camp for families of Nazi leaders. One day an American officer in a big Mercedes stopped to ask Heider directions. Then he kindly offered the ten-year-old boy a lift home. When they arrived, Heider behaved as he always had when thanking an officer: "I raised my hand and said, 'Heil Hitler!' Of course, I hadn't thought where I was. The officer just laughed. 'My boy,' he said, 'forget about that. You don't need that anymore!' "

The war was over.

In Germany itself, the formal end of the war was scarcely noticed by many civilians, benumbed as they had become by the long grinding years of war and disintegration. Every memoirist of that time notes the profound apathy and despair felt by the survivors of the ruined Reich. Even people who yearned for the defeat of the Nazis had become physically and spiritually exhausted long before the fighting stopped. The resulting pervasive anomie did not find expression, however, because any sign of "defeatism" brought immediate punishment. The Austrian-American writer Ingeborg Day (*9½ Weeks*, *Ghost Waltz*) recalled that on the day of the surrender not one person in her family said a word about it.

Yet after enduring years of forced overtime work, severe food and housing shortages, increasingly intrusive police surveillance, saturation bombings, and annihilating losses on the battlefield, most Germans longed for nothing more than the end of "total" war.

The combined effect of invasion and Hitler's scorched-earth policy had destroyed harvests throughout Europe; coal supplies had vanished, roads were often impassable, and electric power only sporadic. With the entire continent facing the danger of famine, the winning countries ruled that the guilty losers should pay the highest price in suffering.

Indeed, in the first few years after the war, many Allied leaders did not really care what became of the Germans. Stunned by the ghastly evidence of mass murder in the death camps—only now becoming widely known and openly photographed—few among the victors bothered to differentiate the SS from other Nazis, or the Nazis as a group from the rest of the populace, including the many millions who had voted against Hitler. To many, all Germans were regarded as somehow tainted, perhaps with a fatal hereditary flaw.

In the earliest American occupation edicts, any fraternizing with the local inhabitants, even patting the head of a German child, was strictly prohibited. At borders throughout the country, signs were posted: "Here ends the civilized world. You are entering Germany."

Germans were forbidden to mail letters or to use the telephone. Their property could be requisitioned at will, often with less than an hour's notice. (Most of the people evicted were, of course, women, old people, and children.) They could be dragooned for forced labor, imprisoned, or shot with no possibility of redress. The British historian Douglas Botting has described the country, with its powerless inhabitants, deprived of civil rights and publicly reviled, as "like a concentration camp." Like such prisoners, they were also slowly starving. In July 1945, the Berlin food ration had fallen to eight hundred calories a day. Ration cards were provided for various groups, depending on the amount of hard labor the recipient provided. All housewives were in the lowest category—cynical Berliners called it "the death card"—even though some of them, the "Rubble women" (*Trümmerfrauen*), were the ones now clearing away rubble with their bare hands. When I asked Lina Heydrich what had happened to her husband's mother after the war, she replied with sudden venom, "She died of a hunger edema. She starved to death! Because she bore the name Heydrich, they let her die! They let her starve!"

Elisabeth Heydrich had fled in 1945 from Jungfern-Breschan to Dresden (in the Soviet zone), but, I discovered, starvation among the older generation was widespread everywhere. Even "good Germans" died in droves. In Hamburg during the month of October 1946 alone, there were a hundred thousand hospitalized cases of hunger edema (swelling associated with the late stages of famine disease).

Only in one area did the immense discrepancies between victor and vanquished somewhat diminish: almost everyone on both sides played the black market.

Very often, for Germans this was the only means to survival. Most passengers on German trains were urban dwellers going to the country to look for food. Without these exhausting trips, on which they traded heirlooms, cameras, cigarettes, and clothes for a piece of meat or a few kilos of fat, many of the travelers would not have stayed alive. As it was, the death rate in the second year of peace, 1946–47—marked by the failure of the autumn harvest and one of the coldest winters in European history—approached that of the Thirty Years' War three hundred years earlier. A new disease sprang up in which people seemed to grow old overnight for no clearly identifiable cause. When some couples were reunited after a few years' absence, neither member even recognized the other.

In this climate of continual dire necessity, many people learned to make choices they would never have considered before the war. Most heads of household were now women, taking over for men who had died in battle or been taken prisoner. In an economy now reduced to barter, one of the few commodities a woman had to trade was herself. It has been estimated that one-sixth of the *total* population of Berlin was engaged in some form of prostitution in the year or so immediately after the war.

Their customers were the men in new uniforms replacing the Nazis as rulers of their lives. Despite Allied directives, fraternization soon became so commonplace that the word *frat* became a widely used synonym for sexual intercourse. British soldiers were so successful in trading their luncheon cheese sandwiches for sex that they named them "frat sandwiches." In the American zone, 90 percent of the troops were estimated to have "gone fratin'."

To fraternization was added widespread financial corruption. In the black market, an American GI might make $6,000 or $7,000 a year trading his standard ration of candy and cigarettes. (By contrast, the normal salary for a professor at the small U.S. college where my father taught was $3,000 a year.)

The exploitive nature of much Allied/German contact caused deep concern among the occupying authorities. Even some of the victims of Nazism fell prey to the prevailing demoralization: former camp inmates and stateless refugees joined with deserters from both the Allied and German armies—including the SS—to form armed bands of robbers that terrorized Berlin. At that time, the former capital of the New Order had the highest crime rate in the world.

The harsh vicissitudes of life in occupied Germany form the essential background against which Lina Heydrich's few terse pronouncements on her postwar experience must be judged. As the American sociology professor Hans Speier has summarized the situation, "In the first years after the war, the Germans suffered severe deprivation: ruins, insufficient housing, a starvation diet, demoralization, widespread misery and the influx of millions of expellees and refugees."

This last problem was of special importance to Lina Heydrich. When she fled from Jungfern-Breschan, she became caught up in what has been called "the greatest ethnic displacement—or involuntary migration—of human beings in modern times." An estimated 16.5 million Germans were expelled from their ancestral homes in the ethnically mixed lands of central Europe. In 1941, Edvard Beneš, president of the Czech government in exile, had proposed that if Germany lost the war, everyone of German origin should be forced out of Czechoslovakia. In the aftermath of brutal war, all the other countries of what would become the Soviet Bloc followed suit.

Once again, trains full of miserable, racially "cleansed" people began to move across Europe. The pitiful state of the deportees reminded the British philosopher Bertrand Russell of "Belsen all over again," but the parallels to Nazi behavior were not limited to the trains. In Czechoslovakia, bands of youths and teenagers formed a "Revolutionary Guard" that imitated the atrocities of the SS, drowning babies in latrines while their mothers watched, beating women to death, systematically breaking the arms and legs of the men. The concentration camp of Theresienstadt, which Heydrich had cynically created to deflect Red Cross attention away from the death camps, was taken over and filled with German youths and children. H. G. Adler, a German-Jewish author and former inmate of Theresienstadt, noted how "frighteningly familiar" it all sounded: "only the word 'Jews' had been changed to 'Germans.'"

Edvard Beneš, once again Czech president, dismissed the whole thing as "some, very few, excesses"—exactly the sort of language the Nazis had always used. At least 2 million Germans died from these "excesses"—something many Westerners ignored, or refused to believe. But whatever the attitude of the outside world, the Germans, of course, were painfully aware of their dramatic plunge into the netherworld of helpless victims of other people's power. The would-be master race now played the parts of desperate émigré, humiliated servant, and wretched prisoner—roles they had once accorded to presumed inferiors.

Even before the war, an SD officer had told the writer Lili Hahn, "If the situation is ever reversed, people like myself will be hanging from the lampposts down there on the street." But at the war's end, few such men were around to receive their just deserts. The former male "heads of the household" were known to their children primarily as pictures hanging on living room walls. Thus, it was soldiers' wives attempting to cope on their own who were the ones to tell their children, "No non-sense now. Losers can't be choosers. They're the ones who give the orders now. Better get used to that, and fast." Later that same woman said to the first American soldier she met, "The fatherland is finished, and so are we. Such is war. You're the victors . . . We have nothing to hope for."

Frau Heydrich told me much the same thing: "It's your world now. I no longer understand it. You are the conquerors now."

The words commonly used to describe this perception of absolute defeat was *Stunde null,* or "hour zero." I found few Germans willing to discuss with an American this hard time in their lives—particularly after they discovered I was studying the SS. For her part, Lina Heydrich told me brusquely, "No! I won't talk about it. We have suffered too much to parade our troubles before you!"

What little she had to say about her experiences at the war's end appeared in *Life with a War Criminal,* the memoir she wrote for a Ger-man audience. Despite the title, she devotes considerable space to her efforts to live without Reinhard Heydrich, and to get out from under the shadow he was to cast over the last forty years of her life. (Perhaps she decided on the title because she never succeeded in escaping it. Other possible titles, she told me, were "My Real Life," or "My Hard Life.")

After Frau Heydrich and her little band of women and children arrived with their trailer at the village of Rottach-Egern, in Bavaria, on the Tegernsee, they were allowed to go no farther. There she encountered other "party wives" or "Nazi women"—both terms are hers—including her old friend Frieda Wolff, ex-wife of Himmler's chief of staff, Karl Wolff, who was living, as Lina put it, in a "henhouse." In this strange new atmosphere, Frau Heydrich wrote, "impossible" things began to happen. She was denounced for storing illegal flour in her trailer and had to submit to a "house search." She says nothing was found, but to the widow of the chief of the Security Police and the SD this seemed an alarming portent of things to come.

Soon the occupying troops arrived, and the party wives watched the local inhabitants greet them as liberators, only to have them steal their wristwatches in exchange. Disquieting rumors began to sweep through the little camp of interned women. When Frau Heydrich heard that Lída Baarová, the Czech actress who had been a mistress of Joseph Goebbels, was about to be "delivered up" to the new government of Czechoslovakia, she decided not to sit around fretting any longer. Instead, she gathered her resolve and went in person to the local government officials and requested a permit to travel back to Fehmarn. Once they found out whose wife she had been, they refused permission.

Later she was to write that it was at Rottach-Egern that she "witnessed for the first time, the rebirth of Reinhard Heydrich." The man whom Hitler had praised as one of the greatest heroes of the Reich had "with a turn of the hand been transformed into a criminal. That word, war 'criminal' . . . has pursued me since then, wherever I have tried to settle down."

Her husband, now suddenly "alive" after three years, was being "made responsible for things about which I was hearing something precise for the first time. That we, my children and myself, are now being pushed to the reckoning as his representatives, I take as a sign of the new times."

Nevertheless, as she seems to have done throughout her life, Frau Heydrich quickly began to adapt to the new era. She was aided greatly by what she called—in quotation marks—"good luck." As if out of nowhere two demobilized soldiers showed up at Tegernsee, claiming to have been sent there by an old school chum of Lina's to be placed at her disposal. Understandably suspicious at first, Lina observed them carefully for several days before deciding to enter "the greatest speculative lottery of my life": to these comparative strangers she gave her trailer, most of her possessions, and her two oldest children, Heider and Silke. The soldiers promised to see that they would all arrive safely in Fehmarn. In the meantime, a former Hitler Youth leader who had also appeared on the scene volunteered to take Lina's remaining valuables—which she says were mostly cigarettes, already worth more than money on the black market—back to Fehmarn concealed in a wooden leg he had worn since losing a limb in the war.

At this point, in a simultaneous stroke of "luck," a young woman from Fehmarn, Lisa Hunger, showed up at Rottach-Egern, having heard of Lina's circumstances and "of course" knowing "who Reinhard Heydrich was." Together the women concocted a daring plan based on the approximate similarity of their names, at least for graphical purposes. Using Lisa's own traveling papers as a model, and a hard-boiled egg as a rubber stamp, the two forged realistic-looking documents giving Lina the same mobility.

Fräulein Hunger then fled to Hamburg with two-year-old Marte Heydrich, whom she passed off as her illegitimate child. Lina Heydrich, now alone and equipped with false papers, borrowed a bicycle and sped away herself. Generally, she traveled by train, using the bike as a prop to bluster her way through the numerous Allied checkpoints where her papers might be carefully perused. Carrying a mesh bag full of cucumbers and lettuce, she pretended to be a local housewife on a domestic errand. "Please, I have no time," she said in English as she dashed by. The harried Allied soldiers allowed her to pass—eighteen different times.

Lina's "lottery" gamble—which was actually an investment in female bonding, Nazi camaraderie, and male chivalry toward "helpless" women—paid off. Lina was reunited with Marte in Hamburg and then managed to hitchhike to Fehmarn, where her two older children were waiting.

Everyone was safe, and the family was once again reunited, but Lina and Marte had not come through their flight unscathed. They had found little food and had spent nights in large, crowded rooms filled with pails of excrement, listening to the sounds of people making love and quarreling. Rarely were they treated as human beings, Frau Heydrich notes in her book. When her little daughter, who had spent her whole life in a "castle," tumbled down a railroad embankment, she hadn't cried or complained, convincing Lina that she too understood the "new situation."

Like many others, they were now home but temporarily homeless. The local British commander had moved into her house, so Frau Heydrich and her three children stayed with her parents in their sturdy two-story home enclosed in a small garden, on a quiet street in the ancient town of Burg-on-Fehmarn.

In a time of desolation and near anarchy, this would seem to have been a peaceful refuge. Indeed, when I saw it more than three decades later, the little house looked both comfortable and charming. But Lina Heydrich insisted it had actually been a sort of peacetime battleground. As she saw it, her troubles were only beginning: after 1945, whenever she tried to hide away from her husband's dreadful political legacies, they would, like the Furies, sooner or later alight to torment her.

After settling into her new lodgings, Lina Heydrich decided to register with the occupation authorities, concluding that "only a fool" would think she could slip into Fehmarn unnoticed. This seems an odd decision for someone who had just used deception and duplicity to escape from the Americans. Yet, in the end, it proved a shrewd decision.

A few weeks after Lina had announced her presence, a British officer appeared at her door. At first, she thought he had come to arrest her, but instead, he wanted to examine her papers. Frau Heydrich seized the moment to regale him with a humorous account of her recent clandestine adventures, using an exaggerated style she described as *blumenreich* ("flowery"; literally, "rich with flowers"). At the end of her tale, both she and the officer burst out laughing. "We don't want to lock you up," he said, as he left. "The Americans *would* have arrested me," she told me, still laughing. "They were much more intrusive!"

Frau Heydrich's "loose tongue" and knack for vivid imagery had caused her trouble in Nazi Germany, but they proved adaptive at Hour Zero, and may have spared her the many months of extremely unpleasant jail time. Yet she wrote that she felt a little sorry to have missed jail, for in other respects, "I was truly spared nothing." "Living from hand to mouth became our motto." There was no coal, so for warmth, she burned their fruit trees, "something like sawing off the branch on which we sat."

Despite such challenges, she tried "to live a normal life without political accent," but the more "un-politically" she behaved, "the more politically I was assessed by others."

Under the impact of the Nuremberg trials, the newspapers were now full of discussions of "the mass murderer, Heydrich": "People who never knew that he had a wife and children, now let out their hatred on us. Most of them did not know that he had been dead for years . . . We had to wear the mark of the murderer on our foreheads."

Frau Heydrich told me many of her oldest friends now crossed the street to avoid meeting her. Another former friend deliberately sat next to her at a gathering at the local museum—but only so he could ask her what it was like to be married to a murderer. Total strangers, some German and some not, would knock on her door, saying they just wanted to see what the wife of Hangman Heydrich looked like.

Yet it was not such "simple people" who drew her ire, but government officials misusing their "power words" to harm the innocent. Her prime target was the regional British commander, a man she called only by his local nickname, "Herr Torture." When I asked her what he had done, she spoke vaguely of wounded men left lying unattended, perhaps to die. It never seemed to cross her mind that her own husband had spoken power words resulting in certain death for millions of people.

She did not, however, shrink from criticizing his former comrades in the SS, including such close associates and former aides to her husband as Walter Schellenberg and Hans Neumann. The reason was not their behavior during the Third Reich, but afterward at Nuremberg, where the International Military Tribunal held court from October 1945 to November 1946. Although much of Nuremberg's populace expressed indifference to the trials—"They should be shot right away," or "I have other worries," were what many said—Lina Heydrich felt passionately about the proceedings, for she realized they had the power to destroy her dream of living a normal life. Like a revolving beacon in a high tower, they were to cast a far-reaching light, both backward into the recent past, and forward, far into the future. Lina claims Hans Neumann had told her that since her husband was already dead, the other SS leaders had decided to place the blame for everything on Heydrich, as he could not defend himself.

She was enraged: "I said to Neumann, tell Schellenberg that we are still alive! That we must pay the penalty if the Allies decide that lacking the major person, they will seize the next best!" Lina Heydrich felt that, unlike the men, she could not just "dive into a hole" and attempt to save herself. "After all, I bore the *name*," she would repeat to me, a constant refrain in her threnody of Hour Zero.

Frau Heydrich felt that after Nuremberg, she was constantly singled out, barred from rights accorded everyone else. For the remaining thirty-eight years of her life, she fought back.

When she heard that new laws would soon be promulgated entitling war widows to pensions from the German treasury, she applied to get one. But there was a catch: the recipient could not have been a "beneficiary of the Nazi regime." Ignoring the years of hunting lodges, suburban villas, and apartments in Prague Castle, Lina felt that since she *now* was virtually penniless, she hadn't benefited. "I am Reinhard Heydrich's widow—otherwise nothing!" she wrote, in furious oversimplification.

Following other attempts to secure her existence—including another unsuccessful attempt at relations with Leopold von Zenetti, the SS officer to whom she had become engaged in 1944, as well as various legal and semilegal attempts to make the most of her poor circumstances—she somehow weathered the worst of the immediate postwar period. Eventually she found an opportunity to benefit from the thaw in anti-Nazi attitudes brought about by the distraction of the Soviet-American Cold War.

In September 1949, the Nazi opponent Konrad Adenauer became the first chancellor of the new Federal Republic of West Germany. In 1953, after undergoing bureaucratic rites of "de-Nazification," Lina Heydrich was allowed to return to her summer house. This enabled her to begin a successful career as the proprietress of a small pension, catering to a yeasty mix of summer tourists, people she had known from "the old days," and occasional scholarly analysts of Nazism. That at least was her situation when I met her, although Bruno Streckenbach said in an interview that the process was actually much more arduous than she ever indicated, either to me or in print:

I have visited Lina Heydrich several times since I returned from [imprisonment in] Russia. It is incredible how hard this woman has worked. She had absolutely nothing. How was she supposed to live? She had to work. And so she ran some kind of fast-food restaurant in a seaside resort, where she did everything. She cooked, served, and who knows what else. She worked like a horse. And when that was not enough, she looked after the kitchen on one of the ferryboats.

Frau Heydrich's hard-won success paved the way for a completely "legal" life—indeed for a life of frequent litigation on her own behalf. In 1953, the same year she regained possession of her summer house, Lina also reapplied for a war widow's pension. This time, the Schleswig district insurance office approved her request, awarding her a monthly stipend of 195 marks. Since Reinhard Heydrich was murdered in wartime by enemy commandos, it could be argued that he had, in effect, fallen in battle. But the question, as posed by one German newspaper, was really *which* war: "that of the German infantryman or Hitler's perfidious racial war?"

The last thing the leaders of the new West German democracy wanted was to sanction the career of Heinrich Himmler's right-hand man. They sought a swift reversal of the earlier decision. Frau Heydrich thereupon hired a lawyer to defend her right to the money. Though the venue was a small local court, the lawsuit touched off a swirl of controversy making headlines all over Germany and propelling both Reinhard and Lina Heydrich back into the limelight.

Because the Nazis' "people's law" had pointedly discriminated among various plaintiffs according to their "political reliability" (determined in the last resort by Reinhard Heydrich), Germany's new laws had been explicitly designed to forestall any consideration of the character of the victims. Personal "unworthiness" or "extralegal considerations" were no longer thought relevant. But was "the Heydrich case" to be an exception? Must the wife and family of a criminal pay the price for his crimes? In a country filled with war widows, these were not negligible issues.

Finally, the federal government summoned an expert witness, Professor Michael Freund, of the University of Kiel. He testified extensively on Heydrich's activities as chief of the Security Police, chief of the SD, and chairman of the Wannsee Conference. In Freund's judgment, Heydrich was a "professional criminal of Luciferian magnitude." It would thus be a travesty of justice to subsume his exceptional case under a law designed for the settling of routine social-insurance claims. In any case, Freund argued, Heydrich's killing was the murder of a tyrant, not an enemy officer: to claim otherwise was to deprive the assassination of its moral significance as a precursor to the judgment at Nuremberg.

Although Freund argued forcefully that there was a world of difference between an ordinary German soldier and a political figure like Heydrich, the case dragged on for two years. Unable to decide whether his death had been an act of war, the court finally took the unusual step of sending to the United States for additional evidence from—of all sources—Heydrich's own Gestapo.

A private archive in New York City contained the final police report concerning the nature of their boss's death. Then, in a last ironic twist, the secret investigators were asked to corroborate their findings. The new expert witnesses said the assassins had carried British guns, used a grenade made only in Britain, and traveled to Czechoslovakia in an English military plane. The policemen stated that the aim of the assassination was to spread civil unrest and thus to disrupt the Czech munitions industry that was so vital to the German war effort. In other words, they were arguing that Heydrich had been killed wearing the hat of Reichsprotektor of Bohemia and Moravia, rather than as SS general or Nazi police leader. In the end, the court agreed, once more awarding Frau Heydrich her pension, and explicitly stating that the case could not be appealed again. In the verdict, the judge reasoned, "While it would certainly be conceivable for such an act of violence to occur with no connection to the Second World War . . . the event as actually played out flowed together with the events of the war and, at least to an essential degree, was an act of the military war leadership."

Freund denounced the judgment as resting on a "fairy tale" invented by the Gestapo, but this time, Heydrich's minions were right. General František Moravec, the Czech resistance leader in London, eventually admitted the murder was intended to provoke massive Nazi reprisals and subsequent Czech resistance—a plan aided throughout by Britain's MI6. Heydrich's war crimes had had little to do with it.

As a lesson in morale building, his death thus proved of dubious value. Indeed, the real, profoundly disturbing lesson of Heydrich's life and career—that he was *both* a war criminal *and* an effective bureaucratic administrator, both a radical political leader and a pragmatic "technocrat of power" playing by rules devised by others—got totally lost in the dispute over the indemnity paid to his wife.

The legal judgment was greeted by a storm of protest in the German press. "Heydrich, the Innocent Boy" blazed one satirical headline. "Is the Bloodbath of Lidice Forgotten?" asked another paper, which printed a cartoon showing Frau Heydrich dressed in a Nazi Frauenshaft uniform, carrying a huge bag of money labeled "state pension for husband's heroic acts."

. . .

At the beginning of the case, everyone had been careful to claim that Frau Heydrich, herself, was not a factor to be considered in any final judgment. Then, in an article written to protest the outcome, Professor Freund speculated, "We do not know and do not want to know how she views herself today in relation to her husband." However, he wrote that it would be "psychologically interesting" to ponder "the spiritual condition of a person who would turn for her protection to the very notions of law and justice which her husband trampled underfoot." A little later, he described her behavior as "insolent."

From this time on, Frau Heydrich no longer went out of her way to avoid publicity. An avowed enemy, Heydrich's adjutant, Kurt Pomme, speculated that she loved being the center of attention. A good friend, Bruno Streckenbach, said,

> She appears cold and hard to outsiders. Many gathered from that [that] she had had influence on Heydrich on official matters. But that is nonsense. She was not permitted to have any say in official matters. Which, by the way, does not keep her nowadays from gladly giving out information on official matters of the Sicherheitsdienst headquarters. I may as well warn you [of this], if you ever meet her.

For her part, Lina Heydrich told me that people would "appear out of nowhere" to ask her opinion or investigate her private life. A valet of Hitler's came to inquire if he should write his memoirs. (She told him she wasn't pleased with the way her own book had turned out.) She also claimed that writers for the German magazine *Stern* visited her, then published an article asserting she was so rich she owned a stable of horses on Fehmarn: "Everyone here could *see* this wasn't true! Around here they think everyone lies, no one tries to tell the truth!"

The combination of her own actions and the public's continual interest in the leaders of Nazism soon locked Lina into her most enduring role—that of Reinhard Heydrich's obstreperous widow.

By the time I met her, in 1976, she had adapted to her position as a semipublic figure, relishing the visits of historians, and fearing the attacks of "journalists." I was something else, a category she couldn't fathom, a female with whom she could freely talk as one woman to another—or could she? As we both wrestled with this issue, safe in her postwar stronghold on isolated, insular Fehmarn, she had a chance, for the last time in her life, to attempt to "draw the balance" of her experiences.

AFTERWORD

by Christopher Lehmann-Haupt

Lina von Osten Heydrich died on August 14, 1985, at age seventy-four, on her island home of Fehmarn, where she is buried. She died only two years after her final talks with Nancy Dougherty, during which she declared her support of what she termed "migration" as a form of warfare, and she divulged her self-excusing dark belief that history would ultimately judge and justify the cutthroat Darwinism implicit in National Socialism and her husband's brutally criminal career.

So, she did not live to witness several historical developments that ran counter to her views. Perhaps most prominent among these was that far from lunging at one another's throats, the countries of Europe would complete the European Union. This was begun in the 1950s, with the Treaties of Paris (1951) and Rome (1957), and finalized with the Maastricht Treaty (1992), which formally incorporated the European Community, with a single currency, the euro, and comprising, by July 2013, twenty-eight member countries.

Moreover, the forces compelling this unification brought about another event that might well have shocked Lina: the collapse of the Berlin Wall, in November 1989. This led to the eventual unification of Germany itself, with long-term results powerful enough to resist successfully, at least for the time being, such counter-unifying forces as Russia's rise again as a hostile autocracy under Vladimir Putin, as well as the anti-European nationalist movements that led the United Kingdom to leave the EC, and the United States, under President Donald Trump, to show signs of wavering in its long-standing commitment as an ally.

What's more, Lina posthumously proved herself ironically correct in denying the resemblance of Germany's extreme right-wing political groups to "people from the old days," as she put it. ("And if there were even one of them, I assure you, I would know," she told Nancy Dougherty.)

While Germany's new right-wing extremists often declared their allegiance to Adolf Hitler's Nazis, especially in their opposition to non-German racial strains, they have so far been unable to achieve significant electoral success, even despite the cyber-meddling of Putin-inspired Russian hackers.

Had she lived to see the twenty-first century, Frau Heydrich might well have claimed vindication of her worldview in Israel's expanding occupation of the West Bank of the Jordan River. But for better or worse this movement has been inspiring louder and louder condemnation throughout the Middle East and the world, even among Israelis on the left, and Jews of the diaspora. And however repugnant their actions, they have not set out to kill an entire race of people.

Finally, while there appears to be no surviving evidence that Lina ever even mentioned the subject with Dougherty, she might well, in keeping with her theory of history's shifting judgments, have pointed to the changed attitude toward Germany's guilt provoked by growing tensions brought on by the Cold War between the United States and the Soviet Union.

She could legitimately have cited the former Nazis among the 1,600 German scientists who came to the U.S. in 1945 as part of Operation Paperclip, designed to help the U.S. compete technologically with its Cold War antagonist. Chief among them was of course Wernher von Braun, the former Nazi rocket scientist who ran the V-2 rocket program at Peenemünde (coincidentally on another island in the Baltic) and ended up leading the American rocket program to put a human on the moon. But many putative war criminals who contributed far less than Braun to the American cause have been reported to have slipped into the U.S. and escaped the judgment of history altogether.

As for how forcefully whatever Frau Heydrich and the legacy of her husband stood for has lived on in her surviving family members, while it's impossible to judge what psychological burdens they may be carrying, the sins of the father do not appear to have been visited on the children.

Or on Reinhard's brother, for that matter, at least in the sense of sharing the same capacity for evil. Heinz Siegfried Heydrich was born September 29, 1905, a year and a half after Reinhard. For a time, he appeared to follow his brother's path, however distantly. When Reinhard was assassinated, Heinz was a lieutenant in the SS, the publisher of the military newspaper *Die Panzerfaust*, and very proud of his older brother, to whom he was so close that frequently when he asked Reinhard to release someone he knew whom the Gestapo had arrested, Reinhard would comply immediately. Heinz was a fervent admirer of Hitler, having joined the Nazi Party even before his older brother knew what it was.

Yet despite their evident closeness, Heinz was altogether different, at least in the views of both Lina and Heinz's son Peter Thomas (1931–2000). While Lina described him to Dougherty as "a sunny boy," she considered him a misfit who never lived up to his potential and committed suicide because of his psychological conflicts. In contrast, Peter Thomas, who became a well-known cabaret performer, recalls his father as a fun-loving, stocky extrovert in contrast to his brother's angular aloofness, a piano-playing, joke-telling life of Gestapo parties, where his brother, after asking him to liven things up, would stand by, skeptically

Reinhard Heydrich (left) and his younger brother, Heinz, circa 1918, ages fourteen and twelve, respectively. Two and a half years after Reinhard's murder, Heinz took his own life out of fear of Gestapo reprisal for his helping Jews escape Germany with papers he forged as publisher of the soldiers' newspaper *Die Panzerfaust*.

withdrawn. Shortly after Reinhard's death, in June 1942, Heinz, while on leave in Berlin from the battlefront, took possession of his brother's personal papers. Following a night of reading them, his wife saw him burning them and judged him to be severely disturbed by their contents.

As Dougherty reports, Heinz's son Peter at first blamed Heinz's suicide in November 1944 on his discovery from reading the papers of his brother's role in the Holocaust. But, it turned out, as a result of what he learned from that night of reading, Heinz undertook to save as many Jews as he could, using the publication he edited, along with its printing press, to create false identities for families to escape to safety. When a commission led by a state attorney announced an investigation of the newspaper's editorial staff, Heinz Heydrich shot himself to death, presumably to protect his family from the Gestapo. It turned out still later, Peter Thomas has written, that the commission knew nothing of Heinz's illicit activities, but was merely investigating why *Die Panzerfaust* was experiencing paper shortages.

As for the next generation of Heydrichs, rather little stands out so far as an attitude toward their Nazi forebears is concerned, at least beyond a struggle between feelings of guilt by association and a sense of the right to start anew. Reinhard's and Heinz's older sister, the reportedly bossy Maria (1901–88)—or "Mausi," as she was called, even by her descendants—married a Wolfgang Heindorf, but he appears to have been a problematic partner, to judge from letters from Maria to Reinhard demanding financial assistance and employment for Heindorf. As one of Heydrich's biographers reports, "Heydrich grudgingly complied and repeatedly found employment" for Heindorf, "first in the Propaganda Ministry, and then in the Volkswagen factory and the German Labour Front." But Heindorf repeatedly got sacked. "As a raging alcoholic who tended to submit falsified expense claims, brag about his influential brother-in-law, and 'borrow' money from subordinates, Heindorf remained a constant source of embarrassment for Heydrich." Eventually, he gave his brother-in-law one final option: "to volunteer for the Wehrmacht and to 'prove his worth in battle.'"

Peter Thomas Heydrich sheds gossipy light on this troubled marriage. Family lore has it that Mausi was what the Germans term a *gefallenes Mädchen* ("fallen woman") and required a husband to forestall potential scandal arising out of her overfamiliarity with numerous men in her hometown of Halle. Heindorf had to be "stuffed with money" and gotten employment, by Reinhard, to be made respectable, because he was "too dumb," says her nephew, to do so on his own. No offspring seem to have resulted.

Among Heinz's five children, the eldest, Peter, seems to have been proudest of his uncle, Reinhard, at least in his youth. But eventually he regretfully came to recognize his family's contributions to the Holocaust. Little has been recorded of his four younger siblings—two sisters, Isa and Ingrid, and two brothers, Heider (b. 1937, and not to be confused with Reinhard's second son, Heider) and Hartmut (b. 1942).

The same can nearly be said of Reinhard's and Lina's children, but not quite. The oldest, Klaus (born in 1933), was, as reported in the foregoing history, killed in a bicycling accident when he was ten, a year after his father died. The youngest, Marte, the daughter born a month after Reinhard's assassination, grew up to help her mother run her pension on Fehmarn, and later, after marrying a Fehmarn farmer, Uwe Beyer, became known as the proprietor there of a ladies' boutique. When interviewed for a (London) *Daily Mail* feature, "Children of the Nazis," appearing in June 1973, she admitted to feeling deeply pained by her father's reputation as "the Third Reich's evil young god of death," and still hoping against hope that history would prove this judgment too harsh.

"Somehow I've never been really convinced that *this* is what happened, *this* is what he was like," she told Anne Leslie, the *Daily Mail*'s reporter. "Perhaps it's too soon for the whole truth to be known."

The infant Klaus Heydrich with his father, circa 1935. Lina Heydrich and her three surviving children remained at Jungfern-Breschan until they, along with other Germans, were forced to flee Prague in April 1945 in advance of the approaching Soviet Red Army. By the time Germany unconditionally surrendered to the Allies on May 7, 1945, Lina, Silke, Heider, and Marte were living in Bavaria.

Marte Heydrich Beyer never knew her father, who was killed before her birth. Even so, the adult Marte told an interviewer, "You have no idea what it means to have such a father." Besides suffering nightmares—"I had to have treatment for a long time"—when she was young "the other children would spit at us."

Marte's elder sister, Silke (born on February 9, 1939), has been described on internet sites as a model, actress, and opera singer, living variously in Germany, America, and South Africa. She is known to have appeared in 1962 in an Italian documentary about the progeny of leading Nazis. In December 1971, the *Boca Raton* [Florida] *News* ran a story, datelined Bonn, Germany, headlined "Nazi Children Reflect on Dad." In it, Silke Heydrich, whose father is known to have doted on her as a child, is quoted: "Was my father an evil man?" She reaches the doubtful conclusion: "If he really was, I should be able to feel this within myself. I have watched myself for a long time and didn't feel anything of the sort."

Two years later, she states this even more defiantly in the *Daily Mail*'s somewhat sensationalized feature. "No, I never thought of changing my name, even when I suffered most from it," Leslie reports Silke telling her, after introducing her as "a big, sexy, loose-limbed blonde of warm and chatty charm," who lounged back in her armchair, sipping her brandy, and speaking cheerfully. "My father was my father. I can't escape that fact. Besides, I hoped maybe that grass would grow over his memory, that people would forget. After all, time heals all wounds, doesn't it?"

As the *Daily Mail* portrays her, the wounds seem to have healed for Silke. "Now 34," she "lives with her two young children and her husband, Gerd, the technical director of a big laundry firm, in a comfortable suburb of Hamburg, sharing the wealth of modern Germany." Still, for all she insists that she has accepted her name, she recounts how

In 1971, the same year Reinhard and Lina's thirty-two-year-old daughter, Silke, told a journalist that she felt no innate sense that her father was evil, her older brother Heider, thirty-seven, said, "I don't want to judge the Third Reich. I want to get ahead and not let myself be held up by the past."

"very hard" it was "for us to get into college," how she was rejected by a half-Jewish "fellow pupil" she had fallen in love with, when he learned of her background, and how she faces the prospect of telling her older daughter's, Helen's, teacher who her grandfather was and hopes "she'll be tactful and understanding with her." And whether because the article's reporter volunteered to protect Silke, or because Silke requested such protection, nowhere in the feature—neither following the given names of her husband, Gerd, nor her older daughter—does Silke's married name appear.

Yet finally, it was left to the oldest surviving offspring of Reinhard and Lina, Heider Heydrich (born in 1934), to appear actually to celebrate his father's role in Czech history at least, when in 2011 he proposed to help raise money to restore Jungfern-Breschan, the sumptuous Mediterranean villa where his family had lived in Prague. Formerly owned by a wealthy Jewish industrialist, Ferdinand Bloch-Bauer, who had bought it in 1909 and then fled the country following the Nazi occupation in 1939, the property had been confiscated by the Nazis and designated the official residence of the Reichsprotektor.

Reinhard Heydrich and his family had moved there early in 1942 and it was from Jungfern-Breschan that Heydrich had departed on the morning of his assassination. Heider Heydrich, perhaps having allowed his idyllic childhood to distort his view of history, found his proposal greeted with outrage among Czechs who were doubtless reminded of his father's brutal regime, not to speak of the mass killing visited by the Nazis on the village of Lidice and elsewhere in reprisal for Heydrich's killing, in which by one estimate as many as five thousand people died.

Even if one grants Heider Heydrich the benefit of every possible doubt and dismisses his suggestion of renovating Jungfern-Breschan as a public relations blunder, the gesture was completely at odds with the tenor of life he had led up to that point. As Lina took pains to explain to Nancy Dougherty, Heider had been a successful unit chief for Dornier aircraft in Munich, in charge of the fastest-growing branch of one of Germany's most successful industries. His unit specialized in repairing damaged aircraft from all over the world, including the American AWACS system. He had once even turned down a promotion, presumably to avoid exposing the reviled family name to the spotlight of history. Following his retirement from his Dornier unit, he ably supervised the company's pensions, and subsequently headed up an independent retirement organization.

With possibly strained generosity, one might conclude that Heider—who incidentally looks much more like a von Osten than a Heydrich—had acted without his customary caution in making his controversial gesture to history. On visiting his former haunts in Prague, he may have experienced a fleeting memory of happy childhood days there, before his father and older brother were killed. He soon withdrew his offer when he saw the outrage it provoked.

Still, by even suggesting that Jungfern-Breschan might deserve veneration, Heider Heydrich seemed to be sharing his mother's fantasy that, at least for a brief time before his assassination, the Butcher of Prague had been capable of something less than total evil. And for doing so he was quickly reminded that if the perhaps half-forgotten name of Reinhard Heydrich were to be brought to public mind once again, it would be deservedly reviled for the unfathomable inhumanity connected with its utterance.

ACKNOWLEDGMENTS

My brilliant, loving wife and author, Nancy Dougherty, died February 6, 2013, after courageously battling early-onset Alzheimer's for thirteen years at our home on Shelter Island. She had been working on this book, writing, researching, taking frequent trips to Germany for interviews and on-site research, since the 1980s. Fortunately, she was near completion when this horrible curse started taking her from us. I'm sure it's unthinkable for a book to be dedicated to its author, but if no one is looking, I may try it.

And there are many others who made invaluable contributions to the successful writing and publication of this important (and still very timely) work.

The late Hayes Jacobs, Nancy's New School literary professor and mentor, tirelessly and wisely counseled and encouraged her in the early days, and discreetly introduced her to publishing insiders.

So many dear friends and fellow members of the writers' world counseled, comforted, and worked with Nancy as they all struggled to realize their dreams—Sally Arteseros, Sally Huxley, the late Wendy Weil, Jo Garfield, and Carole Klein to mention a few. Gratitude also to the MacDowell Colony, which welcomed Nancy as a happy resident in the early 1990s.

Nancy was terribly fortunate to have Victoria Wilson as her editor. Particularly in recent years, Victoria worked tirelessly and brilliantly with a diverse cast to shape the work and push it toward publication. And it was inspiring to me to see Victoria's compassion as she struggled to continue to work with Nancy for a time, when Nancy's skills were beginning to slip away.

The late Christopher Lehmann-Haupt, a teenage resident of Berlin when the Red Army arrived in 1945 (and recommended to me by the late Richard Baron after Nancy's death), did some extensive and important editing, compiled the source notes, and wrote the foreword before his untimely death in 2018, when Stephen M. Silverman took over his role.

There are others, to be sure. I'm an unlucky man, losing my Nancy. But like many of us, I am also a lucky man, as you can see. Thank you, thank you, to the recognized and unrecognized.

—Jim Dougherty

A NOTE ON SOURCES

As I made my way through the editing of Nancy Dougherty's text of *The Hangman and His Wife*, I would often stop to note a passage or quotation that needed sourcing, and I would place a marker to remind me to do future referencing. In the process, I accumulated more than eight hundred such markers. I then faced the prospect of tracking down the several hundred books that the author must have consulted as her sources, and checking their texts and notes for more original documentation. Considering the libraries and bookstores I would need to visit to get this task completed, I feared I faced the prospect of months or even years more work.

Luckily, I then received from the author's family several dozen of the books she had used in her research and a file that contained some 250 of her own footnotes. This reduced the size of my task by about a quarter. More usefully still, I began to learn the power of such internet research tools as Google and Google Books. These appeared to make the job more practical in terms of the time it would take—months rather than years. Unfortunately, as things turned out, they also created handicaps that limited the thoroughness of my research.

Most of these handicaps arose from the fact that the internet allows only partial access to the contents of books and articles, for the obvious reason that full access would make it unnecessary to buy them. But such limited access makes it impossible to properly compare their merits, by riffling through their pages to check out their full contents and their bibliographies, source notes, and indexes.

Because what one can access online usually doesn't include a full view of the works' source notes, one is restricted to reading the author's versions and interpretations of those notes, meaning that one is mainly dependent on what can be termed secondary sources rather than primary ones.

Next, because of Dougherty's facility with German, she understandably relied on many German texts, freely translating the material herself if she felt the need to quote them. Although I have a fair amount of German myself, in order to track down her German-language sources through Google Books, I would inevitably have to figure out how to translate Dougherty's English back into German. This exercise often depended on my hitting on just the right word or idiom that would trigger digital recognition of the exact correct text I might be looking for. I was not always successful at finding the right words.

Finally, I was tripped up by Dougherty's very occasional inclination to infer spoken utterances in descriptive text. That is, when an original text might mention that an individual asked for certain information or stated such and such, she might actually quote the words of the question or the statement. For instance, where the German historian Günther Deschner states in his biography *Reinhard Heydrich: Statthalter der totalen Macht* that Heydrich once asked Franz Josef Huber "which Huber he was," Dougherty in her translation actually quotes Heydrich, "Which Huber are you?" Translating the resulting quotation back into German and googling the result is bound to prove hopeless. The original text of Deschner's book does not recognize even the question mark.

Happily, my later acquiring of Dougherty's partial library and footnotes did serve to lower somewhat the hurdles I faced. Her books gave me some sense of the volumes she valued most highly, though certain key ones were still missing, such as Lina von Osten Heydrich's postwar memoir, *Leben mit einem Kriegsverbrecher* (*Life with a War Criminal*), which had to be bought at considerable cost. And the relatively few footnotes she did leave behind gave me by way of example a strong sense of the direction, depth, and thoroughness of her research.

Still, the various handicaps I encountered do limit in important ways the value of what follows. First, besides too often referring to secondary sources rather than primary ones (for the reasons explained above), one can't even be certain that one is reading the best secondary source available, because of the relatively narrow window that the internet affords. Moreover, occasionally when, after a lengthy search, a text responding to one's description does show up, some details may still be missing, leading one to believe that while the history may be correct, nevertheless this may not be the source that Dougherty actually relied on. And finally, although very rarely, when no source at all shows up after dozens of attempts to describe an event or translate a quote, one is left with no option except to mark the reference as "unsourced."

All the same, any shortcomings in the notes I have compiled do not really reflect any overall failure on the author's part to research thoroughly the facts she has worked with. Quite the contrary, these notes are shot through with signs of Dougherty's impressive conscientiousness. For instance, while inserting her own footnotes to the chapter on Heydrich's deputy Dr. Karl Rudolf Werner Best (chapter 13, "The Expert on the Forms of Words"), I several times found references that read "Werner Best, *Betr.: Reinhard Heydrich*, unpublished monograph dated October 1, 1949, my translation." ("*Betr.*" is the German equivalent of "Concerning" or "Re.")

But when I googled "Werner Best: 'Betr.: Reinhard Heydrich,'" the only relevant result was the footnote to a 1988 anti-Nazi book by Herbert Taege, the German title of which translated into English is *NS-Perestroika?: Reform Goals of National Socialist Leaders.*

A footnote in this volume, translated into English, cites an "unpublished typescript" from a source called "Copenhagen 1.10.1949," "copy in author's archive," from "correspondence of Dr. Werner Best with L.W. Stockholm from 9/15/1977 to 1/29/1979." As near as I could determine, "Copenhagen 1.10.1949" refers to a file created when Best was imprisoned in Denmark for crimes committed when he supervised civilian affairs in Nazi-occupied Denmark. (I refer to it in the foregoing notes with the abbreviation KT:wb, for Copenhagen Typescript: Werner Best.)

My point is that the author took the trouble to read and translate this and other unpublished monographs by Best. Presumably, she traveled to Copenhagen to do so. This is only one example of the lengths she went to in order to gain access to out-of-the-way sources. One therefore has to assume that just because my research failed now and then to turn up satisfactory sources for Dougherty's material, this does not mean she didn't have them.

Of course, her interpretations of the facts she unearthed are not always indisputable. So, where contradictory conclusions occasionally rear their heads, I have tried to note in these sources the details of conflicting opinions.

Still, the extent to which what follows remains unsatisfactory must be blamed on my handicaps as a researcher and not on Dougherty's shortcomings. Or better, on the unhappy circumstances that led the creator of this work to leave her task too soon, and this editor to arrive too late.

—Christopher Lehmann-Haupt

NOTES

A note to the reader: The source notes for *The Hangman and His Wife* are incomplete due to the deaths of the author, Nancy Dougherty, as she succumbed to Alzheimer's disease, and of Christopher Lehmann-Haupt, who was finishing the manuscript, including the source notes, at the time of his sudden death. What appears here represents Mr. Lehmann-Haupt's best efforts in the search for, and assembling of, Ms. Dougherty's vast sources for this ambitious, and ambitiously researched, book.

ABBREVIATIONS

KTwb	Kopenhagen Typoskript: Werner Best
SAwb	Shlomo Aronson: Werner Best
IMTd	International Military Tribunal documents (Nuremberg Trials)
LHI	Lina Heydrich interview
NYT	*New York Times*
NDI	Nancy Dougherty interview
ND translation	Nancy Dougherty translation

INTRODUCTION: THE HANGMAN'S WIFE

The main sources for this introduction are Nancy Dougherty's recollections and firsthand impressions. In addition: Eicke jailed for murder: McNab, p. 137. he told an interviewer: Minnich, p. 27, fn. 6. "I took a large glass of brandy": Sereny, *The Healing Wound*, p. 123. had never killed anyone: Arendt, p. 264. "a symbol": Fest, *The Face of the Third Reich*, part 2: pp. 109ff. "think in slogans": Orwell, p. 188. "a politicizing widow": Heydrich, *Leben*, p. 132. claim the pension: Gerwarth, pp. 29–91. TV interview: NYT, 2/7/79, A2. quoted her extensively: Deschner, *Pursuit*, or *Biographie eines Reichsprotektors*.

1. THE FACE OF NATIONAL SOCIALISM

Wannsee Conference: Roseman. "total and permanent check": Ward, *Law, Philosophy and National Socialism*, p. 65. "Führer order": Hilberg, *Destruction*, vol. 2, p. 418. "the puppet master": Schellenberg, *Memoirs*, p. 31. "technologist of power": Höhne, p. 163. candidate to succeed Hitler: Fest, p. 109. Part Two: *Reinhard Heydrich: The Successor*, fn. 41. "He was one of the best": Dederichs, p. 149. "He was the man with the iron heart": Ibid., p. 150. "What a handsome couple": NDI: Lena Heydrich. obsession with the ideal human form: Spotts, p. 23; Barron. "German men in the Nordic mold": Epstein, p. 56. Paul Schultze-Naumburg: Taylor and van der Will, pp. 66, 253, and 270. most SS men resembled: Longerich, p. 303, fns. 24, 25, and 26. SS specialists eventually produced: Ibid., pp. 303–304. "Then I can't help you": Breitman, p. 195, fn. 40. later turned out to be a pimp: Bleuel, p. 199. He must have seen a lot of something: Evans, pp. 506–36. the freedom and splendor: Rempel, p. 173. "If National Socialism had looked in the mirror": Hayes, p. 150. "perverted beauty": Höhne, *Death's Head*, p. 495, fn. 68. "formed for slow strangling": Butler, p. 55. "iciness": Speer, p. 478. "like polished steel": Fest, *The Face of the Third Reich*, p. 98. "In his Luciferian coldness": Ibid. "both men": Höttl, p. 32. "many more of him": Hoberman, p. 100, fn. 67; Krausnick et al., pp. 339–40; Buchheim. What good is blackmail?: NDI: Lena Heydrich. "Which Huber are you?": Deschner, *Statthalter*, p. 86. Willrich equated salvation: Yenne, p. 117. the insecurity it betrays: von Lang, *Top Nazi*, p. 97. Heydrich got to the point: https://portal.ehri. "Herr Willrich was traveling": von Lang, *Top Nazi*, pp. 96–97. into the Reichsführer's lap: Institut für Zeitgeschichte-Archiv. "without express permission": Ibid. "with décolleté": Hinz, p. 162, fn. 177.

2. CHILD OF UNCERTAINTY

The major sources for this chapter are biographies of Heydrich by Dederichs, Deschner, and Gerwarth, as well as Lina Heydrich's recollections. Also: " 'Knowledge is power' ": Jaeckel, p. 152; NDI: Lena Heydrich. "I, Reinhard Heydrich": Aronson, *Frügeschichte*, p. 311 (ND translation). "Never trust a Saxon": Kent, p. 118. turned to ashes: Ibid., pp. 74ff. "of the scherzo": Ibid. p. 125. Luckily, he possessed: Dederichs; Aronson, *Anfangen*, pp. 11–17. In a rigidly: Whiting, *Search*, p. 79. became a confessed: Čalić, pp. 15–16. Wagner also led: Watson. "Heydrich's father played": Deschner, *Pursuit*, p. 295. wrote two more operas: Gerwarth, p. 17; Dederichs, p. 22. more intimate gifts: NDI: Lena Heydrich. joined a Masonic lodge: Deschner, p. 18. The odd coupling: Aronson, *Frühgeschichte*, pp. 1–16; Gerwarth, ch. 2; Dederichs, ch. 1; Deschner, *Pursuit*, ch. 2. One day he scaled: Deschner, *Statthalter*, p. 22. in French: Ibid., p. 21, fn. 15. In the end, the future Führer claimed: Erikson, p. 329. "Please, try the other side": Deschner, *Pursuit*, p. 18. "Get yourself back": Schellenberg, p. 400. joked about being a Jew: Dederichs, p. 54.

3. THE HONOR OF AN OFFICER

The major sources for this chapter are Shlomo Aronson's *Reinhard Heydrich und die Anfangen des SD und der Gestapo*, Lina Heydrich's *Leben mit einem Kriegsverbrecher*, and her personal recollections. Indeed, despite Aronson's dismissive judgment of Heydrich's naval career, Dougherty credits Aronson's "elegant and meticulous study." Also: Charles Wighton: Wighton, pp. 27 and 31. his years in the navy: Aronson, *Frühgeschichte*, p. 25. Brown House in Munich: Čalić, pp. 50–55. very bad luck: Deschner, ch. 17. "His relationship to the navy": KTwb. the new Halle Freikorps: Ibid., p. 23. On the contrary: Ibid., pp. 21–22. a form of rebirth: Bill Moyers interviewing Joseph Campbell in the TV series *The Power of Myth*, episode 1, "The Power of Myth," PBS, 1988. "with his violin": Graber, p. 1. "For them there had been no fears": Heydrich, *Leben*, p. 23 (ND translation). "not to have a friend": Aronson, p. 27, fn. 68 (1971 edition, ND translation). "somehow womanly and effeminate": Ibid., p. 27. "You have given me peace": Deschner, *Heydrich*, pp. 25–26. "racial types of the East": Ibid., p. 26. "Let's shoot down Walter Rathenau": Wette, p. 59. "classified Heydrich as a liberal": Aronson, *Frühgeschichte*, pp. 26 and 260, fn. 71. "Somehow he was different": Aronson, *Anfangen*, p. 45, Deschner, *Heydrich*, p. 28, and Heydrich, *Leben*, p. 23. Canaris, who was also teased: Höhne, *Canaris*, p. 6, fn. 52. "Whenever he ran into Reinhard": Heydrich, *Leben*, p. 23. They saw a man: Aronson, *Frühgeschichte*, pp. 27ff (1971 edition; ND translation). The opposite of ascription: Anderson, Taylor, and Logio, p. 172. "decisive": Aronson, *Anfangen*, p. 47. "I asked Heydrich": Ibid., p. 47 (ND translation). "How could I stand up for my father": Aronson, *Frühgeschichte* (1971 edition), p. 30 (ND translation). "No one knows for sure": NDI: Peter Thomas Heydrich. "Truth is for children": KTwb. "formally comrade-like, cool": Heydrich, *Leben*, p. 24. "to fortify his personality": Aronson, *Frühgeschichte,* p. 25 (ND translation). "haunt him like a nightmare": Höhne, *Canaris*, p. 85. "Music is just something for musicians": Ibid., p. 86. new acquaintances: Aronson, *Anfangen*, p. 51. He practiced and he practiced: Aronson, *Frühgeschichte*, p. 31. North Sea champion: Graber, p. 26. pentathlon competitions: Op. cit. "not shy at all": Ibid., p. 32. "good at everything": Ibid. Personal notes and communication: Lebram, pp. 27–33. Lebram speculates: Ibid. (1971). He later told his wife: Heydrich, *Leben*, p. 24. favorable reports from his organizational superiors: Deschner, pp. 34–35, fn. 23 (ND translation). "dismissed from the service": Aronson, *Frühgeschichte*, p. 311 (ND translation). Somewhat at odds with Nancy Dougherty's high estimation of Aronson's *Frühgeschichte*, Joachim Fest, in *The Face of the Third Reich*, casts doubt on Aronson's characterization of Heydrich as of average intelligence and ability. In footnotes 11 and 41 (pp. 335 and 339) of his chapter on Heydrich, Fest dissects what he implies may have been Heydrich's concerns about his possibly Jewish ancestry and its effect on his self-confidence and demeanor.

4. THE HONOR OF A WOMAN

The major sources for this chapter are the author's interviews with Lina Heydrich, and her memoir, *Leben mit einem Kriegsverbrecher*. Also: he dived in to rescue her: Whiting, p. 63. "with his pigs and hens": NDI: Lena Heydrich. "In that sphere too": KTwb, p. 10. more problematic: Aronson, *Frühgeschichte*, p. 32. "know him better": Heydrich, *Leben*, p. 9 (ND translation). "it has changed me": Ibid. only going to the theater: Ibid., p. 10. all about her parents: Ibid., p. 11. brought along a translator: Professor Thomas Baylis, University of Wisconsin. "such an answer!": NDI: Lena Heydrich. "O Sov'reign": Wagner, *Tristan and Isolde*, pp. 102–103. reluctant democrats: Mann, *Essays*. During his Christmas leave: Heydrich, *Leben*, pp. 11ff. "fit into the landscape": Ibid., p. 12. "Please, please permit this": Ibid., pp. 32ff. "This report irritated me": Ibid., p. 20. According to Reitlinger: Reitlinger, p. 37. dishonorable to marry: Höttl, p. 14. Commenting on this, the historian Joachim C. Fest, in *The Face of the Third Reich*, writes, "However, this seems to be an invention inspired by caricatures of the German reserve lieutenant, such as Heinrich Mann's [*Der*] *Untertan* [*Man of Straw*] London: Penguin. 1984]" (Fest, *The Face of the Third Reich*: Part Two, "Reinhard Heydrich—The Successor" fn. 12.) According to Günther Deschner: Deschner, *Pursuit*, p. 35. told an English journalist: As told to David Irving, and quoted in Deschner, p. 39 and ch. 4, fn. 4 and 6b. "Even today I don't know": Heydrich, *Leben*, p. 21.

5. HEINRICH HIMMLER—THE GREAT ENIGMA

The major sources for this chapter are Frischauer's *Himmler: The Evil Genius of the Third Reich*, Manvell and Fraenkel's *Heinrich Himmler: The Secret Life of the SS and Gestapo*, Loewenberg's *Decoding the Past*, and the website Spartacus Educational. In particular, Dougherty cites Bradley F. Smith's *Heinrich Himmler: A Nazi in the Making: 1900–1926*, from which she has taken "many of the examples in this chapter," as being "an excellent book, a pioneer work to which I am greatly indebted." Himmler as a virtual incompetent: Fest, *The Face of the Third Reich*, chapter on Himmler, fn. 3; Fest elaborates here, shedding light on Lina's confusion: "Speer's judgement is reported by Alexander Dallin, *German Rule in Russia 1941–1945*. Walter Schellenberg notes in *The Labyrinth* that Himmler in fact used to give marks." Fest adds that similar observations are made by "Friedrich Hossbach, *Zwischen Wehrmacht und Hitler*, and Graf Folke Bernadotte, *The Curtain Falls* (British title: *The Fall of the Curtain*; New York and London, 1945). See also the various assessments collected by Gerald Reitlinger in his book *The SS: Alibi of a Nation*. Actually, one would suspect that a person of stronger susceptibility than Himmler would probably have been incapable of perfecting this type of extermination system. See Conrad-Martius, *Utopien der Menschenzüchtung*. "He was our biggest problem": NDI: Lena Heydrich. to divorce his outspoken wife: Höhne, *Death's Head*, pp. 164–65, fn. 20. resolved the situation: Heydrich,

Leben, pp. 58ff. "almost every important man": Kersten, pp. 28–29; as wording here is different, quote may be ND's translation from German original. Himmler was never arrested: King, Notes and Sources; Genese, p. 38. Himmler as a mildly eccentric schoolmaster: Frischauer; Manvell and Fraenkel; Padfield. "he was the leader, after all": NDI. Data on Himmler: Spartacus Educational. Technologist of power: NDI: Gunter d'Alquen. When he wrote to his idol: Smith, *Heinrich Himmler*, p. 20. learn to dance: Longerich, p. 35. Hanfstängl: "a terrible snob": Loewenberg, pp. 216–18. "the whole pattern of his life": Smith, *Heinrich Himmler*, p. 75. "his father was the only person": Loewenberg, p. 227. "a lack of motherly love": Reitlinger, pp. 15–16. "I was really very bad": Smith, *Heinrich Himmler*, p. 41. "character" and "energy": Ibid., p. 107. war-torn generation: Ibid., pp. 34–35. "Father is so good": Loewenberg, pp. 227–28. "inner unconscious sadism": Ibid., p. 217. "constantly retreated behind": Smith, *Heinrich Himmler*, p. 113. "I have experienced": Manvell and Fraenkel, pp. 9–20. "rage against the Jews": Op. cit., p. 92. "these terrible Jews": Ibid., p. 122. "Rathenau is murdered": Loewenberg, p. 233. "because she is so weak": Manvell and Fraenkel, p. 7. must be broken off: Longerich, pp. 75–77; Smith, *Heinrich Himmler*, pp. 149–52. accepting Nazism: Fromm, *Anatomy*, pp. 346–50. volume Himmler liked best: Günther. "A book which expresses in pleasing words": Smith, *Heinrich Himmler*, p. 142. "Hitler surprised a circle of friends": Heiden, p. 308. "He's no world-beater": Manvell and Fraenkel, p. 16. "a school for good citizenship": Frischauer, ch. 4.

6. FATE, OR "WORK IN RELATION TO LIFE'S POSSIBILITIES"

The chief source for this chapter is Lina Heydrich's recollections as recorded in her memoir and expressed directly to the author. In addition: Unemployment in 1929: Dimsdale, Horsewood, and van Riel. "tears of despair": Gerwarth, *Hitler's Hangman*, p. 45, fn. 125: Heydrich, *Leben*, pp. 21 and 26ff; Aronson, *Frühgeschichte*, p. 35; Deschner, *Heydrich*, 40. his honor in the eyes of the world: Ibid., pp. 45ff. Lina told a British journalist: Wighton, p. 35. "the brown-shirted Storm Troopers were rabble": Deschner, *Pursuit*, p. 38–40. Little house named "Snowflake": LHI. The *Kampfzeit* was the best time ("Die Kampfzeit war die beste Zeit"): Koehl, p. 36, fn. 1. made clear the separateness and independence of his tiny organization: Browder, p. 108. Richard Walther Darré: Reider, pp. 142ff. new marriage code for the SS: Manvell and Fraenkel, p. 22. "Mother" Viktoria Edrich: Deschner, *Pursuit*, p. 49. "exhaustive re-thinking on all fronts": Ibid., p. 46. Heydrich "a great reader of detective stories": Allen, p. 203. "we were comrades": NDI: Gunter d'Alquen. "Get wealth and power": Alexander Pope, *Imitations of Horace: Epilogue to the Satires*, Dialogue 1, 103 (Horace: Rem facias, rem; Si possis, recte; si non, quocunque modo rem). Heydrich king of the underworld: NDI: Gunter d'Alquen. "the most dreaded man in the Third Reich": Wighton, p. 47.

7. BITTER YOUNG MEN, BRIGHT YOUNG MEN: HEYDRICH'S SD

Leading sources for this chapter are Höhne's *The Order of the Death's Head: The Story of Hitler's SS*; Schellenberg's *Memoirs*, and Arendt's *Eichmann in Jerusalem*. Heydrich's one "idealism": Graber, p. 69. "Heydrich's bright young men": Crankshaw, ch. 10. SD the sole intelligence service: Paehler, p. 37, fn. 43: "Hess Decree of June 9, 1934, NA, RG 242, T-580/93, Ordner 457X": Aronson, pp. 196. SD "the refuge for National Socialism's most intelligent men": Höhne, p. 211. Studying the lexicon: Lerner, pp. 3ff. Browder has analyzed: Browder, *Foundations*, esp. ch. 2, "The Roots of the SD," pp. 21–35. "organizational statesman": Kagan, Krygier, and Winston, p. 310. Hans Kobelinsky: Ingrao, p. 85, fn. 75. Alfred Naujocks: Levy, *Wanted*, pp. 14ff; Browder, *Hitler's Enforcers*. Naujocks later wrote: Peis, Foreword. "you resent authority": Ibid., ch. 13. "a glib-tongued egoist": Ibid., Index. "I cannot deny": Schellenberg, *Memoirs*, p. 21. Schellenberg recruited by the SD: Ibid., p. 20. "through the complex channels of this huge machine": Ibid., p. 25. "Heydrich likes your reports": Ibid., p. 26. "the reports cross-indexed": Ibid., p. 28. "he himself stayed in the background": Ibid., p. 31. "any one of 500,000 cards within easy reach": Ibid., p. 28. "the puppet master of the Third Reich": Ibid., p. 31. "the legs of a spider": Ibid., p. 29. Otto Ohlendorf: He was the chief defendant in the Nuremberg Einsatzgruppen trial, covered in chapter 2, "A Judge, a Prosecutor, and a Mass Murderer: Courtroom Dynamics in the SS-Einsatzgruppen Trial," in Priemel and Stiller. He joined the Nazi Party at eighteen. Lewy, p. 47. arrested by the Gestapo: Browder, p. 224. he wrote to his wife: Höhne, p. 213. Höhn actually praised Ohlendorf: The exact ultimate sources of the following paragraphs on Otto Ohlendorf (and Heinz Höhn) are difficult to trace, as the conversations are either inferred from reports or loosely translated from the German. Still, the material is encompassed by Aronson's *Frühgeschichte*, pp. 212–16; Browder's *Hitler's Enforcers*, II. Inside the SD, pp. 103–231; Höhne's *Death's Head* (esp. "Statement by Otto Ohlendorf, 8 October 1947, in the official record Case X, Nuremberg Trials 2nd series (Reference: American Military Tribunal, M-IL-I-ICaming (int Lea) Court IIa Case X)"; Frau Käthe Ohlendorf's private papers. Ohlendorf's career is summarized on the website Holocaust Education and Archive Research Team. Adolf Eichmann: See Arendt, Browder, and Höhne. "I lost interest in selling": "Eichmann Interrogated," *Granta*, 1985. "So I joined the SS": Levy, ch. 11. Robert Gellately . . . has written: *The Gestapo*, p. 66.

8. THE EVIL TWINS

Leading books on the Gestapo are Aronson's *Frühgeschichte*, Browder's *Hitler's Enforcers*, Crankshaw's *Gestapo*, Delarue's *The Gestapo*, Gellately's *The Gestapo*, and Manvell and Fraenkel's *Heinrich Himmler*. Specific sources: Göring liked to proclaim: Noakes and Pridham, p. 314. Heydrich had officially resigned: Browder, *Hitler's Enforcers*, p. 93. Himmler himself received nothing: Ibid., p. 63. "obedient servant": Ćalić, *Schlüsselfigur*, p. 129 (ND translation). Absolute proof: Kitchen, p. 235. he had to phone home: Dederichs, p. 59. sifting through piles of garbage: LHI. former enemies into obedient subordinates: Read, pp. 312ff; Browder, *Hitler's Enforcers*, p. 226. Peterson writes: Peterson, p. 86. secretly to undermine: Meyer, p. 270, fn. 253. Max Weber argued: Eliaeson, p. 88. *Beamte* acting too slowly: Peterson, pp. 177ff. Heydrich and Nazi Party members: LHI. Streckenbach on Heydrich: NDI: Streckenbach. "Müller was irreplaceable": Ibid. against the trade unions: Gerwarth, p. 67. arrest clergymen: Ibid., p. 103. deceitful arrogance: Aronson, *Frühgeschichte*, p. 62. Heydrich denounced Strassner: Ibid., p. 123. turned to Theodore Eicke: Ibid., p. 105. protective custody: Ibid., pp. 185 and 238. "legend of terror": Ibid., p. 155.

9. THE ROAD TO BERLIN

Leading sources for this chapter are Browder's *Foundations of the Nazi Police State* and Höhne's *The Order of the Death's Head*. Others: "permanent revolution": Rauschning, *Germany's Revolution*, p. 83. "Nazification at the top": Steiner, p. 39. good Nazis into petty bureaucrats: Lozowick, ch. 1, cf. footnotes. Heydrich had to recall Oberg: Bajohr. "*that* situation soon reversed itself": NDI: Streckenbach. a clash between: Browder, *Foundations*, p. 93. Yet the SD had also succeeded: Ibid., ch. 8, "The SD Emergent." "he recognized each Reichsstaathalter": Ibid., p. 115, fn. 68. convinced the governor: Browder, *Hitler's Enforcers*, p. 121, fn. 62. "The fifth column did not begin in Spain": Crankshaw, p. 40. "But at least I shoot": Blandford, p. 28. "I am not afraid": Ibid., p. 247. "my mission is only to destroy": Manvell and Fraenkel, p. 106, fn. 15. "all excesses, lies or infringements of the law": Gisevius, p. 141. "a den of murderers": Ibid., p. 291. Arthur Nebe thus epitomized: Gisevius, *Wo ist Nebe?* side to side: Höhne, pp. 76–77. Göring and Diels: Ibid., pp. 84–89. Diels "in all his dark and horrible glamour": Dodd, p. 52. "an awkward assemblage": Browder, *Foundations*, pp. 127-8. "Himmler detested": Ibid., p. 121. "he will kill us all": Ibid., p. 117, fn. 1. "Diels became more neurotic": Dodd, p. 53. "head of the Gestapo": Wighton, p. 64. "a reliable bodyguard": Metcalfe, p. 238.

10. THE RULES OF THE GAME

Hitler's writings, speeches, and utterances are the sources of most of what appears in this chapter, though their original expressions are not always obvious. "indescribable": Deschner, *Pursuit*, p. 45. "He who would live must fight": Hitler, *Mein Kampf*, p. 214. accusing both groups: Ibid., p. 52. "historical events": Ibid., p. 15. he lists exceptions to the rule: Hitler, *Table Talk*, pp. 507ff. "I'm a politician, not a writer": Op. cit., p. 758. "concentrates on present reality": Hitler, *Mein Kampf*, pp. 229–32; cf. Kershaw, p. 157, and Maser, p. 235. "We will keep it!": Steffahn, p. 93 (ND translation). Politics is a game: Rauschning, p. 280. "Our program is expressed in two words—Adolf Hitler": Fest, *Hitler*, p. 252. Tessenow told Speer in 1931: Speer, p. 15, ch. 2, fn. 2. "My first demand": Rauschning, p. 145. "We each possess just so much power": Fest, *The Face of the Third Reich*, p. 75. "There may be only one single rule": Speer, p. 359. "Who is to blame when the cat eats the mouse?": Hitler, *Monologe*, p. 148, or Chamayou, ch. 11, p. 132, fn. 24. "is ruthless, hard as iron": Payne, p. 484. "make use of all forces": Hitler, *Table Talk*, p. 16. "so theatrically stage-managed": NDI: Speer. "Hácha-ized": Ibid. "Clarification would mean division": Van Vrekhem, p. 348. more were employed in factories: Kolinsky and van der Will, p. 124. "warmth is energy": Fest, *Hitler*, p. 436. leaders would gradually emerge: Unterseher, p. 95. "on purely personal grounds": Op. cit. p. 354. "choose a weaker opponent": Rauschning, p. 76. "exact calculation of all human weaknesses": Op. cit. p. 325. "a flaw in the weave": NDI: Speer. "We are brawling our way to greatness": Op. cit. p. 125. "common ideals and common scoundrelism": Ibid., p. 146. "using blackmail": NDI: Speer. "whether or not he has told the truth": Op. cit. p. 595. "If there were no Jew, we would have to invent him": Gordon, *Hitler*, p. 129. "immune to advice": Fest, *The Face of the Third Reich*, p. 141; Röhm, *Die Geschichte*. the tough Fritz Todt: NDI: Speer. "Criticism would be the worst kind of democracy": Ibid. "the age of faits accomplis!": Ibid. "impotence or cunning": Speer, p. 207. "ruled by fear": Rauschning, p. 81. "The rabble has to be scared": Gillespie, p. 16. "I hate the masses": Lengyel, p. 11. Hitler envisioned a postwar world: Schoenbaum. "True aristocracy": Rauschning, p. 40. "These are the men": Wiesenthal, p. 63 (ND translation). "The impossible always succeeds": Fest, *Hitler*, p. 167. "the correct psychological moment": NDI: Speer. "Attack! Attack! Always Attack!": Op. cit., p. 271. "the categorical imperative of the Third Reich": Golsan and Misemer, p. 65. "We must never allow our differences to be bared": Fest, *Hitler*, p. 473. "I can rule them": Rauschning, *Hitler Speaks*, p. 208. "a special, secret pleasure": Murray.

11. A LESSON IN LIFE

Many books have been devoted to the Night of the Long Knives, but the details of this chapter come by and large from broader histories. "my dear Ernst Röhm": Darman, p. 6. "the great drama": Reitlinger, *The SS*, p. 64. "Since I am an immature and wicked man": Röhm, *Die Geschichte*, p. 363. "a skyscraper erected over the Brown House": One can find countless citations of the alleged excesses of SA men, but this statement by Röhm, which likely originally appeared in German, has not yielded to any search, in English or German. "'Führer' personality": Holborn, pp. 226ff. "an association of men for a political purpose": Fest, *Hitler*, p. 307. "Are we revolutionaries or not?": Fried, p. 270. chaos would destroy Germany: Collier and Pedley, p. 169. the return of the Kaiser monarchy: Holborn, pp. 223ff. "no less than five problems": Fest, *Hitler*, p. 493. "doing away with a man": Carlton, p. 125. Walter von Reichenau: Holborn, p. 237. Heydrich relayed their instructions: Höhne, *Death's Head*, p. 100. gathering to plan a coup: Maracin, p. 117.

wielded like a knife to finish him off: Caruthers, p. 17. Heydrich power behind the scenes: Höhne, *Death's Head*, p. 98. "Heydrich's plan": Gallo, p. 100. Heydrich followed up the order: Op. cit., pp. 110ff; Cimino. Udet survived: *Liberty*, vol. 21, no. 2, p. 43. "we heard nothing but raucous laughter": Gisevius, *To the Bitter End*, p. 152. "It's too late now": Höhne, *Death's Head*, p. 127. Röhm and his SA leaders were denounced: Evans, p. 41. "unfathomable ramifications": Reck-Malleczewen, p. 19. "thirty-seven ghosts": Fromm, *Blood*, p. 173. "talked too much": Ibid., p. 174. "Whoever fails": Rauschning, p. 171. "Let the swine bleed to death": Gisevius, *To the Bitter End*, p. 158. "that murderer-in-chief": Op. cit., p. 187.

12. TRANSFORMATIONS OF OUR STRUGGLE: THE INVISIBLE APPARAT

Probably the most comprehensive source for this chapter is Höhne's *The Order of the Death's Head*. For details: "inevitably corrode the character": Dodd, p. 53. "the clarion of an ominous new theme": Heydrich, "Wandlungen unseres Kampfen." "raped mentally": Dederichs, p. 68. an unpolitical naval officer: Gerwarth, p. 47. doubts about Nazism: LHI. "The work on ourselves": Heydrich, "Wandlungen unseres Kampfen" (ND translation). "The duty of the Gestapo": Avalon Law Project, part 6. "murderous ambition": NDI: Thomas Heydrich. "the total and permanent police coverage": NDI: Speer. major categories: Browder, *Hitler's Enforcers*, pp. 47ff. code letters indicating appropriate action: Höhne, *Death's Head*, pp. 183–84. "major ideological questions": Höhne, *Canaris*, p. 181. Hartl was still trying to answer it: Gerwarth, p. 103. a serial killer: Wagner, *Monster of Düsseldorf.* scandalous von Fritsch affair: Deschner, *Pursuit*, p. 135. promoted him instead: NDI: Schellenberg. Himmler announced: Longerich, p. 470. finally got the job: Delarue, p. 360. RSHA now consisted of six divisions: Höhne, *Death's Head*, p. 256. bombed out of existence, Ward, p. 48. "Der C": Wighton, p. 181. "valid for internal purposes only": Höhne, *Death's Head*, p. 356.

13. THE EXPERT ON THE FORMS OF WORDS

The most thorough sources for this chapter are Shlomo Aaronson's two histories, *Heydrich und die Anfänge des SD und der Gestapo*, which Heinz Höhne, in his *The Order of the Death's Head*, identifies as Aronson's "Inaugural Dissertation of Faculty of Philosophy I the Free University of Berlin 1966," and Aronson's *Reinhard Heydrich und die Frühgeschichte von Gestapo und SD*, a slightly shorter version, published by Deutsche Verlags-Anstalt, in Munich. Inconveniently, many of the writings by Werner Best cited in these texts remain unpublished, some of them transcripts in Danish custody in Copenhagen (cited in these notes as Kopenhagen Typoscript Werner Best, or KTwb). Heinz Höhne too makes extensive use of "unpublished sources" by Dr. Best, mainly what are identified as monographs, as well as Best's single published book, *Die deutsche Polizei*. While Nancy Dougherty seems to have had access to this material, this editor has not. It has therefore proved impossible to cite the exact source of references to Best's writings, except in the rare cases where the author did leave notes behind. More specifically: One day [Best]: Gisevius, p. 184. "decisive event": Ingrao, pp. 11 and 13. "fatherless generation": Elsewhere, on p. 61, Koonz cites Peter Merkl's study *Violence Under the Swastika*, noting that about a quarter of early party members, both male and female, had lost a parent, usually the father, during their childhoods. "talking about God and the world": Aronson, *Frühgeschichte*, pp. 144–52 (ND translation). "blood and spirit": Ibid. "not the man": LHI. asked to become a legal adviser: Op. cit., p. 150. "Boxheim Documents": Ibid., p. 150. "resistance will be punished with death": Ibid., p. 292, fn. 41. Hitler "like an older comrade": Ibid., p. 292, fn. 42. a good Nazi: Ibid., p. 145 (ND note: "Best even coined a term for this: 'Völkische Lebensauffassung,' roughly translated as 'interpretation of the people's life' "). "totally unnecessary people": LHI. "negative charisma": Koehl, p. 55. "most demonic personality": KTwb. "Heydrich was very tall": KTwb, p. 2 (ND translation). "admiration mixed with fear": Ibid. Frau Heydrich said, LHI. Werner Best was mixing: Krausnick et al., p. 325. Best rebuked him: ND notes: "From a letter from Friedrich Hielscher to Shlomo Aronson, as quoted in *Heydrich und die Anfangen des SD und der Gestapo*, p. 203, my translation." complained to Himmler: Krausnick et al., p. 444 (ND: "Eicke's letter is quoted in Martin Broszat, "The Concentration Camps, 1933–45," in *Anatomy of the SS State*, p. 444). "the more perfect the state": Höhne, *Death's Head*, p. 180, fn. 119. "Under the leadership": Op. cit., p. 162. "loss of power on the other": Op. cit., p. 180, fn. 119; Parsons, chs. III, IV, and V. "Any attempt to gain recognition": Op. cit., p. 427. "every other threat to the state": Op. cit., p. 427. "We fought lawyers with lawyers": Kersten, p. 104. "the subjective wishes of its supporters": Op. cit., p. 427. "Who will care": KTwb. not subject to judicial review: Dams and Stolle, p. 17. really working together: Höhne, *Death's Head*, p. 197 and ch. 9, fn. 9. Himmler gleefully noted: Kersten, p. 105. Freud's image: Freud, ch. 1. Best divided the spheres of government: Krausnick et al., p. 156. found the right words: Best, *Die deutsche Polizei*, p. 15. "It was the intelligence": KTwb, p. 13. "The acceptance of the stateless person": Höhne, *Death's Head*, p. 185, fn. 143: "Letter of 26 July from Best to Regierungspräsidenten and Police Presidents, RfSS Microfilm 403." "special conditions" of war: Krausnick et al.; "The Concentration Camps," by Martin Broszat; translated by Marian Jackson, p. 468. "fussy, neat, orderly, and correct": NDI: Streckenbach. "sick to death": LHI. a "dilettante": KTwb. "superfluous": Ibid. "always" on hand: Ibid. "his monitoring function in every sphere": Höhne, *Death's Head*, p. 255, fn. 196; Deutsche Recht, Folio 8–9, 15 April 1939 (ND: "From Best's article, 'Kritik und Apologie des Juristen.' Probably also RFSS Microfilm, 239"). "arrogance of the expert": Höhne, *Death's Head*, p. 255, fn. 197; "Letter from Schellenberg to Heydrich, 25 Apr. 1939, RFSS Microfilm 239." "Best handed over his office and disappeared": NDI: Streckenbach. [45]: "I risked that you would cross me up": Ibid. needs a break: Ibid. "fighting against each other as enemies": KTwb, p. 7. "My disagreement with Dr. Best": Krausnick et al., p. 194; Hans Buchheim, "The SS: Instrument of Domination," translated by Richard

Barry. [49]: "you want a subordinate": Höhne, *Death's Head*, p. 258, fn. 214; "Letter from Best to Heydrich, 15 April, 1942 (in Wulf's papers)." Paris in 1942: Ulrich, Best, p. 341 [51]: "It must be remembered": Best, possibly "Grossraumordnung und Grossraumverwaltung," pp. 406–12 (ND translation).

14. "GARBAGE CAN OF THE THIRD REICH"

refused to discuss: Huss, pp. 152–56. "Well, we'll have to change your mind": Sereny, *Albert Speer*, pp. 325–26. arrest of Bishop Galen: Griech-Polelle, p. 47. "I used to know a Berlin family": Köhler, pp. 8–9. "fat apple": Smith, p. 165. [6]: "spiritual effects": Op. cit. p. 9. "a senseless dummy": Ibid., pp. 28–29. "bordering on the sadist": Crankshaw, p. 103. "Power Behind the Throne": Op. cit., p. 28. "I am sending you to a concentration camp": Ibid., p. 81. "We know some people become sick": Himmler, p. 29 (ND translation). "in a bad light": Huss, p. 153. [13]: Dams and Stolle, p. 7 (ND translation). by way of dismissal: Kater, p. 161. [15]: read his confession before signing it: Bielenberg, p. 228. "nothing more than a petty official": Schellenberg, *Memoirs*, p. 210. "an unwavering scrutiny": Crankshaw, ch. 10.?? "terror into the heart of the beholder": Payne Best, p. 27. "Give Mr. Best what he wants": Ibid., pp. 41ff. "At this Heydrich went off the deep end": Ibid., p. 42. [21]: "Jewish inventions": Ibid., p. 108. took him back to Germany: Isenberg, ch. 9. [23]: favored by military men: Dederichs, *Das Gesicht*, p. 103 (ND translation). "the lord of this prison": Ibid. and released Jacob: Palmier, p. 433. The green forms said *DISMISS!*: Krüger, pp. 136–49. [27]: fog of fear: Ibid., p. 151. [28]: "Recsek actually became one of my close friends": Haas, p. 52. "my ability to think quickly": Ibid., p. 145. "until I have your confession": Ibid., p. 148. But did the Führer sanction torture?: Schnabel, p. 52. "severity is essential": Hitler, *Table Talk*, p. 484. "to add to the deterrent effect": Manvell and Fraenkel, p. 36. [IMTd: PS-778; Trial!!, pp. 371–72.] "he considered any abuses quite out of the question": IMTd, XX, 123–26. he beat to death the leader of the French resistance: Parker, p. 45, fns. 63–66. "always smelled of fresh medicine": NDI: Hartl. to describe it in some detail: Rhodes, pp. 258ff. "Go outside before you start to laugh": NDI: Streckenbach. "get over it quicker": NDI: Streckenbach. "It was obviously a Heydrich family joke": NDI: Peter Thomas Heydrich. "I want to say one more thing": NDI: Streckenbach. "people will thank us": Metaxas, p. 170.

AFTERWORD

Heinz Siegfried Heydrich: NDI: Peter Thomas Heydrich. Lina described him to Dougherty: NDI: Lena Heydrich. paper shortages: Dederichs, pp. 165–66. In footnotes 19, 20, and 21, Dederichs cites page 12 of an unpublished manuscript: Hans-Georg Wiedemann's *Peter Thomas Heydrichs Erinnerungen an seinen Onkel Reinhard Heydrich*, 2002. "Heydrich grudgingly complied": Gerwarth, pp. 81,

114–15. "Heindorf remained a constant source of embarrassment": Ibid., fn. 117. "'prove his worth in battle'": Ibid., p. 115, fn. 120. "too dumb": NSI: Peter Thomas Heydrich, Oct. 1993. "Perhaps it's too soon": [London] *Daily Mail*, June 11, 1973, p. 19. As the *Daily Mail* portrays her: Ibid., pp. 18–22. five thousand people died: Phillips, p. 44.

SELECT BIBLIOGRAPHY

BOOKS CITED IN THE TEXT

Allen, Peter. *The Crown and the Swastika: Hitler, Hess and the Duke of Windsor.* London: Hale, 1983.

Anderson, Margaret L., Howard F. Taylor, and Kim A. Logio. *Sociology: The Essentials.* 9th edition. Boston: Cengage Learning, 2017.

Arendt, Hannah. *Eichmann in Jerusalem.* New York: Viking Compass, 1965.

Aronson, Shlomo. *Reinhard Heydrich und die Anfangen des SD und der Gestapo, 1931–1935.* Berlin: Ernst-Reuter-Gesellschaft, 1967.

———. *Reinhard Heydrich und die Frühgeschichte von Gestapo und SD.* Stuttgart: Deutsche Verlags-Anstalt, 1971.

Avalon Law Project. *Nazi Conspiracy and Aggression.* Vol. 2, chap. X, part 6: *The Geheimer Staatspolizei (Gestapo) and Sicherheitsdienst (SD).*

Bancroft, Mary. *Autobiography of a Spy.* New York: Morrow, 1983.

Barron, Stephanie, ed. *"Degenerate Art": The Fate of the Avant-Garde in Nazi Germany.* New York: Abrams, 1991.

Bartz, Karl. *The Downfall of the German Secret Service.* London: Kimber, 1956.

Bendix, Richard. *Max Weber: An Intellectual Portrait.* New York: Doubleday Anchor, 1962.

Best, Herbert Ulrich. *Biographie Studien über Radikalismus, Weltanschauung und Vernunft, 1903–1989.* Munich: C. H. Beck, 1996.

Best, Payne S. *The Venlo Incident: A True Story of Double-Dealing, Captivity, and a Murderous Nazi Plot.* New York: Skyhorse, 2009.

Best, Werner. *Die deutsche Polizei.* Darmstadt: L. C. Wittich Verlag, 1941.

———. "Die Schutzstaffel der NSDAP und die deutsche Polizei." *Deutsches Recht* (edition A), 9 (1939).

Bielenber, Christabel. *When I Was a German, 1934–1945: An Englishwoman in Nazi Germany.* Lincoln: University of Nebraska Press, 1998.

Blandford, Edmund L. *SS Intelligence: The Nazi Secret Service.* Ramsbury: Airlife, 2000.

Bleuel, Hans Peter. *Strength Through Joy: Sex and Society in Nazi Germany.* New York: Dorset, 1996.

Botting, Douglas. *From the Ruins of the Reich: Germany 1945–1949.* New York: Crown, 1985.

Breitman, Richard. *The Architect of Genocide: Himmler and the Final Solution.* New York: Knopf, 1991.

Brissaud, André. *Canaris: The Biography of Admiral Canaris, Chief of German Military Intel-*

ligence in the Second World War. Translated by Ian Colvin. New York: Grosset and Dunlap, 1974.

Browder, George C. *Foundations of the Nazi Police State: The Formation of Sipo and SD.* Lexington: University of Kentucky Press, 1960.

———. *Hitler's Enforcers: The Gestapo and the SS Security Service in the Nazi Revolution.* New York and Oxford: Oxford University Press, 1996.

Browning, Christopher R. *The Origins of the Final Solution in Nazi Jewish Policy, September 1939–March 1942.* With contributions by Jürgen Mathäus. Lincoln and Jerusalem: University of Nebraska Press and Yad Vashem, 2004.

———. *The Path to Genocide: Essays on Launching the Final Solution.* Cambridge: Cambridge University Press, 1992.

Bullivant, Keith, ed. *Culture and Society in the Weimar Republic.* Manchester: Manchester University Press; U.S.: Rowman and Littlefield, 1977.

Butler, Rupert. *An Illustrated History of the Gestapo.* Osceola, WI: Wordwright Books, 1992.

Čalić, Edouard. *Heydrich: Schlüsselfigur des Dritten Reiches.* Düsseldorf: Droste Verlag, 1982.

———. *L'homme clé du IIIe Reich.* Paris: Nouveau Edition, 2010.

———. *Reinhard Heydrich: The Chilling Story of the Man Who Masterminded the Nazi Death Camps.* Translated by Lowell Bair. New York: Morrow, 2014.

Campbell, Joseph, and M. J. Abadie. *The Mythic Image.* Princeton, NJ: Bollingen-Princeton University Press, 1974.

Carlton, Eric. *The State Against the State: The Theory and Practice of the Coup d'État.* Aldershot: Scholar Press, 1997.

Caruthers, Bob, ed. *The SS on Trial: Evidence from Nuremberg.* South Yorkshire: Pen and Sword, 2014.

Chamayou, Grégoire. *Manhunts: A Philosophical History.* Translated by Steven Rendall. Princeton, NJ: Princeton University Press, 2010.

Cimino, Al. *The Story of the SS: Hitler's Infamous Legions of Death.* London: Arcturus, 2017.

Collier, Martin, and Phillip Pedley. *Hitler and the Nazi State.* Oxford: Heinemann, 2005.

Conner, T. D. *Demolition Man: Hitler: From Braunau to the Bunker.* Writeplace Press, 2015.

Crankshaw, Edward. *Gestapo: Instrument of Tyranny.* New York: Viking, 1956.

Craig, Gordon A. *The Germans.* New York: G. P. Putnam's Sons, 1982.

Dams, Carsten, and Michael Stolle. *Die Gestapo: Herrschaft und Terror im Dritten Reich.* Munich: C. H. Beck, 2008.

———. *The Gestapo: Power and Terror in the Third Reich.* Oxford: Oxford University Press. 2014.

Darman, Peter, ed. *The Holocaust and Life Under Nazi Occupation.* New York: Rosen, 2013.

Dawidowicz, Lucy S. *The War Against the Jews 1933–1945.* New York: Holt, Rinehart and Winston, 1975.

Dederichs, Mario R. *Heydrich: Das Gesicht des Bösen.* Munich: Piper Verlag, 2006.

———. *Heydrich: The Face of Evil.* Translated by Lionel Levanthal Ltd. Philadelphia: Casemate, 2006.

Delarue, Jacques. *The Gestapo: A History of Horror.* Translated by Mervyn Savill. New York: Morrow, 1964.

Deschner, Günther. *Heydrich: The Pursuit of Total Power.* London: Orbis, 1981.

———. *Reinhard Heydrich: Biographie eines Reichsprotektors.* Munich: Universitas Verlag, 2008; Esslingen am Neckar: Bechtle Verlag, 1977.

———. *Reinhard Heydrich: Statthalter der Totaler Macht: Biographie.* Esslingen am Neckar: Bechtle Verlag, 1977.

Deuel, Wallace R. *The People Under Hitler.* New York: Harcourt, Brace and Co., 1942.

Dodd, Martha. *Through Embassy Eyes.* New York: Harcourt, 1952.

Dollmann, Eugen. *The Interpreter: Memoirs of Doctor Eugen Dollmann.* London: Hutchinson, 1967.

Domarus, Max. *Hitler: Speeches and Proclamations, 1932–1945: The Chronicle of a Dictatorship.* Volume II. Translated by Chris Wilcox and Mary Fran Gilbert. Wurzburg: Domarus Verlag, 1997.

Eliaeson, Sven. *Max Weber's Methodologies: Interpretation and Critique.* Cambridge and Malden, MA: Blackwell Publishers, 2002.

Engelman, Bernt. *In Hitler's Germany: Daily Life in the Third Reich.* Translated by Krishna Winston. New York: Pantheon, 1986.

Epstein, Catherine. *Nazi Germany: Confronting the Myths.* Malden, MA: Wiley, 2015.

Erikson, Erik. *Childhood and Society.* New York: Norton, 1963.

Evans, Richard J. *The Third Reich in Power.* New York: Penguin Press, 2005.

Farago, Ladislas. *Burn after Reading: The Espionage History of World War II.* New York: Walker, 1961.

Fest, Joachim C. *The Face of the Third Reich: Portaits of Nazi Leadership.* Translated by Michael Bullock. New York: Pantheon, 1970.

———. *Hitler: A Biography.* Translated by Richard and Clara Winston. New York: A Helen and Kurt Wolff Book, Harcourt Brace Jovanovich, 1974.

Freud, Sigmund. *Civilization and Its Discontents.* Translated by James Strachey. New York: W. W. Norton, 1962.

Fried, John Ernest. *The Guilt of the German Army.* New York: Macmillan, 1942.

Frischauer, Willi. *Himmler: The Evil Genius of the Third Reich.* Boston: Beacon Press, 1953.

Fritz, Stephen. *Ostkrieg: Hitler's War of Extermination in the East.* Lexington: University Press of Kentucky, 2011.

Fromm, Bella. *Blood and Banquets: A Berlin Social Diary.* New York: Harper and Brothers, 1942.

Fromm, Erich. *The Anatomy of Human Destructiveness.* New York: Holt, Rinehart and Winston, 1973.

Gallo, Max. *The Night of the Long Knives.* Translated by Lily Emmet. New York: Harper and Row, 1972.

Gellately, Robert. *The Gestapo and German Society: Enforcing Racial Policy 1933–1945.* Oxford: Clarendon Press, 1990.

Genese, Cecil. *Nazi Germany and British Guilt: The German Victory.* Dorset: Purbeck Publications, 1995.

Gerwarth, Robert. *Hitler's Hangman: The Life of Heydrich.* New Haven, CT: Yale University Press, 2011.

Gilbert, Martin. *The Holocaust: A History of the Jews of Europe During the Second World War.* New York: Holt, Rinehart and Winston, 1985.

Gillespie, William. *Dietrich Eckart: An Introduction for the English-Speaking Student.* 2nd edition. Gillespie, 1976.

Gisevius, Hans Bernd. *To the Bitter End.* Translated by Richard and Clara Winston. Boston: Houghton Mifflin, 1997.

———. *Wo ist Nebe?: Erinnerungen an Hitlers Reichskriminaldirektor.* Zurich: Droemer, 1966.

Goldensohn, Leon. *The Nuremberg Interviews.* New York: Vintage, 2005.

Golsan, Richard J., and Sarah M. Misemer, eds. *The Trial That Never Ends: Hannah Arendt's Eichmann in Jerusalem in Retrospect.* Toronto: University of Toronto Press, 2017.

Gordon, Harold J., Jr. *Hitler and the Beer Hall Putsch*. Princeton, NJ: Princeton University Press, 1972.

Gordon, Sara Ann. *Hitler, Germans and the "Jewish Question."* Princeton, NJ: Princeton University Press, 1984.

Graber, G. S. *The Life and Times of Reinhard Heydrich*. Philadelphia: McKay, 1980.

Greenberger, Richard. *The 12-Year Reich: A Social History of Nazi Germany 1933–1945*. New York: Da Capo Press, 1995.

Griech-Polelle, Beth A. *Bishop von Galen: German Catholicism and National Socialism*. New Haven, CT: Yale University Press, 2002.

Günther, Hans. *Ritter, Tod und Teufel: Der heldische Gedanke*. Munich: J. J. Lehmanns, 1920.

Haas, Albert, MD. *The Doctor and the Damned*. New York: Avon, 1985.

Hagen, Walter (Wilhelm Höttl). *Die geheime Front: Organisation, Personen und Actionen des deutschen Geheimdienstes*. Berlin and Leipzig: Nibelungen-Verlag, 1950.

Hangftängl, Ernst. *Hitler: The Memoir of the Nazi Insider Who Turned Against the Führer*. New York: Arcade Publishing, 1957.

Hansen, Ron. *Hitler's Niece*. New York: Harper Perennial, 2000.

Hayes, Peter. *Why?: Explaining the Holocaust*. New York: W. W. Norton, 2017.

Heiden, Konrad. *Der Führer: Hitler's Rise to Power*. Boston: Houghton Mifflin, 1944.

Heydrich, Lina. *Leben mit einem Kriegsverbrecher*. Pfaffenhofen an der Ilm: Verlag W. Ludwig, 1976.

Heydrich, Reinhard. "Wandlungen unseres Kampfen" [Transformations of Our Struggle]. Munich: World Future Fund, 1935.

Hilberg, Raul. *The Destruction of the European Jews*. Vol. II. New Haven, CT: Yale University Press, 2003.

———. *Perpetrators Victims Bystanders: The Jewish Catastrophe, 1933–1945*. New York: Aaron Asher Books, HarperCollins, 1992.

Himmler, Heinrich. *Die Schutzstaffel als antibolschewistische Kamporganisation*. Munich: Zentralverlag der NSDAP, Franz Eher II, 1936.

Hinz, Berthold. *Art in the Third Reich*. Translated by Robert and Rita Kimber. New York: Pantheon, 1979.

Hitler, Adolf. *Mein Kampf*. New York: Reynal and Hitchcock, 1940.

———. *Mein Kampf: English Edition*. Translated by Marco Roberto and James Murphy. New York: Create Independent Publishing Platform, 2017. (Kindle edition.)

———. *Monologe im Führer-Hauptquartier, 1941–1944*. Hamburg: A. Knaus, 1980.

———. *Table Talk, 1941–1945: His Private Conversations*. Translated by Norman Cameron and R. H. Stevens, introduction by Hugh Trevor-Roper. New York: Enigma Books, 2000–2008.

Hoberman, John M. *Sport and Political Ideology*. Austin: University of Texas Press, 1984.

Höhne, Heinz. *Canaris: Hitler's Master Spy*. London: Secker and Warburg, 1979.

———. *The Order of the Death's Head: The Story of Hitler's SS*. Translated by Richard Barry. New York: Coward-McCann, 1970.

Holborn, Hajo, ed. *Republic to Reich: The Making of the Nazi Revolution: Ten Essays*. New York: Pantheon, 1973.

Höttl, Wilhelm (Walter Hagen). *The Secret Front: Nazi Political Espionage 1938–1945*. New York: Enigma Books, 1954.

Hulme, George. *The Life and Death of Adolf Hitler*. Buckinghamshire: Smythe, 1975.

Huss, Pierre J. *The Foe We Face*. New York: Doubleday, Doran, 1942.

Ingrao, Christian. *Believe and Destroy: Intellectuals in the SS War Machine*. Translated by Andrew Brown. Malden, MA: Polity, 2013.

Irving, David. *Göring: A Biography.* New York: A Thomas Congdon Book, Morrow, 1989.

Isenberg, Sheila. *A Hero of Our Own: The Story of Varian Fry.* New York: Random House, 2001.

Jaeckel, Gerhard. *Kriminalzentrale Werderscher Markt: Die Geschichte des "Deutschen Scotland Yard."* Bayreuth: Hestia, 1963.

Joffroy, Pierre. *A Spy for God: The Ordeal of Kurt Gerstein.* New York: A Helen and Kurt Wolff Book, Harcourt Brace Jovanovich, 1971.

Johnson, Eric A. *Nazi Terror: The Gestapo, Jews, and Ordinary Germans.* New York: Basic Books, 1999.

Kagan, Robert A., Marin Krygier, and Kenneth Winston. *Legality and Community: On the Intellectual Legacy of Philip Selznick.* New York and Oxford: Rowman and Littlefield, 2002.

Kater, Michael H. *Composers of the Nazi Era: Eight Portraits.* New York: Oxford University Press, 2000.

———. *The Nazi Party: A Social Profile of Members and Leaders, 1919–1945.* Cambridge, MA: Harvard University Press, 1983.

Kent, Madeleine. *I Married a German.* New York: Harper and Brothers, 1939.

Kershaw, Ian. *Hitler: A Biography.* New York: Norton, 2008.

———. *Hitler: Profiles in Power.* New York: Routledge, 2013.

Kersten, Felix. *The Kersten Memoirs, 1940–1945.* Translated by Constantine Fitzgibbon and James Oliver. New York: Macmillan, 1957.

King, David. *The Trial of Adolf Hitler: The Beer Hall Putsch and the Rise of Nazi Germany.* New York: Norton, 2017.

Kirk, Russell, ed. *Modern Age.* Vols. 14–15. Ann Arbor, MI: Foundation for Foreign Affairs, 1969.

Kitchen, Martin. *A History of Modern Germany: 1800 to the Present.* Hoboken, NJ: Wiley, 2011.

Klee, Ernst. *Das Personen Lexikon zum Dritten Reich: Wer war was vor und nach 1945?* Koblenz: Edition Kramer, 2011.

Klee, Ernst, Willi Dressen, and Volker Riess, eds. *"The Good Old Days": The Holocaust as Seen by Its Perpetrators and Bystanders.* Translated by Deborah Burnstone. New York: Free Press, 1991.

Koch, H. W. *In the Name of the Volk: Political Justice in Hitler's Germany.* New York: Barnes and Noble, 1989.

Koehl, Robert Lewis. *The Black Corps: The Structure and Power Struggles of the Nazi SS.* Madison: University of Wisconsin Press, 1983.

Koehn, Ilse. *Mischling, Second Degree: My Childhood in Nazi Germany.* New York: Bantam Books, 1977.

Köhler, Hansjürgen. *Inside the Gestapo: Hitler's Shadow Over the World.* London: Pallas Publishing Co. Ltd., 1940.

Kolinsky, Eva, and Wilfried van der Will. *The Cambridge Companion to Modern German Culture.* Cambridge: Cambridge University Press, 1998.

Koonz, Claudia. *Mothers in the Fatherland: Women, the Family, and Nazi Politics.* New York: St. Martin's Press, 1987.

Krausnick, Helmut, Hans Buchheim, Martin Broszat, and Hans-Adolf Jacobsen. *Anatomy of the SS State.* Translated by Richard Barry, Marian Jackson, and Dorothy Long. New York: Walker and Co., 1968.

Krüger, Horst. *A Crack in the Wall: Growing Up Under Hitler.* Translated by Ruth Hein. New York: Fromm International, 1982.

Landau, Ronnie D. *The Nazi Holocaust.* Chicago: Ivan R. Dee, 1994.

Lehrer, Steven. *Wannsee House and the Holocaust.* Jefferson, NC: McFarland, 2000.

Lengyel, Emil. *The New Deal in Europe.* New York: Funk and Wagnalls, 1934.

Lerner, Daniel. *The Nazi Elite.* Stanford: Stanford University Press, 1951.

Letters of Thomas Mann, 1889–1955. Selected and translated by Richard and Clara Winston. Berkeley and Los Angeles: University of California, 1975.

Levy, Alan. *Nazi Hunter: The Wiesenthal File.* London: Constable and Robinson, 2002.

———. *Wanted: Nazi Criminals at Large.* New York: Berkley, 1962.

Lewy, Guenter. *Perpetrators: The World of the Holocaust Killers.* New York: Oxford University Press, 2017.

Loewenberg, Peter. *Decoding the Past: The Psychohistorical Approach.* New York: Routledge, 2017.

Longerich, Peter. *Heinrich Himmler.* Translated by Jeremy Noakes and Lesley Sharpe. Oxford: Oxford University Press, 2012.

Lozowick, Yaacov. *Hitler's Bureaucrats: The Nazi Security Police and the Banality of Evil.* Translated by Haim Watzman. London: Bloomsbury, 2002.

Lumsden, Robin. *Himmler's SS: Loyal to the Death's Head.* Gloucestershire: History Press, 2009.

Mann, Thomas. *Essays of Three Decades.* Translated by H. T. Lowe-Porter. New York: Alfred A. Knopf, reprinted as Vintage book, 1957.

Manvell, Roger, and Heinrich Fraenkel. *Heinrich Himmler: The Secret Life of the SS and Gestapo.* London and New York: Greenhill Books and Skyhorse Publishing, 2007.

Maracin, Paul H. *The Night of the Long Knives: 48 Hours That Changed Europe.* Guilford, CT: Lyons Press, 2007.

Maser, Werner. *Hitler: Legend, Myth and Reality.* New York: Harper and Row, 1973.

Mastny, Vojtech. *The Czechs Under Nazi Rule: The Failure of National Resistance, 1939–1942.* New York and London: Columbia University Press, 1971.

McDonough, Frank. *The Gestapo: The Myth and Reality of Hitler's Secret Police.* New York: Skyhorse, 2017.

McKale, Donald M. *Nazis After Hitler: How Perpetrators of the Holocaust Cheated Justice and Truth.* New York: Rowman and Littlefield, 2012.

McNab, Chris. *The SS: 1923–1945.* London: Amber Books Ltd., 2009.

Merkl, Peter. *Violence Under the Swastika.* Princeton, NJ: Princeton University Press, 1975.

Messenger, David A., and Katrin Pähler, eds. *A Nazi Past: Recasting German Identity in Postwar Europe.* Lexington: University of Kentucky Press, 2015.

Metaxas, Eric. *Bonhoeffer: Pastor, Martyr, Prophet, Spy.* Nashville, TN: Thomas Nelson, 2010.

Metcalfe, Philip. *1933.* Sag Harbor, NY: Permanent Press, 1988.

Methvin, Eugene, H. *The Rise of Radicalism: The Social Psychology of Messianic Extremism.* New York: Arlington House, 1973.

Meyer, Beate. *A Fatal Balancing Act: The Dilemma of the Reich Association of Jews in Germany, 1939–1945.* Translated by William Templer. New York and Oxford: Beghahn Books, 2016.

Milgram, Stanley. *Obedience to Authority: An Experimental View.* New York: Harper and Row, 1974.

Minnich, Elizabeth K. *The Evil of Banality: On the Life and Death Importance of Thinking.* Lanham, MD: Rowman and Littlefield, 2017.

Mueller, Michael. *Nazi Spymaster: The Life and Death of Admiral Wilhelm Canaris.* New York: Skyhorse Publishing, 2017.

Murray, Henry A., MD. *Analysis of the Personality of Adolph Hitler: With Predictions of His*

Future Behavior and Suggestions for Dealing with Him Now and After Germany's Surrender. Prepared for the Office of Strategic Services. Kodselim Square: 2017. [Murray cites as sources for Hitler's comments: H. G. Baynes, *Germany Possessed* (London, 1941); data supplied by the OSS; K. Heiden, *Hitler: A Biography* (London, 1936); Adolf Hitler, *Mein Kampf* (New York: Reynal and Hitchcock, 1939) and *My New Order* (New York: Reynal and Hitchcock, 1941); H. Rauschning, *Voice of Destruction* (New York).]

Nicholas, Lynn H. *The Rape of Europa: The Fate of Europe's Treasures in the Third Reich and the Second World War.* New York: Alfred A. Knopf, 1994.

Noakes, Jeremy, and Geoffrey Pridham. *Nazism, 1919–1945: State, Economy and Society, 1933–1939.* Exeter: University of Exeter Press, 2000.

Orwell, George. *Coming Up for Air.* New York: Harcourt Harvest, 1950.

Owings, Alison. *Frauen: German Women Recall the Third Reich.* New Brunswick, NJ: Rutgers University Press, 1993.

Padfield, Peter. *Himmler: Reichsführer SS.* New York: Henry Holt and Co., 1990.

Paehler, Katrin. *The Third Reich's Intelligence Service: The Career of Walter Schellenberg.* Cambridge: Cambridge University Press, 2017.

Palmier, Jean-Michel. *Weimar in Exile: The Antifascist Emigration in Europe and America.* Translated by David Fernbach. New York: Verso, 2006.

Parker, Danny S. *The Life and Wars of SS Colonel Jochen Peiper.* Boston: Da Capo, 2014.

Parsons, Talcott. *The Social System.* Oxfordshire: Routledge, 1991.

Payne, Robert. *The Life and Death of Adolf Hitler.* London: Jonathan Cape, 1973.

Peis, Günter. *The Man Who Started the War.* New York: Popular Library, 1960. (Also available as e-book.)

Peterson, Edward Norman. *Limits of Hitler's Power.* Princeton, NJ: Princeton University Press, 1969.

Petropoulos, Jonathan. *The Faustian Bargain: The Art World in Nazi Germany.* New York: Oxford University Press, 2000.

Peukert, Detlev J. K. *Inside Nazi Germany: Conformity, Opposition, and Racism in Everyday Life.* Translated by Richard Deveson. New Haven, CT, and London: Yale University Press, 1987.

Phillips, Russell. *A Ray of Light: Reinhard Heydrich, Lidice, and the North Staffordshire Miners.* Stoke-on-Trent: Shilka Publishing, 2016.

Priemel, Kim C., and Alexa Stiller, eds. *Reassessing the Nuremberg Military Tribunals: Transition Justice, Trial Narratives, and Historiography.* New York and Oxford: Berghahn Books, 2012.

Rauschning, Anna Schwarte. *No Retreat.* Indianapolis, IN: Bobbs-Merrill, 1942.

Rauschning, Hermann. *Germany's Revolution of Destruction.* Germany: Heinemann, 1939.

———. *Hitler Speaks: A Series of Political Conversations with Adolf Hitler on His Real Aims.* Whitefish, MT: Kessinger Publishing, 2006.

———. *The Voice of Destruction.* Gretna, LA: Pelican, 2003.

Read, Anthony. *The Devil's Disciples: Hitler's Inner Circle.* New York: Norton, 2003.

Reck-Malleczewen, Fritz Percy. *Diary of a Man in Despair.* New York: Macmillan, 1970.

Reider, Frederic. *The Order of the SS.* Tucson, AZ: Aztex Corporation, 1975.

Reitlinger, Gerald. *The SS: Alibi of a Nation.* New York: Viking Press, 1957.

———. *The SS: Alibi of a Nation.* 2nd revised and augmented edition. New York: Thomas Yoseloff, 1968.

Rempel, Gerhard. *Hitler's Children: The Hitler Youth and the SS.* Chapel Hill: University of North Carolina Press, 1989.

Rhodes, Richard. *Masters of Death: The SS-Einsatzgruppen and the Invention of the Holocaust.* New York: Vintage, 2003.

Röhm, Ernst. *Die Geschichte eines Hochverätters.* Munich: Centralverlag des NSDP, 1934.

———. *The Memoirs of Ernst Röhm.* Translated by Geoffrey Brooks. London: Frontline, 2012.

Roland, Paul. *The Secret Lives of the Nazis: The Hidden History of the Nazis.* London: Arcturus, 2017.

Roseman, Mark. *The Wannsee Conference and the Final Solution: A Reconsideration.* New York: Picador, 2002.

Schellenberg, Walter. *The Labyrinth: Memoirs.* Translated by Alan Bullock. New York: Harper and Brothers, 1956.

———. *The Schellenberg Memoirs.* London: Andre Deutsch, 1956.

Schnabel, Reimund. *Macht ohne Moral: Eine Dokumentation über die SS.* Frankfurt: Röderberg Verlag, 1957.

Schoenbaum, David. *Hitler's Social Revolution: Class and Status in Nazi Germany, 1933–1939.* New York: W. W. Norton, 1980.

Sereny, Gitta. *Albert Speer: His Battle with Truth.* New York: Vintage, 1996.

———. *The Healing Wound: Experiences and Reflections on Germany, 1938–2001.* New York: W. W. Norton, 2001.

———. *Into That Darkness: From Mercy Killing to Mass Murder.* London: Andre Deutsch, 1974.

Shirer, William L. *Berlin Diary: The Journal of a Foreign Correspondent, 1934–1941.* New York: Alfred A. Knopf, 1941.

Smith, Bradley F. *Heinrich Himmler: A Nazi in the Making, 1900–1926.* Stanford: Hoover Institution Press, 1971.

Smith, Howard K. *Last Train from Berlin.* New York: Alfred A. Knopf, 1942.

Snyder, Louis L. *Hitler's Elite: Biographical Sketches of Nazis Who Shaped the Third Reich.* New York: Hippocrene Books, 1989.

Speer, Albert. *Inside the Third Reich: Memoirs.* Translated by Richard and Clara Winston. New York: Simon and Schuster, 1970.

Speier, Hans. *From the Ashes of Disgrace: A Journal from Germany 1945–1955.* Amherst: University of Massachusetts Press, 1981.

Spotts, Frederick. *Hitler and the Power of Aesthetics.* Woodstock, NY: Overlook, 2009.

Stangneth, Bettina. *Eichmann Before Jerusalem: The Unexamined Life of a Mass Murderer.* New York: Alfred A. Knopf, 2014.

Steffahn, Harald. *Adolf Hitler: In Selbstzeugen und Bilddokumenten.* Berlin: Rowohlt Verlag, 1983.

Stein, Marcel. *Field Marshal von Manstein: A Portrait—The Janushead.* Translated by Marcel Stein. Edited by Gwyneth Fairbank. Solihull, West Midlands: Helion and Company, 2007.

Steiner, John Michael. *Power Politics and Social Change in National Socialist Germany: A Process of Escalation into Mass Destruction.* Atlantic Highlands, NJ: Humanities Press, 1976.

Taylor, Brandon, and Wilfried van der Will. *The Nazification of Art: Art, Design, Music, Architecture and Film in the Third Reich.* Winchester, ON: Winchester Press, 1990.

Taylor, Telford. *The Anatomy of the Nuremberg Trials.* New York: Alfred A. Knopf, 1992.

Trevor-Roper, H. R. *Hitler's Secret Conversations 1941–1944.* Translated by Norman Cameron and R. H. Stevens. New York: Farrar, Straus and Young, 1953.

Unterseher, Lutz. *Hitlers System oder die Zerstörung der Gesellschaft.* Berlin: Lit Verlag, 2017.

Van Vrekhem, Georges. *Hitler and His God: The Background to the Nazi Phenomenon.* Seattle: CreateSpace Independent Publishing Platform, 2012.

von Lang, Jochen. *Der Adjutant: Karl Wolff: Der Mann zwischen Hitler und Himmler.* Munich: Herbig, 1985.

———. *Top Nazi: SS General Karl Wolff, the Man Between Hitler and Himmler.* Translated by MaryBeth Friedrich. New York: Enigma Books, 1985 (2013).

Wagner, Margaret Seaton. *The Monster of Düsseldorf: The Life and Trial of Peter Kürten.* London: Faber and Faber, 1932.

Wagner, Richard. *Tristan and Isolde.* Translated by Stewart Robb. New York: E. P. Dutton, 1965.

Ward, Ian. *Law, Philosophy and National Socialism: Heidegger, Schmitt and Radbruch in Context.* New York, Paris, and Vienna: Lang, 1992.

Ward, Mark. *Deadly Documents: Technical Communication, Organizational Discourse, and the Holocaust.* New York: Routledge, 2017.

Watson, Derek. *Richard Wagner: A Biography.* New York: Schirmer Books, 1981.

Weale, Adrian. *Army of Evil: A History of the SS.* New York: New American Library, 2010.

Weber, Max. *From Max Weber: Essays in Sociology.* Translated, edited, and with an introduction by H. H. Gerth and C. Wright Mills. New York: Oxford University Press, 1946.

Wette, Wolfram. *The Wehrmacht: History, Myth, Reality.* Translated by Deborah Lukas Schneider. Cambridge, MA: Harvard University Press, 2006.

Wheeler-Bennett, John W. *The Nemesis of Power: The German Army in Politics 1918–1945.* New York: St. Martin's Press, 1954.

Whiting, Charles. *The Search for "Gestapo" Müller: The Man Without a Shadow.* South Yorkshire: Barnsley, 2001.

———. *The War in the Shadows.* New York: Ballantine Books, 1973.

Wiesenthal, Simon. *Die gleiche Sprache: Erst für Hitler—jetzt für Ulbricht.* Bonn: R. Vogel, 1968.

Wighton, Charles. *Heydrich: Hitler's Most Evil Henchman.* Philadelphia: Chilton, 1962.

Wistrich, Robert. *Who's Who in Nazi Germany.* New York: Macmillan, 1982.

Yahil, Leni. *The Holocaust: The Fate of European Jewry.* Translated by Ina Friedman and Haya Galai. New York and Oxford: Oxford University Press, 1991.

Yenne, Bill. *Hitler's Master of the Dark Arts: Himmler's Black Knights and the Occult Origins of the SS.* Minneapolis, MN: Zenith Press, 2010.

Ziegler, Herbert F. *Nazi Germany's New Aristocracy: The SS Leadership, 1925–1939.* Princeton, NJ: Princeton University Press, 1989.

UNPUBLISHED SOURCES

Best, Werner. *Reinhard Heidrich.* Monograph dated October 1, 1949. Translated by Nancy Dougherty. [Identified as Kopenhagen Typoskript, Werner Best: KTwb.]

Wiedemann, Hans-Georg. *Peter Thomas Heydrichs Erinnerungen an seinen Onkel Reinhard Heydrich.* Unpublished manuscript. 2002.

Wikipedia: *Inside the Gestapo: Hitler's Shadow Over the World* is a 1939 book partially published in serial form in the *Manchester Guardian*, and then in full by Pallas, 1940, under the pseudonym Hansjurgen Koehler by the German political exile Walter Korodi (1902–1983). In part the work contained the genuine manuscript "Hinter den Kulissen des 3. Reiches" by Heinrich Pfeifer (1905–1949), a former Gestapo official, which Pfeifer had sent to Pallas, but had never received a reply. A second volume by Korodi as Hansjürgen Koehler entitled *Inside Information* appeared in 1940. The books gained significant press coverage in Britain in 1939 and 1940.

ARTICLES CITED IN THE TEXT

Bajohr, Frank. "Gauleiter in Hamburg: Zur Person und Tätigkeit Karl Kaumanns." *Viertel-jahreshefte für Zeitgeschichte* 43, no. 3 (1995).

Best, Werner. "Grossraumordung und Grossraumverwaltung." *Zeitschrift für Politik* 32 (1942).

Broszat, Martin. "The Concentration Camps 1933–45." In Helmut Krausnick et al., *Anatomy of the SS State.* New York: Walker and Co., 1968.

Browder, George C. *Die Anfänge des SD Dokumente aus der Organisationsgeschichte des Sicherheitsdienstes des Reichsfühers SS.* Munich and Berlin: Quarterly for Contemporary History.

Buchheim, Hans. "Command and Compliance." In Helmut Krausnick et al., *Anatomy of the SS State.* New York: Walker and Co., 1968.

Dimsdale, N., N. Horsewood, and A. van Riel. "Unemployment and Real Wages in Weimar Germany." University of Oxford: Discussion Papers in Economics and Social History, no. 56, October 2004.

"Eichmann Interrogated." *Granta*, nos. 6–7 (1985).

Elwart, N. G. *Zeitschrift für Ostforschung* 23, nos. 3–4 (1974).

Kirk, Russell. "Foundations for Foreign Affairs, 1969." *Modern Age* 24–15, p. 318.

Leslie, Anne. "Children of the Nazis." (London) *Daily Mail*, June 11, 1973.

Liberty magazine, vol. 21, no. 2, p. 43.

Mau, Hermann. "Die zweite Revolution—der 30. Juni 1934." *Viertel-jahreshefte für Zeitgeschichte* 1 (1953): 119–37.

WEBSITES CITED IN THE TEXT

www.ifz-muenchen.de/das-archiv/: Correspondence Heydrich, Willrich, Himmler, Race and Settlement Office, January 13–27, April 1937. Abusive publication of the portrait of Frau Heydrich by Willrich in "Volk und Rasse" 8 379-8 384.

www.holocaustresearchproject.org/einsatz/ohlendorf.html

http://spartacus-educational.com/GERhimmler.htm

http://www.colingolvan.com.au/downloads/plays/eichmann-in-haifa-sample.pdf

http://www.historyplace.com/worldwar2/biographies/eichmann-biography.htm

http://avalon.law.yale.edu/imt/chap15_part06.asp

http://www.wikiwand.com/de/Werner_Best_(NSDAP)

INDEX

Page numbers in *italics* refer to photos.

PHOTOGRAPHIC CREDITS

5 Pictorial Press Ltd / Alamy
4 Süddeutsche Zeitung Photo / Alamy
19 Chronicle / Alamy
88 INTERFOTO / Alamy
95 Keystone Press / Alamy
105 Alamy
127 (top) Getty Images
149 (bottom) Süddeutsche Zeitung Photo / Alamy
162 Süddeutsche Zeitung Photo / Alamy
177 Corbis / Getty Images
196 agefotostock
284 (right) Popperphoto / Getty Images
309 Getty Images
316 United Archives GmbH / Alamy
341 Getty Images
361 PJF Military Collection / Alamy
388 Corbis / Getty Images
397 Alamy
405 World History Archive / Alamy
411 Alamy
457 Getty Images
461 Alamy
491 Alamy

All other images are from the author's collection or in the public domain.

A NOTE ON THE TYPE

This book was set in Adobe Garamond. Designed for the Adobe Corporation by Robert Slimbach, the fonts are based on types first cut by Claude Garamond (c. 1480–1561). Garamond was a pupil of Geoffroy Tory's and is believed to have followed the Venetian models, although he introduced a number of important differences, and it is to him that we owe the letter we now know as "old style." He gave to his letters a certain elegance and feeling of movement that won their creator an immediate reputation and the patronage of Francis I of France.

Composed by North Market Street Graphics, Lancaster, Pennsylvania

Printed and bound by Berryville Graphics, Berryville, Virginia

Designed by Maggie Hinders